Population Change and Rural Society

THE SPRINGER SERIES ON

DEMOGRAPHIC METHODS AND POPULATION ANALYSIS

Series Editor

KENNETH C. LAND

Duke University

In recent decades, there has been a rapid development of demographic models and methods and an explosive growth in the range of applications of population analysis. This series seeks to provide a publication outlet both for high-quality textual and expository books on modern techniques of demographic analysis and for works that present exemplary applications of such techniques to various aspects of population analysis.

Topics appropriate for the series include:

- General demographic methods
- Techniques of standardization
- Life table models and methods
- Multistate and multiregional life tables, analyses, and projections
- Demographic aspects of biostatistics and epidemiology
- Stable population theory and its extensions
- Methods of indirect estimation
- Stochastic population models
- Event history analysis, duration analysis, and hazard regression models
- Demographic projection methods and population forecasts
- Techniques of applied demographic analysis, regional and local population estimates and projections
- Methods of estimaion and projection for business and health care applications
- Methods and estimates for unique populations such as schools and students

Volumes in the series are of interest to researchers, professionals, and students in demography, sociology, economics, statistics, geography and regional science, public health and health care management, epidemiology, biostatistics, actuarial science, business, and related fields.

The titles published in this series are listed at the end of this volume.

Population Change and Rural Society

Edited by

William A. Kandel
Economic Research Service,
U.S. Department of Agriculture
Washington, DC, USA

and

David L. Brown
Department of Development Sociology,
Cornell University,
Ithaca, NY, USA

Springer

A C.I.P. Catalogue record for this book is available from the Library of Congress.

ISBN-10 1-4020-3901-8 (PB)
ISBN-13 978-1-4020-3901-0 (PB)
ISBN-10 1-4020-3911-5 (HB)
ISBN-13 978-1-4020-3911-9 (HB)
ISBN-10 1-4020-3902-6 (e-book)
ISBN-13 978-1-4020-3902-7 (e-book)

Published by Springer,
P.O. Box 17, 3300 AA Dordrecht, The Netherlands.

www.springer.com

Printed on acid-free paper

Printed in the Netherlands.

Dedication

For

James Copp

An intellectual leader in the discipline of Rural Sociology, and our friend and longtime colleague

CONTENTS

CONTRIBUTORS

Calvin Beale is senior demographer with the Economic Research Service, U.S. Department of Agriculture.

E. Helen Berry is professor of sociology in the Department of Sociology, Social Work, and Anthropology, and affiliate with the Population Research Laboratory, at Utah State University.

Dwight B. Billings is professor of sociology at the University of Kentucky and editor of the *Journal of Appalachian Studies*.

Joan Brehm is assistant professor of sociology at Illinois State University.

David Brown is professor of development sociology at Cornell University and director of the Polson Institute for Global Development.

John Cromartie is geographer with the Economic Research Service, U.S. Department of Agriculture.

Katherine J. Curtis White is NICHD postdoctoral fellow at the Center for Demography and Ecology, University of Wisconsin-Madison.

Joe D. Francis is associate professor of development sociology at Cornell University.

Nina Glasgow is senior research associate in the Department of Development Sociology at Cornell University.

Stephan J. Goetz is professor of agricultural and regional economics and director of the Northeast Regional Center for Rural Development at Pennsylvania State University.

Roger B. Hammer is assistant professor of rural sociology at the University of Wisconsin-Madison and land-use specialist with University of Wisconsin-Extension.

Douglas Jackson-Smith is associate professor of sociology at Utah State University.

Brian Jennings is graduate student in sociology at Utah State University.

Eric Jensen is graduate student in sociology at Utah State University.

Leif Jensen is professor of rural sociology and demography and director of the Population Research Institute at Pennsylvania State University.

Kenneth M. Johnson is professor of sociology at Loyola University-Chicago.

William A. Kandel is sociologist with the Economic Research Service, U.S. Department of Agriculture.

Annabel R. Kirschner is professor and chair of the Department of Community and Rural Sociology at Washington State University.

Richard S. Krannich is professor of sociology and professor of environment and society at Utah State University.

M. A. Lee is assistant professor of rural sociology and sociology at the University of Wisconsin-Madison.

Elgin Mannion is assistant professor of sociology at Western Illinois University.

Peter Nelson is assistant professor of geography at Middlebury College.

Emilio Parrado is assistant professor of sociology at Duke University.

Peggy Petrzelka is assistant professor of sociology at Utah State University.

Max J. Pfeffer is professor of development sociology, Cornell University and associate director of the Cornell University Agricultural Experiment Station.

Richard Rathge is professor of agribusiness and applied economics and sociology at North Dakota State University. Dr. Rathge is also director of the North Dakota State Data Center.

Zev Ross is president of ZevRoss Spatial Analysis.

Gundars Rudzitis is professor of geography in the American Studies Program and the Environmental Science Program at the University of Idaho.

Joachim Singelmann is professor of sociology at Louisiana State University.

Richard C. Stedman is assistant professor of rural sociology at Pennsylvania State University.

Hema Swaminathan is economist with the International Center for Research on Women.

Alexander Vias is associate professor of geography at the University of Connecticut.

Christiane von Reichert is associate professor of geography at the University of Montana.

Paul R. Voss is professor of rural sociology at the University of Wisconsin-Madison.

Benjamin Weagraf is associate economist at Economy.com

Leslie Whitener is sociologist and former branch chief of the Rural Economy Branch, Food and Rural Economy Branch, of the Economic Research Service, U.S. Department of Agriculture.

Richelle Winkler is associate researcher in the Applied Population Laboratory at the University of Wisconsin-Madison.

ACKNOWLEDGEMENTS

This book is a cooperative undertaking of social scientists participating in the Western Regional Committee on Population Change in Rural Communities (W1001). During our 2002 annual meeting in Portland, Oregon, and following USDA's approval of our five year proposal, we decided to produce an edited volume that would address central demographic issues facing rural communities. At that meeting, we outlined a book that would analyze four major rural demographic issues in detail and report results of case studies of relationships between population dynamics and community organization and change to illustrate those issues in different regions throughout the country. We also decided that to the extent possible, our book would feature original research, and we invited authors outside of our committee to contribute. As editors, we would like to thank all of our authors for their dedication, multiple revisions, and enthusiastic cooperation.

As a committee, we would like to express our appreciation to Linda Fox, Associate Dean and Associate Director of the Cooperative Extension at Washington State University and our administrative advisor, for her dedicated and sustained support. We gratefully acknowledge financial and administrative assistance from the Cooperative State Research, Education, and Extension Service of the U.S. Department of Agriculture, the Economic Research Service of the U.S. Department of Agriculture, and the Department of Development Sociology at Cornell University. Jim Bjork, a post-doctoral fellow in Cornell's Institute for European Studies, copy-edited the entire manuscript. We would also like to thank our editors, Myriam Poort, Susan Jones, and Evelien Bakker, first at Kluwer Plenum and then at Springer, for their helpful advice, patience, and continuing support.

FOREWORD

CALVIN L. BEALE

In considering how to introduce the subject of rural population change in the 21st Century, I find myself reflecting on my own experience as a demographer for the U.S. Department of Agriculture. When I arrived at the Department, the post-World War II modernization of farming was well under way. Each year, my colleague Gladys Bowles and I had the unpopular task of announcing how much the farm population had decreased in the prior year. It was hard to say that the phenomenon was someone's fault. Dramatic reductions in labor requirements per unit of agricultural output were occurring everywhere and not just in the United States. But politically, blame had to be assigned, and whichever political party was not in the White House was certain to place the blame squarely on the current administration.

The demographic consequences of this trend were major. In a 22-year period from 1941 to 1962, the net loss of farm population from migration and cessation of farming averaged over a million people per year. It took eight years after the war before an administration was willing to begin to talk about the need to diversify rural employment. By that time, farm residents had already become a minority of rural people. However, well into the 1970s, I continued to receive inquiries from people who still equated rural with farm or who could not envision what rural-nonfarm people did for a living. So, much of our research task, it seemed, was to provide the public and policy makers with an accurate picture of current reality so that policy could be made within a valid knowledge context. That continues to be the case today.

Although there have always been gradations of rurality, the vastness of the United States and the complexity of modern society make it increasingly impossible to define rural precisely. Indeed, my colleagues and I at USDA's Economic Research Service are frequently called on to assist other agencies to define rural for program purposes. Rural means different things to different people. To public officials in North Dakota, it has to include Slope County, where the total population is a still-dwindling 767, much of the land is in National Grassland and Badlands Parks, a majority of the workforce remains in agriculture, and the county seat of Amidon has all of 26 residents. However, for a USDA rural development office, the definition would encompass the 144,000 rural-by-census-definition residents of metropolitan Worcester County, Massachusetts, the largest of all county rural populations, whose median income greatly exceeds the national average and whose poverty rate is just 3.7 percent. This population may not be of interest to those concerned with rural social issues, but its settlement patterns are central to rural-urban fringe land use questions.

It is not just that rural-urban borders are no longer as discrete as they may have been in the past but that the daily urban systems of rural and urban residents are so enmeshed, whether physically or in communication. In the 2000 Census, the proportion of employed people who live in one county but work in another reached a new high (over 26 percent), as about 5,000 more people each week made inter-county commutes during the previous decade.

Furthermore, because of the decline in employment in all rural extractive industries, almost all growth in nonmetropolitan employment—with the exception of outdoor recreation—has had to come from businesses or functions that were once more urban in character. In recent decades, thousands of white-collar office tasks have spread to small town settings, enabled by advances in telecommunication and computing technology. For instance, if you want to subscribe to *The New Yorker*, you may be an urban sophisticate, but you have to deal with a subscription office in Boone, Iowa. If you have more plebeian tastes and want the *Readers Digest*, you contact Red Oak, Iowa, and if you are just a news junkie, you subscribe to *Newsweek* through Harlan, Iowa. All are nonmetro towns. These subscription offices together employ well over a thousand people but prove to be branches of just one New York City entity, the Hearst Corporation. There are numerous analogous examples in mail-order and electronic shopping, telephone call centers, claims processing, motel reservations, and other customer services. But even this welcome niche now shows distinct strains of competition from foreign outsourcing as firms continue to look for cheaper labor.

The agricultural population plays a supporting, but not a main, role in the chapters presented in this volume, reflecting, I suspect, just how diminished the demographic role of agriculture has become. But even here, changes in the structure of farming continue to be dramatic, further affecting the size of farm units and the number and composition of farm people.

In this connection, a recent event that caught my eye is a social context of the discovery of "mad cow" disease last year that went unmentioned in all the publicity over that matter. The herd of cattle that included the affected animal was brought first to a large dairy enterprise in Mattawa, Washington that boarded the cows. The cow that later proved infected was then sent to a very large dairy at Mabton, in the Yakima Valley, that had 4,000 head. Mattawa and Mabton are both small, incorporated towns, with populations of 2,600 and 1,900, respectively. Ninety percent of the population in each of these highly farm-dependent towns is now Mexican Hispanic. The median age is 22 years (the level of the United States in 1890), only a fourth of adults have been through high school (compared with the national average of 80 percent) and the poverty rate is 34 percent. This clearly speaks of a great social transformation in these communities, a transformation associated with industrial-scale agriculture. Does this suggest that we need to boost our farm labor research, a topic that was very active in the past?

With regard to farm operators, media reports have described substantial infusions of Hmong refugees as producers in the broiler poultry industry of Arkansas and Oklahoma. Other refugees have been documented as new entrants into truck farming around the Twin Cities of Minnesota. I recently learned, to my astonishment, that South Dakota has actively recruited in Europe for dairy farmers to insure enough milk production to supply a very large cheese plant currently under construction. The situation is not static.

In the economic boom of the 1990's, the nonmetro poverty rate declined more than the metro rate. The incidence of poverty is much less than it was a generation ago. But for that reason it seems incongruous that in a time of almost unprecedented prosperity, there were still about 440 nonmetro counties in 2000 where poverty rates exceeded 20 percent. In the great majority of them, low income is rooted in the past and, with minor exceptions, is the product of conditions among Blacks, Hispanics, Native Americans and non-Hispanic Whites of the Southern Highlands. Poverty is still very much a critical rural issue. The most active sense of rural crisis seems to be in the declining Great Plains areas. What will happen to the numerous counties where the age structure is so undercut that deaths regularly exceed births, and thus natural decrease alone will bring future population decline, even in the absence of out-migration?

Yet some nonmetro counties, especially in recreation and retirement areas, are attracting such rapid growth that they could not turn it off if they wanted. So much of rural America with the proper attractiveness has become a playground for our huge urban population, and now a burgeoning wave of retirees looms ahead. In 1943, demographers marveled at the fact that there were 3 million births in that year after the lows of the Great Depression years. In 2003, that cohort became 60, an age by which many people retire and move. Retirement and recreation aside, I continue to be impressed by how frequently informants who reside in nonmetro counties that have rebounded from population loss to growth give non-economic reasons for their growth. They speak of people moving in, even in the absence of job growth, to get away from the cities, often out of concern for their children.

In sum, there may not be anything occurring in rural and small-town America as dramatic as the earlier exodus from farming but there are still many policy-relevant rural demographic issues that need useful research attention. This volume provides a fresh look at various aspects of these topics and at research approaches assessing them.

PART I

INTRODUCTION AND DEMOGRAPHIC CONTEXT

CHAPTER 1

RURAL AMERICA THROUGH A DEMOGRAPHIC LENS

DAVID L. BROWN AND WILLIAM A. KANDEL

INTRODUCTION

Rural people and communities play a critical role in 21st century American society. The 2000 Census revealed that while eight of 10 Americans live in urban areas, the 56 million rural residents who reside in nonmetropolitan counties exceed the total population of all but 22 of the world's 200 plus nation-states (Population Reference Bureau, 2000). As Brown and Swanson (2003, p. 1) have commented, "while rural people comprise a minority of the U.S. population, they are a very large minority indeed." Moreover, this population quintile resides on 80 percent of the nation's territory that contains most of America's farmland, energy resources, water, metals, timber, fisheries, wildlife, and open space.

This book uses a comprehensive perspective to examine dynamic relationships between contemporary population change and rural society along four dimensions: rural society as a cultural and demographic entity; rural economic life and its continued restructuring; rural territory as a contested natural environment; and rural society as a repository of poverty and economic privilege. Because the work that follows focuses on nonmetropolitan demographic change, it seems fitting that this introductory chapter explore the changing nature of rurality as both cultural conception and official definition.

THE MYTH OF RURAL STABILITY

Content and Origins

The term "rural America" typically evokes an image of a stable cultural bedrock, a repository of unchanging structures and values, a buffer against rapid social and economic change occurring elsewhere in society (Rowley, 1996; Willits et al., 1990). Recent ethnographic research illustrates the degree to which new rural in-migrants from urban areas rely upon such conceptions for their migration

W.A. Kandel & D.L. Brown (eds.), Population Change and Rural Society, 3–23.

and settlement decisions (Salamon, 2003). Yet other scholarship suggests a more nuanced perception involving both normative and structural dimensions. While rural norms and values tend to resist change (Beale, 1995), economic and institutional structures have transformed alongside those in urban areas. As Fuguitt and his colleagues (1989, p. 425) demonstrated in their comprehensive examination of rural and small town demography, "the American population has undergone gradual but profound changes in demographic composition, socioeconomic attributes, and residential distribution. These changes have been pervasive, affecting people in rural and small town settings as well as those who live in more highly urbanized and densely settled locales." The "myth of rural stability," then, arises because many Americans conflate the relative stability of norms and values with more structural realms where social and economic change have, in fact, been pervasive.

How can one understand this myth of rural stability? How and when did it originate? Why does it persist? What purpose does it serve? According to agricultural historian David Danbom (1996) popular notions about American rurality developed during the first half of the 19th century when ruralism provided the emerging nation with a cultural identity distinct from England. Rural areas became celebrated for what they *were not*—not urban, not industrial, and most of all, not England. Rurality served as an anti-urban critique that strengthened in inverse relation to America's burgeoning industrialism and urbanization, a counterweight to its own rapid social and economic transformation that characterized urban life during the nation's first century. Danbom's hypothesis coincides with William Howarth's (1996) observation that pastoralism—the idea of agricultural purity—accelerates during periods of rapid social change. His examination of American literary themes argues that periods of rapid progress generate nostalgia and sentimentality in American writing in which writers often portray rural areas as "wells of permanence and stability" that stem fears of cultural loss.

These myths about rurality and rural life persist in our highly urban and suburban nation because while our national identity and separateness from our colonial forebears have long since been settled, the pace of social and economic change has not diminished. Accordingly, people continue to seek symbols that confer a sense of security in the midst of fundamental societal transformations. As Willits and her colleagues (1990) conclude, rurality continues to involve an aura of treasured and almost sacred elements. Their empirical research showed that contemporary Americans perceive rural communities as the antithesis of the modern urban world—more moral, virtuous, and simple.

How do people obtain their knowledge and attitudes about rural people and communities? John Logan (1996) argues that rural life appeals to many because it is generally known only from a distance. Most people acquire knowledge about rural areas through interacting with American culture—art, music, literature, television, theatre, and film—not by living or working there. The disconnect between perceptions of rural life and its increasingly infrequent firsthand experience frees Americans to construct images of rurality that filter out facts related to changing ethnic composition, industrial restructuring, environmental conflict, entrenched poverty, relative underdevelopment, depopulation, and growing economic inequality. Logan concludes that "a large share of what we value is the mythology and symbolism of rural places, rather than their reality" (p. 26). Accordingly, Americans gain a sense of security by perceiving that rural places are stable and unchanging repositories of what we believe has been lost during our nation's urban and industrial transformations. In reality, however, *change, rather than stability, most accurately characterizes rural America*. This volume examines the demographic determinants and consequences of fundamental demographic and economic transformations affecting rural people and communities in the 21st century.

Change in Contemporary Rural America

Compared to urban areas, social and economic change in rural America tends to be relatively long term and gradual (Castle, 1995; Flora et al., 1992; Fuguitt et al., 1989; Hawley & Mazie, 1992). While some changes occur quickly and have rather limited effects, the subject of this book represents fundamental transformations that have far-ranging manifestations on community organization, economic opportunity, and institutional structure. Examples include well-established economic transitions from extractive industries to goods production to service activities, changed concepts of distance resulting from innovations in communication and transportation technology, and alterations in rural land use from gradual metropolitan area expansion.

Some changes affect specific rural or urban environments, while others occur society-wide. For example, natural decrease—the excess of deaths over births resulting from prolonged out-migration of persons of child-bearing age—only affects rural communities in the United States; exceptions aside, most urban areas and their suburbs continue to experience natural increase. In contrast, the expansion of the Internet affects social and economic relationships throughout society. Interestingly, international migration used to have most of its impact in urban areas, but in-migration from South America and Asia is now a society-wide phenomenon. Society-wide changes do not necessarily affect urban and rural communities in the same way. Hispanic population growth will be experienced quite differently in a small, previously ethnically homogeneous rural community than it is in a large multi-ethnic city that has seen historical waves of immigration. Likewise, industrial downsizing will have different impacts in a rural area where one manufacturing plant dominates the local economy compared with a loss of the same number of industrial jobs—in absolute or proportional terms—in an economically diverse metropolitan or nonmetropolitan labor market. In this volume we view such long-term changes in rural society through the vantage point of social demography, a perspective emphasizing interrelationships between population, community, and environment that are inextricably bound in a set of mutually reinforcing relationships.

Rural Population Change in International Perspective

Before we describe the social demographic perspective, we draw some comparisons with the demographic experience of Western Europe, Australia, and other postindustrial nations. As Rodney Stark (2001, p. 556) has observed about these regions: "Industrialization both caused and depended on urbanization. Neither could have occurred without the other." Moreover, the contemporary United States and other highly developed nations share similar urban structures. Power and control are concentrated in a system of nationally and internationally linked metropolises, and people increasingly live and work in suburban hinterlands. Most rural residents no longer work in traditional economic activities linked to natural resources except as they are associated with leisure pursuits, and many rural workers commute to jobs in nearby (and not so nearby) urban labor markets.[1] Hence, although the present volume focuses on the United States, many of our analyses apply to the experiences of other more developed nations.

Perhaps the clearest evidence of this common experience can be gleaned from studies of "counterurbanization" conducted in the United States, Great Britain, and other more developed countries. As Champion (1989), Vining and Kontuly (1978), and others have shown, population losses began to be sustained by large cities in at least 14 western European countries, Japan, and Australia during the 1960s and 1970s, and more rural parts of these nations achieved growth through net in-migration. For most of these countries this reversed a process of continuous urban concentration that commenced during the industrial revolution some 100 years earlier. While the specific factors reducing population deconcentration in particular nations differed, most analysts reported that the redistribution trends were the product of both structural changes in a nation's economic system and non-pecuniary factors that could be characterized in the most general sense as residential preferences for less highly urbanized locations. This research consistently finds that, economic circumstances permitting, a portion of the people who are living in places that differ from their preferred place size tend to move to smaller and more remote locations.[2] In other words, the number of persons moving from urban to rural areas exceeded the reverse flow, resulting in counterurbanization.

Contemporary rural society in the United States and in other more developed nations share many similarities over and above these deconcentration trends that are reflected in this volume's thematic structure. Rural economies have been transformed along similar lines, with dependence on agriculture and extractive industries declining significantly and dependence on service sector employment increasing substantially. Moreover, the types of service jobs represented in rural economies typically consist of relatively low-wage and low-skill positions in personal services, leisure and recreation, and retail trade. High-wage producer services are under represented in rural economies throughout the more developed world.

In all developed nations, rural populations are aging more rapidly than in urban areas, because decades of chronic out-migration by younger persons have produced populations with relatively low fertility and relatively high mortality. In addition, population aging is exacerbated in many rural regions by net in-migration of retirement age persons. Hence, rural aging is often the result of both aging in place and retirement in-migration.

Metropolitan expansion also yields similar impacts on land use in more developed countries, most notably the conversion of agricultural land and open space into built up uses. Many developed nations have stronger traditions of land use controls and more clearly articulated growth management strategies than the United States, yet concern for farm land and open space protection is also more common in these nations. Finally, economic development has been spatially unequal in all of today's more developed nations, and economic disadvantage, poverty, and social exclusion are disproportionately concentrated in rural regions. Moreover, the special needs of the rural poor are seldom considered in national policies focused on ameliorating economic disadvantage (Dalton et al., 2003).

THE SOCIAL DEMOGRAPHIC PERSPECTIVE

"Demography is the study of the size, territorial distribution, and composition of population, changes therein, and components of such changes . . ." (Hauser & Duncan, 1959, p. 31). This classic definition frames much demographic analysis and focuses attention on the so-called "balancing equation," which examines spatio-temporal variation in population change as a function of changes in natality, mortality, and migration. Social demography, in comparison, does not have such a coherent conceptual framework. Rather, as Hauser and Duncan (1959, p. 3) recognized nearly 50 years ago, "population studies [*aka social demography*] is not a single 'theoretical discipline' with a coherent frame of reference of its own. Instead, it is best characterized as an area of substantive inquiry in which any number of frames of reference may be employed."

Social demography was first articulated through a path-breaking and influential United Nations study in 1953, *The Determinants and Consequences of Population Trends*, which emphasized reciprocal relationships between population change and the social and economic environment. In other words, it situated demographic analysis in a multidisciplinary framework where the components of population change affect, and are affected by, changes in social institutions, the natural environment, economic development, culture, and public policy. Consider the example of urbanization, which can be studied as a strictly demographic phenomenon by examining how relative rates of migration and natural increase in urban and rural areas contribute to more rapid population growth in cities than in the countryside (Tisdale, 1942). However, in addition to this strictly demographic analysis, social demographers examine factors that account for the spatio-temporal changes in demographic processes that result in urbanization. This includes how population concentration affects people's life chances, health, and social norms, for instance, and how these changes in turn affect natural increase and the net flow of migration.

In the most general sense, social demography is concerned with the reciprocal association between population and society. Since no single discipline can provide a sufficiently inclusive framework to examine this broad domain, social demography is an inherently multidisciplinary enterprise. Stycos (1987), who referred to demography as an "interdiscipline," observed that by the nature of its subject matter, demography draws heavily on sociology and biology to examine fertility, geography and economics to study migration, and the health sciences to analyze mortality. This volume's examination of the population of rural America adopts the social demographic perspective, deploying a variety of conceptual frameworks and empirical literatures to examine determinants and consequences of population change in rural America at the start of the 21st century.

The Perspective of Rural Demography

Rural demography is a sub-field within social demography, and many of this book's contributors identify as rural demographers. Rural demographers are particularly well known for their research on internal migration, including studies of out-migration from agricultural regions, Black migration from rural communities in the U.S. South, the rural population "turnaround" and its subsequent rebounds and reversals, amenity-based migration, including that of retirees to rural destination communities, and the role of residential preferences in migration decision making (see Beale, 1975; Brown & Wardwell, 1980; Brown et al., 1993; Fuguitt et al., 1989; Hathaway et al., 1968; Jobes et al., 1992; Swanson & Brown, 1993; Wardwell & Copp, 1997). However, rural demography is broader, and recent studies have examined such diverse topics as natural population decrease (Johnson, 1993), gender inequality (Cotter et al., 1996), racial/ethnic outmarriage (Cready & Saenz, 1997), labor market restructuring (Adamchak et al., 1999), economic restructuring and female-headed families (McLaughlin et al., 1999), underemployment (Jensen et al., 1999; Slack & Jensen, 2002), community-level determinants of educational attainment (Isreal et al., 2001), income inequality (McLaughlin, 2002), and the impacts of welfare reform (Lee et al., 2002).

Rural demographic research often highlights spatial issues, reflecting a realization that place affects life chances. Fuguitt and his colleagues (1989) argue that residential differences persist in contemporary American society and that they structure the lives people live and the opportunities available to them. Another hallmark of rural demography is a predilection toward aggregate-level analysis where the intellectual project is to explain inter-area variation in particular phenomena such as migration, poverty, educational attainment, resource utilization, or economic development. Multi-level approaches, however, are becoming more common as rural demographers seek to examine the joint effects of individual or household characteristics, as well as community or labor market contexts, on various aspects of social, demographic, and economic change.

Rural demography has strong ties to human ecology and in particular to the reciprocal link between population change and local community structure (Brown, 2002). However, contemporary rural demographic research is cognizant of human ecology's theoretical shortcomings. For example, rural demographers are critical of the concept of *adaptation*, the process by which organized populations respond to changes in their natural and institutional environments. They critique adaptation as mechanistic, a black box that obscures social relationships and the agency of actors. Hence, they attempt to unpack the adaptation concept and explore the complementary roles played by individual agency and local social and economic structures as determinants of migration, resource utilization, community organization, and other social outcomes of interest to rural people and communities.

Finally, rural demography is an applied, policy-oriented approach to social science. In part, this is because rural demography's institutional home has been in the U.S. Department of Agriculture (USDA) and in the land grant university system. The Division of Farm Population and Rural Life, established in 1919 and located in USDA's Bureau of Agricultural Economics (BEA), was one of the first federal government units established to conduct research on sociological issues (Larson & Zimmerman, 2003; Larson et al., 1992). Although the agency has experienced several incarnations, sociological and demographic research on rural America continues to thrive in the Economic Research Service, a successor agency of the BEA. Rural studies and policy analysis are also an integral part of the research and extension programs conducted by land grant universities. Programs focused on individual and community well-being are specifically recognized in the Hatch Act of 1887 and the Smith-Lever Act of 1914 that support research and extension conducted by land grant universities in cooperation with the USDA. As part of this cooperative research program, the USDA promotes the development of multi-state research committees to examine issues that span state lines. By their very nature population change and redistribution fill this bill. Accordingly, rural demographers have formed a number of USDA-funded multi-state research projects during the last 30 years to conduct cooperative rural population analysis (Wardwell & Copp, 1997). Hence, while rural demographers seek to advance social science knowledge, they are also concerned with producing research-based knowledge that informs rural public policy more broadly.

This edited volume is also a product of the USDA research system. In October 2002, the USDA, through its Cooperative State Research, Education, and Extension Service, approved a five-year, multi-state project for conducting research on population change in rural communities. Initial findings were presented at a 2004 conference in Washington, DC, entitled "Population Change and Rural Society" sponsored by the USDA's Economic Research Service (ERS) and Cornell University. Hence, the volume can be viewed as the latest product of a USDA-land grant university partnership to inform the nation about the size, socioeconomic composition, and distribution of its rural population, and how these demographic changes affect rural America.

WHAT IS MEANT BY RURAL AMERICA?

The Concept of Rurality

The concept of "rural" emerged with industrialization in the late 19th century, and its statistical recasting continues as of this writing. Seminal sociological theorists, including Durkheim, Weber, and Tönnies, dichotomized the two social spheres of rural and urban according to somewhat abstract characteristics they considered critical for making such distinctions, using terms such as social solidarity, rationality, and community connectedness. From this classical tradition, Wirth's (1938) conceptualization of rurality—developed within the context of examining the impacts of urbanization and industrialization on American society—contrasted the socially fluid, impersonal, and compartmentalized social relations of urban areas with those of rural areas that he characterized as stable, integrated, and inflexible. Wirth's conceptualization remains influential in contemporary sociological research and consistent with popular images of rurality.

Social phenomena can rarely be adequately explained using polarized types. Moreover, social transformations from rapid U.S. urbanization beginning in the 1930s cast Wirth's "urbanism as a way of life" into doubt (Friedland, 2002). Shortly thereafter, Redfield (1941, 1947) expressed a widely held realization that such dichotomies could not properly characterize the distinction between rural and urban societies, and he promoted the concept of a rural-urban continuum. This characterization has been empirically supported by some scholars (Duncan & Reiss, 1976; Frankenberg, 1966) and refuted by others (Newby, 1986; Pahl, 1966).

With technological change, industrial transformation, population growth, and demographic and economic expansion into suburbs and exurbs, it became increasingly important to revise formal definitions of rural space in order to track urbanization and rural population change accurately. Debate over the nature of rurality continues among rural sociologists attempting to demarcate the boundaries and agendas of their subdiscipline (DuPuis & Vandergeest, 1996; Farmer, 1997). Within other disciplines, geographers continue their attempts to delimit economic and social space (Morrill et al., 1999), and policy analysts are entrusted with the task of providing definitions with clear fiscal, legal, and political implications at all levels of government (Butler & Beale, 1994; Cook & Mizer, 1994).

While the term "rural" has an intuitive meaning replete with pastoral imagery, few definitions can fulfill most or all requirements of researchers, program managers, and policy analysts who rely upon them. Halfacree's (1993) extensive review of such attempts allocates 34 descriptive and analytical rural definitions produced between 1946 and 1987 into six categories: statistical, administrative, built-up area, functional regions, agricultural, and population size/density. All are critiqued for different reasons, including historical relativism, lack of robustness, data quality and methodology, geographic scale, and lack of qualitative context. Halfacree concludes that these definitions' narrow functions limit their usefulness as broader delineations of rurality. Moreover, judging from the international origins of the definitions Halfacree reviewed, it is clear that no international consensus on the definition of rural currently exists.

The span between rural stereotypes and rural realities has as much to do with "symbolic landscapes" of economic activity as it does with the dichotomous social relations noted above (Logan, 1996; Willits et al., 1990). The first characteristic that comes to mind for most people when they consider rural America is agriculture, not surprisingly, because agricultural land is its most visible and salient physical characteristic. What does not come to mind are manufacturing plants, distribution centers, jails, solid waste facilities, retirement communities, or, for that matter, large scale agriculture as currently practiced. What also has failed to take hold in the public consciousness since the end of World War II is that agriculture and other extractive activities account for a minor portion of all *nonmetropolitan* county employment; current figures range from 8 to 15 percent, depending on what activities are included in this industrial sector.

Perpetuation of agrarian rural stereotypes may benefit some groups more than others. Recent public policies, such as the phasing out of estate taxes beginning in 2001 and the passage of the Farm Security and Rural Investment Act of 2002, relied in part on images of small farm America. Such imagery, however, does not accurately reflect the organization of agriculture in contemporary America. Rural (and urban) America now possess what is essentially a dual farm structure, divided between 85 percent of smaller farm owners who rely on off-farm earnings for most of their family income and the remaining 15 percent of agri-businesses that produce 80 percent of all agricultural wealth (Mishra et al., 2002; Rural Policy Research Institute, 1995). The latter group, composed of corporations and farm interests, receives far more political attention than most other rural constituencies. Non-farm interest groups that focus on environmental issues, worker and food safety, sustainable agriculture, and rural development have become increasingly vocal yet often lack the ability to politically mobilize sizable numbers of diverse constituents (Stauber, 2001).

Official Statistical Definitions of Rural

How is "rural" defined in U.S. federal statistics? Although different states may construct their own classifications, such as those used for categorizing school districts, highways, and counties, the production of a universal definition of rural is a national responsibility. This is because federal statistical analysis requires comparability across state lines, and universalistic standards are required for program administration and the geographic targeting of federal assistance. Two official definitions predominate currently. The first consists of all *nonmetropolitan counties* as specified by the Office of Management and Budget (2000). The second consists of *rural areas*, or the residual territory that follows from the Census Bureau's delineation of urban areas (U.S. Department of Commerce, 2002). Both terms are defined as residual counties or territory *left behind* after metropolitan counties or urban areas have been defined according to minimum population and geographic thresholds.

These parallel definitions have yielded somewhat different estimates of rural population over time, but most current research favors the OMB county-based definition of nonmetropolitan areas because of its compatibility with other county-based sources of data and because county geography is relatively consistent from one decennial census to the next. Hence, nonmetropolitan counties lend themselves more readily to longitudinal analysis than rural areas, which are more likely to change over time. Finally, it should be recognized that the rural/urban and metropolitan/nonmetropolitan categorizations do not describe mutually exclusive territory. In fact, by 2000 almost half of all census-defined "rural" residents lived in OMB-defined "metropolitan" counties, while one third of "metropolitan" residents lived in "rural" areas (Brown & Cromartie, 2003; Brown et al., 2004).

The Census Bureau's urban-rural classification system emerged at the beginning of the 20th century as rapid industrialization and urbanization occurred throughout the nation, and it has been revised repeatedly ever since. In 1990, the Census Bureau defined "urban" either as places situated outside of urbanized areas that contained at least 2,500 persons or as urbanized areas containing a central place and its contiguous census block groups that together included at least 50,000 persons and a population density of at least 1,000 persons per square mile. This definition of urban appropriately captured the population extending beyond the borders of incorporated cities, but it did not adequately capture similar population density located farther away, since the population density requirement excluded many less densely populated areas that were situated apart from cities but had clear ties to them.

The revised 2000 Census Bureau definition has addressed this issue. As in 1990, it classifies rural as residual territory, population, and housing not located in "urban" territory. Urban, however, now consists of formal urban areas (UAs) or urban clusters (UCs), defined as contiguous census blocks encompassing populations of over 50,000, and between 2,500 and 50,000, respectively. The Bureau defines UAs and UCs using a geographic sequencing algorithm applied to its geographic TIGER file data, which initially selects a core with population density of at least 1,000 persons per square mile and extends through continuous blocks that possess densities exceeding 500. In some cases, less densely populated areas may also be included. Because the new 2000 definitions are based on census blocks—the smallest official geographic units—they ignore geographic boundaries such as census tracts, places, counties, and metropolitan areas. Large but sparsely populated places with populations over 2,500, previously classified as urban, may now possess urban and rural populations, thereby more accurately reflecting their precise character.

Regardless of these improvements, the OMB county-based definition of metropolitan and nonmetropolitan areas is more frequently used than its urban-rural counterpart. Established in 1950 and revised in each succeeding decade, the regulation defines nonmetropolitan counties as the residual of the 3,141 counties which are not metropolitan, meaning they contain neither cities of over 50,000 residents, nor urbanized areas of over 100,000 residents, nor counties integrated economically with the former.

To the extent such definitions become publicly contentious, they do so not for cities and metropolitan areas, where definitions and urban character coincide, but for adjacent and surrounding counties. The 1990 OMB definitions assigned such counties to metropolitan status based on commuting patterns and "metropolitan character." The former could be as low as 15 percent of employed workers commuting to a metropolitan county, as long as the latter—comprising population density, percentage of urban population, and population growth rate—compensated to produce a sufficiently metropolitan county. Five different combinations of commuting and settlement structure qualified counties as metropolitan. Although revisions to the OMB definition are conducted with public input, they invariably arouse negative responses from counties and regions that object to outcomes that assign their county into an undesired metropolitan category or a particular statistical area. The 1990 definitions of metropolitan and nonmetropolitan were also heavily criticized for their complexity regarding the status of counties surrounding metropolitan areas.

In response to these critiques, the OMB produced a new core-based statistical area (CBSA) system for 2000, which represents a significant improvement over the previous set of definitions. A CBSA consists of the county or counties possessing one or more cores of 10,000 or more persons along with adjacent counties that are heavily integrated socially and economically, as measured by commuting ties. As in previous decades, CBSAs are defined as metropolitan statistical areas if they have more than 50,000 persons. In addition, they also comprise a new category, micropolitan statistical areas, which have between 10,000 and 50,000 persons. Both micropolitan areas and the undifferentiated residual designated as "Outside Core Based Statistical Areas" make up what in 1990 were grouped as nonmetropolitan counties.

The revised metro county definition for 2000 primarily affects surrounding counties because it contains only a commuting threshold of 25 percent and no further stipulations. In the case of metropolitan counties, less complex definitions have produced categories that increasingly reflect labor market activity. The 2000 definition increases the ranks of metropolitan counties by approximately 100 counties with strong commuting patterns but with visual landscapes that most persons would characterize as rural. Georgia's Lowndes County exemplifies this situation. It consists of a relatively small metropolitan county, population 92,200, whose surrounding Echols, Lanier, and Brooks Counties do indeed have 25 percent of their employed populations working in Lowndes County, but which to most observers look unmistakably rural.

While this new core-based system significantly improves the earlier set of definitions, some researchers believe that it continues to suffer from using counties as the unit of analysis. If county boundaries were determined according to uniform criteria, such as size, population density, or total population, the OMB metro/nonmetro dichotomy would have more practical relevance to what is experienced, or thought of, as rural or urban. However, counties vary significantly in size and population, and their historical evolution has more to do with urban population growth and local politics than with the proper characterization of rural and urban landscapes, functions, or other systematic criteria (Morrill et al., 1999). Yet the OMB definition continues to categorize territory according to population and commuting patterns and fails to take into account social, economic, institutional, and cultural dimensions used to characterize and differentiate human settlement in either rural or urban areas (Brown & Cromartie, 2003).

In recent decades, the USDA's ERS has created a series of typologies to examine diversity within the nonmetropolitan category. The Rural-Urban Continuum Codes (Butler & Beale, 1994), for example, reflect distinctions among nonmetropolitan counties that are adjacent to large metropolitan counties, possess sizable urban places themselves, or are unambiguously rural. Another series of ERS economic and policy typologies distinguishes among counties dependent upon farming, mining, manufacturing, government, and service employment, as well as those characterized by housing stress, low education, persistent population loss, and retirement settlement (Economic Research Service, 2004).

Clearly, the current systems devised by both the OMB and the Census Bureau do not adequately account for the enormous variety of rural areas. On the basis of population and commuting patterns, for example, one can assemble groups of nonmetropolitan counties that economically, socially, politically, or even visually have virtually nothing in common with one another. While it is not practical (or desirable) to have a separate category for every kind of rural area, the ERS typologies allow researchers and policy analysts to aggregate areas into categories that recognize the main dimensions of rural diversity and that relate to particular public responsibilities and substantive concerns. Failure to account for rural diversity contributes to the political fragmentation described above, and it limits government's ability to target state and federal programs accurately and for maximum effectiveness.

Despite the shortcomings of OMB and Census definitions of rural and urban areas, alternative geographic options may not always yield the best analytic results possible for many practical research purposes. Tolbert and colleagues (2002), for instance, compared the utility of places, minor civil divisions, census county divisions, and census tracts with that of the current OMB county-based classification. Evaluating these units of analysis on the basis of data accessibility, scope of spatial coverage, and applicability for longitudinal analysis, the authors concluded that counties actually present fewer problems than most other geographies.

Conventions Used in this Volume

We wish to emphasize to the reader that throughout this volume, the authors frequently use the terms "nonmetro" or "nonmetropolitan" and "rural" interchangeably.[3] However, unless otherwise specified, use of the term "rural" in this volume always refers to OMB-defined nonmetropolitan counties and not to Census-defined rural areas. We apply this convention so that we may have some flexibility with the language.

We have also chosen to apply the 1990 OMB county-level definition of nonmetropolitan status. Given the extent to which the 1990 and 2000 definitions differ, a choice was necessary to make all chapters consistent. Had our primary charge been to describe and explain current conditions, we would have applied the most recent metro area definition and focused on cross-sectional analysis of the 2000 census data. However, this monograph stresses change over time—particularly what transpired during the 1990s—which supports using a start-of-period definition. Ideally, we might have used both definitions, because the change from nonmetro to metro status is itself an important measure of urbanization, and a critical component of rural and urban change (Fuguitt et al., 1988). Unfortunately, as of this writing, no "bridge" exists to connect past classifications with the new metro/micro classification as well as with new definitions of urbanized areas and urban clusters, which determine the core counties of metro and micro areas, respectively. Hence, for most chapters in the book, "rural" consists of the set of nonmetro counties as defined in June 1993.

ORGANIZATION OF THIS VOLUME

Although many aspects of rural organization affect and are affected by changes in rural population size and composition, we consider four aspects of social and economic change that we consider particularly salient at this time in the nation's history. We selected these features of population-society interaction because each is linked with critical social policy domains that affect rural people and communities. Clearly, these four issue areas do not exhaust the list of problems and opportunities facing rural society, but we contend that the issues we have identified are widely recognized as high priority concerns as rural society enters the 21st century. We summarize these four elements as distinct yet interrelated research questions, each of which forms a major theme of this book:

What characterizes the population of rural America at the start of the 21st century? In focusing our attention on changing rural population size and composition, we emphasize determinants of differential population growth in varying rural contexts, as well as causes and outcomes of changes in the rural population's race, ethnic, age, and gender compositions.

How have rural livelihoods changed, particularly in the past two decades? This question addresses how rural employment has been affected by economic and political globalization, changes in national and international policies, technology, and new forms of economic organization.

Where do rural Americans live, and how do their activities affect the natural, built, and institutional environments? We focus attention on the social and physical spaces where population and the environment intersect, emphasizing urban expansion into previously rural territory, rural tourism, the siting of infrastructure, and other forms of rural development that create contestation over land use and political conflicts among competing interests.

How well-off are rural Americans, and how does their well-being vary across different geographic regions and demographic groups? This question examines why some rural places have prospered in the past several decades while others remain chronically disadvantaged. One of rural America's central ironies is that new forms of development have emerged in some areas that possess characteristics not entirely distinct from other areas plagued perpetually by distress and disenfranchisement.

Our book presents two kinds of analyses: national-level examinations of each of the four critical themes, and case studies that highlight how such themes play out in particular regions of the United States. In selecting topics and regions, we strove for geographic and thematic diversity. Consequently, our volume examines topics on social and structural change for virtually all regions of the country. Contributors have produced original analyses in their own areas of expertise but with the caveat that such work reflects a social demographic perspective. Earlier in this chapter, we discussed prevalent myths and stereotypes of rurality and rural stability that are critically addressed and, in the course of analysis, often debunked in the following chapters.

Thematic Chapters

Johnson and Cromartie (Chapter 2) provide the demographic context for our volume. They examine changes in rates of natural increase and net migration since 1950 to provide a detailed region-specific picture of recent population redistribution trends and their determinants in nonmetropolitan America. Their analysis demonstrates that rural population growth resulted primarily from urban-rural migration during the past three decades, implying that the demographic future of nonmetropolitan America increasingly depends on social, economic, and political factors that integrate rural America into a larger national and international system.

The next two chapters emphasize this linkage between nonmetro areas and the nation as a whole. In their discussion of shifts in rural demographic composition, Kirschner, Berry, and Glasgow (Chapter 3) document both the rapid population aging and growing ethnic diversity of nonmetro America. One major policy implication of these two trends is that a relatively young, heavily Latino immigrant workforce will play an increasingly important economic and social role amid a retirement-age non-minority population. The very processes of globalization and economic restructuring that are profoundly affecting rural livelihoods also foster international migration that contributes to such ethnic change in rural areas. Vias and Nelson (Chapter 4) describe how increasing economic competition from abroad, as well as sectoral employment shifts in the United States, means that fewer than one in ten people living in rural areas still have farming-related jobs. Moreover, while prospects for local economic development remain uncertain, processes beyond the control of local officials, such as exchange rate volatility and the persistent erosion of service sector employment wages, are likely to determine the fate of rural economies in the coming decades.

Nationally, as metropolitan areas expand, the "rural/urban fringes" that connect metro and nonmetro counties become increasingly contested spaces where urban development and environmental preservation compete. Pfeffer, Francis, and Ross (Chapter 5) evaluate the link between changes in farmland utilization since the mid-century and metropolitan status, population change, and the declining number of farms. They show that farm loss in metropolitan counties typically results in farmland conversion, while the declining number of nonmetropolitan farms does not produce a loss of farmland because of farm consolidation.

While these demographic pressures imply that some rural areas are being bolstered by the economic benefits of exurban-urban commuters, retirement migration, and natural-amenity-related growth, many persistently poor counties throughout rural America remain uninfluenced by such developments. Jensen, Goetz, and Swaminathan (Chapter 6) examine the book's fourth theme—persisting rural poverty in the midst of affluence. They examine changes in poverty rates during the unusually long economic expansion of the 1990s and find that persistent poverty remains both spatially clustered and concentrated among rural minority populations. Social and economic forces improving well-being in other nonmetro areas have not alleviated long term entrenched disadvantage in these areas. These five overview chapters provide the foundation for the geographically diverse set of case studies that follows.

Case Studies

Changing Population Composition

Kandel and Parrado, and Glasgow and Brown address two salient nonmetro demographic trends: increasing ethnic diversity and aging, respectively. Kandel and Parrado (Chapter 7) document how numerous public policy implications of rapid rural Hispanic population growth stem from differences in age composition between non-Hispanic Whites, the dominant racial and ethnic category of nonmetro America outside of the south, and the relatively small but rapidly growing Hispanic population. Their analysis distinguishes between established and recent nonmetro Hispanic settlement to highlight Latino population growth in the South and Midwest and its implications for social integration of this rapid, and largely unexpected, demographic influx. In contrast, Glasgow and Brown (Chapter 8) show that elderly in-migrants to rural retirement destinations have levels of social integration comparable to longer-term older residents despite their recent arrival. Moreover, their research indicates that retiree in-migrants have almost as many children and other relatives close by as older persons who have lived in the retirement destinations for a longer period of time. This bodes well for elderly involvement and well-being in new rural communities and bolsters the argument for rural development policies aimed at attracting retirees.

Employment and Economic Restructuring

Johnson and Rathge (Chapter 9) focus on how increasing agricultural productivity and declining natural increase in the Northern Great Plains exert enormous pressure on local labor markets and social service provision in the region. Some rural localities have responded with alternative economic development strategies, including gaming, an approach yielding mixed results. Using a case study of the Nez Perce reservation in Idaho, for example, Rudzitis (Chapter 10) documents the uneven distribution of economic benefits resulting from opening and operating casinos in opposition to state government mandates.

Land Use and Settlement Structure

The economic prosperity of the 1990s had pronounced effects on the demand for rural land, particularly in the Intermountain West, which witnessed some of the most dramatic population increases in the United States. Conventional approaches to understanding these changes argue that the "Old West" of ranchers, miners, and loggers is being transformed into a "New West" of amenity-migrants, retirees, and tourists. Jackson-Smith, Jensen, and Jennings (Chapter 11) examine impacts of nonmetropolitan demographic changes in the region on patterns of rural land use, with a particular emphasis on agriculture, and they find remarkably little overlap between these two county profiles. Their results suggest that in some areas of the Intermountain West, amenity migration may not conflict with agriculture and other traditional rural land uses as much as expected. However, in areas of the region with greater population density, demographic change may have more invasive effects on nonmetro counties. Stedman, Goetz, and Weagraff (Chapter 12) tackle another rural land use issue by analyzing how seasonal home ownership in the Northeast influences resource-based employment and civic participation of newcomers. Their findings suggest a mixed prognosis for maintaining a quality of life associated with rural culture. Similarly, in the third chapter in this section, Hammer and Winkler (Chapter 13) explore the impact of recreational development on housing affordability and competition in the increasingly developing northern Midwest. They find that such development has deleterious effects on the housing market for low and moderate income residents, but given the fact that this result stems from economic growth rather than stagnation or decline, they also offer several policy prescriptions rooted in planned growth strategy as well as homeownership. The final chapter in this section focuses on the impact of metro expansion on nonmetro growth and economic change in the South. Cromartie's analysis of commuting and net migration change on the metro periphery (Chapter 14) characterizes economic development as an unplanned form of infiltration occurring through a series of stages: increased commuting, gradual suburbanization, and eventual full integration into the metro sphere. The study implies considerable variation at each stage of rural land use change, varying levels of social conflict, a variety of economic benefits and costs of rural commuting, and environmental concerns associated with unmanaged growth.

New Opportunities and Persistent Disadvantage

Population growth in nonmetro areas often corresponds with natural amenity environments, yet the implications of amenity-based growth for social and community well-being have received little systematic research. Krannich, Petrzelka, and Brehm's comparative case study of four distinct Utah localities (Chapter 15) illustrates how community satisfaction, social integration, community participation, and attitudes toward development among both newcomers and longer term residents vary according to the degree of amenity-based growth. These researchers caution against typical generalizations made regarding rural development and social disintegration, even for communities in the same region. Their findings reinforce the value of collaborative processes and broad-based engagement in community planning and decision making for ameliorating the more salient negative impacts of amenity-based growth. Von Reichert (Chapter 16), on the other hand, explores resident satisfaction in the Northern Great Plains, a region of persistent population loss since the 1950s. Her analysis of dissatisfaction with social relations in the Northern Great Plains suggests that the social fabric is being tested in a region long known for strong community ties. Her results suggest that disillusionment with the social climate actually ranks higher than dissatisfaction with the harsh natural climate typically perceived as the region's main disadvantage. Policy implications from her work include paying greater attention to non-economic strategies, such as fostering qualities of respect, tolerance, neighborliness, political fairness, and inclusion for the vital populations of newcomers and young people.

Despite extended economic growth and its correlated real estate boom throughout most regions of the country, a significant number of rural regions continue to experience pervasive and protracted levels of poverty. Mannion and Billings (Chapter 17) question the efficacy of federal economic development efforts of the past thirty years by analyzing measures of income convergence and inequality in Appalachia, one of the regions most often associated with persistent rural poverty. Their analysis of economic indicators for the region over the past three decades argues for continued federal involvement and income maintenance for rural counties, and calls into question the ability of market forces alone to alleviate rural-urban poverty and income differentials. Lee and Singlemann's analysis (Chapter 18) follows this research theme south to the Mississippi Delta, another classic setting of protracted rural inequality. They examine impacts of the 1996 federal welfare reform legislation (PRWORA) on welfare caseload and employment outcomes for selected nonmetro and metro parishes in northeastern Louisiana. They find surprisingly little difference in employment outcomes for metro and nonmetro welfare leavers and contend that concerns about rural disadvantage associated with PRWORA may be exaggerated.

Methodology and Policy

The volume concludes with a methodological chapter and a chapter that explores policy implications of demographic change for rural areas. The case studies presented in this volume often describe social processes that are embedded within a spatial context, a focus that, according to Voss, Hammer, and Curtis-White (Chapter 19), has attracted the attention of the scholarly community after decades micro-demographic dominance. The authors review the role of geography within demography during the past century and describe recent methodological advancements, including ways of bridging the chasm between macro- and micro-demography through multilevel models. Special attention is given to spatial autocorrelation, a key violation of the standard regression model, which the authors illustrate by modeling county-level population change in the Great Plains. Whitener (Chapter 20) concludes this volume by outlining a series of public policy issues gleaned from the studies presented, and emphasizes how knowledge of the volume's four critical themes of demographic and socioeconomic change can help to shape the policy agenda for rural America.

This volume contributes original research to scholarly disciplines concerned with spatial and particularly rural issues, and provides a comprehensive picture of an ever-changing rural population. By applying a social demographic perspective, it demonstrates how demographic changes affect a number of policy domains. The various chapters not only contribute to understanding rural residents in their own right, but they also illuminate the association between rural fortunes and metropolitan growth and decline as well as links to globalization processes that are integrating rural peripheries with metropolitan centers in the United States and throughout the world.

ENDNOTES

1. While the American experience and that of western Europe have much in common, this mutually interdependent process is not being replicated currently in many developing nations where rapid urbanization occurs in the absence of industrial growth.

2. Research on residential preferences indicates that the vast majority of persons reside in places consistent with their preferences, but persons whose size of place of residence differs from their preferred size are twice as likely to prefer a smaller rather than a larger place (Brown et al., 1997).
3. Similarly, the terms metropolitan, metro, and urban are used interchangeably in this volume.

REFERENCES

Adamchak, D., Bloomquist, L., Bausman, K., & Qureshi, R. (1999). Consequences of population change for retail/wholesale sector employment in the nonmetropolitan Great Plains, 1950–1996. *Rural Sociology, 64*(1), 92–112.

Beale, C.L. (1975). *The revival of population growth in non-metropolitan America* (ERS Report 605). Washington, DC: U.S. Department of Agriculture, Economic Research Service.

Beale, C.L. (1995). *Non-economic value of rural America.* Paper presented at the USDA experts workshop on the Value of Rural America, Washington, DC.

Brown, D.L. (2002). Migration and community: Social networks in a multilevel world. *Rural Sociology, 76*(1), 1–23.

Brown, D.L., & Cromartie, J. (2003). The nature of rurality in postindustrial society. In T. Champion & G. Hugo (Eds.), *New forms of urbanization: Beyond the urban-rural dichotomy* (pp. 269–284). Aldershot, England: Ashgate Publishers.

Brown, D.L., Cromartie, J., & Kulcsar, L.J. (2004). Micropolitan areas and the measurement of American urbanization. *Population Research and Policy Review, 23*, 399–418.

Brown, D.L., Field, D., & Zuiches, J.J. (Eds.). (1993). *The demography of rural America.* University Park, PA: Northeast Regional Center for Rural Development.

Brown, D.L., Fuguitt, G.V., & Waseem, S. (1997). Continuities in size of place preferences in the United States, 1972–1992. *Rural Sociology, 62*(4), 408–428.

Brown, D.L., & Swanson, L.E. (2003). Rural America enters the new millennium. In D. L. Brown & L. E. Swanson (Eds.), *Challenges for rural America in the 21st century* (pp. 1–15). University Park, PA: Penn State University Press.

Brown, D.L., & Wardwell, J.M. (Eds.). (1980). *New directions in urban-rural migration: The population turnaround in rural America.* New York: Academic Press.

Butler, M.A., & Beale, C.L. (1994). *Rural-urban continuum codes for metropolitan and nonmetropolitan counties, 1993* (Staff Report No. 9425). Washington, DC: U.S. Department of Agriculture, Economic Research Service.

Castle, E.N. (1995). *The changing American countryside.* Manhattan: University Press of Kansas.

Champion, A.G. (1989). *Counterurbanization.* London: Edward Arnold.

Cook, P.J., & Mizer, K.L. (1994). *The revised ERS county typology* (Rural Development Research Report No. 89). Washington, DC: U.S. Department of Agriculture, Economic Research Service.

Cotter, D., Defiore, J., Hermsen, J., Marsteller Kowalewski, B., & Vanneman, R. (1996). Gender inequality in metropolitan and nonmetropolitan areas. *Rural Sociology, 61*(2), 272–288.

Cready, C., & Saenz, R. (1997). The nonmetropolitan context of racial/ethnic outmarriage: Some differences between African Americans and Mexican Americans. *Rural Sociology, 62*(3), 335–362.

Dalton, G., Bryden, J., Shucksmith, M., & Thompson, K. (2003). *European rural policy at the crossroads.* Aberdeen, Scotland: Arkelton Institute.

Danbom, D.B. (1996). Why American's value rural life. *Rural Development Perspectives, 12*(1), 19–23.

Duncan, O., & Reiss, A. (1976). *Social characteristics of rural and urban communities 1950*. New York: Russell and Russell.

DuPuis, E.M., & Vandergeest, P. (Eds.). (1996). *Creating the countryside: The politics of rural and environmental discourse*. Philadelphia: Temple University Press.

Economic Research Service, U.S. Department of Agriculture. (2004). *Briefing room: measuring rurality: 2004 county typology codes*. Retrieved February 2005, from http://www.ers.usda.gov/Briefing/Rurality/Typology/

Farmer, F. L. (1997). The conceptualization and measurement of rural. In *Encyclopedia of rural America* (pp. 623–626). Santa Barbara, CA: ABC-CLIO.

Flora, C., Flora, J., Spears, J., & Swanson, L. (1992). *Rural communities: Legacy and change*. Boulder, CO: Westview Press.

Frankenberg, R. (1966). *Communities in Britain*. Harmondsworth, England: Penguin.

Friedland, W.H. (2002). Agriculture and rurality: Beginning the 'final separation?' *Rural Sociology, 67*(3), 350–371.

Fuguitt, G.V., Brown, D.L., & Beale, C.L. (1989). *Rural and small town America*. New York: Sage.

Fuguitt, G.V., Heaton, T.B., &. Lichter, D.T. (1988). Monitoring the metropolitanization process. *Demography, 25*(1), 115–128.

Halfacree, K.H. (1993). Locality and social representation: Space, discourse, and alternative definitions of the rural. *Journal of Rural Studies, 9*(1), 23–37.

Hathaway, D.E., Beegle, J.A., & Bryant, W.K. (1968). *People of rural America*. Washington, DC: U.S. Bureau of the Census.

Hauser, P., & Duncan, O.D. (1959). The nature of demography. In P. Hauser & O. D. Duncan (Eds.), *The study of population* (pp. 29–44). Chicago, IL: University of Chicago Press.

Hawley, A.H., & Mazie, S.M. (1992). *Nonmetropolitan America in transition*. Chapel Hill: University of North Carolina Press.

Howarth, W. (1996). The value of rural life in American culture. *Rural Development Perspectives, 12*(1), 6–12.

Isreal, G., Beaulieu, L., & Hartless, G. (2001). The influence of family and community social capital on educational achievement. *Rural Sociology, 66*(1), 43–68.

Jensen, L., Findeis, J., Hsu, W.L., & Schacter, J. (1999). Slipping into and out of underemployment: Another disadvantage for nonmetropolitan workers? *Rural Sociology, 64*(3), 417–438.

Jobes, P.C., Stinner, W.F., & Wardwell, J.M. (Eds.). (1992). *Community, society, and migration: Noneconomic migration in America*. Lanham, MD: University Press of America.

Johnson, K.M. (1993). When deaths exceed births: Natural decrease in the United States. *International Regional Science Review, 15*, 179–198.

Larson, O., Moe, E., & Zimmerman, J. (1992). *Sociology in government*. Boulder, CO: Westview Press.

Larson, O., & Zimmerman, J. (2003). *Sociology in government: The Galpin Taylor years in the U.S. Department of Agriculture, 1919–1953*. University Park, PA: Penn State University Press.

Lee, M., Henry, M., & Neustrom, A. (2002). Local labor markets and case load decline in Louisiana in the 1990s. *Rural Sociology, 67*(4), 556–577.

Logan, J. (1996). Rural America as a symbol of American values. *Rural Development Perspectives, 12*(1), 24–28.

McLaughlin, D. (2002). Changing income inequality in nonmetropolitan counties, 1980 to 1990. *Rural Sociology, 67*(4), 512–533.

McLaughlin, D., Gardner, E., & Lichter, D. (1999). Economic restructuring and the changing prevalence of female-headed families in America. *Rural Sociology, 64*(3), 394–416.

Mishra, A.K., El-Osta, H.S., Morehart, M.J., Johnson, J.D., & Hopkins, J.W. (2002). *Income, wealth, and the economic well-being of farm households* (AER-812). Washington, DC: U.S. Department of Agriculture, Economic Research Service.

Morrill, R., Cromartie, J., & Hart, G. (1999). Metropolitan, urban, and rural commuting areas: Toward a better depiction of the United States settlement system. *Urban Geography, 20*(8), 727–748.

Newby, H. (1986). Locality and rurality: The restructuring of rural social relations. *Regional Studies, 20*, 209–215.

Office of Management and Budget. (2000). Standards for defining metropolitan and micropolitan statistical areas; notice. *Federal Register, 65*(249), 82228–82238.

Pahl, R.E. (1966). The rural-urban continuum. *Sociologia Ruralis, 6*, 299–327.

Population Reference Bureau. (2000). *1999 world population data sheet*. Washington, DC: Author.

Redfield, R. (1941). *The folk culture of Yucatan*. Chicago, IL: University of Chicago Press.

Redfield, R. (1947). The folk society. *American Journal of Sociology, 52*, 294–308.

Rowley, T. (1996). The value of rural America. *Rural Development Perspectives, 12*(1), 2–5.

Rural Policy Research Institute. (1995). *Opportunities for rural policy reform: Lessons learned from recent farm bills*. Retrieved June 2, 2003, from http://www.rupri.org/pubs/archive/old/rupolicy/P95-2.html

Salamon, S. (2003). *Newcomers to old towns: Suburbanization of the heartland*. Chicago, IL: University of Chicago Press.

Slack, T., & Jensen, L. (2002). Race, ethnicity and underemployment in nonmetropolitan America: A 30 year profile. *Rural Sociology, 67*(2), 208–233.

Stark, R. (2001). *Sociology*. Belmont, CA: Wadsworth.

Stauber, K. (2001). Why invest in rural America—And how? A critical public policy question for the 21st century. *Economic Review, 86*(2), 33–63.

Stycos, J.M. (1987). Demography as an interdiscipline. *Sociological Forum, 2*(4), 616–617.

Swanson, L., & Brown, D.L. (Eds.). (1993). *Population change and the future of rural America: A conference proceedings* (Staff Report AGES 9324). Washington, DC: U.S. Department of Agriculture, Economic Research Service.

Tisdale, H. (1942). The process of urbanization. *Social Forces, 20*, 311–316.

Tolbert, C., Blanchard, T., & Nucci, A. (2002, November). *The plausibility of place and other sub-county typologies*. Paper presented at the Economic Research Service conference on Measuring Rural Diversity, Washington, DC.

United Nations. (1953). *The determinants and consequences of population trends* (Population Studies No. 17). New York: United Nations Population Division.

U.S. Department of Commerce, Bureau of the Census. (2002). Urban area criteria for census 2000. *Federal Register, 67*(51), 11663–11670.

Vining, D., & Kontuly, T. (1978). Population dispersal from major metropolitan regions: An international comparison. *International Regional Science Review, 3*, 182.

Wardwell, J., & Copp, J. (1997). *Population change in the rural west*. Washington, DC: University Press of America.

Willits, F., Bealer, R., & Timbers, V. (1990). Popular images of rurality: Data from a Pennsylvania survey. *Rural Sociology, 55*(4), 559–578.

Wirth, L. (1938). Urbanism as a way of life. *American Journal of Sociology, 44*, 1–24.

CHAPTER 2

THE RURAL REBOUND AND ITS AFTERMATH

Changing Demographic Dynamics and Regional Contrasts

KENNETH M. JOHNSON[1] AND JOHN B. CROMARTIE

INTRODUCTION

Data from the 2000 Census confirm that the 1990s were a period of renewed growth in rural America. Nonmetropolitan areas gained more than 5 million residents during the period, compared with less than 1.3 million during the 1980s. This "rural rebound" was fueled primarily by migration. Most migrants came from metropolitan areas, but rural areas also receive some immigrants from abroad. These widespread population gains represent yet another twist in the complex pattern of demographic change in rural America during the latter half of the 20th century. Population redistribution trends in the U.S. during this period were extremely fluid.

Through most of the 20th century, nonmetropolitan (nonmetro) areas experienced modest population growth because the excess of births over deaths was sufficient to offset migration losses. The magnitude of the migration loss varied from decade to decade but the pattern was quite consistent: more people left rural areas than came to them. This changed abruptly in the 1970s when rural America experienced a remarkable demographic turnaround, with population gains in nonmetropolitan areas exceeding those in metropolitan areas for the first time in at least 150 years. The rural turnaround appeared to wane in the 1980s as widespread out migration and population decline reemerged. Rural demographic trends rebounded again in the 1990s. However, recent findings suggest that the rebound diminished in the late 1990s, adding yet another twist to the complex pattern of population change in rural America (Beale, 2000; Cromartie, 2001; Johnson, 2000).

Research on nonmetropolitan demographic trends suggests that a process of selective deconcentration is occurring in the U.S., continuing a trend first evident during the nonmetropolitan turnaround of the 1970s (Frey & Johnson, 1998; Long & Nucci, 1997). Selective deconcentration refers to the spatial unevenness of rural population growth. Rural America is a big place, encompassing over 75 percent of the land area of the United States and 56 million people. Population

W.A. Kandel & D.L. Brown (eds.), Population Change and Rural Society, 25–49.

changes in this vast area are far from monolithic. Some regions have experienced decades of sustained growth, while large segments of the agricultural heartland continue to lose people and institutions. Not only has deconcentration been selective (Frey & Johnson, 1998), it has also been affected by a variety of cyclical forces. However, the overall trend reflects a consistent flow from more densely settled to less densely settled areas (Boyle & Halfacree, 1998; Long & Nucci, 1997; Vining & Strauss, 1977). Findings from other developed nations indicate deconcentration (often labeled "counterurbanization") is underway there as well (Champion, 1998).

In this paper, we analyze county-level population data, including information on natural increase and net migration, to provide a detailed picture of recent population redistribution trends in nonmetropolitan America. Our research focuses on three questions:

- What changes have occurred in the contributions of net migration and natural increase to the population redistribution trends of recent years?
- What significant regional differences exist in the patterns of population redistribution?
- What county-level factors are associated with the spatial pattern of population redistribution in nonmetropolitan areas, and have these factors shifted in importance over time?

Demographic change does not occur in a vacuum. It is a direct response to prior organizational, technological, and environmental changes. Thus, globalization, economic restructuring, innovations in farming, and the diminishing friction of distance fostered by communications and transportation improvements all have implications for the demographic future of rural America. Nor is demographic change merely a response to these forces. It is also a causal agent fostering future changes in the social, economic, and political landscapes of rural America. In this regard, the protracted outflow of young adults characteristic of so many rural counties (Johnson & Fuguitt, 2000; Johnson et al., 2003) diminishes the available human capital of the area, thereby sapping the prospects of future economic development and reducing the available residents to staff the myriad of social, cultural, and civic organizations that form the social fabric of communities. Thus, policymakers charged with planning for the future of the people and institutions of rural America must attend to the population redistribution underway there and to the demographic and economic forces that underlie these trends.

DATA AND METHODS

Population data for each county come from the decennial Census of population and from the Federal-State Cooperative Population Estimates (FSCPE) program. This FSCPE program estimates the population on an annual basis as of July 1, and here we include the period from April 1, 1990 through July 1, 2003. The FSCPE also provides data on the number of births and deaths in each year. The estimates of net migration used here were derived by the residual method whereby net migration is what is left when natural increase (births minus deaths) is subtracted from total population change. Net migration includes net international migration, net internal migration, and differences in coverage of the various censuses.[2]

Historical data used in this report include population statistics from decennial censuses and estimates of components of change back to 1930 (Johnson, 1985; U.S. Census Bureau, 1978, 1984, 1992). Recently released age-specific net migration data for 1990–2000 (Johnson et al., 2003) combined with previous research following similar methodologies (Bowles & Tarver, 1965; Bowles et al., 1975; Fuguitt & Beale, 1993; White et al., 1987) provide a comprehensive picture of the age structure of rural migration since 1950.

Counties are the units of analysis because they have historically stable boundaries and are a basic unit for reporting fertility, mortality, and census data. Counties are also appropriate units of analysis because metropolitan areas are built up from them (county-equivalents are used for New England).[3] Counties are designated as metropolitan or nonmetropolitan using criteria developed by the U.S. Office of Management and Budget. County-level typologies developed by the Economic Research Service are used to identify factors associated with rural population redistribution (Cook & Mizer, 1994; McGranahan, 1999).

The number of counties identified as nonmetropolitan changes following each census. The reclassification of counties has important implications for our research. Metropolitan territory increases as a result of two processes: (1) expansion of existing metropolitan settlements and (2) growth of smaller settlements to a size that causes them to be redefined as metropolitan. A few metropolitan counties also revert to nonmetropolitan status each decade. For our primary analysis examining population change during the 1990's (including comparisons with the 1980's), we use a constant 1993 metropolitan-nonmetropolitan classification. Using this same metropolitan definition understates the magnitude of nonmetropolitan population gain in prior decades, so in our historical analysis we employ metropolitan definitions from earlier periods.

To highlight geographical differences in the scale and timing of nonmetropolitan population change, we use the Census Bureau's division of states into four regions—Northeast, Midwest, South, and West—a simple and widely-used scheme that allows for comparison with a long series of census publications and other research on rural demography (Cromartie, 1993; Frey & Speare, 1988; Fuguitt et al., 1989). Subsequent chapters in this book specifically focus on important sub-regions, such as the Great Plains or the Pacific Northwest, that are not separately identified here.

HISTORICAL CONTEXT

To appreciate the causes and implications of recent demographic changes in rural America, it is important to view them in the context of three protracted population redistribution trends that have overlapped one another for several decades: rural-to-urban migration, suburbanization, and interregional migration from "Rustbelt" to "Sunbelt." All three movements contributed to massive population shifts affecting the balance of population among communities, states, and regions. Along with changes in fertility and mortality, these overriding migration flows determined the ebb and flow of rural population growth over time.

Urbanization has been a constant throughout this nation's history, but the contribution of rural out-migration reached unprecedented levels from roughly 1940 to 1970. During this period, the farm population declined by over 700,000 per year, due mostly to enormous productivity increases that lowered labor demands (Banks & Beale, 1973; Beale, 1989). Many farm-dependent counties continue to lose population, but the continuation of rural-to-urban migration today is less tied to labor surpluses in agriculture and more to geographic conditions, such as lack of access to urban services, that inhibit the emergence of other economic activities (McGranahan & Beale, 2002).

As out-migration depleted the farm population, suburbanization fueled rapid growth in rural areas on the metropolitan periphery. From the end of World War II to the present, economic prosperity, investments in transportation infrastructure, and other factors have contributed to a residential development boom on the ever-expanding metropolitan fringe, transforming the countryside and raising debates on the pros and cons of "urban sprawl" (Heimlich & Anderson, 2001). As suburbanization progressed, it increasingly reached across metropolitan boundaries into adjacent nonmetropolitan counties and was therefore labeled "exurbanization" or "incipient suburbanization" (Beale, 2000, p. 27). The fastest-growing nonmetropolitan counties have been those in the path of metropolitan expansion. However, the inevitable reclassification to metropolitan status of many fringe counties each decade diminishes the nonmetropolitan population base and dampens subsequent population growth attributed to nonmetropolitan areas (Elliott & Perry, 1996; Fuguitt et al., 1989).

Interregional migration in the United States since 1950 has caused a major redistribution of population out of states in the Northeast and Midwest into the South and West. The percentage of Americans living in the South and West grew from 44 to 58 percent from 1950 to 2000 (Hobbs & Stoops, 2002). Factors contributing to this on-going demographic shift include the regional deconcentration of manufacturing jobs, the emergence of a service-based economy, public investment in transportation and communication infrastructure that disproportionately benefited the South, and the growing importance of amenity-based migration. Population growth in the Sunbelt has been mostly urban-centered, but these states also captured the majority of nonmetropolitan growth through metropolitan spillover, the expansion of small-town labor markets, and the increasing attraction of recreation and retirement areas.

These three major migration trends, along with changes in fertility and mortality, help explain the scale and pace of rural population change over time as well as regional variations. In each decade from 1930 to 1970, the population of

Figure 2.1. Nonmetropolitan Demographic Trends, 1930–2003

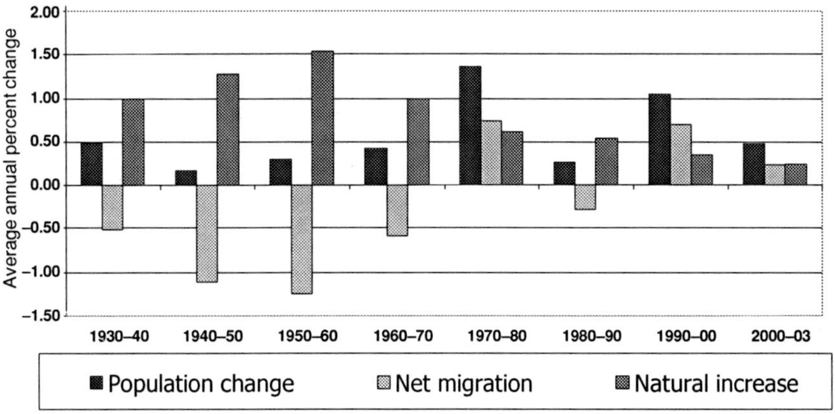

Source: Kenneth M. Johnson, using data from the U. S. Census Bureau.

nonmetropolitan America as a whole grew modestly (Figure 2.1). This population gain was fueled entirely by natural increase. Although population growth along the metropolitan fringe was increasing throughout this period and especially after 1950, it was overshadowed by out-migration from more isolated settings. Rural America experienced a net exodus of migrants in each of the four decades from 1930 to 1970. During the 1940s and 1950s, the net migration loss was particularly pronounced, and the small population gains only occurred because the large birth cohorts of the baby boom were sufficient to offset deaths plus the substantial out-migration.

Toward the end of the 1960s, rural-to-urban migration declined precipitously (though it has never ceased altogether) and suburbanization accelerated. Net migration losses moderated, resulting in a somewhat larger population gain. But the significance of these historical shifts became apparent during the nonmetropolitan turnaround of the 1970s. During that remarkable decade, nonmetropolitan population gains exceeded those of the previous four decades combined. Of even greater importance was the fact that most of this growth resulted from net inmigration. Thus, after at least four decades of substantial migration loss, nonmetropolitan areas actually received a net influx of migrants from metropolitan areas in the 1970s.

The turnaround waned in the 1980s because of renewed rural out-migration and diminishing natural increase. An exceptionally severe farm crisis and economic recessions heavily focused on goods-producing industries made it harder for rural areas to retain current residents or attract new migrants. Also, the pace of suburbanization fell slightly as household formation slowed (Heimlich & Anderson, 2001). Though some researchers suggested that this downturn reflected a return to historical redistribution trends (Frey, 1993), the reversal proved to be short lived. As the 1990s dawned, rural population gains rebounded as rural areas again received an influx of migrants.

The nonmetropolitan turnaround and rural rebound were widespread geographically, as was the protracted era of rural migration loss that preceded them. However, the persistent movement of people and jobs to the South and West, starting in the 1950s, was strong enough to cause a significant redistribution of the nonmetropolitan population. The scale and timing of rural-to-urban migration shifted during each decade and contributed to differential growth patterns. In addition, metropolitan expansion was not uniform but varied regionally according to metropolitan size and growth rates (McGranahan & Salsgiver, 1992).

Regional differences in rural concentration largely disappeared during the past century (Figure 2.2). In 1930, the South was by far the most rural of the four regions, with close to 80 percent of its residents living in nonmetropolitan counties, compared with only 20 percent in the Northeast. Migration trends since that time created a significant convergence in regional residential patterns. All regions became more urbanized over the years as the number of U.S. residents living in nonmetropolitan areas dropped to 20 percent in 2000. But the decline in the percent rural was more pronounced in the South and West, in part because Sunbelt migration brought so many new residents to those regions' metropolitan centers. Today, the Midwest has the largest nonmetropolitan percentage, while

Figure 2.2. Percentage of Population Nonmetropolitan by Region, 1930–2000

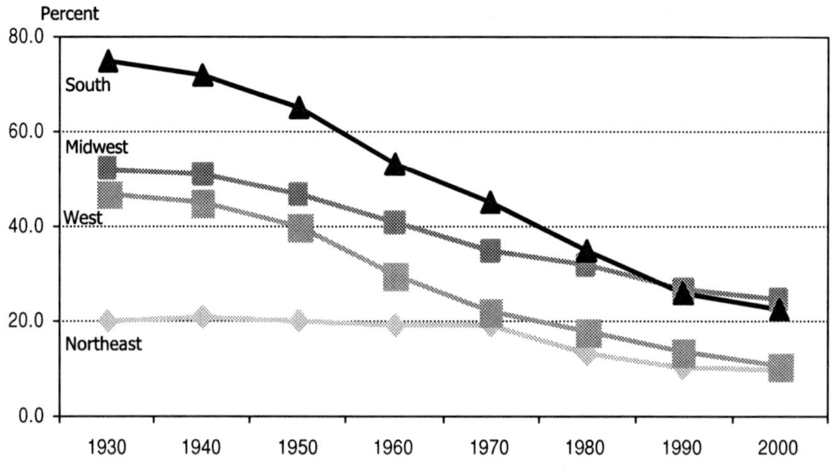

Source: Economic Research Service, U. S. Department of Agriculture, using data from the U. S. Census Bureau.

the Northeast percentage declined by the smallest amount, with all of the change coming after 1970.

The nonmetropolitan turnaround of the 1970s had its greatest impact in the Sunbelt. Although rural out-migration related to farm sector restructuring reappeared in the 1980s and has never completely disappeared, it does not shape the pattern of current regional redistribution trends today. Rather, nonmetropolitan population growth is now determined largely by the dynamics of metropolitan expansion, urban growth below the metropolitan level, and amenity-based migration. In terms of destinations for new rural and small town residents, these migration trends largely, though not exclusively, favor Sunbelt locations in the South and West.

THE RURAL REBOUND AND AFTERMATH: DEMOGRAPHIC PATTERNS

Data from the 2000 census substantiate earlier reports that a rural population rebound occurred during the 1990s. The nonmetropolitan population was 56.1 million in April 2000, a gain of 5.3 million (10.3 percent) since April 1990 (Table 2.1). This is a striking contrast to the 1980s when nonmetropolitan areas grew by fewer than 1.3 million. Net migration now plays the most important role in redistributing the U.S. population because of recent reductions in natural increase and rising immigration.

Net Migration

Migration gains accounted for 67 percent of the total population increase between 1990 and 2000. Nonmetropolitan areas had a net inflow of 3.5 million people during the 1990s compared to a net outflow of 1.4 million during the 1980s. The nonmetropolitan net migration gain (7.0 percent) between 1990 and 2000 was greater than that in metropolitan areas (6.1 percent). This is in sharp contrast to the 1980s when metropolitan areas had net inmigration, whereas nonmetropolitan areas had a net outflow. The only other recent period during which nonmetropolitan migration gains exceeded those in metropolitan areas was during the population turnaround of the 1970s.

Net migration to nonmetropolitan areas has always been age selective (Fuguitt & Heaton, 1995). In each decade from 1950 to 2000, nonmetropolitan counties experienced a significant outflow of young adults ages 20–29 (Figure 2.3). This loss was greatest during the 1950s and 1960s, a period when the rural exodus was near its peak. Young adult losses moderated considerably during the turnaround of the 1970s and again during the rural rebound of the 1990s. For those in their 30s and 40s, net migration losses moderated (1950s, 1960s, 1980s) or were replaced by population gains (1970s, 1990s). Among those over the age of 50, nonmetropolitan counties received a net influx in all but the 1950s. In general, the 1990s and 1970s

Table 2.1. Population Change, Net Migration, and Natural Increase by Adjacency and Metropolitan Status, 1970–2000

			Population Change			**Net Migration**			**Natural Increase**		
	No. of Cases	Initial Population	Absolute Change	Percent Change	Percent Growing	Absolute Change	Percent Change	Percent Growing	Absolute Change	Percent Change	Percent Growing
1970–1980:											
All nonmetropolitan	2,280	43,484	5,868	13.5	79.6	3,159	7.3	66.9	2,631	6.1	88.1
Nonadjacent	1,278	19,991	2,540	12.7	72.1	1,223	6.1	60.5	1,249	6.2	85.9
Adjacent	1,002	23,573	3,328	14.1	89.1	1,936	8.2	75.1	1,381	6.3	90.8
Metropolitan	835	159,514	17,280	10.8	88.6	5,948	3.7	73.4	11,198	7.0	97.8
Total	3,115	202,998	23,147	11.4	82.0	9,107	4.5	68.7	13,829	6.8	90.7
1980–1990:											
All nonmetropolitan	2,303	49,520	1,296	2.6	45.1	−1379	−2.8	27.4	2,675	5.4	89.5
Nonadjacent	1,296	22,554	110	0.5	36.3	−1184	−5.2	20.9	1,294	5.7	86.7
Adjacent	1,007	26,966	1,186	4.4	56.3	−195	−0.7	35.9	1,381	5.1	93.0
Metropolitan	837	177,019	20,871	11.8	81.0	6,585	3.7	57.7	14,286	8.1	97.7
Total	3,141	226,542	22,168	9.8	54.7	5,206	2.3	35.5	16,962	7.5	91.7
1990–2000:											
All nonmetropolitan	2,303	50,816	5,262	10.4	73.9	3,535	7.0	68.4	1,727	3.4	70.9
Nonadjacent	1,296	22,663	1,853	8.2	64.4	1,092	4.8	59.9	762	3.4	64.1
Adjacent	1,007	28,152	3,409	12.1	86.1	2,443	8.7	79.6	966	3.4	79.6
Metropolitan	837	197,890	27,456	13.9	90.1	12,124	6.1	77.5	15,332	7.7	94.9
Total	3,141	248,710	32,716	13.2	78.2	15,659	6.3	70.8	17,059	6.9	77.3

Notes: 1993 Metropolitan Status used for all periods. Initial population and absolute change reported in ’000s.
Source: Kenneth M. Johnson, using data from the U.S. Census Bereau.

Figure 2.3. Nonmetropolitan Age-Specific Net Migration, 1950–2000

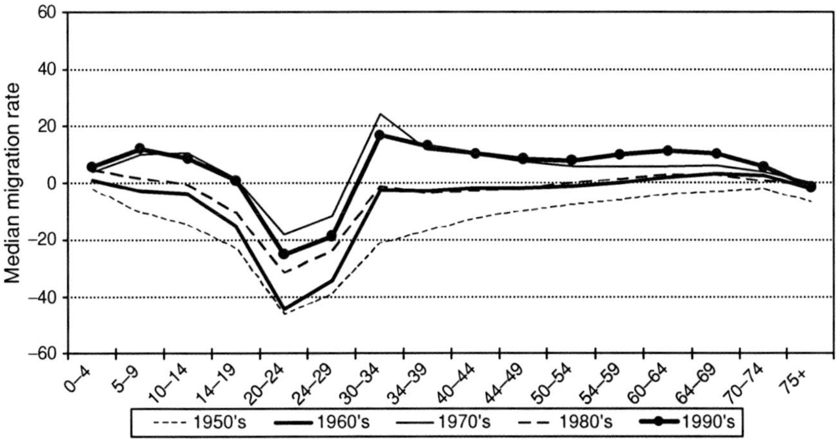

Source: Johnson et al., 2003.

show considerably larger population gains (or smaller losses) for virtually every age group when compared to the other three decades.

Prior research (Johnson & Fuguitt, 2000) suggested that the significant difference between age-specific migration trends in the 1970s and those in other decades (using data through 1990) supported the argument that the nonmetropolitan turnaround of the 1970s represented a significant break from prior rural demographic trends. These new estimates for the 1990s document for the first time that the age-specific migration trends of the 1990s more closely approximate the trends of the 1970s than those of any other decade. The trends of the 1990s are generally more moderate than those of the 1970s among those under the age of 40. However, at older ages the migration gains in nonmetropolitan areas were generally greater than in any previous decade. The cumulative impact of these age-specific net migration trends has important implications for natural increase as well.

Natural Increase and Decrease

The impact of natural increase is often neglected in the study of population redistribution. In contrast to net migration, which can rapidly transform the size and structure of a population, the impact of natural increase is subtle and gradual. For example, when a young adult migrates, the loss is immediately reflected as a net migration loss of one person. However, the longer-term impact for the area is that the loss of the migrant diminishes future population gains from the descendents of the departed migrant. Over the course of several generations, the impact of such age-specific out migration on natural increase can be substantial. The minimal natural increase in nonmetropolitan counties in the 1990s reflects just such a culmination of decades of young adult out migration as documented above. These migration trends have now produced an age structure in many nonmetropolitan counties that includes few young adults of childbearing age and many older adults at greater risk of mortality. In addition, rural and urban birth rates have converged recently (Long & Nucci, 1998), eroding the historical fertility advantage nonmetropolitan areas once enjoyed. The overall result of these trends has been low levels of natural increase (or natural decrease) in many nonmetropolitan counties in the 1990s.

Natural increase accounted for only 33 percent of the nonmetropolitan population increase between 1990 and 2000. In all, births exceeded deaths by an estimated 1.7 million in nonmetropolitan areas. The gain through natural increase in nonmetropolitan areas diminished during the 1990s from what it had been during the 1970s and 1980s (Table 2.1). The reduced contribution of natural increase to nonmetropolitan population redistribution trends in the 1990s underscores the changing relationship between it and net migration. Historically, natural increase fueled rural population change. Yet in recent decades, it has been migration that has fueled growth. Migration accounted for 54 percent of the population gain during the turnaround of the 1970s, and it accounted for more than 67 percent of the gain during the rebound of the 1990s.

Diminished natural increase in nonmetropolitan areas is also reflected in a sharp rise in the incidence of natural decrease there since 1990. Natural decrease is a function of a complex interaction between fertility, mortality, and migration over a protracted period of time. Most natural decrease is a product of the prolonged out-migration of young adults from an area (Johnson, 1993; Johnson & Beale, 1992). Eventually, the dwindling number of young adults can no longer produce sufficient births to offset deaths among the larger older cohorts who remain in the area. In essence, natural decrease is the ultimate demographic consequence of the longitudinal, age-specific net migration patterns that characterize a considerable part of rural America.

Evidence of the rising levels of natural decrease is clearly reflected in the data considered here. Some 670 nonmetropolitan counties (29.1 percent) experienced overall natural decrease between 1990 and 2000. This is up from approximately 10 percent in the 1980s. The incidence of natural decrease is highest in nonmetropolitan counties that are remote from metropolitan areas. More than a third of the nonadjacent counties experienced natural decrease between 1990 and 2000. Prior research suggests that natural decrease is particularly common in sparsely settled, agriculture-dependent counties (Johnson, 1993; Johnson & Beale, 1992) such as those concentrated on the Great Plains (see also chapter 9). Natural decrease reflects an aging population that places higher demands on local services, especially health care, which are limited in areas of low population density.

Figure 2.4. Nonmetropolitan Demographic Change 1990–2003

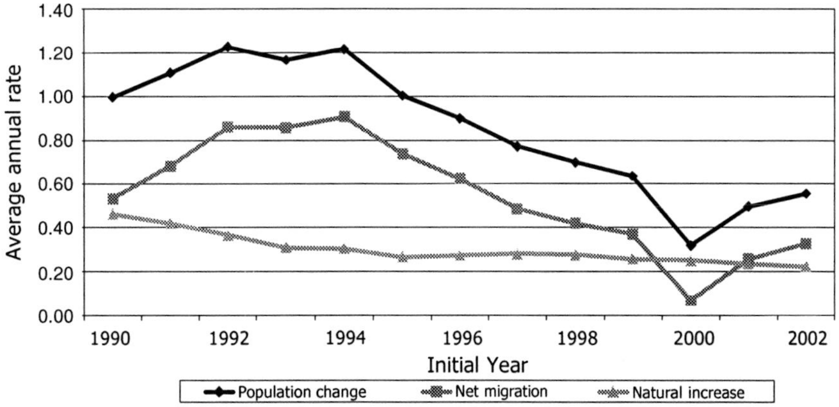

Source: Kenneth M. Johnson, using data from the U. S. Census Bureau.

The Uneven Pace of Demographic Change in the 1990s

Annual population estimates for the 1990s suggest that the amount of population change in nonmetropolitan areas varied from year to year during the 1990s. Such variation in nonmetropolitan migration has been common, with the population growth slowdown in the late 1990s closely resembling the pattern of the 1970s. Figure 2.4 compares the annual percentage change in population throughout the 1990s and the first years of the new century using the Census Bureau's recently revised FSCPE estimates. The data point for a given year reflects the percent change between July 1 of that year and July 1 of the subsequent year.

Growth rates were higher during the early and middle 1990s reflecting the rural rebound. Later in the decade, the nonmetropolitan population growth rates diminished, reaching a low point in 2000–2001. These findings are consistent with prior research suggesting that the rebound weakened in the late 1990s (Beale, 2000; Cromartie, 2001). In 2001–2003, the population growth rate turned up again, though it remains quite modest.[4]

The significant impact that migration had on overall population change is clearly evident in the annual migration data. Migration gains were substantial in the first years of 1990s. However, beginning in 1994–1995 nonmetropolitan migration rates began to diminish and continued to do so through the first year of the new century, after which they turned up. The close correlation between changes in magnitude of net migration and population change underscore the importance of migration to recent population change.

In contrast to the variability in net migration trends during the 1990s, the contribution of natural increase sharply diminished over the course of the 12 year period. By historical standards, the contribution of natural increase was very modest throughout the 1990s, but the rate near the end of the decade may well have been the lowest in history. The nonmetropolitan percentage gain from natural increase dropped from 0.46 in 1990–1991 to 0.26 in 2001–2003. This lower rate of natural increase resulted from a 2 percent drop in births between 1990 and 2001 and by a 15 percent increase in the number of deaths.

Considering natural increase and net migration simultaneously helps to explain the patterns of population change during the 1990s. Nonmetropolitan counties had very modest natural increase and were, therefore, more dependent on net migration to fuel population gains. Rural population and migration gains began to diminish in the late 1990s and post-censal estimates through July of 2003 suggest the slowdown continued in the first year of the new century. As a result, when net migration subsided near the end of the decade, population growth rates in nonmetropolitan areas sharply diminished. Thus, the slowdown in nonmetropolitan population increase in the late 1990s resulted from diminished net migration coupled with a reduction in the rate of natural increase. However, there is some evidence of an upturn in migration beginning in 2001–2002 resulting in slightly higher population gains. Given the temporal variation in nonmetropolitan growth rates during the past thirty years, it is too early to ascertain whether the upturn represents the end of the temporary lull in rural growth.

In sum, the population patterns for nonmetropolitan counties derive both from the current trend toward selective deconcentration and a prior history of out-migration by young adults. The complex interaction of these trends supplemented by social and economic period effects produced the redistributive patterns evident in our data. With natural increase in nonmetropolitan areas now at historically low levels, migration will dominate future rural demographic trends. As a result, the fortunes of rural America in this new century are ever more closely intertwined with events beyond its boundaries and with the social, economic, technological, and political forces that shape those events.

THE RURAL REBOUND AND AFTERMATH: GEOGRAPHIC PATTERNS

The geographic unevenness of population redistribution is perhaps the most common theme in rural demography. Here we apply the term "selective deconcentration" to denote the county-level deviation in rates of nonmetropolitan population change. In any time period, population change rates deviate more among nonmetro than metro counties, so the issue of demographic "winners" and "losers" is a more salient one in rural America. Questions remain concerning whether and how selective deconcentration changes over time. Has the gap between declining and growing counties diminished over time, as some regional economic theories

Figure 2.5. County Population Change, 1990–2000

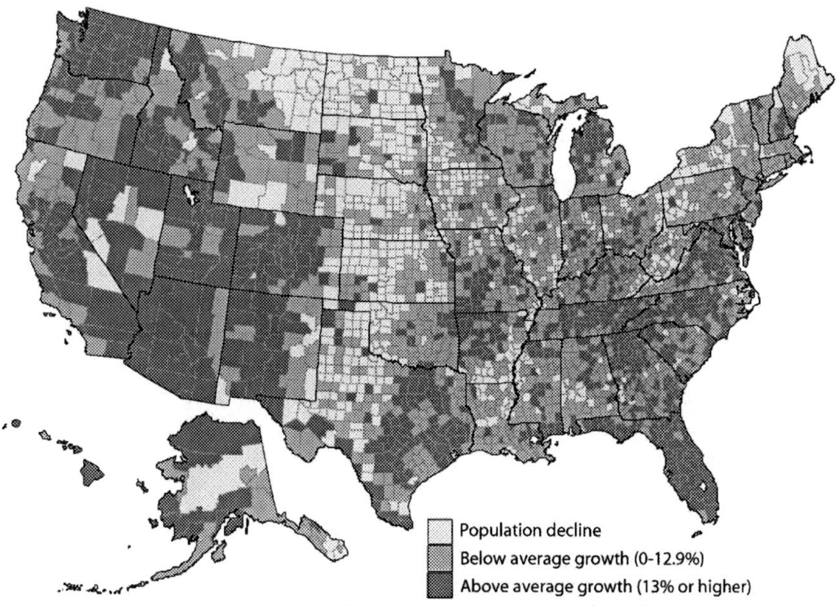

Source: Economic Research Service, U. S. Department of Agriculture, using data from the U.S. Census Bureau.

predict, has it widened, or has it tended to stay fixed? Here we explore this question in the context of the rural rebound of the 1990s and its aftermath.

County-level Population Change, 1990–2000

Even during a decade of heightened population deconcentration, county growth rates were highly uneven and geographically clustered (Figure 2.5). Counties with above-average rates of population growth (higher than the 13 percent pace for the country as a whole) covered large sections in the Mountain West, the Pacific Northwest, California's Central Valley, the Upper Great Lakes, the southern Highlands and Piedmont, Florida and the eastern half of Texas. The vast majority of nonmetropolitan counties located in these sub-regions benefited demographically from scenic landscapes, mild climates, proximity to rapidly-growing metropolitan areas, or a combination of these amenities. For instance, six of the ten fastest-growing nonmetropolitan counties in the 1990s were located in Denver's commuting shed, within or alongside the spectacular Front Range of the Rocky Mountains.

At the other extreme, a distinct swath of counties experiencing population decline extends through the Great Plains from the Canadian border to south Texas. Here population densities are typically quite low and the pattern of decline has often persisted for several decades. Most of these counties have struggled to develop an economic base outside of agriculture. More densely settled areas of decline are found in the lower South, typically in places where Blacks are a large proportion of the population. Other clusters of population decline occurred in coal-mining sections of Appalachia and in parts of the Northeast from western Pennsylvania to northern Maine. Manufacturing losses have contributed to out-migration from many of these locations as well as from smaller clusters in the Midwest.

Compared with the previous decade, the rural rebound at the county level was widespread. The number of declining nonmetropolitan counties fell from 1,200 during the 1980s to just under 600 during the 1990s. However, the distinct regional clustering did not shift significantly. Rapid-growth areas were not as extensive in the West or South during the 1980s, and the area of decline in the Great Plains was much larger, extending farther west into Montana, Wyoming and Colorado, and through much of the Corn Belt to the east. Other areas of nonmetropolitan population loss, especially in Appalachia and the lower South, were also much larger in the 1980s, but the general geographic pattern for the country as a whole was remarkably similar to the map shown here.

The Geographic Character of the Rural Rebound and Aftermath

The spatial consistency of growth and decline suggests that the rural rebound was not confined to high-growth areas but affected the vast majority of counties to some degree. With some important regional exceptions, counties tended to move up and down together as the rural rebound emerged and then diminished. Overall, 84 percent of nonmetropolitan counties experienced some level of population rebound during the 1990s. An even higher number (93 percent) of counties that were losing population in the 1980's had a rebound in the 1990s, either losing fewer people or experiencing a turnaround from population decline to growth. This indicates that deconcentration became less selective and more geographically widespread to some degree in the 1990s, but it did not come close to smoothing out the significant geographic differences in population redistribution that remain regionally entrenched across America.

The widespread nature of the rebound and its aftermath indicates that factors influencing migration were, in part, national in scale. The economic recessions of the 1980s were more severe and longer-lasting in rural areas, and the upturn in migration flows into nonmetropolitan areas began in the late 1980s, just as this period of low employment growth was ending. The rural rebound experienced its peak just after the "white collar" recession in the early 1990s that caused relatively lower job growth in metropolitan areas. Similarly, its aftermath coincided with the sustained recovery that was led by the strongly urban-focused technology sector.

These macroeconomic period effects tend to have a nationwide impact, as do cohort effects related to the aging of the population. The 1970s nonmetropolitan turnaround was influenced by the entry into the labor force of a large baby boom cohort, which increased competition for metropolitan jobs (Plane, 1992). Similar research ties the emergence of the rural rebound with the increased economic ability of an older baby boom generation to act on preferences for living in high-amenity areas, building second homes and engaging in mid-life career shifts and even early retirement (Nelson et al., 2004). In contrast, the small size of the depression-era cohort placed far fewer people in the traditional retirement age ranges in the 1990s, which partially explains why the high levels of amenity-based migration were not sustained throughout the decade.

Regional Variation in the Rebound and Aftermath

There were, of course, exceptions to the generalized ebb and flow of nonmetropolitan redistribution. Regions varied somewhat in the timing and strength of net migration during the years 1990–2003 (Figure 2.6). Most prominent is the unique profile of the Northeast. The small number of nonmetropolitan counties in this highly urbanized region experienced the lowest rates of population growth

Figure 2.6. Nonmetropolitan Net Migration by Region, 1990–2003

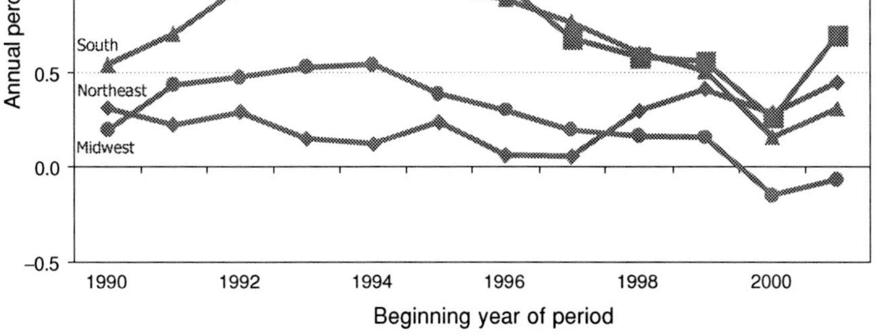

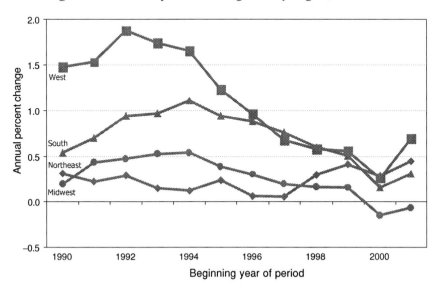

Source: Economic Research Service, U.S. Department of Agriculture, using data from the U.S. Census Bureau.

from migration through most of the decade and showed no discernable pattern of rebound until after 1997. Low migration for the Northeast and Midwest reflect the on-going job loss associated with deindustrialization in the nation's Rustbelt. But the delayed timing of the rebound in the nonmetropolitan Northeast follows the trend seen in the region's metropolitan areas in general, indicating a higher degree of rural-urban integration. In the Northeast, the spatial separation of rural and urban areas is smaller than elsewhere, the density of the urban settlement structure is higher, and the transportation and communications infrastructure is well developed. In contrast to other regions, urban and rural sections of the Northeast tend to respond similarly to recessions and other period effects.

The rebound pattern is evident in the other three regions, though much more pronounced in the Sunbelt, especially the West. At its peak in 1992, the nonmetropolitan West was attracting migrants at twice the rate of the South, prompting much speculation on the emergence of a "New West" economy based on quality-of-life factors. A major flow contributing to the phenomenal pace of rural and small town inmigration originated in California, and the rather precipitous decline in nonmetropolitan population growth after 1994 coincides with that sub-region's economic recovery as well as the expansion of other metropolitan economies throughout the region.

In sum, the rural rebound of the 1990s and the subsequent decline in net migration rates exhibited a fairly high level of geographic consistency. Nationwide economic and demographic forces were strong enough to be felt quite broadly, causing a general tendency for nonmetropolitan counties to move up and down together. The Northeast represents the only exception to the rural rebound pattern visible at the broad regional scale examined here. A more detailed analysis undoubtedly would reveal other divergent sub-regional and local trends. Nonetheless, the persistent character of selective deconcentration appears to be an important rural demographic trait.

FACTORS ASSOCIATED WITH SELECTIVE DECONCENTRATION

Given the general geographic consistency of the rebound and its aftermath, it is likely that factors determining the unevenness over space have not changed either, or at least tended to change slowly. The historical description above shows that a demographic "competitive advantage" has long been held by areas with mild climates and high scenic qualities, areas with access to urban amenities (either their own or ones nearby), and to areas less dominated by traditional rural economic activities. The fastest-growing nonmetro counties in the country typically score high on the first two factors and exhibit a diversified, services-based employment base. A large portion of the differential regional trends outlined above can be attributed to regional contrasts in these endowments. The Sunbelt regions of the South and West have warmer climates along with a wealth of landscape amenities and rapidly expanding, economically booming metropolitan areas. Here we examine whether any shifts in the influence of these factors occurred during the rural rebound and beyond.

Natural Amenities

Counties with significant landscape amenities or quality of life advantages have been particularly prone to rapid growth. Research consistently finds climate to be a primary factor explaining the persistence of southward and westward migration flows since the mid-1950s. Using a county-level index combining measures of climate, topography, and presence of bodies of water, McGranahan (1999) showed that basic natural amenity endowments explained a larger percentage of the variation in nonmetropolitan 1970–1996 population growth rates than urban influence and economic structure combined.

Updating this analysis using the same index confirms that no significant shift occurred over the course of the 1990s in this basic relationship (Figure 2.7). During the 1980s, counties scoring in the lower half on the natural amenities scale lost population while those in the highest quartile grew at over 1 percent per year, higher than the overall national rate. The rural rebound shows up quite clearly as

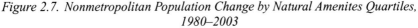

Figure 2.7. Nonmetropolitan Population Change by Natural Amenites Quartiles, 1980–2003

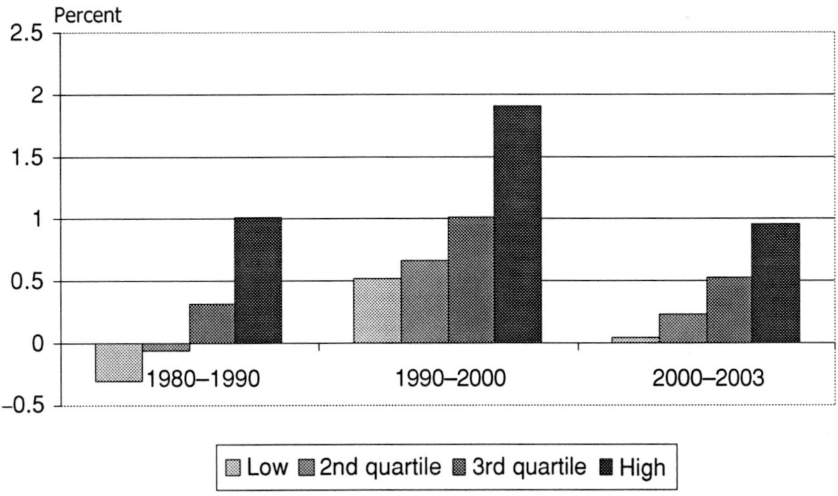

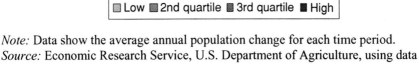

Note: Data show the average annual population change for each time period.
Source: Economic Research Service, U.S. Department of Agriculture, using data from the U.S. Census Bureau.

all four quartiles experienced some level of population growth during the 1990s, but the relative position of these county groups changed little. All four groups continue to show growth during the post-rebound period, but at half or less the pace shown during the 1990s.

Other measures capture distinct aspects of amenity-based migration to rural areas. The population in 190 "retirement destination" counties grew by 28.4 percent during the 1990s, with virtually all the growth due to net immigration. Such areas are located in the Sunbelt, coastal regions, parts of the West and in the Upper Great Lakes (Cook & Mizer, 1994). Population and migration gains were also substantial in nonmetropolitan "recreational" counties (Beale & Johnson, 1998; Johnson, 1999; Johnson & Beale, 1994; McGranahan, 1999). Such counties were prominent growth nodes during the 1970s and 1980s and this trend has persisted in the 1990s. Counties where much of the land is federally owned also had substantial growth in the 1990s. Most of these counties are concentrated in the West and many have experienced significant net inmigration in recent years with migrants attracted by the scenic and recreational amenities.

Urban Influence

It has long been recognized that the spillover of population from proximate metropolitan areas has contributed to growth in adjacent nonmetropolitan counties (Fuguitt, 1985). More than 86 percent of these counties gained population between 1990 and 2000. Counties adjacent to large metropolitan areas grew at a rate higher than metropolitan areas during the 1990s, a position they did not hold either before or after the rebound (Figure 2.8). In all three time periods, the distinct advantages of adjacency in attracting new residents is clear; as a group, nonadjacent counties have maintained a low-growth profile since at least 1980.

In addition, nonmetropolitan counties with their own urban centers have a distinct advantage in providing access to jobs and services, and therefore are better able to retain population and attract new residents compared with more rural counties. This was certainly the case in the 1980s and in the post-rebound period (Figure 2.9). During the 1990s it appears that urban advantage temporarily faded with a more widespread deconcentration; population growth rates evened out along this dimension as a large number of more sparsely populated rural counties experienced a turnaround from decline to growth.

The evenness of growth rates across the urban hierarchy during the 1990s is due, in large part, to differences in initial population size; it requires a much smaller increase in the number of new residents for small counties to record higher growth rates. Nonetheless, to the extent that percentage change is an accurate proxy for the impact that demographic events are having on a given local area, these smaller areas felt the effects of the rebound as much or more than larger nonmetropolitan counties.

Figure 2.8. Population Change by Urban Influence, 1980–2003

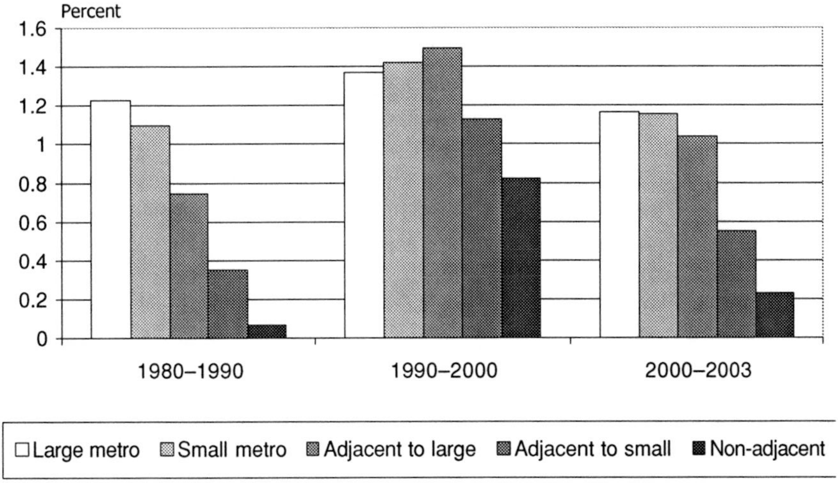

Note: Data show the average annual population change for each time period.
Source: Economic Research Service, U.S. Department of Agriculture, using data from the U.S. Census Bureau.

Figure 2.9. Nonmetropolitan Population Change by Level of Urbanization, 1980–2003

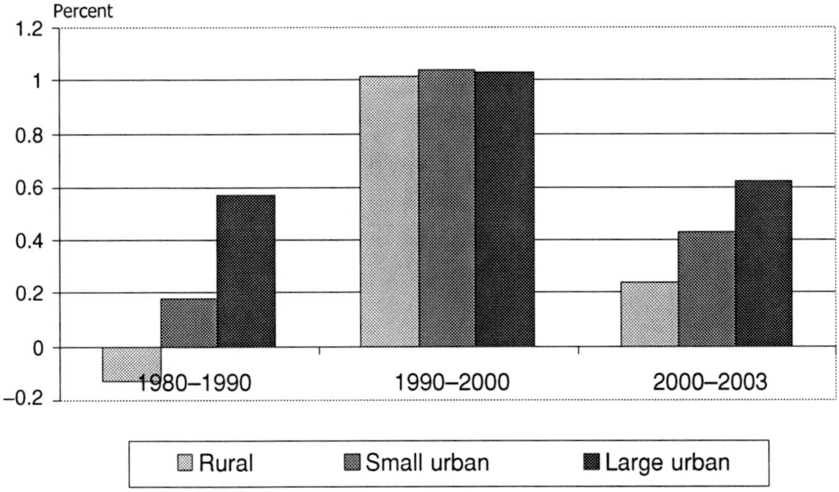

Note: Data show the average annual population change for each time period.
Source: Economic Research Service, U.S. Department of Agriculture, using data from the U.S. Census Bureau.

Economic Structure

Migration into and out of rural areas is strongly tied to employment opportunities. Productivity gains in farming fueled rural out-migration for several decades prior to 1970 as rural competitive advantage shifted towards low-skill manufacturing and services. Agriculture is still a dominant industry throughout much of rural America but not in terms of jobs or new job creation; continued restructuring has only a small impact on population redistribution. Most new jobs in nonmetropolitan areas, as elsewhere, are in services. Today, rural areas struggle to maintain a strong manufacturing base as that industry takes on a high-skill, high-technology orientation.

County-level employment profiles show a strong and persistent demographic advantage to diversified economies, areas that provide a high share of service-sector jobs or that are non-specialized (Figure 2.10). Counties dependent on farming or mining experienced a turnaround from overall decline to growth during the rural rebound, but still had the lowest rates of growth among economy typology groups. The resumption of overall decline for these types of counties since 2000 reflects a general difficulty in building an alternative economic base.

Figure 2.10. Nonmetropolitan Population Change by Economic Typology, 1980–2003

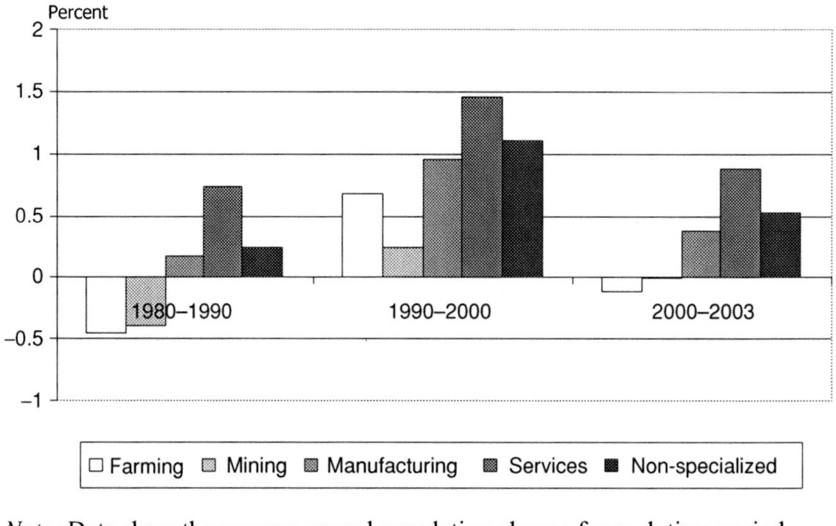

Note: Data show the average annual population change for each time period.
Source: Economic Research Service, U.S. Department of Agriculture, using data from the U.S. Census Bureau.

In addition, natural decrease is now a common contributor to population decline in farm-dependent counties.

This analysis does not take into account the interaction of population redistribution factors. Counties with high natural amenities and those adjacent to metropolitan areas also tend to have rapidly-growing, diversified economies. Many high-growth counties score well on all three attributes. Counties that remain dependent on agriculture typically have fewer urban or scenic amenities upon which to attract new livelihoods. We have been able to show that, throughout the latest period of rural rebound and its aftermath, the underlying factors influencing rural population redistribution did not shift significantly. Selective deconcentration appears to remain firmly rooted in the same types of places over time.

SUMMARY AND CONCLUSION

From a strictly demographic viewpoint, the rebound in rural population growth in the 1990s was caused by an increase in migration from metropolitan areas. It took place despite a persistent drop in population growth from natural increase. With nonmetropolitan birth rates now at historically low levels and death rates on the rise due to an aging population, migration will dominate future rural demographic trends. As a result, the fortunes of rural America in this new century are ever more closely intertwined with events beyond its boundaries and with the social, economic, technological and political forces that shape those events. For example, economic factors, including the relative cost of labor and transportation in China's burgeoning manufacturing sector, affect the future employment prospects of workers in U.S. rural manufacturing plants. Technological innovations influence the extent of outsourcing of back office and customer service functions to the Philippines or India and thus the viability of the many call-back centers located in rural America. Political decisions about immigration policy influence the number of immigrants settling in rural areas near meat-and-poultry processing centers on the Great Plains, in the Carolinas, and elsewhere.

The 1990's rural population rebound was a demographic tide that lifted all boats. The vast majority of counties experienced elevated growth rates; even those still losing population did so at a lower pace. The widespread impact of changing migration trends—the fact that counties tend to move up and down together—suggests separate findings regarding how population redistribution changes over time and how it changes over space. On the one hand, the timing of the rebound and its aftermath seems to be influenced by cyclical economic and demographic forces that have had a nationwide impact. On the other hand, the selective deconcentration of the population is held in place by fixed spatial endowments that have a fairly steady impact over time.

Rural areas attractive to new residents typically have some combination of scenic amenities, proximity to metro areas, and high degree of service-sector employment. Clear regional variations in the timing and strength of net migration, featuring a fast-growing Sunbelt and a slow-growing Rustbelt, emerged during the rebound, then disappeared in its aftermath. The nonmetropolitan West showed the strongest "boom and bust" cycle, as it has in the past. The Northeast did not participate in the rebound, instead following a metropolitan pattern; that is, slower population growth in the first half of decade followed by recovery. However, these regional differences were not large enough to alter the overall geographic pattern of growth and decline, which has remained remarkably stable over time.

If largely external forces influenced the timing of the rebound and its subsequent demise, and fixed geographical features channel selective deconcentration, the potential for local areas to address population-related challenges is slim. Counties that are sparsely populated, isolated, and without scenic landscapes face tough choices in trying to stem continued out-migration. The only development strategies that appear to be working currently under these conditions include the addition of large-scale food-processing operations, casinos, or prisons (McGranahan & Beale, 2002). These alternatives often add social costs as well as income benefits.

It is important for policy makers to be aware of the geography of demographic change as well as its underlying causes. Economic and social problems related to persistent population decline endanger the future of many rural communities, but not all. In fact, rural areas with persistently high inmigration face their own set of population-related challenges, including inadequate planning, environmental degradation, traffic congestion, and temporary shortages of services as population outruns supply. Persistent out-migration is the more dire condition and has been the focus of federal rural policy for several decades. Entrenched out-migration erodes the population base, contributes to business closures, and increases the per capita cost of delivering needed services. These problems are exacerbated by an aging population. Programs developed to help ameliorate these conditions need to be geographically targeted and adapted to today's economic and social realities.

ENDNOTES

1. Kenneth Johnson wishes to acknowledge research support from the North Central Research Station of the US Forest Service, and the Economic Research Service, USDA.
2. Most analyses of population redistribution trends in the 1990s relied on the original Federal State Cooperative Population estimates (FSCPE). The release of the 2000 decennial census raises questions about the robustness of these data. The 2000 Census revealed significantly more residents in the United States than was suggested by the original FSCPE population estimates released during the 1990s. Our analysis uses the revised population estimates for the 1990s (those that incorporate information from the 2000 Census). Analysis of these data suggest considerably greater population and net migration gains in nonmetropolitan areas than was suggested by the original population estimates for the 1990s.
3. Independent cities are combined with the counties surrounding them.

4. It may be pertinent that data for 2001–2002 are the first to reflect the impact of the September 11 tragedy. Because the tragedy had both economic and non-economic repercussions, it may have implications for population redistribution trends. It is widely believed that part of the explanation for the nonmetropolitan turnaround of the 1970s and the rebound of the 1990s was the rising importance of non-economic factors in migration decision-making among some parts of the population. If such non-economic factors became even more salient to some groups following September 11, it could impact decisions about whether to migrate or not. In addition, the events of September 11 further weakened an already faltering economy, which still plays a significant role in migration and childbearing decisions for a broad cross-section of the population (especially those in the labor force). It will be some time before the demographic implications of September 11 are fully understood, but certainly they deserve further study.

REFERENCES

Banks, V.J., & Beale, C.L. (1973). *Farm population estimates, 1910–70* (Statistical Bulletin No. 523). Washington, DC: U.S. Department of Agriculture, Rural Development Service.

Beale, C.L. (1989). Significant recent trends in the demography of farm people. *Proceedings of the Philadelphia Society for Promoting Agriculture, 1987–1988*, 36–50. Philadelphia, PA.

Beale, C.L. (2000). Nonmetro population growth recedes in a time of unprecedented national prosperity. *Rural Conditions and Trends, 11*, 27–31.

Beale, C.L., & Johnson, K.M. (1998). The identification of recreational counties in nonmetropolitan areas of the USA. *Population Research and Policy Review, 17*, 37–53.

Bowles, G.K., Beale, C.L., & Lee, E.S. (1975). *Net migration of the population 1960–70, by age, sex and color*. Washington, DC: U.S. Department of Agriculture, Economic Research Service, and Athens, GA: University of Georgia.

Bowles, G.K., & Tarver, J.D. (1965). *Net migration of the population 1950–60 by age, sex and color.* Washington, DC: U.S. Department of Agriculture, Economic Research Service.

Boyle, P., & Halfacree, K. (1998). *Migration in to rural areas*. Chichester, England: Wiley.

Champion, T. (1998). Studying counterurbanization and the rural population turnaround. In P. J. Boyle & K. H. Halfacree (Eds.), *Migration into rural areas: Theories and issues* (pp. 21–40). London: Wiley.

Cook, P.J., & Mizer, K.L. (1994). *The revised ERS county typology: An overview* (Rural Development Research Report No. 89). Washington, DC: U.S. Department of Agriculture, Economic Research Service.

Cromartie, J.B. (1993). Population. *Rural Conditions and Trends, 4*, 12–31.

Cromartie, J.B. (2001). Nonmetro out-migration exceeds in-migration for the first time in a decade. *Rural America, 16*, 35–37.

Elliott, J.R., & Perry, M.J. (1996). Metropolitanizing nonmetro space: Population redistribution and emergent metropolitan areas, 1965–90. *Rural Sociology, 61*, 497–512.

Frey, W.H. (1993). The new urban revival in the United States. *Urban Studies, 30*, 741–774.

Frey, W.H., & Johnson, K.M. (1998). Concentrated immigration, restructuring, and the selective deconcentration of the U.S. population. In P. J. Boyle & K. H. Halfacree (Eds.), *Migration into rural areas: Theories and issues* (pp. 79–106). London: Wiley.

Frey, W.H., & Speare, A. (1988). *Regional and metropolitan growth and decline in the United States.* New York: Sage.

Fuguitt, G.V. (1985). The nonmetropolitan turnaround. *Annual Review of Sociology, 11*, 259–280.

Fuguitt, G.V., & Beale, C.L. (1993). The changing concentration of the older nonmetropolitan population, 1960–90. *Journal of Gerontology: Social Sciences, 48*, S278–S288.

Fuguitt, G.V., Brown, D.L., & Beale, C.L. (1989). *Rural and small town America*. New York: Sage. Fuguitt, G.V., & Heaton, T.B. (1995). The impact of migration on the nonmetropolitan population age structure, 1960–1990. *Population Research and Policy Review, 14*, 215–232.

Heimlich, R.E., & Anderson, W.D. (2001). *Development at the urban fringe and beyond: Impacts on agriculture and rural land* (Agricultural Economic Report No. 803). Washington, DC: U.S. Department of Agriculture, Economic Research Service.

Hobbs, F., & Stoops, N. (2002). *Demographic trends in the 20th century* (Census 2000 Special Reports, Series CENSR-4). Washington, DC: U.S. Census Bureau.

Johnson, K.M. (1985). *The impact of population change on business activity in rural America*. Boulder, CO: Westview Press.

Johnson, K.M. (1993). When deaths exceed births: Natural decrease in the United States. *International Regional Science Review, 15*, 179–98.

Johnson, K.M. (1999). *The rural rebound* (PRB Reports on America, Vol. 1, No. 3). Washington, DC: Population Reference Bureau.

Johnson, K.M. (2000, September). *Migration to rural America: Historical trends and future prospects*. Paper presented at the Conference on Changing Landscapes of Rural America, Yellowstone Park, WY.

Johnson, K.M., & Beale, C.L. (1992). Natural population decrease in the United States. *Rural Development Perspectives, 8*, 8–15.

Johnson, K.M., & Beale, C.L. (1994). The recent revival of widespread population growth in nonmetropolitan areas of the United States. *Rural Sociology, 59*, 655–667.

Johnson, K.M., & Fuguitt, G.V. (2000). Continuity and change in rural migration patterns, 1950–1995. *Rural Sociology, 65*, 27–49.

Johnson, K.M., Fuguitt, G.V., Hammer, R., Voss, P., & McNiven, S. (2003, May). *Recent age-specific net migration patterns in the United States*. Paper presented at the Population Association of America Meeting, Minneapolis, MN.

Long, L., & Nucci, A. (1997). The "clean break" revisited: Is U.S. population again deconcentrating? *Environment and Planning A, 29*, 1355–1366.

Long, L., & Nucci, A. (1998). Accounting for population turnarounds in nonmetropolitan America. *Research in Rural Sociology and Development, 7*, 47–70.

McGranahan, D.A. (1999). *Natural amenities drive population change* (Agricultural Economics Report No. 718). Washington, DC: U.S. Department of Agriculture, Economic Research Service.

McGranahan, D.A., & Beale, C.L. (2002). Understanding rural population Loss. *Rural America, 17*, 2–11.

McGranahan, D.A., & Salsgiver, J. (1992). Recent population change in adjacent nonmetro counties. *Rural Development Perspectives, 8*, 2–7.

Nelson, P.B., Nicholson, J., & Stege, E.H. (2004). The baby boom and nonmetropolitan population change, 1975–1990. *Growth and Change, 35*, 525–544.

Plane, D. (1992). Age composition change and the geographical dynamics of interregional migration in the U. S. *Annals of the Association of American Geographers, 82*, 283–299.

Vining, D.R., Jr., & Strauss, A. (1977). A demonstration that the current deconcentration of population in the United States is a clean break with the past. *Environment and Planning A, 9*, 751–758.

U.S. Census Bureau. (1978). *County and city data book: Consolidated file: County data, 1947–1977* http://webapp.icpsr.umich.edu/cocoon/ICPSR-STUDY/07736.xml Washington, DC: Author.

U.S. Census Bureau. (1984). *Intercensal estimates of population by counties, 1970–1980.* Washington, DC: Author.

U.S. Census Bureau. (1992).*Revised estimates of the population by county, 1980–1989.* Washington, DC: Author.

White, M.J., Mueser, P., & Tierney, J.P. (1987). *Net migration of the population of the United States 1970–1980, by age, race and sex: United States, regions, divisions, states and counties* http://webapp.icpsr.umich.edu/cocoon/ICPSR-STUDY/08697.xml. Ann Arbor, MI: University of Michigan, Inter-university Consortium for Political and Social Research.

PART II

FOUR CRITICAL SOCIO-DEMOGRAPHIC THEMES

CHAPTER 3

THE CHANGING FACES OF RURAL AMERICA[1]

ANNABEL KIRSCHNER, E. HELEN BERRY, AND NINA GLASGOW

THE STORY WE WANT TO TELL

Rural Americans can still be Norwegian bachelor farmers. They can also be Hmong seamstresses, Latino businessmen, Pakistani landlords, and Filipino computer programmers. The Norwegians, meanwhile, are buying radicchio at the co-operated by newly retired women lawyers or organic basil grown by hobby farmers living on 20-acre ranchettes. Nonmetropolitan (nonmetro) places in the 21st century are very different than they were just 30 years ago. Rural populations have also changed as a significant number of retirees have moved into nonmetro places, while increasing tourism has helped to shift the nature of rural livelihoods. Simultaneously, as young people leave high schools in some rural areas to move to cities, schools and businesses are closing due to a lack of students and customers. In other places, rural schools and hospitals now must provide bilingual teachers and nurses to educate and care for new immigrants' children. As a result, nonmetro people are now older, more likely to be female, and more ethnically diverse than in the recent past.

Why did rural populations transform so dramatically in the latter part of the 20th century? Partly these changes had been coming for more than 30 years. As the economy shifted from resource extraction and manufacturing to services, and as family farms were replaced by corporate farms, the types of employment that could be found in nonmetro places was transformed. The need for low wage labor on corporate farms and in processing plants greatly augmented already existing streams of immigrant labor. At the other end of the spectrum, these technological developments, in association with rising personal affluence, also allowed people with higher incomes to move to rural places for non-economic reasons. For example, an IBM employee could have her phone ring in Atlanta; her secretary could answer the phone in Boston; and transfer the call to her actual location in Logan, Utah. Finally, while the total U.S. population was aging because of declining fertility rates and increasing life expectancy, the overall age of people in nonmetro places increased even more rapidly than in metropolitan (metro) areas

W.A. Kandel & D.L. Brown (eds.), Population Change and Rural Society, 53–74.

due to the long-established tendency of young adults to leave rural areas after high school graduation and the newer phenomenon of retirement migration.

This chapter examines changes in age, gender, and race/ethnic composition and discusses implications of these changes for personal and community well being. The chapter is organized in three distinct, integrated sections. We first examine trends in aging, which affect housing, work, Social Security, care-giving (for both young and old) and community services, and which have important implications for individual well-being among rural residents. Fluctuations in age composition are tied to changes in relative numbers of males and females, and thus the next section focuses on how age and gender interact to alter characteristics of rural labor markets as well as family and household structure. Third, we consider how the rapidly transforming ethnic and racial makeup of rural places affects, and is affected by, both age and gender. These three variables—age, sex, and race/ethnicity—are so closely intertwined that it is difficult to discuss developments in one without discussing changes in the others. Many of these dynamic processes occur in urban places as well, but they have distinctive causes and consequences in rural America.

HOW THE AGE STRUCTURE OF RURAL PLACES IS CHANGING AND WHY IT MATTERS

Fertility, mortality and immigration determine the age structure of a country's population, and these variables along with internal migration affect the age composition of different geographic areas within that country (e.g., rural versus urban). In the past, fertility exerted a stronger influence on a population's age composition than mortality or migration, but over time declining mortality rates concentrated in the older ages have played an increasingly important role in changing the age structure of the U.S. population (Siegel, 1993).

Fertility rates began a sharp decline in both rural and urban areas after 1960 following the post-World War II baby boom, which peaked at 3.58 children per woman. Currently the rate hovers around the replacement level of 2.1 children per woman. In recent years, fertility has declined even more rapidly in rural than in urban areas (see Chapter 2). In 1940 the child to woman ratio for women 20–44 years old was 44 percent higher in nonmetro than metro areas. In 1980 it was 18 percent higher and by 2000 metro and nonmetro child to woman ratios had equalized (data not shown).

Concurrent with declines in fertility, life expectancy in the 20th century alone increased from just 47 years in 1900 to over 75 years in 2000. Crude death rates are somewhat higher in nonmetro than metro areas, but the median age is also higher and consequently the literature is inconsistent on whether there is a difference in mortality after adjusting for age composition (McLaughlin et al., 2001; Morton, 2004). The important point is that metro and nonmetro areas have been on largely parallel paths relative to declining fertility and increasing longevity, and these trends have fueled the rapid aging of the population. Recent waves of immigrants, especially Hispanic and Southeast Asian immigrants, have been a countervailing force. Immigrants are younger and have higher fertility than other nonmetro or metro residents. Immigration is primarily focused on metro areas, but nonmetro areas have also become the destinations of a substantial number of immigrants in recent years. Accordingly, immigration increases the share of the total population in younger age groups and thus over time may diminish the proportion but not the number of the population that is elderly. The result is that the rapidity of aging in nonmetro areas is historically unprecedented in the United States. This phenomenon is examined by comparing the age structures of metro and nonmetro areas in 1990 and 2000 and then by examining long-term trends in median age. Finally, aging is considered by region.

The population pyramids in Figure 3.1 illustrate the aging of the metro and nonmetro populations (using the 1993 metro definition) during the last decade. As the median age on each pyramid shows, both sectors have become older, but the aging of the nonmetro population (from 33.8 to 37.0) was more dramatic than that of the metro population (from 32.6 to 34.9). In 1990, nonmetro areas still had a slightly greater percent of their population between 5 and 19 than their metro counterparts. However, even then, nonmetro areas had proportionately fewer children less than five years of age. While the baby boom affects both metro and nonmetro areas, it is more exaggerated in metro areas, with nonmetro areas having a notably smaller proportion of adults between the ages of 25 and 44.[2] On the other hand, nonmetro areas had a higher proportion of older adults starting in the 55–59 age group.

This pattern repeats in 2000, but with two important shifts. First, by 2000 there were proportionately fewer children in the 0–4 and 5–9 age groups in nonmetro areas, and the proportion of 10–14-year-olds was about the same for both metro and nonmetro areas. Second, nonmetro areas had a greater proportion of older adults starting with the 50–55-year-old age group.

Figure 3.2 examines median age from a longer-term perspective by two types of geographic areas—metro/nonmetro and urban/rural (in each case the area definitions are those that were current at the time of the census.)[3] Between 1920 and 1940, the rural population was on average five years younger than the urban population, although both were increasing in age. After 1950, the age gap between rural and urban areas began to narrow. In 1980, for the first time in the 20th century, the median age of the rural population was older than that of the urban population. This was also true comparing nonmetro to metro areas.

This narrowing of the metro/nonmetro age gap between 1950 and 1980 was due to several factors. Rural fertility declined more rapidly and more closely approximated that of urban women (Fuguitt et al., 1989). This was also a time of heavy out-migration of rural youth to urban areas. Note that the median age declined in both urban and metro areas between 1960 and 1970 but not in rural or nonmetro areas as baby-boom youths began to graduate from rural/nonmet high schools and move to urban/metro areas.

Figure 3.1. Age Distribution of the Metro and Nonmetro Population by 5-year Age Groups: 1990 and 2000

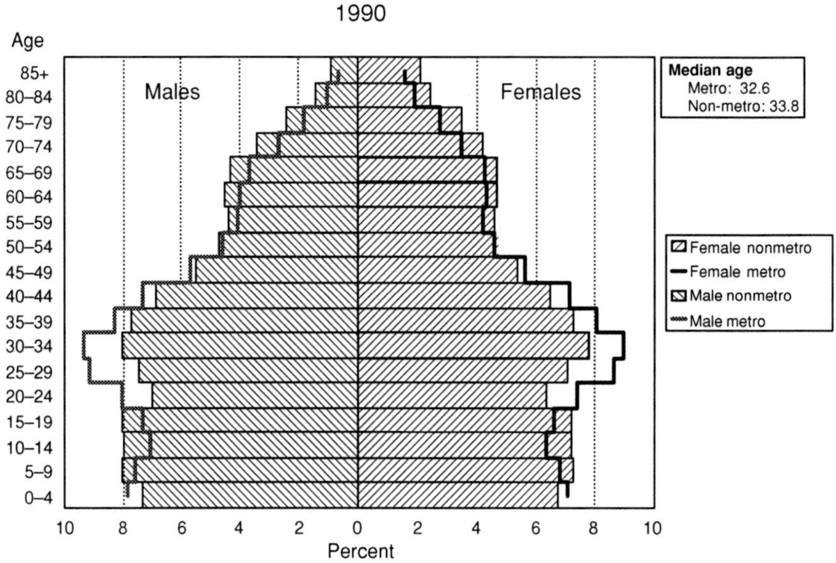

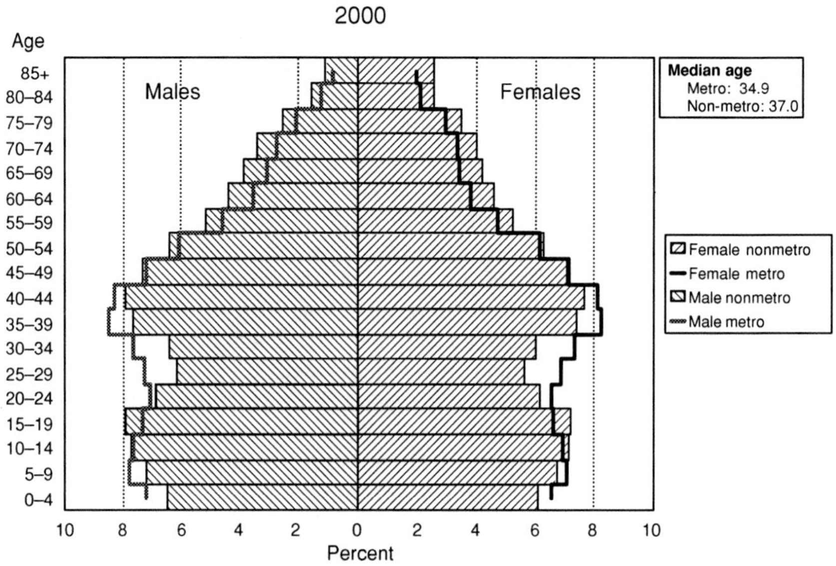

Figure 3.2. Median Age 1920 and 2000

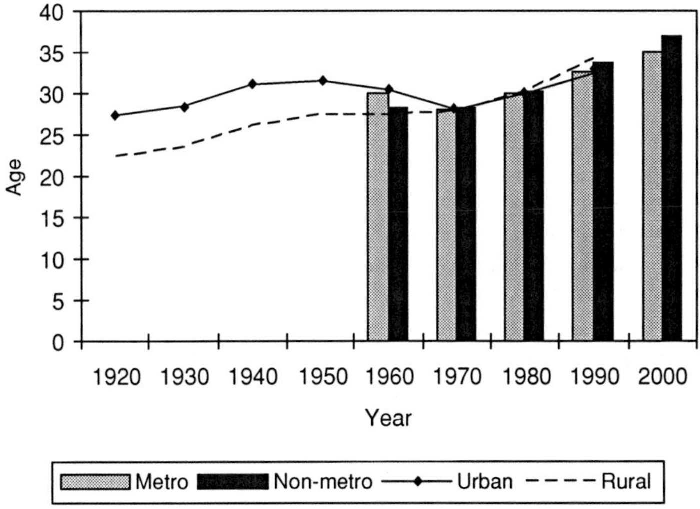

Despite the much-heralded "rural turnaround" of the 1970s, which saw the rural population increase at a faster rate than the urban population for the first time in decades, nonmetro areas continued to lose young adults—and their childbearing capacity—at the same time that they gained older adults. During the 1970's turnaround, net migration to nonmetro areas became positive after decades of net out-migration. Examining migration rates by age for the four years between 1975–76 and 1992–93, Fulton and colleagues (1997) found that 18–24-year-olds had net out-migration rates from nonmetro areas in every period, while persons 60 and over had net in-migration rates for every period. Nonmetro areas were not only losing young adults and their childbearing capacity but were gaining older adults throughout this period of renewed overall growth.

Although out-migration of rural youth to urban areas has been the pattern for over 100 years, this pattern became more important at the end of the 20th century (especially when coupled with the in-migration of older adults). This is because differences in rural and urban fertility narrowed throughout the 20th century and became negligible by 2000. In the past, higher rural birth rates helped offset the out-migration of rural youth. In the 21st century, migration will be the primary determinant of differential growth between rural and urban areas. Thus the continued out-migration of rural youth is likely to contribute to differentially higher aging in nonmetropolitan areas. These long-term historical trends were behind the jump in median age in nonmetro areas between 1990 and 2000.

The rapid aging of the population is a major trend affecting all areas of the United States, but, as noted above, the nonmetro population is aging more rapidly than the metro population. In 2000, 14.6 percent of the nonmetro population was age 65 or older compared to only 11.8 percent of the metro population. Moreover, trends affecting the age distributions of the metro and nonmetro populations vary by region of the country. For decades, the Great Plains and parts of the Midwest have experienced heavy out-migration of young people of childbearing age, which had a strong negative effect on fertility. It is now common for nonmetro counties in those regions to have natural decrease—an excess of deaths over births (McGranahan & Beale, 2002)—and they have the highest concentrations of older people of any nonmetro region of the United States (Glasgow, 1998). Nonmetro retirement migration has been channeled primarily to the South and West. Sunbelt migration has been a widespread phenomenon affecting all age groups, however, so that the South (except for Florida) and the West have not become disproportionately old. In the first quarter of the 21st century, both rural and urban areas will be affected by the aging of baby boomers because the leading edge of the baby boom will reach retirement age by 2010. Baby boomer aging will necessitate significant increases in health care, but it is more difficult and expensive to provide health services in rural than urban areas (Glasgow et al., 2004; Krout, 1998). Migration and/or a continuation of long-established residence patterns will determine the extent to which the aging of the baby boom generation affects different regions and metro versus nonmetro areas of the country.

An examination of the proportions of the population in different age groups by metro and nonmetro residence across the four broad census regions (Northeast, Midwest, South and West) shows roughly comparable proportional shares in each age group (data not shown). This suggests that variations in age composition by metro/nonmetro status are a subregional rather than a regional phenomenon. In other words, while rural areas in the Midwest as a whole may not be older than their counterparts in other regions, Plains counties with persisting dependence on agriculture are much older than the regional average. Moreover, percent change in the population by age group and residence shows regional variations between 1990 and 2000. To gain a better perspective on how rural population age composition is changing, we examine the differences and implications of those changes.

First, it is worth noting that, regardless of region, metro/nonmetro differences in population change by age group between 1990 and 2000 were substantial (Table 3.1). In all regions among all age groups, metro population gains were greater or declines were smaller than was the case for nonmetro areas. Nonmetro areas showed declines in the proportionate size of the less than 20 years of age population everywhere except in the West, whereas metro areas in all regions of the country gained younger persons. Nonmetro declines in this age segment will contribute to the further aging of the rural population. The 35–54 age group, comprised of baby boomers, had the largest increase in size of any age group, regardless of region or residence, yet in all regions metro areas showed larger population gains among baby boomers than did nonmetro areas. This suggests that the aging of the

Table 3.1. Percent Change in Metro/Nonmetro Population by Age and Region: 1990–2000

Age Group	United States	Northeast		Midwest		South		West	
	Total	Metro	Nonmetro	Metro	Nonmetro	Metro	Nonmetro	Metro	Nonmetro
Under 20	12.8	10.8	−13.3	10.9	− 5.1	23.9	−5.3	24.3	2.9
20–34	−5.4	−13.7	−29.1	−7.1	−16.8	3.9	−11.8	1.5	−8.2
35–54	31.9	26.0	11.3	30.7	19.4	43.9	17.1	38.5	26.4
55–64	14.8	3.9	−1.6	9.8	2.6	28.1	6.5	27.0	18.5
65–74	1.6	−5.5	−13.4	−0.4	−8.8	13.9	−6.4	8.9	−1.8
75 and older	26.4	23.9	5.5	26.9	6.2	39.9	6.7	42.3	23.0

baby boom will affect metro areas more than nonmetro areas, unless baby boomers migrate to rural areas in large numbers upon their retirement. Between 1990 and 2000, the population in the 65–74 age category shrank in size in all nonmetro regions and did so as well in metro areas of the Northeast and Midwest but not the South and West. The Depression-era birth cohorts entered this age group during the previous decade, which accounts for the drop off in growth of the 65–74 years population. The 75 and older segment showed large gains in population size, however, providing further indication of the rapid aging of the population. For that age group, proportional gains were considerably larger in metro than nonmetro areas, which over time would tend to equalize metro and nonmetro concentrations of older people.

Regional differences are apparent in that, between 1990 and 2000, the South and West continued to have higher population growth than the Northeast and Midwest (Table 3.1). This comparison pertained more to metro than nonmetro areas. Among nonmetro areas, the West had higher growth or smaller declines at each age group than did the other three regions. Overall, the South and West are more likely to experience the pluses and minuses of population growth than the Northeast and Midwest. Parts of the Northeast and Midwest are more likely to face issues related to population decline.

The currently middle-aged baby boomers will turn age 65 and older between 2010 and 2030. During that period, the number of older persons is projected to increase from 39 to 65 million, with the older population expected to comprise 20 percent or more of the national total population by 2030 (Siegel, 1993). After 2030, the older population will slowly decline as a proportion of the total, and the U.S. population is expected to reach zero population growth.

Baby boomers are approaching old age, and a large increase in the number of older people in the population between 2010 and 2030 is projected. This change will have implications for the types of housing, health care and transportation services that communities need to provide. Older people occupy smaller housing units than do younger families, and at some point in older people's lives they may need housing combined with personal and health care services (such as that provided in assisted living, continuing care retirement communities and nursing homes). Unfortunately, rural areas often do not have the capacity to meet increased demands for these types of services (Brown & Glasgow, 1991; Krout, 1998).

Presently, nonmetro areas are relatively more aged than metro areas, but, should trends of the previous decade continue into the 21st century, concentrations of older people in metro versus nonmetro areas may even out. Services for older people are relatively more difficult to provide in nonmetro than metro areas due to distance, sparse settlement patterns and lower capacity among rural governments to provide services (Krout, 1998). Moreover, in those rural areas characterized by chronic out migration of younger people, elderly parents are less likely to live in near proximity to their adult children than are metro older parents (Glasgow, 2000). Not only are formal services less available in rural areas, informal services provided by adult children and others in the informal network are also limited. Policies pertaining to the aging of baby boomers should pay particular attention to how formal services can bolster and support informal services.

HOW AGE RELATES TO GENDER

Age affects the gender makeup of rural places, which, in turn, affects family and household structure. First, since it is women who bear children, the presence of women of childbearing age in a population is associated with larger numbers of children. The fewer the women of childbearing age, the less likely there will be large numbers of children, and the population age structure will be older. As with the age structure of the population, gender affects the types of services required in nonmetro places, such as the need for obstetricians and childcare in populations with large proportions of younger women. In addition, most occupations are dominated by either males or by females. As a result, gender also affects the likelihood of employment. Men are less often employed in service occupations, so that the increase in service employment in rural places tends to favor women.

Second, as shown in Figure 3.3, regardless of race or ethnic background, the percentage female increases with age. Hence the proportion female in nonmetro places is highest in the oldest age groups. Simply put, women live longer than men even though more boys are born than girls. That is, if one thinks of the proportion

Figure 3.3. Nonmetro Percent Female by Race/Ethnicity and Age

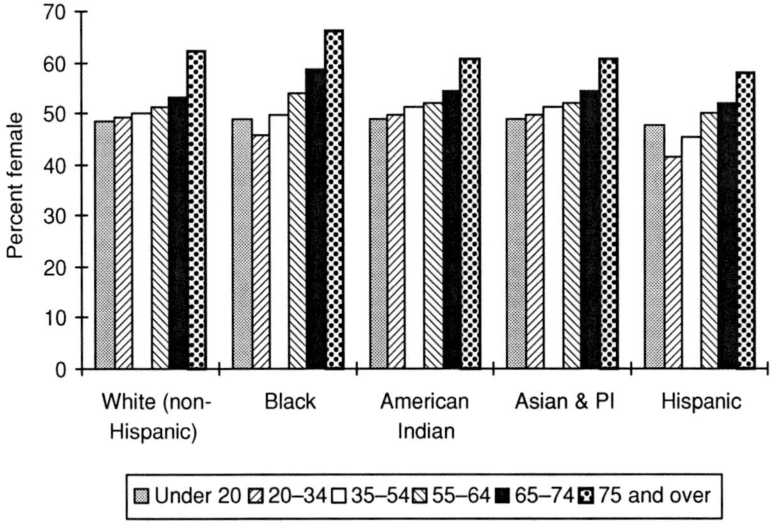

of males and females as a ratio, at birth there are about 105 male babies born for every 100 female babies. Over the life course, however, males are more likely to die at younger ages from accidents and certain illnesses, slowly eroding their numerical advantage. At age 35 there are equal numbers of males and females, and by age 65, there are only 70 males for every 100 females.

Historically, more urbanized places have had more women, while rural areas have had more men. This differential was in part due to higher birth rates in rural places, themselves a result of younger age structures. Moreover, rural places were frontier areas that attracted more male than female in-migrants and harbored employment opportunities like mining or forestry that were open primarily to men, not women. As family sizes declined, the age structure of rural places became increasingly older and the gender structure of rural places changed, although not as dramatically as age and race/ethnic structure changed (Fuguitt et al., 1989). The traditional pattern of youth leaving rural places for education and jobs in more urban settings persisted, ensuring that nonmetropolitan places grew older and became increasingly female.

This close relationship between aging and gender composition explains why the decline of the young adult population (20–34 years of age) in nonmetro counties in all four regions from 1990 to 2000 resulted also in changes in the proportion of men compared to women. The population pyramids in Figure 3.1 show that the percentage of the nonmetro population that is female and over age 34 increased while the percentage female in younger age groups did not.

Why does gender composition matter? Rural labor markets are and have long been more sex-selective of males than females. Rural economies were historically defined by male-oriented employment, whether in mining, fishing or other extractive industries. In the 1960s and '70s, however, the economic restructuring of rural places drew more women into the rural labor force, albeit into the lowest paying jobs (Fuguitt et al., 1989). An increasingly service-oriented economy means that rural employment tends to be more open to women now than in the past. However, rural female workers generally have less education and fewer work skills than do their urban counterparts, which tends to segregate them into low wage jobs. In addition, the greater gender segregation of rural labor markets further reduces the returns to education or employment training among women in rural than urban places (Bokemeier & Tickamyer, 1985; Gorham, 1992; McLaughlin & Perman, 1991; Lichter & McLaughlin, 1995; Sachs, 1996; Wells, 2002).

The gender make-up of nonmetro and rural places affects and is affected by family and household structure. In 1990, 70 percent of the older population lived alone or with a spouse, whereas, in 1850, 70 percent of elderly people resided with their adult children (Ruggles & Brower, 2003). Given increasing life expectancies and the greater predominance of women at older ages, nonmetro older females are at risk of becoming socially isolated. Hence, service providers and businesses in rural areas will have a growing role in supporting the needs of the greater presence of older rural women.

WHERE RACE AND ETHNICITY COME INTO PLAY

Racial and ethnic change in rural America has complicated the gender and age differentials described above. While rural America has always been racially and ethnically diverse, the racial and ethnic character of rural areas has evolved and changed since the settling of the first colonies. Historically, Native Americans were forcefully pushed further and further west onto reservations. African-origin slaves were brought to all of the original colonies, but for centuries they formed the backbone of the rural work force in the South's plantation economy. Spanish-speakers were absorbed when the United States wrested control of Florida from Spain and part or all of what would become the states of Texas, California, New Mexico, Arizona and Colorado from Mexico. Immigrants from China and the Philippines, a territory of the United States from 1898 to 1946, helped build the railroads of the West while Japanese immigrants established farms in many rural areas of the West. Western and Eastern European immigrants homesteaded in areas of the Midwest and West.

Immigration is often seen as targeting primarily urban areas, but this has never been completely true. In the latter part of the 20th century, both legal and illegal immigrants have migrated to or been recruited by industry to work throughout the rural United States. They have taken jobs as low wage laborers to tend and harvest crops and work in processing plants for fruits, vegetables, and in meat and poultry packing plants (Broadway, 1990; Griffith, 1990; Martin, 1984). In short, America's rural areas have never been racially and ethnically homogeneous, and many formerly homogeneous areas have been swept into the increasing diversity of the U.S. population.

These historical forces have been significantly modified by changes in U.S. immigration policy since the 1960s. These new laws have opened immigration to an increasingly diverse set of countries of origin and accelerated immigration to both urban and rural areas. In 1965, Congress passed a bill that replaced a national origins system favoring Western Europe with a system of family reunification without preference to particular countries or regions. In 1980, it eased restrictions on the admittance of refugees, many of whom were from Southeast Asia. In 1986, the Immigration Reform and Control Act legalized the status of 2.7 million unauthorized aliens, many from Latin America. The Special Agricultural Worker provision of the 1986 act made it easier for those who worked in agriculture, most of whom were in rural areas, to qualify for legal status. In contrast, between 1996 and 2002, the nation tried to tighten its borders, and several pieces of legislation were passed to try to stem the flow of illegal immigrants. (See Martin & Midgley, 2003 for a more complete discussion.)

Changing definitions of race and ethnicity across time complicate the comparability of data from census to census.[4] The major racial categories on the decennial census and those used in this chapter are: White; African American or Negro (referred to as Black in this chapter); American Indian or Alaska Native (referred to as American Indian); and Asian and Pacific Islander. Prior to 2000, persons were allowed to check only one category on the race question, but in 2000 persons were allowed to check more than one. Thus data on race are not strictly comparable between the 1990 and 2000 censuses. Because Hispanic Origin (considered an ethnic identity) and race were separate questions in both 1990 and 2000, it is possible to select out persons of Hispanic Origin from their racial group.

The census data presented in Table 3.2 reflect the increased racial and ethnic diversity that occurred in just one decade, from 1990 to 2000. In all regions, the metro population was more diverse than the nonmetro population—a smaller percent of the population was non-Hispanic White. Throughout the United States, in all regions and in both metro and nonmetro areas, the non-Hispanic White population grew more slowly than all other racial/ethnic groups and consequently declined as a percent of the population.

With the 2000 Census, the Black population remained by far the largest minority in nonmetro America at over four and a half million. In the United States as a whole during the last decade, however, the Hispanic population became the largest minority. In nonmetro areas, the Hispanic origin population rapidly gained ground on the Black population, growing by over a million compared to less than half that for Blacks. Should this trend continue, Hispanics would be the largest nonmetro minority by 2010.

With its history of slavery and, more recently, return migration of Northern Blacks to both the metro and nonmetro South (Frey, 2001; Stack, 1996), over 90 percent of the nonmetro Black population lived in the South in 2000. Over 17 percent of the South's nonmetro population was Black, far higher than in any other region in the United States. The growth of the nonmetro Black population in the South also accounted for 77 percent of the growth of the nonmetro Black population overall.

The nonmetro American Indian population was about one-fifth the size of the nonmetro Black population in 2000, but it was more evenly distributed regionally. Given the history of the reservation system, it is not surprising that the largest number, 523,000, or about half of the nonmetro American Indian population, lived in the West, where they made up fewer than 6 percent of nonmetro residents. In the South, the American Indian population was numerically larger than in the Midwest, but in each region it made up 1.2 percent of the nonmetro population. Only small numbers of American Indians remain in the Northeast. However, in all nonmetro areas, the proportion of American Indians grew faster than the non-Hispanic White population. This was due to higher fertility, a younger age structure, and a growing tendency for American Indians to self-identify starting with the 1970 census (Eschbach et al., 1998).

The Asian and Pacific Islander population was the smallest nonmetro minority in 2000. Prior to WWI, representatives of this group were often driven out of rural areas, and large amounts of land were confiscated from rural Japanese Americans at the beginning of WWII. More recent arrivals have tended to settle in

*Table 3.2. Race/Ethnicity by Region: 1990–2000**

	United States		Northeast		South		Midwest		West	
	Metro	Nonmetro	Metro	Nonmetro	Metro	Nonmetro	Metro	Nonmetro	Metro	Nonmetro
Non-Hispanic White										
Population 1990 (thousands)	145,032	43,393	35,351	5,089	44,215	17,213	35,925	15,313	29,540	5,778
Population 2000 (thousands)	148,564	45,989	34,138	5,189	47,436	18,492	36,642	15,744	30,347	6,564
Percent 1990	73.3	85.3	77.6	96.6	70.1	77.0	82.2	95.8	64.9	79.2
Percent 2000	66.0	81.9	71.0	94.3	63.0	74.1	77.1	93.2	55.8	74.5
Percent change 1990–2000	2.4	6.0	−3.4	2.0	7.3	7.4	2.0	2.8	2.7	13.6
Black										
Population 1990 (thousands)	24,955	4,329	5,180	70	11,718	3,955	5,419	241	2,638	64
Population 2000 (thousands)	29,162	4,786	5,687	98	14,449	4,318	6,148	289	2,879	81
Percent 1990	12.6	8.5	11.4	1.3	18.6	17.7	12.4	1.5	5.8	0.9
Percent 2000	12.9	8.5	11.8	1.8	19.2	17.3	12.9	1.7	5.3	0.9
Percent change 1990–2000	16.9	10.5	9.8	40.8	23.3	9.2	13.5	19.8	9.1	27.3
American Indian										
Population 1990 (thousands)	962	904	90	18	297	268	169	166	406	453
Population 2000 (thousands)	1,028	1,041	93	20	335	302	167	195	433	523
Percent 1990	0.5	1.8	0.2	0.3	0.5	1.2	0.4	1.0	0.9	6.2
Percent 2000	0.5	1.9	0.2	0.4	0.4	1.2	0.4	1.2	0.8	5.9
Percent change 1990–2000	6.8	15.1	2.8	11.0	12.8	13.0	−1.5	17.9	6.7	15.6

(cont.)

Table 3.2. (Continued)

	United States		Northeast		South		Midwest		West	
	Metro	Nonmetro	Metro	Nonmetro	Metro	Nonmetro	Metro	Nonmetro	Metro	Nonmetro
Asian and PI										
Population 1990 (thousands)	6,607	388	1,260	30	997	74	673	69	3,677	215
Population 2000 (thousands)	10,005	472	2,076	40	1,822	120	1,113	93	4,994	219
Percent 1990	3.3	0.8	2.8	0.6	1.6	0.3	1.5	0.4	8.1	2.9
Percent 2000	4.4	0.8	4.3	0.7	2.4	0.5	2.3	0.5	9.2	2.5
Percent change 1990–2000	51.4	21.7	64.8	35.1	82.8	61.8	65.5	33.9	35.8	2.0
Hispanic Origin										
Population 1990 (thousands)	20,036	1,864	3,581	58	5,824	838	1,475	185	9,156	784
Population 2000 (thousands)	32,130	3,176	5,154	100	10,115	1,472	2,715	409	14,146	1,194
Percent 1990	10.1	3.7	7.9	1.1	9.2	3.7	3.4	1.2	20.1	10.7
Percent 2000	14.3	5.7	10.7	1.8	13.4	5.9	5.7	2.4	26.0	13.6
Percent change 1990–2000	60.4	70.4	43.9	73.8	73.7	75.7	84.0	121.8	54.5	52.3

* Percents do not sum to 100 because the "some other race" and "two or more races" categories have been omitted. In 2000 only a small number of people were in these categories. However, it will be very important to follow trends in the "two or more races" category (an option available for the first time on the 2000 Census).

metro areas, primarily on the west coast. In 2000, the largest number of nonmetro Asian and Pacific Islanders was located in the West (2.5 percent of the nonmetro population), but their numbers grew slowly during the last decade, resulting in a percentage decline from 55 percent of all nonmetro Asians and Pacific Islanders in 1990, to just 46 percent by 2000. The nonmetro South experienced the greatest numeric increase in Asian and Pacific Islanders during the last decade, followed by the Midwest and the Northeast. This reflects the trend of Southeast Asian refugees to settle in selected nonmetro counties to work in poultry processing and meat packing plants and other low wage industries.

The Hispanic population was by far the most rapidly growing minority in the United States during the last decade. Their growth was so rapid that, by 2000, they outnumbered Blacks in metro areas. They are quite likely to outnumber Blacks in nonmetro areas by the end of this decade as well. The South experienced the largest increase in the number of nonmetro Hispanics and had the largest number in 2000, 1.4 million or 5.9 percent of its nonmetro population. The number of Hispanics in the West was only slightly smaller than in the South but represented 13.6 percent of this region's nonmetro population. In addition, both the Northeast and the Midwest witnessed substantial increases in the number of Hispanics.

HOW RACE AND ETHNICITY INTERSECT WITH GENDER AND AGE

Gender

As noted earlier, the number of males exceeds females at birth, but these numbers are essentially equal in the young adult years, with the preponderance of females increasing at older ages. Imbalances from this expected pattern should be examined to determine why they have occurred and the policy implications for areas where they occur. In 2000, the pattern described above characterized the non-Hispanic White, American Indian, Asian and Pacific Islander and two or more races populations for both metro and nonmetro areas and for all regions (data not shown). By contrast, the nonmetro Black population in the Northeast, Midwest and West varied markedly from this pattern and from the metro population, as did the Hispanic population in all regions. Figure 3.4 shows that, with the exception of the South, the relative lack of Black females in nonmetro areas for 20–54 year olds is striking. In the Northeast and West, only about a quarter of 20–54-year-old Blacks were female. As Figure 3.4 shows, this pattern is also apparent, although not as markedly, for the Hispanic population in all regions. In each region the percent female in nonmetro areas is below the percent female in metro areas.

To understand these gender imbalances, we examine, in Figure 3.5, the percent of male Black and Hispanic 18–64-year-olds (more detailed age groups were not available) living in correctional facilities in 2000 by metro and nonmetro areas, one possible reason for the deficit of young females shown in Figure 3.4. In 2000, in all regions of the United States, including the South, nonmetro Blacks

Figure 3.4. Percent Female by Race/Ethnicity, Ages 20–54

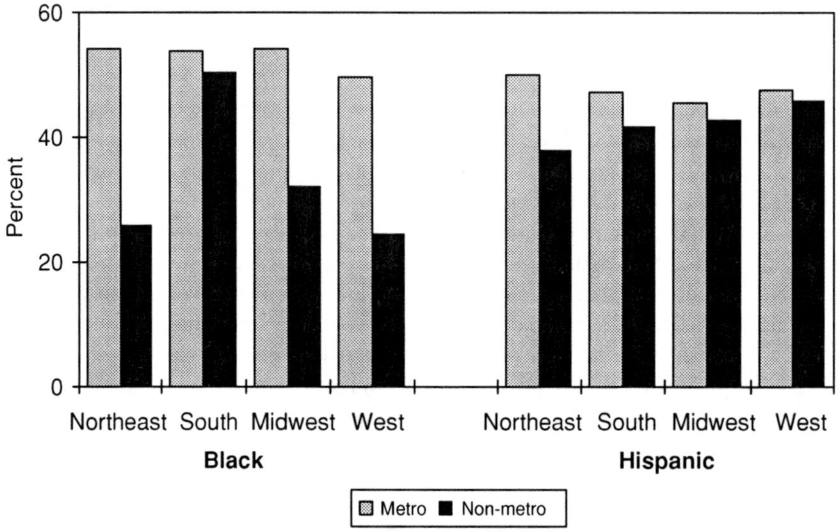

Figure 3.5. Percent of Males in Correctional Institutions by Race/Ethnicity, Ages 18–64

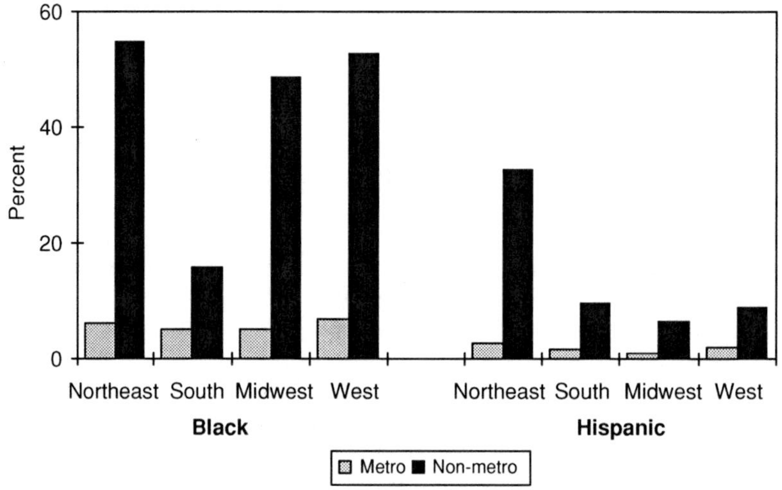

were more likely to live in prisons than metro Blacks, but this difference was extreme in the Northeast, Midwest and West. In those regions, around half of nonmetro Black males 18–64 years of age lived in correctional institutions.[5] Many nonmetro areas have pursued a policy of recruiting correctional facilities to offset job losses in resource-based industries. These data probably reflect such policies. However, these high figures must be understood in the context of low overall Black population living outside the nonmetro South.

Nonmetro Hispanic males 18–64 were also more likely to live in prisons than metro Hispanics. The most extreme case was in the Northeast, where one-third of nonmetro Hispanic males lived in such institutions. The rates of incarceration were higher for nonmetro than metro Hispanics in other regions as well, but probably not enough to account for the preponderance of young males in the general population. Immigration and labor trends probably account for that preponderance. A culture of Mexican migration to the United States, especially among young males (Kandel & Massey, 2002), would lead to a greater preponderance of Hispanic males. In addition, in 2000 Hispanic males far outnumbered females in two of the most important rural industries, agriculture (5:1) and food processing (2:1) (U.S. Bureau of the Census, 2000).

Age Composition

Changes in the age composition of metro and nonmetro areas overall were described earlier. It is also important to consider whether there are differences in age by race/ethnicity, which could lead to inter-ethnic tensions over the distribution of needed services. As Figure 3.6 shows, the median age of the non-Hispanic White population in nonmetro areas was around 40 years. The median age of nonmetro minorities was younger, generally substantially younger. On average, American Indian and Asian and Pacific Islander populations were around nine years younger. But the nonmetro Black population was more than 12 years younger than non-Hispanic Whites, and the Hispanic population was fully 15.6 years younger. Similar differences exist in metro areas as well, but they are more muted mainly because the metro, non-Hispanic White population is somewhat younger. Historical factors already described, including the decline of fertility overall, equalization of metro-nonmetro fertility rates, and out-migration of rural youth, primarily affected the non-Hispanic White population. In addition, international migrants are concentrated in the young-adult, childbearing years (McFalls, 2003).

Are these trends in diversity important to rural America? In an article titled "The Diversity Myth," Frey contends that immigrants tend to concentrate in a few areas, and that "multiethnic counties are few and far between" (Frey, 1998; p. 39). It is true that many rural areas are not racially and ethnically diverse, and they are likely to remain primarily non-Hispanic White, especially those in the Midwest experiencing population loss. But to talk of diversity only in terms of current immigration trends ignores the nation's history. The nonmetro South has

Figure 3.6. Median Age for White (non-Hispanic) and Minority Populations: 2000

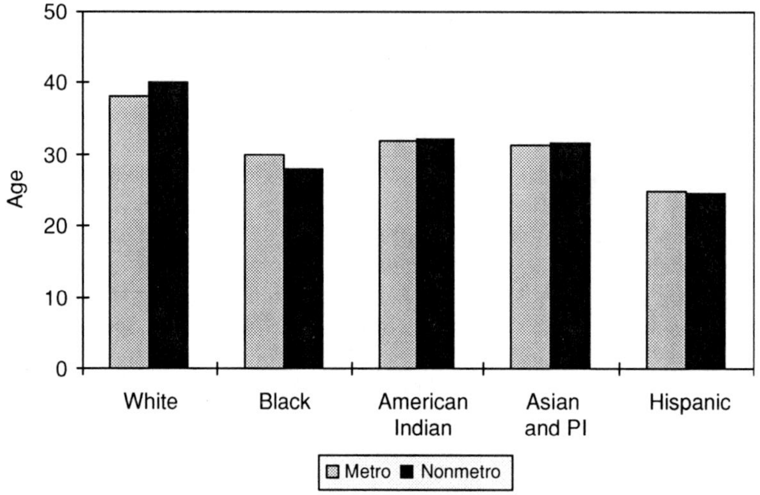

always been racially diverse, and most of the nation's American Indian reservations are located west of the Mississippi River. Descendants and cousins of the diverse Asian and Pacific Islanders who helped build the intercontinental railroad and farm California's Central Valley are also concentrated in the West. Moreover, with the absorption of Mexican territory in the 19th century, western and southwestern counties have historically had Spanish-speaking populations. These populations grew more rapidly in nonmetro areas than the non-Hispanic White population during the 1990s and will probably continue to do so in the coming decade. Policies that ignore the growing importance of racial and ethnic diversity in the rural population are increasingly likely to be inappropriate.

THE DENOUEMENT TO THE AGE, SEX, RACE/ETHNICITY STORY

This chapter has examined three important aspects of nonmetro population composition: age, gender and race/ethnicity. Major changes in all three of these characteristics have important policy implications. Nonmetro America is aging more rapidly than metropolitan America. Because of the out-migration of rural youth throughout the 20th century, the impact of the baby boom has been more limited in nonmetro areas. Moreover, birth rates, rather than exceeding those in metro America, as was the case for much of the 20th century, are now at parity. This is coupled with the attractiveness of many nonmetro areas for retirement living since the 1970s. Although these trends will be exacerbated or muted in specific counties depending on their history, natural amenities, economic base and proximity to metro areas, the analysis here shows that nonmetro areas in all regions of the United States experienced a continued loss of young adults, which contributed to a rapid aging of the nonmetro population.

The aging of the nonmetro population comes in spite of the fact that growth of the 65–74-year-old age group slowed during the 1990s in nonmetropolitan areas because these were the small cohorts born during the Great Depression. As their children, the baby boomers, age into the retirement years beginning in 2008, nonmetro areas will likely see rapid growth in this age group through both aging in place and continued retirement migration. During the 1990s, the 75 and over population increased in all regions of the United States. This increase was generally slower in nonmetro than metro areas, but service provision for the oldest adults in nonmetro areas often lags behind that in more urban areas.

In addition, as populations age, they become more female. The non-Hispanic White population makes up the largest number of nonmetro older adults 75 and over and is approximately 63 percent female, except in the West (58 percent). Rather than live with adult children as they did a century ago, older adults are now more likely to live alone. Many women over age 75 who were living alone in 2000 may be doing so for the first time in their lives. These women were born in 1925 or earlier, when it was customary for young women to live at home or with relatives until they were married. The small size of informal social supports in many rural communities challenges their capacity to supply essential services (Glasgow, 2000). Both the public and private sector are needed to provide substitute services for older people that would typically be provided by kin and friendship networks were these structures stronger.

Finally, nonmetro racial/ethnic diversity is increasing through immigration and through the large share of immigrants who are of childbearing age. The influx adds to a historically diverse mix of Blacks, primarily in the South; American Indians, often connected with reservations, primarily in the South and West; an increasing Asian and Pacific Islander population, particularly in the South but also in the Midwest and Northeast; and a Spanish-speaking culture in the South and West that was absorbed when the United States conquered parts of Mexico in the 19th century and has been augmented by immigration since the end of the Bracero Program. This growing diversity complicates the picture of nonmetropolitan areas. Some counties will remain primarily White, but others already have notable non-White minorities that have lived there for generations. Still others are experiencing the rapid growth of Hispanics or South East Asians as industries seek low wage labor and as individuals and families seek to improve their standard of living.

The young Black and Hispanic populations are more heavily male in several regions of the country. Many nonmetro areas actively sought the building of prisons to replace job losses in other sectors, and a large percent of the nonmetro Black population in all regions but the South was incarcerated in 2000. This attempt by rural areas to make up for job losses suffered by more traditional industries needs further examination, among other reasons to determine if persons incarcerated where it may be difficult for families to visit have higher or lower rates of recidivism.

Immigration streams that draw more heavily on males have increased the proportions of young Hispanic males in nonmetro areas. If past demographic trends persist, wives and children will join many of these men and/or they will marry and have children. Hispanics are already the youngest segment of the nonmetro population and these trends will ensure that this situation continues in the coming decades.

All of the changes related to the composition of the population raise challenges and opportunities that rural areas will face in the decades to come. For example, older adults are wealthier, more active, and healthier than in the past. When they are in-migrants, they bring incomes earned outside the area. Jobs that are related to this retirement population should do well in the future. Such jobs may range from low-wage jobs such as housecleaning and yard work to much better-paying employment in specialty health, medical, dental and vision services.

But it is up to individual communities to make sure that the types of services as well as the goods that this population would like to purchase are available in the area. A healthier population of older adults means that this population is more likely to travel to metro areas if the goods they need are not available in rural areas. And, as an increasing number of computer-literate older adults retire in rural areas, they can easily make purchases on-line. Given that the older population is more heavily female than other age groups, it is important to make sure that older women feel they have service providers and businesses that they see as safe and reliable.

An important question that will confront aging individuals as well as the nonmetro communities in which they live is the extent to which those communities can provide the specialty medical and housing needs of the oldest old. Will the very elderly find it more convenient to leave rural communities for urban ones to have access to these services? And to what extent do or can communities provide services for this population?[6]

All of this is complicated by changes in race/ethnicity and gender. Nonmetro areas have witnessed the pervasive out-migration of high school graduates for many decades. While birth rates have fallen for all racial and ethnic groups, the non-Hispanic White population has the lowest birth rate. Birthrates for minority groups are somewhat higher, and they have a higher proportion of young adults in the childbearing years. Many rural areas have an older non-Hispanic White female population and a younger minority population with a higher proportion of younger males.

This relatively young minority population has service needs as well. Most importantly, pregnant and nursing mothers need routine pre- and postnatal care if they and their children are to be healthy. Young children need routine vaccinations as well as doctor visits to avoid serious and costly health emergencies, and these children need good schooling to move into jobs with benefits and above-poverty-level pay scales. Older adults, the population most likely to vote, however, are sometimes hesitant to support tax increases, especially for property taxes. Many local services, such as schools, rely heavily on local taxes.

Many rural communities will be facing issues related to this bifurcation of the population—an older non-Hispanic White population with a greater proportion of females, and a younger minority, often proportionately more male population with a rapidly growing number of young children—a generation gap reinforced by a culture gap. The ongoing viability of rural communities has always depended on how well residents work together. Thus, it is important for rural places to make sure that the Latino businessmen, Hmong seamstresses, Filipino computer programmers, Norwegian farmers, retired female attorneys and organic hobby farmers are all included in community decisions and all benefit from community services. Cooperation and understanding between an older White population, and a younger minority population will enhance the viability of rural areas. Without this, many rural areas could see increasing rates of rural minority poverty, failing education systems and increasing tensions that will be detrimental to all segments of the population.

ENDNOTES

1. Anabelle Kirschner acknowledges support from the Washington State University ARC Project 0981 and the assistance of Julie Rice. E. Helen Berry acknowledges support from Utah Experiment Station grants #UAES0843 and UAES0835. Nina Glasgow's work on this chapter was supported by a grant from the USDA's National Research Initiative and by Hatch Grant #159-7925 from the New York State Agricultural Experiment Station at Cornell University.
2. The baby boom took place between approximately 1945 and 1965. The youngest of the baby boomers would have been 25 and the oldest 45 years of age in 1990.
3. The metro/nonmetro time series begins in 1960 because this category was established after the 1950 census. Using an urban/rural definition (urban places are those with populations greater than 2,500) produces a longer time series.
4. A question on race has been on the census since 1790. While the wording of this evolved over time, important changes have occurred since 1970. In that year, a question on Hispanic Origin (considered an ethnic identity) was added because a rapidly growing number of persons from Spanish speaking countries did not identify with any one racial group and checked the "other" category under race.
5. It should be remembered that the Black population is small in these regions Beale (1996).
6. Glasgow (1998) found that migration of older-old people from nonmetro-to-metro areas was equal to their rate of migration from metro-to-nonmetro areas.

REFERENCES

Beale, C. (1996). Rural prisons: An update. *Rural Development Perspectives, 11*, 25–27.

Bokemeier, J.L., & Tickamyer, A.R. (1985). Labor force experiences of nonmetropolitan women. *Rural Sociology, 62,* 1–20.

Broadway, M. (1990). Meatpacking and its social and economic consequences. *Urban Anthropology, 19,* 321–344.

Brown, D.L., & Glasgow, N.L. (1991). Capacity building and rural government adaptation to population change. In C. B. Flora & J. A. Christenson (Eds.), *Rural policies for the 1990s* (pp. 194–221). Boulder, CO: Westview.

Eschbach, K., Supple, K., & Snipp, C.M. (1998). Changes in racial identification and the educational attainment of American Indians, 1970–1990. *Demography, 35,* 35–43.
Frey, W. (1998). The diversity myth. *American Demographics, 20,* 38–43.
Frey, W. (2001). Migration to the south brings blacks full circle. *Population Today, 29*(1), 4–5.
Fuguitt, G.V., Brown, D.L., & Beale, C.L. (1989). *Rural and small town America.* New York: Sage.
Fulton, J.A., Fuguitt, G.V., & Gibson, R.M. (1997). Recent changes in metropolitan-nonmetropolitan migration streams. *Rural Sociology, 62,* 363–385.
Glasgow, N. (1998). *The nonmetro elderly: Economic and demographic status* (Rural Development Report No. 70). Washington, DC: U.S. Department of Agriculture, Economic Research Service.
Glasgow, N. (2000). Rural/urban patterns of aging and caregiving in the United States. *Journal of Family Issues, 21,* 611–631.
Glasgow, N., Morton, L.W., & Johnson, N.E. (Eds.). (2004). *Critical issues in rural health.* Ames, IA: Blackwell.
Gorham, L. (1992). The growing problem of low earnings in rural areas. In C. M. Duncan (Ed.), *Rural poverty in America,* 21–40. New York: Auburn.
Griffith, D. (1990). Consequences of immigration reform for low-wage workers in the southeastern U. S. *Urban Anthropology, 19,* 155–184.
Kandel, W., & Massey, D.S. (2002). The culture of Mexican migration: A theoretical and empirical analysis. *Social Forces, 80,* 981–2004.
Krout, J.A. (1998). Services and service delivery in rural environments. In R.T. Coward & J.A. Krout (Eds.), *Aging in rural settings: Life circumstances and distinctive features* (pp. 247–266). New York: Springer.
Lichter, D.T., & McLaughlin, D.K. (1995). Changing economic opportunities, family structure, and poverty in rural areas. *Rural Sociology, 60*, 688–706.
Martin, P. (1984). *Migrant labor in agriculture: An international comparison.* Berkeley, CA: Giannini Foundation.
Martin, P., & Midgley, E. (2003). Immigration: Shaping and reshaping America. *Population Bulletin, 58,* 1–44.
McFalls, J.A. (2003). Population: A lively introduction.*Population Bulletin, 58,* 1–40.
McGranahan, D.A., & Beale, C.L. (2002). Understanding rural population loss. *Rural America, 17,* 2–11.
McLaughlin, D.K., & Perman, L. (1991). Returns versus endowments in the earnings attainment process for metropolitan and nonmetropolitan men and women. *Rural Sociology, 56,* 339–365.
McLaughlin, D.K., Stokes, C.S., & Nonoyama, A. (2001). Residence and income inequality: Effects on mortality among U. S. counties. *Rural Sociology, 66,* 579–598.
Morton, L.W. (2004). Spatial patterns of rural mortality. In N. Glasgow, L.W. Morton, & N.E. Johnson (Eds.), *Critical issues in Rural Health,* 37–45. Ames, IA: Blackwell.
Ruggles, S., & Brower, S. (2003). Measurement of household and family composition in the United States, 1850–2000. *Population and Development Review, 29,* 73–101.
Sachs, C. (1996). *Gendered fields: Rural women, agriculture, and environment.* Boulder, CO: Westview.
Siegel, J.S. (1993). *A generation of change: A profile of America's older population.* New York: Sage.
Stack, C.B. (1996). *Call to home: African Americans reclaim the rural south.* New York: Basic Books.
U.S. Dept. of Commerce, Bureau of the Census. Census of Population and Housing 2000 [United States]: Summary File of Washington, D.C.: U.S. Dept. of Commerce, Bureau of the Census.
Wells, B. (2002). Women's voices: Explaining poverty and plenty in a rural community. *Rural Sociology, 67,* 234–254.

CHAPTER 4

CHANGING LIVELIHOODS IN RURAL AMERICA

ALEXANDER C. VIAS AND PETER B. NELSON

INTRODUCTION

Globalization and economic restructuring have profoundly affected the rural economy over the past 30 years (Glasmeier & Conroy, 1994). As noted in the introductory chapter, the notion of a rural economy reliant on a stable farming sector has been outmoded for decades. Today, fewer than one in 10 people living in rural America has a job directly related to farming. New competitive pressures will continue to change the rural economy and have significant impacts on the livelihoods of rural Americans, as workers in virtually all industries scramble to maintain a reasonable and sustainable standard of living in an increasingly volatile global market. At the same time, the ways in which globalization and economic restructuring play out both across geographic regions and within economic sectors is far from uniform. Impacts of these macro-scale processes on rural livelihoods merit examination at various levels of analysis.

The nature of rural economic change over the past few decades is an active topic of research (Barkley, 1993; Falk & Lobao, 2003; Galston & Baehler, 1995; McGranahan, 2003), as are the linkages between economic, demographic and social change (Castle, 1995; Fuguitt et al., 1989). However, the increasing pace of global change, especially over the past 10 years, presents new challenges to rural Americans and their way of life. In this chapter we consider the nature of nonmetropolitan economic change in the last 30 years by examining links between the rural and global economies, exploring internal restructuring in specific sectors of the rural economy, and outlining repercussions of these changes for employment and income in various U.S. regions.

The last 30 years brought significant sectoral shifts in rural employment within the United States (see Figure 4.1). Using data from the Regional Economic Information System (REIS) throughout our analysis, we identify three broad sectors that now comprise well over three quarters of all nonmetropolitan employment (Bureau of Economic Analysis, 2003). These include agriculture, manufacturing, and the tertiary sector consisting of transportation, communications and public

W.A. Kandel & D.L. Brown (eds.), Population Change and Rural Society, 75–102.

Figure 4.1. Composition of Nonmetropolitan Employment

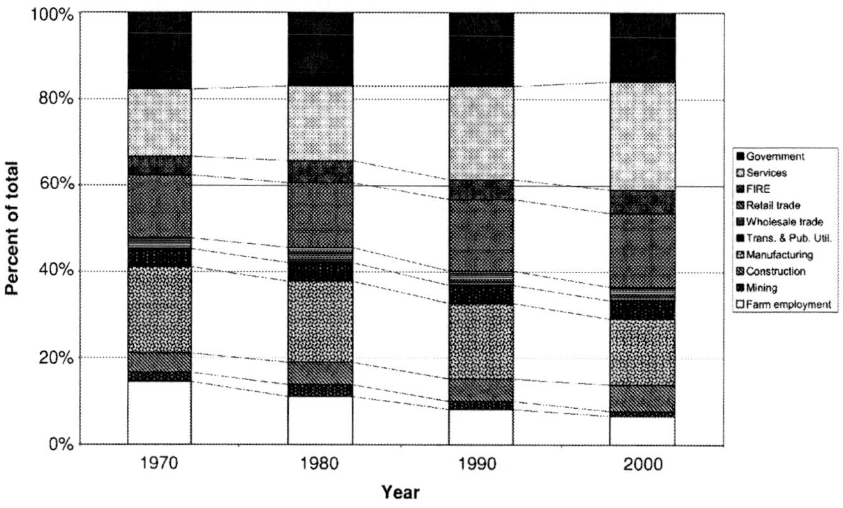

Source: REIS 2003.

utilities; wholesale and retail trade; finance, insurance and real estate; services; and public administration/government. However, the trajectory of these three principle sectors has been quite different over the last 30 years. Since 1970, there has been a dramatic decrease in the share of total employment within agriculture, from nearly 15 percent to less than 7 percent. In contrast, the broadly defined tertiary sector now accounts for nearly 50 percent of all nonmetropolitan employment. Manufacturing's share of total employment has dropped modestly, but shares for both 1970 and 2000 remain between 15 and 20 percent. Through our examination of these key economic sectors, we illustrate some of the fundamental processes of globalization and economic restructuring and their impacts on rural livelihoods.

The section on agriculture illustrates how globalization radically alters the competitive environment farmers now face. It further explores the internal restructuring of the sector as more and more output comes from fewer but larger farms, and it describes changes in the spatial distribution of agriculture around the United States over the past 30 years. The section concludes with a brief discussion of how farmers respond to this new economic environment. The section on manufacturing highlights regional trends in employment and income in the manufacturing sector. It illustrates how nonmetropolitan economies have benefited as manufacturing jobs move down the urban hierarchy, while rural manufacturing workers struggle relative to their urban counterparts to earn comparable wages. In contrast to agriculture and manufacturing, the tertiary sector is by far the largest part of the rural economy today. The section devoted to the tertiary sector emphasizing retail trade, services, public administration/government, and finance, insurance and real estate illustrates how structural shifts in the developed economies of the world increase the significance of the tertiary sector, especially compared to traditional rural economic staples such as agriculture and manufacturing. Unlike agriculture, however, we find the tertiary sector operates on a different spatial scale driven primarily by local demand. Moreover, individual components of the tertiary sector are quite different from each other (e.g., consumer services versus producer services), and the spatial impact of increasing or decreasing employment in one sub-sector as opposed to another will be quite different. In an era characterized by widely varied experiences across space in terms of growth and decline in local populations, an unstable customer base will create prosperous and difficult times for people relying on these sectors for their livelihood.

AGRICULTURE

Despite dramatic growth in other segments of the rural economy and its relative decline in the share of total rural employment, agriculture remains a critical sector in rural America for several reasons. First, agriculture is often the primary link between the rural countryside and the global economy. Second, agriculture still dominates rural areas in terms of land use. Finally, agriculture and farming are deeply embedded in conceptions of American rurality. This section focuses on three substantive questions surrounding agriculture in the rural United States at different geographic scales. First, how is United States agriculture connected to the global economy? Second, how has the structure of farming changed across different regions of rural America? Third, how have the economics of farming been transformed over the last 30 years? The final segment of this section briefly describes some ways in which farm operators respond to the increased challenges posed by globalization and restructuring.

Placing Agriculture on the Global Stage

Agriculture in the United States is intricately linked to the global economy and is one of the few sectors of the economy consistently showing a trade surplus (ERS, 2003b). Figure 4.2 presents the agricultural trade balance and exchange rate for the United States for the 1970–2002 period. Figure 4.2 illustrates how the last 30 years have been characterized by an increasing trend towards export-oriented agriculture and increased integration into the global economy. Prior to the 1970s, U.S. agricultural imports and exports were roughly equal, resulting in a trade balance hovering around zero. This situation changed dramatically in the 1970s. Beginning in 1970, agricultural exports greatly exceeded imports, generating an increasing agricultural trade surplus. After peaking in 1981, however, the agricultural surplus dropped for seven consecutive years before recovering in 1987. The late 1980s

Figure 4.2. Trade Balance and Exchange Rates

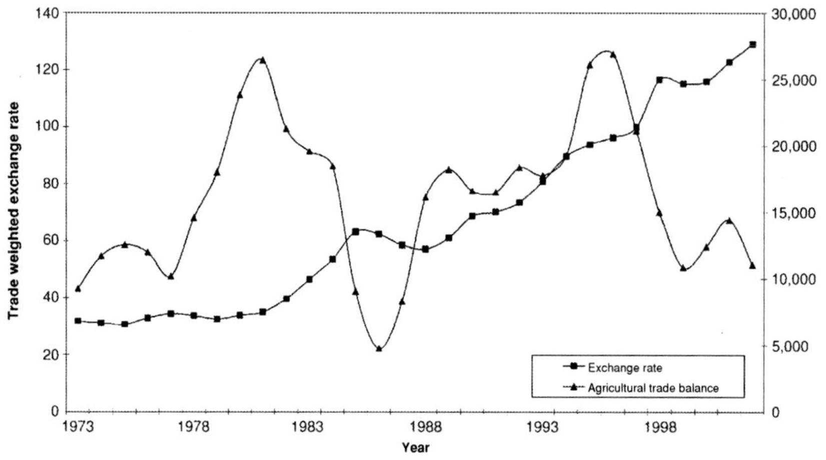

Source: Economic Research Service, http://www.ers.usda.gov/data/FATUS/DATA/XMScy1935.xls, Federal Reserve Bank.

and early 1990s brought an increasing surplus that spiked again in 1997 before experiencing more volatility in the most recent years.

Explanations behind these agricultural trends highlight the myriad connections between U.S. agriculture, federal policy, and markets overseas. Briefly, the peaks and valleys of the last 30 years result from fluctuations in interest rates, inflation, and global economic conditions. In the early 1970s, the Nixon administration devalued the dollar, making U.S. agricultural exports less expensive on the global market. This devaluation coincided with opening of trade relations with China and reduced harvests in the Soviet Union (Barnett, 2000). The combination of these three factors created tremendous opportunity for the U.S. farm sector in the 1970s, as agricultural exports increased six-fold while imports increased barely three-fold. Figure 4.2 clearly shows a link between the increased agricultural trade surplus and the value of the U.S. dollar. As the dollar increased in value in the late 1970s, the trade balance plummeted.

As the declining value of the dollar and conditions in foreign markets combined to create favorable export conditions, further processes of economic change on the domestic front contributed to increased levels of domestic production. High nominal interest rates and high inflation in the early 1970s created extremely low *real* interest rates. Low interest rates provided the mechanism for many farm operators to expand their operations through increased land purchases and increased capital intensification (Barnett, 2000). During the 1970s and 1980s, farm debt-to-equity ratios increased from a low of 19.28 percent in 1974 to 29.84 percent in 1985, as farmers took advantage of these low real interest rates and borrowed money (ERS, 2003a).

Yet, the agricultural boom of the 1970s began to crumble in the early 1980s. Steadily decreasing inflation coupled with high interest rates created rising real interest rates. At the same time, global production levels increased alongside domestic production, creating an oversupply of agricultural products on the global market. Prices dropped, and those producers saddled with high levels of debt found it increasingly difficult to meet their debt obligations (Hobbs &Weagley, 1995). In addition, beginning in 1980, the value of the U.S. dollar rose, making U.S. exports more expensive in international markets. This convergence of both international and domestic factors contributed to the widely discussed farm crisis of the 1980s.

Agricultural exports rebounded in the late 1980s and early 1990s as the farm crisis came to an end and the trade balance stabilized. More recently, however, the agricultural trade balance has dropped once again, and continues to be more volatile. Once more, the value of the dollar has steadily risen against foreign currencies, making U.S. agricultural exports comparatively more expensive. Further difficulties emerge from foreign markets. The early 1990s marked a significant economic crisis in East Asia, a major trading partner for U.S. agriculture. Sluggish demand in East Asia coupled with dropping prices for Asian agricultural products greatly reduced the value of U.S. exports to Asia, and increased the flow of Asian imports. Between 1995 and 2002, the value of U.S. exports dropped 6 percent while imports have increased 38.6 percent (ERS, 2003).

The Changing Shape of U.S. Farms—Regional Perspectives

The peaks and valleys of agricultural trade over the last 30 years have reshaped the structure of U.S. agriculture both nationally and regionally. These changes can be summarized at the national level as an overall decline in the number of farms, a drop in the amount of land in farming, and an increased capitalization of farming. While these trends at the national scale are well documented, they mask significant regional variations in agricultural restructuring. Figures 4.3 and 4.4 present changes in the number of farms and land in farms by region for the last 30 years. Nationally, it appears that the number of farms after dropping dramatically during the 1970s and 1980s, stabilized by the 1990s, indicating a possible end to the decline (see also Chapter 5).

The regional variations evident in Figures 4.3 and 4.4 suggest that the farm experience is anything but uniform across space. Farm numbers dropped most precipitously in the Plains, Great Lakes, and Southeast regions, decreasing at rates faster than the national decrease. The 1980s farm crisis was felt most strongly in these three regions. In contrast to the struggles of these regions, the Far West, Rocky Mountains, and Southwest all enjoyed stable or expanding numbers of farms, with accelerated growth in the early 1990s.

Figure 4.3. Relative Change in the Number of Farms by Region, 1970–2000

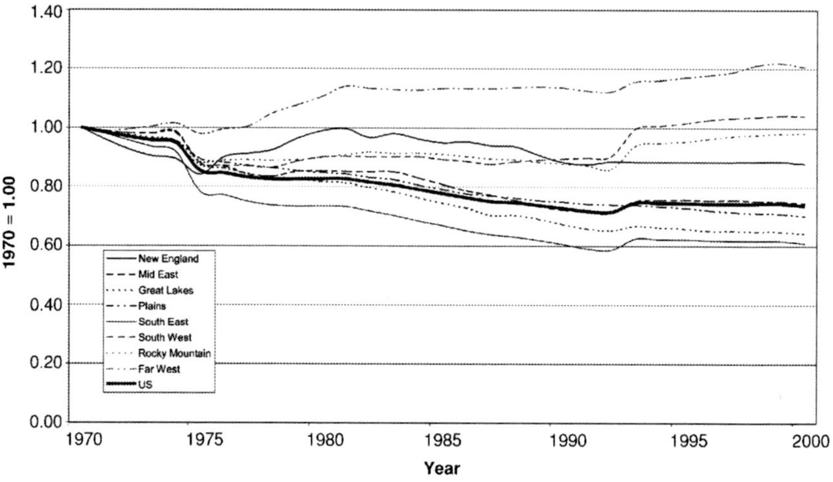

Source: Economic Research Service, 2003.

Figure 4.4. Relative Change in Farmland by Region, 1970–2000

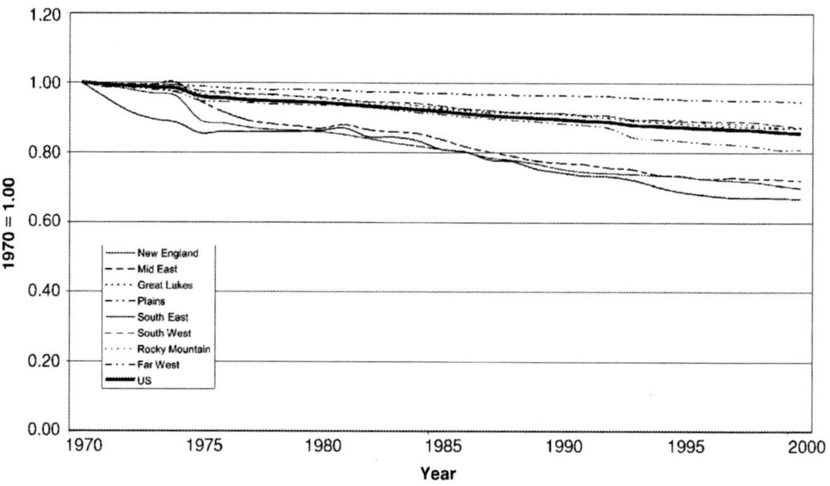

Source: Economic Research Service, 2003.

Significant regional variation in farmland data is illustrated in Figure 4.4. The Plains, Great Lakes, and Southeast experienced the greatest amount of farm consolidation, but the New England, Mid East, and Southeast regions lost the most land in farms. It is possible that the rapid decline in the amount of land in farms can be attributed to the suburban expansion of "Bos-Wash," the megalopolis spanning these three regions (Borchert, 1992; Gottman, 1961). The Plains region had by far the smallest loss of land in farms, yet one of the most rapid declines in numbers of farms. The combination of these forces suggests a pronounced increased size of farms and increased capitalization (in terms of land) of farm operations on the Plains. In contrast, three regions with stable or increasing numbers of farms (Far West, Southwest, and Rocky Mountains) had losses in farmland, perhaps indicating the popularity of hobby farms in these regions. Indeed, farms with gross sales under $10,000 per year were the fastest growing category in states like Montana (Bohrer, 2003).

The Changing Farm Economy—Regional Perspectives

While farming still is a major activity within the U.S. involving more than 2 million operations and occupying nearly a billion acres of land (ERS, 2003a), employment and income data demonstrate that the economic impact of farming is declining. Table 4.1 presents the relative importance of farm employment for the nonmetropolitan portions of each BEA region compared with the United States as a whole.[1] In the United States, farm employment accounts for only 1.85 percent of total employment in 2000, down from 4.34 percent in 1970. Not surprisingly,

Table 4.1. Farming Share of Total Employment (in Percentages) for Nonmetropolitan Territory, 1970–2000

Region	1970	1975	1980	1985	1990	1995	2000
U.S. Total	4.3	4.0	3.3	2.8	2.3	2.1	1.9
U.S. Nonmetro	14.4	12.9	11.0	9.7	8.0	7.1	6.5
Far West	11.7	10.6	8.8	7.8	6.6	6.0	5.6
Rocky Mountain	16.5	13.2	10.7	9.7	8.5	7.1	6.6
South West	17.9	15.5	12.9	11.7	11.1	10.9	10.3
South East	14.2	12.2	10.1	8.6	6.9	6.1	5.5
Plains	20.7	19.3	16.5	15.4	13.1	11.2	10.0
Great Lakes	12.3	11.9	10.6	9.4	7.4	6.3	5.7
Mid East	6.1	6.2	5.7	5.0	3.9	3.7	3.4
New England	4.5	3.5	3.6	2.6	2.0	2.0	1.8

Source: REIS 2003.

farm employment is more important in nonmetropolitan regions, accounting for 6.5 percent of total employment in 2000, yet this share is also less than half of what it was 30 years prior.

Regionally, there have been interesting shifts in the importance of farm employment to nonmetropolitan economies. Every nonmetropolitan region in Table 4.1 shows a decline in the relative importance of farm employment, yet certain regions maintain higher relative concentrations than others. In 1970, one in five jobs in the Plains was in farming, making it the most farm-dependent region, though by 2000, only one in ten jobs in this region was in the farming sector. This decline in farm dependence in the Plains reflects the trends discussed above, with the Plains losing relatively large numbers of farms and experiencing some of the most rapid capitalization in farming. In 2000, the Southwest was the region most dependent upon farm employment, with 10.3 percent of its nonmetropolitan employment coming in the farming sector. In contrast, the nonmetropolitan Mid East and New England had relatively low employment concentrations in farming. In fact, in 2000, nonmetropolitan New England has a lower concentration of employment in farming than the United States as a whole. The other four regions roughly mirror the U.S. nonmetropolitan employment profiles. These trends in employment, coupled with the shifts in agricultural land use discussed above clearly reflect regional variations in the degree of agricultural mechanization. For example, the Plains had relatively small losses of land in farms yet relatively large declines in agricultural employment, suggesting higher degrees of mechanization. In contrast, the Mid East experienced relatively large declines in farm employment, land in farms, and numbers of farms suggestive of land use conversion from agricultural to nonagricultural uses.

While the last 30 years have brought steady decreases in the importance of farm employment across regions, farm earnings have been more volatile. Table 4.2 presents the average wage per agricultural job for the United States and the nonmetropolitan United States.[2] First, the U.S. total average agricultural earnings and the average agricultural earnings of nonmetropolitan territory are very similar, as most of the agricultural jobs are located in nonmetropolitan regions. That said, in all years except for 1975, earnings in nonmetropolitan regions lagged

Table 4.2. Average Earnings (Constant 2000 Dollars) Per Agricultural Job, 1970–2000 (in 1000s of Dollars)

Region	1970	1975	1980	1985	1990	1995	2000
U.S. Total	17.5	20.6	10.8	13.0	17.3	12.9	16.1
U.S. Nonmetro	17.4	20.9	8.3	11.7	16.7	11.5	15.0

Source: REIS 2003.

behind the national averages. These average earnings data clearly illustrate several of the key periods in U.S. agricultural history over the last 30 years. The 1970s saw rising agricultural earnings, as market conditions were favorable and operating costs low. Table 4.2 also illustrates clearly the difficulties presented by the farm crisis of the 1980s. Nonmetropolitan agricultural earnings dropped by more than 50 percent during the 1980s, and they have still not recovered to their peaks in the 1970s. These earnings data also highlight the difficulties that farming in the United States experienced in the mid 1990s, as the agricultural trade balance dropped as a result of the rising value of the dollar and the East Asian economic crisis.

Responses on the Farm

The agricultural economy of the United States has been anything but smooth over the last 30 years. Significant turmoil brought on by changes in domestic and international economic conditions has created periods of relative prosperity followed by episodes of decline for U.S. farmers. Larger farms are becoming more competitive and better able to weather these fluctuations by drawing on their larger economic reserves and wielding their political weight to influence policies that better suit their positions. That said, other farmers have adopted strategies to enhance their economic well-being. Just as retailing and manufacturing have benefited from changing consumer preferences for more differentiated products, so too has agriculture, as farmers produce more niche-oriented products in this post-Fordist era (Harvey, 1989). In addition, farmers are increasing their ability to capture value added and expanding farm operations to include nontraditional activities.

Hawaiian farmers, for example, are faced with several challenges when forced to compete with other agricultural producers. Increased transport costs, operating costs, and limited land inputs put Hawaiian farmers at a distinct economic disadvantage when competing with other domestic and international producers. Hawaii does, however, possess a unique climate and a certain cultural allure that some Hawaiian farmers have tapped. Over the last decade, Hawaii has developed a small but growing exotic flower sector for export markets. Hawaiian farmers have been able to tap this niche created by climate and the marketing panache of "from the islands of Hawaii" to their advantage (Suryanata, 2002). Similarly, cattle producers in North Dakota have faced increasing international competition from Canadian and Mexican beef growers as NAFTA has opened U.S. beef production up to international competition. Rather than trying to compete on an economic field tipped against them some North Dakota beef operations have shifted towards the growing bison niche market (Sell et al., 2001). Accordingly, bison now ranks fourth in North Dakota's livestock industry.

Co-operatives have a long history in agricultural communities stemming back to the days of collectively owned grain elevators. Today, co-ops offer farmers an opportunity to capture greater amounts of value-added from their commodities.

In the Dakotas, a group of Durum wheat growers have established a co-operative to use their wheat in a pasta-producing operation. Most Durum wheat in the United States is used in pasta production, yet this production has historically taken place outside the wheat-growing regions. Through this co-operative, members are able to increase the value they extract from their crops by producing a higher-value processed product. Likewise, Vermont's Department of Agriculture has created the Vermont Fresh Network, a consortium of farmers, restaurants and small food stores that work together to create local markets for farm commodities. Member restaurants agree to purchase locally grown produce, effectively keeping more dollars in the Vermont economy, enhancing multipliers. Both of these examples demonstrate how farmers can respond to economic challenges and continue growing the same products.

A final example of how farmers have enhanced their economic situation is through expansion into nontraditional farm-related activities. Most often, this strategy incorporates tourist activities that couple farm operations with a distinct regional identity or culture. Sonoma and Napa Valleys have developed successful agricultural activities in conjunction with tourist endeavors. Other regions have followed this example, and there are now thriving agro-tourist activities centered on wine growing in eastern Washington, eastern Oregon, and the Finger Lakes region of New York. Agro-tourism can also be seen in the farm tours of northeastern Connecticut, which couple traditional farming with tours of the "quintessential" New England experience (Bender & Davis, 2000). It is important to note, however, that these niche agricultural activities often most benefit areas either inside or adjacent to metropolitan areas (Heimlich & Anderson, 2001).

Therefore, while farming in the United States has been tumultuous over the last 30 years, and increased globalization only indicates an increase in the competition and volatility U.S. farmers are likely to face, there is hope. As the future continues to bring challenges for U.S. farmers, the shape of U.S. farm economy will continue to respond, and farmers will adapt in creative ways to these inevitable forms of restructuring. One of the most substantive forms of restructuring that has affected U.S. rural economies over the last 30 years has been the decentralization of manufacturing, the topic to which we now turn.

RURAL MANUFACTURING

It comes as no surprise that manufacturing in the United States has struggled to maintain high levels of employment and earnings over the last 30 years. Media accounts of layoffs, plant closings, and the geographic shifts of manufacturing jobs took center-stage in the 2004 Presidential Campaign (Nagourney, 2004). Beginning in the 1970s and up to the present, we have been reminded constantly of the increasingly global economy as neoliberal trade policies have enabled manufacturing jobs to move to lower-cost locations, often overseas or in rural locations in the United States. This process is well documented in Bluestone and Harrison's seminal work, *The Deindustrialization of America* (1982, 1987). While the dominant thread in this manufacturing discourse is one of losing manufacturing jobs to overseas competition, there has also been a significant shift down the urban hierarchy of manufacturing employment. To illustrate, between 1970 and 2000, while the U.S. economy increased its total employment 83 percent, it lost 3 percent of its manufacturing jobs. In contrast, manufacturing employment in the nonmetropolitan United States *grew* 23 percent. By 2000, nonmetropolitan economies in the United States had become more dependent upon manufacturing than the total US economy. In 2000, manufacturing accounted for 15 percent of all nonmetropolitan jobs, compared with 11 percent of jobs throughout the entire economy. Clearly there have been different experiences in the manufacturing sectors of urban and rural places over the last 30 years. This brief section examines the trends in rural manufacturing employment and income at the regional level.

Table 4.3 presents rates of change for manufacturing employment for the United States, U.S. nonmetropolitan territory, and the nonmetropolitan portions of the eight BEA regions. Examining the rates of change over the 30-year period, one sees tremendous variation in the manufacturing sector across space and over time. While the entire U.S. economy lost manufacturing jobs during every time period except the late 1970s, the nonmetropolitan United States gained manufacturing jobs in four of the six five-year intervals between 1970 and 2000. Furthermore, the changes in manufacturing employment reflect the periodization of other demographic and economic trends in rural America. Between 1975 and 1980, every region shown in Table 4.3 enjoyed a growing manufacturing sector, and this period coincides with the well-documented rural renaissance. In contrast, the early 1980s, the time period marking the end of this renaissance, brought more difficult times for manufacturing employment in nonmetropolitan territories. Only the Rocky Mountain region enjoyed positive growth during this period, at a meager 0.92 percent. The Rocky Mountain and the Plains regions appear to be the big winners in generating manufacturing employment. The Rocky Mountains enjoyed positive manufacturing growth in every five-year interval, while the Plains enjoyed positive growth in every period but the early 1980s. Manufacturing in the Rocky Mountain and Plains regions expanded 72 percent and 62 percent respectively over the 30-year period—more than double the rate of US nonmetropolitan manufacturing growth overall. The Far West, Southwest, Southeast and Great Lakes regions also enjoyed positive manufacturing growth over the 30-year period, but this growth is much more consistent with the entire nonmetropolitan manufacturing experience. In contrast, the Mid East and New England regions appear to be at a distinct disadvantage in generating manufacturing employment. With the exception of the late 1970s, these two regions lost manufacturing employment in every time period shown in Table 4.3. Between 1970 and 2000, the Mid East and New England lost manufacturing jobs at a rate three to five times faster than the US as a whole.

Just as the rates of change in manufacturing employment demonstrate marked geographic variation, so too does the relative dependence on manufacturing

Table 4.3. Percent Change in Manufacturing Employment for Nonmetropolitan Portions of Regions, 1970–2000

Region	1970–1975	1975–1980	1980–1985	1985–1990	1990–1995	1995–2000	1970–2000
U.S. Total	−5.3	11.4	−4.8	−0.4	−2.6	−0.4	−3.0
U.S. Nonmetro	1.4	12.9	−3.2	8.2	5.9	−2.9	23.3
Far West	5.6	11.2	−5.1	11.3	−1.6	−3.7	17.5
Rocky Mountain	15.8	12.0	0.9	14.6	12.0	2.5	72.1
South West	17.9	20.9	−7.3	1.4	6.2	−5.2	34.9
South East	2.0	15.0	−1.1	7.6	4.3	−10.0	17.1
Plains	9.7	14.4	−4.2	16.2	14.9	1.0	62.1
Great Lakes	−3.0	6.8	−2.9	11.2	11.0	0.4	24.8
Mid East	−7.5	5.6	−10.2	1.3	−5.4	−2.1	−17.7
New England	−8.0	24.8	−3.9	−6.4	−4.5	−6.9	−8.2

Source: REIS 2003.

Table 4.4. Manufacturing Share of Total Employment (in Percentages) for Nonmetropolitan Territory, 1970–2000

Region	1970	1975	1980	1985	1990	1995	2000
U.S. Total	21.6	18.9	18.2	15.9	14.1	12.9	11.4
U.S. Nonmetro	19.8	18.5	18.6	17.4	17.3	16.7	15.0
Far West	15.9	13.9	13.0	11.8	11.0	9.8	8.5
Rocky Mountain	8.8	8.5	7.8	7.5	7.9	7.4	6.6
South West	9.5	10.2	10.6	9.1	9.2	8.8	7.6
South East	25.2	23.9	24.4	23.4	23.1	21.8	18.4
Plains	11.5	11.7	12.3	11.7	13.0	13.7	12.9
Great Lakes	23.8	21.7	21.4	20.3	20.7	20.7	19.4
Mid East	26.1	22.8	22.4	19.1	17.2	15.8	14.3
New England	24.7	21.7	22.8	19.6	16.3	15.1	12.7

Source: REIS 2003.

at the regional level. Table 4.4 presents manufacturing's share of regional employment over the 30-year period. Comparing Table 4.4 with Table 4.1 demonstrates that rural economies at the regional level have become much more manufacturing dependent than farm dependent. In 2000, rural economies at the national level had more than twice the concentration of jobs in manufacturing (~15 percent) compared with farming (6.5 percent), and this difference has widened since 1970. That said, every region except the Plains is less dependent on manufacturing in 2000 than in 1970, and this is clearly the result of the growing service economy in nonmetropolitan regions (see discussion below). Despite this uniformity in the declining importance of manufacturing for rural economies, regional variations do exist.

In 1970, four of the eight regions (Southeast, Great Lakes, Mid East, and New England) had higher shares of employment in manufacturing than the U.S. nonmetropolitan totals. By 2000, the losses of manufacturing employment in New England and the Mid East had pulled these regions below the U.S. nonmetropolitan total, leaving only the Southeast and Great Lakes as having higher than average manufacturing dependence. The Far West, Mid East, and New England regions had the greatest relative drops in manufacturing dependence, each greater than 45 percent. Despite the rapid growth of the Rocky Mountain and Plains regions in the number of manufacturing jobs, these two regions still lag behind the U.S. average nonmetropolitan dependence on manufacturing. Similarly, the Far West and Southwest have lower than average shares of employment in manufacturing, suggesting other segments of these regional economies must be expanding at faster rates.

Table 4.5. Average Earnings (Constant 2000 Dollars) Per Manufacturing Job, 1970–2000 (in 1000s of Dollars)

Region	1970	1975	1980	1985	1990	1995	2000
U.S. Total	33.0	35.0	38.8	39.8	42.1	44.9	50.2
U.S. Nonmetro	25.7	27.0	30.6	30.6	31.3	32.7	35.2
Nonmetro/Total	0.78	0.77	0.79	0.77	0.74	0.73	0.70

Source: REIS 2003.[3]

The interest scholars have in manufacturing employment stems from both its connection to the economic base of regions and its tendency to pay high wages (Tiebout, 1962). For example, in 2000, average earnings per manufacturing job in the United States were over $50,000. Table 4.5 presents average earnings per manufacturing job for the entire U.S. economy as well as the total U.S. nonmetropolitan economy. In contrast with the experience in farming, where real earnings have declined slightly since 1970, earnings in nonmetropolitan manufacturing have increased from $25,660 to $35,180, a 40 percent increase. However, this increase in manufacturing earnings lags behind the 52 percent increase enjoyed nationwide. These earnings data suggest that manufacturing earnings in the nonmetropolitan United States are eroding slightly in relative terms, as in 1970 the rural manufacturing worker earned $78 for every $100 dollars earned nationally. This ratio dropped to $70 per $100 by 2000, a greater than 10 percent decline.

This brief section highlights the changes taking place in rural manufacturing across the United States and across different geographic regions. Over the last 30 years, manufacturing employment in the nonmetropolitan United States has enjoyed positive growth as the sector struggled nationwide. Explanations for the significant regional variations in manufacturing dependence are elusive, as no work to date has comprehensively examined rural manufacturing from a regional perspective. The small literature that does exist on the subject emphasizes a variety of factors, including lower costs, higher quality of life, access to resources, proximity to "parent plants" and the emergence of rural manufacturing clusters (Erickson, 1976; Beyers &Nelson, 2000; Goetz & Rupasingha, 2002). While nonmetropolitan manufacturing earnings remain high relative to farm earnings, these data suggest that nonmetropolitan manufacturing workers are at a disadvantage compared with manufacturing workers for the entire country. Finally, even though manufacturing employment has grown at positive rates in most regions, manufacturing is declining in relative importance, indicating that other sectors of the rural economy are expanding at more rapid rates. The next section in this chapter examines the recent history of the retail, finance, insurance, real estate, service, and public administration/government sectors to illuminate the rising importance of these tertiary economic sectors in the increasingly dynamic rural economy.

THE TERTIARY OR "SERVICE" SECTOR

While the primary and secondary economic sectors of rural America have declined in relative size or remained stagnant, the tertiary sector experienced continuous growth over the past 30 years (Garnick, 1984; Gatrell, 2002). It is difficult to overestimate the significance and size of the tertiary sector in today's economy. Needless to say, for rural America, this is a starkly different picture of the economy than the one that existed a hundred or even 30 years ago (Smith, 1993). The extraordinary growth in this sector stems from a number of broad changes in the economy in general and from changes within certain parts of the economy. At the broadest level, economies in the developed parts of the world have matured and incomes have risen, increasing the demand for the retail goods and services provided by the tertiary sector (Mawson, 1987). Moreover, productivity gains common in the primary and secondary sectors do not translate as readily to the tertiary sector, keeping labor demand high, especially in the face of increased overall demand (Kahan, 1990). Changes within sectors such as manufacturing also precipitate growth in the tertiary sector. As manufacturing firms faced increasing competition from abroad over the past few decades, many sought to eliminate tertiary-sector activities once done in-house (O'Farrell et al., 1993; Scott, 1988). This led to outsourcing many functions and the creation of tertiary-sector firms, especially in producer services. Finally, the nature of manufacturing itself has changed and now often requires new specialized services to run complex manufacturing processes, computer systems and databases, a requirement which did not exist decades ago (Beyers, 1989; Goe, 2002).

These factors hint at the complex processes involved in this large and diverse portion of the economy. As a result, a simple aggregate analysis of growth or decline in service employment ignores variations within the sector and obscures the uneven spatial impacts of a restructured economy where the tertiary sector often provides over 50 percent of total employment in many rural communities (Smith, 1993). For example, producer services offer great potential for employment and income growth, but many researchers argue that only a small percentage of rural counties can take advantage of these opportunities (Glasmeier & Howland, 1995). Additionally, while employment in some tertiary activities like retail has not changed much relative to other sectors in rural America as a whole, stores and jobs are disappearing in many isolated areas as retail restructuring continues, and the most remote counties lose population (Adamchak et al., 1999; Vias, 2003). Clearly, as the tertiary sector grows, an investigation needs to unpack this large section of the economy to find which parts are able to promote economic growth, or at least to maintain the economic health and viability of rural communities (Smith, 1993; USDA, 1996a).

In this section, we investigate three aspects of the tertiary sector that are important to rural America. First, what does the literature tell us about the potential for rural economic development as a result of growth in the size of the tertiary sector and its individual constituents? Second, what are the employment and income trends of the tertiary sector over the past 30 years? Third, what opportunities are still available for rural America in terms of utilizing growth in the tertiary sector to sustain or promote economic development?

In discussing this literature, we apply a slightly modified hybrid scheme for the tertiary sector developed by Singelmann (1978) that uses four categories: producer services (e.g., business and legal services; finance, insurance and real estate); consumer services (e.g., all retail, repair shops, entertainment); social services (e.g., health services, education, public administration/government); and distributory services (e.g., wholesale trade and transportation, communications and public utilities). Because of data limitations, the empirical analysis presented later relies on the simple aggregate standard industrial classification (SIC) system used by the federal government, with a focus on retail trade (RTRAD); finance, insurance, and real estate (FIRE); services (SERV); and public administration and government (PADAM). Although wholesale trade (WTRADE) is a part of the tertiary sector as well, the above components of the tertiary sector are of most interest to scholars because they either employ the largest number of people or they grew the fastest over the past 30 years.

The Potential for the Tertiary Sector in Rural America

Over the years, one of the primary reasons why the tertiary sector was treated as a residual part of the economy and never the central focus of rural economic research was the notion that this sector was not part of the export base of a community (Tiebout, 1962). It was the primary and secondary sectors of agriculture, mining, and manufacturing alone that had the potential to bring outside income into a community and to induce further growth. Although tertiary activities, especially retail and services, always employed a large segment of the local population, this sector's perceived inability to promote growth led to its inferior status among most scholars and local economic development specialists (Galston & Baehler, 1995; Glasmeier & Howland, 1995).

In recent decades, scholars have reevaluated the role of the tertiary sector. Today, strong evidence suggests that several tertiary activities can act as part of the export base (Smith, 1984; Vias & Mulligan, 1997). That is to say, many types of tertiary activities do not derive all their income from local sources. Additionally, new ideas on the role of tertiary sector in the local economy as a whole emerged, arguing that export potential aside, the same types of goods and services are crucial for keeping the entire economy vibrant (Goe, 2002). Despite this optimistic reassessment of the tertiary sector, there is a lively debate on the specific value of tertiary jobs for the employees themselves, especially the low income associated with sectors like retail (Power, 1996; Vias, 1999). While ongoing research on the role of tertiary activities remains contentious, the subject is too broad and extensive to examine in detail here. However, several aspects of these debates are particularly relevant to rural economic growth and development and are worthy of further elaboration in this section.

Consumer services are often viewed as having the least potential for improving the export base of communities and thus inducing economic development because they usually rely on local sources of income (Anding et al., 1990). A well-developed literature on central place theory supports this idea, arguing that these activities are closely linked to local demand and the size of settlements (Christaller, 1966). That said, the number of people employed in providing consumer services increased in recent decades as rural consumers began to demand the same types of goods once only available in cities (Power, 1996; USDA, 1996a). Besides serving the needs of residents, a healthy consumer services sector serves a broader function as well. As long as there are stores providing consumer services within the community, income as well as tax revenue will stay local, an important consideration with respect to the provision of local government services.

However, aggregate growth in consumer services really hides a spatially uneven geography of consumer-related activities. With many remote areas losing population (e.g., the Great Plains), local demand for consumer services has evaporated in many small communities, and the central business districts are declining (Adamchak et al., 1999). This contrasts with regions gaining population and maintaining healthy consumer service sectors (e.g., the Sunbelt). In recent decades, restructuring in retail trade has dramatically affected rural communities as well (Hornbeck, 1994). Specifically, the development of "big box" stores and giant general merchandisers like Wal-Mart that take advantage of huge economies of scale create a difficult economic environment for locally-owned small businesses. In most rural areas, stores like Wal-Mart tend to locate in one or two large, service center towns. In these fortunate towns, small stores not directly competing with these retail giants can actually do quite well (Stone, 1995). However, retailers in the small towns in surrounding hinterlands cannot compete with the low prices and the variety of goods offered by these large stores. As customers drive to shop in distant towns, local retail withers and eventually disappears. Thus, although employment in retail can remain constant or even grow for a large region, the spatial distribution of this employment may be highly uneven, with a cluster of retail in a few large, successful centers, and a host of smaller towns with little or no retail activity.

Compared to consumer services, many researchers believe that producer services (services provided to other businesses) offer better prospects for growth and development, especially as these services decentralize much in the way manufacturing moved from urban areas over 30 years ago (Goe, 2002; Porterfield & Pulver, 1991). This is a result of communications technologies that now permit some of these producer services to locate outside of major cities (Galston & Baehler, 1995; Goe, 2002). A classic example often cited by scholars was the move of Citibank's credit card processing unit to South Dakota in the 1980s (Glasmeier & Howland, 1995; Trigaux, 1981). Another example of decentralization often cited is the shift of small and individual proprietor service companies (high fliers and lone eagles) to remote high-amenity areas (Beyers & Lindahl, 1996). Besides offering better employment prospects, especially for those with minimal skills, producer services can diversify local tax bases, and provide environmentally sound development as opposed to certain types of extractive industries.

The research on producer services does support the notion that this part of the tertiary sector can act as an export base, bringing significant outside income and promoting economic development (Beyers & Alvine, 1985; Daniels, 1993). In spite of this evidence, many scholars are skeptical that most rural communities can benefit from new firms and employment of this sort (Glasmeier & Howland, 1995). Of those that are moving out of cities, most seem to locate near metro areas, with more rural areas still vastly underrepresented (Garnick, 1984; Glasmeier & Howland, 1995). Perhaps a more alarming concern is that some of these new footloose producer services requiring modest to no skills will eventually join many manufacturing firms in continuing the decentralization process offshore (Glasmeier & Howland, 1995).

Even if the export potential for producer services is limited to a few select areas of rural America, there is evidence that rural producer services can still play an important role for a variety of rural centers (Goe, 2002; Hansen, 1990). Like a healthy consumer service sector, a good variety of local producer services can reduce the leakage of business spending to other more urban communities. More importantly, providing producer services locally can make a community and its firms more competitive, while making it more attractive to new firms.

Finally, social services, which include tertiary sector employment in education and health services, along with public administration, remain an important part of the rural economy. Throughout rural areas, social services are among the more stable parts of the economy in terms of employment (USDA, 1996b). This stability is partly a result of the external nature of many of these jobs, which are often supported through funds from state and federal sources. In some cases employment is actually increasing in the social services as states push for increased educational opportunities in rural areas, including institutions such as community colleges (Rubin, 2001). Also, as the population ages (see Chapter 3), there is an increased need for health care for the elderly, although it is unclear whether the funds will be available to provide these services in rural areas (Bull, 1998). In the long run, growth in the social services is limited because most employment in these tertiary activities is still dependent on the size of the local population, so for areas experiencing out-migration, employment losses in these types of establishments are still likely.

Underlying this entire debate on employment and growth in the tertiary sector is the nature of the jobs available in this sector. Specifically, scholars note that employment in this sector is more likely to be part-time, have lower wages and have few if any benefits (Applebaum & Albin, 1990; Kassab, 1992; Smith 1993). This is especially true of jobs in the consumer services. Hence, even if the tertiary sector represents an area of employment growth, the overall impact on the economic well-being of the community may be minimal. However, there are many scholars who disagree with these findings and still see some important economic benefits from a broad range of tertiary sector activities (Kassab, 1992; Power, 1996). In producer services, the situation is more complex because employment is more segmented in terms of skills and wages (Glasmeier & Howland, 1995; Kassab, 1992). Unfortunately, many of the lower-paying back office operations include the types of jobs most likely to locate in rural areas, with the higher paying producer services remaining in major urban centers (Glasmeier & Howland, 1995).

Overall, the picture that emerges from the literature on the tertiary sector in the rural economy is mixed. While the sector grew considerably over the past 30 years, unevenness remains both across the different tertiary activities and across space. Consumer services grew the most, but restructuring within this sector has led to "service-rich" towns and "service-poor" towns. Furthermore, these jobs are generally lower paying, limiting their potential to stimulate rural economic growth and development. In contrast, producer services tend to offer higher paying jobs, yet rural places seem increasingly less suited to attract and retain a substantial amount of this employment.

Aggregate Trends in the Tertiary Sectors, 1970–2000

The increasing importance of the tertiary sector in the rural economy is easily shown with the REIS data set (Bureau of Economic Analysis, 2003). Table 4.6 shows the percentage of total employment in four of the most important

Table 4.6. Employment of Tertiary Sectors as a Percentage of All Employment

Region	SIC Sector	1970	2000	% Change 1970–2000
U.S. Nonmetro	RTRAD	14.5	16.7	88.1
	FIRE	4.2	5.2	99.2
	SERV	15.2	24.2	160.6
	PADAM	17.6	15.7	45.9
	TOTAL %	51.5	61.8	
U.S. Total	RTRAD	15.0	16.3	99.6
	FIRE	6.7	8.1	120.3
	SERV	18.7	31.8	212.8
	PADAM	17.6	13.6	41.5
	TOTAL %	58.0	69.8	

(RTRAD–Retail Trade; FIRE–Finance, Insurance and Real Estate; SERV–Services; PADAM–Public Administration/Government).
Source: REIS 2003.

single-digit SIC sub-sectors of the tertiary sector (RTRAD, FIRE, SERV and PADAM). Percentage of total employment is an aggregate statistic derived by summing all employment for each of the four sub-sectors for nonmetropolitan counties and all U.S. counties (based on 1998 metropolitan areas designation) for 1970 and 2000. While the data based on SIC delineations do not match up perfectly with the hybrid sectors outlined above, the data still provide some useful insights into the significance of the tertiary sector in rural America and how this sector is changing over time. For example, most consumer services sector employment comes from retail trade (SIC 52–RTRAD in REIS data); all finance, insurance and real estate sector employment (SIC 60–FIRE) falls into the producer services category; and all public administration sector employment (no SIC sector–PADAM) is in the social services category. Thus, analysis of these three SIC sectors provides information on three of the important services categories discussed above. Only the services sector (SIC 70 and 80–SERV), where employment is fairly evenly spread across producer, social, and consumer services, makes analysis of specific sub-sectors impossible. However, because this is the single largest tertiary sector, growth and change in this sector still provides information on the role of tertiary activities in general over the past 30 years.

Examining Table 4.6, we see that the four sub-sectors together increased their share of total employment in nonmetropolitan areas from 51.5 percent to 61.8 percent between 1970 and 2000, compared with an increase from 58 percent to 69.8 percent in the United States as a whole. The only sub-sector that decreased as a percentage of total employment was public administration and government (PADAM). Clearly, the increasing dominance of the tertiary sector is a broad trend affecting all parts of the U.S. economy. The restructuring process is even more startling considering that the total U.S. population only grew by 38.9 percent over that same time period. While nonmetropolitan counties were a part of this restructuring process, these counties remain under-represented in the tertiary sector compared to all U.S. counties. The largest contributor to this gap is employment in services (SERV), which accounts for 31.8 percent of total employment in all U.S. counties but only 24.2 percent in nonmetropolitan counties. Nonmetropolitan areas have lower employment concentrations in finance, insurance and real estate (FIRE), a sub-sector that falls completely within producer services. Finally, nonmetropolitan counties lagged behind U.S. counties with respect to employment growth in the same SIC sub-sectors that comprise the producer and consumer service categories. Only in public administration (PADAM), a segment of social services, did the nonmetro areas show greater employment growth and concentration than U.S. counties as a whole. This suggests that nonmetro counties are investing extra money in such areas as health care and education in an effort to match the services found in more urban areas.

Besides the smaller footprint of tertiary sector employment in nonmetropolitan counties compared to all U.S. counties, average income for these jobs in nonmetropolitan counties lags as well, especially when data are broken

Table 4.7. Average Income (Constant 2000 Dollars) for Tertiary Sector Jobs

Region	SIC Sector	1970	2000	% Change 1970–2000
U.S. Nonmetro	RTRAD	17,382	15,439	−11.2
	FIRE	13,806	20,081	45.5
	SERV	16,801	21,405	27.4
	PADAM	21,904	33,062	50.9
U.S. Total	RTRAD	19,506	19,357	−0.8
	FIRE	21,102	42,743	102.6
	SERV	22,744	33,327	46.5
	PADAM	28,109	41,557	47.8

(RTRAD–Retail Trade; FIRE–Finance, Insurance and Real Estate; SERV–Services; PADAM–Public Administration/Government).
Source: REIS 2003.

down into SIC sub-sectors. Table 4.7 shows average income in 2000 dollars for the same four SIC sub-sectors used in Table 4.6. A significant and growing income discrepancy exists for these same jobs between nonmetropolitan counties and the entire country. Besides differences in the average income in the vital producer service sectors (all of FIRE and a third of SERV), average earnings in all U.S. counties grew about twice as fast as those in nonmetropolitan counties. Although metropolitan counties (which dominate U.S. statistics) do have a higher cost of living than nonmetropolitan counties, differences in these earnings probably also reflect differences in the types of producer service jobs found in these economies. As Glasmeier and Howland (1995) argue, the higher-paying producer service jobs are likely to remain in and around major urban centers, with the lower-paying back-office operations the most likely to move into rural areas or abroad. Hence, while growth in employment between all counties and nonmetropolitan counties may be similar in many ways, there are startling contrasts in the kinds of jobs each type of area is gaining.

The increasing divergence between the economic fortunes of all U.S. counties versus nonmetropolitan counties is particularly evident when we examine the ratio of average income levels for the two populations over time. Figure 4.5 graphs the ratio of nonmetropolitan to total U.S. average earnings for all four SIC sectors from 1970 to 2000. The strong downward trend for three of the four sub-sectors illustrates the weakness in the rural service economy compared to the U.S. economy. Especially disturbing is the significant drop in relative income levels in the finance, insurance, and real estate (FIRE) sub-sector, part of producer services that many assume will provide quality jobs that have been lost in manufacturing

Figure 4.5. Nonmetro/U.S. Ratio of Average Earnings for Tertiary Sectors (Constant 2000 Dollars)

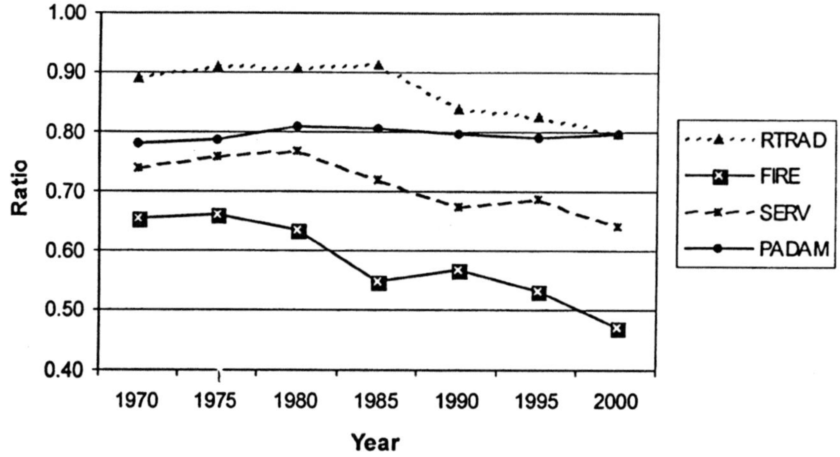

Source: REIS 2003.

and agriculture. Only in public administration (PADAM) did average income levels not lose ground compared with U.S. counties as a whole, although nonmetropolitan workers still earn less than the average U.S. worker in this sub-sector.

On the whole, these aggregated data still demonstrate clearly the growing dominance of the tertiary sector in nonmetropolitan economies. As we move into the post-industrial era, more of rural America reflects these processes through changing livelihoods. Still, rural America lags behind the rest of the United States in the pace of this transition. Moreover, the nature of the transition appears to differ as well, with strong empirical evidence suggesting that tertiary-sector jobs emerging in rural areas are less desirable and lower-paying than those found in urban areas, the foci of high-end producer service employment.

Potential Areas of Service Growth

Even as the tertiary sector increases in importance in the economy as a whole, the data show us that rural areas lag behind the rest of the United States. This is especially apparent for the few parts of the tertiary sector (e.g., producer services) that can act as sources of growth for the entire economy. While chances of attracting activities such as producer services to rural areas remain slim, a few niches of tertiary sector activities can serve as an important component of a vibrant rural economy.

For example, one advantage many parts of rural America have over urban areas, especially in the western United States, is the availability of scenic environmental locales that are especially attractive for tourism and recreational development (Drabenstott & Smith, 1996; Gibson, 1993). Where these high-amenity areas exist, there is an increasing demand for a broad spectrum of consumer services that cater to visitors. Although wages for these jobs are low, and these opportunities are limited to certain parts of rural America, they still represent new jobs that would not otherwise exist. Additionally, most of the jobs generated through tourism and recreation represent export earnings (i.e. visitors from outside the region) and thus are a direct source of growth in the local economy.

Besides short-term visitors, many high-amenity areas experienced population growth as a result of permanent migration (Rudzitis & Johansen, 1989; Vias, 1999). These migrants include people of working age moving to more desirable areas in the Sunbelt, especially exurban areas not far from major cities. Another component of this migration are certain types of producer service workers who can take advantage of improved communications technologies (e.g., "lone eagles" and "high fliers") to live in dispersed locations. Finally, many rural parts of the United States experienced population growth as people permanently left the workforce and moved to many areas dominated by retirees (Longino, 1994). Whatever the origins or age of these migrants, they often bring income with them (e.g., nonemployment income, pensions, etc.) and spend most of it locally on consumer services and health care (Galston & Baehler, 1995; Reeder et al., 1993).

Finally, rather than chasing after new tertiary sector jobs or the "New Buffalo Hunt," as Kassab and Luloff (1993) put it, rural communities may try to keep tertiary jobs already in place. As noted earlier, many tertiary activities are lost as a result of depopulation trends, a situation that represents much more than an economic problem. However, in numerous cases, local stores are simply becoming less competitive, especially compared to consumer service giants like Wal-Mart. As indicated earlier, these large companies are rearranging the geography of consumer services by clustering these activities in a few service-center towns (Stone, 1997). Some scholars feel that small stores can remain competitive by targeting specific niches the retail giants deem too small or by developing better marketing tools and business practices (Stone, 1995). In many ways, retaining these types of stores and jobs within local economies is optimal because they represent assets already in place that can work in conjunction with more traditional export sectors as important tools for economic development (Galston & Baehler, 1995).

DEMOGRAPHIC AND SOCIAL IMPACTS OF CHANGING RURAL LIVELIHOODS

The agriculture, manufacturing, and tertiary sectors offer different scenarios of change in rural America, but these changes ultimately lead to similar and often disturbing outcomes. For centuries, the bedrock of the rural economy had been agriculture, with additional support from manufacturing in recent decades. However, the forces of agricultural restructuring, both domestic and international suggest that agriculture's relative importance within the rural economic base will continue to decline. While farm output and exports have increased dramatically over the past 30 years, albeit with significant year-to-year volatility, farm employment, farm numbers, and farm earnings have eroded. These trends illustrate a redistribution of agricultural resources as fewer but significantly larger farms dominate the rural agricultural economy. Manufacturing, once an important part of economic growth and development in many rural areas, experienced a small relative decline in percentage of sectoral employment. As the global economy continues to restructure, the relative size of manufacturing compared to the tertiary sector will further wane. For rural areas especially, the persistent loss of many low-skill, low-wage manufacturing jobs to offshore locations is also likely to continue (Galston & Baehler, 1995; Nelson, 1999). The rise of the service economy is evident in employment trends in the nonmetro areas of the United States, but the quality of the work available makes getting by, even on two incomes, a difficult chore for many rural residents. Except for limited opportunities in certain regions and within certain sectors, prospects appear bleak for sustainable and locally derived economic development based on employment in agriculture and manufacturing.

These economic changes will have significant demographic repercussions. Many rural areas, especially those regions heavily reliant on traditional small family farms, will continue to experience depopulation as farms disappear. Additionally, as manufacturing jobs continue to migrate offshore, the declining manufacturing employment will also drive people out of rural areas. Those rural communities likely to maintain or increase population are those with geophysical amenities and proximity to large urban employment centers. In both situations, sources of income external to rural areas foster local economic growth and development.

Other issues warrant consideration apart from economic impacts on population distribution. Sociologists working from a human ecology perspective have long investigated the impact of population change on rural economies (Hawley, 1968), but as impacts of broad economic changes discussed above ripple through rural America, long-term effects on how people live and earn livelihoods will also be significant (Albrecht & Albrecht, 1996). For example, a major area of research in rural sociology since the 1930s has been the Goldschmidt hypothesis concerning the negative social impact of restructuring in the farm sector, especially the development of corporate farms and the decline of small family farms. Goldschmidt (1978) and several others have shown that as the proportion of small family-owned farms declines, social stratification in rural communities becomes more pronounced and rigid, civic involvement declines, and quality of life is diminished. In recent years, scholars extended research on the impact of these types of changes in the rural economy to other sectors, including communities and regions dominated by manufacturing or retail trade and services (Lyson & Tolbert, 1996; Vias, 2004).

Change in a community need not take place at the gradual pace implied above. For rural economies dominated by a single industry such as mining or manufacturing, change often comes abruptly and with no warning (Freudenberg, 1992). Increased foreign competition and industry consolidation can lead to the sudden closure of important plants and facilities that employ a very large percentage of the community, an event that can result overnight in high rates of unemployment and poverty and a range of social ills as depressed conditions persist.

Finally, as small family farmers face an increasingly difficult competitive environment, those who wish to remain in rural areas must rely on off-farm sources of income, usually low-wage, part-time service jobs that lack benefits (Kassab, 1992). Increasingly, other members of the household have to join the workforce to make ends meet. In the long-run, as part-time and low-wage employment becomes the principal source of work, scholars expect that some rural areas will look increasingly like high-poverty urban areas, with more divorces, single-parent families, and other aspects of social dislocation (Coward & Smith, 1982). Clearly, the types of economic changes discussed above have impacts that reverberate throughout the social and demographic rural landscapes. These processes of social and demographic restructuring precipitated by economic change are the foci of many of the chapters that follow.

ENDNOTES

1. Agricultural jobs include hired laborers as well as farm owners, sole proprietors, and partners. Rough estimates based on census microdata indicate that 75 percent of workers in agricultural industries (crop production and livestock production) are hired laborers.
2. Because of nondisclosure requirements, income data for farming at the regional scale are suppressed. Therefore, it is not possible to examine average earnings per job for the eight BEA regions separately.
3. Because of nondisclosure requirements, income data for manufacturing at the regional scale is suppressed. Therefore, it is not possible to examine average wage per job for the eight BEA regions separately.

REFERENCES

Adamchak, D., Bloomquist, L., Bausman, K., & Qureshi, R. (1999). Consequences of population change for retail/wholesale sector employment in the nonmetropolitan great plains: 1950–1996. *Rural Sociology, 64,* 99–112.

Albrecht, D.E., & Albrecht, S.L. (1996). Changing employment patterns in nonmetropolitan America: Implications for family structure. *Southern Rural Sociology, 12* (1), 43–59.

Anding, T., Adams, J., Casey, W., de Montille, S., & Goldfein, M. (1990). *Trade centers of the upper Midwest: Changes from 1960–1989.* Minneapolis: University of Minnesota, Center for Urban and Regional Affairs.

Applebaum, R.P., & Albin, P. (1990). Shifts in employment, occupational structure, and educational attainment. In T. Noyelle (Ed.), *Skills, wages and productivity in the service sector* (pp. 31–66). Boulder, CO: Westview.

Barkely, D.L. (Ed.). (1993). *Economic adaptations: Alternatives for nonmetropolitan areas.* Boulder, CO: Westview.

Barnett, B.J. (2000). The U.S. farm financial crisis of the 1980s. *Agricultural History, 74* (2), 366–380.

Bender, N., & Davis, N. (2000). Developing agricultural and nature-based tourism in eastern Connecticut. In P. Schaeffer & S. Loveridge (Eds.), *Small town and rural economic development* (pp. 99–106). Westport, CT: Praeger.

Beyers, W. (1989). *The producer services and economic development in the United States: The last decade.* Washington, DC: U.S. Department of Commerce.

Beyers, W., & Lindahl, D. (1996). Lone eagles and high fliers in rural producer services. *Rural Development Perspectives, 11*, 2–10.

Beyers, W., & Nelson, P.B. (2000). Contemporary development forces in the nonmetropolitan west: New insights from rapidly growing communities. *Journal of Rural Studies, 16,* 459–474.

Beyers, W.B., & Alvine, M.J. (1985). Export services in postindustrial society. *Papers of the Regional Science Association, 57,* 33–45.

Bluestone, B., & Harrison, B. (1982). *The deindustrialization of America: Plant closings, community abandonment, and the dismantling of basic industry.* New York: Basic Books.

Bluestone, B., & Harrison, B. (1987). The impact of private disinvestments on workers and their communities. In R. Peet (Ed.), *International capitalism and industrial restructuring* (pp. 72–104). Winchester, MA: Allen & Unwin.

Bohrer, B. (2003, February 23). Service: Farm numbers up. *Associated Press Wire.* Posted February 28, 2003. (accessed through LexisNexis)

Borchert, J.R. (1992). *Megalopolis: Washington D.C. to Boston.* New Brunswick, NJ: Rutgers University Press. http://web.lexis-nexis.com

Bull, C.N. (1998). Aging in rural communities. *National Forum, 78* (2), 38–42.

Bureau of Economic Analysis. (2003). *REIS—Regional Economic Information System, 1969–2000* [CD]. Washington DC: Department of Commerce.

Castle, E.M. (Ed.). (1995). *The changing American countryside.* Lawrence: University of Kansas Press.

Christaller, W. (1966). *Places in southern Germany* (C. W. Baskin, Trans.). Englewood Cliffs, NJ: Prentice Hall.

Coward, R.T., & Smith, W.J. (1982). Families in a rural society. In D. A. Dillman & D. J. Hobbs (Eds.), *Rural society in the United States: Issues for the 1980s* (pp. 45–66). Boulder, CO: Westview.

Daniels, P.W. (1993). *Service industries in the world economy.* Cambridge, MA: Blackwell.

Drabenstott, M., & Smith, T. (1996). *The changing economy of the rural heartland.* Kansas City, MO: Federal Reserve Bank of Kansas.

Economic Research Service, U.S. Department of Agriculture. (2003a). *Farm balance sheet.* Retrieved March 23, 2003, from http://www.ers.usda.gov/Data/FarmBalanceSheet/fbsdmu.htm

Economic Research Service, U.S. Department of Agriculture. (2003b). *Agricultural trade, calendar year.* Retrieved May 27, 2003, from http://www.ers.usda.gov/Data/FATUS/DATA/XMScy1935.xls

Erickson, R. (1976). The filtering-down process: Industrial location in a nonmetropolitan area. *The Professional Geographer, 28,* 254–260.

Falk, W., & Lobao, L. (2003). Who benefits from economic restructuring? In D. L. Brown & L. E. Swanson (Eds.), *Challenges for rural America in the twenty-first century* (pp. 152–165). University Park, PA: Penn State Press.

Freudenberg, W.R. (1992). Addictive economies: Extractive industries and vulnerable localities in a changing world economy. *Rural Sociology, 57,* 305–332.

Fuguitt, G., Brown, D.L., & Beale, C. (1989). *Rural and small town America.* New York: Sage.

Galston, W.A., & Baehler, K.J. (1995). *Rural development in the United States: Connecting theory, practice, and possibilities*. Washington DC: Island Press.

Garnick, D. (1984). Shifting balances in U.S. metropolitan and nonmetropolitan area growth. *International Regional Science Review, 9*(3), 257–273.

Gatrell, J. (2002). Business services, productivity, and wages: Metropolitan and nonmetropolitan Michigan counties, 1977–1997. *Professional Geographer, 54*(3), 365–376.

Gibson, L.J. (1993). The potential for tourism development in nonmetropolitan areas. In D.L. Barkley (Ed.), *Economic adaptations: Alternatives for nonmetropolitan areas* (pp. 29–48). Boulder, CO: Westview.

Glasmeier, A., & Conroy, M. (1994). *Global squeeze on America: Opportunities, threats, and challenges from NAFTA, GATT, and processes of globalization*. University Park, PA: Penn State University, Institute for Policy Research and Evaluation.

Glasmeier, A., & Howland, M. (1995). *From combines to computers: Rural services and development in the age of information technology*. Albany, NY: State University of New York Press.

Goe, W.R. (2002). Factors associated with the development of nonmetropolitan growth nodes in producers service industries, 1980–1990. *Rural Sociology, 67*(3), 416–441.

Goetz, S., & Rupasingha, A. (2002). High-tech firm clustering: implications for rural areas. *American Journal of Agricultural Economics, 84,* 1229–1236.

Goldschmidt, W. (1978). *As you sow: Three studies in the social consequences of agribusiness*. Montclair, NJ: Allanheld, Osman.

Gottman, J. (1961). *Megalopolis: The urbanized northeastern seaboard of the United States*. Cambridge, MA: MIT Press.

Hansen, N. (1990). Do producer services induce regional economic development. *Journal of Regional Science, 30,* 465–476.

Harvey, D. (1989). *The condition of post-modernity*. Cambridge, MA: Blackwell.

Hawley, A. (1968). Human ecology. In D. Sills (Ed.), *International encyclopedia of the social sciences* (pp. 328–332). New York: Macmillan.

Heimlich, R., & Anderson, W. (2001). *Development at the urban fringe and beyond: Impacts on agriculture and rural land* (Agricultural Economic Report no. 803). Washington DC: U.S. Department of Agriculture, Economic Research Service.

Hobbs, D., & Weagley, R. (1995). The agricultures of the Midwest and their demographic and economic environments. In P. Lasley, L. Leistritz, L. Lobao, & K. Meyer (Eds.),*Beyond amber waves of grain: An examination of social and economic restructuring in the heartland* (pp. 28–49). Boulder, Westview.

Hornbeck, J.F. (1994). *The discount retail industry and its effects on small towns and rural communities*. Washington DC: Library of Congress, Congressional Research Services.

Kahan, S. (1990). The service economy - At present, employment tells the whole story. *The Service Economy, 4*(2), 1–8.

Kassab, C. (1992). *Income and inequality: The role of the service sector in the changing distribution of income*. New York: Greenwood Press.

Kassab, C., & Luloff, A.E. (1993). The new buffalo hunt: Chasing the service sector. *Journal of the Community Development Society, 24*(2), 175–195.

Longino, C.F. (1994). From sunbelt to sunspots. *American Demographics, 11,* 23–31.

Lyson, T. & Tolbert, C. (1996). Small manufacturing and nonmetropolitan socioeconomic well-being. *Environment and Planning A, 28,* 1779–1794.

Mawson, J. (1987). Services and regional policy. *Regional Studies, 21,* 471–475.

McGranahan, D. (2003). How people make a living in rural America. In D.L. Brown & L.E. Swanson (Eds.), *Challenges for rural America in the twenty-first century* (pp. 135–151). University Park, PA: Penn State Press.

Nagourney, A. (2004, February 24). Edwards says NAFTA is important but needs change. *The New York Times*, p. A22.

Nelson, M. (1999). Economic restructuring, gender, and informal work: a case study of a rural community. *Rural Sociology*, *64* (1), 18–43.

O'Farrell, P.N., Moffat, A.R., & Hitchens, D.N. (1993). Manufacturing demand for business services in a core and peripheral region: Does flexible production imply vertical disintegration of business services? *Regional Studies, 27,* 385–400.

Porterfield, S.L., & Pulver, G.C. (1991). Exports, impacts, and locations of services producers. *International Regional Science Review, 14,* 41–59.

Power, T.M. (1996). *Lost landscapes and failed economies: The search for a value of place*. Washington DC: Island Press.

Reeder, R.J., Schneider, M.J., & Green, B.L. (1993). Attracting retirees as a development strategy. In D. L. Barkley (Ed.), *Economic adaptations: Alternatives for nonmetropolitan areas* (pp. 127–144). Boulder, CO: Westview.

Rubin, S. (2001). Rural colleges as catalysts for community change: The RCCI experience. *Rural America, 16* (2), 12–19.

Rudzitis, G., & Johansen, H. (1989). *Amenities, migration, and nonmetropolitan regional development* (Report to the National Science Foundation). Moscow: University of Idaho, Department of Geography.

Scott, A.J. (1988). *New industrial spaces*. London: Pion Press.

Sell, R.S., Bangsund, D.A., & Leistritz, L. (2001). Contribution of the bison industry to North Dakota's economy. *American Journal of Alternative Agriculture, 16* (3), 106–113.

Singelmann, J. (1978). *From agriculture to services*. Beverly Hills, CA: Sage.

Smith, S.M. (1984). Export orientation of non-manufacturing businesses in nonmetropolitan communities. *Journal of the Agricultural Economics Association, 66,* 145–155.

Smith, S.M. (1993). Service industries in the rural economy: The role and potential contributions. In D. L. Barkley (Ed.), *Economic adaptations: Alternatives for nonmetropolitan areas* (pp. 105–127). Boulder, CO: Westview.

Stone, K.E. (1995). *Competing with the retail giants: How to survive in the new retail landscape*. New York: Wiley.

Stone, K.E. (1997). *Impact of the Wal-Mart phenomenon on rural communities*. Chicago: Farm Foundation.

Suryanata, K. (2002). Diversified agriculture, land use, and agrofood networks in Hawaii. *Economic Geography, 78*(1), 71–86.

Tiebout, C. (1962). *The community economic base study*. Seattle: University of Washington, Committee for Economic Development.

Trigaux, R. (1981). Citibank opens its Sioux Falls credit card center. *American Banker, 146*, 3–5.

U.S. Department of Agriculture. (1996a). Service industries expected to dominate 1994–2005 job growth. *Rural Conditions and Trends*, *7* (1), 10–12.

U.S. Department of Agriculture. (1996b). Government plays significant role in nonmetro employment. *Rural Conditions and Trends, 7*(1), 48–51.

Vias, A.C. (1999). Jobs follow people in the rural Rocky Mountain West. *Rural Development Perspectives, 14*, 14–23.

Vias, A.C. (2004). More stores, bigger stores or no stores: Paths of retail restructuring in rural America: 1988–1999. *Journal of Rural Studies, 20* (3), 303–318.

Vias, A.C., & Mulligan, G.F. (1997). Disaggregate economic base multipliers in small communities. *Environment and Planning A, 29* (6), 955–974.

CHAPTER 5

FIFTY YEARS OF FARMLAND CHANGE

Urbanization, Population Growth, and the Changing Farm Economy

MAX J. PFEFFER, JOE D. FRANCIS, AND ZEV ROSS[1]

INTRODUCTION

Metropolitan areas of the United States are diverse landscapes that often include substantial tracts of agricultural and open land. This landscape of diverse activities is often referred to as the "rural/urban fringe." These tracts are becoming increasingly contested spaces given conflicting pressures for urban development and environmental preservation. In this context, farmland preservation has become an important issue. For the environmental community, it is often a tool for preserving open space, habitat for wildlife, and functioning ecosystems. Land owners may see farmland preservation measures as a potential source of remuneration for environmental services they provide. Residents of the area see farmland and some forms of farm production as an amenity and as an asset in preserving property values.

This chapter is intended to inform policy discussions about farmland preservation. While numerous state and local policies have been implemented to preserve farmland, evidence of their effectiveness is not strong. With a better understanding of the factors related to farmland change, we can examine how policy can preserve farmland most effectively and how scarce resources can be used to greatest effect to preserve farmland. In addition, we consider whether an emphasis on the protection of farmland is appropriate and whether greater attention should be given to the proximate causes of farmland change.

Our analyses focus on farmland change at the county level in the continental United States. We evaluate this change for the period between 1949 and 1997, almost a half century, using agriculture and population census data. Our empirical analyses attempt to determine how much county-level variation in farmland change is accounted for by selected variables, including metropolitan status and changes in population and farm numbers. As we discuss below, these factors

W.A. Kandel & D.L. Brown (eds.), Population Change and Rural Society, 103–129.

are indicators for aspects of urbanization and structural change in agriculture. We also take into account spatial and temporal effects. To account for spatial effects we control for regional location and test for spatial autocorrelation. To account for temporal effects of cyclical swings in the farm economy we analyze farmland change for each of the 10 intervals between agricultural censuses beginning in 1949. We conclude the chapter with a discussion of the policy implications of our findings.

FARMLAND, URBANIZATION, AND THE CHANGING FARM ECONOMY

Farmland change has been a matter of concern over the past few decades, but the nature of that concern has changed over time. Beginning in the 1960s and continuing into the 1970s, some observers warned of the deterioration of soil quality and the conversion of fertile farmland to alternative uses. They pointed to the loss of the productive potential of the farmland base as a major issue. The National Agricultural Lands Study completed in 1981 affirmed many of these concerns, but it was later severely criticized for overstating the extent and negative consequences of farmland loss. Subsequent studies concluded that most of these losses were of marginally productive land and that even with the level of farmland change witnessed in the 1960s and 1970s, the supply of actively and potentially cultivated land was adequate to meet projected increases in demand for farm produce (Brown et al., 1982). Nevertheless, the interest in farmland has persisted, and trends in the stock of farmland and other non-federal lands are monitored regularly in the USDA's National Resources Inventory (USDA/NRCS, 2000; Vesterby & Krupa, 2001).

Despite the overall abundance of farmland, its loss in urbanizing areas has generated concern about maintaining these areas' rural character and quality of life. With the spread of non-farm residences across the countryside, land use has become more diversified, and farmland and related habitats have become fragmented. By the 1970s, rapidly expanding urban areas, especially on the east and west coasts, were encroaching on agriculture and raising concerns about the negative environmental impacts of continued low-density development—what is sometimes referred to as sprawl. For example, in 1950 officially designated metropolitan areas encompassed 136 million acres. By 1993 they covered 438 million acres, an increase of more than 200 percent in 40 years. A 124 percent increase in population accompanied this increase in metropolitan area. In some areas, the dispersal of residences across the countryside has occurred without population growth (Pendall, 2003). In any case, low-density development has led to population dispersal across the landscape, as evidenced by declines in metropolitan population density beginning in the 1960s in conjunction with the creation of dispersed "edge" cities and loosely organized clusters of residential housing (Altobelli & Pfeffer, 2000; Daniels, 1999; Garreau, 1988).

Development of a Multi-Functional Agriculture

Development patterns that emerged in the 1970s created geographically extensive metropolises encompassing a wide variety of land uses. Metropolitan areas have become increasingly made up of expanses of agricultural, forested, or otherwise "undeveloped" land that have significant and growing transportation and communication linkages to urban areas, such that a substantial portion of the population living in these areas is oriented to urban occupations and markets (Daniels, 1999; Pfeffer & Lapping, 1994). Metropolitan areas expanded spatially to include extensive rural territories as people commuted to work across greater distances. This development created a more varied and complex "rural/urban fringe" landscape that reduced the spatial separation between the non-farm population and agriculture and expanded the rural/urban interface. This form of development has been described as "leap frog" development or as a rural/urban fringe because it does not create a smooth or consistent pattern of land loss. Houses are often built on large lots and isolated from other dwellings, creating a fragmented landscape peppered with residences. Daniels (1999, p. 9) characterizes this development as follows:

> Like a fringe, strips of urban and suburban 'fabric' have extended into the countryside, creating a ragged settlement pattern of 'subdivisions, single-family housing on five- to ten-acre lots, shopping centers, retail strips, schools and churches all separated by farms, forests, or other urban spaces.'

Both the number of farms and acres of farmland in metropolitan areas decreased between 1949 and 1997. Farm numbers in the metropolitan United States hit a low in the 1960s and then climbed slightly over the following two decades. Between 1949 and 1997 the mean acreage of farms increased, but averages mask the structure of metropolitan agriculture.

In the metropolitan context, farmland serves a number of purposes extending beyond agricultural production per se (Daniels, 1999; Pfeffer et al., 2001). It takes on new "multifunctional" significance. Multifunctional agriculture provides benefits from both the production of agricultural commodities for markets as well as a variety of non-market benefits. Non-market benefits of farmland preservation include the limitation of urban sprawl, the protection of high quality soils and open space, and air and water quality (Batie, 2003; Lapping & Pfeffer, 1997; Pfeffer & Lapping, 1995). However, there are also problems associated with increasing encounters between non-farm residents and agricultural enterprises. Non-farm residents sometimes complain of odors, chemical drift, noise and other conditions attributed to agricultural production (Pfeffer & Lapping, 1995).

Metropolitan expansion has also created consumer demand for high-quality locally produced farm produce. This demand, for example, has been the basis for the increasing importance in the 1980s and 1990s of roadside stands and farmers' markets (Pfeffer & Lapping, 1995). Metropolitan farms nationwide tend to operate intensively on smaller acreages and specialize in high-value horticultural products while large-scale crop and animal farms remain concentrated in nonmetropolitan areas (Heimlich & Anderson, 2001).

Costs and Compensation for Services

Although metropolitan expansion creates certain market opportunities, it also creates production challenges. Farm operators must contend with difficult operating conditions, including high costs for land, labor, and other inputs, and interference in farm operations from competing land uses. Despite its intensive nature and potential to profit from high-value urban niche markets, the costs of doing business in this environment are considerable. Under these circumstances, farm operations are challenged by high production costs, and improvements in the quality of life that these farms contribute—fresh air, clean water, and open space—are not directly compensated. While agriculture's importance is acknowledged through preferential taxation of farmland, some feel farmers are inadequately compensated for their non-market goods and services, especially in peri-urban areas where agriculture satisfies needs beyond the production of food (Altobelli & Pfeffer, 2000; Heimlich & Anderson, 2001; Pfeffer & Lapping, 1994; Pfeffer et al., 2001). Preferential taxation of farmland is common in much of the United States, but it is intended to protect landowners from disproportionate tax burdens resulting from property tax-financed public infrastructure and services. Typically property tax relief is not provided as compensation for non-market goods and services. The non-market value of agriculture is difficult to establish, and there is little economic research documenting such value. Nevertheless, economists have indicated the potential importance of these non-market resources (Batie, 2003).

Metropolitan agriculture is also faced with skyrocketing prices for land (Adelaja & Schilling, 1999; Daniels & Bowers, 1997; Schnidman et al., 1990). The increasing economic value of farmland is a two-edged sword. While farmland may represent great potential personal wealth to a farm household, it can also create impediments to continued farming. Higher appraised values lead to increased taxes that farmland owners must pay in the face of stagnant or declining farm income. On the other hand, the land may serve as collateral for obtaining loans for investments to increase production and income (Daniels & Bowers, 1997). Thus, in the context of metropolitan population growth and associated residential and commercial developments, the continued economic viability of farming depends on the maintenance of a delicate balance between market opportunities and increasing production costs.

A variety of production conditions also make this context unfavorable to the economic viability of farming. Machine transport and repair become more difficult and time consuming. Farm support businesses are in short supply.

Vandalism and nuisance complaints become a problem. Under these circumstances, farmers may begin to explore alternatives to continued farming, and potential farmers are discouraged from entering the business, leading to changes in structure of the metropolitan farm sector.

The decrease in farm numbers resulting from low entry levels of younger farmers is true regardless of geographic location and has been true throughout the post-World War II period. Because of skill requirements and high initial investment costs, intergenerational transfer of farms is a common method by which younger individuals enter into the industry, but such transfers have become less common during the last 50 years. Farms are most likely to go out of business as established farmers retire without offspring willing to take over the farm operation (Keating, 1996; Stover & Helling, 1998). However, we expect such tendencies to be most pronounced in metropolitan areas because of the more difficult and expensive operating conditions. Farmers may shorten their planning horizons and consider non-farm investment and employment opportunities. As they attempt to keep their options open, they might reduce long-term investments in their farm operations. As such investments decline and farms fall behind competitors in adopting technological and market innovations, the economic viability of the enterprises erodes and the farms become more vulnerable to price fluctuations and natural conditions limiting production. In this context, farmers faced with low commodity prices, rising costs of production, or crop failure may simply give up farming and sell their farmland. This complex of factors leading to disinvestment in agriculture has been termed the *impermanence syndrome* (Daniels, 1999; Daniels & Bowers, 1997; Lynch & Carpenter, 2003; Pfeffer & Lapping, 1995).

The conversion of farmland to alternative uses tends to be most pronounced when certain factors like the proximity of public sewers, water, shopping, job centers and major roads increase the demand for land (Daniels & Bowers, 1997). In the rural/urban fringe, developers of alternative uses of the land are likely to outbid farmers, and in this context we expect decline in farm numbers to be more directly associated with a decrease in farmland than in less densely populated areas. In contrast, nonmetropolitan farm enterprises under economic duress would likely be sold to other farmers capable of investing in competitive technologies, hence keeping the land in production. Thus, farmland in metropolitan rural/urban fringe areas is especially vulnerable to being converted. The notion of the impermanence syndrome attempts to capture this vulnerability.

It should be noted that our focus is on farming as a land use. Given the positive outcomes associated with it, some consider it a preferred land use. This chapter is concerned with the perpetuation of this land use and does not deal with the fate of the land once farming on it ceases. Farmland could be converted to a variety of uses, including residential, commercial, or recreational development, as well as being left unmanaged (Vesterby & Krupa, 2001).

Farmland Preservation Policy

Farmland preservation measures are usually state and local initiatives intended to mitigate the effects of population growth and associated development. State and local governments began to adopt farmland preservation measures in the 1970s and 1980s in reaction to metropolitan development pressures. Expanding metropolitan development brought many rural/agricultural areas into the sphere of influence of the "urban growth machine." Molotch (1976) and Logan and Molotch (1987) characterize urban development as a growth machine that centers on the exchange of land. The land market allows property owners to realize the land's speculative value, and this aim is best achieved in conditions of economic growth.

Controls which limit development pose a direct challenge to the growth machine. Growth controls include limits on the total amount of construction permitted, down-zoning, utility restrictions and open space requirements. While some observers are skeptical about their effectiveness, these controls have the potential to significantly alter growth machine dynamics and shift development away from a singular focus on exchange values to one that considers the importance of the varied use values of land. One expression of this re-orientation is the interest in the fate of farmlands in rural/urban fringe areas and the generally strong public support for the preservation of farmlands.

Ironically, the concern to protect this farmland in rural/urban fringe areas is partly an outgrowth of the urbanization of rural/agricultural areas. As Logan and Molotch (1987, p. 226) conclude, "the dynamic is identical to that underlying the urban growth machine, but in a rural context." Real estate interests want to develop open lands and realize speculative values through an active real estate market. In this context, farmers and other established residents who hold land sometimes want development so as to realize the exchange value of their property, while newcomers, on the other hand, are often interested in farmland preservation to protect the "rural way of life" they sought in moving into the area in the first place (Pfeffer & Lapping, 1994).

According to Daniels (1999, p. 215), "farmland protection methods are frequently the primary means local governments use to try to manage growth in the fringe countryside." These measures include preferential taxation of farmland, agricultural zoning, agricultural districts, right-to-farm laws, and purchase and transfer of development rights. The effectiveness of these measures is a significant public policy issue because they are costly and difficult to fund and implement. Moreover, evidence suggests that in rural/urban fringe areas these measures are only effective in the short run (Daniels & Bowers, 1997; Diaz & Green, 2001; Pennington, 1999). This observation raises the question of whether or not these measures are properly targeted. Is the emphasis on land appropriate, or should greater attention be given to the proximate causes of farmland change?

In metropolitan areas we expect farmland change to be most strongly associated with change in farm numbers, but the relationship between changes in population and farmland is less clear. While numerous observers assert that there is a clear direct effect of population growth on farmland change, research has rarely provided direct evidence of this link. Several studies that explicitly examined this connection found population growth's impact on farmland change was relatively weak (Hirschl & Bills, 1994). However, this conclusion may be context specific. Lynch and Carpenter (2003) recently found a clear and fairly strong effect of population growth on farmland change in the mid-Atlantic region.

Contradictory findings on the effects of population change are not surprising. Population growth, especially low-density growth, as already mentioned, may create short-run challenges *as well as* opportunities for agriculture. As traditional farm operations face increasing costs of doing business like the ones described above, farm enterprises catering to specialized demands for food and local services may find additional opportunities for profitable operations (e.g., niche markets or specialty products produced for sale to target consumers). Thus, population change may have some positive effects on farming as well as negative ones, and under certain circumstances they may cancel each other out. The practical significance of these observations is that different farmland protection measures might be most effective at different levels of population growth. Evidence suggests that farmland protection measures are most effective when population growth and associated development pressures are less pronounced. Daniels and Bowers (1997, p. 133) observe:

> Farmland protection efforts have most often succeeded in areas located some distance from development. There, farmers can see a future for farming and often feel they can live with a combination of incentives and land-use controls designed to encourage farming and limit non-farm development . . . But at the edge, where city or suburb meets countryside, these incentives and land-use controls have not succeeded in protecting farmland for more than a few years.

The limited effectiveness of farmland protection efforts under certain conditions has prompted some to point out the importance of farm economic viability. Daniels and Bowers (1997, p. 102) assert, "If farming is not profitable, farmland protection programs ultimately will not be successful. Both farmland protection and economic development measures are needed to bolster the future prospects of agriculture as an industry." Daniels (1999, p. 150) presses this point further:

> Non-farmers in the fringe often perceive farmland . . . as valuable only for its scenic views and open space amenities. In fact, many farmland protection efforts in fringe areas are aimed at preserving open space rather than maintaining agriculture as an economically viable industry. This strategy misses the simple point that there can be no farms without farmers. The need for integrated farmland and agricultural policies is especially evident in the fringe because land use restrictions alone do not guarantee the financial success of a farm, and the value of farmland is usually much higher for home sites, a mall, or an office park.

Temporal and Geographical Contexts

While local forces may be the proximate causes of the conversion of farmland to other uses, a variety of macro-economic and natural forces also influence the farm economy and the economic viability of farms. Production failures associated with natural disasters may drive farms out of business. The variability of farm commodity prices due to fluctuations in domestic and international production levels or changes in trade policies also have major impacts on local farm economies. As indicated above, in the metropolitan context of strong demand for alternative uses of farmland, the cessation of farming is likely to result in farmland decline rather than the concentration of farmland in fewer enterprises—the more likely situation in nonmetropolitan counties. A number of observers have noted the central importance of macro-economic forces in driving farmland change and have argued for national-level policies that address the impacts of these forces at the local level (Hirschl & Bills, 1994; Schnidman et al., 1990). An understanding of the relative importance of periodic effects of farm crises and population growth on farmland change can inform the development and targeting of an appropriately balanced set of policy measures that address both the effects of economic crisis and land use change associated with urbanization.

Farmland change also needs to be placed in the appropriate geographical context, given the pronounced regional variation in natural environments and historical patterns of development (Castle, 2003; Vesterby & Krupa, 2001; Schnidman et al., 1990). Farmland may play substantially different roles in the local ecology depending on the features of the natural and built environments in different regions. For example, differences in soil quality are an important determinant of variation in farm productivity. Historical patterns of settlement also create different conditions that may or may not favor farm viability. For example, a historically fragmented configuration of land holding may limit the potential for farm consolidation.

Forces Inducing Farmland Change

The following analyses focus on three factors that are thought to drive farmland change: (1) metropolitan location and the level of urbanization, (2) population change, and (3) change in farms. In the metropolitan context of competing demands for land use, farmland is particularly vulnerable. Hence we expect changes in farm numbers to be more strongly related to farmland change in metropolitan counties. The effects of population change are less clear since population growth creates both constraints and opportunities for specialized farm production. With these points in mind, we address the following empirical questions:

- What is the relative importance of metropolitan location, population change, and the number of farms in accounting for variation in farmland change?

- Do the effects of population change and farm numbers on farmland change vary according to metropolitan versus nonmetropolitan settings?
- Do these factors have an effect on farmland change net of controls for period effects that attempt to account for the cyclical effects of macro-economic and natural conditions?

DATA AND METHODS

To address these questions we completed two phases of analysis. First, we addressed the empirical questions listed above through an examination of change across 50 years of observation as a whole with no cyclical or period effects. That is, we calculated and included variables that reflected overall change between 1949 and 1997. We refer to this as the "overall effects" model. Second, as overall models like this often mask important dynamics of change during periods associated with significant farming industry events, we conducted a second modeling activity to address the possibility that changes during the period 1949–1954 may not have been the same as during the period 1954–1959 and so forth. We refer to this second modeling activity as the "period effects" model.

Study Area and Units of Observation

We restricted our analyses to the coterminous United States, using as primary data sets the Censuses of Agriculture for the years 1949 through 1997, and the U.S. Census of Population for the decades 1950–1990. As of this writing, data from the 2002 Census of Agriculture were not available. The decision to restrict the study to the continental United States reflects the fact that farming differs significantly in Alaska and Hawaii, and that key farming and farmland data were less consistently available and reliable for these states over the 50-year period of this study, particularly the earlier years.

Our units of observation and analysis are counties or county equivalents. Counties are the lowest geographical unit for which the Census of Agriculture reports information on a consistent and systematic basis and Census of Population data are available for all counties. County units are not the standard reporting unit in all parts of the United States and some new counties were created between 1949 and 2000. For consistency across the 1949–1997 period, the base data file we used consisted of the 3,088 county equivalent units identified by Fuguitt and colleagues (1989).

To ensure accuracy, a small number of counties with missing or suspect data were removed prior to analysis.[2] A small number of counties that appeared to represent non-viable farming situations (e.g., ultra-urbanized environments) were also removed. Based on a careful inspection of the county data, we estimated that counties with both a particularly small farming acreage (less than 100,000) and a small proportion of total land devoted to farming (less than 10 percent) were atypical and might skew our analyses. These non-viable farming counties represent less than 2 percent of total counties and a comparison of models with and without these counties suggests that they have very little influence on the results. The effective number of county units for the overall (1949–1997) model analysis was 2,982, while the effective number of observations for the period modeling, based on 10 five-year intervals, was 29,993. The difference in these two numbers reflects differences in data availability for specific agricultural censuses.[3]

FIFTY YEARS OF FARMLAND CHANGE

The Outcome Variable Analyzed

The main outcome variable being modeled in this chapter is farmland change from 1949 to 1997 for the overall model and within each of the ten intervals between agricultural censuses for the period effects model. We used Census of Agriculture definitions of land in farms as a basis for determining the amount of farmland in each county. Like counties and metropolitan status, the definition of farmland has changed over the years. For purposes of the analyses presented in this chapter, it was assumed that the amount of farmland reported in each census year was sufficiently accurate and no attempt was made to adjust for definitional differences.

Overall Farmland Change 1949–1997

The amount of total farmland in the continental United States declined significantly over the past 50 years. In 1949 the Census of Agriculture reported 1,151 million acres of farmland, while the comparable figure in 1997 was 921 million, a decrease of 230 million. Farmland change over the past half century has not been uniform across the American landscape. Figure 5.1 shows rather marked regional differences in the rate of farmland change. Areas east of the Mississippi display some of the most pronounced change during this period. Some of the largest decreases in farmland are concentrated in the "Old South," the southeast Piedmont, the Ozark Ouchita Plateau, the Ohio Valley, New England, and the northern reaches of Michigan, Wisconsin and Minnesota. High rates of change are also found in the far West, but areas with high rates of change are more scattered than they are in the East. One area of concentrated farmland decrease in the West is the Seattle metropolitan area. The least change occurred across the American heartland of the Midwest and the Great Plains. All regions of the United States experienced some farmland decline between 1949 and 1997, but the greatest decreases occurred in the New England and South Atlantic Census Divisions. The lowest rates of decline are found in three Central and the Mountain Census Divisions.

*Figure 5.1. Percent Farmland Change, 1949–1997**

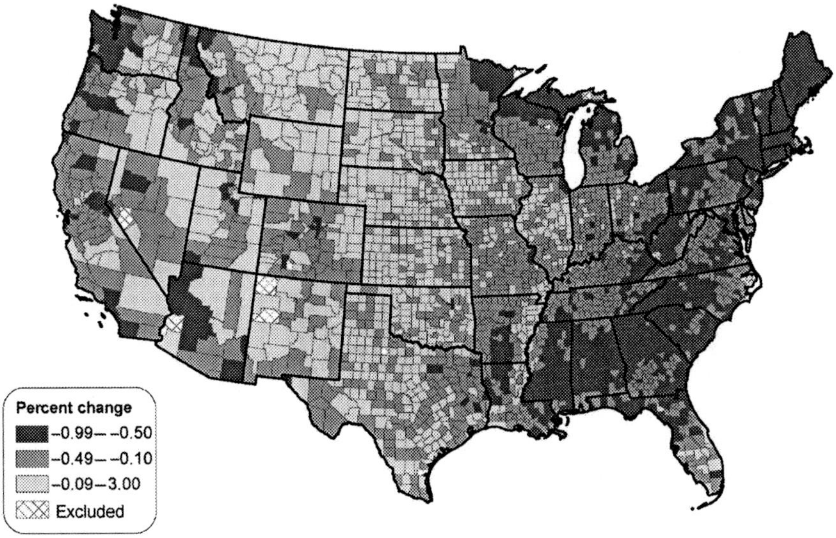

Predictor Variables

Predictor variables employed to account for systematic differences in change of farmland among the counties across time included: metropolitan status, size of metropolitan area, regional location (Census Divisions), population change, and change in the number of farms. To control for initial differences, we used population, the number of farms and amount of farmland in 1949. To reflect regional location we employed the U.S. Bureau of the Census's 10 Divisions. In an examination of how metropolitan areas related to the divisions, we found that metropolitan areas were almost always contained in a single division.

Concerning the metropolitan county classification, the primary source of information was the U.S. Office of Management and Budget's designations of metropolitan status for 1993. We distinguished metropolitan counties by total population and nonmetropolitan counties by whether they were adjacent to a metropolitan area. We delineate six categories: (1) greater than one million; (2) 500,000 to one million; (3) 250,000 to 499,999; (4) less than 250,000; (5) nonmetropolitan and adjacent to a metropolitan area; (6) nonmetropolitan and non-adjacent to a metropolitan area. This classification scheme has proven to be a useful and widely used means of categorizing rural and urban areas. Rural and nonmetropolitan, however, are far from synonymous; nonmetropolitan areas include urban population, and there is considerable rural population inside areas designated metropolitan. Background and justification for these classifications are given by Fuguitt and colleagues (1989, p. 6).

To insure backward comparability, we imposed the 1993 metropolitan status designations of the counties retrospectively for all census years back to 1949. Previous research by Altobelli and Pfeffer (2000) demonstrated that the trends in farms and farmland by metropolitan status do not change appreciably when the status is fixed either by the 1950 designation or the 1993 designation. Consequently, the trends observed over time and presented below are not solely a function of how metropolitan status was determined.

Another important variable in the analyses is the number of farms in the county. We used the Census of Agriculture's definition of a farm as a basis for determining the number of farms in each county. Although the census definition of farms changed in 1959 and in 1974, our analysis operates under the assumption that changes in farm definition would have little impact on the broad trends under consideration, and thus we made no attempt to adjust census reported data on farm numbers.[4]

Population change, the last of the predictor variables, was computed in a straightforward manner: the population in the county as of the 1990 census minus the population in 1950. Mid-term population estimates by county were calculated by assuming a constant rate of change between decennial censuses. Mid-term values were assigned by multiplying the total population change across the decade by the proportion of the number of years elapsed.

In addition to the predictor variables mentioned above (metropolitan location, population change and change in the number of farms), both the overall effects model (1949–1997 change) and the period effects model (five year changes) contained variables to represent and control for initial conditions. For the overall model, we included total farms and farmland in the county in 1949, as well as the county 1950 population.

Relationship between Farmland Change and Metropolitan/Nonmetropolitan Status

Farmland change over the past half century took place in the context of considerable urbanization. Table 5.1 shows counties grouped by size of metropolitan area. Counties classified as metropolitan with populations greater than one million grew five-fold, and the number of smaller metropolitan counties more than doubled, while there were only about half as many nonmetropolitan counties not adjacent to metropolitan areas in 1993 compared with 1950. Moreover, as shown in Table 5.2, the largest metropolitan areas experienced the highest rates of farmland change. In fact, counties in the largest metropolitan areas had rates of farmland decrease almost four times greater than in nonmetropolitan non-adjacent counties. In 1949 farmland was more uniformly part of the American landscape. Further, Table 5.2 indicates that in 1949 the majority of the total land in each category of counties was farmland, but by 1997 farmland as a proportion of total land in the

Table 5.1. Counties by Size of Metropolitan

	1950		1993	
Size of Metropolitan Area	N	Percent	N	Percent
Greater than 1,000,000	53	1.8	268	9.0
500,000–999,999	99*	3.3	142	4.8
250,000–499,999			173	5.8
Less than 250,000	97	3.2	198	6.6
Non-Metropolitan, Adjacent to Metropolitan	767	25.7	1,147	38.5
Non-Metropolitan, Not Adjacent to Metropolitan	1,966	66.0	1,054	35.3
TOTAL	2,982	100.0	2,982	100.0

* In 1950, the size of metropolitan area combines the 250,000 to 499,999 and the 500,000 to 999,999 categories.
Source: Glenn V. Fuguitt, University of Wisconsin.

largest metropolitan areas was about half that in nonmetropolitan non-adjacent ones.

As indicated earlier, the classification of a county as metropolitan reflects both population increase and the growth of commuting between outlying counties and core population centers. Both factors can have an independent impact on farmland. As mentioned above, Pendall (2003) recently observed urban sprawl in conditions of little or no population growth. Under such circumstances, residential development, not population growth, may be the cause of farmland change. On the other hand, the data in Table 5.3 show that there were, overall, clear differences in population growth by the size of the metropolitan area. The largest metropolitan areas grew at a rate of almost eleven times that of nonmetropolitan non-adjacent areas. As the rate of population growth increases, the rate of farmland loss increases, but the slope of this relationship is fairly flat (not shown). This result is not surprising given the intermingling of positive and negative impacts of population growth on the farm economy as noted earlier.

Farmland Change and Change in Number of Farms

Farmland change during the last half century also took place in the context of a profound re-structuring of the farm sector. By 1997 the nation had only about one-third the farms it had in 1949. Unlike farmland change, which varied across metropolitan areas of different sizes, the rate of decline in farms was fairly constant across these areas (Table 5.3).

Table 5.2. Farmland and Total Land by Size of Metropolitan Area, United States, 1949 and 1997

Size of Metropolitan Area	Farmland Acres 1949	Farmland Acres 1997	Total Acres	Percent Farmland 1949	Percent Farmland 1997	Farmland Percent Change 1949–1997
1,000,000+	69,008,110	37,903,340	124,852,356	55	30	−45
500,000–999,999	48,991,586	31,562,128	93,163,236	53	34	−36
250,000–499,999	52,112,120	35,754,543	82,744,930	63	43	−31
Less than 250,000	83,235,870	64,006,597	127,262,409	65	50	−23
Nonmetro, Metro- Adjacent	427,151,192	336,609,998	702,652,200	61	48	−21
Nonmetro, Not Metro-Adjacent	470,039,991	415,176,845	691,165,221	68	60	−12
TOTAL (000)	1,150,539	921,013	1,821,840	63	51	−20

Source: U.S. Census of Agriculture, 1949 and 1997.

Table 5.3. Population and Farm Numbers by Size of Metropolitan Area

	Population			Farm Numbers		
Size of Metropolitan Area	1950	1990	Percent Change 1950–1990	1949	1997	Percent Change 1949–1997
1,000,000+	49,814,809	114,059,822	129	591,165	194,204	−67
500,000– 999,999	15,154,319	30,262,368	100	316,813	105,218	−67
250,000– 499,999	13,461,239	28,262,368	110	404,642	147,301	−64
Less than 250,000	12,048,838	21,864,677	81	450,012	168,239	−63
Nonmetro, Metro- Adjacent	25,795,600	34,703,041	35	2,093,898	750,332	−64
Nonmetro, Not Metro-Adjacent	16,153,085	18,061,946	12	1,499,774	531,862	−65
TOTAL (000)	132,409,890	247,234,569	87	5,356,304	1,897,156	−65

Source: U.S. Census of Population, 1950 and 1990; U.S. Census of Agriculture 1949 and 1997.

Figure 5.2. Scatterplot of Percent Change in Farmland and Farms

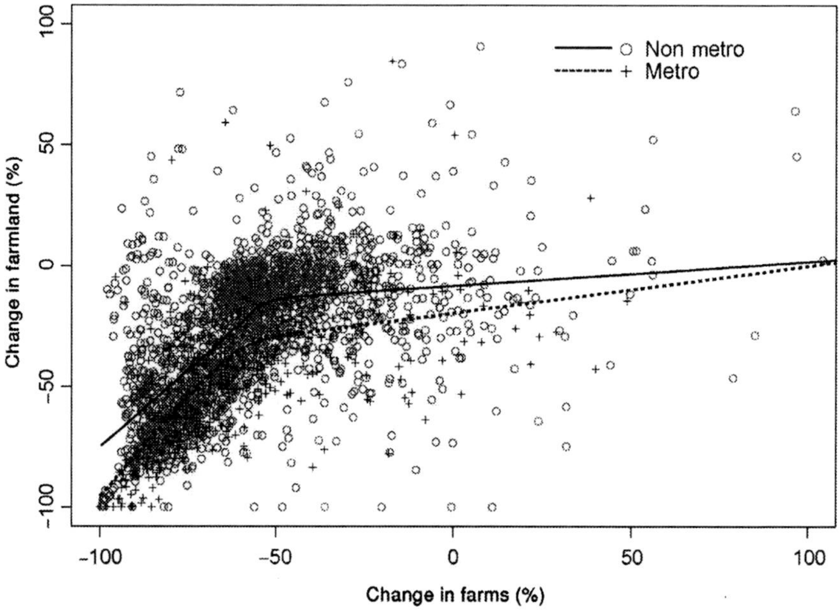

The relationship between change in the number of farms and farmland decline cannot be adequately characterized as a linear relationship, as shown in Figure 5.2. When the rate of decrease in the number of farms in a county is greater than 50 percent, there is a fairly steep positive relationship with farmland change. When farm loss is less pronounced, the positive relationship with farmland change is more muted, as indicated by the relatively flat slope for the curve to the right in Figure 5.2. Another important point about the relationship between change in farm numbers and farmland change is that this relationship is more pronounced in metropolitan than nonmetropolitan areas. As farmers leave farming in metropolitan areas, the land is less likely to pass on to other farmers. As mentioned above, metropolitan areas are characterized by both greater demands for the conversion of farmland to other uses and increasing costs of farming. Under these circumstances, farmers may be less likely to make long-term commitments to continue farming and invest in farmland. This combination of strong demand for the conversion of farmland to alternative uses and lack of incentives to continue farming was referred to earlier as the impermanence syndrome. Thus, although the same factors may be driving farmers' exits from farming (e.g., farm population aging, sectoral pressures from technical change, changes in farm product demand, foreign competition), decline in the number of farms, whatever the reason, affects farmland change more in metropolitan than in nonmetropolitan areas.

Figure 5.3. Farmland Change for 10 Intervals Between Agricultural Censuses Since 1949

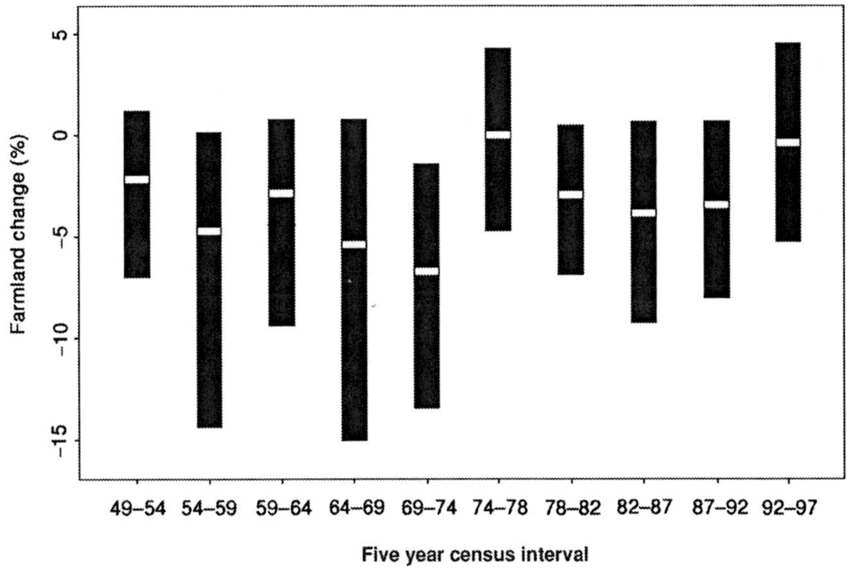

Period Differences in Farmland Change, 1949–1997

So far we have discussed overall changes between 1949 and 1997, but the rate of change for shorter time periods within this span varied considerably. This variation reflects the changing fortunes of the volatile farm economy. The data in Figure 5.3 show that the highest rates of farmland change occurred between 1964 and 1974. Some of the farmland loss over this time period reflects recurring farm crises. In the 1960s and late 1970s farm crises stimulated protests like the "holding actions" of the National Farmers Organization in 1967 and the "tractorcade" in Washington, DC instigated by the American Agricultural Movement in the late 1970s (Morgan, 1980; Walters, 1968). The growing post-World War II economy created numerous employment opportunities for farmers who left farming and ceased farming marginal lands. In the eastern United States, much of this abandoned farmland was allowed to return to forest (Vesterby & Krupa, 2001). On the other hand, the stabilization of farmland changes reflects the export boom of the early 1970s, when Secretary of Agriculture Earle Butz encouraged farmers to "plant fence row to fence row." The period effects shown in Figure 5.3 are likely associated with macro-economic factors and appear to be related to variation in the rate of farmland change. We will return to a consideration of these period effects in conjunction with the effects of changes in population and farm numbers in our description of the multivariate analyses.

MODELLING 50 YEARS OF FARMLAND CHANGE

To assess the relationship between changes in farmland and our predictor variables for the 50-year interval (1949–97), we used ordinary least squares regression (OLS). In all cases, the change variables (farmland change, change in number of farms, and population change) are computed as a proportion of the beginning value (e.g., $(X_{97}\text{-}X_{49})/X_{49}$). We used deviation (sum-to-zero) contrasts for the categorical variables (Census divisions, metropolitan status). Deviation scoring is similar to the more familiar dummy coding (0, 1), except that with deviation coding (1, 0, −1) each coefficient associated with the category or level of the factor compares that level to the average of all the levels rather than to some arbitrary reference category of the variable. As with all categorical coding structures, the last level is considered redundant and no coefficient is estimated for that category. However, with deviation (or effect) coding, since the sum of the coefficients is constrained to sum to zero, the final level can easily be computed by summing the coefficients for all other levels and multiplying by −1.[5]

The Overall Model

Each variable accounts for a statistically significant share of the variance, but the largest share of the variance by far is accounted for by change in the number of farms and the associated squared term that we included in the model to approximate the nonlinear relationship demonstrated in Figure 5.2. Size of metropolitan area and Census Division were the next most important variables and of about equal predictive power, while the control variables were the least important. The results in Table 5.4 are for the sequential analysis of variance.

Parameter estimates for our regression are shown in Table 5.5. Coefficients for metropolitan areas with populations less than 500,000 are very small (i.e., farmland change was not significantly different from the national average). Metropolitan areas with populations greater than 500,000 were likely to have experienced higher rates of farmland decline than average (i.e., greater population growth is related to a decline in farmland). Nonmetropolitan areas experienced less farmland change than average.[6] Population change has a statistically significant effect on farmland change. Farm change stands out as the principle proximate cause of farmland decline. These results are net of the effects of geographic region. The parameter estimates for Census Division are consistent with the regional variation described in Figure 5.1 above. The parameter estimates in Table 5.5 show that New England had the greatest farmland loss of all Census Divisions, while farmland loss was least in the West North Central Census Division. It should be remembered that the effects of the size of the metropolitan area and population and farm change are net of the effects of spatial variation across Census Divisions.

Table 5.4. Results of Sequential Analysis of Variance

Variable	Degrees of Freedom	Sum of Squares	Mean Squares	*F*-Statistic	*p*
Size of Metro Area	5	23.30	4.66	137.27	.000
% Population Change	1	.55	.55	16.21	.000
% Number of Farms Change	1	66.03	66.03	1,945.17	.000
% Number of Farms Change-Squared	1	19.77	19.77	582.40	.000
Farms 1949	1	3.85	3.85	113.51	.000
Farmland 1949	1	.34	.34	9.98	.002
Population 1950	1	1.24	1.24	36.60	.000
Census Division	8	23.82	2.98	87.73	.000
Residuals	2,962	100.54	.034	—	—

Source: Analysis performed by the authors.

Mixed Effects and Five Year Time Periods Model

The ordinary least squares approach, used to model the overall 50-year change, is appropriate in situations where the data and errors can be assumed independent. However, in our detailed analysis of farmland change, where we include ten observations (representing the ten time intervals) for each county, this assumption is violated. To address the issue of correlated error, we used a mixed effects approach to model periods of farmland change. Mixed effects models offer the flexibility of modeling within-group correlation present in a repeated measure analysis where we have multiple measurements of a response on the same unit of observation (i.e., counties) (Laird & Ware, 1982). The mixed effects model treats the fixed effects (i.e., our predictors and controls) as before but treats the random effects (in this case counties) as random variations around a mean of zero. The random effects and the error are assumed to follow a normal distribution.[7,8]

Results of Mixed Effects Model for Five Year Periods

Once again the sequential analysis of variance indicates that all of the variables in the model were statistically significant (results not shown). Taking into account the period effects reveals slightly greater than average farmland losses in the largest metropolitan areas and slightly lower losses in nonmetropolitan non-adjacent counties. However, these effects are very small. The effects for change in the number of farms and population change are larger. Comparing the equivalent

Table 5.5. Results of Ordinary Least Squares Regression to Estimate Mean Percentage Farmland Change, 1949–1997

Variable	Coefficient	Standard Error	t-Value	p
Metropolitan, 1 Million +	−.044	.011	−3.871	.000
Metropolitan, 500,000–999,999	−.031	.014	−2, 26	.023
Metropolitan, 250,000–499,999	.011	.012	.859	.390
Metropolitan, Less than 250,000	.002	.012	.194	.846
Non-Metropolitan, Adjacent to Metro	.016	.007	2.28	.023
Non-Metropolitan, Not Adjacent to Metro (Ref.)*				
% Change in Population	−.025	.002	−11.766	.000
% Number of Farms Change	.402	.017	24.155	.000
% Number of Farms Change-Squared	−.189	.014	−14.073	.000
Farms 1949 (000)	.030	.003	9.072	.000
Farmland 1949 (00000)	.001	.001	.951	.341
Population 1950 (00000)	−.014	.003	−5.627	.000
New England	−.227	.021	−10.770	.000
Middle Atlantic	−.093	.015	−6.142	.000
East North Central	.072	.009	7.890	.000
West North Central	.175	.009	20.515	.000
South Atlantic	−.079	.009	−8.613	.000
East South Central	−.055	.010	−5.339	.000
West South Central	.116	.009	12.809	.000
Mountain	.111	.013	8.381	.000
Pacific (reference)*				
Constant	−.093	.014	−6.64	.000
R-Squared	.580	—	—	—
F	215.4	—	—	.000
Degrees of Freedom	2, 962	—	—	—
N	2, 982	—	—	—

** Deviation (sum-to-zero) contrasts for the categorical variables compare each coefficient compares the level of the factor to the average of the all levels. As with all contrasts, the last level is considered redundant and is omitted. However, since the sum of the coefficients is constrained to sum to zero, the final level can easily be computed by summing all other levels and multiplying by −1.

Source: Analysis performed by the authors.

coefficients in the OLS and mixed effects models shows that the effects of farm loss and population growth are strengthened by taking into account period effects that are strongly associated with macro-level forces affecting the farm economy. This observation has important implications for discussions about farmland protection policy. Macro-economic factors accentuate more secular trends in the farm economy like the overall process of concentration and intensification of farm production. Most important, there is less farmland loss in times of agricultural economic prosperity. As indicated in Table 5.6, farmland loss was lowest in the late 1960s and 1970s and during the early to mid-1980s. On the other hand, regional differences appear to be diminished after taking into account temporal variation. This suggests that regional changes are not constant across time, but are more pronounced at particular times and places. The policy implication of this observation is that farmland protection efforts need to be tailored to specific historical and local conditions since farmland loss is not uniform across time and space.

Evaluating Spatial Autocorrelation

Like many socioeconomic phenomena, changes in population components and the farming industry within a given county are significantly related to changes in nearby counties (see Chapter 19 for a fuller discussion). This spatial relationship can be a function of a major dynamic, like rapid growth of a core city and the surrounding areas resulting in either the emergence of a new metropolitan area or the expansion of an existing one. Spatial autocorrelation can also result from many minor changes over time, like the decline of farming due to the aging of farm operators or the deterioration of soils. To account for possible spatial autocorrelation, we identified for each county all counties that were adjacent to it. We then constructed a matrix of weights to reflect this adjacency.

A visual inspection of the map of the dependent variable and the residuals shows an indication of spatial autocorrelation (counties near to each other tend to be more similar than counties further away). Spatial autocorrelation violates the OLS statistical assumption of independent error, and significant spatial autocorrelation can lead to an underestimation of variation in statistical models, which in turn affects confidence intervals and conclusions about parameter significance (Cressie, 1993). In order to evaluate the autocorrelation levels and to assess how well our independent variables account for the autocorrelation, we computed the Moran's I statistic on our dependent variable before analysis (i.e., before introducing the predictor variables) and again on the residuals after running our model (Odland, 1988). Moran's I is a statistic that provides an indication of the type and degree of spatial autocorrelation among neighboring observations. Moran's I ranges from 1 (perfect positive correlation, neighboring areas are extremely similar) to zero (no correlation) to -1 (perfect negative correlation, neighboring areas are extremely dissimilar).

Table 5.6. Results of Mixed Effects Model Estimating Mean Percentage Change for Ten Periods between 1949 and 1997

Variable	Coefficient	Standard Error	*t*-Value	*p*
Metropolitan, 1 Million +	−.008	.002	−3.980	.000
Metropolitan, 500,000–999,999	−.003	.002	−1.355	.175
Metropolitan, 250,000–499,999	.001	.002	.666	.505
Metropolitan, Less than 250,000	.003	.002	1.636	.109
Non-Metropolitan, Adjacent to Metro	.003	.001	2.158	.031
Non-Metropolitan, Not Adjacent to Metro (ref.)*				
% Change in Population	−.104	.008	−12.493	.000
% Number of Farms Change	.444	.005	82.665	.000
% Number of Farms Change-Squared	−.043	.001	−51.256	.000
Farms 1949 (000)	−.009	.000	9.741	.000
Farmland 1949 (00000)	−.000	.000	−.549	.583
Population 1950 (00000)	−.003	.000	−8.382	.000
New England	−.043	.004	−11.414	.000
Middle Atlantic	−.019	.003	−7.166	.000
East North Central	.011	.002	6.395	.000
West North Central	.022	.001	14.332	.000
South Atlantic	−.008	.002	−5.411	.000
East South Central	−.001	.002	−.772	.440
West South Central	.019	.002	11.704	.000
Mountain	.016	.002	6.703	.000
Pacific (reference)*				
1949–1954	.020	.002	10.354	.000
1954–1959	.021	.002	10.183	.000
1959–1964	.022	.002	11.919	.000
1964–1969	−.018	.002	−9.446	.000
1969–1974	−.007	.002	−3.821	.000
1974–1978	.007	.002	3.850	.000
1978–1982	−.028	.002	−14.809	.000
1982–1987	−.018	.002	−9.511	.000
1987–1992	−.003	.002	−1.805	.071
1992–1997 (reference)*				
Constant	−.013	.002	−7.589	.000
N	3, 003	—	—	—

* Deviation (sum-to-zero) contrasts for the categorical variables compare each coefficient compares the level of the factor to the average of the all levels. As with all contrasts, the last level is considered redundant and is omitted. However, since the sum of the coefficients is constrained to sum to zero, the final level can easily be computed by summing all other levels and multiplying by −1.

Although the results of the Moran's I computations suggest that the predictor variables account for a significant proportion of the spatial autocorrelation, residuals from our OLS model were still auto-correlated (Moran's I on change in farmland is 0.70, and on the residuals from the full OLS model it is 0.37). In order to ensure that this residual autocorrelation was not leading to underestimated standard errors or changes in our coefficients, we compared the OLS results with those from a spatial linear model. A spatial linear model uses generalized least squares regression to fit a linear model with spatial dependence. We used a conditional spatial autoregressive covariance structure and specified a neighborhood based on first-order adjacency (Kaluzny & Vega, 1998). Both the coefficients and the standard errors from the spatial linear model (not shown here) are nearly identical to those from the OLS model, suggesting that the residual autocorrelation is having little effect on our results and that an OLS model is appropriate.

CONCLUSIONS

When a variety of factors is considered, a county's location within an officially designated metropolitan area accounts for relatively little of the farmland change variation between counties. In our analyses, the most important factor accounting for variation in farmland change was decline in the number of farms. This effect was robust across fitted models.

The estimated effects of metropolitan status, population change and change in farm numbers on farmland change vary depending on the time frame for which one measures change. The overall patterns of results were similar for both the overall and the period effects models, but the size of our parameter estimates differed noticeably. Analyzing farmland change for the four- and five-year intervals between agricultural censuses accentuates the estimates of the effects of changes in both farm numbers and population compared with the analysis of overall change for the 1949–1997 period. The parameter estimates for the mixed effects model are about two and four times larger for farm loss and population change respectively. Thus, the results of this model strengthen our conclusions that macro economic factors related to changes in the farm economy are most important in accounting for farmland change, and that farmland protection efforts need to be tailored to specific historical and local conditions.

We began this paper with two questions. How can policies to preserve farmland be most effective? How can scarce resources be used to greatest effect to preserve farmland? Our findings are consistent with other analyses that call for greater attention to farm economics and assert that farmland preservation efforts that do not address the economic viability of farms are likely to fail (Daniels, 1999; Daniels & Bowers, 1997; Hirschl & Bills, 1994).

Given these observations, policies should be designed to help farmers take advantage of multiple income-earning opportunities. These opportunities are most abundant in metropolitan areas and include the sale of products and services that cater to the growing urban population. As indicated above, population growth bears both opportunities and constraints for agriculture. However, with careful local planning, population growth can be channeled in ways that buffer farmland and create additional economic opportunities for farm enterprises (Daniels, 1999). In some cases this may involve recognizing the multi-functionality of agriculture and compensating farmers for the economic value of non-market goods that they provide (Pfeffer & Lapping, 1995; Pfeffer et al., 2001). While this approach has potential, little is known about it and how it might work (Batie, 2003).

ENDNOTES

1. The authors acknowledge helpful comments from Nelson Bills and participants in the USDA/ERS Conference on Population Change and Rural Society, Economic Research Service, U.S. Department of Agriculture, Washington, DC, January 29. Partial support for this research was provided by the Polson Institute for Global Development at Cornell University and by the USDA multi-state research project NE-1011. The authors are entirely responsible for the contents of this chapter.
2. "Suspect" refers to three counties with farmland gains greater that 200 percent. In these instances farmland and total land values were unreasonable and suspected to be inaccurate.
3. After removing a small number of counties with missing data, limited farmland or gains in farmland of more than 200 percent, we were left with 2,982 counties. We also removed a small number of counties with missing values, little farmland, and gains in farmland of more than 200 percent. Due to differences in data availability from census to census, certain five-year periods had fewer counties. As a result, our mixed model used different numbers of counties across the five-year intervals. The numbers of counties in any interval ranged from a low of 2,982 to a high of 3,006.
4. Censuses of agriculture used three definitions of farms during the period covered in this chapter:
   1) 1949, 1954. Places with three or more acres were counted as farms if the value of farm products (excluding products from home gardens) was at least $150. These farm products could have been used for home consumption or could have been sold; the determining factor was a set value of at least $150. Also counted were those considered farms if the *value of sales* was at least $150, and those places that normally would meet these minimum production thresholds but that did not either because of unusual circumstances (such as crop failure) or because the farm was in its first year of operation.
   2) 1959, 1964, 1969. New minimum thresholds were established. Places with less than 10 acres were counted only if the estimated *sales* of agricultural products was at least $250. If the place had more that 10 acres, *sales* of agricultural products had to be at least $50 for the farm to be counted. Here also, places that would normally meet these criteria but did not, due to unusual circumstances or first year of operation, were still counted.
   3) 1974 to 1997. The acreage requirement was discontinued, and any place that actually had or normally would have had $1,000 in agricultural product sales during the census year was counted as a farm.

5. Our dependent variable showed an overall normal distribution, exhibiting a slight bimodal distribution and a slight right skew. Our model is specified in the usual way: $Y = X\beta + \varepsilon$, where Y is a column vector of responses, X is a data matrix and $\varepsilon \sim N(0, \sigma^2)$. The X data matrix includes an intercept, change in population, change in the number of farms, change in the number of farms squared, number of farms 1949/1000, land in farms 1949/100,000 acres, population in 1949/100,000, five dummy variables representing the six metropolitan county designations, and nine dummy variables representing the 10 Census divisions. Residuals from the full model were normally distributed with a slight right tail. An investigation of these residuals suggests that, while the model produced a good fit overall, the model was less adequate for the limited number of counties with significant *gains* in farmland during this 50 year period. All relationships between the predictor variables and farmland change were linear except for a somewhat nonlinear relationship between the change in the number of farms and change in farmland. Variance inflation factors were all below 5, indicating low multicollinearity, and an evaluation of the Cook's distances suggested that there were no overly influential counties in the fit.
6. As mentioned above, we used deviation (sum-to-zero) contrasts for the categorical variables where each coefficient compares the level of the factor to the average of the all levels. As with all contrasts, the last level is considered redundant and is omitted. However, since the sum of the coefficients is constrained to sum to zero, the final level can easily be computed by summing all other levels and multiplying by -1.
7. In general, a mixed effects model is specified by:

$$Y_i = X_i\beta + Z_i b_i + \varepsilon_i$$
$$b_i \sim N(0, \sigma_b^2),\ \varepsilon_i \sim N(0, \sigma^2)$$

   where the Y_i are the response vectors for the ith county, $X_i\beta$ represent the fixed effects for county i and the $Z_i b_i$ represent the random effects for county i. The σ_b^2 represents the between-county variability while the σ^2 represents the within-county variability.
8. We chose to fit the mixed effects model using restricted maximum likelihood. Our data has a small number of missing values (slightly unbalanced), however, the *lme* function in S-PLUS statistical software produces accurate restricted maximum likelihood estimates under these conditions (Pinheiro & Bates, 2000). A plot of the standardized residuals against the fits showed no departures from our assumption of constant variance. Normal plots and histograms of the residuals and random effects justify the Gaussian assumption but did show significantly heavier tails than expected under normality. Given that these tails are symmetric around zero, however, estimates of the fixed effects would not be expected to be affected. The within-group standard error ($\hat{\sigma}$) would likely be inflated under heavy tailed conditions but would result in more *conservative* fixed effects tests (Pinheiro & Bates, 2000). An ANOVA comparing the model described above to a model with a specified covariance structure confirmed that accounting for temporal autocorrelation using an autoregressive covariance function did not improve the model.

REFERENCES

Adelaja, A.O., & Schilling, B.J. (1999). Innovative approaches to farmland preservation. In M.B. Lapping and O.J. Furuseth (Eds.), *Contested countryside: The rural urban fringe in North America* (pp. 113–136). Aldershot, UK: Ashgate.

Altobelli, J., & Pfeffer, M.J. (2000). *Metropolitan agriculture: A chart book of trends and statistics for the United States, the northeast region, and New York state*. Ithaca: Cornell University Agricultural Experiment Station.

Batie, S.S. (2003). The multi-function attributes of northeastern agriculture: A research agenda. *Agricultural and Resource Economics, 32*(1), 1–8.

Brown, D.L., Brewer, M., Boxley, L., & Beale, C. (1982). Assessing prospects for the adequacy of agricultural land. *International Regional Science Review, 7*(3), 273–284.

Castle, E.N. (2003). Land, economic change, and agricultural economics. *Agricultural and Resource Economics, 32*(1), 18–32.

Cressie, N.A.C. (1993). *Statistics for spatial data*. New York: Wiley.

Daniels, T. (1999). *When city and country collide: Managing growth in the metropolitan fringe*. Washington, DC: Island Press.

Daniels, T., & Bowers, D. (1997). *Holding our ground: Protecting America's farms and farmland*. Washington, DC: Island Press.

Diaz, D., & Green, G.P. (2001). Growth management and agriculture: An examination of local efforts to manage growth and preserve farmland in Wisconsin cities, villages, and towns. *Rural Sociology, 66*(3), 317–341.

Fuguitt, G.V., Brown, D.L., & Beale, C.L. (1989). *Rural and small town America*. Beverly Hills, CA: Sage.

Garreau, J. (1988). *Edge city*. New York: Anchor Books.

Heimlich, R.E., & Anderson, W.D. (2001). *Development at the urban fringe and beyond: Impacts on agriculture and rural land* (Agricultural Economic Report No. 803). Washington, DC: U.S. Department of Agriculture, Economic Research Service.

Hirschl, T., & Bills, N. (1994). Urban influences on farmland use in New York state. *Population Research and Policy Review, 13*(2), 179–194.

Kaluzny, S.P., & Vega, S.C. (1998). *S+ spatial stats: User's manual for Windows and UNIX*. New York: Springer.

Keating, N.C. (1996). Legacy, aging and succession in farm families. *Generations, 20*(3), 61–64.

Laird, N.M., & Ware, J.H. (1982). Random-effects models for longitudinal data. *Biometrics, 38*, 963–974.

Lapping, M.B., & Pfeffer, M.J. (1997). City and country: Forging new connections through agriculture. In W. Lockeretz (Ed.), *Visions of American agriculture* (pp. 91–104). Ames, IA: Iowa State University Press.

Logan, J.R., & Molotch, H.L. (1987). *Urban fortunes: The political economy of place*. Berkeley: University of California Press.

Lynch, L., & Carpenter, J. (2003). Is there evidence of a critical mass in the mid-Atlantic agriculture sector between 1949 and 1997? *Agricultural and Resource Economics, 32*(1), 129–144.

Molotch, H.L. (1976). The city as a growth machine. *American Journal of Sociology, 75*, 226–238.

Morgan, D. (1980). *Merchants of grain*. New York: Penguin Books.

Odland, J. (1988). *Spatial autocorrelation*. Newbury Park, CA: Sage.

Pfeffer, M.J., & Lapping, M.B. (1994). Farmland preservation, development rights and the theory of the growth machine: The views of planners. *Journal of Rural Studies, 10*(3), 233–248.

Pendall, R. (2003). *Sprawl without growth: The upstate paradox*. Washington, DC: Brookings Institution.

Pennington, M. (1999). Free market environmentalism and the limits of land use planning. *Journal of Environmental Policy and Planning, 1*, 43–59.

Pfeffer, M.J., & Lapping, M.B. (1995). Prospects for a sustainable agriculture in the Northeast's rural/urban fringe. *Research in Rural Sociology and Development, 6*, 68–93.

Pfeffer, M.J., Stycos, J.M., Glenna, L., & Altobelli, J. (2001). Forging new connections between agriculture and the city. In O. T. Solbrig, R. Paarlberg, & F. di Castri (Eds.), *Globalization and the rural environment* (pp. 419–446). Cambridge: Harvard University Press.

Pinheiro, J.C., & Bates, D.M. (2000). *Mixed effects models in S and S-PLUS.* New York: Springer.

Schnidman, F., Smiley, M., & Woodbury, E.G. (1990). *Retention of farmland for agriculture: Policy, practice and potential in New England.* Cambridge: Lincoln Institute of Land.

Stover, R.G., & Helling, M.K. (1998). Goals and principles of the intergenerational transfer of the family farm. *Free Inquiry in Creative Sociology, 26*(2), 201–212.

U.S. Department of Agriculture, National Resources and Conservation Service (NRCS), & Iowa State University Statistical Laboratory. (2000). *Summary report, 1997 national resources inventory* (revised, December 2000). Washington, DC: Author.

Vesterby, M., & Krupa, K.S. (2001). *Major uses of land in the United States* (Statistical Bulletin No. 973). Washington, DC: U.S. Department of Agriculture, Economic Research Service, Resource Economic Division.

Walters, C., Jr. (1968). *Holding action.* New York: Halcyon House.

CHAPTER 6

CHANGING FORTUNES

Poverty in Rural America[1]

LEIF JENSEN, STEPHAN J. GOETZ, AND HEMA SWAMINATHAN

INTRODUCTION

Go to the website for the Tunica County, Mississippi Chamber of Commerce, and the clues are pretty obvious. The clickable icons show that shopping can be done at the "Casino Factory Shoppes," the logo for which features three bright red cherries in a row, and a click on a pair of dice (showing 6 and 5) will take you to opportunities for "gaming and tourism." It turns out that of all nonmetropolitan (nonmetro) counties in the contiguous United States, Tunica County had the fastest declining poverty rate over the 1990s. A local official, in response to our question about why that might be, responded:

> In 1991 the state authorized gaming, and Tunica is a gaming community. We're just south of Memphis and bring in people from a three-state area. This was an extremely poor county prior to gaming, and we were very far behind in terms of infrastructure. But we've had wise leadership, and gaming revenue has been reinvested into the county's roads and such. We created 14,000 jobs and have nine casinos. We used to be a drain on the state's economy, but we now provide 5 percent of the state budget.

While we did not verify these numbers, one thing is clear: the 1990s were good to Tunica County, Mississippi. In fact, the 1990s were good to a lot of people. The decade began amidst recession, but this was followed by an economic expansion unprecedented in its length and strength. Between 1989 and 2000 the poverty rate for all Americans declined from 13.1 percent to 12.4 percent, the rate for children declined from 18.3 percent to 16.6 percent (Bishaw & Iceland, 2003), and *mean* family income rose about 20 percent from $49,902 to $59,664 in constant (2002) dollars (DeNavas-Walt et al., 2003). As good as this sounds, times of prosperity inevitably lead to questions about whether everyone is sharing in the wealth, or whether some people are being left behind. While poverty rates were down and income up, income inequality was on the rise over this period. That the

W.A. Kandel & D.L. Brown (eds.), Population Change and Rural Society, 131–152.

rise in *median* family income was only about 10 percent ($39,949 to $43,848) is one indication that the well-to-do were benefiting disproportionately. Also, between 1990 and 1998, the share of aggregate income going to the households in the bottom 20 percent of the income distribution (the lowest quintile) declined from 3.9 to 3.6 percent, or a decline of 7.7 percent in relative terms (Jones & Weinberg, 2000). The share enjoyed by the second quintile dropped from 9.6 to 9.0 percent (−6.3 percent). By contrast, the top quintile enjoyed a 5.6 percent relative increase (46.6 percent to 49.2 percent), and the top 5 percent of all households enjoyed a 15.1 percent relative increase (18.6 percent to 21.4 percent).[2] Apparently the rising tide was not lifting all boats.

Our concern in this chapter is less with individual people and families per se than with the places in which they reside. Specifically, we explore the changing economic fortunes of U.S. nonmetro counties and the determinants of those changes. We question whether the rising tide lifted all counties, and if not, why did some prosper but others falter? In fact, there *were* winners and losers over the decade. As noted, Tunica County had the fastest declining poverty rate of all nonmetro counties, and it had seized on gaming as an emerging opportunity. In order, Tunica County was followed by Guadalupe County, NM; East Caroll Parish, LA; Issaquena County, MS; and Billings County, ND. For some of these counties, examination of websites and casual telephone interviews with local officials also revealed potential clues to why poverty rates declined substantially.

The website for Guadalupe County in northeast New Mexico shows a picture of the Pecos River, which "flows gently through the hills, mesas and rolling grassland" of the county, "creating a fertile oasis." This suggests natural amenities as a potential explanation. However, a local official was surprised to learn of the economic improvement in Guadalupe County, saying, "I'm baffled really. Businesses are family owned. Kids leave and don't come back until they retire, if at all. A lot of kids do leave, maybe they take the poverty with them?" A county official in East Caroll Parish, Louisiana was similarly at a loss for an explanation, though here too its website indicates amenities may be at play, and its location directly across the Mississippi River from a number of new Mississippi gaming counties suggests commuting to new jobs may be a factor. On the other hand, since East Carroll Parish is among the poorest in Louisiana, perhaps they had nowhere to go but up. Finally, a county worker in Issaquena County, Mississippi commented, "In the mid-1990s a correctional facility went in which gave several folks something to do. And we do have some folks driving to Vicksburg to work in gaming. We have some tourism too, mostly around commercial hunting."

As alluded to above, however, some counties lost ground during the 1990s. The nonmetro counties with the fastest increasing poverty rates were, in order, Buffalo County, SD; Clark County, ID; Echols County, GA; King County, TX; and Clark County, KS. Perhaps not surprisingly, it was harder to find websites describing *these* counties. Those we did find tended to be oriented to people seeking genealogical or historical information, perhaps suggestive of the former but not ongoing vitality of these places. When asked to speculate why poverty might have increased so rapidly in Buffalo County, SD, one local expert said, "farmers have retired and moved or have died, and several have sold the land to those who don't live here. Also about two-thirds of the county is reservation." An antique map on their website confirms the presence of a large American Indian reservation there. A local from Echols County, Georgia, along the Florida border, felt that "the influx of Hispanics" might be a factor. From Clark County, Kansas, the speculation was, "we have a high elderly population, with a lot of folks in their 80s and 90s. There was a lot of money in ranching and banking. But the well-to-do folks have left, some ranches have gone out and banks are foreclosing. Plus we've had a lot of low-income folks moving in, attracted by our lower taxes and cost of living, low crime, decent schools, and such. And some of the wealthy ranchers and a doctor left money to support local kids with college."

This cursory exercise suggests a variety of reasons why the fortunes of counties rise and fall. These include race/ethnic composition (e.g., Indian country), other demographic factors (e.g., aging in place and migration), industrial structure (e.g., agricultural dependence), proximity to jobs in neighboring counties (e.g., gaming), or reasons that are rather idiosyncratic (e.g., a benevolent physician). As seen, even local experts may not be aware of the considerable changes in poverty rates going on around them. They would likely be even less aware of more macro-level forces that have captured the attention of scholars examining these issues. Such forces include continued industrial restructuring, globalization, and NAFTA and other free trade initiatives that have been implicated in the deterioration of the job prospects of those who are less skilled and less well educated. That industries are not distributed randomly across space raises questions about the spatial distribution of economic improvement and decline. Our overall purpose is to describe the spatial distribution of poverty and change in poverty in the nonmetro United States, and to evaluate empirically an array of explanations for why some counties prospered over the 1990s, while others declined. In so doing, we hope to describe the contours of emerging opportunities and economic erosion in rural America.

REVIEW OF PREVIOUS RESEARCH

If rural poverty has not figured prominently on the national agenda in the last four decades, the same is true of the attention given to rural poverty by academics (Albrecht et al., 2000; Cotter, 2002; Tickamyer & Duncan, 1990). Rural demography (Brown & Kandel, this volume) and sociology are the fields of study that have contributed the most to our understanding of issues surrounding rural poverty. Economists have focused on national-level time series analyses of aggregate poverty over the business cycle (e.g., Schoeni & Blank, 2000) on measurement issues regarding the use of consumption- versus income-based measures of poverty (e.g., Cox & Alm, 1999; Jorgenson, 1998; Slesnick, 1993), or on cross-country comparisons (Smeeding et al., 2001). With few exceptions (e.g., Levernier et al., 2000), economists have not concerned themselves with spatial variation in poverty at the sub-state level. Other social scientists have primarily studied urban poverty, investigating, for example, whether poverty is becoming more concentrated at the neighborhood level (e.g., Kingsley & Pettit, 2003, using 2000 Census data; Madden, 2003, using pre-2000 Census data). An emerging literature in the political sciences and planning fields presents compelling evidence of how urban sprawl is perpetuating poverty in the urban African-American community (Jargowsky, 2002). This, in turn, raises the possibility that different forces cause poverty in urban as opposed to rural areas.

A number of authors have recently examined issues of rural poverty, including the roles of changes in natural-resource-based industries and de-industrialization in causing poverty, as well as reasons why rural industrialization policies have generally failed to reduce rural poverty rates (Tickamyer & Duncan, 1990). More specifically, the lessons from the decades studied (pre-1990s) are that targeted economic policies alone were not necessarily sufficient to lift all individuals out of poverty (Tickamyer & Duncan, 1990, p. 77):

> Large-scale economic growth, if it is not well distributed or if it is imbedded in a repressive political economy, may do little to change patterns of persistent poverty of rural areas, as has been found in the Deep South and Appalachia.

This is especially noteworthy in light of the fact that some authors have concluded, for urban areas, that economic growth tends unequivocally to benefit the "residents of the ghettos" (Jargowsky, 1997; Kingsley & Pettit, 2003). The question of whether poverty is caused by individual- or community-level (structural) forces is important in poverty studies and revisited below. Tickamyer and Duncan (1990, p. 81) conclude their review by pointing to the need for more research on changes in poverty over time, along with research on the role of local markets for labor and the structure of local political systems.

Duncan (1999) has documented through case study research in three rural communities that so-called "political influence" and social or civic capacity are essential to the perpetuation or amelioration of poverty over time. A key empirical challenge in confirming or refuting her hypothesis in large-scale econometric studies that control for other determinants of poverty has been measuring these subtle political influences consistently and systematically across different geographic units such as counties. Cotter (2002) similarly suggests that it is important to consider civic infrastructure and the local political (or capitalist) economy to understand fully the determinants of local poverty. Recent and ongoing work by Rupasingha and Goetz (2003) shows some promise in this regard.

Also, more recently, Albrecht and colleagues (2000) point out that poverty rates are not only higher in nonmetro than in metro areas but also more severe, a finding that is contested, at least for 2000 data, by Jolliffe (2003), who uses alternative measures of poverty, such as a gap index. Albrecht and colleagues (2000) maintain that structural change affecting all sectors of the economy is more important than individual-level characteristics in explaining both rural and urban poverty. Like Tickamyer and Duncan, Albrecht and others note that studies of changes in poverty over time are needed, and that the focus on a single time period is "an obvious weakness" of their study.

Levernier and colleagues (2000) also found that changes in economic structure contributed to higher short-term poverty levels, but that the effect dissipated after five years, although not necessarily in communities with large minority shares, or large population shares with less formal education. Their study also raises questions of potential endogeneity bias, because the poverty rate and regressors are measured contemporaneously. An alternative approach is either to lag regressors by a decade (as in Rupasingha & Goetz, 2003) or to regress changes in poverty over the 1990s on regressors measured in 1990 (as in Goetz & Rupasingha, 2003).

This brief and necessarily selective synopsis highlights a number of gaps in the literature, which we address in this chapter. First, poverty data are now available from the 2000 US Census. While updating studies based on poverty data from earlier decades is important in its own right, the implementation during the 1990s of two major federal policies with spatial implications—the North American Free Trade Agreement of 1994 (NAFTA) and the Personal Responsibility and Work Opportunity Restoration Act of 1996 (PRWORA)—heightens the urgency of studying changes in poverty rates over the decade. In particular, it is essential for an informed public policy debate to know how these national policies have impacted individual rural counties. Second, an important gap identified in the literature is that prior studies have focused more on poverty levels than changes in poverty rates over time. By focusing on the latter, we also avoid the problem of spatial variation in living costs. A third issue is that while the spatial clustering of poverty is well recognized (e.g., Nord, 1997), researchers have, with few exceptions, ignored the statistical implications of such clustering. Fourth, for the first time it is possible to include measures of political influence or the lack of democratic governance as well as civic capacity or engagement in large-scale econometric studies of county-level poverty. Finally, we simultaneously explore the effects of population characteristics and structural factors within counties, which allows us to contribute to the debate surrounding the relative importance of the independent effects of each type of factor.

RESEARCH METHODS AND FINDINGS

In this analysis we address the following very fundamental research questions. How is poverty distributed across space in nonmetro America? How is the *change* in poverty distributed across space? And what factors account for changes in poverty rates over time among nonmetro U.S. counties? To answer our research questions, we follow the method briefly summarized here. The units of analysis for this study are nonmetropolitan U.S. counties, which we describe principally through data from the summary files of the 1980, 1990, and 2000 U.S. Censuses of Population and Housing. As noted below, additional county-level indicators are retrieved verbatim or constructed from alternative sources and then merged with our census data for counties. We use both descriptive and multivariate techniques to analyze these data. Specifically, we use maps to provide geographic visualization of the spatial distribution of poverty and of changes in poverty rates. We also estimate a series of multivariate regression models to document causes of changing poverty rates over time.

Our principal measure of county economic well being is the family poverty rate, as defined by the U.S. government. In brief, a family consists of two or more people living in the same household who are related by blood, marriage or adoption. A family is defined as poor if their annual pre-tax cash income from employment and all other sources is below the official poverty threshold.[3] Individuals living alone, or who are otherwise unrelated to others living in their household, have their poverty status defined separately. Since the early 1960s, poverty thresholds have been set at three times the cost of a minimally sufficient diet and are adjusted to account for family size and composition, as well as changes in the cost of living over time (i.e., inflation). In recent years the official definition of poverty has come under fire because it fails to account for cost-of-living differences across space, in-kind (non-cash) income, changes in consumption patterns that have made food a smaller proportion of the cost of all necessities, and other reasons (Citro & Michael, 1995). While superior alternatives have been proposed, they have not found their way into official statistics. In any event, two aspects of our analysis obviate some of the more notable problems with the official definition. First, most of the concern about cost-of-living differences has focused on variation between metro and nonmetro areas, or between central cities and elsewhere. Our analysis, however, is restricted to nonmetro counties only. Second, while some quibble with the official definition's ability to capture validly the true prevalence of poverty, there is less reason to question the substantive meaning of *changes* in county poverty rates as an indicator of economic improvement or decline, since the definition is consistent over time.

The Geographic Distribution of Nonmetro Poverty

Map 6.1 shows the spatial distribution of poverty across counties in the contiguous United States as of 1989. Metropolitan counties are in white, while nonmetro counties are placed in two categories and are shaded light and dark, denoting increasing poverty rates. A number of well-known geographic clusters of economic deprivation are clearly evident. A classic image of rural poverty is that which is found among the white folks in the hills and hollows of the Appalachian

Map 6.1. Nonmetro Family Poverty Rates, 1989

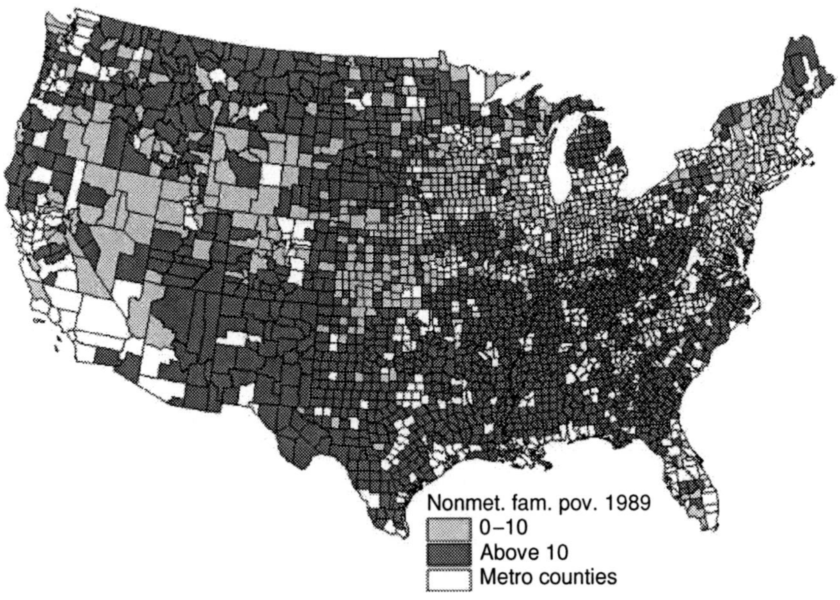

Mountains. As late as 1989, this image was apparently consistent with the statistical reality portrayed in this map. As noted by Beale (2004, p. 26), other pockets of high rural poverty where whites predominate are found in the Ozark Plateau and the Ouachita Mountains west of the Mississippi River. These pockets are in evidence in Map 6.1. Another band of high nonmetro poverty arcs from the rural Carolinas southwest into the Deep South and reflects very high poverty rates among the African Americans concentrated in this so-called Black Belt. Clearly visible nearby and to the west is the concentrated poverty of the Mississippi Delta, also dominated numerically by rural African Americans. Another swath of rural poverty is seen stretching from the lower Rio Grande Valley in Texas, northwest into New Mexico and the four corners region. This band of rural poverty likewise reflects the double jeopardy of rural minorities, as it captures the higher poverty rates among rural Latinos and, more so in the four corners, of American Indians (see Beale, 2004). Scattered elsewhere in the Northern Plains and west into the high country of Montana and the northern Rockies, are additional places of high rural poverty, likely reflecting the presence of Indian reservations as well as natural resource dependence.

Essentially the same portrait emerges in Map 6.2, which shows the distribution of nonmetro poverty a decade later, in 1999. The high poverty of Appalachia, the Black Belt and Mississippi Delta, the Rio Grande Valley, and of Indian country

Map 6.2. Nonmetro Family Poverty Rates, 1999

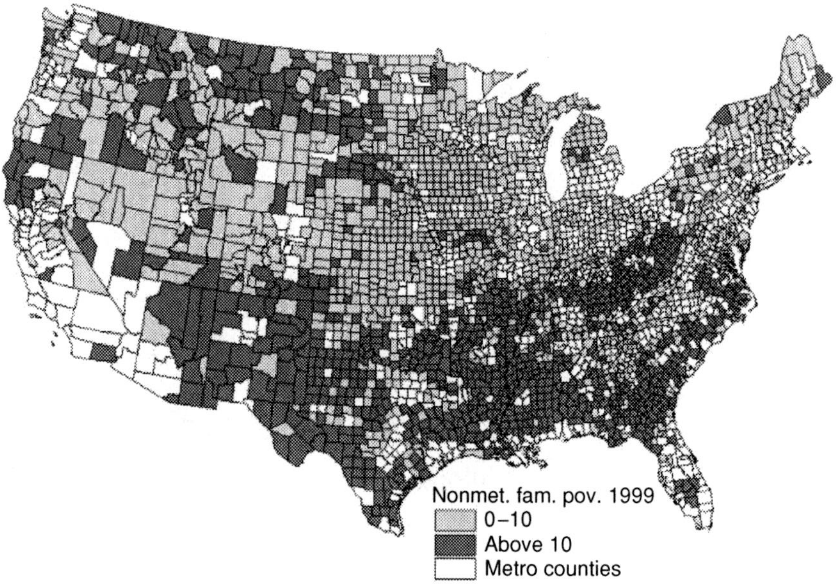

did not change despite the prosperity of the 1990s. Instructive, however, is a visual comparison of 1989 and 1999 (Maps 6.1 & 6.2), a period of rapid economic expansion. Because these maps use the same cut points, the overall decline in poverty over the 1990s, both nationwide and in rural areas, is evidenced by the declining number of counties with rates of 13 percent or higher. As noted by Goetz and Rupasingha (2003), the greatest improvement in nonmetro areas seemed to take place in counties at the fringes of concentrated pockets of rural poverty. For example, like a shrinking tumor, the blight of Appalachian poverty gets smaller, yet remains readily apparent among the core counties. The same geographic pattern is seen in the Black Belt and the Delta. This pattern reflects the fact that poverty rates are highest in the cores of these rural poverty clusters, that conditions are somewhat better at the fringes, and therefore that the booming economy of the 1990s was able to tip more of the latter counties under the arbitrary 10 percent cutoff.

The poverty *rate* of a place is obviously important since it reflects the percent of a population that may be in need and have associated social and economic problems, while its inverse reflects the percentage of the population that might be called upon to help. Crudely, a high poverty rate indicates high need and low capacity to meet that need. However, often forgotten in portrayals of poverty is the geographic distribution of the absolute number of poor individuals. On this question a somewhat different picture emerges. Map 6.3 shows nonmetro counties categorized by the sheer size of their poverty populations in 1999. While some

Map 6.3. Nonmetro Population Below Poverty Level, 1999

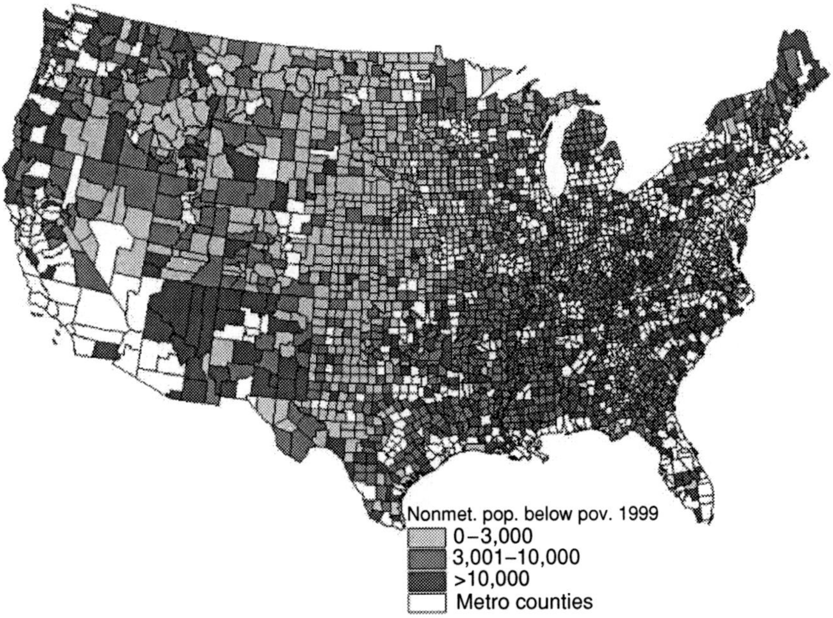

of the same clusters of rural poverty can be discerned (e.g., Appalachia), they are much less distinct. Rather, in terms of numbers the nonmetro poverty population is spread out more in relation to the nonmetro population generally. Interestingly, in this case the nonmetro counties straddling the New York—Pennsylvania border stand out, as do several counties in northern New England. If a policy goal is to target resources where the rural poor live, this map suggests somewhat different priorities than those that obtain when high poverty rates are the issue.

Mapping Poverty Rate Change

Just as the benefits of economic growth or the penalties of decline are unevenly felt across demographic groups, so too is growth and decline distributed unevenly across geographic space. Maps 6.4 and 6.5 show counties with the greatest improvement and greatest deterioration in measured poverty rates over the decade of the 1980s and 1990s, respectively. With counties sorted in terms of relative change (arithmetically: (poverty rate 1989–poverty rate 1979) / poverty rate 1979), Map 6.4 shows the top and bottom deciles of this distribution. Those counties in the bottom decile are those 10 percent of counties with the greatest improvement (i.e., decline) in their poverty rates, while those in the top decile are those 10 percent of counties with the greatest deterioration (i.e., increase). The map reveals that over

Map 6.4. Change in Family Poverty Rates, 1979–1989

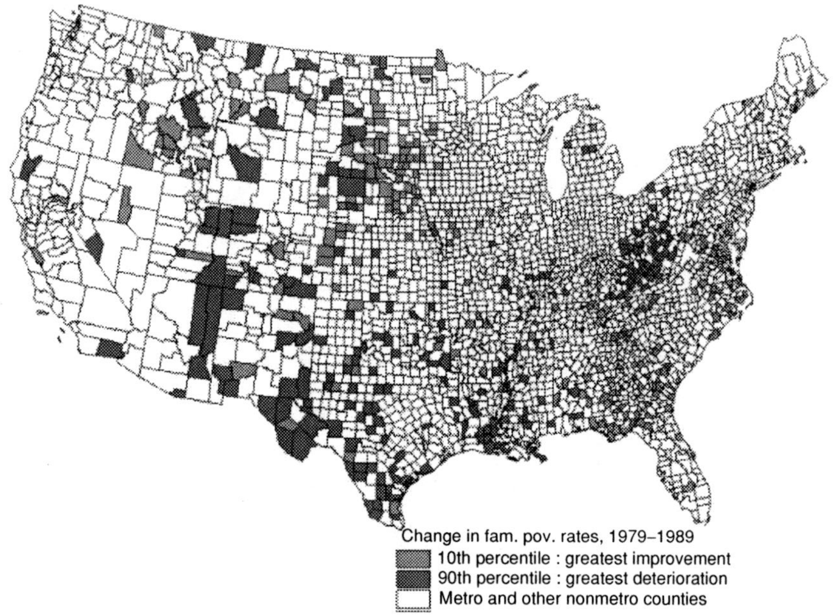

Map 6.5. Change in Family Poverty Rates, 1989–1999

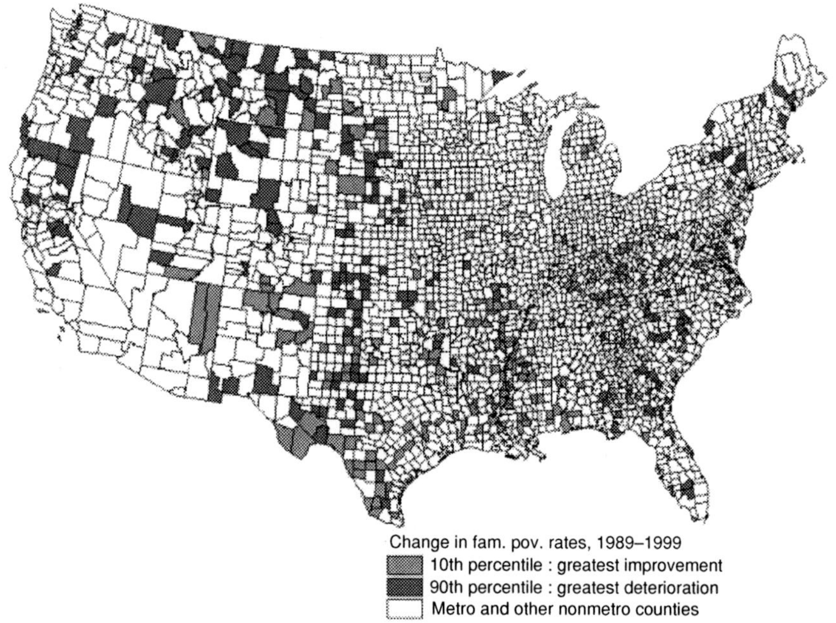

the 1980s, improvement and deterioration were rather clustered. Improvements were seen through the Black Belt, in the northern Plains, and scattered through the mountain West. Deterioration was clearly seen in Appalachia, the Mississippi Delta, along the Rio Grande Valley, and in the four corners region. The geographic pattern of changing fortunes over the economically strong 1990s (Map 6.5) is somewhat more scattered (with areas of improvement intermingling more with areas of deterioration), but to some degree the opposite pattern obtains. That is, over the 1990s the counties with the greatest improvement were clustered in Appalachia, in the Rio Grande Valley, and in the Delta, which, again, were the most in decline during the 1980s. This pattern is consistent with our earlier observation drawn from the comparison between Maps 6.1 and 6.2, that the improvement over the 1990s seemed to be in areas peripheral to core poverty areas. Over the 1990s, several nonmetro counties in New England, in the Black Belt, in the northern Rockies, and in resource-dependent northern California showed the greatest deterioration or increases in poverty rates. With this spatial descriptive portrait as a backdrop, we next turn our attention to a multivariate analysis of changing fortunes.

The Etiology of Changing Poverty

What county-level characteristics are associated with changing poverty rates over time? In this section we present results of a series of regression models. The dependent variable is the percentage point change in county poverty rate, calculated as the 1999 rate minus the 1989 rate. As such, positive values reflect *increasing* poverty, while negative values denote *decreasing* poverty. That the mean for this variable is negative (−2.76) reflects the fact that on average, county-level poverty rates declined by 2.76 percentage points. Also, the coding of this change variable means that positive coefficient estimates reflect detrimental impacts of a given variable (higher values of this variable are associated with *increasing* poverty), while negative coefficient estimates indicate beneficial effects of a variable. To avoid confusion, we use the terms detrimental (+) and beneficial (−) effects.

Table 6.1 shows operational definitions, central tendencies, and expected effects (signs) of the variables we use in our models of changing poverty rates. Variables are measured in 1990 (or before) to reduce problems of endogeneity. There are four groups of predictors. The first group includes the *economic and structural conditions* of counties. Family poverty rate in 1989 is expected to have a negative effect due to "regression toward the mean," a statistical force that will tend to see observations with extreme values at time 1 move toward the middle of the distribution at time 2.[4] Employment growth, employment rates (i.e., the inverse of the unemployment rate), and female labor supply all are expected to have beneficial (−) effects, the latter all the more so in view of the 1996 welfare reform, which placed unprecedented emphasis on work as a route out of poverty. A measure of industrial distribution change in the period immediately preceding the 1990s

Table 6.1. Variable Definitions, Descriptive Statistics, and Expected Effects on Change in Poverty

Description	Mean	Std.Dev.	Expected
Change in family poverty rate between 1989 and 1999[a]	−2.76	2.98	
Economic and Structural Conditions			
Family poverty rate 1989[a]	14.51	7.12	−
Growth of private employment between 1988–1990[c]	0.03	0.06	−
Employment rate: Civilian employed labor force/total civilian labor force 1990[c]	93.09	3.33	−
Female labor force participation in 1990 (total female labor force/females 16 years and over*100)[d]	50.11	6.53	−
Industrial change 1988–1990: Sum of absolute changes in the share of one-digit industry employment between 1988 and 1990, divided by two[c]	0.84	6.14	+
Pct. Agriculture, forestry, and fisheries employment 1990[d]	13.04	9.92	+
Pct. Manufacturing, mining, construction employment 1990[d]	27.38	10.98	?
Pct. Transportation and public utilities employment 1990[d]	6.32	2.06	?
Pct. Wholesale and retail trade employment 1990[d]	18.94	3.56	?
Pct. Finance, insurance, and real estate employment 1990[d]	3.79	1.25	?
Pct. Services employment 1990[d]	27.95	5.55	+
Big-box retailers per 10,000 people 1990[f]	0.78	0.90	?
Jobs lost due to NAFTA, 1994–1999, as a percent of total workforce in 1999[h]	0.31	1.20	+
Population Composition Variables			
Pct. 0–17 years old persons 1990[d]	27.12	3.52	+
Pct. 18–24 years old persons 1990[d]	8.82	3.30	+
Pct. 65 years and over persons 1990[d]	16.00	4.12	+
Pct. African American 1990[d]	8.07	15.08	+
Pct. Other minorities 1990[d]	3.85	8.19	+
Pct. Female-headed households 1990[d]	12.69	5.40	+
Pct. High school plus some college 1990[d]	55.88	8.01	−

(cont.)

Table 6.1. (Continued)

Description	Mean	Std.Dev.	Expected
Pct. 4-year college or more 1990[d]	11.74	4.83	–
Pct. Non-movers: Persons in 1990 who lived in the same county in 1985–1990[e]	0.76	0.05	+
Pct. Foreign-born population in a county 1990[d]	1.63	2.66	+
Pct. Self-employed: Nonfarm proprietors in a county in 1990[c]	17.60	5.25	?
Residential Status			
Urban population of 20,000 or more, adjacent to a metro area[b]	0.06	0.23	Ref.
Urban population of 20,000 or more, not adjacent to a metro area[b]	0.05	0.21	+
Urban population of 2,500 to 19,999, adjacent to a metro area[b]	0.27	0.44	?
Urban population of 2,500 to 19,999, not adjacent to a metro area[b]	0.29	0.45	+
Completely rural or less than 2,500 urban population, adjacent to a metro area[b]	0.11	0.31	?
Completely rural or less than 2,500 urban population, not adjacent to a metro area[b]	0.23	0.42	+
Commuter county (≥ 40% of workers commute out of county)	0.17	0.37	–
Political Influence Variables			
Income Inequality: Family mean income/Family median income 1989[d]	1.46	0.11	+
Per capita Direct federal expenditures or obligations – grant awards 1990[d]	487.20	474.09	?
One-party dominance index (see text), 1988[d]	8.41	6.15	+
Social Capital index (see text) 1990[a,f,g]	0.12	1.41	–
Local Consumption Spending: Ratio of current (consumption) local government expenditure to total expenditure in a county in 1987[a]	89.35	6.73	+

Data Sources: [a]U.S. Census Bureau. [b]Based on Beale codes. [c]Regional Economics Information System (BEA). [d]USA Counties. [e]County-to-County Migration Files. [f]County Business Patterns. [g]National Center for Charitable Statistics. [h]NAFTA-TAA database.

is expected to have a detrimental effect due to adjustment costs facing workers shifting between industries (Rupasingha & Goetz, 2002). Employment shares in six key industries are included to capture the local industrial structure. Apart from expected disadvantages for places dominated by agriculture and services, we have no *a priori* expectations for the signs of these coefficients. Much popular press has attended the so-called "Wal-Marting" of America. There is no question that large retail establishments have affected rural communities, though the direction of impact is unclear as they do offer employment opportunities (albeit at low wages) but also tend to negatively impact "downtown." We measure the prevalence of "big-box" retailers as the number of retail establishments per 10,000 population employing 100 or more people. Finally, job loss due to NAFTA during the period 1994–1999 is expected to have a detrimental (+) effect.

We also include *population composition variables* that aggregate demographic, human capital, and other characteristics customarily included in individual-level analyses of poverty. These variables include percentages in three age categories to capture age dependency within counties. Counties with highly youthful or elderly populations are expected to be at a disadvantage. The prevalence of African Americans, other racial/ethnic minorities, and the foreign-born are expected to put upward pressure on poverty rates. Educational attainment of the local population should have beneficial effects. The percentage of non-migrant residents ("stayers") likely reflects economic stagnation and should have a positive (detrimental) association with poverty rate change. Finally, given the importance of entrepreneurship, the prevalence of self-employment is included, though its expected effect is unclear.

Residential status includes dummy variables for the rural-urban continuum ("Beale") codes for nonmetro counties, which are sensitive to both the size of the urban population within nonmetro counties and their adjacency to metro areas. In general, we expect smaller and more distal counties to be at a disadvantage. We also include a dichotomous identifier for commuter counties that send 40 percent or more of their workers to other counties for employment, and expect this to have a beneficial (−) effect.

Finally, *political influence variables* seek to capture important socio-political characteristics of counties. Income inequality is expected to have a detrimental effect (+). A measure of Federal grants obtained could either reflect initiative or need, so its relationship with change in poverty is unclear. Political dominance by one party or another, measured as the divergence between a county's vote and the national average, is expected to have a detrimental effect (Levitt & Poterba, 1999). An index measuring the level of local social capital (indicated by the percentage voting in national elections, number of social-capital-generating institutions per capita, charitable organizations per capita, and participation in the decennial census) is expected to have a beneficial (−) effect. Finally, the share of local spending that is on short-term consumption (e.g., snow removal) versus more long-term investments is expected to have a detrimental impact.

Our modeling strategy is to enter and remove the above sets of variables in blocks before entering them all in a full model. We also estimate the full model with corrections for spatial autocorrelation (not shown). Specifically, the full model was re-estimated as a spatial autoregressive error model (SEM) (see Rupasingha & Goetz, 2003). Results confirmed that the errors were spatially correlated. With only one exception, however (described below), the parameter estimates were substantively identical to those estimated via OLS.

Model I in Table 6.2 shows effects of economic and structural conditions. First, the effect of the county family poverty rate in 1989 (in other words, at time 1) is negative, meaning that places with higher initial poverty rates experienced greater poverty rate declines. Because of the regression toward the mean that this likely reflects, family poverty rate in 1989 is included in all subsequent models. Following Levernier and others (2000), all models also include state-level fixed effects (not shown), operationalized as dummy variables for each state in the analysis (less the reference state, Wyoming), to account for missing state-specific variables. We concentrate on those predictors that are significant at a liberal but conventional p value of 0.1 or lower as a way to direct attention to those predictors with potential substantive importance. We recognize that because we have a total sample of nonmetro counties in the lower 48 states, statistical significance is moot. Other significant predictors in Model I include initial employment rate, suggesting that places with higher rates (lower unemployment) in 1990 experienced greater declines in poverty. Change in employment over the 1990s, female labor supply in 1990, and industrial dissimilarity did not have significant effects. Only two industry variables were significant: nonmetro counties with more employment in agriculture were disadvantaged in terms of changing poverty, while those with proportionately more employment in finance, insurance and real estate were advantaged. The prevalence of big-box retailers (e.g., Wal-Mart) proves to be detrimental to nonmetro counties; those with more such outlets in 1990 fared worse in terms of changing poverty rates over the decade. Not surprisingly, but no less alarmingly, job losses due to NAFTA had a detrimental effect on nonmetro poverty.

Model II shows the effects of the socio-demographic and economic composition of the local population. High age dependence (a proportionately large number of children) has a detrimental effect, as does presence of non-black minorities. The prevalence of African Americans in 1990 had no effect on changing poverty rates, but a higher prevalence of female-headed households in 1990 proved detrimental.[5] Having proportionately more adults who have graduated high school is beneficial. Interestingly, however, over and above that, the presence of college graduates is not significant. Having a high proportion of non-migrants (stayers) is detrimental; such places were more likely to have increasing poverty and less likely to have decreasing poverty. As noted, this likely reflects the economic stagnation of places that are losing the native born while not attracting newcomers. That the prevalence of workers who are self-employed is beneficial bodes well for localities

Table 6.2. OLS Regressions of Change in Family Poverty Rates (Nonmetro Counties), 1989–1999, by Select County Characteristics

	I Coefficients	II Coefficients	III Coefficients	IV Coefficients	V Coefficients
Constant	20.574	−5.646	1.575	−0.125	13.164
Economic and Structural Conditions					
Family poverty rate, 1989	−0.359*	−0.454*	−0.274*	−0.306*	−0.619*
Growth in employment, 1988–1990	1.873				1.292
Employment rate, 1990	−0.219*				−0.059+
Female labor force partic., 1990	0.016				−0.118*
Industrial change, 1988–90	−0.002				0.010
Pct. Agr., For., Fish., 1990	0.072*				0.042*
Pct. Mfg., Min., Const., 1990	0.003				−0.030*
Pct. Transpo., Util., 1990	−0.034				−0.059+
Pct. Wholesale/Retail Trade, 1990	0.003				−0.021
Pct. Finance, Insur., Real Est., 1990	−0.190*				−0.096*
Pct. Services, 1990	0.023				0.003
Big-box retailers/10K pop., 1990	0.168+				0.022
Job loss from NAFTA, 1994–99	0.074+				0.061+
Population Composition Variables					
Pct. Aged < 17		0.171*			0.127*
Pct. Aged 18–24		0.007			−0.024
Pct. Aged 65+		0.017			−0.074*
Pct. African American, 1990		0.010			−0.003
Pct. Other Minority, 1990		0.063*			0.055*

Pct. Female-Headed HH, 1990		0.119*			0.273*
Pct. High School Plus, 1990		−0.069*			−0.075*
Pct. 4-Year College +, 1990		0.013			0.012
Pct. Non-movers, 1990		9.804*			5.771*
Pct. Foreign-born, 1990		0.059			0.054
Pct. Self-employed, 1990		−0.032*			−0.017
Residential Status					
Large urban, not adjacent			0.068		0.194
Medium urban, adjacent			−0.446*		−0.098*
Medium urban, not adjacent			−0.104		0.372*
No urban, adjacent			−0.609*		−0.090
No urban, not adjacent			−0.098		0.703*
Commuter county			−0.492*		−0.298*
Political Influence Variables					
Income inequality, 1989				0.155	−0.166
Federal expenditures, 1990				0.000	0.000
One-party dominance, 1988				0.043*	0.023*
Social Capital, 1990				−0.348*	−0.243*
Local consumption spending, 1987				0.013	−0.004
Adjusted R^2	0.435	0.489	0.410	0.418	0.544

* and + denote significance at $p < 0.05$ and $p < 0.1$, respectively.

that promote entrepreneurship as an economic development strategy. Mode III includes dummy variables for five of the six Beale codes for nonmetro counties. That all but one of the coefficients is negative suggests some disadvantage for the reference group (adjacent to metro with a large urban population). Relative to counties in this category, smaller adjacent counties tended to have favorable changes in their poverty rates over the 1990s. Finally, counties with higher proportions of workers who commute to a neighboring county for work were relatively advantaged.

Model IV shows the effects of political influence variables, two of which reach significance. Places characterized by one-party dominance were disadvantaged. This is consistent with other research showing that, other things equal, states with a more even competition between parties enjoy faster income growth (Levitt & Poterba, 1999). Importantly, greater social capital had a beneficial effect on change in poverty rates over the 1990s.

Model V is a full model. Almost all coefficients significant in Models I–IV maintain their significance and direction, though some weaken, while some insignificant coefficients in the block models become significant. Among the economic and structural conditions, the presence of big-box retailers slips to insignificance. In this full model female labor supply becomes negative and significant, suggesting places with greater proportions of women in the labor force in 1990 enjoyed greater improvement (or less deterioration) in their poverty rates over that decade. Also, employment shares in two industries—goods producing and transportation—become significant and negative (beneficial). Among the population composition effects, a higher percentage elderly becomes significant and negative in the full model, suggesting the relative presence of elders in 1990 actually had a beneficial effect on poverty rate change over the 1990s. The prevalence of self-employment becomes insignificant in model V. Finally, residential status effects again suggest that adjacency to metro areas is beneficial, while non-adjacency has a significant and detrimental effect. No changes in political influence effects are found between the block and full models.[6]

To conclude, some of these results were perfunctory and fully expected, such as the detrimental effect of agricultural dependence or youth age dependency on changing poverty rates. Other results, however, bear emphasis. First, the significant effect of the initial poverty rate (in 1989) on subsequent change illustrates that in analyses of this sort regression toward the mean is occurring and needs to be taken into account. The beneficial effects of female labor supply on economic trajectories is noteworthy and underscores the importance of emphasizing economic development strategies aimed at improving employment opportunities for women. While not significant in the full model, the intriguing finding of a detrimental impact of big-box stores in the block model requires careful further study, especially given ongoing trends toward increasing market share for such retail outlets while formerly vibrant downtowns of rural communities languish. Likewise, the detrimental effects of job loss due to NAFTA suggests the need to be attentive to possibly negative effects of ongoing free trade movements. With respect to population composition, that the prevalence of elders is beneficial stands in some contrast to individual-level findings of increasing poverty risks with age and needs to be explored more deeply. And the significant and detrimental impact of the prevalence of female-headed households on subsequent trends in county-level poverty is a concern. Regarding residence, it is noteworthy that counties that are adjacent to metro areas are clearly advantaged over those that are not adjacent, suggesting both that the engine for nonmetro improvement seems to be centered in metro areas and that the most remote counties deserve special political consideration. Finally, it is important to stress that higher levels of social capital in a county have clear beneficial effects on changing poverty rates over time.

CONCLUSIONS AND DISCUSSION

The adage, "when you've seen one rural community, you've seen one rural community," underscores the diversity that characterizes rural America both yesterday and today.[7] Nonmetro counties and communities differ sharply from one another along demographic, economic, ecological, and political lines, and these differences directly shape patterns of growth and decline as well as mitigate impacts of global forces on these patterns. We have anchored our analysis of this complex dynamic around the poverty rates of counties and have focused on changes in those rates as a key indicator of changing fortunes.

By way of conclusion, we underscore the following findings. Rural poverty remains a significant problem worthy of special concern due its prevalence, diversity, and relative obscurity in mainstream political conversations about poverty. Rural poverty also is spatially clustered, with some of the most persistent pockets found in places of high racial and ethnic minority concentration (e.g., the "Black Belt" and "Indian Country"), in Appalachia and in places of significant natural resource dependence. That said, the 1990s were characterized by an extraordinary economic expansion, and average poverty rates for nonmetro counties declined over the decade. However, just as patterns of economic inequality at the individual level suggest that rising tide of the 1990s was not lifting all boats, our analysis shows that there was a mixture of winners and losers. Some counties were benefiting from emerging opportunities, while others were in decline. The balance of our analysis was an attempt to shed light on factors associated with improvement and deterioration.

A review of websites and informal interviews with officials from those counties with the most rapid increases and decreases in poverty rates confirmed the diversity of experiences and explanations for changing fortunes. For example, the introduction of gaming in many Mississippi counties clearly had beneficial effects on prevailing economic opportunities there. Interviewees also speculated variously about race/ethnic composition, age structure, industrial structure, and social climate as possible reasons why poverty rates increased or decreased rapidly in their counties.

Our multivariate analysis of changing fortunes provided some empirical confirmation for these casual observations. We estimated multivariate models of changing poverty rates, focusing on economic and structural conditions, population composition, residential variables, and political influence variables. Together, what do these results imply for community leaders who are trying to position their localities positively for the future? First, leaders need to be mindful of the quality and full impact of outside opportunities that present themselves. While we did not measure it in our multivariate models, the introduction of gaming has been beneficial in some areas. On the other hand, our results suggest there may be reason to be wary of the emergence of "big-box" retailing as a local economic development strategy. While the detrimental impact of job loss due to NAFTA is a concern, we recognize that any job loss is apt to have negative effects. And we certainly have not measured job gains from NAFTA. Still, local leaders need to be mindful of their own communities' industrial composition and future directions in this regard vis-à-vis the world economy and free trade initiatives. Second, an emphasis on building local human capital (a sufficiently educated workforce) will help rural places attract and take advantage of endogenous opportunities and will enhance chances for the development of meaningful economic opportunity from within, say through self-employment and entrepreneurship. Third, localities need to recognize the critical and increasing importance of female labor supply for the well being of families. Counties with higher female labor force participation had higher economic trajectories over the 1990s. Of course, anything to increase overall labor demand will help women workers, but localities need to do what they can to reduce barriers to employment among women (e.g., provision of affordable and quality day care). This is especially true given the drastically reformed welfare system. Fourth, net of other characteristics, counties with greater measured social capital enjoyed more rapid declines in poverty. The social science literature on social capital is still relatively new, and even less is known about the viability of strategies to increase social capital. But our results are clear and provocative: if localities could increase their stock of social capital, they would be better off in the long run. Fifth, counties that are not adjacent to metropolitan areas seem to be at a disadvantage. Political discourse is needed to enhance the economic opportunities available to more remote locales, and officials in these areas need to be aggressive in pursuing new and emerging opportunities.

ENDNOTES

1. This research was supported by a National Research Initiative Competitive Grants Program (USDA) project titled, "Structural Determinants of Rural Poverty: An Expanded Analysis" (NRIGCP 03-35401-12936, Stephan J. Goetz, Principal Investigator). Additional infrastructural support was provided by the Population Research Institute, Pennsylvania State University, which has core funding from the National Institute of Child Health and Human Development (HD041025-03). We thank Anil Rupasingha for

invaluable assistance in constructing the data file analyzed here, and Pamela Hileman for map creation. We also benefited from the helpful comments of the editors and anonymous reviewers. We alone are responsible for any errors that remain.

2. We note that a significant portion of this increase in inequality is due to a change between 1992 and 1993 in the way in which income data were collected by the Current Population Survey, the source of these statistics. However, even if attention is restricted to 1993–1998, a vastly disproportionate share of the rise in income over this period was enjoyed by the highest income quintile, and the top five percent in particular (Jones & Weinberg, 2000).
3. Poverty status is based on family income for the calendar year prior to the given Census Bureau survey used to gather income data. We refer to the poverty rate derived, for example, from the 2000 Census, as being that for 1999. Also, while we could have used individual-level county poverty rates, the latter are very highly correlated with the family-level rates and would yield results that are substantively identical to those reported here.
4. Like East Caroll Parish, LA, places near the bottom of the economic hierarchy of counties have nowhere to go but up, controlling for other factors.
5. When Model II is estimated without female headship, the prevalence of African Americans in 1990 has a significant and positive (detrimental) effect, suggesting higher prevalence of single headship among African Americans is at play.
6. We also estimated models with a limited number of two-way interactions (results not shown). Interestingly, these results suggest that greater social capital can compensate for lower aggregate levels of human capital in the population. Earlier we mentioned that we re-estimated the full model with corrections for spatial homogeneity. The results were substantively identical with only one exception. The effect for living in a non-adjacent county with a medium-sized urban population maintained the same strength and direction but slipped just below significance ($p = .122$).
7. The saying is attributed to rural sociologist Daryl Hobbs (Brown & Swanson, 2003, p. 397).

REFERENCES

Albrecht, D.E., Albrecht, C.M., & Albrecht, S.L. (2000). Poverty in nonmetropolitan America: Impacts of industrial, employment and family structure variables. *Rural Sociology, 63*(1), 87–103.

Beale, C.L. (2004, February). Anatomy of nonmetro high-poverty areas: Common in plight, distinctive in nature. In *Amber waves*. Washington, DC: U.S. Department of Agriculture, Economic Research Service. Retrieved from http://www.ers.usda.gov/amberwaves

Bishaw, A., & Iceland, J. (2003). *Poverty: 1999, Census 2000 brief* (U.S. Census Bureau Report C2KBR-19). Washington, DC: U.S. Census Bureau. Retrieved from http://www.census.gov/prod/2003pubs/c2kbr-19.pdf

Brown, D.L., & Swanson, L.E. (2003). *Challenges for rural America in the twenty-first century*. University Park, PA: Penn State Press.

Citro, C.F., & Michael, R.T. (1995). *Measuring poverty: A new approach*. Washington, DC: National Academy Press.

Cotter, D.A. (2002). Poor people in poor places: Local opportunity structures and household poverty. *Rural Sociology, 67*(4), 534–555.

Cox, W. M., & Alm, R. (1999). *Myths of rich & poor – Why we're better off than we think.* New York: Basic Books.

DeNavas-Walt, C., Cleveland, R.W., & Webster, B. H., Jr. (2003). *Income in the United States: 2002* (Current Population Report P60-221). Washington, DC: U.S. Census Bureau. Retrieved from http://www.census.gov/prod/2003pubs/p60-221.pdf

Duncan, C.M. (1999). *Worlds Apart – Why poverty persists in rural America.* New Haven, CT: Yale University Press.

Goetz, S.J., & Rupasingha, A. (2003 July). *Spatial poverty dynamics in U.S. counties in the 1990s.* Paper presented at the Joint AAEA-RSS meeting, Montreal, Quebec.

Jargowsky, P.A. (1997). *Poverty and place: Ghettos, barrios, and the American city.* New York: Sage.

Jargowsky, P.A. (2002). Sprawl, Concentration of poverty, and urban inequality. In G.D. Squires (Ed.), *Urban sprawl: Causes, consequences and policy responses* (pp. 39–71). Washington, DC: Urban Institute.

Jolliffe, D. (2003, June). *Comparisons of metropolitan-nonmetropolitan poverty during the 1990s* (Rural Development Research Report No. 96). Washington, DC: U.S. Department of Agriculture, Economic Research Service. Retrieved from http://www.ers.usda.gov/publications/rdrr96/

Jones, A.F., Jr., & Weinberg, D.H. (2000). *The changing shape of the nation's income distribution, 1947–1998* (Current Population Report P60-204). Washington, DC: U.S. Census Bureau. Retrieved from http://www.census.gov/prod/2000pubs/p60-204.pdf

Jorgenson, D.W. (1998). Did we lose the war on poverty? *Journal of Economic Perspectives, 12*(1), 78–96.

Kingsley, T.G., & Pettit, K.L.S. (2003). *Concentrated poverty: A change in course* (Neighborhood Change in Urban America, No. 2). Washington, DC: Urban Institute.

Levernier, W., Partridge, M.D., & Rickman, D.S. (2000). The causes of regional variation in U.S. poverty: A cross-county analysis. *Journal of Regional Science, 40*(3), 473–497.

Levitt, S.D., & Poterba, J.M. (1999). Congressional distributive politics and state economic performance. *Public Choice*, 99, 85–216.

Madden, J.F. (2003). The changing spatial concentration of income and poverty among suburbs of large US metropolitan areas. *Urban Studies,* 40(3), 481–503.

Nord, M. (1997, July). *Where are the rural poor? A geography of poverty in nonmetropolitan America* (Rural Poverty Information Series, Working Paper No. 14). Madison: University of Wisconsin, Department of Sociology.

Rupasingha, A., & Goetz, S.J. (2002, November). *Social and political forces as determinants of poverty: A spatial analysis.* Paper presented at the International Regional Science Association annual meeting, San Juan, Puerto Rico.

Schoeni, R.F., & Blank, R.M. (2000, February). *What has welfare reform accomplished? Impacts on welfare participation, employment, income, poverty, and family structure* (NBER Working Paper 7627). Washington, DC: National Bureau of Economic Research.

Slesnick, D.T. (1993). Gaining ground: Poverty in the postwar United States. *Journal of Political Economy, 101*(1), 1–38.

Smeeding, T.M., Rainwater, L., & Burtless, G. (2001). United States poverty in a cross-national context. In S. Danziger & R. Havemen (Eds.), *Understanding poverty* (pp. 162–189) (chap. 5). New York: Sage.

Tickamyer, A.R., & Duncan, C.M. (1990). Poverty and opportunity structure in rural America. *Annual Review of Sociology, 16,* 67–86.

PART III

CASE STUDIES OF POPULATION AND SOCIETY IN DIFFERENT RURAL REGIONS

CHAPTER 7

RURAL HISPANIC POPULATION GROWTH

Public Policy Impacts in Nonmetro Counties[1]

WILLIAM A. KANDEL AND EMILIO A. PARRADO

INTRODUCTION

Data from Census 2000 reveal dramatic increases in the Hispanic population in new destinations throughout all areas of the country. Since the end of the Second World War, the majority of Hispanics have resided in a handful of large cities. Recent attention to new Hispanic destinations has examined the extraordinary Hispanic population growth in Birmingham, Alabama; Louisville, Kentucky; and other unexpected harbingers of urban multiculturalism (Suro & Singer, 2002). However, Hispanics are also becoming a widely felt presence throughout many rural regions of the nation. In fact, over the past decade, their *rates* of increase in nonmetro counties exceeded that in metro counties as well as the rates of all other racial and ethnic groups in both county types (Cromartie & Kandel, 2002). This unusual growth has, for the first time in U.S. history, shifted half of all nonmetropolitan Hispanics outside the nonmetropolitan portion of the Southwest, comprised of Arizona, California, Colorado, New Mexico, and Texas.

These patterns have attracted scholarly attention because of the new geography of recent migration flows and because of public policy issues raised by such population influxes. Unlike traditional urban destinations with histories of integrating new immigrants, new rural destinations are often unprepared to deal with new demands for social services from ethnic minorities (Grey, 1995; Horowitz & Miller, 1999). Fundamental differences in demographic profiles lie at the root of these policy issues, and they represent a considerable social transformation of rural and small town America in their own right. We therefore address the following three research questions:

- How do Hispanic demographic profiles compare across different types of rural settlement areas, as well as to non-Hispanic Whites in these areas?
- How has rapid Hispanic population growth in nonmetro counties altered the demographic profiles of these counties?

W.A. Kandel & D.L. Brown (eds.), Population Change and Rural Society, 155–175.

- What public policy implications for social service demand stem from rapid rural Hispanic population growth?

We proceed by reframing recent migration to rural areas of the country as a demand-driven phenomenon stemming from industrial restructuring that helps shape the demographic composition of migration flows into new destinations. We show this by documenting demographic divergence not only between Hispanics and non-Hispanic Whites, but also between Hispanics residing in new versus established destinations. We use a typology of nonmetro counties that highlights differences in Hispanic composition to assess impacts of Hispanic in-migration on local socioeconomic conditions and new demands for public services, such as schooling, health care, and housing. Our findings suggest that rapid growth rates combined with substantial demographic differences from a relatively small Hispanic population have measurable impacts on county level socioeconomic profiles and social service demand.

THE DEMAND-DRIVEN HYPOTHESIS

If the demographic composition and profile of the recent rural Hispanic population were similar to those of native residents, changes in social services would reflect the quantity demanded from a growing population. However, the demographic profile of new rural Hispanics is distinct from that of the native population, a difference that stems from self-selection embedded in the process of international migration from Latin America to the United States. As a result, rapid Hispanic growth alters the population profile of receiving counties in ways that trigger new public policy demands.

Two trends motivating Hispanic migration to new rural destinations affect the demographic selectivity of this flow. First, industrial restructuring has increased labor demand in industries employing low-skilled, low-wage workers (Kandel & Parrado, 2003, 2004). Growing consumer demand for value-added food products has increased labor-intensive processes that utilize low-skilled workers, and the concentration of production in large, vertically integrated firms has shifted rural production away from small producers employing domestic workers. In addition, some industries, such as beef processing, have relocated to rural areas (MacDonald et al., 2000; Ollinger et al., 2000). The relative unattractiveness of these emerging forms of employment within a limited wage structure has fostered labor recruitment of Hispanic and immigrant workers (Carlin, 1999; Johnson-Webb, 2002; Katz, 1996a, 1996b; Smothers, 1996; Taylor & Stein, 1999). Consequently, during the past decade, traditional rural-based industries such as meat processing, carpet manufacturing, oil refining, and forestry have employed an increasing share of Hispanic workers (Barboza, 2001; Broadway, 1994; Engstrom, 2001; Gouveia & Stull, 1995; Griffith, 1995; Hernández-León & Zúñiga, 2000; McDaniel & Casanova, in press).

As migration flows evolve, networks of friends and family members perpetuate population flows, contributing to growth in new destinations (Massey, 1990). This pattern is instrumental for growing industries since firms can rely on informal social channels rather than more visible recruitment practices to ensure a continuous supply of low-wage workers. In addition, acquaintance and familial networks at places of destination facilitate additional migration by providing information, transportation financing, initial settlement arrangements, and other elements necessary to overcome barriers to employment in a foreign country.

These two processes help explain the demographic structure of the recent Hispanic population and its impact on nonmetro counties. The arduous and dangerous process of international migration itself, combined with narrow requirements of most migrant jobs means that labor migrants will be self-selected for "positive" characteristics such as initiative and youth, as well as "negative" characteristics, such as lower levels of education (Borjas, 1999, Massey et al., 2002). The logic of migration has changed little over the past several decades in the case of Mexico, the source of most Latino immigration (Durand et al., 2001). New labor migrants are primarily young males, often initiating their U.S. work experience as single teenagers or young adults. Most originate from rural communities in economically depressed regions of Mexico and other Latin American countries and are neither well off nor extremely poor (Massey et al., 1987). On average, they have fewer than 10 years of formal education, speak little English, and often begin migrating without documentation. As young adults, most migrants tend to be at the early stages of family formation, and if they do not eventually bring their spouses and children with them after residing in the United States for several years, they may marry and have children in this country.

It is international migration's self-selecting logic regarding migrants' demographic characteristics, and the resulting differences in migrant-receiving societies that create public policy challenges and attendant economic, social, and political impacts in new rural destinations. Our focus on public policy impacts stems from the growing concern among government officials and the public in general about rapid population change. To the extent that we clarify the demographic basis of some of these changes, we hope to contribute to the formulation of more even-handed policies.

ANALYTIC STRATEGY AND COUNTY TYPOLOGY

To disentangle demographic influences accompanying Hispanic growth from its policy impact, we compare counties with different population trajectories between 1990 and 2000. We place these population trends within economic and employment-related contexts before analyzing characteristics with significant local policy implications for public health, education, and housing. Because county-level data broken down by race and ethnicity are difficult to obtain for the entire nation, we base our analyses on Decennial Census and Area Resource File data.[2] Our main expectation is that cross-county comparisons will help identify what is unique about new Hispanic destination areas and how their policy demands have been changing.

We create a nonmetro county typology that derives from three factors: the Hispanic proportion of 1990 county population, its change during the 1990s, and total county population change during the 1990s. When combined, these factors produce a typology that allows us to compare counties with rapid Hispanic population growth in new regions of the country with counties that have always had a sizeable Hispanic population, counties whose populations have grown without significant Hispanic influence, and counties that are demographically stagnant. We use counties as the unit of analysis because they represent relatively small geographic and legal entities for which Census data can be compared consistently across decades. More formally our typology is specified as follows:

Table 7.1. Criteria for Nonmetro County Typology

County Type	Hispanic Composition, 1990	Percent Change, Hispanic Composition, 1990–2000*	Percent Change, Total Population, 1990–2000*
Substantial Hispanic Representation	≥3%		
Rapid Hispanic Growth	<3%	≥1%	
Rapid Growth Non-Hispanic	<3%	≤1%	≥2%
Slow Growth & Declining Non-Hispanic	<3%	≤1%	≤2%

* Rates of change computed over entire decade.

After reviewing the distributions for the demographic variables, this typology captures our underlying assumption of differential policy demands based on population composition. To avoid confounding our analysis with misleading mean and median values, we exclude from our analysis counties whose total populations in 2000 numbered less than 5,000 persons. This removes counties for which minor absolute changes in Hispanic population translate into unusually high proportions and growth rates.

Although our typology reduces the great variation of nonmetro counties to a handful of mutually exclusive types, Figure 7.1, which maps out this schema, reflects the distinct demographic trajectories of the Hispanic population that we would expect from our understanding of recent population geography. Established

Figure 7.1. Map of County Typology, 2000

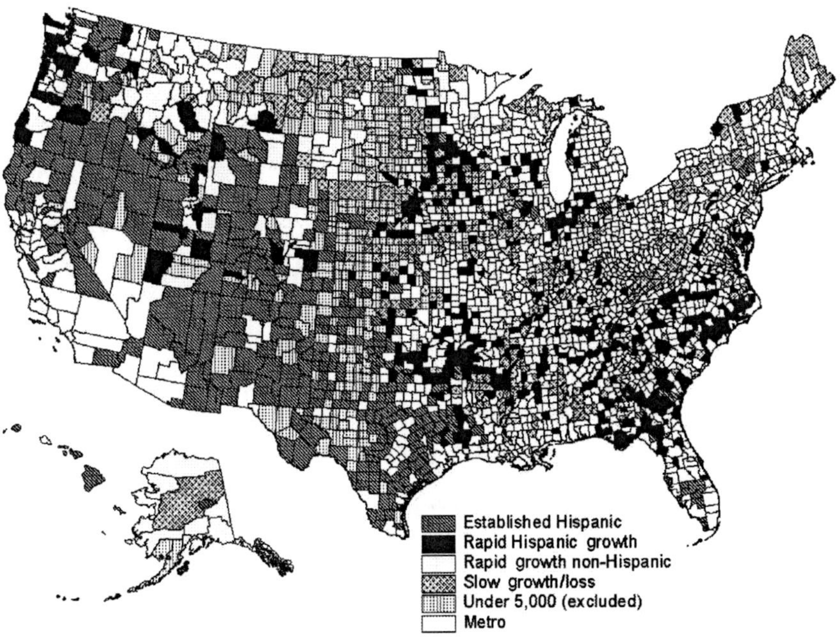

Hispanic counties predominate in traditional rural Hispanic settlement areas of the Southwest. Rapid Hispanic Growth counties tend to be concentrated in the Midwest and Southeast, where industrial transformations in beef processing during the 1980s and poultry processing in the 1990s generated significant new Hispanic population growth (Kandel & Parrado, 2003). They also appear north of the group of Established Hispanic counties. Slow Growth and Loss counties extend into the Central Plains and Texas but are concentrated in the Northern Great Plains which have lost population continuously since the 1950s (see Johnson & Rathge, and von Reichert, in this volume).

We present median values of demographic variables in Table 7.2 to further illustrate the clear differences between county types. With the exception of Slow Growth or Loss counties, total populations in 2000 and population growth rates over the decade were comparable for the first three county types, at roughly 20,000–22,000 persons and 10–12 percent, respectively. Differences appear in the size of the Hispanic population stemming from our definition. Despite similarly sized total populations, Established Hispanic counties exhibited the largest median number of Hispanics in 2000 but the lowest Hispanic population growth rate of any county type. This is largely a function of how growth rates are computed, as the same-size

Table 7.2. Descriptive statistics for Hispanic and Total County Populations by County Type, 1990–2000

		Total Population		Hispanic Population		Hispanic Composition	
	Number of Counties	In 2000	Percent Change, 1990–2000	In 2000	Percent Change, 1990–2000	1990	2000
Established Hispanic	362	20,351	12%	3,474	42%	9.6%	14.5%
Rapid Hispanic Growth	468	22,792	11%	707	308%	0.8%	3.0%
Rapid Growth Non-Hispanic	756	20,119	10%	192	105%	0.5%	1.0%
Slow Growth or Loss	415	15,305	−2%	132	75%	0.4%	0.8%

Source: Computed by authors from Census 1990 and 2000 data, SF1.

Hispanic influx will yield higher growth rates for smaller Hispanic populations. Even in Slow Growth and Loss counties, Hispanics grew in proportion and absolute numbers, ameliorating and in numerous instances reversing total population loss (Kandel & Cromartie, 2004). Differences also appear in the form of changes in county Hispanic population composition. Although Established Hispanic counties exhibit the highest Hispanic proportion, Rapid Hispanic Growth counties saw the largest increase in this proportion over the decade, almost four times the proportion in 1990 (0.8 to 3.0 percent). The following analysis demonstrates how this relatively modest 3 percent population composition can significantly influence county-level statistics and indicators.

AGE EFFECTS

The crux of our thesis stems from differences between Hispanic and non-Hispanic White age composition. Figures 7.2.A and 7.2.B compare population pyramids for Hispanics (left side of graphs) and non-Hispanic Whites (right side of graphs), and each bar indicates the percentage of the total population within indicated five-year age groups. Figure 7.2.A, which shows the age structures of both groups for Established Hispanic counties, resembles a population pyramid for both groups for the entire U.S. population (not shown). Because the Hispanic population

Figure 7.2. A. and B. Population Pyramids of Hispanics and Non-Hispanic Whites for Established Hispanic and Rapid Hispanic Growth Counties, 2000

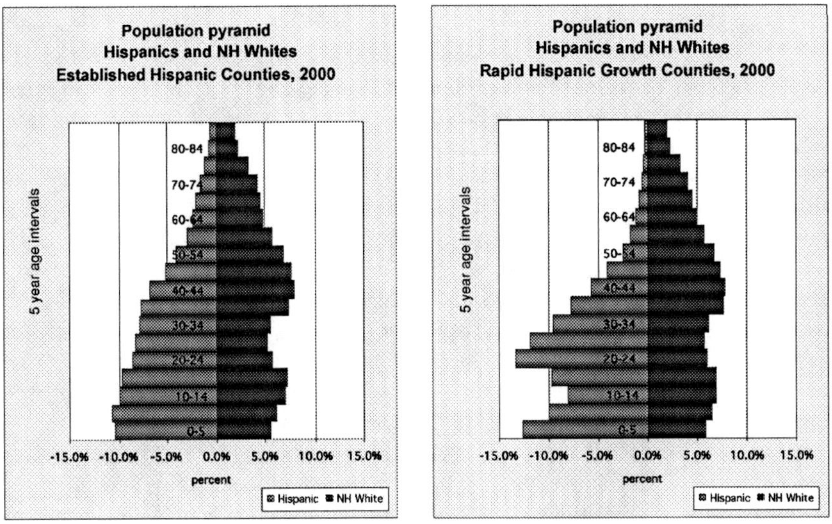

is significantly younger than the non-Hispanic White population, proportions of Hispanics in younger age groups exceed those of non-Hispanic Whites. The situation reverses at age 40, with non-Hispanic Whites displaying higher proportions than Hispanics in older age groups.

Figure 7.2.B, representing the age composition for Rapid Hispanic Growth counties, shows a much sharper contrast between the two groups. While the age structure of non-Hispanics Whites differs little from other county types, that for Hispanics is heavily tilted toward prime working ages and young children. Higher proportions of the population pyramid in younger age brackets reflect both family-forming ages of Hispanic parents and slightly higher fertility rates of first-generation Hispanics. Such differences can significantly affect county indicators such as median age. In Established Hispanic counties, with relatively high average Hispanic composition, median age actually declined during the 1990s from 37.04 to 36.04 years. However, the most interesting comparison is between Rapid Hispanic Growth and Rapid Growth, Non-Hispanic counties, where the 1990 median ages of 36.26 and 35.87, respectively, increased to 37.18 and 37.78. Both county types saw their median ages increase over the decade, but the impact of Hispanic population growth among the former actually retarded population aging that continues throughout most nonmetro counties outside the Southwest.

PUBLIC POLICY CHALLENGES

Employment and Poverty

What do shifts in age composition imply for public policy? A first glance at employment statistics suggests that Rapid Hispanic Growth counties appear relatively prosperous. Census data in Table 7.3 indicate that unemployment rates were considerably lower in Rapid Hispanic Growth counties than in other county types for both 1990 and 2000. Moreover, when we distinguish by ethnicity, the results show that in 2000 Rapid Hispanic Growth counties had lower unemployment rates for both Hispanics and Non-Hispanic Whites than any other county type, 8.6 and 4.5 percent respectively. Especially interesting is the comparison with Established Hispanic counties, in which Hispanics exhibit a significantly higher 9.7 percent unemployment rate. At the other end of the distribution, Slow Growth and Loss counties exhibit the highest unemployment levels for Non-Hispanic Whites (5.3 percent). These results are consistent with the expectation that employment opportunity drives new rural Hispanic population growth.

A closer look at these employment data, however, reveals a mixed portrait. Greater employment opportunity does not translate automatically into improved living conditions. While Rapid Hispanic Growth counties exhibit lower overall poverty levels than other county types, ethnic differences highlight considerable disparities. In 2000, Rapid Hispanic growth counties had the highest Hispanic (25.1 percent) as well as the lowest non-Hispanic White (10.4 percent) poverty rates of all other county types. More notably, during the job creation years of the 1990s, all nonmetro Whites and Hispanics in all other nonmetro county types saw their proportions of adults with poverty-level incomes decline, yet Hispanics in Rapid Hispanic Growth counties saw their proportions increasing. This growing ethnic inequality appears in the changing per-capita income gap between Hispanics and non-Hispanic Whites across county types. In 1990 Rapid Hispanic Growth counties exhibited the second lowest gap between the two groups, but by 2000 their average gap of $8,576 exceeded that of all other county types.

Thus, while employment opportunities appear greater in new destinations, the relatively low incomes earned by Hispanics in these counties have done little to alleviate their relative disadvantage. Moreover, their economic fortunes and those of the non-Hispanic White population appear to be diverging. The social processes undergirding such trends can be traced back to the concentration of Hispanics at the less-skilled and lower-paid ends of the occupational scale (Newman, 2003) as well as to the occupational and industrial transformation of industries attracting Hispanics to these new destinations (Kandel & Parrado, 2004). From a policy perspective, these results suggest that while rapid Hispanic growth is not putting obvious strains on the employment structures of non-metro counties, low income levels associated with new jobs available to Hispanics are retarding poverty declines and increasing Hispanic representation among the poor. As a result, social

Table 7.3. Economic Indicators by County Type, 1990–2000

		Established Hispanic	Rapid Hispanic Growth	Rapid Growth Non-Hispanic	Slow Growth or Loss
Unemployment Rate	Total, 1990	7.3%	6.2%	7.7%	7.7%
	Total, 2000	6.7%	5.6%	6.2%	6.6%
	NH White	4.9%	4.5%	5.3%	5.5%
	Hispanic	9.7%	8.6%	8.8%	9.7%
Poverty Rate	Total, 1990	16.9%	15.3%	16.4%	17.1%
	Total, 2000	14.4%	13.0%	13.3%	14.3%
	NH White	10.5%	10.4%	11.5%	11.9%
	Hispanic	23.5%	25.1%	21.2%	21.0%
Change in Poverty Rate, 1990–2000	NH White	−1.7%	−2.1%	−2.8%	−2.4%
	Hispanic	−5.8%	0.5%	−3.0%	−4.7%
Per-Capita Income Gap between Hispanics and NH Whites	1990	$5,076	$4,052	$3,445	$4,348
	2000	$8,088	$8,576	$6,932	$7,302

Source: Computed by authors from Census 1990 and 2000 data, SF3 and SF4 files.

services towards the poor might need to be expanded and especially tailored towards Hispanics.

Health: Fertility, Mortality, and Emergency Room Utilization

Rapid population change is likely to affect health policy demands, which have considerable impacts on state and local budgets. Hospitals tend to receive significant amounts of funding from government agencies, and rural areas often struggle to provide a relatively complete range of health services for a dispersed population (Capalbo & Heggem, 1999). Hispanic population growth yields positive and negative health policy outcomes that differentially affect the mix of health service provision. Hence, if significant numbers of relatively younger Hispanics move to a county with an aging population—a typical scenario for nonmetro counties—they will likely alter specific demands for health services, triggering a gradual restructuring of local health care systems.

For foreign-born residents, legal status influences the interaction between population change and health service demand, because it can restrict access to or inhibit the use of public social services. Following our assumption that health demand reflects the particular demographic characteristics of Hispanic groups, we concentrate on three public health dimensions: fertility, mortality, and emergency health service demand.

Health indicators presented in Table 7.4 relate directly to median ages recorded by the 2000 Census, which are shown in the first row. Median ages for all Hispanic populations are substantially lower than those of non-Hispanic Whites, a difference with clear health policy impacts among women in their child-bearing years. The difference between Hispanic and non-Hispanic White women's median ages is considerable by any measure, ranging from 15 years in Rapid Growth non-Hispanic counties to 18.6 years in Rapid Hispanic Growth counties. In light of the 15–44 age range of childbearing years used to compute general fertility rates, Hispanic women, on average, have far more childbearing years ahead of them than non-Hispanic White women, and this is particularly the case in Rapid Hispanic Growth counties.

Changes in fertility rates have responded accordingly. Table 7.4 reports changes in general fertility rates between 1989 and 1999 by county type. They indicate that in Rapid Hispanic Growth counties, average absolute numbers of total births over the decade increased by roughly 16, double that of Established Hispanic counties and a sharp contrast with declining numbers of average births in Rapid Growth non-Hispanic and Slow Growth or Loss counties.

Total births result from the population size of women in their childbearing years and the average number of births per woman. As in other industrialized nations, American women are increasingly delaying marriage and childbearing to

Table 7.4. Age and Health Indicators by County Type, 1989–1999

	Established Hispanic	Rapid Hispanic Growth	Rapid Growth Non-Hispanic	Slow Growth or Loss
Median Age, Non-Hispanic White Women, 2000	41.9	40.8	40.3	41.9
Median Age, Hispanic Women, 2000	24.4	22.2	25.3	25.7
Change, Average Absolute Number of Total Births Per County, 1989–1999	8.1	16.2	−5.6	−46.2
Percent Change, General Fertility Rate, 1989–1999	−6.3%	−3.8%	−6.6%	−8.9%
Percent Change, Crude Death Rate, 1989–1999	1.2%	−1.0%	0.4%	5.2%
Percent Change, Crude Death Rate from Chronic Diseases,* 1989–1999	−2.2%	−5.8%	−4.4%	−0.4%
Percent Change, Emergency Room Visits, 1990–2000, Per 1,000 Residents–Mean Values	38.8%	38.5%	27.4%	35.1%
Percent Change, Emergency Room Visits, 1990–2000, Per 1,000 Residents–Median Values	21.7%	11.2%	14.4%	14.8%

Chronic lower respiratory disease, chronic liver disease and cirrhosis, malignant neoplasms, and other cardiovascular and cerebrovascular diseases.
Source: Figures computed from Area Resource Files using three-year averages, 1988–1990 and 1998–2000.

invest in their education and careers and are having fewer children within marriage (Downs, 2003). Accordingly, the general fertility rate, measuring the number of children born to every 1,000 women aged 15–44, declined throughout nonmetro counties during the past decade, as it has in every one since 1960. While this trend appears for every nonmetro county type shown in Table 7.4, the fertility decline for Rapid Hispanic Growth counties (−3.8 percent) was substantially less than in all other county types. Once again, a relatively small proportion of the population appears to have a disproportionate impact on the demographic profile of the total county population.[3]

Similar trends also influence death rates but with the opposite effect on health services demand. By introducing greater numbers of relatively younger persons with lower mortality risk into nonmetro counties, Hispanic population growth effectively reduces mortality rates. Crude death rates in the U.S. have been rising for decades due to population aging (see Kirschner, Berry, & Glasgow in this volume), and Table 7.4 shows these rates increasing during 1989–1999 for Established Hispanic, Rapid growth Non-Hispanic, and Slow Growth or Loss Counties. However, the reverse is true for Rapid Hispanic growth counties, which experienced declines in crude death rates over the past decade.

Hispanic population growth also affects the distribution of mortality by cause of death, potentially altering the cost of per-capita health service provision. American life expectancy continues to increase from advances in medical technological and public health policies. Consequently, death rates from heart disease, diabetes, and other chronic diseases have declined continuously over the past century. While all nonmetro county types show decreases in mortality rates from chronic diseases, the rate has declined the most for Rapid Hispanic growth counties. While not conclusive, the implication we draw from these data is that rapid Hispanic population growth can reduce per-capita health service demand for medical services geared toward aging rural populations.

Fertility and mortality rate changes, in turn, influence the allocation of public health resources. Regardless of whether public and/or private health facilities expand the availability of such resources to meet the demands of a growing population, they must confront the impact of demographic compositional change on service delivery allocation. Hospitals with stable caseloads of patients with chronic diseases may need to reallocate resources to meet greater demand for obstetrics and gynecology services. However, if health care resources expand on a per-capita basis, and if the cost of treating chronic diseases significantly exceeds that of maternity-related services, some municipalities may find their public health spending declining with an influx of younger residents.

Public health policy makers must also concern themselves with the growing reliance on hospital emergency rooms as medical providers of last resort for those lacking documentation, sufficient income, or health insurance (National Center for Health Statistics, 2003, Table 77). Counties with sizable numbers of recent Hispanic in-migrants—many of whom face the above disadvantages—would be expected to experience increases in local emergency hospital visits. Yet, a comparison of Area Resource File data for all county types, averaged across 1988–1990 and 1998–2000, reveals no such relative increase (Table 7.4). All county types except Rapid-growth Non-Hispanic counties showed increases in mean emergency hospital visits per 1,000 residents at roughly 35–40 percent, reflecting broader national trends.[4] While recent Hispanic arrivals in new destinations may be utilizing some public health services, the data presented here suggest that the demand

Table 7.5. Education Indicators, 1990–2000

		Established Hispanic	Rapid Hispanic Growth	Rapid Growth Non-Hispanic	Slow Growth or Loss
Percent Change in Enrollment Rates, 1990–2000	Grades K–8	8%	10%	7%	−9%
	NH White	−2%	9%	10%	−8%
	Hispanic	96%	525%	246%	122%
	Grades 9–12	38%	31%	28%	14%
	NH White	31%	25%	26%	11%
	Hispanic	98%	472%	177%	106%
Hispanic Proportion of School-Age Population	1990	22.8%	1.4%	0.9%	0.9%
	2000	28.1%	4.7%	1.5%	1.4%

Source: Computed by authors from Census 1990 and 2000 data, SF1 and SF4 files.

for relatively costly emergency room services may occur independently of their concentrated population growth.

Education

School enrollment rates provide some of the most pronounced evidence of public policy impacts associated with changing rural Hispanic demography. Lower median ages and relatively higher fertility rates of Hispanic in-migrants have yielded a Hispanic school-age population that has grown more rapidly than the non-Hispanic White school-age population, a demographic contrast with considerable implications for rural school districts. Table 7.5 presents mean enrollment rates by county type for pre-school to middle school and high school. In Rapid Hispanic Growth counties, enrollment rates for all students attending preschool through middle school as well as high school are only slightly higher than in Rapid Growth non-Hispanic counties. However, if we examine these enrollment rate data by race and ethnicity, dramatic differences emerge. During the 1990s, enrollment rates for Hispanic children increased more rapidly than for non-Hispanic White children in every county type. In Rapid Hispanic Growth counties, for example, enrollment rates for Hispanic children increased by about 500 percent at both schooling levels.

Although Hispanics, on average, still comprise a relatively small proportion of the total school-age population in nonmetro counties (Table 7.5), high rates of enrollment growth foreshadow considerable challenges facing rural schools that must devote substantial resources to address this population's distinct needs. These needs include additional classroom space and English as a Second Language (ESL) classes, as well as orientation seminars and translation services for their parents. Moreover, schools facing state and national mandates for instructional performance, such as the recent "No Child Left Behind" policy, are at a distinct disadvantage for achieving such standards during periods of limited or declining public education budgets.

Housing

Influxes of new residents in predominantly low-wage and/or unstable employment, including many who limit consumption to maximize earnings or remittances to family members in countries of origin, are likely to affect local housing availability, affordability, and quality. We focus on rental housing because employees in relatively low-paying and unstable jobs are less likely to possess the residential stability and financial capital necessary for homeownership. Ethnographic accounts of migrants living in new rural destinations routinely describe substandard and exploitative living conditions characterized by overcrowding, poor housing quality, and excessive rents (Atiles & Bohon, 2003; Fennelly & Leitner, 2002).

Nevertheless, housing quality is difficult to measure because of its subjectivity, despite the extent of housing data available from the Census. For example, Census measures of housing quality include the existence of phone service, plumbing, and electricity, utilities found in the most shoddy rental unit. More accurate gauges of rental unit quality—whether the plumbing functions adequately or the walls contain insulation—remain unrecorded. Therefore, in this analysis, we focus on housing tenure, rental costs, and overcrowding.

Data from Table 7.6 indicate that in nonmetro counties, which have relatively high rates of home ownership compared to metro counties, one fourth of all residents rent their homes. During the 1990s, this proportion declined by only 1 to 2 percent in all nonmetro county types. Among Hispanics, however, declines were more pronounced. In Established Hispanic counties with significant numbers of Hispanics who settled prior to 1990, and who benefited from status legalization provisions of the Immigration Reform and Control Act (IRCA) of 1986, the proportion of renting residents declined by 20 percentage points. While changes in legal status for a sizable proportion is not the only factor influencing homeownership, it remains a significant determinant (Ray et al., 2004). In all other county types, declines ranged between 8 and 12 percentage points. What stands out in Rapid Hispanic growth counties, however, is the relatively high proportion of Hispanic renters which remained above 40 percent in 2000, in sharp contrast not only with non-Hispanic Whites in the same counties but also with Hispanics in other nonmetro counties. Hence, Hispanics are more likely to have to contend with rental housing market fluctuations in Rapid Hispanic growth counties than in other nonmetro counties.

Table 7.6. Housing Indicators, 1990–2000

	Established Hispanic	Rapid Hispanic Growth	Rapid Growth Non-Hispanic	Slow Growth or Loss
Proportion of Total Population Renting in 1990	29.7%	26.0%	24.4%	26.4%
Proportion of Total Population Renting in 2000	27.9%	25.1%	23.2%	24.9%
Proportion of Hispanics Renting in 1990	47.2%	47.8%	39.1%	43.3%
Proportion of Hispanics Renting in 2000	27.2%	41.9%	30.9%	31.4%
Percent Change, Median Gross Rent, 1990–2000[a]	37.3%	42.7%	40.6%	35.4%
Percent Change, Aggregate County Rent, 1990–2000	53.5%	71.4%	64.9%	37.1%
Proportion of Rental Units "Crowded"[b], 1990	9.8%	5.5%	5.2%	4.5%
Proportion of Rental Units "Crowded"[b], 2000	10.6%	6.4%	4.8%	3.8%
Percent Change in Absolute Number of Crowded Rental Units, 1990–2000	26.0%	38.9%	6.7%	−15.6%
Proportion Hispanics in Crowded Housing, 2000	22.8%	27.3%	12.2%	10.1%
Proportion NH Whites in Crowded Housing, 2000	2.8%	1.9%	2.1%	1.5%

[a] For comparability, median gross rent is adjusted by the Census Bureau to exclude utilities.
[b] We define crowded rental housing units as those with 1.01+ persons per room.
Source: Computed by authors from Census 1990 and 2000 data, SF3 and SF4 files.

Rent increases may be more revealing than absolute rent levels themselves. During the 1990s, median gross rents increased throughout the country, but counties with rapid Hispanic population growth exhibited increases several percentage points higher than in other county types, a trend even more pronounced for aggregated rents (the total for each county) averaged for each county type. Although not shown in Table 7.6, actual average rents in 2000—at just over $400—differed only slightly across county types. Moreover, upper limits on rents that landlords can charge stem from corresponding wage levels and local affordability.

Shared housing and overcrowding are a function of income as well as a critical element of migrants' strategy to maximize financial remittances and savings. The Census Bureau does not formally define crowding, but many housing studies use more than one person per room as a conventional measure (U.S. Census Bureau, 2002, p. B58). Although this threshold fails to differentiate, for instance, a family with two children sharing a large room from a dozen temporary workers sleeping in shifts in a mobile home, we assume such differences are randomly distributed over time across all county types. Data in Table 7.6 indicate that only a small percentage of rental units are classified as crowded, but this percentage increased from 1990 to 2000 in Established and Rapid Hispanic Growth counties and declined in the other two. Moreover, Rapid Hispanic Growth counties experienced the largest percentage growth in the absolute number of crowded rental units. These aggregate measures by county type reflect the influence of a relatively minor portion of the total population and accordingly mask substantial differences by race and ethnicity. When compared, Hispanics and non-Hispanic Whites show very different rates of overcrowding, with the highest levels for Hispanics occurring in Rapid Hispanic Growth counties.

PATTERNS OF HISPANIC ADAPTATION IN RURAL COUNTIES

Thus far, our discussion has emphasized impacts of rapid Hispanic population growth on county-level measures of fiscal and public policy. Yet, policy demands arising from rapid Hispanic growth change over time with greater adaptation of foreign-born Hispanics to the United States. We now consider indicators of social and economic incorporation and compare results across county types to highlight the association between policy demands and Hispanic in-migrants' characteristics.

Hispanic in-migrants' duration of residence in the United States differs substantially across counties. Two census measures include foreign birth and previous residence. Almost half of all Hispanics living in Rapid Hispanic Growth counties were born outside of the U.S., roughly double the rate of Hispanics in Established Hispanic counties. However, foreign birth does not necessarily imply lack of U.S. experience. Sizable proportions of Hispanic newcomers to nonmetro counties possess substantial U.S. experience in other parts of the country, and some relocate to rural destinations because of a higher perceived quality of life (Fennelly & Leitner, 2002; Hernández-León & Zúñiga, 2000; Salamon, 2003). Census 2000 data indicate that a significantly larger proportion of Hispanics in Rapid Hispanic Growth counties resided in another state or country in 1995 than did Hispanics in other nonmetro county types.

English language proficiency, a critical mechanism of social and economic adaptation, is a function of education attainment and U.S. experience. To

Table 7.7. Social and Economic Incorporation Indicators, 1990–2000

		Established Hispanic	Rapid Hispanic Growth	Rapid Growth Non-Hispanic	Slow Growth or Loss
Percent of Foreign-Born Hispanics	2000	26%	48%	20%	16%
Where Hispanics in the 2000 Census Resided in 1995	Other State	6%	18%	17%	15%
	Other Country	5%	17%	5%	2%
Linguistic Isolation[a] among Foreign Language-Speaking Households	1990	19%	8%	5%	6%
	2000	21%	19%	7%	6%

[a] Defined by Census as when no one in household over age 12 speaks English "very well."
Source: Computed by authors from Census 1990 and 2000 data, SF3 and SF4 files.

measure it, we use Census data on "linguistic isolation," defined for individuals living in households where no member over age 12 speaks English "very well." In 1990, Hispanics living in Established Hispanic counties had, by far, the highest proportion of linguistic isolation of any county type, roughly one in five individuals. However, by 2000, Hispanics living in Rapid Hispanic Growth counties averaged roughly the same proportion, a singular increase of this measure among county types. Apart from labor market outcomes, English skills have particular policy relevance not only for public services, such as language translation in courts, schools, and hospitals, but because of what they imply about newcomers' ability to acquire information about living in the United States.

DISCUSSION

Policy implications of rapid Hispanic population growth can be captured in the types of newcomer assistance programs undertaken by community organizations. For instance, a North Carolina elementary school that saw its proportion of Hispanic students increase from less than 5 percent to over 50 percent within a decade formed El Guia Family Center,[5] with assistance from the local Chamber of Commerce, with the intention of acclimating recent Hispanic immigrant parents. Services provided include information tours to the local public institutions, such as hospitals, courts, churches, and public transit facilities. Families can obtain the services of immigration lawyers and domestic violence counselors, acquire parenting skills, and take ESL, GED, and computer classes. Their childcare program involves both parents to emphasize family-oriented support, and for older children having academic difficulty, the center offers tutorial programs during and after school.

In sum, recent Hispanic population growth in new nonmetro county destinations represents one of the more profound social transformations affecting rural places, altering their social, economic, and political profiles as well as the broader national perception of rural and small town America. Hispanics in new nonmetro destinations are likely to possess different sociodemographic characteristics from Hispanics in other county types; they are generally younger and possess a number of economic disadvantages. In Rapid Hispanic Growth counties, highlighted in this chapter, they experienced higher rates of poverty as well as poverty growth over the past decade, despite lower unemployment rates, compared to Hispanics living in nonmetro counties with different demographic profiles. In addition, we emphasize Hispanic age composition as a critical factor underlying social service needs and influencing local public policy. Younger Hispanic populations alter the per-capita calculus for health care delivery, raise significant needs and opportunities for public education, and place substantial demands on local housing markets. Despite small absolute numbers, high rates of Hispanic population growth have altered demographic profiles of counties throughout rural and small town America, implying future shifts in public service spending and provision.

Nevertheless, while this analysis has emphasized disadvantage, economic hardship, and consequent public policy demands associated with rural Hispanic population growth, it has not addressed the advantages, economic benefits, and opportunities that such growth has produced for many rural communities. It is important to keep in mind that rural Hispanic population growth is often a response to actual labor shortages in industries that either cannot or do not pay wages that attract native workers. Moreover, economic contributions of migrant workers, including payroll tax and Social Security withholdings, low rates of social service usage for undocumented workers, and local economic multiplier effects from consumption should not be overlooked. In light of the economic forces that generate Hispanic population growth in new rural destinations of the country, precise measures of fiscal impacts, state and federal support, and the economic contribution of newcomers would be fruitful areas of research.

ENDNOTES

1. Opinions expressed herein do not reflect those of the Economic Research Service or the U.S. Department of Agriculture.
2. The Area Resource File is a compendium of county-level statistical data from a variety of government agencies, including the National Center for Health Statistics and the

National Center for Education Statistics. It is compiled by the Health Resources and Services Administration, U.S. Department of Health and Human Services.
3. Two competing explanations for substantial increases in fertility in Rapid Hispanic Growth counties might be that total population increases produced higher populations of non-Hispanic White women, but population change figures from Table 7.1 that show comparable changes across county types make this unlikely. Another explanation is that nonmetro Blacks with relatively higher fertility might be relocating to the same new destinations. Again, this explanations loses power when one considers the declining fertility rates among metro and nonmetro Blacks over the past several decades and the fact that the Black populations in these counties have growth rates similar to those of non-Hispanic Whites.
4. Median values for the same statistic, a more conservative measure, actually indicate relatively smaller increases for counties with rapidly growing populations.
5. Based upon fieldwork conducted by both authors in October 2002. A pseudonym is used to protect the identity of interviewees.

REFERENCES

Atiles, J. H., & Bohon, S. A. (2003). Camas calientes: Housing adjustments and barriers to adaptation among the South's rural Latinos. *Rural Southern Sociology, 19*, 97–122.

Barboza, D. (2001, December 21). Meatpackers' profits hinge on pool of immigrant labor. *New York Times*.

Borjas, G. J. (1999). *Heaven's door: Immigration policy and the American economy*. Princeton: Princeton University Press.

Broadway, M. J. (1994). Hogtowns and rural development. *Rural Development Perspectives, 9*, 40–46.

Capalbo, S. M., & Heggem, C. N. (1999). Innovations in the delivery of health care services to rural communities. *Rural Development Perspectives, 14*, 8–13.

Carlin, M. (1999, July 28). Even tougher on farm labor? *Raleigh News and Observer*.

Cobb, J. C. (1982). *The selling of the South: The Southern crusade for industrial development, 1936–1990*. Baton Rouge: Louisiana State University Press.

Cromartie, J. (1999). Race and ethnicity in rural areas. *Rural Conditions and Trends, 9*, 9–19.

Cromartie, J., & Kandel, W. (2002, May 8–11). *Did residential segregation in rural America increase with recent Hispanic population growth?* Poster presented at the Meetings of the Population Association of America, Atlanta, GA.

Downs, B. (2003). *Fertility of American women: June 2002* (Current Population Reports P20–548). Washington, DC: U.S. Census Bureau.

Durand, J., Massey, D. S., & Zenteno, R. (2001). Mexican immigration to the United States: Continuities and changes. *Latin American Research Review, 36*, 107–126.

Engstrom, J. (2001). Industry and immigration in Dalton, Georgia. In A. Murphy, C. Blanchard, & J. A. Hill (Eds.), *Latino workers in the contemporary South*, 44–56. Athens: University of Georgia Press.

Fennelly, K., & Leitner, H. (2002). *How the food processing industry is diversifying rural Minnesota* (Working Paper No. 59). Lansing, MI: Michigan State University, Julian Samora Research Institute.

Gouveia, L., & Stull, D. D. (1995). Dances with cows: Beefpacking's impact on Garden City, Kansas, and Lexington, Nebraska. In D. D. Stull, M. J. Broadway, & D. Griffith (Eds.), *Any way you cut it: Meat processing and small-town America*, 85–108. Lawrence, KS: University Press of Kansas.

Grey, M. A. (1995). Pork, poultry, and newcomers in Storm Lake, Iowa. In D. D. Stull, M. J. Broadway, & D. Griffith (Eds.), *Any way you cut it: Meat processing and small-town America*, 109–128. Lawrence, KS: University Press of Kansas.

Griffith, D. (1995). Hay trabajo: Poultry processing, rural industrialization, and the latinization of low-wage labor. In D. D. Stull, M. J. Broadway, & D. Griffith (Eds.), *Any way you cut it: Meat processing and small-town America*, 129–152. Lawrence, KS: University Press of Kansas.

Guthey, G. (2001). Mexican places in southern spaces: Globalization, work and daily life in and around the North Georgia poultry industry. In A. Murphy, C. Blanchard, & J. A. Hill (Eds.), *Latino workers in the contemporary South*. Athens: University of Georgia Press.

Hernández-León, R., & Zúñiga, V. (2000). "Making carpet by the mile": The emergence of a Mexican immigrant community in an industrial region of the U.S. historic South. *Social Science Quarterly, 81*, 49–66.

Horowitz, R., & Miller, M. J. (1999). *Immigrants in the Delmarva poultry processing industry: The changing face of Georgetown, Delaware and environs* (Occasional Paper No. 37). Lansing, MI: Michigan State University, Julian Samora Research Institute.

Johnson-Webb, K. D. (2002). Employer recruitment and Hispanic labor migration: North Carolina urban areas at the end of the millennium. *Professional Geographer, 54*, 406–421.

Kandel, W., & Cromartie, J. (2004). *New patterns of Hispanic settlement in rural America* (Rural Development Research Report 99). Washington, DC: U.S. Department of Agriculture, Economic Research Service.

Kandel, W., & Parrado, Emilio (2003, May 1–3). *U.S. meat processing industry restructuring and new Hispanic migration*. Paper presented at the Annual Meeting of the Population Association of America, Minneapolis, MN.

Kandel, W., & Parrado, Emilio (2004). Industrial transformation and Hispanic migration to the American South: The case of the poultry industry. In D. D. Arreola (Ed.), *Hispanic spaces, Latino places: A geography of regional and cultural diversity*. Austin, TX: University of Texas Press.

Katz, J. (1996, November 10–12). The chicken trail (three articles). *Los Angeles Times*.

Katz, J. (1996, December 8). Poultry industry imports labor to do its dirty work. *Los Angeles Times*.

MacDonald, J., Ollinger, M., Nelson, K., & Handy, C. (2000). *Consolidation in U.S. meatpacking* (Agricultural Economic Report 785). Washington, DC: U.S. Department of Agriculture, Economic Research Service.

Massey, D. S. (1990). Social structure, household strategies, and the cumulative causation of migration. *Population Index, 56*, 3–26.

Massey, D. S., Alarcón, R., Durand, J., & González, H. (1987). *Return to* uniform *Aztlan*. Berkeley, CA: University of California Press.

Massey, D. S., Durand, J., & Malone, N. (2002). *Beyond smoke and mirrors: Mexican immigration in an era of economic integration*. New York: Sage.

McDaniel, J. M., & Casanova, V. (2003). Pines in lines: Tree planting, H2B guest workers, and rural poverty in Alabama. *Southern Rural Sociology, 19*(1), 73–96.

National Center for Health Statistics, U.S. Department of Health and Human Services. (2003). *Health, United States, 2003*. Hyattsville, MD: Author.

Newman, C. (2003). *Impacts of Hispanic population growth on rural wages* (Agricultural Economic Report 826). Washington, DC: U.S. Department of Agriculture, Economic Research Service.

Ray, B., Papademetriou, D., & Jachimowicz, M. (2004). *Immigrants and homeownership in urban America: An examination of nativity, socioeconomic status and place*. Washington, DC: Migration Policy Institute.

Salamon, S. (2003). *Newcomers to old towns: Suburbanization of the heartland*. Chicago: University of Chicago Press.
Smothers, R. (1996, January 30). Unions head South to woo poultry workers. *New York Times*.
Studstill, J. D., & Nieto-Studstill, L. (2001). Hospitality and hostility: Latin immigrants in Southern Georgia. In A. Murphy, C. Blanchard, & J. A. Hill (Eds.), *Latino workers in the contemporary South*, 68–81. Athens: University of Georgia Press.
Suro, R., & Singer, A. (2002). *Latino growth in metropolitan America: Changing patterns, new locations*. Washington, DC: Brookings Institution, Center on Urban and Metropolitan Policy, and Pew Hispanic Center.
Taylor, M., & Stein, S. (1999, July 4). Network helps recruit immigrants for U.S. job market. *The Fort Worth Star-Telegram*.
U.S. Census Bureau. (2002). *Technical documentation, summary file 3, 2000 census of population and housing*. Washington, DC: Author.

CHAPTER 8

SOCIAL INTEGRATION AMONG OLDER IN-MIGRANTS IN NONMETROPOLITAN RETIREMENT DESTINATION COUNTIES:

Establishing New Ties[1]

NINA GLASGOW AND DAVID L. BROWN

INTRODUCTION

Migration is closely associated with various life course transitions, and, as Longino (1990) and others have shown, retirement and migration are frequently linked. While the 2000 CPS showed that older persons tend to have a relatively low propensity to migrate (only 2.0 percent crossed county lines from 1995 to 2000 compared with 8.6 percent of persons aged 30–34), when they do move, they are more likely to move to nonmetropolitan (nonmetro) destinations.[2] As a consequence, older persons have made a positive contribution to nonmetro population change in each decade since the 1960s. Regardless of the overall direction of metro to nonmetro migration—positive in the 1970s and 1990s and negative in the 1980s—more older persons have moved to nonmetro areas than in the opposite direction in each decade since the 1970s (Fulton et al., 1997).[3] Counties with higher than average net in-movement of older persons are among the most rapidly and consistently growing types of nonmetro area. During the 1990s, for example, nonmetro counties with 15 percent or higher net in-migration of persons aged 60 or older grew by 28 percent compared with 8 percent for other nonmetro counties. Retirement destination counties, by definition, attract older migrants, but they also attract working-age persons who obtain jobs in economic activities induced by the in-flow of retirees (Johnson & Fuguitt, 2000). Hence, retirement migration has been an engine of nonmetro economic and demographic growth, and many states and localities have developed explicit strategies to attract retirees (Reeder, 1998; Stallman & Siegel, 1995).

While a substantial amount of research has examined the geographic mobility of older Americans (De Jong et al., 1995; Litwak & Longino, 1987) and the social and economic effects of retiree migration on destination communities

W.A. Kandel & D.L. Brown (eds.), Population Change and Rural Society, 177–196.

(Glasgow & Reeder, 1990; Siegel et al., 1995), few studies have focused on the social adjustment of older in-migrants in nonmetro retirement destinations. Our research seeks to fill this gap by examining migrants' formal and informal social relationships and comparing their degree of social integration with that of longer-term older residents of retirement destination counties. This chapter contributes to a larger study of social integration and well-being of older in-migrants to nonmetro retirement counties. The overall hypothesis motivating the work is that older in-migrants to nonmetro counties who establish extensive and meaningful social relationships are expected to age more successfully than their counterparts who fail to establish effective social relationships and involvements.

Our goals in this chapter are: (a) to examine the selectivity of migration to nonmetro retirement destination counties by describing the social, economic, and health characteristics of a sample of older in-migrants and comparing them with longer-term older residents of the same counties; (b) to examine migrants' degree of formal and informal social integration, and compare their social involvement with that of longer-term older residents; and (c) to examine the determinants of social participation among elders in nonmetro retirement destinations. This analysis sheds light on the process by which older migrants build social ties and establish social relationships and participation in their new communities. We will not examine the link between social integration and social well-being *in this paper* because this depends on the availability of data from a re-contact survey that was just conducted in 2005. Rather, our purposes in this paper are to establish a baseline of information of migrants' and non-migrants' health, socioeconomic status, and social participation, and to examine the process by which older in-migrants become socially integrated subsequent to moving to nonmetro retirement counties.

Newcomers' integration is important from both the community's and individual migrants' perspectives. More effective integration into the community contributes to migrant health, longevity, and overall quality of life. From the destination community's point of view, better-integrated migrants provide time, experience and know-how that can contribute to accomplishing important communal goals.

CONCEPTUAL FRAMEWORK: MIGRATION AND SOCIAL INTEGRATION

Migration and Social Networks

Migration is a permanent or semi-permanent change of residence that disrupts everyday social relationships (Long, 1988). Hence, even when migration is voluntary, which is usually the case with retirement migration, it is initially disruptive of long term social involvements. Older in-migrants to nonmetro retirement destinations face the challenge of establishing new social relationships, and some persons are more successful in doing this than are others. As indicated earlier, few studies have focused on the adaptation of older migrants to nonmetro retirement areas, even though migrant adjustment has been a major focus of research on international migration. Such studies demonstrate that social networks are a critical element in the migrant incorporation process (Alba & Nee, 1999; Zhou & Logan, 1991). They show that having access to co-ethnic social capital in the destination facilitates migrant adjustment and that maintaining social relationships with one's community of origin can also affect the adaptation experience. Accordingly, in addition to examining the usual socioeconomic correlates of social integration, our study examines the extent to which older in-migrants to nonmetro retirement counties had pre-existing social relationships in destination communities and whether they maintain contacts in their origin community subsequent to moving to a nonmetro retirement destination. The presence of pre-existing relationships might facilitate older migrants' success in becoming socially integrated in nonmetro retirement destinations, and, conversely, maintaining contact with one's origin might diminish one's inclination to become socially involved in a new area of residence.

Social Integration

We follow Pillemer, Moen, Wethington, and Glasgow in conceptualizing social integration as "the entire set of an individual's connections to others in his or her environment" (2000, p. 8). This broad definition of social integration refers to both participation in meaningful roles and the network of social contacts. Hence, to say that an individual is highly integrated in this sense means being embedded in a network of social ties, the most proximate of which are family, friendships, and affiliations with community organizations (Booth et al., 1991; Glasgow & Sofranko, 1980). This usage differs from narrower conceptualizations simply involving the personal support that people gain through family and friendship networks. In contrast, our concept also includes participation in clubs, volunteer agencies, and other organizations. While family and friendship relationships tend to yield emotional support, information, and various resources and services (such as caregiving and transportation), formal organizations serve as educational arenas where participants become better problem solvers, and they provide bridging ties linking persons to a constellation of community organizations that provide information and supportive services. Both formal and informal social integration have been shown to enhance older people's well-being (Glasgow, 2004; House et al., 1988; Moen et al., 1989; Young & Glasgow, 1998).

THE RETIREMENT MIGRATION SURVEY

This research examines survey data obtained from recent older migrants to nonmetro retirement destination counties and a matched sample of longer-term older residents of these same counties. Nonmetro retirement destination counties

Figure 8.1. Nonmetropolitan Retirement Destination Counties as Defined in 1990

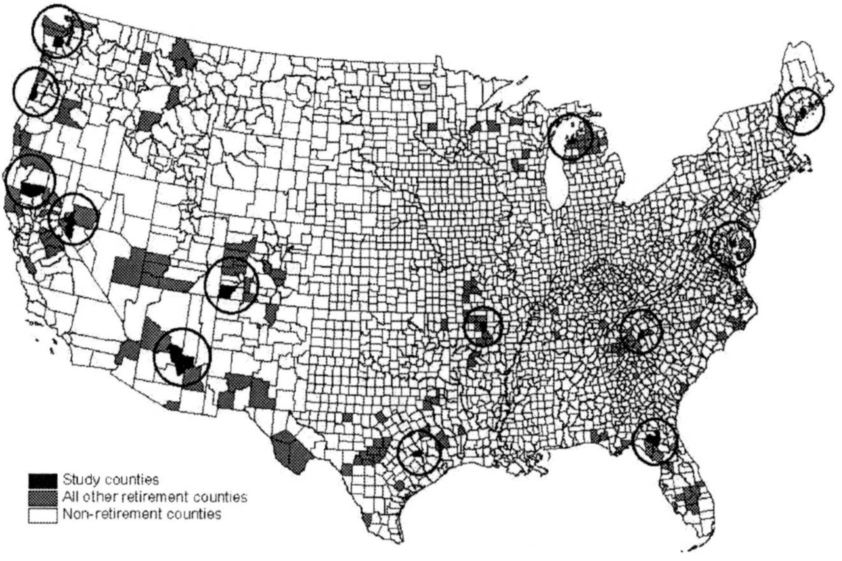

Source: ERS-USDA, based on the results of the 1990 Census of Population.
Note: A nonmetro retirement destination county is defined as having 15% or greater increase in population aged 60+ from in movement between 1980 and 1990.

are defined as having a 15 percent or greater increase in population age 60+ from in-movement between 1980–1990 (Cook & Mizer, 1994).[4] From the list of 190 nonmetro retirement destination counties, we selected 14 counties that reflect the diversity of contexts represented in this analytical category. Even though nonmetro retirement destinations are concentrated in the South and Southwest, we purposely selected study sites in other regions where retirement migration is also well established (see Figure 8.1). Hence, while our survey data are not statistically representative of the older population living in the 190 nonmetro retirement destination counties, they do reflect the broad diversity of local conditions contained in areas that attract older persons to nonmetro America.

Data were collected by Cornell University's Survey Research Institute in the fall of 2002 using computer-assisted telephone survey techniques. Age-targeted samples for the 14 study counties were obtained from a commercial vendor, and respondents were screened with respect to residence in a study county,[5] age 60 to 85, and length of residence. Migrants were defined as persons who had lived in the county for five or fewer years. The sample was stratified to obtain approximately equal numbers of migrants (368) and longer-term residents (420). The resulting sample represents the population age 60–85 in these 14 counties. When a contacted household contained more than one person age 60–85, one older household member was chosen randomly to be the respondent. Each telephone interview lasted approximately 30 minutes.

NONMETRO RETIREMENT DESTINATION COUNTIES

Definition and Location

While only 190 counties meet the nonmetro retirement destination criteria, past research indicates that retiree in-migration at somewhat lower rates is a widespread phenomena throughout much of nonmetropolitan America. In other words, achieving the status of a retirement destination may be somewhat rare, but older migrants are moving to rural counties throughout the nation at somewhat lower rates. Hence, our examination of retiree adjustment has relevance far beyond the small set of counties where the rate of older in-migration is highest.

Nonmetro retirement destination counties are disproportionately located in the Southeast, Southwest, Mountain, and Pacific Coast sub-regions (see Figure 8.1). They are most likely to be located in amenity-rich retirement areas with warm climates, especially those with lakes, coastal areas, and other scenic resources. However, some nonmetro retirement destinations are located in Michigan and Wisconsin, the Missouri Ozarks, and in New England. Many retirement areas have recreation- and resort-based economies which may have been well established prior to the initiation of retirement in-migration.

Comparative Profile of Retirement Destination Counties

The data in Table 8.1 show that retirement destinations are areas of growth and socioeconomic advantage. Retirement destination counties grew by 28.4 percent between 1990 and 2000 compared with only 8.3 percent for other nonmetro counties (Table 8.1). Moreover, almost one out of every four residents of retirement counties lived elsewhere five years prior to the 1990 and 2000 censuses compared to only about 18 percent in other nonmetro areas.

Compared with other nonmetro counties, retirement destinations had a slightly lower percentage of their population aged less than 20, and a slightly higher share above age 65. This is unsurprising given the fact that this category of counties had relatively high in-migration at age 60 and above during the previous decade. The percent 65 and above remained constant during the 1990s in both retirement and non-retirement counties because new entrants to these age groups were relatively few since they are members of small depression-era birth cohorts. However, the percentage 65 and above will increase rapidly in the near future when the large baby boom cohorts begin entering this age group.

Table 8.1. Comparative Profile of Retirement Destination and Other Nonmetro Counties, 1990–2000

	Retirement Counties (N = 190)		Other Nonmetro Counties (N = 2115)	
	1990	2000	1990	2000
Percent of Population				
Under age 20	28.4	25.9	30.2	28.5
Ages 20–64	54.8	56.3	54.1	56.1
Ages 65+	18.8	18.8	15.7	15.5
Median Per Capita Income in 1999 (USD)	$11,305	$17,807	$10,194	$16,046
Median Household Income in 1999 (USD)	$22,732	$34,490	$21,637	$32,258
Percent Below Poverty Level	15.0	13.3	18.0	14.9
Percent of Population Employed (Age 16+)	52.0	52.5	55.2	56.1
Percent of Population Unemployed (Age 16+)	3.9	3.4	4.0	3.5
Percent of Population Age 5+ Years Lived In A Different County In 1995	25.3	24.3	18.0	18.8
Percent of Population Change, 1990–2000		28.4		8.3

Source: 1990 and 2000 US Census of Population.

Retirement destination counties are substantially better off financially than other nonmetro counties. Retirement counties have higher income and lower poverty rates than their counterparts with lower rates of retiree in-migration. The relative income of retirement destinations and other nonmetro counties was essentially unchanged between 1990 and 2000, although retirement destinations increased their advantage slightly with respect to median household income (the ratio increased from 1.05 to 1.07). Relative income examined through the lens of personal income and poverty, however, was the same in both 1990 and 2000. Employment-related measures are very similar in both county types. Residents of non-retirement counties are only slightly more likely to be employed than persons living in retirement destinations, and this difference has remained essentially constant since 1990. Similarly, unemployment rates do not vary between retirement and non-retirement counties.

These data are consistent with previous research (Longino & Crown, 1990; Glasgow & Reeder, 1990) demonstrating that retirement in-migration has a positive impact on nonmetro economies. Hence, it is understandable that state and local areas have devoted significant resources to attracting retirees as an economic development strategy (Reeder, 1998). Given the expectation of rapid aging during the next several decades, this further underlines the importance of understanding the retiree migration process as an aspect of rural social and economic change during the 21st century.

WHO MOVES TO NONMETRO RETIREMENT DESTINATIONS, AND WHERE DO THEY COME FROM?

Metro-Nonmetro Origin

Previous research had shown that older in-migrants to nonmetro retirement destinations came overwhelmingly from metropolitan places. In fact, Glasgow's (1995) study of service utilization among older in-migrants to nonmetro retirement destinations in the Middle Atlantic region showed that nine of ten originated in metropolitan areas. In contrast, our data show that a much lower share of older in-migrants originate in metropolitan counties. As shown in Table 8.2, over one quarter of in-migrants come from other nonmetro counties.[6] Moreover, nonmetro-origin in-migrants are more likely to cross state boundaries while metro-origin in-migrants are evenly split between the same and a different state. Glasgow's data were collected in 1993 when the "rural rebound" was in full swing, while our survey was conducted in 2002 when the volume of migration of older people to nonmetro areas had diminished (Johnson & Fuguitt, 2000).[7] Hence, the geographic pattern of older migration to nonmetro areas may have changed during this time as well. In addition, Glasgow's earlier survey was restricted to the Middle Atlantic region with its plethora of large metro areas, and this may account

Table 8.2. Metro-Nonmetro Origin of In-Migrants to Nonmetro Retirement Destinations, 2002

	Residence Category		
	Metro	Nonmetro	Total
Same State	35%	11%	54%
Different State	37%	16%	46%
TOTAL	73%	27%	100%

Source: Cornell Retirement Migration Survey.

for the somewhat different origins of older migrants in the present study which was conducted in 14 different nonmetro locations throughout the United States.

Characteristics of In-Migrants to Nonmetro Retirement Counties

The data in Table 8.3 show a comparative profile of migrants and longer-term older residents. These data reconfirm the results of previous research indicating that older migrants to nonmetro retirement destinations are positively selected (Glasgow, 1995; Longino, 1990). In-migrants are younger, more likely to be male (because they are younger and more likely to be married and living with their spouse), and more highly educated. The education data for longer-term residents are higher than expected. While longer-term residents have less education than in-migrants, over one third of longer-term residents have completed college, and only 8 percent have less than a high school education. The unexpectedly high percentage of college graduates among longer-term residents may reflect the fact that nonmetro retirement destinations have been attracting older migrants for some time, and hence many longer-term residents may themselves have been migrants at a previous time. This would diminish the socioeconomic differences between older in-migrants and longer-term older residents.

Nine out of ten in-migrants have retired at least once in their life compared with 83 percent of longer-term older residents. However, between 35 and 40 percent of both migrants and longer-term older residents currently work for pay. Some of these persons are labor force re-entrants, while others have worked continuously without ever retiring. The importance of current earnings, however, should not be over-emphasized. Less than two out of ten respondents reported that earnings from work were an important component of their current total household income. By comparison, 60 percent of longer-term residents and in-migrants indicate that Social Security is important, and over half of in-migrants and 40 percent of longer-term residents state that savings are a very important component of their total income (data not shown here). In summary, while these data show the familiar selectivity of in-migrants, differences between migrants and longer-term older residents of nonmetro retirement destinations are less than expected.

Similar to the socioeconomic data shown above, the data in the lower part of Table 8.3 indicate that in-migrants are in somewhat better health than longer-term residents, but the differences are modest.[8] The most important conclusion that can be drawn from these data is that older residents of the 14 nonmetro retirement destination counties are in remarkably good health, regardless of their migration status. This lack of difference is surprising since longer-term residents are significantly older, on average, than their in-migrant counterparts. Still, over 80 percent of both groups rate their health good or excellent, less than one third have been diagnosed with a new medical condition during the past two years, and fewer than one in four have stayed overnight in a hospital during this time. Predictably, respondents report a very low level of activity limitation, with longer-term residents

Table 8.3. Comparative Profile of In-Migrants vs. Longer-Term Older Residents in Nonmetro Retirement Destinations, 2002

	Migrants	Non-Migrants
Demographic and Socioeconomic Characteristics:	*(Percent unless otherwise noted)*	
Median Age (years)	68.1	71.0
≥70 yrs	36.8	56.6
Female	48.6	66.2
<High School	3.5	8.1
High School Graduate	23.9	28.5
College or Post-Graduate	43.5	34.7
Ever retired	91.0	82.7
Currently working for pay	36.9	34.8
Median years in county	2.9	22.1
Health Status:		
Rating health good or excellent compared to others	85.8	81.9
Having illness or injury during past two years	28.3	31.4
Utilization of Medical Care:		
Visited doctor ≥10 times in past yr.	15.1	18.5
Stayed overnight in hospital in last 2 yrs.*	21.6	23.8
More than 1 overnight stay	29.5	38.0
Activity Limitation:		
Limited with respect to:		
Walking 6 blocks	22.0	29.0
Climbing stairs	19.0	21.1
Doing household tasks	12.8	16.0
Going shopping	8.1	10.2
Volunteering	9.1	16.4
Driving a car	8.1	9.1
Participating in recreation	18.8	25.5
Bending, kneeling, or stooping	26.9	26.3
	(N = 368)	(N = 420)

* Respondents with at least one stay.
Source: Cornell Retirement Migration Survey.

experiencing slightly more limitations but for the most part still being able to participate in the activities of daily living.

LEVEL OF SOCIAL PARTICIPATION AMONG MIGRANTS AND LONGER-TERM OLDER RESIDENTS OF RETIREMENT DESTINATIONS

Our general expectation was that in-migrants would be substantially *less* well integrated in the retirement destination communities than longer-term residents. Simply comparing persons who have lived in a place for five or fewer years (migrants) and persons who have lived there for more than five years (non-migrants), however, could be problematic if a substantial number of non-migrants moved in a couple of years before the somewhat arbitrary five-year cut off. Fortunately, this is not a problem in the present research because while some longer-term residents did move to the retirement destination during the past decade, most have lived there far longer. In fact, longer-term residents have lived in their current county for an average of 22.1 years (Table 8.3); 46 percent have lived in their current county for 20 years or longer, and less than 25 percent have lived there for 10 or fewer years (data not shown).

Informal Social Relationships

As expected, the data in Table 8.4 show that longer-term residents are more likely to have primary group relationships in the retirement destination counties than is true of in-migrants. However, in-migrants also have a considerable number of family and friend connections in their new communities. Half of longer-term older residents have at least one child within a half hour drive, and a quarter have two or more children close by. Grandchildren and other relatives are also quite

Table 8.4. Informal Social Relationships of In-Migrants and Longer-Term Residents of Nonmetro Retirement Destination Counties, 2002

	Migrants	Non-Migrants
Percent with at least 1 child within 1/2 hour	34.9	49.7
Percent with 2 or more children within 1/2 hour	8.4	24.2
Percent with at least 1 grandchild within 1/2 hour	28.6	39.7
Percent who see their children 5 or more times per year	41.7	51.8
Percent with other relatives within 1 hour*	31.8	42.0
Frequency of visits with friends	1–2 times/wk	1–2 times/wk.

* Other than children and/or grandchildren.
Source: Cornell Retirement Migration Survey.

accessible to longer-term residents. Similarly, a fairly large number of recent migrants to nonmetro retirement destinations have family members living nearby. While their level of access to family is less than that of longer-term residents, over one third of migrants have a child within a half hour drive, 29 percent have grandchildren nearby, and 32 percent have other relatives in their immediate vicinity. These findings are in contrast to Litwak and Longino's (1987) developmental theory of elderly migration which hypothesizes that retirees move to amenity-based locations at the time of retirement and subsequently make a second move to be close to their children later in life, especially if they experience declining health or an adverse life course event such as the loss of their spouse. In contrast, our data seem to indicate that many older persons consolidate their family ties much earlier in life during their first move after retiring.

These data provide insights into the destination selection process among older persons who move to nonmetro retirement destinations. It seems obvious that, in addition to amenities, the location of family and friends is an important consideration in their destination choice. Our survey (data not shown here) show that four of ten migrants visited friends in their new communities prior to moving there, and 48 percent of migrants with relatives in the destination county visited them prior to moving in. Thus, for many migrants, destination choice is steered by the location of friends and relatives. Physical access to friends and family is reflected in visitation patterns. Both migrants and longer-term residents report average visiting of once or twice per week. From the standpoint of informal social integration, older residents of nonmetro retirement counties, both recent migrants and longer-term residents, appear to have ample opportunities to interact with and obtain support from friends and family.

Formal Social Participation

Participation in formal organizations and community activities is shown in Table 8.5. Over two-thirds of longer-term older residents participate in at least one type of formal organization compared with 58 percent of in-migrants. Longer-term residents are somewhat more likely to participate in service, political, and volunteer organizations, but migrants and non-migrants are equally likely to participate in social clubs (although longer-term residents belong to more clubs). Similarly, participation in community activities does not vary much between migrants and longer-term older residents. Longer-term older residents attend religious services more regularly, but in-migrants are more likely to participate in team or individual sports, to attend cultural events, and to use a gym or health club or take an exercise class. Hence, while the data in Tables 8.4 and 8.5 show that longer-term older residents are somewhat more integrated in both informal social relationships and formal organizations, migrant vs. non-migrant differences in participation are modest. Clearly, *migration status is not the principal factor explaining why some older residents of nonmetro retirement counties are more socially integrated than others.*

Table 8.5. Formal Social Participation of In-Migrants and Longer-Term Residents of Nonmetro Retirement Destination Counties, 2002

	Migrants	Non-Migrants
Participation in Formal Organizations:		
Percent participate in at least 1 type of formal organization	58.5	63.4
Percent participate in service organizations	22.8	31.0
Median number of organizations	(1)	(2)
Percent participate in political organizations*	8.9	13.1
Percent participate in social clubs	32.3	32.6
Median number of clubs	(1)	(2)
Percent participate in organized volunteer activity*	38.1	42.6
Participation in Community Activities:		
Average frequency of attendance at religious services	Monthly	2–3 times/ month
Percent never attend:	36.3	32.1
Percent attend sometimes or often:		
Senior Center	12.3	12.6
Adult Education	16.6	18.4
Team or Individual Sports (participate)	21.7	16.2
Cultural Events	49.2	34.0
Gym/Health Club/Exercise Class	22.0	19.0

* Median number of political organizations is less than 1 for both groups.
Source: Cornell Retirement Migration Survey.

Why Are Some Older Residents of Retirement Destinations More Likely to Participate in Formal Organizations?

In this section we examine factors associated with variability in participation in formal social organizations among migrants and longer-term older residents in nonmetro retirement destinations. Even though our data indicate that migrants and longer-term residents have similar levels of participation in formal social organizations, they also show a substantial amount of variation in participation within both the migrant and non-migrant groups. We focus on three types of factors that have been shown in previous research to be associated with social participation: (a) socio-demographic status, (b) health and activity limitation, and (c) involvement in close primary social relationships (Young & Glasgow, 1998). Logistic regression provides a multivariate technique for examining factors that are associated with the likelihood of participation in formal organizations, with the outcome variable coded 1 = participates, and 0 = does not participate. Three logistic regression

Table 8.6. Factors Associated with Organizational Participation among Older Persons in Nonmetro Retirement Destinations, 2002

	Participation Index (0, 1)		
	Non-Migrants	Migrants	Migrants
Currently Married	0.1894	0.2832	0.5632
Age (Yrs.)	−0.0077	−0.0185	−0.0271
Male	−0.1087	0.1024	0.0482
Adult Kids Close	−0.2670*	−0.1487	−0.1051
Relatives Close	−0.0046	−0.0519	−0.0693
Years in County	0.0189*	0.0224	0.1205
Education (Yrs.)	0.2790***	0.1633***	0.1886***
Currently Working	−0.4697	−0.6961*	−0.6456
Good Health	0.4302*	0.0244	0.001
Problem Walking 6 Blocks	−0.4088	−0.6598*	−0.5204
Problem Driving	0.2248	−0.3789	−0.7673
Metro Origin			−0.1948
Owned Land			−0.0002
Vacationed Here			0.314
Not Visited Friends			−0.559
No Friends Here			−0.1693
Not Visited Relatives			−0.2914
No Relatives Here			−0.0322
Returned to Origin			−0.3341
Constant	−4.138	−0.8929	−0.3718
−2 Log Likelihood	451.979	435.530	344.059
Pseudo R^2	.224	.121	.154

$p < .05$, $^{***}p < .001$.

models were run, and their results are shown in Table 8.6. The first model examines factors associated with participation in formal organizations among non-migrants in the 14 retirement destination counties. The second model examines the same set of variables but only among migrants. The third migrant model includes additional independent variables that were only asked of migrants and reflect their contact and associations in the retirement destination prior to their move there, as well as contact with their origin community subsequent to their move.

Prior research on social participation among older persons has shown that participation is higher among the young-old, healthier persons, those with few activity limitations, and persons with more education (Young & Glasgow, 1998). Conversely, participation has been shown to be lower among persons with dense networks of close ties that result in frequent interaction with friends and family and among persons who work for pay outside of the home (Moen et al., 2000). The rationale for expecting greater social activity among younger and healthier persons is straightforward. Simply put, these older people are more physically able to participate than the old-old and persons with physical limitations on their activities. Better-educated older people are more likely to participate in community activities because education promotes the value of community service and participation. In addition, more highly educated older people have more financial resources and can afford to pay dues and participation fees, and they can better afford transportation and other costs associated with involvement in service, political, social, and/or volunteer organizations. In contrast, participation in formal organizations has been shown to be lower among older people with frequent primary group involvements because interaction with family and friends is thought to substitute for social involvements in the wider community. Finally, employed persons are less likely to participate because of time constraints associated with their work schedules, although on-the-job social connections may bridge people to other social involvements (Moen et al., 2000).

The non-migrant analysis reconfirms some of these earlier findings, but the results seldom reach the level of statistical significance. Education has the most consistent positive association with organizational participation.[9] Better health is also positively associated with participation. Having children close by has the expected negative association with organizational participation. In contrast, while older age, having relatives nearby, currently working, and being physically limited are in the expected negative direction in association with organizational participation among older residents of nonmetro retirement destinations, these effects fail to reach statistical significance.

We included length of residence in the logistic regression even though our previous cross tabular analysis did not demonstrate substantial differences in organizational participation between migrants and older residents who have lived in the retirement destination five or more years. While the five-year migration cut off is somewhat arbitrary, previous research has shown that residential stability is positively associated with community involvement (Sampson, 1988). Hence, regardless of the absence of a migrant/non-migrant difference in the cross tabular analysis, we wanted to examine whether duration of residence makes a difference once other variables are controlled. The data in Table 8.6 show the expected positive relationship between length of residence and participation in formal organizations among longer-term residents of retirement destination counties.

Why Are Some Recent Migrants to Retirement Destinations More Likely to Participate in Social Organizations?

While the five-year migration cut off may be somewhat arbitrary, it identifies a subgroup of older residents of retirement destinations who have lived there relatively briefly. Why are some of these newer residents more socially involved than others? In addition to the factors shown for non-migrants in Table 8.6, research indicates that contact with the retirement destination prior to moving there should increase a migrant's knowledge of the destination community and enhance the chances that in-migrants will become socially involved in a relatively brief amount of time (Glasgow & Sofranko, 1980). As indicated earlier, recent migrants to the 14 nonmetro retirement destinations had a variable amount of prior contact with destination counties before they moved there. Over one-quarter owned property in the destination prior to moving, about half had vacationed there, and about one-third had visited friends or relatives who lived in the destination county prior to their move.[10] These types of prior contacts have been shown to be important factors in steering migrants to particular nonmetro destinations (Williams & McMillen, 1980; Williams & Sofranko, 1979). Everything else being equal, one would expect that in-migrants with prior experience in their new residences should have more information about the community, more knowledge of opportunities to become involved, and perhaps a stronger commitment to the place than recent in-migrants who had little or no prior connection to the place previous to moving and/or who had never been there before.

In contrast, maintaining contact with one's previous community might be expected to reduce social participation in the destination during the first several years of residence. Old ties that are maintained might substitute for new involvements and reduce one's inclination to join new organizations. This would be especially true if migrants belonged to "cosmopolitan" organizations in their origin communities. Such organizations have primarily non-local membership that would facilitate continued participation after migration (Richmond, 2003) and a reduced inclination to join new organizations in the destination. Seven out of ten in-migrants in our study have visited their origin community at least one time during the year prior to the survey, and nine of ten who made such visits did so to visit friends (the next most likely reasons for visiting were to obtain medical or dental care, 41 percent, and to shop, 39 percent). Accordingly, it seems that older in-migrants to nonmetro retirement destinations maintain fairly strong connections with their previous places of residence, and there is reason to believe that those who visit their previous home might be less likely to become socially involved in their new communities.

Migrants Compared with Non-Migrants

The logistic regression analysis displayed in the migrants' column in Table 8.6 examines factors related to variability in organizational participation among older persons who have lived in a retirement destination county for five years or less. Considering the variables examined for both longer-term older residents and migrants (Model A), these data show that among recent migrants, education has a strong positive effect on organizational involvement, while the likelihood of involvement is depressed by currently working and by activity limitations.

Other variables show expected relationships with participation, but none of these relationships reaches the level of statistical significance. For example, older migrants are less likely to participate in organizations; having children and other relatives close by reduces one's propensity of becoming involved in formal organizations; good or excellent health enhances participation in organizations; length of residence in the retirement destination is positively related to involvement in community organizations; and migrants who have problems driving are less likely to participate.

Prior Contact with the Destination

The analysis in Model B examines whether prior contact with the destination enhances the chances that a migrant will be socially involved in formal organizations after moving to the new community. While most of the relationships shown in this model are consistent with our expectations, none of these relationships reaches the level of statistical significance. Moreover, this model examines whether returning to one's origin community depresses the likelihood of participation among migrants. Again, the relationship is not statistically significant, and in fact it is in the opposite direction from our expectations. Hence, we find no statistically persuasive evidence that prior contact with the destination or continuing contact with the origin affects migrants' likelihood of becoming involved in formal organizations in retirement destination counties. As was true in the two previous models, education is the only variable to increase consistently and strongly the likelihood of participation in formal organizations among older residents of nonmetro retirement destinations.

SUMMARY AND CONCLUSIONS

This analysis presents a picture of who is moving to nonmetropolitan retirement destination counties, where they come from, their primary group ties, and their post-move levels of organizational participation. Our analysis reconfirms some findings of previous research on retirement migration, but some of our results are at variance with previous research. Consistent with previous studies, in-migrants to the 14 retirement destination counties are positively selected with respect to younger age, higher education, greater health, and absence of activity limitation. As with previous research, we found that longer-term residents are somewhat more likely to be embedded in informal social relationships with family and friends, although in-migrants are not lacking in these types of social connections. The fact that in-migrants have substantial kin and friendship ties in nonmetro retirement destinations prior to moving there makes us re-examine theories of migration among older populations in the United States. Prior research indicated that retirement migration is primarily motivated by the presence of amenities in destination communities (Litwak & Longino, 1987). Our research suggests that family reunification may also be a motive shaping retirees' destination choice. Moreover, previous research indicated that amenity-seeking older migrants are likely to make a subsequent move later in life to be closer to their children. Our research suggests that family reunification often occurs earlier in the life course, not later in life as a result of declining health, loss of a spouse, or other adverse circumstances. In contrast to previous research, older in-migrants in our survey are less likely to originate in metropolitan areas, and their level of participation in organizations is greater than we had expected.

Our analysis of factors associated with organizational participation among older residents in nonmetro retirement destination counties showed that educational attainment is the only consistent predictor of organizational participation. In addition, we found modest evidence that having children close by depresses participation (especially among non-migrants), duration of residence increases the likelihood of participation, currently working depresses participation (especially among migrants), and health and lack of activity limitations are positively associated with involvement in formal organizations. Contrary to our expectations, having prior experience in one's new community does not enhance the ease of becoming involved in community organizations, and maintaining contacts in one's origin community does not have a depressive effect on participation in one's new residence.

Therefore, while this study has helped us think systematically about the process by which older in-migrants to nonmetro retirement communities become socially integrated, it has raised as many questions as it has resolved. Reconfirming the education effect is reassuring, but why does education have such a strong and pervasive impact on participation? Perhaps better-educated persons are more likely to participate in organizations because they develop "bridging social capital" in school (e.g., the longer one attends school, the wider is one's network of affiliations). Or perhaps students are socialized to appreciate the value of social participation, and the longer one studies, the stronger the lesson. Understanding education's effect on participation is a theoretical challenge that we have not fully surmounted at this time. We also need to examine the reasons why age does not have a depressive effect on participation. The association between informal social relationships with family and friends and participation in the formal organizational sphere is not fully understood. Recent migrants to nonmetro retirement destinations have a substantial amount of prior experience in their new communities prior to moving there. However, contrary to our expectations, we found that prior contact does not enhance the chances that one will become organizationally involved soon after arrival. These questions await further analysis. This paper has provided some insights into the process through which new residents become socially involved in retirement destinations, but further research is needed to elaborate this process. Only after we understand how in-migrants become socially integrated, and how longer-term older residents maintain their social connections, will we be able to understand whether and how social integration makes a positive contribution to the health and well-being of older residents in nonmetro retirement destination communities.

ENDNOTES

1. Acknowledgement: This research was supported by a grant from the USDA's National Research Initiative and by Hatch grant #159-7925 from the New York State Agricultural Experiment Station at Cornell University. The authors wish to acknowledge Bharat Pathak and Laszlo Kulcsar for conducting the computer analysis reported in this paper and William Kandel for his constructive comments.
2. This is true of the "young old" population. In contrast, when the oldest old move they are more likely to move toward metropolitan areas to be close to their children or better medical care (Glasgow & Beale 1985; Litwak & Longino, 1987).
3. Older in-migrants made a relatively small contribution to the 1990s nonmetro population rebound because the number of new entrants to the older age groups was diminished as a result of the aging of relatively small depression era birth cohorts (Johnson & Fuguitt, 2000).
4. In-migration rates among retirement destinations ranged from 15 percent to 121 percent. Age-specific net migration data for counties during 1990–2000 were unavailable when this analysis was conducted. Hence, we relied on 1980–90 data to identify nonmetro retirement destination counties. The number and location of such counties has changed marginally since 1990.
5. Age-targeted samples are based on telephone area codes that sometimes span more than one county. Hence, it is possible that some persons in the age-targeted sample could actually live in a contiguous county and not in the study county. Individuals who did not live in one of our study counties did not meet our residence criterion and were screened out.
6. Origin patterns differ among the 14 retirement counties. Less than two thirds of in-migrants come from metropolitan counties in Baxter, Arkansas; Lincoln, Maine; and Lincoln, Oregon, but more than 80 percent have metropolitan origins in Gila, Arizona; Talbot, Maryland; and Tehema, California.
7. As shown in chapter 2 of this book, net migration rates among persons 60+ increased during the 1990–2000 decade even though the volume of migration at these ages declined because potential migrants were drawn from small depression-era cohorts.
8. Some people question the reliability of self reported health, but a substantial body of literature has substantiated the accuracy of such measures (Idler & Kasl, 1991; Wolinsky & Johnson, 1992).
9. Income also had a positive association with participation in previous bivariate analyses, but we deleted it from the multivariate analysis because more than one third of respondents failed to answer the income question. Accordingly, retaining income in the multivariate analysis would have substantially diminished the number of cases with information for all respondents.
10. In contrast, only 8.7 percent had ever lived in the destination previously.

REFERENCES

Alba, R., & Nee, V. (1999). Rethinking assimilation theory for a new era of immigration. In C. Hirschman (Ed.), *The handbook of international migration* (pp. 137–160). New York: Sage.

Booth, A., Edwards, J., & Johnson, D. (1991). Social integration and divorce. *Social Forces, 70*(2), 201–244.

Cook, P., & Mizer, K. (1994). *The revised ERS county typology* (Rural Development Research Report, 89). Washington, DC: U.S. Department of Agriculture, Economic Research Service.

De Jong, G., Wilmoth, J., Angel, J., & Cornwall, G. (1995). Motives and the geographic mobility of very old Americans. *Journal of Gerontology: Social Sciences, 50B*(6), S395–S404.

Fulton, J., Fuguitt, G., & Gibson, R. (1997). Recent changes in metropolitan-nonmetropolitan migration streams. *Rural Sociology, 62* (3), 363–384.

Glasgow, N. (1995). Retirement migration and the use of services in nonmetropolitan counties. *Rural Sociology, 60*(2), 224–243.

Glasgow, N. (2004). Healthy aging in rural America. In N. Glasgow, L. Wright-Morton, & N. Johnson (Eds.), *Critical issues in rural health* (pp. 271–281). Ames, IA: Blackwell.

Glasgow, N., & Beale, C. (1985). Rural elderly in demographic perspective. *Rural Development Perspectives, 2*, 22–26.

Glasgow, N., & Reeder, R. (1990). Economic and fiscal implications of nonmetropolitan retirement migration. *Journal of Applied Gerontology, 9* (4), 433–451.

Glasgow, N., & Sofranko, A. (1980). Migrant adjustment and integration in the new residence. In A. Sofranko & J. Williams (Eds.), *Rebrith of rural America: Rural migration in the Midwest* (pp. 87–104). Ames, IA: North Central Regional Center for Rural Development.

House, J., Landis, K., & Umberson, D. (1988). Social relations and health. *Science, 241*, 540–545.

Idler, E.L., & Kasl, S. (1991). Health perceptions and survival: Do global evaluations of health status really predict mortality? *Journal of Gerontology, 46*, S55–S65.

Johnson, K., & Fuguitt, G. (2000). Continuity and change in rural migration patterns. *Rural Sociology, 65*(1), 27–49.

Litwak, E., & Longino, C. (1987). Migration patterns among the elderly: A developmental perspective. *Gerontologist, 27*(3), 266–272.

Long, L. (1988). *Migration and residential mobility in the United States.* New York: Sage.

Longino, C. (1990). Geographic distribution and migration. In R. Binstock & L. George (Eds.), *Handbook of aging and the social sciences* (pp. 45–63). San Diego, CA: Academic Press.

Longino, C., & Crown, W. (1990). Retirement migration and interstate income transfers. *Gerontologist, 30*(6), 784–789.

Moen, P., Dempster-McClain, D., & Williams, R. (1989). Social integration and longevity: An event history analysis of women's roles and resilience. *American Sociological Review, 54*, 635–648.

Moen, P., Fields, V., Quick, H.E., & Hofmeister, H. (2000). A life-course approach to retirement and social integration. In K. Pillemer, P. Moen, E. Wethington, & N. Glasgow (Eds.), *Social integration in the second half of life* (pp. 75–107). Baltimore: Johns Hopkins University Press.

Pillemer, K., Moen, P., Wethington, E., & Glasgow, N. (2000). *Social integration in the second half of life.* Baltimore: Johns Hopkins University Press.

Reeder, R. (1998). *Retiree-attraction policies for rural development* (Agriculture Information Bulletin 741). Washington, DC: U.S. Department of Agriculture, Economic Research Service.

Richmond, D. (2003). Embeddedness in voluntary organizations and the timing of geographic moves. *Sociological Forum, 18* (2), 295–322.

Sampson, R. (1988). Local friendship ties and community involvement in mass society: A multilevel systematic model. *American Sociological Review, 53*(5), 766–759.

Siegel, P., Leuthold, F., & Stallman, J. (1995). Planned retirement/recreation communities are among development strategies open to amenity-rich rural areas. *Rural Development Perspectives, 10*(2), 8–14.

Stallman, J., & Siegel, P. (1995). Attracting retirees as an economic development strategy: Looking into the future. *Economic Development Quarterly, 9*(4), 372–382.

Williams, J., & McMillen, D. (1980). Migration decision making among nonmetropolitan-bound migrants. In D. Brown & J. Wardwell (Eds.), *New directions in rural-urban migration* (pp. 189–212). New York: Academic Press.

Williams, J., & Sofranko, A. (1979). Motivations for the inmigration component of population turnaround in nonmetropolitan areas. *Demography, 16*(2), 239–255.

Wolinsky, F.D., & Johnson, R.J. (1992). Perceived health status and mortality among older men and women. *Journal of Gerontology, 47*, S304–S312.

Young, F., & Glasgow, N. (1998). Voluntary social participation and health. *Research on Aging, 20*(3), 339–362.

Zhou, M., & Logan, J. (1991). In and out of Chinatown: Residential mobility and segregation of New York City's Chinese. *Social Forces, 70*(2), 387–408.

CHAPTER 9

AGRICULTURAL DEPENDENCE AND CHANGING POPULATION IN THE GREAT PLAINS[1]

KENNETH M. JOHNSON AND RICHARD W. RATHGE

The Great Plains hold a special place in the history of the United States. Sweeping in a broad swath from the Canadian border down to Texas and New Mexico, they represent one of the most productive agricultural regions in the world. The region is also one of the most thinly settled areas of the country. On the Great Plains, technological innovations and a changing organizational structure have allowed fewer and fewer farmers to produce more and more food. One consequence has been a persistent displacement of farmers and those in the agricultural support infrastructure, together with their families, from the rural Heartland. A lack of alternative employment for those displaced has set in motion an unprecedented movement of residents from rural areas to the region's metropolitan centers. Our interest here is in exploring the linkage between agricultural dependency and population redistribution in the Great Plains and its relevance for public policy.

Human ecology offers a useful theoretical perspective to guide our discussion because it recognizes the interdependence between change in organization, technology, and population (Adamchak et al., 1999; Johnson, 1985). Such a theoretical model provides a context for examining how the remarkable technological and organizational innovations that have made Great Plains agriculture so productive have dramatically realigned the settlement patterns within the region. It also allows us to consider how the region's shifting population has influenced and will continue to influence the organizational and technological structure of the Great Plains. In particular, the protracted loss of young adults from rural areas has significant implications because both organizational and technological innovations depend on human capital. Likewise, the vitality and entrepreneurial spirit that drives technology is compromised by decades of dwindling youth. In turn, the smaller tax base created by population loss forces key government functions and private sector businesses to shut down or consolidate. In short, organizational structures from communities to volunteer services lose critical mass and can no longer be sustained.

W.A. Kandel & D.L. Brown (eds.), Population Change and Rural Society, 197–217.

Our goal in this paper is twofold. First, we examine the complex interplay of fertility, mortality and migration across time and space that produced the initial widespread population gains in the Great Plain, but later caused highly differential patterns of population growth and decline across the region. Second, we explore the policy implications of these population redistribution trends. Looking beyond the fundamental flaw of existing policy, which equates policy for the Great Plains with agriculture, we argue that the Great Plains are not homogeneous and that future policy for the region must offer an array of solutions to address its diverse needs.

DATA AND METHODS

Scholars differ in their delineation of the Great Plains (Adamchak et al., 1999; Gutmann et al., 1998; Rathge, 1995). Typically, the territory is bounded by Montana and Minnesota on the north and New Mexico and Texas on the south. The area of the Great Plains is usually defined using an ecological or agricultural context. For example, Gutmann and his colleagues delineated the Great Plains based on precipitation and elevation as well as geography (Gutmann et al., 1998). The United States Department of Agriculture defines the territory as having lower and more erratic rainfall, less timber, and less suitability for corn, cotton, and other crops without irrigation or periodic fallowing of land (Bogue & Beale, 1961). Our version is one suggested by Calvin Beale and includes 490 counties in 11 states (Figure 9.1). It is slightly more exclusive than other delineations of the Great Plains because its eastern boundary is west of other classification systems.

Counties are the units of analysis because they have historically stable boundaries and are a basic unit for reporting demographic, social, and economic data. We subdivide counties into metropolitan and nonmetropolitan based on the 1993 Office of Management and Budget definition. To avoid problems of longitudinal compatibility, any county classified as metropolitan in 1993 was considered metropolitan throughout the entire study period, even though it might have been nonmetropolitan under an earlier definition. Among the 490 Great Plains counties, 449 are classified as nonmetropolitan and 41 as metropolitan.

Nonmetropolitan counties are further subdivided to separate farming dependent counties from other nonmetropolitan counties. We use the USDA Economic Research Service definition to identify farming dependency. It identifies a county as farming dependent if farming contributed a weighted annual average of 20 percent or more of total labor and proprietor income over the three years from 1987 to 1989 (Cook & Mizer, 1994). In all, 278 nonmetropolitan Great Plains counties are farming dependent and 171 are not. Some of this latter group were once primarily agricultural counties but have since diversified their economies. Some non-farm counties benefit from their proximity to the metropolitan areas in the region (notably Denver), while others have recreational and scenic amenities that have become increasingly attractive as the transportation network improved

Figure 9.1. The Great Plains by Metro Status, Farm Status, and Population Change, 1950–2000

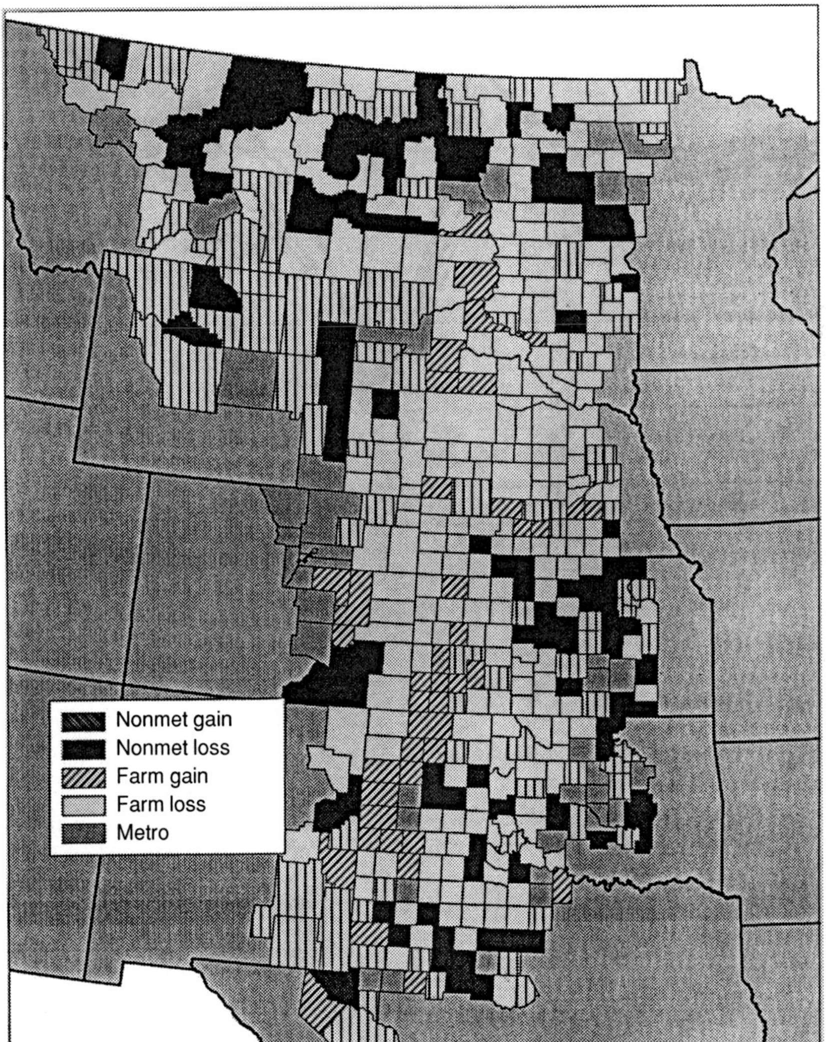

and interest in leisure increased. The remainder diversified their local economies through locational advantages, the efforts of local entrepreneurs, the influences of outside institutions (e.g., colleges, prisons, food processing facilities), or historical accident.

Most of the 41 metropolitan counties within the Great Plains lie on the region's periphery, such as Denver on the west, or Oklahoma City on the southeast.[2] Major metropolitan centers such as Dallas-Ft. Worth and Kansas City are just beyond the boundaries of the Great Plains, but they may also exert some influence on its closely located counties.

Population data for each county come from the United States Bureau of the Census. Births and deaths are from the Federal-State Cooperative Population Estimates. Estimates of overall net migration used here were derived by the residual method, whereby net migration is what is left when natural increase (births minus deaths) is subtracted from total population change (Johnson et al., 2003). Net migration includes net internal migration, net international migration, and differences in coverage of the various censuses.

POPULATION REDISTRIBUTION TRENDS ON THE GREAT PLAINS

The patterns of population change on the Great Plains over the past 130 years have been complex. Nonetheless, three distinct periods are evident and directly tied to advancements in technology. The first period, ending in the 1940s, was marked by initial rapid growth brought on by a flood of settlers to the region. The second period began after World War II with a significant agricultural restructuring that escalated the decline of rural agricultural counties. The last period began with a unique nonmetropolitan revival that was short-lived in the region but highlighted the significance of rural residential preference.

The Rural Growth Period on the Great Plains

In 1870, the Great Plains were very sparsely settled: fewer than 127,000 people, including a considerable number of Native Americans, lived in the Great Plains.[3] The population grew rapidly over the next six decades. By 1930, more than 6.8 million people resided in the area. Migration fueled much of this population gain as the relentless westward movement of the population and the great agricultural potential of the region attracted millions. Throughout this period, the vast majority of the population on the Great Plains resided in nonmetropolitan areas. In 1870, nearly 80 percent of the Great Plains residents lived in areas that remain nonmetropolitan to this day. Little had changed by 1930, when almost 74 percent of the Great Plains population still lived in nonmetropolitan areas. Such areas gained more than 4.9 million residents during the period. Territory that was metropolitan or would soon become so grew by 1.8 million during the same period. However, after 1930 the growth patterns in metropolitan and nonmetropolitan areas diverged. The nonmetropolitan population peaked in 1930, whereas the metropolitan population continued to grow.

Between 1930 and 1940, the Great Plains suffered a population loss of approximately 200,000. More than 75 percent of the counties in the region lost population during the decade. Most of the loss resulted from net out-migration. The Great Depression and severe drought forced many rural families to abandon farms, stores, and enterprises. The difficult situation also diminished fertility levels, resulting in less natural increase. The losses were most severe in the nonmetropolitan areas of the Great Plains, which lost 360,000 residents. In contrast, the metropolitan counties of the region gained more than 150,000.

Growth resumed during the 1940s, with the region as a whole gaining 558,000 residents. Natural increase fueled all of this growth. Migrants continued to leave the nonmetropolitan areas of the Plains, attracted by the recovering industrial sector of the nation's cities. Almost all the growth that did occur was in metropolitan areas. Overall, such counties gained over 630,000 residents, whereas nonmetropolitan counties lost more than 70,000.

Technology and the Bust Period

The year 1950 is an appropriate moment to pause to take stock of the demographic situation on the Great Plains. By that point the initial settlement surge was complete, and the Great Depression and Second World War were over. Against this historical backdrop of population change on the Great Plains, we can begin to examine the linkage between farm dependency and demographic change in the last half of the 20th century. Technological advances in farming were dramatically increasing productivity and efficiency. Between 1940 and 1989, agricultural output per hour of farm work rose 1,300 percent (Beale, 1993), and productivity per acre more than doubled (Albrecht & Murdock, 1990). In North Dakota, the average farm size expanded from roughly 500 acres to nearly 1,300 acres, reducing the number of farms in the state from 86,000 to approximately 30,000 (Rathge, 2002). For nearly 85 percent of the farm counties in the region, their peak population was reached prior to 1950. Nonetheless, farm counties still contained 26.9 percent of the 7.3 million people who resided on the Great Plains in 1950 (Table 9.1). This percentage would dwindle as the 20th century continued. Nonmetropolitan counties that were not farm dependent were home to nearly 2.7 million Great Plains residents in 1950, some 36.8 percent of the region's population; slightly fewer than half (47 percent) of these counties reached their peak population before 1950.

Masking the problems in the rural farm counties was an accelerated growth period for the region's metropolitan counties. Natural increase associated with the baby boom fueled all of this gain, offsetting net migration losses. Though the region as a whole gained population, farm counties sustained a 7.6 percent population decline (Table 9.2); even the surge of natural increase resulting from the baby boom was not sufficient to offset the net migration losses sustained in such counties. Nonmetropolitan counties that were not farm dependent grew by 4.7 percent during the 1950s. In contrast to the experience of nonmetropolitan counties, metropolitan areas of the Great Plains grew by 1.1 million (42 percent) between 1950 and 1960 (Table 9.2). The growth was fueled by the fertility gains

Table 9.1. Population in the Great Plains Counties by Year and County Type, 1950–2000

	Farm Counties		Other Nonmetropolitan Counties		Metropolitan Counties		Total Population of the Great Plains Counties (in 000's)	Great Plains as a Percent of the U.S. Population
Year	Number (in 000's)	Percent	Number (in 000's)	Percent	Number (in 000's)	Percent		
1950	1,957	26.9	2,676	36.8	2,647	36.4	7,280	4.8
1960	1,809	21.6	2,801	33.5	3,760	44.9	8,370	4.7
1970	1,617	18.5	2,707	30.9	4,432	50.6	8,757	4.3
1980	1,592	16.0	2,976	29.8	5,404	54.2	9,972	4.4
1990	1,439	13.9	2,921	28.2	5,992	57.9	10,352	4.2
2000	1,418	12.2	3,024	26.1	7,138	61.6	11,580	4.1

Source: United States Department of Agriculture, Economic Research Service; United States Census Bureau.

Table 9.2. Population Change in Great Plains Counties by Year and County Type, 1950–2000

Year	Total Population Change in the Great Plains Counties		County Type					
			Farm Counties		Other Nonmetropolitan Counties		Metropolitan Counties	
	Number	Percent	Number	Percent	Number	Percent	Number	Percent
1950–1960	1,090,206	15.0	−148,505	−7.6	125,091	4.7	1,113,620	42.1
1960–1970	386,746	4.6	−191,510	−10.6	−93,580	−3.3	671,836	17.9
1970–1980	1,215,855	13.9	−25,308	−1.6	268,979	9.9	972,184	21.9
1980–1990	379,806	3.8	−153,079	−9.6	−55,237	−1.9	588,122	10.9
1990–2000	1,227,514	11.9	−20,745	−1.4	102,896	3.5	1,145,363	19.1
1950–2000	4,300,127	59.1	−539,147	−27.5	348,149	13.0	4,491,125	169.7

Source: United States Department of Agriculture, Economic Research Service; United States Census Bureau.

of the baby boom and by a substantial influx of migrants. As a result, metropolitan counties contained nearly 45 percent of the region's population in 1960, up from 36 percent just 10 years earlier (Table 9.1).

Between 1960 and 1970, the population of the Great Plains grew by only 385,000 (Table 9.2). Aside from the loss of the 1930s, this was the smallest decade gain to this point. Natural increase was sufficient to offset net out-migration from the region, but only 23 percent of the counties experienced population gain. In all, the net migration loss from the Great Plains was over 611,000 during the 1960s. While the nonmetropolitan population declined by 285,000, the metropolitan population grew by 672,000. Metropolitan gain was fueled primarily by natural increase, though metropolitan areas did receive a net inflow of migrants as well. Farm-dependent counties suffered a loss of 10.6 percent during the 1960s; in all, migration losses exceeded gains from natural increase by nearly 192,000 during the decade. Even among non-farm nonmetropolitan counties, the gain from natural increase was not sufficient to offset out-migration. As a result, nonmetropolitan counties that did not depend on farming sustained a 3.3 percent loss. By the end of the 1960s, the population residing in metropolitan areas of the Great Plains exceeded that in nonmetropolitan areas for the first time in history.

The Nonmetropolitan Turnaround and Beyond

At the national level, the 1970s witnessed a remarkable nonmetropolitan demographic turnaround characterized by widespread inmigration and substantial population increase (Beale, 1975). The Great Plains participated in this reversal to a certain extent; however, gains there were considerably smaller than elsewhere in nonmetropolitan America. Consistent with national trends, nonmetropolitan areas of the Great Plains gained population in the 1970s. This was the first decade of nonmetropolitan gains in this area since at least the 1920s. However, contrary to the national trend, the nonmetropolitan gain in the Great Plains came entirely from natural increase. In contrast, metropolitan areas grew at a substantial rate. This substantial metropolitan gain coupled with modest nonmetropolitan growth produced an overall population gain of nearly 1.2 million in the 1970s (Table 9.3).

In contrast, farm counties actually lost population during the 1970s. The gain of 68,000 from natural increase was insufficient to offset a migration loss of 94,000 (Table 9.3). Only 30 percent of the farm dependent counties grew during the period. In contrast, some 75 percent of the nonmetropolitan counties that were not dependent on farming grew. They enjoyed nearly a 10 percent gain fueled by net in-migration and natural increase. Growth was even more pronounced in metropolitan areas, with a gain of nearly a million. This was fueled both by a substantial natural increase of 485,000 and continued migration gains of 484,000. In all, some 95 percent of the metropolitan counties grew during the decade.

The turnaround on the Great Plains did not last long. The 1980s were a difficult time for all of rural America, but agricultural areas like those on the Great

Table 9.3. Population Change, Net Migration, and Natural Increase in the Great Plains Counties by Year and County Type: 1970–2000

		Population Change			Net Migration			Natural Increase		
County Type and Year	Initial Population (in '000s)	Absolute Change (in '000s)	Percent Change	Percent of Counties Growing	Absolute Change (in '000s)	Percent Change	Percent of Counties Growing	Absolute Change (in '000s)	Percent Change	Percent of Counties Growing
Farm										
1970 –1980	1,618	−26	−1.6	30.2	−94	−5.8	20.1	68	4.2	78.4
1980–1990	1,592	−153	−9.6	8.3	−225	−14.1	2.2	71	4.5	80.2
1990 to 2000	1,439	−21	−1.5	27.7	−36	−2.5	27.7	15	1.0	43.9
Other Nonmetropolitan										
1970–1980	2,708	268	9.9	74.9	78	2.9	54.4	191	7.1	84.2
1980–1990	2,976	−55	−1.8	30.4	−295	−9.9	9.9	240	8.1	89.5
1990–2000	2,921	103	3.5	53.2	−22	−0.8	48.0	125	4.3	69.6
Metropolitan										
1970–1980	4,436	969	21.8	95.1	484	10.9	73.2	485	10.9	100.0
1980–1990	5,405	588	10.9	78.1	−45	−0.8	39.0	632	11.7	100.0
1990–2000	5,992	1,145	19.1	95.1	609	10.2	73.2	537	9.0	100.0
Total										
1970–1980	8,762	1,211	13.8	51.2	467	5.3	36.5	744	8.5	82.2
1980–1990	9,973	379	3.8	21.8	−565	−5.7	8.0	944	9.5	85.1
1990–2000	10,352	1,228	11.9	42.2	550	5.3	38.6	677	6.5	57.6

Notes: 1993 Metropolitan Status used for all periods; The number of counties in each category were constant over time: Farm = 278, Metropolitan = 41, Other Nonmetropolitan = 171.
Source: Census 1970–2000 and Federal State Cooperative Estimates (rev. 7/01/03).

Plains were hit particularly hard. The region only grew by 379,000 during the 1980s (Table 9.2), the lowest decade growth in the 20th century. Only 22 percent of the counties gained population during the decade, the fewest in history. Out-migration was again common in the 1980s, with a net loss of 565,000 (Table 9.3). Both metropolitan and nonmetropolitan areas of the Great Plains suffered migration losses during the 1980s. However, the magnitude of the farm losses was much greater. The farm counties lost nearly 10 percent of their 1980 population by 1990. Migration losses of 14 percent were only partially offset by natural increase. Nearly 92 percent of the farm counties lost population in the 1980s, and even fewer experienced net in-migration. Nor were the population losses restricted to the farm counties. With a migration loss of nearly 10 percent in non-farm counties, even the substantial natural increase failed to fend off population losses (Table 9.3). Nearly 70 percent of the non-farm counties lost population. Even metropolitan counties were not immune to migration losses. Though natural increase was more than sufficient to offset the modest migration losses, the overall metropolitan population gain of approximately 11 percent was the smallest of the five decades examined in detail here.

As the 1990s began, the fortunes of nonmetropolitan America changed yet again with another unexpected rebound. In the Great Plains, the nonmetropolitan population grew by only 80,000 during the 1990s and continued to experience net out-migration, albeit at a rate considerably slower than that of the 1980s. Some 35 percent of the nonmetropolitan counties of the Great Plains did experience net migration gains in the 1990s, far more than the 5 percent that gained migrants in the 1980s. But net migration gains in nonmetropolitan areas of the Great Plains remained far less widespread than in the rest of the country. Only in metropolitan areas was there robust growth and net in-migration.

Overall population declines from farm areas during the 1990s were similar in magnitude to those during the turnaround of the 1970s. However, the combination of demographic components that produced this change was quite different. Loss from out migration from farm counties in the 1990s was considerably smaller than had been the case in the 1970s. However, the natural increase that has historically offset out-migration did not occur in the 1990s. *In fact, in the majority of farm counties, more people died than were born.* We shall return to natural decrease in the next section of this paper, but its implications for future population growth in farm areas is a matter of serious concern. Nonmetropolitan counties that were not dependent on farming gained population again in the 1990s, but neither the extent nor the magnitude of the gains rivaled those of the turnaround. In fact, the continued out migration of population from such counties runs contrary to national trends for the decade. The magnitude and extent of natural increase in such counties also diminished sharply in the 1990s. The metropolitan counties of the Great Plains did experience a substantial rebound in the 1990s. Such counties gained 1.2 million people during the decade with the growth coming both from substantial net in-migration and significant and extremely widespread natural increase (Table 9.2).

In sum, the patterns of population growth on the Great Plains over the past 130 years have been complex. From 1870 to 1930, the population of the region grew significantly. And, most of the growth occurred in areas of the Great Plains that remain nonmetropolitan to this day. As late as 1930, 75 percent of the Plains population remained nonmetropolitan. After 1930, the nonmetropolitan population diminished, while the metropolitan population grew dramatically. In 2000, nearly 62 percent of the 11.6 million people of the Plains resided in metropolitan areas. Only 4.4 million remained in nonmetropolitan areas, down from a peak of 5 million in 1930. Population losses have been most pronounced in the 278 farm counties of the Great Plains. Between 1950 and 2000, the population of farm counties diminished by nearly 28 percent (Table 9.2). By 2000, only about 1.4 million people resided in farm counties (Table 9.1). In contrast, the metropolitan population of the Great Plains grew by 170 percent to 7,138,000 in 2000 (Table 9.1). So, while the metropolitan areas of the Great Plains thrived, the nonmetropolitan areas that once dominated this vast expanse of the nation's heartland have slowly diminished.

DEMOGRAPHIC COMPONENTS OF CHANGE

Population redistribution results from the complex interaction of migration, natural increase, and age structure shifts played out over both temporal and spatial dimensions. Here we examine how this interplay has produced distinctly different patterns of growth and decline in metropolitan and nonmetropolitan areas of the Great Plains. Migration patterns are of particular interest because they have the capacity to rapidly alter the size and composition of a population. In contrast, natural change generally has a more gradual, though sometimes more profound, impact on the population of an area. For example, the movement of a young migrant out of the area immediately reduces the local population by one. However, because the locality loses not only the young migrant but also all potential offspring and their descendants as well, the eventual impact on natural increase may be much greater.

Neither migration nor natural increase is a random event. The probability of migration, birth, or death is linked with age. Such age-specific net migration has significant implications for future demographic trends. Previous research suggests both continuity and change in age-specific net migration patterns across decades (Johnson & Fuguitt, 2000). Examining net migration patterns during the last half-century for the Great Plains reveals extremely consistent age-specific migration signatures for the three groups of counties of interest.

The farm dependent counties suffered significant losses of young adults in each of the last five decades. The loss is most pronounced among those who would have been 20–24 years old at the end of each decade (Figure 9.2). In the typical Great Plains farm county, the loss of 20–24 year olds was about 50 per 100 in four of the last five decades. Even during the turnaround of the 1970s, the loss of young adults was substantial. Overall, median age-specific net migration

Figure 9.2. Age-Specific Net Migration, Farm

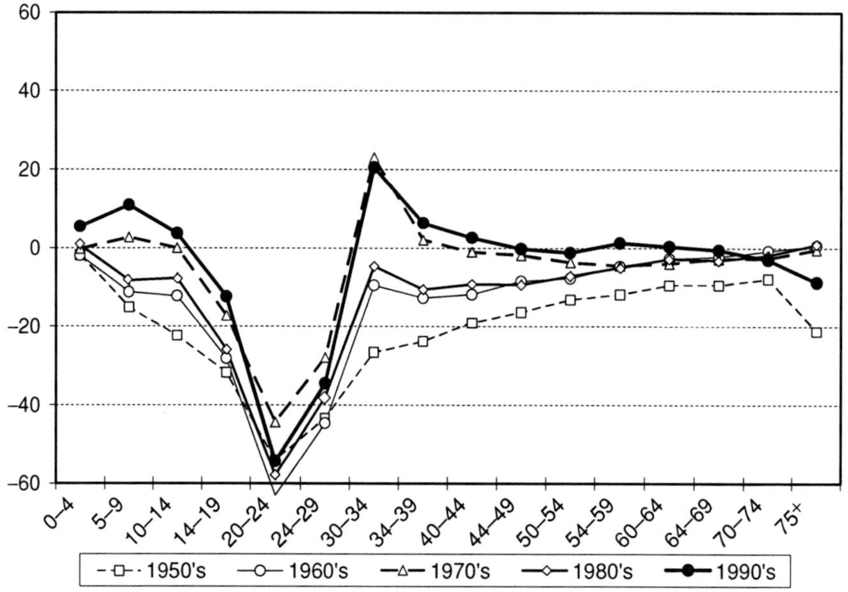

rates for farm counties exhibit a distinct signature that is consistent across the five decades. Losses are greatest for young adults, diminish (or are replaced by growth) for those in their 30s, and further diminish for older adults. The migration patterns for children closely resemble those of their parents (assumed to be 20–25 years older). There are also temporal variations in the rates across the decades. Losses were greatest during the 1950s, when the adjustment to the diminished demand for labor in agriculture was still strong, and losses were smallest during the turnaround of the 1970s and the rebound of the 1990s.

The age-specific net migration patterns for nonmetropolitan counties that were not farm dependent are similar in form to those of farm counties but are more moderate in magnitude. Thus while 20–24 years olds are still the most likely to leave, the rate of loss is less than in farm counties (Figure 9.3). Losses moderated (or gains occurred) for those in their 30s as well as for their children. Temporal variation is also evident with the turnaround and rebound clearly differentiated by smaller losses or greater gains.

The age-specific net migration patterns in metropolitan counties are distinctly different from those in nonmetropolitan areas of the Great Plains (Figure 9.4). The typical metropolitan county experienced net migration gains across a broad spectrum of the age structure. Migration gains are generally greatest for young adults 20–24 years old. As this is the age group prone to leave nonmetropolitan areas, it appears that at least some of the young adult out-migrants

Figure 9.3. Age-Specific Net Migration, Other Nonmetro

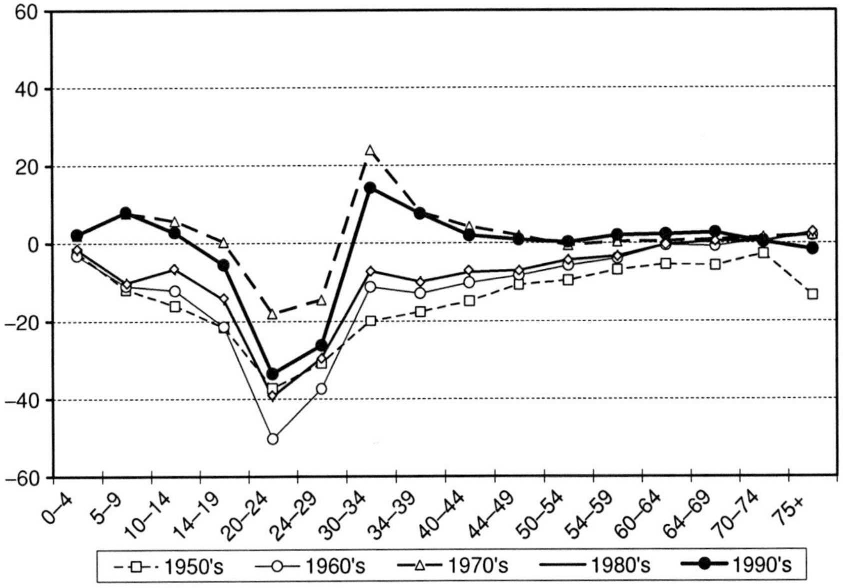

Figure 9.4. Age-Specific Net Migration, Metro

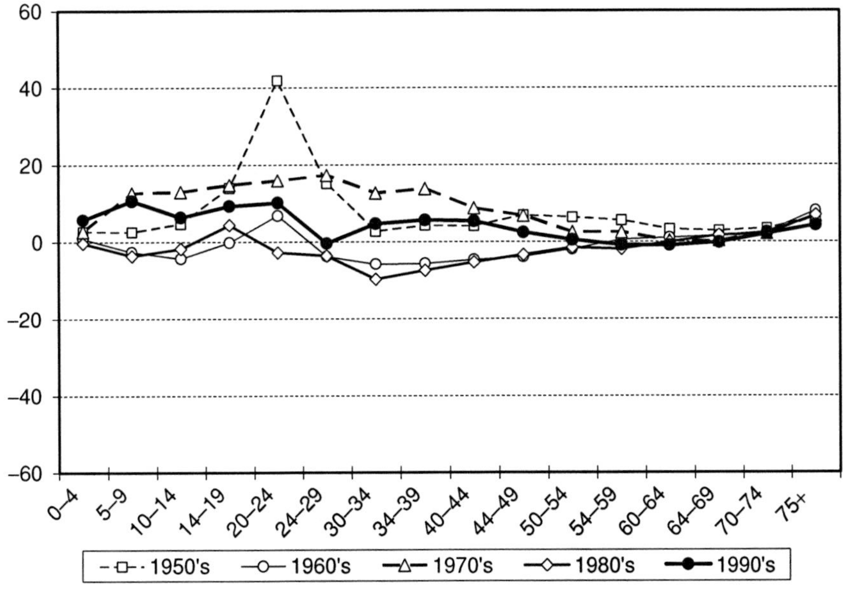

from nonmetropolitan areas are settling in the metropolitan areas of the region. The magnitude of the young adult movement should not be underestimated. For example, during the 1950s, when nonmetropolitan areas lost 122,000 20–24-year-olds, metropolitan areas of the Plains gained 86,000 young adult migrants. Thirty years later, during the 1980s, nonmetropolitan Great Plains counties suffered a net migration loss of 96,000 20–24 year olds, whereas metropolitan areas of the Great Plains gained 55,000 of the same age (Table 9.3). This represents a considerable loss of human capital from nonmetropolitan areas that has persisted for decades.

The most significant demographic implication of the persistent outflow of young adults from nonmetropolitan areas of the Great Plains is the influence it exerts on natural change. Because young adults produce most of the children born in an area, their loss reduces the number of births locally. The eventual consequence of this is a greater probability of natural decrease, which occurs when the number of deaths in a county exceeds the number of births. It was infrequently observed in the United States at the county level before 1960 (Beale, 1969). Since then the incidence of natural decrease in United States counties has varied. It reached an early peak in the 1970s, diminished in the 1980s, and then rose to unprecedented levels in the 1990s (Johnson, 1993).

Research suggests that the primary cause of natural decrease is an age structure that contains too few young adults and too many older adults. Such age structure distortion is the result of protracted age-specific net out-migration by young adults (Johnson, 1993). In some areas the outflow of young adults has been supplemented by an influx of older adults, although this is relatively uncommon in the Great Plains. The probability of natural decrease also increases as temporal declines in the birth rate result in women having fewer children. However, research clearly shows that women in natural decrease counties do not have fewer children than their contemporaries in other counties (Johnson, 1993). In essence, natural decrease in the Great Plains is not due to low fertility, but rather to a dearth of women of child-bearing age. Over time, the outflow of young adults coupled with the "aging in place" of older generations also increases the death rates. The process often takes several decades to emerge, but eventually the number of deaths begins to rise, while the number of births continues to fall.

The linkage between migration and natural increase underscores the complex interplay between demographic components that produced the population redistribution trends evident on the Great Plains. The age-specific net migration trends produce an immediate population loss of young adults. In the intermediate term this diminishes the number of births and eventually (after several decades) produces an excess number of deaths. Only in the 1990s did the full impact of these processes combine to produce widespread natural decrease. The proportion of Great Plains counties with natural decrease is greater than in any region of the country at any time in history.

The loss of young adults has been greatest and has persisted longest in the farm counties, where the incidence of natural decrease is most pronounced.

Nearly 56 percent of these counties had more deaths than births in the decade of the 1990s. This compares with fewer than 30 percent with natural decrease during the 1980s. Moreover, the situation deteriorated during the decade. In 1991, 46 percent of the counties had more deaths than births. By 2000, this rose to nearly 60 percent. In 2000, there were only 18,123 births in Great Plains farm counties compared to 17,440 deaths. Thus, for every 100 deaths there were only 104 births, an exceedingly low ratio. The linkage between age structure shifts and natural decrease is clearly evident in the farm counties. The number of young adults (20–34) in farm counties diminished from 20.1 percent of the farm population in 1980 to only 14.9 percent in 2000. In comparison, the Great Plains as a whole had 20.6 percent of its population in their prime childbearing years in 2000. While the proportion of younger adults is diminishing, the older population is growing. In 2000, 18 percent of the farm county population was over the age of 65, up from 16.5 percent in 1980. In comparison, 12.5 percent of the population of the Great Plains as a whole was over the age of 65 in 2000. In farm counties the proportion of the population at high risk of mortality now exceeds the proportion capable of producing the next generation of children.

Natural decrease is somewhat less common in nonmetropolitan areas that are not dependent on farming. However, by historical standards the incidence of natural decrease is high there as well. More than 30 percent of the nonmetropolitan non-farm counties experienced natural decrease in the 1990s, up from just 10 percent in the 1980s. And the situation worsened over the course of the decade. The proportion with natural decrease grew from 21 percent in 1991 to nearly 37 percent in 2000. Here also the proportion of young adults is diminishing (from 24.8 percent in 1980 to 18.8 percent in 2000), while the proportion of older adults is rising (from 13.3 percent in 1980 to 14.6 percent in 2000). In 2000, there were 130 births for every 100 deaths in these counties.

In stark contrast to the situation in nonmetropolitan areas of the Great Plains, natural decrease is not a concern in the region's metropolitan counties. Fueled by decades of young adult in-migration, the metropolitan age structure has a much larger proportion of young adults and a smaller proportion of older adults. As a result, it produced a healthy surplus of births over deaths throughout the 1990s. In 2000, for example, there were 206 births for every 100 deaths.

Such natural decrease is the inevitable demographic consequence of decades of out-migration by young adults. With natural increase at such low ebb in nonmetropolitan areas of the Great Plains, the future of the region depends increasingly on net migration. Without an influx of migrants, many nonmetropolitan counties simply cannot replenish their populations. Human ecology suggests that change in one element of the ecological complex causes changes in other segments of the complex. Thus, the population change underway on the Great Plains will affect the future organizational and technological structure of the region. A primary way in which this will be transmitted is through the region's labor force of the region, which we now examine.

THE LABOR FORCE CONSEQUENCES OF POPULATION REDISTRIBUTION

One of the latent and more serious consequences of population redistribution in the region is the dramatic change in the labor pool. Age-selective migration is systematically draining the entry labor pool from the nonmetropolitan counties within the region. Between 1980 and 1990, the entry labor pool (i.e., persons age 20 to 34 years old) in the farm counties of the region dropped nearly 19 percent or by roughly 60,000 residents (Table 9.4). A somewhat less severe decline of approximately 12 percent was reported among the other nonmetropolitan counties in the region. In contrast, the region's metropolitan counties lost less than 2 percent of their entry labor pool during that period, mainly due to the aging of the baby boomers.

The long-term accumulative effect of selective out-migration in the region is sobering. Between 1980 and 2000, entry labor dropped by more than 34 percent in farm counties and nearly 23 percent in other nonmetropolitan counties of the region. During the same 20-year period, the metropolitan entry labor pool managed a slight upswing, even though this was a transition period from the bulge of the baby boom to a much smaller baby bust cohort (i.e., those born after 1964). Overall, the size of the entry labor pool in the Great Plains dropped by slightly more than 10 percent across the last two decades.

A similar trend exists for those in the labor pool who were nearing retirement (Table 9.4). The pre-retirement labor pool (i.e., those between the ages of 55 and 64) declined by 19.2 percent within the farm counties of the region over the past two decade, while the drop for other nonmetropolitan counties was less than 3 percent. Metropolitan counties, on the other hand, grew their pre-retirement labor pool by 28.0 percent during that period.

The economic crisis facing the Great Plains is best highlighted by shifts in the much larger segment of the labor pool, those in their prime working years (i.e., ages 35 to 54). Farm counties of the region, which represent 57 percent of all counties, grew its prime labor pool by nearly 23 percent or 72,059 potential workers over the past two decades (Table 9.4). In contrast, the 41 metropolitan counties in the region, which represent less than 10 percent of all counties but 62 percent of the region's population base in 2000, grew their prime labor pool by 88 percent or by nearly 1 million over the same time period. The other nonmetropolitan counties expanded their prime labor pool by 45 percent.

The persistent drain of labor pools has serious consequences for the viability of nonmetropolitan communities. The business community makes key decisions based on available labor. Losses, especially in the entry labor pool, send very negative signals to potential employers and business leaders. Continued farm consolidations and production efficiencies will further reduce labor requirements to produce agricultural goods. In addition, farm-related employment through value-added industries peripheral to agriculture has not offset the number of jobs lost in farming (Majchrowicz, 2000). This strongly suggests the need to explore solutions

Table 9.4. Change in the Labor Pool by Age Cohort in Great Plains Counties by Year and County Type, 1980–2000

Age Cohort and Year	Total Population Change in the Great Plains Counties		County Type: Farm Counties		County Type: Other Nonmetropolitan Counties		County Type: Metropolitan Counties	
	Number	Percent	Number	Percent	Number	Percent	Number	Percent
Entry Labor Pool (Ages 20–34)								
1980–1990	−178,873	−6.7	−60,040	−18.8	−91,380	−12.4	−27,453	−1.7
1990–2000	−90,396	−3.7	−48,881	−18.8	−77,484	−12.0	35,969	2.3
1980–2000	−269,269	−10.2	−108,921	−34.1	−168,864	−22.9	8,516	0.5
Prime Labor Pool (Ages 35– 54)								
1980–1990	503,989	24.7	6,555	2.0	92,323	15.9	405,111	35.6
1990–2000	825,783	32.5	65,504	20.0	169,054	25.2	591,225	38.3
1980–2000	1,329,772	65.2	72,059	22.5	261,377	45.1	996,336	87.6
Pre-Retirement (Ages 55–64)								
1980–1990	−14,240	−1.6	−25,215	−14.9	−19,739	−7.2	30,714	7.0
1990–2000	96,826	11.2	−7,279	−5.1	12,098	4.8	92,007	19.6
1980–2000	82,586	9.4	−32,494	−19.2	−7,641	−2.8	122,721	28.0

Source: United States Department of Agriculture, Economic Research Service; United States Census Bureau.

to employment opportunities in farming communities in economic sectors not related to agriculture. Whitener and McGranahan (2003) argue that diversity through locally tailored initiatives offers important promise in the new economy. The key is to build innovatively on existing community assets. These might be natural amenities, unique skills within the labor pool, proximity to key resources, or strong public/private networks.

POLICY OPTIONS

These dramatic trends show the restructuring that has occurred in the nonmetropolitan Great Plains. Indeed, the prospects for the future viability of many Great Plains counties are not encouraging. A public commitment needs to be made to break the downward cycle of population loss. In addition, investment in the rural Great Plains is good public policy. According to Stauber (2001), such investment is necessary to maintain and protect the environment, ensure reliable sources of high-quality food and fiber, equalize population distributions to prevent urban overcrowding, and uphold the social contract made to those who helped settle this territory for the betterment of the larger society. This can be accomplished through very aggressive economic development policies that diversify rural economies and enhance employment potential. An important starting point, based on ecological theory, is the interplay between organizations and technology. If we view rural areas from an organizational perspective, the first conclusion we should reach is that rural areas are not homogeneous. Therefore, we should be considering an array of solutions. Ironically, the fundamental undercurrent to existing policy strategies assumes that rural is synonymous with agricultural and that one standardized solution is appropriate for all (Stauber, 2001). Currently, the single largest governmental support of rural areas is agricultural subsidies. Between 1996 and 1998, farm subsidies totaled nearly $23 billion, with over half that amount going to only 7.2 percent of the farmers (Fluharty, 2003). The notion that agriculture is the economic engine for rural America perpetuates current policy and serves as a major barrier to exploring alternatives that may be equally vital (Freshwater, 1997).

Our findings suggest that one of the greatest challenges for rural communities in the Great Plains is overcoming the region's remoteness and sparse population base. Although, the landmass of the rural Great Plains is quite large, the political power base is relatively small because of a lack of people. As a result, rural communities have limited voice and a culture of independence that restricts coalition building. One solution offered by Galston and Baehler (1995) is to utilize technology to create a new organizational structure that links remote rural areas to urban or metropolitan centers. This is being accomplished with greater frequency in the new information age. For example, interactive video or other forms of immediate-response broadcast are connecting urban and remote rural communities in the delivery of an increasing range of services from education to health. In North Dakota, one-third of the emergency consults from a hospital in one of the state's metropolitan centers is conducted via Tel-Medicine. This partnership is allowing satellite health clinics to remain viable, thereby offering employment opportunities to health professionals in small rural communities. Similarly, data and resource sharing via computer technologies allow small rural firms to be more competitive by keeping abreast of new advances as well as expanding their reach to distant markets.

Perhaps the greatest advantage of the new information age for rural communities is its emphasis on niche markets. The economic development philosophy of the industrial era focused on mass-production in an attempt to create economies of scale in order to produce a profit. Thus, success was defined in terms of consistency and scalability, which required manufacturing to be done in one place. In contrast, the goal of production in the information age is serving a niche rather than a mass market. Profits, therefore, are acquired by creating the niche and supplying a product or service to that niche audience more quickly than one's competitor. In this case, success is a function of one's vision and speed in delivery. As Stauber (2001) suggests, successful communities will be those that find and maintain a competitive advantage.

An approach that centers on small rural entrepreneurship and that has registered a growing amount of success is micro-enterprises. For example, Hassebrook (2003) reports that over 70 percent of the net job growth in Nebraska's agriculture-dependent counties is a result of non-farm self-employment. He cites the state's deliberate efforts to cultivate small business development as the key to this success. An important aspect of micro-enterprises is that their entrepreneurs are invested in their rural communities and are therefore less likely to move regardless of the economic conditions of those communities (Bailey & Preston, 2003). In addition, a fundamental principle that underlies micro-enterprises is interdependence. The most successful micro-enterprises are a result of public/private partnerships that link nonprofit organizations, rural communities, and entrepreneurs, typically with the assistance of partial government funding. Nebraska's Center for Rural Enterprise Assistance Program (REAP) is the best example of such a government-sponsored linkage program. Its success story includes more than 2,000 rural businesses that range from woodcraft and pottery makers to caterers, day care centers, and fitness centers (see www.microenterprisesworks.org).

The next step in improving success among rural micro-enterprises is to link them with metropolitan markets. This can be accomplished by electronic commerce, which is at the heart of the new information age. Training or technical assistance in the use of electronic commerce through small business development programs will help increase success (Hassebrook, 2003). Moreover, collaborative efforts among small rural businesses can be linked to form larger regional supply networks via electronic commerce. This allows small rural businesses to take advantage of shared infrastructure, resources, and professional staff. A common example of this concept is a shared website that markets products from numerous businesses in a multi-county area.

Government incentives can be used to encourage such linkages. For example, Stauber (2001) suggests that for-profit companies can be enticed by direct support efforts, risk minimization, or tax incentives to develop and market technologies aimed at enhancing community interdependence. At the federal level, an exciting initiative that holds promise is the New Homestead Act of 2003 (S.602). In brief, its philosophy is similar to the original Homestead Act of 1862 that stimulated population growth in the Great Plains through a one-time incentive (i.e., free land if you worked and improved it over a five-year period). This legislation offers similar short-term incentives aimed at new residents and the business sector. To attract new residents, it offers loan repayment, tax credits for home purchases, and targeted savings programs. Similarly, to attract business it provides various investment tax credits and venture capital programs. The major hurdle to this type of legislation, however, is to convince the bulk of the members of Congress why it is important to save the rural heartland. Given the limited voice of the rural Great Plains, this is a daunting task.

ENDNOTES

1. Johnson's research support was received from the North Central Research Station, US Forest Service and Economic Research Service, USDA. Rathge's research support was received from the USDA North Dakota Rural Development Center as part of regional project W1001.
2. Great Plains metropolitan areas include: Abilene, Amarillo, Billings, Bismarck, Casper, Colorado Springs, Denver, Fargo, Fort Collins, Grand Forks, Great Falls, Laramie, Lawton, Lubbock, Midland, Oklahoma City, Pueblo, Rapid City, Tulsa, Wichita, Wichita Falls.
3. This section draws heavily on our previous research on Great Plains demographic trends (Rathge, 2002; Johnson, in press).

REFERENCES

Adamchak, D.J., Bloomquist, L.E., Bausman, K., & Qureshi, R. (1999). Consequences of population change for retail/wholesale sector employment in the nonmetropolitan Great Plains: 1950–1996. *Rural Sociology, 64*(1), 92–112.

Albrecht, D.E., & Murdock, S.H. (1990). *The sociology of U.S. agriculture.* Ames, IA: Iowa State University Press.

Bailey, J.M., & Preston, K. (2003). *Swept away: Chronic hardship and fresh promise on the rural Great Plains.* Walthill, NE: Center for Rural Affairs.

Beale, C.L. (1969). Natural decrease of population: The current and prospective status of an emergent American phenomenon. *Demography, 6*, 9199.

Beale, C.L. (1975). *The revival of population growth in nonmetropolitan America* (ERS-605). Washington, DC: U.S. Department of Agriculture, Economic Research Service.

Beale, C.L. (1993). Salient features of the demography of American agriculture. In D.L. Brown, D.R. Field, & J.J. Zuiches (Eds.), *The demography of rural life* (pp. 108–127). University Park, PA: Northeast Regional Center for Rural Development.

Bogue, D.L., & Beale, C.L. (1961). *Economic areas of the United States*. New York: Free Press of Glencoe.

Cook, P.J., & Mizer, K.L. (1994). *The revised ERS county typology: An overview* (RDRR-89). Washington, DC: U.S. Department of Agriculture, Economic Research Service.

Fluharty, C.W. (2003, October). *Toward a community based rural policy for our nation*. Paper presented at the Annie E. Casey Foundation's Forum on Children and Families, Omaha, NE.

Freshwater, D. (1997). Farm production policy versus rural life policy. *American Journal of Agricultural Economics, 79*(5), 1515–1525.

Galston, W.A., & Baehler, K.J. (1995). *Rural development in the United States: Connecting theory, practice, and possibilities*. Washington, DC: Island Press.

Gutmann, M.P., Peri, A., & Deane, G.D. (1998). *Migration, environment and economic change on the Great Plains, 1930–1990*. Paper presented at the Annual Meetings of the Population Association of America, Chicago, IL.

Hassebrook, C. (2003, January). Rural economic development depends on small entrepreneurship. In M. Powell (Ed.), *Center for rural affairs newsletter* (pp. 6–8). Walthill, NE: Center for Rural Affairs.

Johnson, K.M. (1985). *The impact of population change on business activity in rural America*. Boulder, CO: Westview.

Johnson, K.M. (1993). When births exceed deaths: Natural decrease in the United States. *International Regional Science Review, 15*(2), 179–198.

Johnson, K.M. (in press). Urban and rural population redistribution on the Great Plains. In D.J. Wishart (Ed.), *Encyclopedia of the Great Plains*. Lincoln: University of Nebraska Press.

Johnson, K.M., & Fuguitt, G.V. (2000). Continuity and change in rural migration patterns, 1950–1995. *Rural Sociology, 65*(1), 27–49.

Johnson, K.M., Fuguitt, G.V., Voss, P., Hammer, R., & McNiven, S. (2003, May 1). *Recent age-specific net migration in the United States*. Paper presented at the Annual Meeting of the Population Association of America, Minneapolis, MN.

Majchrowicz, A. (2000). Farm employment losses outstrip job gains in farm-related industries in some nonmetro areas. *Rural Conditions and Trends, 10*(2), 22–26.

Rathge, R.W. (1995). Population dynamics and their implications for the ecosystems of the Great Plains. In S.R. Johnson & A. Bouzaher (Eds.), *Conservation of Great Plains ecosystems* (pp. 49–62). London: Kluwer.

Rathge, R.W. (2002, April 11–12). *The changing population profile of the Great Plains*. Paper developed for the Great Plains Population Symposium, North Dakota State University, North Dakota Rural Development Center, Fargo, ND.

Stauber, K.N. (2001). Why invest in rural America—and how? A critical public policy question for the 21st century. *Economic Review, 86*(2), 57–87.

Whitener, L., & McGranahan, D. (2003). Rural America: Opportunities and challenges. *Amber Waves, 1*(1), 14–21.

CHAPTER 10

GAMING, POPULATION CHANGE, AND RURAL DEVELOPMENT ON INDIAN RESERVATIONS

An Idaho Case Study[1]

GUNDARS RUDZITIS

INTRODUCTION

Indians are almost an invisible part of rural America. While reservations represent a significant feature of the American West, they are not centrally featured in rural policy discussions. Many Indian reservations have extreme levels of poverty, unemployment rates that exceed 50 percent, and the highest suicide rates in the nation. By most economic indicators, American Indians rank among the most disadvantaged population groups in the United States (Gitter & Reagan, 2002; Young, 1990). Recently, however, the introduction of casino gaming has brought hope and income to some Indian reservations, yet it remains unclear whether casino gambling will provide a lasting economic solution for Indians individually or collectively.

In this chapter, I consider the following questions: (1) What are the social and economic impacts of what appears to be a "successful" economic development strategy on a disadvantaged population? (2) How does gaming compare with other economic development strategies employed by various tribes? (3) How might gaming affect the size and composition of the Native American population in northern Idaho? (4) What is, or should be, the relationship between gaming, economic development and nation building on Indian reservations? The discussion begins at the national level and later uses a case study of impacts of casino gaming on the Nez Perce tribe in Idaho.

SIZE, CHANGE AND LOCATION OF THE INDIAN POPULATION

The demography of Indian tribes has been a subject of continuing controversy, particularly the number of Indians in North America before European conquest with estimates ranging from 4 to over 20 million (Churchill, 1993; Denevan,

W.A. Kandel & D.L. Brown (eds.), Population Change and Rural Society, 219–232.

Figure 10.1. American Indian Population and Proportion Living on Reservations, 1800–2000

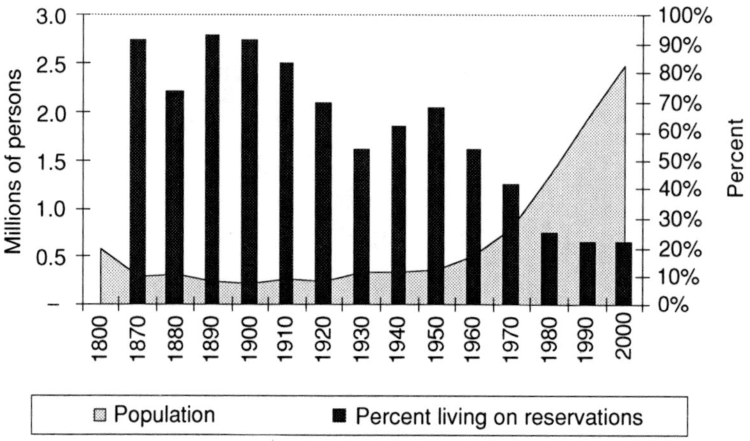

Source: U.S. Census, various years, Franz, 1999.

1992; Dobyns, 1983). The exact number is controversial because of the genocidal impact of European-introduced diseases associated with Indian population change, with larger Native American populations experiencing greater absolute and percentage declines. Whatever the precise number, the Indian population declined to the point where terms such as the "vanishing Indian" were used as the Indian population came close to disappearing in the United States.

If somewhere between 4 and 25 million indigenous peoples lived in current U.S. boundaries when Europeans arrived, the population was estimated to have dropped to around 600,000 by 1800, comprising at that time about 5 percent of the total U.S. population.[2] By 1900 the Indian population dropped further, to below 240,000 or less than 1 percent of the total U.S. population. During the first half of the 20th Century the total Indian population fluctuated, and by 1950 it numbered just over 357,000 or 0.3 percent of the total population.

The decades since 1950 have seen dramatic increases in the Indian population. By 1990 the U.S. Census counted over 1.9 million American Indians, and in 2000 the population was almost 2.5 million. Part of this increase has been attributed to improved socioeconomic conditions on reservations and improvements in census estimates that had frequently undercounted Indians, but much of it was the result of more people self-identifying as Indians (Nagel, 1996; Snipp, 1989, 1997). As a percentage of the U.S. population, however, American Indians remained below 1 percent. In 2000 people were allowed on census forms to designate themselves as belonging to more than one race, and if those persons are included in the Indian total, the Indian population increases from 2.5 to over 4.1 million. According to Census 2000, four out of 10 Native Americans reside in the West (43 percent), three out of ten (31 percent) live in the South, and the remainder lives in the Midwest (17 percent) and the Northeast (10 percent). With a few exceptions, such as the states of Arizona and New Mexico, Indians comprise a small segment of the total population, and in the Northeast, Midwest and South (with the exception of North Carolina) they make up less than 1 percent of the population.

The land base of the more than 500 tribes in the United States has been reduced to 4 percent of total U.S. territory (LaDuke, 1999). The ten most populous Indian nations include the Cherokee, Navaho, Choctaw, Sioux, Chippewa, Apache, Blackfeet, Iroquois, and Pueblo. Indian reservations vary widely in geographic size with the Navaho reservation being the largest at over 24,000 square miles. This is the exception rather than the rule; only 7 percent of reservations contain more than 1,000 square miles, 19 of these account for about 75 percent of all Indian reservation lands, and two thirds of all reservations cover areas of less than 50 square miles (Frantz, 1999). On many reservations, non-Indians own much of the land due to federal government re-allocation policies. The number and percentage of Indians on reservations has also decreased over time because the rural-to-urban migration typical of other groups in rural America also effects Indians. However, rural-to-urban migration of the Indian population lagged behind that of the non-Indian population. By 1929 more than half of the U.S. population lived in cities, whereas even in 1940, most American Indians still lived in rural areas (Frantz, 1999).

Historically, federal government policies to assimilate Indians and efforts to eliminate reservations also encouraged the migration of Indians off reservations. In 1870, 92 percent of Indians lived on reservations, dropping to 54 percent by 1930 and to just 22 percent by 2000. The dramatic decreases in the Indian population, combined with federal programs to encourage them to leave reservations and integrate with the larger population, have not been conducive to the maintenance and building of successful sovereign Indian nations.

ECONOMIC DEVELOPMENT ON RESERVATIONS

The very nature of settling Indians on reservations put them at a disadvantage in the context of economic development. The land base upon which most Indian tribes depended was diminished, and tribes were required to move to more marginal lands. When Euro-American settlers began appropriating land on Indian reservations, they did so by renegotiation or seizure, diminishing the size of many reservations.

Much of the early interest in "civilizing" Indians and promoting economic development on reservations involved turning them into farmers. While these policies generally failed, in some cases where reservations were opened up to white settlement, they ironically broke up successful Indian farms and gave land to European "pioneer" settlers.[3] Indians, in turn, were often moved to more marginal lands.

Many Indian reservations lack natural resources and have the geographical disadvantage of being isolated from major transportation routes, urban centers, and large shopping facilities. Because of this remoteness, as well as their low socioeconomic status, and low education levels, reservations are not usually attractive to outside investment. Nor is there much capital on reservations to invest in internal development. Nonetheless, there is a history of attempts at economic development on Indian reservations, though the question of who has benefited from these efforts and by how much remains contentious.

The most notable examples of past development efforts on Indian reservations have involved natural-resource extraction, including mining and oil development. Unfortunately, only a small number of tribes have benefited from such efforts. There is also a history of corruption and collusion between mineral and energy corporations and the U.S. Bureau of Indian Affairs in minimizing royalties paid to Indian tribes. Instances of tribal government corruption and misallocation of funds have also occurred (LaDuke, 1999). The lack of control over resource decisions has alienated many tribes and strained government-to-government relations at the state and national level. Indian relations with agencies such as the Army Corps of Engineers, the Forest Service, and the Bureau of Land Management have often yielded conflict.

While development strategies in many rural areas that involve attracting small manufacturing firms or branch plants of larger firms often yield mixed results, they have been rarely successful on Indian reservations. Tourism remains limited to larger reservations or those able to develop ski resorts and other recreational activities (Lew & Van Otten, 1998). Moreover, some Southwestern tribes with little interest in tourists observing them in their daily lives have posted signs cautioning against entering their reservations or taking photographs. Other pueblos such as the Taos or Acoma in New Mexico allow only Indian guided tours, and restrict areas where tourists may visit. It is against this backdrop that gambling entered the context of economic development for American Indians.

Gambling and Indian Economic Development

Gambling and casinos first appeared as an economic development strategy in Las Vegas in the 1950s, transforming the state of Nevada into the fastest growing state in the nation, both demographically and economically (Raento, 2003). Since then, gambling has become a part of the American way of life, generating over $ 600 billion in gross revenues since its inception, and becoming legally ensconced in over 31 states in various forms. Relative to the entire gaming industry dominated by Las Vegas and other centers of state-approved gaming, Indian gaming is relatively recent and comprises roughly 20 percent of all gaming revenues. From the perspective of Indian reservations, gaming revenues clearly possess considerable economic development potential.

Indian tribes, which tried to introduce gambling in the 1960s and 1970s, had more success following a Supreme Court ruling in the 1980s permitting the establishment of Indian bingo operations where states already allowed them. At the time, 45 states allowed bingo operations, and the Supreme Court's decision arose from conflicts where states had attempted to shut down high stakes bingo operations on reservations that were attracting many non-Indians (Winchell et al., 1998). Yet, the Court's decision did not resolve a fundamental conflict between state and federal laws. Indian gaming was only allowed if it did not conflict with state law (i.e. if the state allowed bingo). If the state did not allow card games or roulette, Indian tribes could not by federal law have them. However, tribes as sovereign nations contended that state laws regulating gambling should not apply to them.

The Indian Gaming Regulatory Act (IGRA) of 1988 was a compromise between states that wanted either to limit or to deny gaming operations and tribes that viewed gaming as a positive economic development strategy that they could deploy legally as sovereign nations. The law kept the requirement that limited Indian gaming activities to those already legal in the state and stipulated that each state and its tribes enter into a compact for the operation of Indian gaming facilities. The requirement for such agreements between tribes and states is controversial because it effectively decreases tribes' sovereign powers (Davis & Hudman, 1998; Gonzales, 2004).

With the passage of the IGRA, the scope of gaming on Indian reservations changed dramatically. In 1980 there were fewer than 20 Class II gaming establishments (bingo halls) on Indian reservations, but by 1990, 14 tribes in 4 states had Class III gaming establishments (casinos), and by 2002, 201 tribes in 29 states had gaming facilities of one type or other (Davis & Otterstrom, 1998). Accordingly, tribal gaming revenue has increased at an exponential rate. In 1988 when the law was passed, it totaled $121,000; by 1993 at had reached $3 million, and in 2002, it had exceeded $13 billion.

The financial success of Indian gaming and the revenues to specific tribes is a function of proximity to large population centers. For example, the Foxwoods Casino on the small Mashantucket Pequot reservation in Connecticut between New York City and Boston is the largest casino in the United States. The tribe has expanded its operations to include a hotel, golf courses, sports complexes, and a theme park, and it also invests in a variety of other businesses (Carmichael, 1998; Carmichael & Peppard, 1998; d'Hauteserre, 2000; Fromson, 2003). Other Indian tribes within driving distance of metropolitan centers have tried to capitalize on their marketable locations by building casinos. Income from Indian casinos also varies depending upon the presence and size of local competing casinos.

Not all casinos are economically successful, and many in rural areas struggle to break even. Montana, Nevada, North Dakota, Oklahoma, and South Dakota—five primarily rural states with almost half of the U.S. Indian population—account for less than 3 percent of all Indian casino revenue. In contrast, California, Connecticut and Florida, with 3 percent of the total Indian population, account for 44 percent of all casino revenues (Davis & Otterstrom, 1998). Consequently, Indian tribes in rural areas may not open casinos if they suspect their location is too risky, but where location is propitious, gaming and associated tourist-related development often reaps large benefits for tribes (Jorgenson, 1998; King & McIntire, 1998).

CASINOS, RURAL DEVELOPMENT AND NATION BUILDING

While casinos can provide one means of economic development, tribes also need to consider what kinds of development they wish to undertake. Previous strategies to attract economic activity to reservations or generate tribal businesses involved those of other rural places, namely landing a branch plant of some large manufacturing or technology-based company. While all government entities, from small towns to states, pursue economic development opportunities by attracting businesses and industries, rural places face particular disadvantages. The number of actual plants relocating is tiny compared to the attempts of tens of thousands of local governments to attract them (Rudzitis, 1996). In the face of this challenging environment, Indian tribal planners often write grant proposals to obtain start-up funding, but evidence of success for this type of "jobs-and-income" approach is weak. As an alternative, Cornell and Kalt (1998) promote a "nation building" approach for Indian tribes that creates an environment where people want to live and invest. The nation-building and the place-based quality-of-life regional development approaches argue that natural, social, and cultural environments provide the means for a development model that goes beyond a reductive focus on economic criteria (Diamond & Tolley, 1982; Power, 1995, 1996; Rasker, 1993; Rudzitis, 1993, 1996, 1999).

Most research, theory, and politics associated with promoting local or regional development is obsessed with economic dimensions of our lives, while the quality-of-life development approach emphasizes individual and company preferences for living environments in determining the location of economic activity. It thereby gives priority to social factors as determinants of local development (Young, 1999). Because entrepreneurs and businesses in the West often place considerable importance in quality-of-life considerations in their decisions to locate or remain where they are (Johnson & Rasker, 1993, 1995), developing a community's unique character can be an important economic development strategy.

Proponents of the quality-of-life approach argue, as do Cornell and Kalt (1998), that too much stress has been placed on economics as the driving force behind regional development efforts in the American West. Often "experts," citizens, and politicians assume that the promotion of local or regional development depends on harnessing the desire of people to make money and of firms to maximize profits. These conventional economic models of regional development don't consider the context of peoples' lives and how they interact with, shape, and are affected by their social, cultural, and natural environments. People often form attachments to a place or region that keep them from moving away during times of economic distress because of a loyalty to landscapes and communities. (Bolton, 1992; Marsh, 1987; Relph, 1986; Rudzitis, 1989, 1996; Rudzitis & Streatfeild, 1993; see also von Reichert in this volume). The unique attachments Indians form to a region following centuries of settlement is rooted in a natural environment with which they have interacted to create "roots" and a "sense of place." Even among non-Indians in the West, there are people who Wallace Stegner refers to as "stickers" or people who remain despite natural, economic or social calamities (Stegner, 1990). Research also shows that people who are more satisfied with where they live feel more attached to their communities and are less likely to move (Bolan, 1997; Fernandez & Dillman, 1979; Samson, 1998; Stinner et al, 1990). Most regional development models ignore loyalties and ties to place and landscapes, although some recent research has attempted to outline and develop models that incorporate sense of place and culture (Rudzitis, 1998; Rudzitis & Tolley, 1999; Tolley et al., 1999).

Table 10.1 compares the jobs-and-income and the nation-building, quality-of-life approaches to reservation development. The former may lead, as with gaming casinos, to short-term successes, but itself may not necessarily provide for a sustainable tribal future. A nation-building approach does not guarantee success, but evidence suggests it improves the chances that development will take root and be holistic and sustainable (Cornell & Kalt, 1998). A nation-building and quality-of-life approach, rooted in preserving, sustaining, and strengthening the physical, social, and cultural environment within which reservations exist, shifts attention to the importance of places and what makes them unique and desirable. However, tribes must decide the approach they want to take and the role that casinos and their revenues should play in promoting nation-building. To illustrate this process, I present a case study of the Nez Perce tribe of rural northern Idaho that chose to use casino gambling as a form of economic development. I discuss how and why they chose to build a casino, the obstacles they faced and continue to face, and the consequences of the strategy they selected.

GAMING AND THE NEZ PERCE RESERVATION

The Nez Perce are more typical of tribes in rural areas that do not have access to large metropolitan areas upon which to draw potential customers to their casino. The reservation, which is located in a relatively low-income region of the state where revitalization is most needed, has changed significantly over time. Historically, the territory of the Nez Perce included over 13 million acres stretching from central Idaho to adjoining areas in present day Washington and Oregon. The arrival of the Lewis and Clark expedition in 1805 prefaced the era of manifest destiny, and later, under the Treaty of 1855, the federal government

Table 10.1. Two Conceptions of Economic Development

"Jobs and Income" (Reactive)	"Nation-Building" (Proactive)
Responds to anyone's agenda, (from the Federal government or off the street)	Responds to one's own agenda (from strategic planning for the long-term future)
Emphasizes short-term payoffs (especially jobs and income now)	Emphasizes long-term payoffs (sustained community well-being)
Emphasizes starting businesses	Emphasizes creating an environment in which businesses can last
Success is measured by economic impacts	Success is measured by social, cultural, political, *and* economic impacts
Development is mostly the tribal planner's job (planner proposes; council decides)	Development is the job of tribal and community leadership (they set vision, guidelines, policy, others implement
Treats development as, first and foremost, an *economic* problem	Treats development as, first and foremost, a *political* problem
The solution is money	The solution is a sound institutional foundation, strategic direction, informed action

Source: Cornell & Kalt (1998).

designated a 7.5 million-acre reservation for the Nez Perce spanning northeastern Oregon and central Idaho. The discovery of gold within the reservation boundary resulted in a renegotiation of the treaty boundaries in 1863, which reduced the reservation to one-tenth its original size (750,000 acres in northern Idaho), and the Dawes Allotment Act of 1887 opened up 500,000 acres on the reservation for white settlement. Consequently, over 85 percent of Nez Perce reservation land is currently owned by non-Indians.

People and towns on or near the reservation have traditionally been tied to resource-extraction industries, especially logging. In the 1990s, the Clinton Administration reacted to charges of large-scale over-harvesting of timber on federal lands in the region and reduced such harvesting by nearly 90 percent. The local logging industry, severely affected, began laying off non-Indians and Indians working in mills near the Nez Perce reservation, resulting in some of the highest unemployment rates in the Idaho.

Some non-Indian towns on the reservation are trying—with limited success—to switch their economic bases from resource extraction to tourism, hoping to benefit from the tourists expected as part of the Lewis and Clark bicentennial celebrations that began in 2004. By contrast, the Nez Perce tribe has limited options for attracting visitors to its reservation town of Lapwai. With its traditional government-built low-income housing, it is not an attractive destination. Before gaming, the tribe had the familiar litany of problems associated with other reservations, including an unemployment rate of over 70 percent (personal interview with J. Matthews, 2004). Not surprisingly, having observed the gaming success of other tribes, the Nez Perce tribe decided to build a gambling casino.

However, gambling in Idaho was, and remains, a controversial issue. The introduction of Indian gaming met with enormous opposition in the state. Although Idaho permitted lottery machines, former Governor Phil Batt initially tried to ban lottery gambling on reservations. Eventually, he dropped his opposition to Indian gaming and tried to work more closely with the Nez Perce, Coeur d'Alene, and Kootenai tribes. Accordingly, the Nez Perce were able to open their gaming casino in 1995. The current Governor negotiated an agreement with the tribes in 2001 under which they would remit a percentage of casino profits to the state, but the legislature would not ratify the compact.

In 2002 the Nez Perce and other Idaho tribes garnered sufficient support to have the issue of Indian gaming placed on the 2002 election ballot as a statewide referendum, and it passed with 58 percent of the vote. The referendum on the Idaho Indian Gaming and Reliance Act stipulates that 5 percent of net profits from Indian casinos go to local schools and education. It also limits Indian gaming growth to 5 percent a year and to a total of 25 percent over 10 years, a rare example of a business enterprise limiting in advance its growth potential.

Despite passage of the referendum, some Idaho State legislators continued to pursue legal challenges in court, claiming that the Indian gaming referendum was invalid. Some tribal leaders raised the issue of racism against Indians (Rudzitis, 2005). Motivations for opposing gaming varied. While some Idaho legislators argued against gaming on moral grounds and on the need to protect the integrity of the family, others raised fears of Indian tribes expanding gambling beyond reservations. Skeptics argued that the state simply wanted to avoid competition with its own lottery. Still other critics of the state charged that opponents to Indian gaming were in the pay of the Nevada gaming association, because Jackpot, Nevada attracts people from southern Idaho who might go to Indian casinos if they were located in the state. Subsequently, the Idaho Supreme Court dismissed the lawsuit and let the results of the referendum stand.[4]

Pragmatism played a role in the eventual outcome. The tribe is a nation whose sole dealings, from its perspective, should be with the federal government. However, the Supreme Court of the United States has a spotty history of interpreting laws and tribal jurisdictional issues in favor of the tribes (Mason, 2000). If the U.S. Supreme Court ruled against the right of the tribe to have gaming, it would most likely foreshadow a devastating financial and legal blow to the tribe by the Idaho Supreme Court. Therefore, the Nez Perce, like other tribes, agreed to give a percentage of the profits to the state and to restrict the extent to which they would expand tribal gaming facilities in the future. The decision by the Nez Perce tribe to put the gaming issue on the statewide ballot also reflected its view that economic benefits from the casino extend beyond the reservation itself. The tribe initiated a policy to apply a portion of casino profits to fund social and health programs on reservations and make contributions to local public schools.

The casino in question is located eight miles from Lewiston-Clarkston, which the Census recently designated as a metropolitan area. As the second largest local business, it employs approximately 400 persons, roughly a third of whom are non-Indians. Unemployment on the reservation has declined from an extraordinary 70 to 30 percent since the casino was opened (personal interview with J. Matthews, 2004). The casino also brings people into surrounding communities since 40 percent of the Nez Perce Indian gaming facility visitors are from out-of-region. These nonresident visitors are estimated to spend $ 80 to $ 130 per person on gasoline, food, and other forms of consumption and shopping outside the Nez Perce casino (Peterson & DiNoto, 2002). At a regional level, a study of tribal gaming by the five tribes in northern Idaho found that it contributed $ 45 million in wages and earnings to the regional economy. Moreover, social welfare payments dropped by over $ 6 million since the casinos opened.

The population on the Nez Perce reservation has increased 44 percent from 1,463 in 1980 to 2,101 in 2000, and tribal members are also more likely to remain on or live near the reservation, with 64 percent doing so in 2000 (Personal interview with A. Miles, 2004). For Idaho as a whole, between 1990 and 2000, the Indian population increased almost 30 percent. The dramatic decrease in unemployment has helped retain tribal members on reservations, stemming a downward trend and also attracting Indians back onto the reservation from metropolitan areas. Not all of the increased population or the greater tendency to stay on the reservation can be attributed to job opportunities and improved conditions from opening the casinos. The Nez Perce tribe has been proactive in trying to provide opportunities in a number of other ways. The tribe created a variety of programs on the reservation, including a sustainable forestry program, wolf reintroduction, fish hatcheries, and horse breeding (Personal interview with A. Miles, 2004).

The income generated by casinos has given tribes a newfound economic freedom, but it can also potentially create social conflict and factionalism within tribal structures, especially over who can be a tribal member and benefit from the casino earnings (Gonzales, 2003). The Nez Perce tribe has, to date, used that money wisely and minimized local and tribal conflicts by making investments both within and beyond their communities.

The Nez Perce tribe recognized the need to diversify its economy since gaming may not prove to be profitable or sustainable in the longer term. The tribe has moved towards diversifying activities at their casino by planning a $ 54 million hotel and entertainment facility expansion. The tribe has created firms that provide jobs in new activities, including retail convenience stores, gift shops, gas stations, logging, and light manufacturing, and has provided various social services such as a new medical clinic. It realizes that Idaho state legislators may find casinos an attractive economic development tool and ultimately decide to allow non-Indian casino gambling, thereby creating direct competition to their own establishment. The investment of tribal casino profits in a variety of diversified activities is one means of anticipating the potentially reduced revenues from tribal gaming sources. In making such investments, the tribe is leading the transformation of the reservation from an economically depressed community into one with more opportunities for future rural economic development and nation building.

CONCLUSIONS

The recent advent of gaming has opened up a new era for economic development on Indian reservations, offering hope to many tribes mired in a poverty-laden past and neglected by the larger non-Indian population. Gaming holds out the real possibility for some tribes to become self-sustaining and has provided them with a means of taking control of their own future economic development. Tribal economic development strategies in the past (and, for many tribes without casinos, still today) have been based on resource extraction or marginal agriculture, development policies which, in rural areas, were typically instigated at the urging of the state or federal government or by private corporations. Given the limited private investment on Indian reservations, as well as financial constraints Indians face to obtain their own investment capital, gaming has opened possibilities in an otherwise bleak economic landscape, with profits from gaming activities allowing tribes to plan more diversified local economies. An indirect consequence of economic development from gaming might well be increased interactions between Indians and non-Indians that would lessen the endemic tensions and increase mutual understanding and respect between the two groups.

As the gap widens between poor and newly wealthy Indian tribes, the unequal distribution of gaming wealth between tribes remains a concern. This income and wealth gap is largely a function of geography and individual cultural-political considerations unique to individual tribes. There is a need to consider possible strategies to cope with the growing differences. However, economic development from gaming activities is clearly a step up from the pervasive poverty that, until recently, characterized the economic situations of many Native American tribes. Finally, gaming and economic development in general are only a means by which tribes have a chance to become self-sufficient, reassert their sovereign rights, and re-establish a vital culture that was almost destroyed. It is hoped that Indian tribes, at the same time, will increasingly contribute their distinctiveness to the larger society of which they are citizens.

ENDNOTES

1. The author gratefully acknowledges Angela Gonzalez, Joe Kalt, Rosemary Streatfeild, and especially Julian Matthews, Aaron Miles and other Nez Perce tribal members who help make this research possible.
2. Historically, American Indians have been undercounted. The U.S. Census only began enumerating American Indians separately in 1860, and those counts excluded Indians living on reservations until 1890. The numbers vary and have been imprecise for reasons related to how census takers defined Indians, how the data methodology changed, and the impact of not allowing people to self identify as Native Americans until the 1960 census.
3. This was the experience of the Coeur d'Alene tribe where Indians had large farms exceeding 1,000 acres and also employed non-Indians. These farms were broken up and the land sub-divided in small 160-acre plots which were allotted to tribal members. The remaining land was opened up for white settlement.
4. The issue of the Nez Perce tribe negotiating with the state of Idaho, or even putting the referendum on the ballot for the voters to decide, was fraught with difficulties and risks for the tribe. Legally, as a nation that signed a treaty with the federal government, the tribe is not bound to, or under, Idaho jurisdiction, and has no need to negotiate or ask approval from the state.

REFERENCES

Bolan, M. (1997). The mobility experience and neighborhood attachment. *Demography, 34,* 225–237.

Bolton, R. (1992). Place prosperity vs. people prosperity revisited: An old issue with a new angle. *Urban Studies*, *29*, 185–203.

Churchill, W. (1993). *Struggle for the land.* Monroe, ME: Common Courage Press.

Carmichael, B.A. (1998). Foxwoods resort casino, Connecticut-a mega-attraction: Who wants it? Who benefits? In K. J. Meyer-Arendt & R. Hartman (Eds), *Casino gambling in America: Origins, trends, and impacts* (pp. 67–75). New York: Cognizant Communications.

Carmichael, B.A., & Peppard, D.M. (1998). The impacts of Foxwoods resort casino on its dual host community: Southern Connecticut and the Mashantucket Pequot tribe. In A.A. Lew & G.A. Van Otten (Eds), *Tourism and gaming on American Indian land* (pp. 128–144). New York: Cognizant Communications.

Cornell, S., & Kalt, J.P. (1998). Sovereignty and nation-building: The development challenge in Indian country today. *American Indian Culture and Research Journal, 23*, 187–214.

Davis, J.A., & Hudman, L.E. (1998). The history of Indian gaming law and casino development in the western United States. In A.A. Lew & G.A. Van Otten (Eds.), *Tourism and gaming on American Indian land* (pp. 82–92). New York: Cognizant Communications.

Davis, J.A., & Otterstrom, S.M. (1998). Growth of Indian gaming in the united states. In K.J. Meyer-Arendt & R. Hartman (Eds.), *Casino gambling in America: origins, trends, and impacts* (pp. 53–66). New York: Cognizant Communications.

Denevan, W.M. (Ed.). (1992). *The native population of the Americas in 1492.* Madison, WI: University of Wisconsin Press.

Diamond, D.B., & Tolley, G.S. (1982). *The economics of urban amenities.* New York: Academic Press.

Dobyns, H.F. (1983).*Their number becomes thinned: Native American population dynamics in eastern North America.* Knoxville, TN: University of Tennessee Press.

Fernandez, R.R., & Dillman, D.A. (1979). The influence of community attachment on geographic mobility. *Rural Sociology, 44*, 345–360.

Franz, K. (1999). *Indian reservations in the United States*. Chicago: University of Chicago Press.

Fromson, B.D. (2003). *Hitting the jackpot: The inside story of the richest Indian tribe in history*. New York: Atlantic Monthly Press.

Gitter, R.J., & Reagan, P.B. (2002). Reservation wages: An analysis of the effects of reservations on employment of American Indian men. *American Economic Review, 92*, 1160–1170.

Gonzales, A.A. (2003). Gaming and displacement: Winners and losers in American Indian casino development. *International Social Science Journal, 55*, 123–133.

Gonzales, A.A. (2004). American Indians: Their contemporary reality and future trajectory. In D. Brown & L. Swanson (Eds.), *Challenges for rural America in the twenty first century* (pp. 53–66). College Station, PA: Pennsylvania State University Press.

d'Hauteserre, A.-M. (2000). Foxwoods casino resort: An unusual experiment in economic development. *Economic Geography, 75*, 112–121.

Johnson, J.D., & Rasker, R. (1993). Local government, local business climate and quality of life. *Montana Policy Review, 3*, 11–19.

Johnson, J.D., & Rasker, R. (1995). The role of economic and quality of life values in rural business decisions. *Journal of Rural Studies, 11*, 405–416.

Jorgenson, J.G. (1998). Gaming and recent American Indian economic development. *American Indian Culture and Research Journal, 22*, 157–172.

LaDuke, W. (1999). *All our relations: native struggles for land and life*. Cambridge, MA: South End Press.

King, J.M., & McIntire, E. (1998). The impact of the Indian gaming regulatory act on tribes in the U.S. In A. A. Lew & G. A. Van Otten (Eds.), *Tourism and gaming on American Indian land* (pp. 48–56). New York: Cognizant Communications.

Marsh, B. (1987). Continuity and decline in the anthracite towns of Pennsylvania. *Annals, Association of American Geographers, 77*, 337–352.

Mason, W.D. (2000). *Indian gaming: Tribal sovereignty and American politics*. Norman, OK: University of Oklahoma Press.

Nagel, J. (1996). *American Indian ethnic renewal: red power and the resurgence of identity and culture*. New York: Oxford University Press.

Power, T.M. (1995). Thinking about natural resource dependent economies: Moving beyond the folk economics of the rearview mirror. In R.L. Knight & S.F. Bates (Eds.), *A new century for natural resource management* (pp. 137–161). Washington, DC: Island Press.

Power, T.M. (1996). *Failed landscapes: The search for an economics of place*. Washington, DC: Island Press.

Raento, P. (2003). The return of the one-armed bandit: Gambling and the west. In G.J. Hausladen (Ed.), *Western places, American myths: How we think about the West* (pp. 225–252). Reno, NV: University of Nevada Press.

Rasker, R. (1993). Rural development, conservation, and public policy in the greater Yellowstone ecosystem. *Society and Natural Resources, 6*, 109–126.

Relph, E. (1986). *Place and placelessness*. Toronto: University of Toronto Press.

Rudzitis, G. (1989). Migration, places, and nonmetropolitan development. *Urban Geography, 10*, 396–411.

Rudzitis, G. (1993). Migration, sense of place, and the American West. *Urban Geography, 14*, 574–584.

Rudzitis, G. (1996). *Wilderness and the changing American West*. New York: Wiley.

Rudzitis, G. (1998, April). *Towards a theory of place in the 'new' American West*. Paper presented at the annual meeting of the Association of American Geographers, Boston, MA.

Rudzitis, G. (1999). Amenities increasingly draw people to the rural West. *Rural Development Perspectives, 14*, 9–13.

Rudzitis, G. (2005). Indigenous Indian populations, racist discourses and ongoing conflicts in the American Northwest. In P. Lagayette (Ed.), *Exchange: practices and representations* (pp. 171–196). Paris: University of Paris Press.

Rudzitis, G., & Streatfeild, R.A. (1993). The importance of amenities and attitudes: A Washington example. *Journal of Environmental Systems, 22*, 269–277.

Rudzitis, G., & Tolley, G.S. (1999, November). *Towards a theory of place and regional development.* Paper presented at annual meeting of the Regional Science Association, Santa Fe, NM.

Samson, R.J. (1988). Local friendship ties and community attachment in mass society: A multilevel systematic model. *American Sociological Review, 53*, 766–779.

Snipp, C.M. (1989). *American Indians: The first of this land.* New York: Sage.

Snipp, C.M. (1997). Some observations about racial boundaries and the experience of American Indians. *Ethnic and Racial Studies, 20*, 667–689.

Stegner, W. (1990). *The American West as living space.* Ann Arbor, MI: University of Michigan.

Stinner, W.F., Van Loon, M., Chang, S.-W., & Byun, Y. (1990). Community size, individual social position and community attachment. *Rural Sociology, 55*, 494–521.

Tolley, G.S., Rudzitis, G., & Baden, B. (1999). *Regional economic theory, sense of place and the American West.* Unpublished manuscript, University of Chicago.

Winchell, D., Lounsbury, J., & Sommers, L. (1998). Indian gaming in the U.S.: Distribution, significance and trends. *Focus, 44*, 1–10.

Young, F.W. (1999). *Small towns in multilevel society.* New York: University Press of America.

Young, I.M. (1990). *Justice and the politics of difference.* Princeton: Princeton University Press.

CHAPTER 11

METRO EXPANSION AND NONMETRO CHANGE IN THE SOUTH

JOHN B. CROMARTIE

INTRODUCTION

Demographic trends over the past several decades reflect a relentless geographic expansion of U.S. metropolitan (metro) areas, a steady rise in the number of long-distance commuters, and rapid population growth in adjacent, nonmetropolitan (nonmetro) counties. As suburbs expand, nearby nonmetro counties enter a period of change marked by increasing economic integration with metro economies, steady losses of rural and small-town landscapes and livelihoods, and eventual reclassification from nonmetro to metro status. Such transitions intensified during the 1990s as migration into nonmetro areas rebounded. Given the complexity of land-use patterns and socioeconomic conditions emerging along the metro-nonmetro boundary, it's important to understand the transition process and its effect on communities and people. In addition, such extensive transitions call into question the use of nonmetro counties to identify rural and small town settlement areas. Researchers and policy makers must apply rural and urban concepts cautiously or even consider new thinking altogether.

In this paper I examine what happens to nonmetro counties and their mostly rural and small-town settlement patterns as they become metro. Previous research assumed no systematic process by which nonmetro counties became integrated into metro areas, and no one has proposed or measured any type of transitional sequence. I attempt to do this by exploring the following questions concerning metro expansion and nonmetro change in the South:

1. Over time, is it possible to describe a consistent developmental pattern followed by a significant portion of nonmetro counties in the process of becoming metro? In particular, would this sequence commonly include a period of increasing commuting from the rural and small town periphery prior to suburban in-migration and the land-use changes associated with sprawl?

2. At any given point in time, is it possible to distinguish counties at different stages in this developmental sequence? In particular, is it possible to

W.A. Kandel & D.L. Brown (eds.), Population Change and Rural Society, 233–252.

distinguish two types of high-commuting counties, those in which long-time residents have simply increased their city-bound job commuting, and those that have experienced suburbanization and sprawl?

To address the first question, I introduce a stages-of-growth model consisting of a sequence of demographic and socioeconomic transitions representing nonmetro-to-metro county assimilation. It is based on demographic transition theory, especially the mobility transition hypothesis explaining changes in migration patterns in response to modernization (Zelinsky, 1971). The sequence begins with a mostly rural, nonmetro county experiencing little or no metro influence and ends with a fully integrated, mostly urban, metro county. Hypothesized sequences are tested using 40 years of population and commuting data for 28 counties surrounding Atlanta, a metro area known for its rapid and widespread deconcentration (Fulton et al., 2001; Galster et al., 2001).

To address the second question, I focus on commuting and population growth in southern, nonmetro counties during the 1990s. Counties with significant increases in commuting to metro areas are identified and compared on the basis of population change from net migration. I use these measures to distinguish counties experiencing suburbanization and those that simply send more workers into metro areas.

In this paper I use "suburbanization" and "sprawl" to denote different aspects of rapidly expanding, residential and retail development on the metro fringe. Suburbanization describes demographic and socioeconomic change and its effect on individuals, families, neighborhoods, and communities (Frey & Speare, 1988; Stanback, 1991). Sprawl applies to physical aspects of metro expansion, specifically to low-density, fragmented patterns of residential and commercial development, most often unplanned and unmanaged (Daniels, 1999; Heimlich & Anderson, 2001; Wolman et al., 2005). The terms do not always coincide. Theoretically at least, suburbanization can occur without sprawl. However, in the context of metro expansion and nonmetro change in the South, the overlap between suburbanization and sprawl is nearly complete. In the 1980s and 1990s, urbanized land in the South expanded at three times the rate of metro population growth, a strong indication that low-density development dominates southern, metro expansion (Fulton et al., 2001). Sprawl causes more counties to undergo nonmetro-to-metro reclassification than would occur with more compact patterns of development, therefore increasing the rate at which nonmetro population declines as a result of reclassification.

BACKGROUND

Forces driving metro expansion shift over time and vary considerably among regions and individual metro areas (Elliott & Perry, 1996; Frey & Speare, 1988; Heimlich & Anderson, 2001; Stanback, 1991). The automobile helped trigger a massive city-to-suburb relocation, resulting in settlement patterns in formerly nonmetro counties that conform more to commuting and less to farming, mining, or logging. The development of interstate highways, high-speed telecommunications, the extension of public utilities, and lifestyle changes oriented toward lower-density settings helped fuel population and settlement deconcentration (Johnson, 1999). Rising incomes have allowed more Americans to act on widely-shared residential preferences for smaller places on the metro fringe (Brown et al., 1997). Social conflict in the 1960s and 1970s led to "white flight" out of many central cities. More recently, the influx of immigrants to some larger metro areas may be stimulating an outflow of domestic migrants, especially those who might compete directly with immigrants in the urban labor market (Frey, 1993; Frey & Johnson, 1998).

All of these explanations of metro expansion derive from an urban perspective. That is, the increase in metro influence, the transformation of rural areas on the periphery, and the eventual reclassification of counties from nonmetro to metro are said to result from the spillover of metro population and economic activity into once rural or small-town settings. Statistics support this viewpoint. According to a recent ERS study, census-defined urbanized areas grew by more than 1 million acres per year between 1960 and 1990 (Heimlich & Anderson, 2001). Most nonmetro population growth occurs in counties adjacent to metro areas; during the "rural rebound" of the 1990s, 75 percent of nonmetro population growth occurred in such areas.

However, other factors emerge when transformation on the urban fringe is viewed from a rural perspective. The process of metro integration can begin before suburbanization. Long-distance commuting to metro jobs, the most widely used empirical measure of metro influence, can increase in an outlying county before any increase in residential development or suburban in-migration. The decline of nearby job opportunities, increased ease of travel to better-paying jobs, and a better-educated nonmetro labor force all contribute to increased long-distance commuting on the part of workers already living near enough to metro areas. The evolving structure of metro central cities, especially the expansion of employment into suburbs, stimulates rural commuting. The fact that a nonmetro county can fall within the sphere of metro influence before suburbanization and sprawl is not fully appreciated.

This analysis demonstrates that metro expansion and its transformative impact on rural and small town America are more complex than previously supposed. Demographers have documented aspects of rural change on the metro periphery and shed light on causes and key socioeconomic effects (Brown, 1979; Elliott & Perry, 1996; Fuguitt et al., 1988; Fuguitt et al., 1989; McGranahan & Salsgiver, 1992). This study adds to these insights by dividing the process into distinct stages and measuring the differing impacts on rural people and landscapes at each stage.

In addition, this research helps address the need to better classify U.S. settlement, at a time when rural-urban boundaries are increasingly blurred. The actual mechanics of the nonmetro-to-metro transition remain understudied, at least from a rural perspective, in part because the end result of the process is the development of an urban landscape and loss of nonmetro status. When hundreds of nonmetro counties are following this transition at any given time, settlement classifications need constant adjustment. Researchers find it difficult to compare metro and nonmetro conditions over time (Fuguitt et al., 1989). Policy makers face a fundamental problem in determining eligibility for rural-based programs, because they must aim at a constantly moving target. This analysis represents one effort to differentiate rural and urban county characteristics along the ever-expanding metro periphery.

DATA AND METHODS

In this paper I examine daily commuting and population growth from net migration for counties in the South, using decennial data from the U.S. Census Bureau. Commuting data derive from a set of journey-to-work questions, appearing since 1960 on the "long-form" questionnaire, administered to a one-in-six sample of the population. The Census Bureau provides aggregated, county-to-county commuting files for each census year, that are calculated by comparing the county of residence and county of work for all individuals in the sample.

I measure increasing metro integration as an increase during a decade in commuting levels from nonmetro counties on the periphery into the "central" counties of metro areas. Defined by the Office of Management and Budget (OMB) after each decennial census, central counties contain the principal cities of metro areas. Additional metro counties are included because their level of commuting to central counties indicates they are already economically integrated into the metro area. This study focuses on counties not yet qualified as metro but clearly heading in that direction.

By definition, suburbanization is a function of migration. I use five sets of 10-year net migration data to measure the onset of suburbanization in counties that are experiencing rising commuting rates. County-level net migration rates have been calculated for each decade since the 1950s, using similar methodologies applied to census data and statistics on births and deaths from the vital registration system (Bowles & Tarver, 1965; Bowles et al., 1975; Fuguitt & Beale, 1993; Johnson et al., 2003; White et al., 1987). Counties that are growing at three times the national average for nonmetro counties are identified as clearly suburbanizing and are compared with counties that continue to experience net out-migration despite rising commuting levels.

To address the first question—exploring nonmetro-to-metro transitions over time—I compare levels of commuting to the central counties of Atlanta for five decennial censuses, 1960–2000, and population change from net migration for five decades, 1950–2000. The analysis includes the 28 counties that comprise the Atlanta metro area as of 2000. In order to account for the expansion of Atlanta's urban core over time, it was necessary to use the changing set of central counties. OMB metro definitions show three central counties in Atlanta in 1960 and 1970, five in 1980 and 1990, and 12 in 2000.

To address the second question—exploring metro expansion in the 1990s—I identify emerging, high-commuting counties on the periphery of all metro areas in the South. I measure the change in the percent of workers commuting from nonmetro counties to metro central cities, using OMB's 1990 definitions. Emerging, high-commuting counties are defined as those with less than 25 percent commuting to the central counties in 1990 that increased their commuting by 5 percentage points or more (twice the national average) from 1990 to 2000.

Why examine the South? By many indicators, the rural South has been most affected by nonmetro-to-metro transitions. The region has shown the steepest decline in the proportion of its population living in nonmetro counties over the past 75 years [see Figure 11.1 in Johnson and Cromartie chapter]. Close to one-third of workers living in the nonmetro South crossed county lines to get to work in 2000, compared to just one-quarter in the rest of the nation's nonmetro counties. The region also leads the nation in low-density sprawl development. Between 1982 and 1997, the built-up portion of metro areas (as measured by census-defined urbanized areas) increased by 60 percent in the South, 20 points higher than elsewhere. At the same time, the overall metro population in the South increased by just 22 percent. The resulting 23 percent decline in population density, from 2.82 to 2.16 people per acre, was the highest drop among the four U.S. census regions (Fulton et al., 2001).

County-level analysis limits the tracking of suburbanization and sprawl because so much change occurs within county boundaries. Average county size in the South is small enough to allow relatively useful analysis at the county level. Being another fast-growing, sun-belt region, the West most likely has similar levels of sprawl, but much more of it is hidden within counties. Smaller geographic units, such as census tracts, would be required to conduct this type of analysis with the same level of detail in many parts of the West. In addition, the South has much more densely-settled rural areas compared to the West, so that as metro areas expand, they more often merge with and transform already established nonmetro towns and cities.

Within the South, Atlanta provides an excellent case study of metro expansion over the past 40 years. The official size of the region grew from 5 to 28 counties since 1960. The original central business district has greatly expanded and now competes with multiple "edge cities" (Garreau, 1991). Extensive, low-density development extends into every corner of the region. Urbanized land grew from 700,000 to 1.3 million acres between 1982 and 1997, at the same time that population density dropped (Fulton et al., 2001). In addition, counties in northern Georgia are small even by southern standards, allowing a more detailed picture of metro expansion.

Table 11.1. Nonmetro-to-Metro County Transitions in the South, 1960–2000

	Number of Counties	Population (Millions) 1960	1990	Population Change (Millions), 1960–1990
South	1,424	55.0	100.2	45.2
Metro Areas, 1960	154	27.1	52.5	25.4
Nonmetro, 1960	1,270	27.8	47.7	19.9
Added to existing metro areas after 1960	165	4.3	11.9	7.6
Formed new metro areas after 1960	88	5.0	11.2	6.2
Remained nonmetro after 1960	1,017	18.6	24.6	6.0

A STAGES-OF-GROWTH MODEL OF THE NONMETRO-TO-METRO TRANSITION

Metro expansion is a well-documented and on-going process, but the actual level of conversion from nonmetro to metro status may not be fully appreciated. Table 11.1 documents the extent of county conversion in the South over a 40-year period. In 1960, the 81 metro areas identified in the South contained 154 counties and little more than half the region's population. By 2000, the metro areas originally identified in 1960 had expanded to include an additional 165 formerly nonmetro counties and contained nearly two-thirds of the region's population. These new, outlying suburban counties were among the fastest-growing in the region (and the country as well). The 7.6 million people added to them between 1960 and 2000 exceeded the 6 million people added to the 1,017 counties that remain nonmetro (last column of Table 11.1). It also exceeded the 6.2 million people added to the 88 counties that formed 45 new metro areas after 1960 (row 5). With the removal through reclassification of 253 counties, the nonmetro population in 2000 (24.6 million) was less than it was in 1960 and little more than half of what it would have been without metro expansion (47.7 million).

Given the extent and intensity of nonmetro change represented by these numbers, it is surprising to find little research on how the process plays out in affected counties. What happens to economic, social, and settlement patterns in these nonmetro counties in the course of becoming metro? Are they merely passive recipients of new population or do more complex interactions occur? Most of the literature on suburbanization and sprawl assumes a one-way process: suburbs expand into rural territory, urban sprawl transforms the landscape. However, nonmetro counties may undergo change themselves, less visible than sprawl itself, as a result of growing metro influence. A key component of that change is an increase in the number of residents already living there who begin commuting to jobs in metro central cities.

A simple increase in commuting causes a number of changes prior to the rapid population growth associated with suburbanization. Incomes increase, unemployment and out-migration decrease, and there may even be a slight shift in population distribution to places with greater access to the newly acquired metro jobs. However, the extent of these changes is small compared to areas undergoing suburbanization, and the rural character of the county—its landscape amenities, industrial structure, and overall settlement patterns—would be largely unaffected.

This scenario suggests that many nonmetro counties pass through a series of stages as they become economically integrated with a metro area (Table 11.2). The stages differ not only in terms of the rise in metro influence through commuting but also in terms of demographic patterns, socioeconomic characteristics, settlement, and land use.

Stage I counties are those most easily identifiable as rural, with little or no commuting to metro centers and landscapes dominated by small towns and cities, farms, woods, open countryside, and scattered rural homesteads. Economic restructuring and technological change in agriculture and other resource-based economies fueled high out-migration in the 1950s and 1960s from most of these types of counties. Population loss or below-average growth persists, except where manufacturing, recreation, or other service economies provide an alternative economic base. These counties typically face higher unemployment and poverty, lower education and job skills, and an aging population compared with metro (especially suburban metro) settings.

As metro areas expand, workers in nearby rural counties gain access to better-paying jobs, especially where new transportation and communications links improve travel time and information flows. Stage II is marked by increased commuting flows to metro central counties prior to large-scale suburbanization. Such increases are caused by a combination of declining job opportunities in the rural counties themselves and increasing ease of access to metro jobs. The deconcentration of metropolitan economic activity into the suburbs, a hallmark of suburban development beginning in the 1960s, brought jobs closer to hinterland populations (Stanback, 1991). Stage II counties show little change in the visible landscape except where residents move from more isolated locations to form dispersed settlement patterns along roads and highways leading to metro areas (Hart, 1995). Incomes improve but the types of jobs available in the county itself continue to be limited. Population loss is mitigated because fewer people need to leave for job-related reasons, but high-level suburban in-migration has not yet begun.

Table 11.2. Stages of Growth in the Nonmetro-to-Metro Transition

	Level of Metro Interaction	Population Change	Socioeconomic Change	Land-Use Change
Stage I Little or no metro influence	Little or no daily commuting to metro central counties; interaction limited to business trips, weekend shopping, and leisure visits	Population loss through out-migration	Traditional, rural industries predominate; lower education rates, higher unemployment, and lower incomes	Small towns and rural landscapes predominate; low overall population densities
Stage II Initial increase in metro influence through an increase in daily commuting	Initial rise in daily commuting to metro central counties; increases in shopping and other forms of interaction	Decreasing out-migration but little growth from in-migration	Rural jobs still predominate within the county; incomes increase for families with commuters; other disadvantages remain	Small towns and rural landscapes continue to predominate; transportation links begin to affect settlement patterns

Stage III Continued increase in metro influence through the emergence of urban sprawl	Daily commuting to metro central counties peaks; local trips begin to replace other forms of metro interaction	Rapid population growth through in-migration and higher natural increase	Rural jobs replaced by construction jobs and a growing service sector; incomes rise, unemployment decreases; new residents are younger and better educated	New homes, subdivisions, roads, and businesses increase sprawl development; rural landscapes fragment
Stage IV Full incorporation into metro sphere	Local commuting and shopping increases; long-distance commuting patterns diversify	Continued population increases but at decreasing rates	Diversified service sector predominates local employment; socioeconomic indicators continue to improve	Residential infill, retail infrastructure, and business expansion completes the urbanization of the landscape

Metro population growth, increasing urban land values, expanding transportation investments, and other factors eventually lead to further population deconcentration. Rural areas on the periphery enter a more familiar and visible process of suburbanization and sprawl. Stage III is characterized by rapid change in settlement patterns and socioeconomic characteristics, a turnaround from net out- to net in-migration, and increasing potential for social conflict between newcomers and longer-term residents. Farmers and other rural landowners face increasing land values and tax assessments but also increasing availability and quality of goods and services. Construction jobs and a growing local service sector improve employment chances and reduce poverty. Population density increases in the suburbanizing county at the same time it decreases in the expanding urban area as a whole. As nonmetro counties enter Stage III, sprawl often decreases their urbanization, defined as the percentage of the population living in urban areas of 2,500 or more. Nonmetro areas in the South are more heavily settled than elsewhere, and large percentages of their populations typically live in small towns and cities. Initially, new suburban residents tend to locate outside these urban settings (Hart, 1995; Heimlich & Anderson, 2001).

Stage IV signifies a county fully incorporated into the metro economy. Large-lot subdivisions compete with higher-density residential infill, office parks, and shopping malls within a greatly transformed, suburban landscape. Daily commuting patterns diversify as local job opportunities keep more workers close to home and also attract reverse commuters. Population continues to increase, and a diversified service sector dominates the economy. The rural landscape declines significantly along with the socioeconomic disadvantages associated with sparse, isolated settlement. Just as Stage I counties are most easily labeled rural, Stage IV counties clearly fall outside such a classification and cease to directly concern rural analysts and policy makers.

DEVELOPMENT OF METRO ATLANTA, 1960–2000

The extent to which this path is followed by counties encountering metro expansion, especially the initial rise in commuting on the part of current residents prior to suburban in-migration, is unknown. Stage II and Stage III describe changes that certainly take place in most nonmetro-to-metro transitions, but how often are they typically sequential and distinct phases? To begin addressing this question, I compare the timing of commuting and net migration increases for 28 counties in the Atlanta metro area during a 40-year period of rapid suburbanization and sprawl. With a few exceptions, Stage I counties were identified as those with less than 15 percent commuting to central counties, the minimum threshold used for many years in identifying outlying counties within the official metro area system. A distinct Stage II for a given decade was marked in counties showing a significant, initial jump in commuting to Atlanta's central counties with little or no population growth from net migration during that decade. Stage II persisted if high commuting continued in subsequent decades with no increase in net migration. A simultaneous increase in commuting and net in-migration signified Stage III. If the initial commuting increase coincided with significant net in-migration, then no Stage II was recorded for that county. Stage IV was marked by the transition to central-county status within the official metro system, an indication of increased urbanization.

For a few counties, a jump from Stage I to Stage II was identified when the percentage of workers commuting to the central counties went from zero to just under the 15 percent threshold, if that was the biggest jump in its development. On the other hand, if a county followed this initial jump with a higher one-decade jump, than the Stage I to Stage II change would be identified with the decade in which this more significant change took place. Also, it was not always easy to pinpoint the decade when suburbanization first appeared, as indicated by a big jump in positive net in-migration. Especially in the 1970s, when all places were growing much more than in previous decades, I judged the growth from net migration as significant in comparison with the average for that decade. Finally, the official set of central counties (to which commuting was measured) increased over the time period examined, reflecting the rapid expansion of Atlanta's urban core. For these reasons, the commuting pattern in each county over all decades had to be examined and judged separately, adding an element of subjectivity and limiting the present application to one metro area.

Even with these caveats, the results clearly confirm the existence of distinct, Stage II changes to many nonmetro counties as they entered the Atlanta metro area (Figure 11.1). A majority of counties that were in Stage I in 1960 followed the stages-of-growth model. The 1970 map in Figure 11.1 shows just how rapidly Atlanta expanded its influence during the 1960s, with 18 counties exhibiting an initial, sharp rise in commuting to the region's central counties, which at the time numbered just three. Seven of the counties closest to the urban core entered directly as Stage III counties (with no distinct Stage II), while the other 11, more peripheral counties, exhibited pre-suburbanization commuting increases on the part of rural and small town residents.

A common pattern (Stage I to II in the 1960s, Stage II to III in the 1970s) is illustrated by Dawson County on the northern edge of the metro area. The percentage of workers commuting out of the county into Atlanta core counties (as defined for 1960) jumped from zero to 11 percent in the 1960s. If you include Forsyth County as part of Atlanta's core (a status it gained in 2000) the jump for Dawson in the 1960s was from zero to 20 percent. This occurred at the same time that Dawson lost 9 percent of its population to net out-migration, following an 18 percent loss in the 1950s. Migration patterns shifted dramatically to 21 percent growth in the 1970s, followed by growth of 85 percent in the 1980s and 58 percent in the 1990s. Commuting into Atlanta core counties peaked at 52 percent in 1990, dropping slightly to 50 percent in 2000.

The commuting and migration trends for Lamar County, at the southern edge of Atlanta's metro area, are somewhat harder to place in a stages-of-growth

Figure 11.1. Stages of Growth in the Atlanta Metro Area, 1960–2000

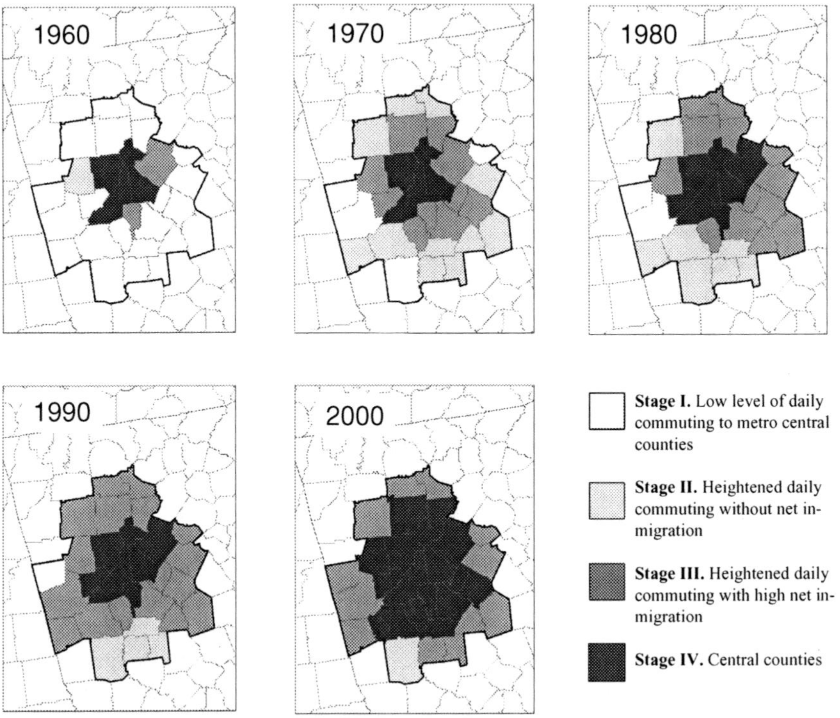

Note: The outer boundary marks the current (2003) Atlanta metro area.

framework. Lamar County showed no significant commuting towards Atlanta until the core of central counties expanded to include neighboring Henry and Spalding Counties in 2000. With these two counties included, the commuting increase was steady and significant throughout the period, from 7 percent in 1960 to 18 percent in 1970, 26 percent in 1980, 34 percent in 1990, and 50 percent in 2000. Net migration turned around in the 1970s, just as it had in Dawson County and hundreds of other nonmetro counties throughout the country. However, the rate of in-migration was just 6 percent, less than one-third the average for Atlanta counties during that decade, and net in-migration dropped to 2.5 percent in the 1980s before rebounding to 17 percent growth in the 1990s. Although the data could be interpreted differently, I found evidence of a Stage II pattern lasting at least 20 years, 1970–1990, with no significant suburbanization until the 1990s.

For Atlanta metro counties, the transition from Stage I to Stage II occurred mostly in the 1960s. Just four counties remained in Stage I in 1970. Three moved directly from Stage I to Stage III in the following decades. Seven counties persisted in Stage II through 1980 and four of these counties still remained there in 1990.

After the number of central (Stage IV) counties doubled in 2000, only one county remained in Stage II, showing net out-migration at the same time that its ties to the urban core increased.

EMERGING, HIGH-COMMUTING COUNTIES IN THE NONMETRO SOUTH, 1990–2000

The map of Atlanta's development clearly demonstrates the stages-of-growth model's value. However, it also raises the possibility that the model is of decreasing relevance to current nonmetro-to-metro transitions. Almost all Atlanta's transitions from Stage I to II occurred during the 1960s, when agricultural restructuring was still causing significant population redistribution. Are identifiable transitions from Stage I to Stage II mostly limited to this period prior to 1970 when rural out-migration peaked, as Atlanta's pattern suggests? Or did net migration patterns continue to vary significantly along the metro-nonmetro boundary elsewhere in the South in the 1990s, indicating a continued complexity in patterns of metro expansion?

Interregional migration and rural-to-urban residential shifts fueled strong urban growth in the South and West starting in the 1950s, causing their metro areas to be the most rapidly expanding in the nation since 1960 (Frey & Speare, 1988; Fulton et al., 2001). Increased immigration to new "gateway" cities, such as Atlanta, Dallas, and Charlotte, bolstered these trends beginning in the 1980s (Singer, 2004). During the 1990s, 120 of the South's nonmetro counties that were adjacent to metro areas saw a five-point increase in the percent of workers commuting to metro central counties. This increase was twice the national average for adjacent counties during the decade. These 126 counties, given the label "emerging, high-commuting" counties, form the leading edge of metro expansion in the South and are found throughout the region in a variety of social and economic settings (Figure 11.2). If demographic and socioeconomic differences also are present among these counties, it would confirm the continued importance of the stages-of-growth approach for understanding nonmetro-to-metro transitions.

Among emerging, high-commuting counties, Figure 11.2 distinguishes between those experiencing population growth through net in-migration and those losing population through net out-migration. Counties in Stage II would more likely fall in the latter group, while Stage III counties would fall into the former group. The 91 net in-migration counties are evenly distributed throughout the South (they are found in all states except Maryland and Delaware), compared with the 35 net out-migration counties that show a higher incidence in western States. Sparsely settled counties in the Great Plains of West Texas were particularly prone to Stage II development during the 1990s, as were counties in less prosperous sections of Louisiana, Mississippi, and Alabama. They adjoin relatively small, slow-growing metro areas and depend to a large degree on economically volatile, resource-based industries, specifically farming, ranching, and oil and gas extraction. Suburban expansion is not strong in these counties but metro jobs are attracting more rural commuters.

Figure 11.2. Two Types of Emerging, High-Commuting Counties in the Nonmetro South, 1990–2000

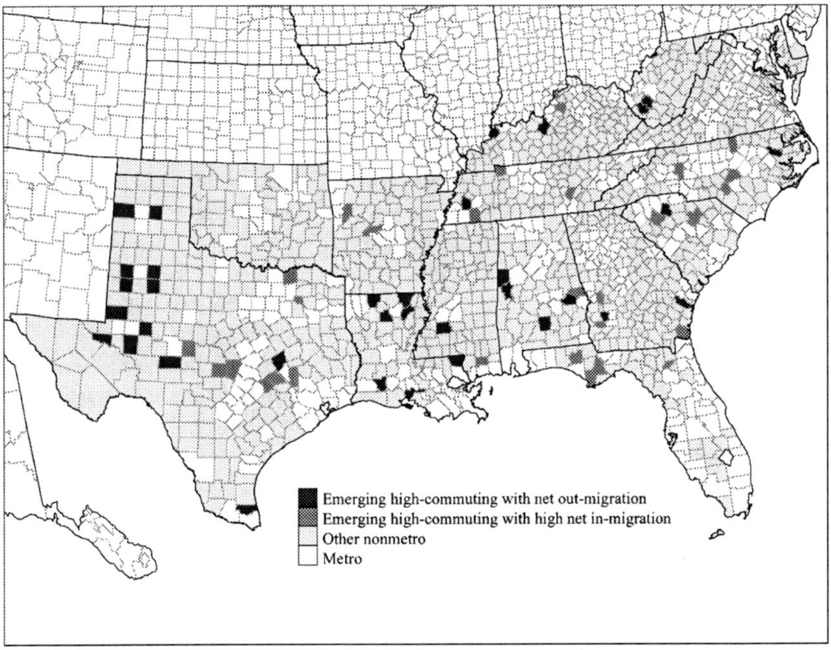

Note: Emerging, high-commuting counties had less than 25 percent commuting to the central counties of a metro area in 1990 and increased their level of commuting by 5 percent or more by 2000; high net in-migration indicates a rate of population growth from net migration of 15 percent or higher.

Stage III suburban expansion prevails around more populous metro areas in the eastern half of Texas. It also shows up in the Piedmont sections of North and South Carolina, an area attracting both workers and retirees to the periphery of its widespread network of small and medium sized metro areas. Only one out of 20 emerging, high-commuting counties in this subregion showed net out-migration.

As expected from our findings in the previous section, only one nonmetro county adjacent to Atlanta shows up as an emerging, high-commuting county in the 1990s. None appear around Washington, DC or in South Florida. In all three areas, population growth and suburban expansion exceeded the national average for several decades. Further expansion into adjacent, nonmetro counties may be slowing simply because sprawl reached such a high level before 1990. Figure 11.1 in the preceding analysis shows that Stage III development already reached 50 miles or more from downtown Atlanta and other "edge city" employment centers in 1990. Beyond this range, metro influence as reflected in additional commuting is still increasing, but at a slower rate.

Despite having similar experiences in terms of increasing commuting patterns, the emerging, high-commuting counties showed a wide range of population growth in the 1990s, confirming the stages-of-growth model. Net out-migration occurred in 25 percent of cases, indicating a Stage II pattern of increasing metro ties with little or no suburbanization. At the other end of the growth spectrum, another 25 percent showed net in-migration above 15 percent, three times the national average, indicating a strong, Stage III pattern of suburban development. The remaining 50 percent experienced net in-migration during the 1990s, but at levels below 15 percent. These counties appear to have begun Stage III during the decade, either simultaneously with Stage II or following an initial Stage II period within the same decade.

A comparison of these three groups shows that counties undergoing metro economic integration in such different ways also experienced different socioeconomic and land-use outcomes, as predicted by the stages-of-growth model (Table 11.3). By definition, all emerging, high-commuting counties increased their level of commuting to metro central counties by at least five percentage points, but I expected to find a higher average increase among Stage III counties (those with high net in-migration) compared with Stage II (net out-migration) counties. Instead, the average increase was 8.1 points in both cases. What distinguished their position in the stages-of-growth model was not their rate of increase but their initial level of commuting. On average, commuting levels jumped from 11 to 19 percent for Stage II counties, compared with a jump from 14 to 22 percent for Stage III counties. In general, Stage III counties are farther along in the metro integration process, as the model predicts. They are closer to reaching the 25 percent commuting level that would cause them to be reclassified as metro under the new OMB criteria adopted in 2000.

The average rate of net out-migration among Stage II counties was low enough (−6.2 percent) to offset gains from natural increase (the surplus of births over deaths). Thus, on average, these counties lost population (−1.4 percent) in the 1990s. This level of net out-migration and overall population loss is higher than expected for a set of counties that were adjacent to metro areas and that showed a sizeable increase in metro interaction during a decade of increased growth for nonmetro counties in general. Equally impressive is the very rapid growth in Stage III counties. By definition, these counties grew by at least 15 percent from net migration during the 1990s, but they averaged a much higher 29.5 percent rate of population growth. The fact that two sets of nonmetro, adjacent counties, in the same region of the country and with identical commuting increases, experienced such different patterns of natural increase and net migration confirms the complexity underlying the process of metro economic integration.

A comparison of socioeconomic characteristics indicates that Stage II counties display disadvantages typically associated with rural and small town settlement. Poverty rates are higher and job opportunities are more scarce compared

Table 11.3. Characteristics of Emerging, High-commuting Counties in the South, by Level of Net Migration, 1990–2000

	Stage II	Transitional	Stage III
	Net Out-Migration	Low Net In-Migration (0.1 to 15 percent)	High Net In-Migration (15.1 percent or higher)
Level of Metropolitan Interaction:			
Percent commuting to central counties, 1990	10.8	13.7	14.2
Percent commuting to central counties, 2000	18.9	21.3	22.3
Change in percent commuting to central counties, 1990–2000	8.1	7.6	8.1
Population Change:			
Population growth rate, 1990–2000	−1.4	9.8	29.5
Net migration rate, 1990–2000	−6.2	6.6	26.1
Rate of natural increase, 1990–2000	16.6	17.6	26.8
Socioeconomic Characteristics:			
Percent in poverty, 1999	21.7	18.3	15.3
Percent unemployed, 2000	8.1	6.6	5.3
Percent 25 years and older without a high school degree, 2000	31.1	31.5	27.6
Settlement Characteristics:			
Population size (1,000s), 2000	22.6	28.6	31.1
Population per square mile, 2000	38.3	58.1	55.6
Percent urban, 2000	35.9	26.2	26.1

Note: Emerging, high-commuting counties were identified as nonmetro counties with less than 25 percent commuting to the central counties of a metro area in 1990 that experienced increases in commuting of 5 percentage points or more by 2000.

with Stage III counties. It is not possible to confirm cause and effect without further analysis. It may be that lower socioeconomic conditions inhibit suburban development, making such counties more likely to remain in Stage II. More likely, the contrasts emerge with suburbanization. Suburban in-migrants during Stage III are less likely to be poor and unemployed. They also tend to be better educated, as indicated by the lower percentage of workers with less than a high school education.

Settlement characteristics and land-use patterns differ considerably among emerging, high-commuting counties. Net out-migration counties have lower overall population size and density, on average, than either category of net in-migration counties. However, the level of urbanization in high net in-migration counties is almost 10 percentage points lower than those in net out-migration counties. This difference confirms an expected, though counterintuitive, characteristic of suburbanization. Few appreciate that sprawl initially shows up as a rural pattern of settlement, prior to the development of a more urbanized landscape in Stage IV. This finding alone demonstrates the value of the stages-of-growth approach for analyzing metro expansion and indicates one of the many reasons why standard urban and rural concepts need to be applied with caution.

CONCLUSIONS

Suburbanization and sprawl, terms used to describe different aspects of metro expansion, continue to fuel the most formidable demographic, socioeconomic, and physical transitions found in rural and small town America. The processes are particularly complex in the South because nonmetro counties enter the transition with relatively large rural populations and long-established towns. Demographic contrasts between new and old residents, economic diversification, and sprawl development reach their peak at the same time that so many counties experiencing change lose their nonmetro status. Due to nonmetro-to-metro reclassification, rural analysts too often shift their attention away from these areas during these critical stages. As a result, underlying suburbanization processes and the policy implications of rural transformation remain understudied.

The mechanics of metro expansion and nonmetro change go beyond the simple picture of migration-induced, suburban spillover. The results presented here confirm the existence of distinct stages in the nonmetro-to-metro transition. In particular, rural areas can increase their interaction with metro areas and begin to change prior to the onset of suburbanization, a fact little noted in previous research. A stages-of-growth approach places a needed focus on the changing conditions of long-term, rural residents as they move through large-scale settlement transitions.

The expansion of the Atlanta metro area over 50 years includes a remarkable period of growth in the 1960s. The number of counties interacting with the area's three-county urban core grew from 3 to 20 in 10 years. These counties fell into two distinct groups—an inner ring of eight counties experiencing suburbanization (Stage I to III) and nine counties farther out that increased commuting but retained much more of their rural character (Stage I to II). Clearly, the stages-of-growth model identifies important distinctions among outlying counties prior to 1970, when agricultural restructuring and other factors caused massive rural out-migration and increased long-distance commuting.

The analysis of net migration during the 1990s shows continued differentiation among emerging, high-commuting counties in line with the stages-of-growth model. More than 25 percent of nonmetro counties with increasing metro influence also exhibited net out-migration, indicative of Stage I to II development. Many of these counties lost some portion of their traditional, rural economic base but had not yet developed subdivisions or otherwise attracted large numbers of urban migrants to bedroom settlements. They are beginning to integrate with the metro economy simply because of work decisions on the part of long-time residents, thus retaining more rural socioeconomic conditions and settlement patterns. Another 25 percent experienced in-migration rates at three times the national average for nonmetro counties, indicating a very strong contrast in development conditions along the expanding metro-nonmetro boundary.

Such distinctions are critical from a policy perspective. Urban and rural characteristics define eligibility for an array of federal programs aimed at alleviating rural disadvantages. Clients for these programs are increasingly difficult to pinpoint accurately, especially on the metro fringe where administrators face a constantly shifting target. This analysis provides one method for improving the process. Although both types of counties show similar increases in metro commuting, more residents in Stage II counties retain the need to access rural-based programs. They leave school earlier, experience higher conditions of poverty, have less access to jobs and services in their home county, and do not necessarily benefit by being labeled metro.

Long-term, nonmetro residents in Stage III counties experience a different set of problems and policy choices. Socioeconomic conditions improve with the emergence of a diversified service sector meeting local demands and services improve. Conditions stimulating out-migration recede. At the same time, the potential for conflicts with newcomers arises because differing demands exist for publicly-provided services and different values are placed on rural landscape amenities. The social, political, and environmental changes associated with sprawl have come under increased scrutiny in recent years by policy makers and by voters at the ballot box. Often occurring with inadequate planning, sprawl increases traffic congestion, pollution, and financial burdens related to infrastructure development. Federal and state initiatives designed to maintain community viability in the face of sprawl, including central-city reinvestment, tax breaks for compact and mixed-use development, and the fostering of regional cooperation among government entities, will have a greater impact in Stage III counties.

Further research applying the stages-of-growth model would help differentiate critical rural and urban characteristics along the metro periphery, especially in relatively new, rapidly growing metro areas where the process is at an early stage. Regional comparisons are essential. Results may vary sharply in other parts of the country, especially in light of rural and small-town settlement differences. Beyond the boundaries of built-up, urbanized areas, the rural West contains a much more sparsely-settled landscape. Changes in urbanization levels may not follow the same, counterintuitive pattern (a declining urban percentage as sprawl increases) in the West as in the South.

Research on suburban expansion and nonmetro change in the West (and elsewhere) would benefit from shifting to sub-county data, beginning with the application of rural-urban classifications developed for census tracts and zip codes (Morrill et al., 1999). Additionally, such a strategy would allow expanding the coverage of this analysis to micropolitan areas, a new classification of cities and towns of 10,000 to 50,000 people that was added to the metro area system in 2000. Counties are too large in most places to adequately measure micropolitan suburbanization and sprawl. Moving to a smaller geographic unit would help test more fully the universality of the stages-of-growth model.

REFERENCES

Bowles, G.K., Beale, C.L., & Lee, E.S. (1975). *Net migration of the population 1960–70, by age, sex and color*. Washington, DC: U.S. Department of Agriculture, Economic Research Service, and Athens, GA: University of Georgia.

Bowles, G.K., & Tarver, J.D. (1965). *Net migration of the population 1950–60 by age sex and color.* Washington, DC: U.S. Department of Agriculture, Economic Research Service.

Brown, D.L. (1979). Metropolitan reclassification: Some effects on the characteristics of the population in metropolitan and nonmetropolitan counties. *Rural Sociology, 44*(4), 791–801.

Brown, D.L., Fuguitt, G.V., Heation, T.B., & Waseem, S. (1997). Continuites in the size of place preference in the United States, 1972–1992. *Rural Sociology, 62*, 408–428.

Daniels, T. 1999. *When the city and the countryside collide*. Washington, DC: Island Press.

Elliott, J.R., & Perry, M.J. (1996). Metropolitanizing nonmetro space: Population redistribution and emergent metropolitan areas, 1965–90. *Rural Sociology, 61*, 497–512.

Frey, W.H. (1993). The new urban revival in the United States. *Urban Studies, 30*, 741–774.

Frey, W.H., & Johnson, K.M. (1998). Concentrated immigration, restructuring, and the selective deconcentration of the U.S. population. In P.J. Boyle & K.H. Halfacree (Eds.), *Migration into rural areas: Theories and issues* (pp. 79–106). London: Wiley.

Frey, W.H., & Speare, A., Jr. (1988). *Regional and metropolitan growth and decline in the United States*. New York: Sage.

Fuguitt, G.V., & Beale, C.L. (1993). The changing concentration of the older nonmetropolitan population, 1960–90. *Journal of Gerontology: Social Sciences, 48*, S278–S288.

Fuguitt, G.V., Brown, D.L., & Beale, C.L. (1989). *Rural and small town America*. New York: Sage.

Fuguitt, G.V., Heaton, T.B., & Lichter, D.T. (1988). Monitoring the metropolitanization process. *Demography, 25*, 115–128.

Fulton, W., Pendall, R., Nguyen, M., & Harrison, A. (2001). *Who sprawls most? How growth patterns differ across the U.S.* Washington, DC: Brookings Institution, Center on Urban and Metropolitan Policy, Survey Series.

Galster, G., Hanson, R., Ratcliffe, M.R., Wolman, H., Coleman, S., & Freihage, J. (2001). Wrestling sprawl to the ground: Defining and measuring an elusive concept. *Housing Policy Debate, 12*, 681–717.

Garreau, J. (1991). *Edge city: Life on the new frontier.* New York: Random House.

Hart, J.F. (1995). Spersopolis. *Southeastern Geographer, 35*, 103–117.

Heimlich, R.E., & Anderson, W.D. (2001). *Development at the urban fringe and beyond: Impacts on agriculture and rural land* (Agricultural Economic Report No. 803). Washington, DC: U.S. Department of Agriculture, Economic Research Service.

Johnson, K.M. (1999). *The rural rebound* (PRB reports on America, Vol. 1, No. 3). Washington, DC: Population Reference Bureau.

Johnson, K.M., Fuguitt, G.V., Hammer, R., Voss, P., & McNiven, S. (2003, May). *Recent age-specific net migration patterns in the United States.* Presented at the Population Association of America meeting, Minneapolis, MN.

McGranahan, D.A., & Salsgiver, J. (1992). Recent population change in adjacent nonmetro counties. *Rural Development Perspectives, 8*, 2–7.

Morrill, R., Cromartie, J., & Hart, G. (1999). Metropolitan, urban, and rural commuting areas: Toward a better depiction of the United States settlement system. *Urban Geography, 20*, 727–748.

Singer, A. (2004). *The rise of new immigrant gateways.* Washington: Brookings Institution.

Stanback, T.M., Jr. (1991). *The new suburbanization: Challenge to the central city.* Boulder, CO: Westview.

White, M.J., Mueser, P., & Tierney, J.P. (1987). *Net migration of the population of the United States 1970–1980, by age, race and sex: United States, regions, divisions, states and counties.* Ann Arbor, MI: University of Michigan, Interuniversity Consortium for Political and Social Research. (Computer file)

Wolman, H., Galster, G., Hanson, R., Ratcliffe, M.R., Furdell, K., & Sarzynski, A. (2005). The fundamental challenge in measuring sprawl: Which land should be considered? *Professional Geographer, 57*, 94–105.

Zelinsky, W. (1971). The hypothesis of the mobility transition. *Geographical Review, 61*, 219–249.

CHAPTER 12

CHANGING LAND USE IN THE RURAL INTERMOUNTAIN WEST

DOUGLAS JACKSON-SMITH, ERIC JENSEN, AND BRIAN JENNINGS

INTRODUCTION

The western United States has long captured the imagination of the American people. As the last frontier for settlement and development in the 19th century (Turner, 1920), the dominant image most people have of the American West is of traditional resource-extractive industries (logging, mining, and ranching) taking place in a largely wild, undeveloped, and sometimes dangerous landscape. Rurality also means something special in the West. Unlike typical small Midwestern farming towns with close community ties, egalitarian property ownership, and a reverent connection between farmers and their land (Berry, 1977), the rural West evokes a picture of isolated ranches, fiercely rugged and independent individuals, and a dominating, extractive relationship between rural residents and their environment (Malone & Etulain, 1989).

Although this stereotypical view of the rural American West has probably never been very accurate, it was remarkably durable through the later half of the 20th century (Athearn, 1986). Moreover, this imagery has permeated much of the recent sociological and geographical academic writing on this region. For example, most analysts utilize a dichotomous framework to make sense of patterns of development and change in the Intermountain West—characterizing these changes as a conflict between the "Old West" of cowboys, extractive industries, and property rights zealots and an emergent "New West" defined by lifestyle inmigrants, high-technology and amenity-oriented industries, and environmentalists (Nelson, 2001; Power, 1996; Shumway & Otterstrom, 2001).

This chapter provides an overview of the changing social, economic, and biophysical landscape of the Intermountain West during the late 20th and early 21st centuries. It critically examines the "New vs. Old West" approach to explaining the trends in the West, and demonstrates the complexity of the relationship between demographic changes and rural land use. Specifically, the results suggest

W.A. Kandel & D.L. Brown (eds.), Population Change and Rural Society, 253–276.

that traditional extractive industries (agriculture, mining, etc.) are more robust in the face of urban pressures than many observers had predicted. In fact, many of the "New West" counties are not important sites of agricultural production. The chapter concludes by linking demographic changes to a growing number of local and regional land use conflicts. How local communities respond to these conflicts will likely affect future trajectories of population change and industrial restructuring.

RURAL RESTRUCTURING IN THE INTERMOUNTAIN WEST

The precise boundaries of the American West are difficult to define. This analysis utilizes a six state region often referred to as the "Intermountain West"—Idaho, Montana, Wyoming, Colorado, Utah and Nevada. This region captures the bulk of the "interior" West and is dominated by interspersed high mountain ranges and relatively dry valleys (McNabb & Avers, 1994).

It can be argued that the Intermountain West is simultaneously one of the most rural and least rural parts of the United States. From a landscape perspective, this is a very rural region. The federal government owns just over half of the land, most of it administered by the Bureau of Land Management and the Forest Service. In 1997, only 1.3 percent of the land was in "developed" uses, by far the lowest proportion in any region of the continental United States; this rises to 2.7 percent of private land when the federal lands are excluded (United States Department of Agriculture [USDA], 2000). However, over 80 percent of residents live in urban areas, and the extent of urban concentration in this region has increased during the 1990s (Otterstrom & Shumway, 2003).

The Intermountain West was one of the most rapidly growing regions in the United States during the 1990s. Like other regions, much of this growth took place in nonmetropolitan areas (Shumway & Davis, 1996). Unlike other regions, however, nonmetropolitan population growth in the West was relatively widespread, affecting more remote regions as well as areas adjacent to urban centers (Otterstrom & Shumway, 2003).

The reasons for rapid growth in the Intermountain West have been the subject of a great deal of scholarly research. Initially, migration patterns reflected the impacts of national and global economic restructuring processes. At the regional level, this has been reflected in the apparent stagnation and gradual demise of the "old" western economy. Employment and personal income in the agriculture, forestry, and mining sectors have been flat or declining since the 1960s (Power & Barrett, 2001; Rasker, 1995). Meanwhile, large numbers of new western residents have found service-sector employment, and many report high levels of unearned income from investments, retirement accounts, and government transfer payments (Nelson & Beyers, 1998; Power, 1996; Smutny, 2002).

Meanwhile, demographic changes and shifting lifestyle choices have contributed to the recent wave of growth. Long viewed as a region with unusually high natural amenities, growing numbers of retirees and mid-career families with high levels of investment income have been drawn to the area (Beyers & Lindahl, 1996; Nelson, 1997, 1999). These inmigrants have selected rural work and residential locations based on scenic amenities, access to recreational opportunities, and a desire to escape perceived urban problems, rather than on the availability of good jobs (Egan & Luloff, 2000; Rudzitis, 1999; Rudzitis & Johansen, 1989; Salant et al., 1997; Vias, 1999).

METHODOLOGICAL APPROACH

This chapter's research design compares population and land use changes during the 1990s across subsets of counties based on their metropolitan character, recent trends in population growth, and the structure of their local economy. The results suggest that there is less overlap between Old and New West counties than most analysts assume. The following sections outline these county typologies and illustrate their spatial location in the Intermountain West.

Metropolitan Adjacent and Rapid Population Growth Counties

Initially, metropolitan (n = 23) and nonmetropolitan (n = 209) counties were identified based on the 1993 U.S. Office of Management and Budget classification scheme (Butler & Beale, 1994). To highlight the impact of proximity to major urban centers on land use, the nonmetropolitan counties were subdivided based on whether or not they are adjacent to a metropolitan county (n = 44 and 165 counties, respectively).

Rapid-population-growth counties were identified by ranking nonmetropolitan counties based on their net increase in population between 1990 and 1996 divided by square miles of private land area available in each county. The top quartile of nonmetropolitan counties in the region that added at least three people per square mile during the six-year period were considered high population growth counties (n = 56). This area-weighted index controls for differences in total county land area and the fact that public lands are unavailable for new population settlement. Unlike traditional percent-growth categories, this type of measure is also unaffected by the size of initial population in 1990. By focusing on the number of new people added per square mile, the index should detect the increases in population most likely to affect rural land use. A map of the high population growth nonmetropolitan counties is provided in Figure 12.1.

"Old West" Counties

Conventional approaches to defining "Old West" counties have relied on "economic dependency" codes developed by the USDA Economic Research Service (ERS) to identify traditional rural land use areas (Cook & Mizer, 1994).

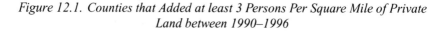

Figure 12.1. Counties that Added at least 3 Persons Per Square Mile of Private Land between 1990–1996

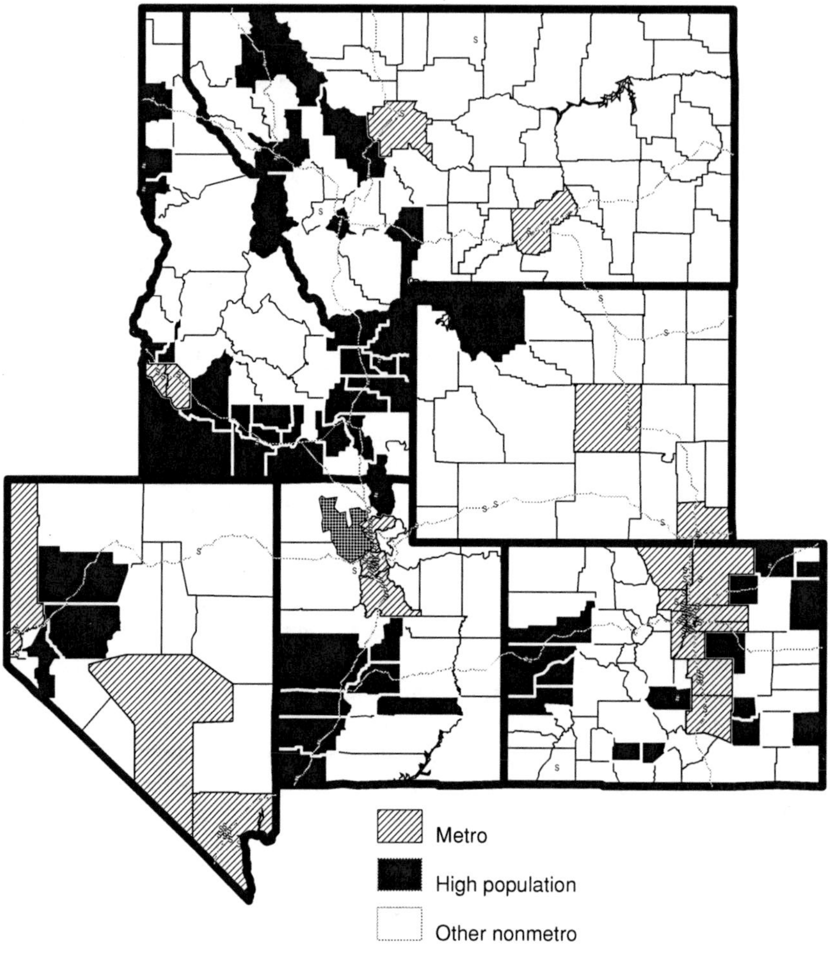

These ERS codes classify nonmetropolitan counties with greater than 20 percent of total labor and proprietor income from farming as "farm dependent". Similarly, "mining-dependent" counties are those with more than 15 percent of income from mining. These dependency codes have been widely used in empirical analysis of population and economic restructuring in the Mountain West.

Because the ERS codes identify counties in terms of the relative share of personal income from traditional extractive industries, they can disguise the actual relationships between traditional uses of rural land and population dynamics.

Methodologically, the choice of sectoral dominance can serve more as a measure of the absence of non-extractive economic activities than as a measure of the size of the extractive industry itself. As such, the ERS codes are imperfect indicators of the importance of extractive industries in local land use patterns.

For this analysis, an alternative measure of the importance of agriculture to a rural county was developed based on the total gross farm sales, weighted by the available land base used for farming and ranching activities.[1] The 51 counties that are deemed "agriculturally important" in this region are those that have the most intense agricultural activity and produce the lion's share of the region's agricultural output. Figure 12.2 shows the spatial relationships between the various indicators of "Old West" counties.

Interestingly, 12 of the 51 "agriculturally important" counties in the Intermountain West are metropolitan in character (more than half of all metro counties). This suggests that even in the more urban environments, significant agricultural activity can continue to take place. Interestingly, there is relatively little overlap between agriculturally important and farm-dependent counties. Among the 39 nonmetropolitan "agriculturally important" counties, only 17 were considered farm dependent. Similarly, only 29 percent of the 59 farm dependent counties in the region were agriculturally important. Only one mining-dependent county was deemed agriculturally important.

New West Counties

Several indicators for "New West" counties were developed for this analysis. Initially, we used McGranahan's Natural Amenity Index (1999) to identify western counties that had unusually high natural amenities associated with rural inmigration. A total of 38 nonmetropolitan counties had natural amenity index scores of 6 or 7 (the highest scores possible). Second, areas with intense seasonal and recreational home construction are often associated with "New West" forms of development (Booth, 2002) (see chapter 13). In our analysis, counties with greater than 15 percent seasonal housing in 2000 (n = 46) were identified as "high seasonal housing" counties. Finally, the top 61 nonmetropolitan counties that had unusually high levels of unearned investment income in 1999 (greater than $2,500 income per capita from dividends, interest rent, and retirement income) were called "high investment income" counties. A map of the location of these types of New West counties is provided in Figure 12.3.

While roughly half of the New West counties are in the same location as farming-and mining-dependent counties (using the traditional measures), only 7 to 10 percent of New West counties were considered agriculturally important in the region. This suggests that the potential for direct conflict between commercial agriculture and the emerging New West rural economy may be lower than is often assumed. The spatial relationships between agriculturally important counties, New West counties, and high-growth counties are illustrated in Figure 12.4.

Figure 12.2. Location of "Old West" Counties

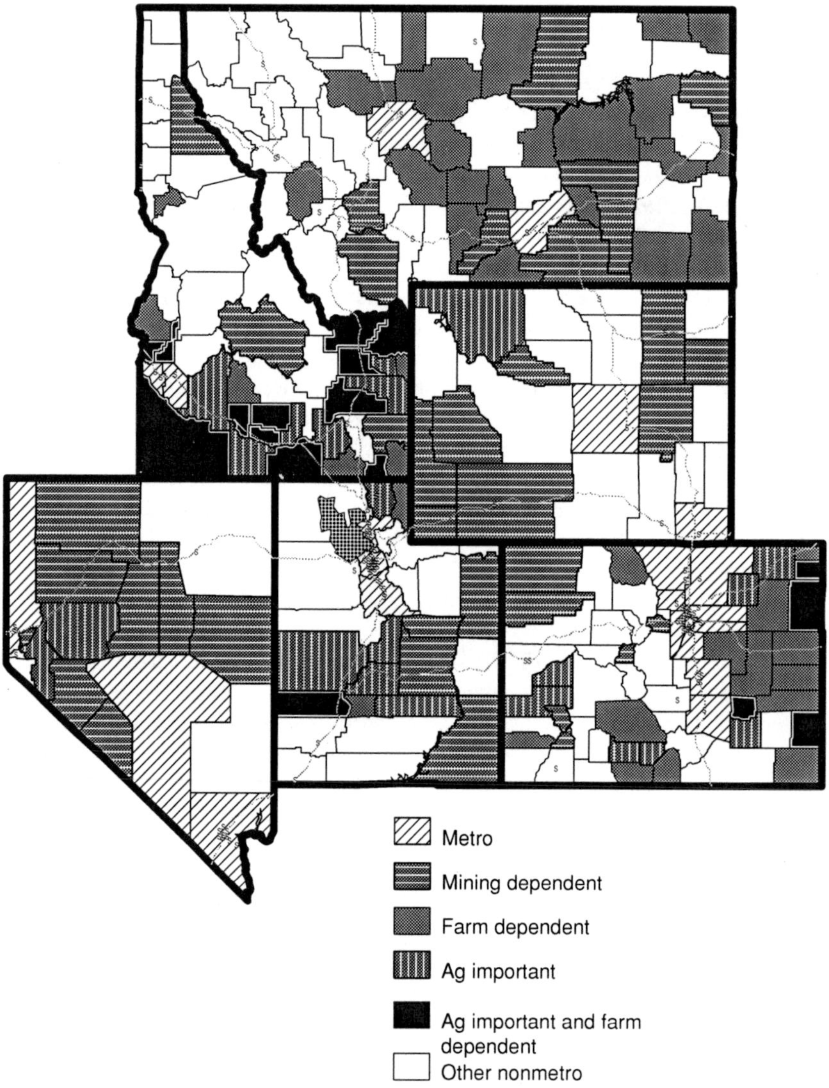

Figure 12.3. Location of "New West" Counties

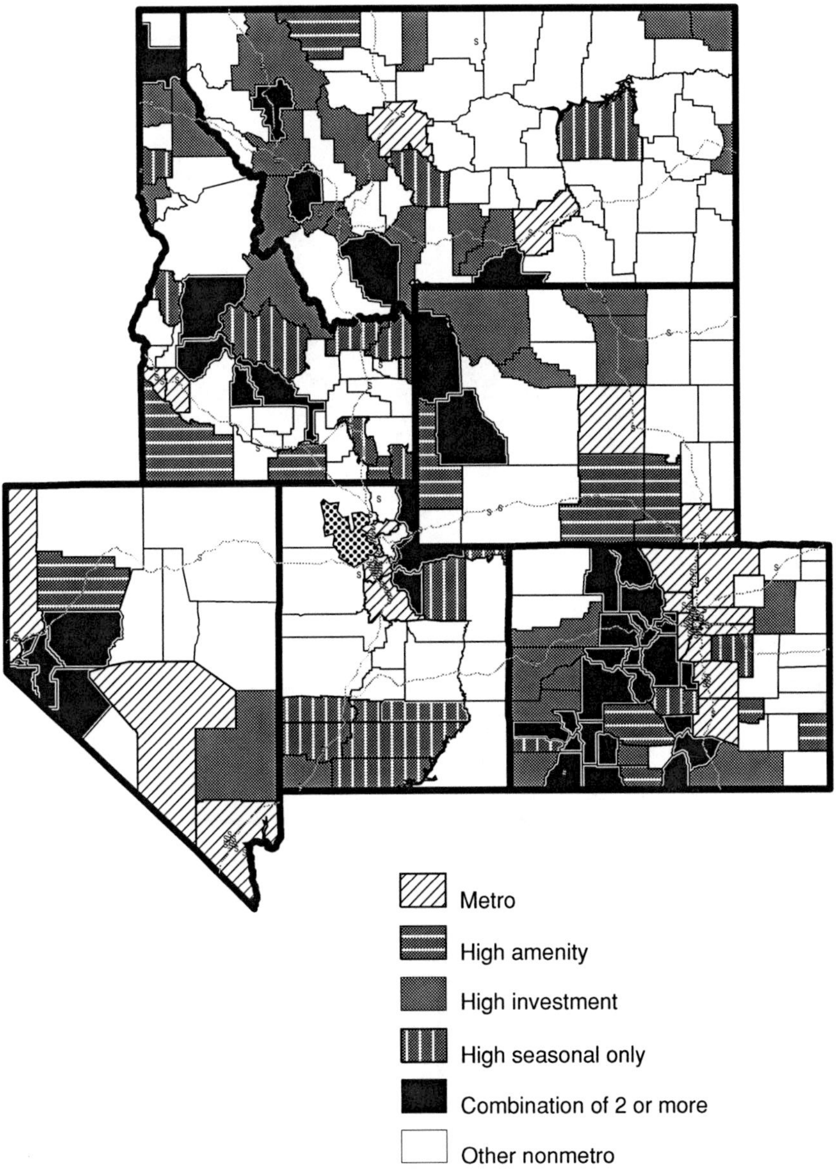

Figure 12.4. Intersection of Agriculturally Important Counties, New West Counties and High Growth Counties

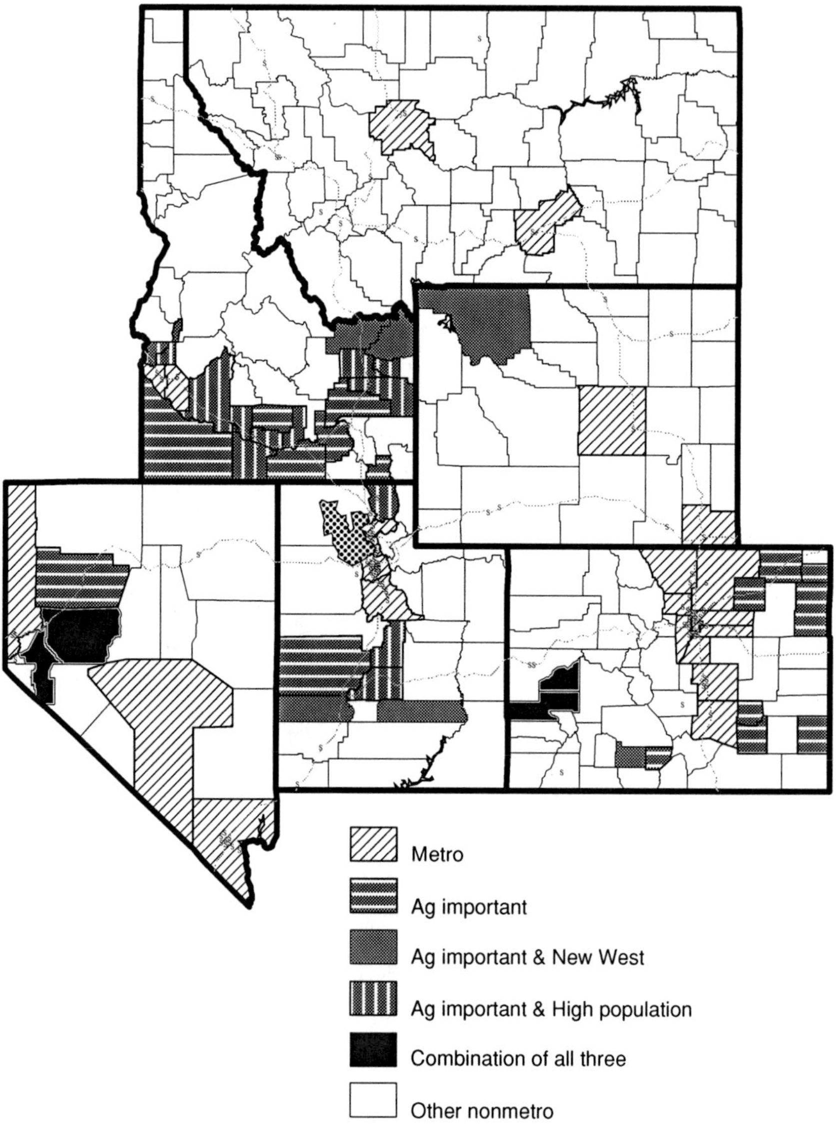

POPULATION CHANGE IN THE INTERMOUNTAIN WEST

Table 12.1 decomposes demographic changes between 1990–2000 for the region as a whole and for various types of counties. Overall, the population in the Intermountain West grew by 32 percent during the decade (more than double the national average). This growth was most rapid in the metropolitan counties, where 75 percent of the total growth occurred. Nonmetropolitan areas grew by over 23 percent. Net migration was the most important source of population growth in the western states during the 1990s, contributing over twice as many people to the region as natural increase.

There was considerable diversity in the pace and character of population change in the region depending on metropolitan proximity and county type. About 40 percent of nonmetropolitan growth occurred in counties adjacent to metropolitan areas. This growth is similar to patterns of urban sprawl throughout

Table 12.1. Population Changes in the Intermountain West, 1990–2000, by Type of County

County Type		Net Change	Percent Change: Overall Change	Natural Increase	Net Migration
All Types (Regional Total)	232	2,696,803	31.6	10.6	21.0
Metropolitan Counties	23	2,037,387	35.8	12.1	23.7
Nonmetropolitan Counties	209	659,416	23.3	7.5	15.7
Adjacent	44	272,300	41.1	9.8	31.3
Non-Adjacent	165	387,116	17.8	6.9	11.0
Nonmetropolitan County Subtypes					
New West					
High Amenity[a]	41	167,270	36.9	6.6	30.3
High Seasonal Housing[b]	50	143,831	41.5	8.6	32.9
High Investment Income[c]	61	357,163	37.7	6.2	31.6
Old West					
Farming Important[d]	39	150,273	21.3	10.0	11.3
Farming Dependent[e]	59	55,449	16.2	6.4	9.9
Mining Dependent[e]	36	27,873	7.9	8.0	−0.2

[a] Index score of 6 or higher on Amenity Index (McGranahan, 1999).

[b] At least 15 percent of housing units were seasonal in 2000.

[c] Counties with at least $2,500 per capita income from investments, dividends, rent, and retirement income in 1999.

[d] Top quartile of counties by intensity of agricultural production and value of output (USDA, 1999).

[e] Based on USDA-ERS Economic Dependency Codes (Cook & Mizer, 1994).

the United States. In addition, rural counties with high levels of investment income, natural amenities, and significant seasonal home construction all witnessed above average rates of population growth and unusually high rates of net migration (Cromartie & Wardwell, 1999; McGranahan, 1999; Nelson & Beyers, 1998; Otterstrom & Shumway, 2003; Shumway & Otterstrom, 2001).

Meanwhile, areas that symbolize the "Old West" appear to be growing more slowly. Traditional farm-and mining-dependent counties experienced lower rates of net population growth, and more of their growth was due to natural increase. By contrast, the 39 agriculturally important counties experienced population growth rates more typical of nonmetropolitan counties in the region, though this was driven more by a relatively high rate of natural increase than by unusual net migration rates.

LAND USE CHANGE IN THE INTERMOUNTAIN WEST

Overall Changes in the Use of Private Lands

The U.S. government estimates that roughly 60 percent of the 190 million acres of private lands in the region is used as rangeland. Roughly a quarter of the land is in cropland and pasture uses, and just over 8 percent is in forest cover. A total of 11.8 million acres of "developed land" account for roughly 6 percent of the total private land area (USDA, 2000).

The dramatic population growth during the 1990s created pressures to change private land use throughout this region. These changes have been linked to shifts in the intensity of traditional agricultural or natural-resource-extraction activities, as well as the transformation of the rural landscape from a locus of production to an object of consumption for residential and recreational purposes (Marsden, 1999).

In fact, a comparison of USDA estimates from 1982 and 1997 suggest that there has been relatively little overall change in the way private lands are used in the Intermountain West.[2] Roughly 95 percent of all private land remained in the same land use category throughout this 15-year period. Total acreage in cropland and pasture actually increased by 2.5 percent, while forest and rangeland acreage declined by 1.8 percent. These are not rates of change that suggest a sudden or radical transformation of the rural landscape as a whole.

Some of the most important region-wide rural land use transformations reflect changes in the intensity of agricultural land use rather than the removal of lands from agricultural production entirely (Reibsame, Gosnell & Theobald, 1996). In the 1980s and 1990s, roughly 6.3 million acres were shifted from intensive crop production to less intensive pastures or cropland enrolled in the Conservation Reserve Program. At the same time, over 1.2 million acres were converted from rangeland to intensive crop production. These shifts reflect the combined influence of federal agricultural policies and changing market conditions.

While not as significant in terms of total acreage, there were notable changes in the use of rural lands for residential and other urban-like uses. Analysis of the NRI trend data suggests that 1.3 million acres were converted from agricultural and forestry uses to new "developed" land uses. Developed lands include dense urban and built-up land uses, as well as lands used for farmsteads and less dense rural housing units.[3] Specifically, urban and built-up acreage in the region increased by almost 30 percent, and the total developed land base grew by 13 percent during this time period. Overall, roughly half of the land developed between 1982 and 1997 had been used as cropland in 1982, with 40 percent coming from rangeland and 10 percent from previously forested lands.

Linking Rural Restructuring with Land Use Changes

Overall shifts in land use patterns in the Intermountain West can mask considerable diversity in the trends within the region. Changes in rural land uses between 1982 and 1997 in the Intermountain West are disaggregated in Table 12.2 for different types of counties depending on metropolitan proximity, population growth rates, and Old and New West areas. The results suggest that urban proximity and in-migrations associated with New West growth areas affect trajectories of land use change.

Initially, it is clear that metropolitan counties in the region experienced the most dramatic changes in land use patterns. Traditional land uses declined more precipitously and developed land uses increased more rapidly than in the nonmetropolitan counties. During this 15-year period, over 5 percent of cropland and pastures and 4 percent of forested land was converted into various types of developed uses.

Among nonmetropolitan counties, the effects of proximity to urban areas present an intriguing picture. Overall, the total land used for cropland and pasture in nonmetropolitan counties increased by 1.3 million acres. Adjacent counties appear to be more hospitable to lower-intensity land uses, with notably slower rates of decline in rangeland and forested acres than nonadjacent counties. By contrast, more intensively managed cropland acres increased most quickly in nonadjacent counties.

Residential development in the West also takes a number of forms (Theobald, 2001). Higher-density developments (such as subdivisions and expansion of urban area boundaries) receive much of the attention from critics of urban sprawl. However, new houses in rural areas typically utilize much larger parcels of land per unit and thus are disproportionately responsible for the conversion of farmland and forests to development each year (Heimlich & Anderson, 2001; Reibsame et al., 1996). Indeed, the larger lot sizes and expansion of farmsteads associated with housing development in nonadjacent counties led to greater increases in developed land per new resident than in the adjacent counties.

Table 12.2. *Land Use Changes by Metropolitan Status, Population Pressure, and County Type, 1982–1997*

	Percent Change 1982–1997							Percent Converted to Developed Uses		
	Traditional Rural Uses			Developed Uses						
	Cropland, Pasture, and CRP	Rangeland	Forestland	Urban, Built-up, and Transportation	Farmsteads	Other Rural	Combined Developed Uses	Cropland, Pasture, and CRP	Rangeland	Forestland
Metropolitan Status										
Metro	−3.6	−2.6	−4.5	43.7	−1.6	6.0	32.0	5.4	2.0	4.2
Nonmetro Adjacent	2.1	−0.8	−0.6	30.8	24.8	2.1	11.3	1.0	0.3	1.5
Nonmetro Non-Adjacent	3.3	−1.8	−2.4	20.8	12.1	1.8	9.0	0.6	0.2	0.6
Population Growth, 1990–1996 (nonmetropolitan counties only)										
High[a]	−2.2	−2.6	−1.3	43.6	17.3	5.9	22.8	3.6	1.6	2.1
Medium	2.3	−0.2	−2.8	18.0	8.5	1.7	6.1	1.5	0.5	0.5
Low[b]	5.2	−2.6	−1.4	9.6	21.5	−0.7	5.3	0.5	0.2	0.2
New West										
High Amenity	−6.4	−0.8	−3.7	44.9	−12.9	9.7	27.6	2.9	1.3	2.5
Seasonal Housing	5.4	−2.4	−1.9	35.6	−15.5	6.7	14.8	1.0	0.5	1.3
High Invest. Income	−2.2	−1.3	−2.2	38.4	5.8	6.0	18.1	2.2	0.9	2.2
Old West										
Farm Dependent	4.2	−2.5	−1.6	10.7	15.7	−6.7	5.1	0.2	0.1	0.1
Agriculturally Important	−0.5	−1.2	−5.0	35.5	9.3	4.1	21.3	2.2	0.8	3.3

[a] Counties in the top quartile of population growth, with 3 or more new residents per square mile of private land.
[b] Counties in the bottom quartile of population growth, with 0.25 or less new residents per square mile of private land.
Source: USDA, 2000.

A comparison of the nonmetropolitan counties by population growth rates reinforces the complexity of the relationships between demographic pressure and land use changes. Not surprisingly, counties with the highest population growth are associated with the most rapid expansion of developed land. These counties also witnessed a net decline in acreage used for all three traditional categories of land use. Interestingly, the rate of rangeland loss was equally fast in both high-and low-population growth areas, with medium-growth counties witnessing the greatest proportionate losses of forested lands. In medium-growth areas, there appears to have been pressure to convert significant amounts of forestland into rangeland and pasture, and in low-growth counties there was a large shift from rangeland into cropland and pasture.

The bottom of Table 12.2 describes land use changes within five different types of nonmetropolitan counties in the region. The first three rows reflect "New West" counties. Between 1982 and 1997, high-amenity areas saw the most rapid expansion of developed land area of any type of rural county. These same counties witnessed a 6.4 percent loss in cropland and pasture and a nearly 4 percent loss in forested acres. Investment-income counties also saw relatively rapid expansion of urban and built-up areas, but had slightly smaller rates of decline in traditional rural land uses. By contrast, in counties with significant numbers of seasonal homes, a much smaller proportion of lands in traditional uses was converted into development. In addition, in these counties there was considerable net growth in the acreage used as cropland, pasture, and Conservation Reserve Program lands (CRP), most of which was converted from lands used as rangeland in 1982.

The last two rows present land-use-change statistics for counties that are either farming-dependent or agriculturally important. Most farming-dependent areas witnessed relatively low rates of development and land conversion. The most notable changes in these counties reflect the conversion of almost 800,000 acres of rangeland into cropland and pasture uses. By contrast, agriculturally important counties experienced a relatively rapid increase in their developed acreage. Nevertheless, land used for crop production and pasture decreased only slightly during the 15-year period. This net loss disguises the fact that 260,000 acres of cropland and pasture were converted into developed uses, balanced by transition of nearly 240,000 acres from rangeland back into cropland and pasture.

Changes in Agricultural Activity

Although the USDA/NRI data provide important insights into shifts among various broad categories of rural land use, they are an imperfect indicator of how the "Old West" economic sectors may be changing in the face of rural restructuring. Data from the U.S. Census of Agriculture are used in Table 12.3 to capture some of the important agricultural trends across different types of counties in the Intermountain West (USDA, 1999).

Table 12.3. Changes in Agricultural Sector, 1987–1997, by Type of County

County Type	Percent Changes in Agriculture, 1987–1997				
	Farm Numbers	Land in Farming	Cropland Acres	Gross FarmSales[a]	Livestock Numbers[b]
All Types (Regional Total)	−1.2	−3.8	−1.5	18.1	5.8
Metropolitan Counties	−0.4	−3.9	−2.2	12.5	2.2
Nonmetropolitan Counties (All)	−1.3	−3.8	−1.4	19.7	6.2
Nonmetro Adjacent	1.2	−3.8	−0.9	10.1	8.2
Nonmetro Nonadjacent	−2.0	−3.8	−1.5	22.6	5.8
Nonmetropolitan County Subtypes					
High Population Growth	0.6	−10.0	−5.1	24.7	8.6
New West					
High Amenity	4.9	−7.3	6.0	1.4	2.3
High Seasonal Housing	0.3	2.7	−0.1	7.3	−1.2
High Investment Income	2.6	−1.4	−3.7	4.2	5.2
Old West					
Agriculturally Important	−6.4	−13.6	−1.8	36.3	16.5
Farming Dependent (1989)	−6.4	−5.0	4.0	28.8	6.4
Mining Dependent (1989)	2.6	−2.6	7.6	−0.5	−13.6

[a] Inflation adjusted for Producer Price Index for all farm commodities.
[b] Weighted index of total cattle and sheep numbers where cattle = 1.0 and sheep = 0.2 animal units.
Source: USDA, 1999.

Overall, the number of farm and ranch operators in the Intermountain West declined by just over 1 percent between 1987 and 1997 (a net loss of roughly 1,200 operations). The total land in farming dropped by 3.8 percent (a net loss of over 6 million acres, mostly rangeland or pasture). Interestingly, these declines in farms and farmland do not reflect trends in the amount of economic activity in the farm sector. For example, agriculture in the region generated almost $12 billion in gross sales in 1997. Adjusting for inflation, this is an 18 percent rise over a decade earlier. Similarly, inventories of cattle and sheep rose by 6 percent during the same period.

Somewhat surprisingly, metropolitan counties in the region still play an important role in the region's agricultural economy. Although less than 10 percent of the region's agricultural lands are located in metropolitan counties, they generate over 20 percent of total agricultural receipts. Similarly, as one moves farther from metropolitan areas, the intensity of sales per acre of farmland declines fairly steadily. Compared to nonmetropolitan counties, the metropolitan counties in the region reported lower rates of decline in farm numbers, higher rates of cropland loss, and slower growth in farm sales and livestock inventories (see Chapter 4 for a nationwide comparison).

Proximity to metropolitan areas appears to have an important impact on the intensity of agricultural production and farm trends. Nonmetropolitan counties adjacent to urban areas were the only areas where farm numbers were increasing, and their livestock inventories grew faster than any other areas (despite small declines in land used for farming). By contrast, total farm receipts increased relatively slowly in these counties, suggesting the growth in small-scale, part-time hobby farms (many raising cattle and horses) side-by-side with relatively high-value, small-acreage specialty farming operations. Meanwhile, nonmetropolitan areas with the highest rates of population growth—many of which are not adjacent to metropolitan counties—witnessed the most rapid declines in farmland acreage but had the fastest rate of increase in gross farm sales. This suggests that intensification of production on surviving farm operations more than compensates for the conversion of farmland into residential uses in these areas.

The bottom half of Table 12.3 illustrates the different agricultural trends in the region's "New" and "Old" West counties. Contrary to claims that amenity migration is incompatible with traditional industries, "New West" counties experienced actual growth in farm numbers and relatively modest rates of farmland loss. However, these counties also reported sluggish growth in farm sales, suggesting a possible shift from commercial-scale operations toward hobby farms. By contrast, in the Old West counties, there was a steep decline in farm numbers and farmland acres. At the same time, in both farming-dependent and agriculturally important areas, farm receipts grew by 29 and 36 percent and livestock inventories increased by 6 and 17 percent respectively. One interesting difference between agriculturally important and farm dependent counties reflects trends in how agricultural land is used. The agriculturally important counties experienced the fastest rate of increase in farm receipts at the same time that they had the most rapid rate of loss in total farmland. This suggests dramatic changes in the intensity of agricultural land use and output. By contrast, farm-dependent counties had lower rates of land loss and maintained their farm income largely by increasing acres used as cropland.

Changes in the Use of Public Lands

The preceding discussion focused on changes in the privately owned segments of the rural landscape in the Intermountain West. Unlike the midwestern and northeastern parts of the United States (where a great deal has been written about rural land use changes), this region is most distinctive because of the large swaths of publicly owned lands managed by the federal government, primarily the U.S. Forest Service and the Bureau of Land Management (BLM). Many have argued that increased demand for recreational use of public lands has threatened the viability of traditional industries dependent on public lands for forage, minerals, energy, and timber (Cawley, 1993; Matthews et al., 2002). Government statistics paint a less alarming picture.

Initially, the role of public lands as a major grazing resource for western livestock operations has attracted considerable attention and political debate (Donahue, 1999; Foss, 1960; Hage, 1990; Jacobs, 1991; Libecap, 1981). However, while the number of federal grazing permittees has declined over the last 30 years, the number of total animal grazing months used on federal grazing allotments in this six-state region has remained fairly steady since the 1980s (US Forest Service, various years; US Department of Interior, various years). Meanwhile, the dramatic booms and busts that have characterized income and employment in the western mining and energy industries belie the fact that production of fossil fuels from federal lands has increased steadily by almost 700 percent in the last 40 years and by over 60 percent just since 1988 (US Department of Energy, 2003). The one extractive industry that experienced real declines in output on federal lands in the 1980s and 1990s was the timber industry, in which the total volume of harvested timber from public lands declined by over 80 percent between 1970 and 2001.

The continued use of public lands by traditional extractive industries has coincided with growing demands by visitors seeking to use federal lands for a wide range of recreational activities. Nationally and regionally, visits to National Parks rose by over 50 percent between 1979 and 2002 (US Department of Interior, 2003). Recreational use on Forest Service and BLM lands is more difficult to track because of inconsistencies in data collection and classification, but evidence suggests large increases in the numbers of people hiking, camping, hunting, fishing, and viewing birds and wildlife on public lands during the same period. According to Watzman (2001), visitors on Forest Service lands increased from 18 million in 1946 to almost a billion in 2000, generating over $110 billion in revenue compared to $3.5 billion from timber sales. Meanwhile, downhill ski resorts in the Rocky Mountains (usually located on land leased from the federal government) hosted over 19 million total skier visits in the 2000/01 season, up by 30 percent from 1982/83 (BBC Research and Consulting, 2003).

One of the most visible changes in the recreational use of public lands in the 1990s is the growing use of snowmobiles and motorized off-road vehicles (Havlick, 2002). Although region-wide estimates are difficult to obtain, in Utah the number of registered all-terrain vehicles (ATVs) grew three-fold between 1988 and 1998 (Knowles, 1999) and almost doubled in the ensuing five years (Wharton, 2002). In Colorado, ATV registrations increased six-fold between 1991 and 2001 ("New ATV rules necessary," 2003). An estimated 36 million Americans now own ATVs (ibid).

Many scholars have linked changes in the use of public lands to the rapid population growth that characterized the region in the late 1980s and 1990s (Baden & Snow, 1997; Booth, 2002; Ringholtz, 1996). It is clear, however, that public lands debates emerged well before the current wave of in-migration and economic restructuring (Francis & Ganzel, 1984). Additionally, since it has been a half-century since many counties in the region were principally economically dependent on timber, mining, or agriculture (Power & Barrett, 2001), it is not surprising that a growing number of regional residents want surrounding federal lands managed to support their recreational interests. What is distinctive about public land changes in the last 15 years is not the long-standing tension between extractive and recreational uses of public lands. Rather, it is a growing conflict among the various types of recreational users—hunters and motorized vehicle users clashing with hikers, backpackers, and naturalists—that is generating most of the headlines.

IMPLICATIONS OF LAND USE CHANGES IN THE INTERMOUNTAIN WEST

Environmental Impacts

The land use changes taking place in the West have important environmental implications for the ecological dynamics of this vast region. Some of these impacts reflect the intensification of traditional "Old West" industries in certain areas, including the concentration of livestock production on new "industrial-scale" farming units (Stiffler, 2002; Stuebner, 2002), growth in coal-bed methane and natural gas drilling (Bohrer, 2003; Soraghan, 2003), and efforts to return timber harvests to levels typical of peak years of the 1980s (Udall, 2003). Meanwhile, the expansion of motorized recreation on public lands has been linked to dramatic negative impacts on soil erosion, biodiversity, and wildlife populations (Shore, 2001; Wilderness Society, 2003).

While traditional extractive industries have a long legacy of adverse environmental impacts (Behan, 2001; Donahue, 1999), the growth of residential development on private lands is likely to generate new stresses for local ecosystems (Booth, 2002; Watzman, 2001). These impacts are often far more extensive than the acreage of developed land might suggest. For example, the fragmentation of rural properties into smaller parcels has created an agricultural landscape that looks relatively undeveloped, but is practically incapable of supporting viable commercial agricultural operations (Theobald et al., 1996). Even low-density housing in rural areas is likely to alter ecosystem dynamics beyond property boundaries by increasing disturbances and creating barriers to seasonal migration for wildlife (Collinge, 1996; Theobald et al., 1997). In some settings, exurban development results in decreased levels of biodiversity compared to traditional rural land uses (Maestas et al., 2001).

Social and Political Conflicts

Beyond their environmental impacts, regional land use changes are associated with a range of emerging social and political conflicts. Where growth occurs in areas with significant agricultural activities, political fights frequently erupt over efforts to preserve agricultural lands and open space. Ironically, these debates often pit newly arrived residents who favor restricting further growth against long-term rural landowners (many of whom are working farmers and ranchers) who seek to protect their ability to profit from the sale of parcels for development (Booth, 2002; Daniels & Bowers, 1997; Wright, 1993). These conflicts often transcend differences between old versus new residents, because the interests of retiring generations of farmers can conflict with younger operators, and long-term residents have mixed feelings about agricultural land conversion (Smith & Krannich, 2000). In addition, subtle changes in the organization of local agricultural operations can alter the political dynamic of rural land use debates. An example is when commercial operations are replaced by trophy ranches and hobby farms operated more to provide lifestyle benefits than as businesses ("Family ranches dying out," 2003).

While farmland preservation debates are typical of other regions, the Intermountain West has a number of rural land use conflicts that are distinctive to the area. Most obvious are growing conflicts over scarce water supplies in this arid region. For historical reasons, most available water is legally controlled by farmers and ranchers and is used for crop production (Schlager & Blomquist, 2001). However, rapidly growing non-farm populations have demanded a greater share for drinking water (Miller, 2000). At the same time, Native Americans and environmental groups have successfully sued to increase water availability to protect populations of endangered fish and other wildlife (McKinnon, 2003). Separately, housing development at the "urban-wildland interface" has increased the potential property damage and loss of human life from wildfires on National Forests (Matthews, 2000). This problem was illustrated by the loss of thousands of homes and billions of dollars of damage when catastrophic forest fires swept through Southern California in 2003 (Wood, 2003). Much of the damage from these fires has been attributed to the inability of local governments to restrict home construction near the boundaries of public forests (Mohan & Smith, 2003).

Perhaps what makes Western land use debates most distinctive are the conflicts over the use and management of the vast tracts of federal land. In the mid-1970s, growing demands by nontraditional users of public lands led to the emergence of a new "multiple-use" management paradigm designed to balance the interests of extractive and recreational users (Fedkiw, 1998; Schuler, 1975). Multiple-use approaches force agencies to consider potential conflicts between extractive and recreational uses and find a balance that best meets the needs of all users. In practice, this balance has been difficult to strike, and federal agencies have become accustomed to intense criticism from all sides in modern debates over the use of public lands.

During the 1990s, the pendulum swung in favor of conservation and low-impact recreation interests at the expense of traditional extractive users. Under the leadership of then Secretary of the Interior Bruce Babbitt, a number of major reforms of grazing, mining, and timber policies toward public lands were proposed.

The pendulum swung back abruptly with the election of George W. Bush as President in 2000. With the support of a Republican legislative majority, the Bush administration implemented a wide range of policy changes to reverse many of the Clinton administration initiatives. One of the most important has been an effort to streamline the regulatory process to accelerate the production of timber, coal, and natural gas from public lands in the West (Raabe, 2003). This push has encountered surprising opposition from traditionally conservative hunting and ranching interests who fear that unregulated energy development will permanently affect their property rights and quality of life (Bohrer, 2003; Harden, 2003).

CONCLUSION

Rapid population growth in the Intermountain West during the last 15 years has contributed to transformations in the way private lands are used in the region. From a macro-landscape perspective, these changes are not particularly dramatic. Farming, ranching, and other traditional uses remain the overwhelmingly dominant forms of land use in the region. Moreover, despite steady losses of jobs and income to local residents in farming, mining, and forestry, the overall level of agricultural output and natural-resource extraction appears to have held steady or increased throughout this period. A more fine-grained analysis reveals more subtle shifts between traditional land uses, such as the growth in acres of less intensively managed cropland (e.g., Conservation Reserve Program fields) at the expense of row crops, rangeland, and forests.

The pace and direction of private land use changes in the region are notably different across various types of rural counties. As traditional geographic theory suggests (Hart, 1991; Sinclair, 1967), urban proximity has a dramatic impact on the use of rural lands. In particular, the intensity of agricultural production in urban areas is rising despite a diminishing land base. In rings of nonmetropolitan counties adjacent to the urban cores, acreage in cropland and pasture actually increased during the last decade, though stagnant farm receipts appear to signal a shift from commercial to more hobby-oriented farming systems in these areas. Despite lower population pressures in more remote nonmetropolitan counties, the conversion of significant amounts of land on a per capita basis to development contributed to relatively high rates of loss of rangeland and forests when compared to metro adjacent areas.

The conventional approach to understanding demographic and economic restructuring in this region has been to frame it as a transition from an "old" western economy based on extractive primary industries to a "New West" based on amenity migration, recreational use of public lands, and service sector employment. The present analysis suggests this old-vs-new frame is too simplistic to capture the complex relationships between traditional and emerging uses of rural lands in the region. For one thing, many of the counties that typify the New West are not located in areas with heavy local economic reliance on extractive industries. This is not to say that rapid population growth is not a threat to the long-run viability of traditional rural land uses—particularly agriculture—in some key areas. However, resort towns, high amenity recreational and seasonal housing communities, and areas with significant amounts of unearned income tend to be physically separated from the places where most of the economic value from farming, timber, and mining is generated. The "cows versus condos" puzzle that has received significant attention by regional environmental and agricultural organizations (Horning, 2002; Marsden, 2002) may well prove to be a false dichotomy. Indeed, cow numbers appear to be increasing fairly rapidly in places where seasonal and recreational housing is most common.

No discussion of land use in the Intermountain West can be complete without a thorough appreciation of the changing demands placed on public lands in the region. Although shifts in national politics have had the most dramatic impacts on recent federal agency efforts to balance competing uses of public lands, the in-migration of millions of new residents seeking high-amenity recreational opportunities has increased the intensity and changed the character of the public lands debate. Moreover, the impact of new residents on public lands occurs regardless of whether or not they choose to live in rural areas.

A final question relates to whether or not the trends observed during the 1990s are typical of what the 21st century will bring to the Intermountain West. Certainly, rates of population growth and net migration were considerably slower during the latter half of the decade and have yet to rebound. Cromartie (2002) has noted that the West led the nation in net migration into nonmetropolitan counties between 1996 and1998 yet had the most rapid rate of out-migration between 1999 and 2001. The lessening of the urban-to-rural migration stream is related to changes in the regional and national economy that increased opportunities for employment in metropolitan areas more rapidly than in rural counties (ibid). Moreover, the crash in the stock market in 2000 can be expected to have greatly reduced the ability of people to rely on investment income to subsidize their residential location choices.

ENDNOTES

1. Specifically, we used 1997 Census of Agriculture data to calculate the total amount of farm receipts per acre of: (a) farmland; (b) cropland; and (c) a weighted index of cropland, pasture, and rangeland that discounted the non-cropland by a factor of 0.2. We ranked counties in the region based on these three farming intensity ratios, as well as a fourth variable reflecting the total county gross farm sales in 1997. Counties ranking in the top quartile on at least two of these measures were determined to be "agriculturally important" since they have the most dense farming activity and contribute the most economic activity to the region's farm economy. Because of the lack of detailed county-level data on timber and mining output, similar codes could not be computed for those particular industries.

2. Regional data from the 1982 and 1997 National Resource Inventory database (USDA 2000) were aggregated according to the county typologies described above, and transition matrices linking the land use category at each sample point in 1982 and 1997 were constructed.
3. The inclusion of farmsteads and "other rural" lands in the development category reflects the authors' view that many low density rural housing developments, including hobby farms, ranchettes, and scattered individual homes are captured by changes in these two classes of land use. See Radeloff, Hagen, Voss, Field, & Mladenoff (2000) and Theobold (2002) for discussions of the strengths and weaknesses of alternative indicators of housing development in the rural landscape.

REFERENCES

Athearn, R.G. (1986). *The mythic West in twentieth century America.* Lawrence: University Press of Kansas.

BBC Research and Consulting. (2003, July 3). *The American ski industry—Alive, well and even growing.* Report prepared for the National Ski Areas Association. Retrieved November 1, 2003, from http://www.nsaa.org/nsaa2002/_media.asp

Baden, J.A., & Snow, D. (1997). *The next West: Public lands, community, and economy in the American West.* Washington, DC: Island Press.

Behan, R.W. (2001). *Plundered promise: Capitalism, politics and the fate of the federal lands.* Washington, DC: Island Press.

Berry, W. (1977). *The unsettling of America: Culture and agriculture.* New York: Avon Books.

Beyers, W.B., & Lindahl, D. (1996). Lone eagles and high fliers in rural producer services. *Rural Development Perspectives, 11*, 2–10.

Bohrer, B. (2003, July 17). BLM accused of failing CBM duties. *Billings Gazette.* Retrieved November 5, 2003, from http://www.billingsgazette.com/index.php?id=1&display=rednews/2003/07/17/build/local/37-cbm.inc

Booth, D.E. (2002). *Searching for paradise: Economic development and environmental change in the Mountain West.* Lanham, MD: Rowman and Littlefield.

Butler, M.A., & Beale, C. (1994). *Rural-urban continuum codes for metro and nonmetro counties, 1993* (Economic Research Service Staff Report No. 9425). Washington, DC: U.S. Department of Agriculture, Economic Research Service.

Cawley, R.M. (1993). *Federal land, western anger.* Lawrence: University Press of Kansas.

Collinge, S.K. (1996). Ecological consequences of See memo for detailed responses for each reference change fragmentation: Implications for landscape architecture and planning. *Landscape and Urban Planning, 36*, 59–77.

Cook, P.J., & Mizer, K.L. (1994). *The revised ERS county typology: An overview* (Rural Development Research Report No. 89). Washington, DC: U.S. Department of Agriculture, Economic Research Service.

Cromartie, J.B. (2002). Nonmetro migration continues downward trend. *Rural America, 17*(4), 70–73.

Cromartie, J.B., & Wardwell, J.M. (1999). Migrants settling far and wide in the rural West. *Rural Development Perspectives, 14*(2), 2–8.

Daniels, T.L., & Bowers, D. (1997). *Holding our ground: Protecting America's farms and farmland.* Washington, DC: Island Press.

Donahue, D.L. (1999). *The western range revisited: Removing livestock from public lands to conserve native biodiversity.* Norman, OK: University of Oklahoma Press.

Egan, A.F., & Luloff, A.E. (2000). The exurbanization of America's forests: Research in rural social sciences. *Journal of Forestry, (March), 99*(3), 26–30.

Family ranches dying out. (2003, July 17). *Billings Gazette*. Retrieved November 5, 2003, from http://www.billingsgazette.com/index.php?id=1&display=rednews/2003/07/17/build/wyoming/38-ranches.inc

Fedkiw, J. (1998). *Managing multiple uses on national forests, 1905–1995: A 90-year learning experience and it isn't finished yet*. Retrieved April 19, 2004, from the U.S. Department of Agriculture Forest Service Web site: http://www.fs.fed.us/research/publications/managing_multiple_uses_on_nation.htm

Foss, P.O. (1960). *Politics and grass: The administration of grazing on the public domain*. New York: Greenwood Press.

Francis, J.G., & Ganzel, R. (1984). *Western public lands: The management of natural resources in a time of declining federalism*. Totowa, NJ: Rowman and Allanheld.

Hage, W. (1990). *Storm over rangelands: Private rights in federal lands*. Bellevue, WA: Free Enterprise Press.

Harden, B. (2003, November 4). Talk of gas drilling splits pro-Bush factions in West. *Washington Post*, page A1.

Hart, J.F. (1991). The perimetropolitan bow wave. *Geographical Review, 81*(1), 35–51.

Havlick, D.G. (2002). *No distant place: Roads and motorized recreation on America's public lands*. Washington, DC: Island Press.

Heimlich, R.E., & Anderson, W.D. (2001, June). *Development at the urban fringe and beyond: Impacts on agriculture and rural land* (ERS Agricultural Economic Report No. 803). Washington, DC: U.S. Department of Agriculture, Economic Research Service.

Horning, J. (2002, December 9). Ranching advocates lack a rural vision. *High Country News, 34*(23). Retrieved November 5, 2003, from http://www.hcn.org/servlets/hcn.Article?article_id=13587

Jacobs, Lynn (1991). Waste of the West: Public lands ranching. Tuscon, AZ: Lynn Jacobs.

Knowles, S. (1999, July 8). New rules for forests appealed. *Salt Lake Tribune*.

Libecap, G.D. (1981). *Locking up the range: Federal land controls and grazing*. San Francisco: Pacific Institute for Public Policy Research.

Maestas, J.D., Knight, R.L., & Gilgert, W.C. (2001). Biodiversity and land-use change in the American Mountain West. *The Geographical Review, 91*(3), 509–524.

Malone, M.P., & Etulain, R.W. (1989). *The American West: A twentieth-century history*. Lincoln, NE: University of Nebraska Press.

Marsden, E. (2002, December 9). Cow-free crowd ignores science, sprawl, *High Country News. 34*(23), Retrieved July 1, 2004, from: http://www.hcn.org/servlets/hcn.Article?article_id=13586

Marsden, T. (1999). Rural futures: The consumption countryside and its regulation. *Sociologia Ruralis, 39*(4), 501–520.

Matthews, M. (2000, August 28). Home is where the heat is. *High Country News. 32*(16), Retrieved July 1, 2004, from: http://www.hcn.org/servlets/hcn.Article?article_id=5972

Matthews, K.H., Ingram, K., Lewandrowski, J., & Dunmore J. (2002). Public lands and rural communities. *Agricultural Outlook, 292*, 18–22.

McGranahan, D.A. (1999). *Natural amenities drive rural population change* (Agricultural Economic Report No. 781). Washington DC: U.S. Department of Agriculture, Economic Research Service, Food and Rural Economics Division.

McKinnon, S. (2003, July 6). Water: Growing demand, dwindling supply. *Arizona Republic*.

McNab, W.H., & Avers, P.E. (1994). *Ecological subregions of the United States* (Report No. WO-WSA-5). Retrieved April 19, 2004, from the U.S. Department of Agriculture Forest Service Web site: http://www.fs.fed.us/land/pubs/ecoregions/ch47.html

Miller, C. (Ed.). (2000). *Water in the West: A high country news reader*. Corvallis, OR: Oregon State University Press.

Mohan, G., & Smith, D. (2003, October 28). Despite risk, hills irresistable to home buyers, *Los Angeles Times*, page A1.

Nelson, Peter. (1997). Migration, sources of income, and community change in the nonmetropolitan Northwest. *Professional Geographer, 49*(4), 418–430.

Nelson, Peter. (1999). Quality of life, nontraditional income, and economic growth: New development opportunities for the rural West. *Rural Development Perspectives, 14*(2), 32–37.

Nelson, Peter. (2001). Rural restructuring in the American West: Land use, family and class discourses. *Journal of Rural Studies, 17*, 395–407.

Nelson, P.B., & Beyers, W.B. (1998). Using economic base models to explain new trends in rural income. *Growth and Change, 29*(Summer), 295–318.

New ATV rules necessary. (2003, October 1). *Denver Post*, Editorial.

Otterstrom, S.M., & Shumway, J.M. (2003). Deserts and oases: The continuing concentration of population in the American Mountain West. *Journal of Rural Studies, 19*, 445–462.

Power, T. (1996). *Lost landscapes, failed economies*. Washington, DC: Island Press.

Power, T.M., & Barrett, R.N. (2001). *Post-cowboy economics: Pay and prosperity in the new American West*. Washington, DC: Island Press.

Raabe, S. (2003, October 12). Rockies' natural gas fuels land-use clash. *Denver Post*, page K1.

Radeloff, V.C., Hagen, A.E., Voss, P.R., Field, D.R., & Mladenoff, D.J. (2000). Exploring the spatial relationship between census and land-cover data. *Society and Natural Resources, 13*(6), 599–609.

Rasker, R. (1995). *An economic overview of the interior Columbia River Basin: Facts, myths, and challenges for ecosystem management*. Bozeman, MT: Wilderness Society.

Riebsame, W.E., Gosnell, H., & Theobald, D.M. (1996). Land use and landscape change in the Colorado mountains I: Theory, scale and pattern. *Mountain Research and Development, 16*(4), 395–405.

Ringholtz, R. (1996). *Paradise paved: The challenge of growth in the new West*. Salt Lake City, UT: University of Utah Press.

Rudzitis, G. (1999). Amenities increasingly draw people to the rural West. *Rural Development Perspectives, 14*(2), 9–13.

Rudzitis, G., & Johansen, H. (1989). Migration to western wilderness counties: Causes and consequences. *Western Wildlands, 15*, 19–23.

Salant, P., Dillman, D., & Carley, L. (1997). *Who's moving into the nonmetropolitan counties? Evidence from Washington State*. Pullman, WA: Social and Economic Sciences Research Center, Washington State University.

Schlager, E., & Blomquist, W. (2001). Water resources: The southwestern United States. In J. Burger, E. Ostrom, R. Norgaard, D. Policansky, & B. Goldstein (Eds.), *Protecting the commons: A framework for resource management in the Americas* (pp. 133–159). Washington, DC: Island Press.

Schuler, A. (1975). Planning resource use on national forests to achieve multiple objectives. *Journal of Environmental Management, 3*(4), 351.

Shore, T. (2001). *Off-road to ruin: How motorized recreation is unraveling California's landscapes*. Retrieved November 1, 2003, from the California Wilderness Coalition Web site: http://www.calwild.org/resources/pubs/ORV_report.pdf

Shumway, J.M., & Davis, J.A. (1996). Nonmetropolitan population change in the mountain west: 1970–1995. *Rural Sociology, 61*(3), 513–529.

Shumway, J.M., & Otterstrom, S.M. (2001). Spatial patterns of migration and income change in the mountain west: The dominance of service-based amenity-rich counties. *Professional Geographer, 53*(2), 492–502.

Sinclair, R. (1967). Von Thünen and urban sprawl. *Annals of the Association of American Geographers, (XLVII)*, 72–87.

Smith, M.D., & Krannich, R. (2000). "Culture clash" revisited: Newcomer and longer-term residents' attitudes toward land use, development, and environmental issues in rural communities in the rocky mountain west. *Rural Sociology, 65*(3), 396–421.

Smutny, G. (2002). Patterns of growth and change: Depicting the impacts of restructuring in Idaho. *Professional Geographer, 54*(3), 438–453.

Soraghan, M. (2003, July 6). Plan taps "Persian Gulf of natural gas" in West. *Denver Post*, page A1.

Stiffler, L. (2002, May 31). As neighbors, cows stink, residents say. *Seattle Post-Intelligencer,* Retrieved November 5, 2003, from http://seattlepi.nwsource.com/local/72704_idaho31.shtml

Stuebner, S. (2002, April 15). Raising a stink: Factory dairies catch Idaho's magic valley by surprise. *High Country News, 1*, 8–11.

Theobald, D.M. (2001). Land-use dynamics beyond the American urban-fringe. *The Geographical Review, 91*(3), 544–564.

Theobald, D.M., Gosnell, H., & Reibsame, W.E. (1996). Land use and landscape change in the Colorado mountains II: A case study of the East River Valley. *Mountain Research and Development, 16*(4), 407–418.

Theobald, D.M., Miller, J.R., & Hobbs, N.T. (1997). Estimating the cumulative effects of development on wildlife habitat. *Landscape and Urban Planning, 39*, 25–36.

Turner, F.J. (1962). *The frontier in American history.* NY: Holt, Rinehart, and Winston. (Original work published 1920).

Udall, M. (2003, November 24). Our publicly owned forests are being subverted, *High Country News. 35*(22), Retrieved July 1, 2004, from: http://www.hcn.org/servlets/hcn.Article?article_id=14410

U.S. Department of Agriculture, National Agricultural Statistics Service. (1999). *1997 census of agriculture.* Retrieved July 22, 2002, from http://www.nass.usda.gov/census/

U.S. Department of Agriculture, Natural Resources Conservation Service. (2000). *Summary report: 1997 national resources inventory*. Retrieved July 22, 2002, from http://www.nrcs.usda.gov/technical/NRI/1997/summary_report/

U.S. Department of Energy. (2003). *Energy information agency report on historical energy use trends.* Retrieved November 3, 2003, from http://www.eia.doe.gov/emeu/aer/txt/ptb0114.html

U.S. Department of Interior, Bureau of Land Management. (various years). *Public land statistics.* Retrieved January 15, 2004, from http://www.blm.gov/natacq/pls03/

U.S. Department of Interior, National Park Service. (various years). *Visitation statistics.* Retrieved September 15, 2004, from http://www2.nature.nps.gov/stats/

U.S. Forest Service. (various years). *Annual grazing statistical reports.* Washington, DC: U.S. Department of Agriculture.

Vias, A.C. (1999). Jobs follow people in the rural rocky mountain west. *Rural Development Perspectives, 14*(2), 14–23.

Watzman, N. (2001, May). Playground or preserve: How the recreation industry has become the newest threat to our public lands. *Washington Monthly*. Retrieved November 5, 2003, from http://www.washingtonmonthly.com/search.html#2001

Wharton, T. (2002, May 6). Dust-up over ATV trail bill. *Salt Lake Tribune.*

Wilderness Society. (2003). *Taken for a ride: How off-road vehicles damage the nation's wildest lands.* Retrieved November 1, 2003, from www.wilderness.org/Library/orv.ctm

Wood, D.B. (2003, October 28). California's blazing density problem. *Christian Science Monitor.*

Wright, J.B. (1993). *Rocky mountain divide: Selling and saving the West.* Austin, TX: University of Texas Press.

CHAPTER 13

DOES SECOND HOME DEVELOPMENT ADVERSELY AFFECT RURAL LIFE?

RICHARD C. STEDMAN, STEPHAN J. GOETZ, AND BENJAMIN WEAGRAFF[1]

INTRODUCTION

Second home ownership is an increasingly common use of rural space and is posited as a viable rural development strategy in many places. Yet some are concerned that the proliferation of second homes may threaten the character of rural places. As a response, we examine in our chapter whether second home development adversely affects traditional rural community life. Theory and research suggest that increases in second homes may be a double-edged sword for rural areas: this growth may bring needed revenues to some rural places, but it may be accompanied by impacts on traditional uses (and definitions) of rural space. Increasingly, high-amenity rural places are seen as "playgrounds" for rich urbanites, changing the notions of what (and for whom) rural places are. Understanding these tensions is critical for understanding the future of many areas of rural America.

Our chapter explores several questions. First, to what degree is second home ownership a rural phenomenon: how does it vary by degree of rurality, and to what extent does this relationship vary by region? Second, we examine the relationship between second home ownership and several phenomena rooted in traditional definitions of rural and rurality: social capital and employment in traditional resource-dependent industries. We ask two questions of each of these dependent variables: (1) to what extent is it really a rural phenomenon (are our images of rurality consonant with the current reality of rural places?), and (2) to what extent are the realities that underlie these images affected or threatened by second home development?

PREVIOUS RESEARCH

Second homes have interested researchers in the U.S. since at least the late 1960's. Increased disposable income, leisure time, and improved transportation

W.A. Kandel & D.L. Brown (eds.), Population Change and Rural Society, 277–292.

have been associated with population growth in nonmetropolitan areas rich in natural amenities such as mild climate, surface water, mountains, and forests (Beale & Johnson, 1998; Cromartie & Wardwell, 1999; Deller et al., 2001; McGranahan, 1999; Rudzitis, 1999). These amenities have become the chief source of comparative advantage for many nonmetropolitan counties in the U.S. (Galston & Baehler, 1995). Natural amenities, especially when located in areas far from urban centers, stimulate population growth primarily by attracting migrants to the area in a progression from recreationists to residents (Bennett, 1996; Godbey & Bevins, 1987; Shumway & Davis, 1996; Stewart & Stynes, 1994). In rural areas closer to metropolitan centers, natural amenities represent a significant draw for permanent residents who commute to work (Fuguitt, 1991).

Linked to this type of rural population growth are concomitant concerns about its impacts on traditional rural life or the rurality of rural spaces (Bealer et al., 1965; Willits & Bealer, 1967). Definitions of rural include (1) ecological: rural places by definition have low population density; (2) sociocultural: rural communities are identified by traditional patterns of social interaction, high density of acquaintanceship, shared values and beliefs, and other indicators of *gemeinschaft* relations; and (3) occupational: rural employment is closely tied to land and other natural resources as factors of production (Bell, 1992; Gilbert, 1982; Jacob & Luloff, 1995). Brown and Cromartie (2004) note that multidimensional approaches that incorporate ecological, sociocultural, occupational, and other factors may have great utility in defining rurality in the context of changing population preferences. Although the urban/rural dichotomy is simpler, this may not always be an accurate representation, nor may it be sufficiently flexible to capture dimensions of rurality that change over time. Accordingly, although studies of the urban-rural continuum have somewhat fallen out of favor (e.g., Buttel et al., 1987) based on increasing recognition that rural spaces and people are more diverse than commonly recognized (e.g., Fortmann & Kusel, 1990; Naples, 1994), others (e.g., Brown & Kandel, this volume; Willits & Luloff, 1995) note that the rural mystique may persist even in the face of contrary evidence.

In this vein, many concerns have been raised about the social impact of increased visitors and second homes in rural America as well as their potential impacts on environmental quality (e.g., Gobster et al., 2000; Radeloff et al., 2001; Wear & Bolstad, 1998; Wear et al., 1998). Amenity-based, recreation-led growth can affect lake ecosystems, forest fragmentation, biodiversity, and other environmental indicators (Huang & Stewart, 1996; Marcouiller et al., 2002; Rudzitis, 1999; Schnaiberg et al., 2002). Gartner (1987) and Stroud (1985) argue that recreational areas that are marketed as consisting entirely of vacation homes have had a history of being poorly regulated. Gartner claims this is due to the fact that these developments are unplanned by any public entity (local government unit). This is a concern because if land use is completely unregulated, environmental damage can be significant.

More germane to our chapter, concerns have also been articulated about impacts to community well-being and community social fabric (Chaplin,

1999; Coppock, 1997; Girard & Gartner, 1993; Rothman, 1978). Stedman (2002, 2003) examined the potential impacts of second home growth on year-round residents' sense of place. Cutting across multiple research traditions is the tendency to consider visitors as potential threats to rural, resource-rich settings. For example, within the sense of place literature, Relph (1976) is careful to differentiate between "authentic" and "inauthentic" sense of place, and he considers visitor perceptions as inauthentic (see also Hay, 1998; Tuan, 1974). By implication, this position suggests that visitors may negatively affect the social fabric of these communities. This perspective is also reflected in tourism-and migration-related research. Buller and Hoggart (1994) note the "outsider" phenomenon in their treatment of British vacation homeowners in rural France. Natives of Jordan's (1980) Vermont host community lump together tourists and seasonal residents into an undifferentiated "summer people" category, linked to cultural value clashes and concerns about vanishing community identity. Allen and others (1988) examine potential tourist impacts on community by studying resident perceptions of community life using a carrying capacity framework (see also Getz, 1983), in which communities have a certain capacity to absorb newcomers before damage is incurred. Community change associated with newcomers may lead to perceived declines in community quality-of-life and well-being (Ringholz, 1996; Wright, 1993). Some researchers have asserted that managing rapid growth while protecting social, ecological, and economic values is now the single most important issue facing rural communities experiencing rapid growth (Beyers & Nelson, 2000). According to Duane (1999), the fundamental question for citizens and planners in high-amenity rural communities is how such places can avoid a development process that will destroy the very features that make the region a desirable place to live.

Regardless of theoretical perspective, second homeowners are clearly perceived by the authors noted above as different in their characteristics and potentially threatening to cherished aspects of rurality. Second homeowners have also been identified as more concerned about environmental protection (Green et al., 1996). This may challenge the viability of local natural resource employment, according to the moral exclusion argument for the link between natural resource employment and rural poverty (RSS, 1993). According to this argument, the social construction of nature and "what it is for" has shifted away from consumptive use. Furthermore, this shift is associated with rural spaces becoming "places to play," as evidenced by the proliferation of second homes. Another key difference between year-round residents and second homeowners is in human capital. According to the National Association of Realtors (2002), second homeowners are older (61 years on average) and wealthier (average income of $76,900) than those who do not own second homes (see also Wolfe, 1978). The reported median value of second homes was $150,000 (NAR, p.11). Using survey data, Stedman (2000) found that in a lake-rich landscape, owners of second homes were nearly four times as likely to have a university degree than year-round residents and over twenty times more likely to report annual household incomes (in 1999) in excess of $100,000. Therefore, although second homeowners may bring revenues to an area (e.g., Brown,

Table 13.1. National Growth in Second Homes, 1980–2000

Year	Total Number of Second-Homes	Percentage of All Housing Units
2000	3,872,468	3.34%
1990	3,081,174	3.01%
1980	1,652,546	1.87%

1970; Stynes et al., 1996), income disparities between second homeowners and local residents, especially when coupled with perceived attitudinal and value differences, may contribute to already heightened tensions between "them" and "us."

RESEARCH QUESTIONS, DATA, AND MEASURES

Characteristics and Locations of Second Homes

Second homes are becoming an increasingly common use of rural space, with the U.S. Census now counting a total of close to four million such residences (Table 13.1). This is especially true in areas with high amenity values, as identified by McGranahan (1999). Other research (e.g., Stedman, 2003) has examined the role of natural resource amenities in fostering growth in second homes. Prior to examining the relationship between second home ownership and our rurality phenomena of interest, we describe the location of second homes to provide context for subsequent analysis.

Figure 13.1 maps second homes as a percent of all homes at the county level. The rural Northeast and northern Great Lakes are well known as summer home destinations, but the map reveals that these regions hardly have a monopoly on second homes. The Rocky Mountain West also stands out as an important region for second home ownership.

The economic boom of the 1990's, coupled with low interest rates, fueled a boom in second home construction in that decade (see also Table 13.1). Figure 13.2 shows that areas with greater second home density in 2000 did not necessarily experience large *relative* increases in second homes as well between 1990 and 2000. Much of the growth in second homes occurred in portions of southern states such as Mississippi, Alabama, Georgia, Arkansas, and West Virginia, in parts of the northern Great Plains and Mid-Atlantic region, and in selected counties of the Mountain West. It is important to note that, on a percentage basis, growth in second homes remains a disproportionately rural phenomenon.

Figure 13.1. Second Homes as a Percent of All Homes

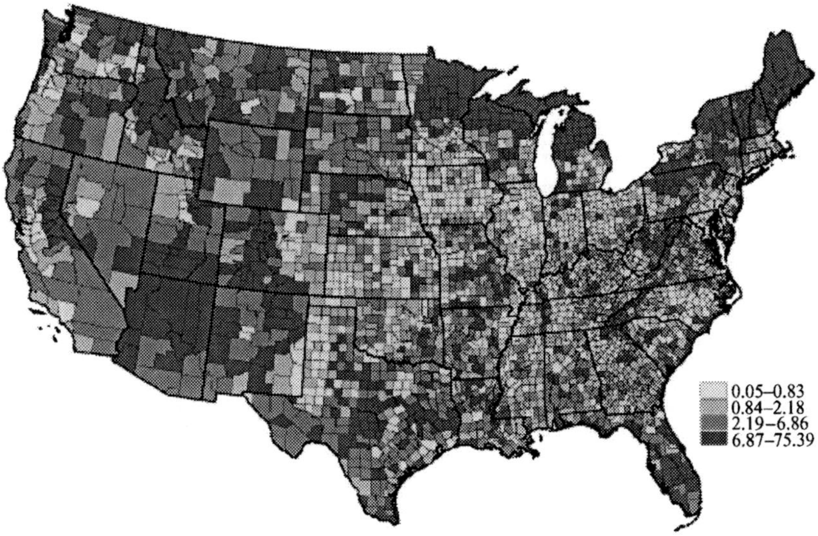

Source: The Northeast Regional Center for Rural Development. ©2003.

Figure 13.2. Percentage Point Change in Second Homes as a Percent of Total Homes, 1990–2000

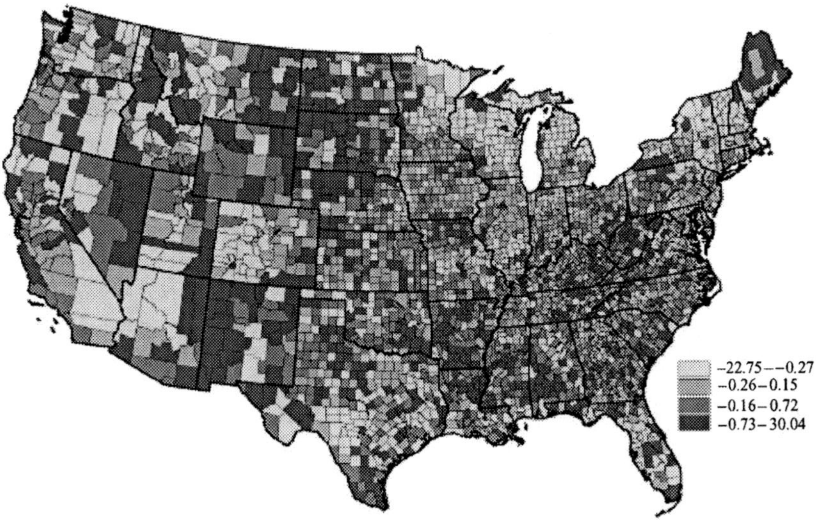

Source: The Northeast Regional Center for Rural Development. ©2003.

Table 13.2. Rural-Urban Continuum Code Specifications

Label	Specifications
RUCC0,1	Metropolitan county with 1,000,000 or more population
RUCC2	Metropolitan county with population of 250,000–999,999
RUCC3	Metropolitan county with less than 250,000
RUCC4	Non-metropolitan, urban population of 20,000 or more, **adjacent** to metropolitan county
RUCC5	Non-metropolitan, urban population of 20,000 or more, **not adjacent** to metropolitan county
RUCC6	Non-metropolitan, urban population of 2,500–19,999, **adjacent** to metropolitan county
RUCC7	Non-metropolitan, urban population of 2,500–19,999, **not adjacent** to metropolitan county
RUCC8	Non-metropolitan, urban population of less than 2,500, **adjacent** to metropolitan county
RUCC9	Non-metropolitan, urban population of less than 2,500, **not adjacent** to metropolitan county

Degree of Rurality and Second Homes

To what degree are the presence and growth of second homes primarily a rural phenomenon, as defined by population density? The relationship between second home ownership and conventional definitions of rural places, as indicated by standard population density criteria, is analyzed using data drawn from the decennial U.S. Population Census. The degree of rurality is defined by the 10 category Rural-Urban Continuum Code (henceforth RUCC), a county level measure that enjoins population size, metropolitan/non-metropolitan status, and adjacency to metropolitan areas (Table 13.2).

Analysis of variance was used to compare, by RUCC, the percent of homes defined as seasonal, recreational, or occasional use. Two variables are presented: the percent of second homes in 2000, to describe current conditions, and the relative change between 1990 and 2000, to assess whether second home ownership became an increasingly rural phenomenon during the 1990s (Table 13.3).

A relatively clear picture emerges by comparing county-level means. Rural, nonadjacent counties have a significantly higher proportion of second homes (11.8 percent of all housing on average) than any other county categorization. RUCC 8 (rural, metro adjacent) and 7 (urban, non metro adjacent) also stand out as significant from other counties. In contrast, more metropolitan counties (RUCC 0-5) do not differ significantly from each other, with the mean proportion

Table 13.3. Summary County Statistics: Percent Second Homes, Social Capital, and Employment in Natural Resource Industries

	0	1	2	3	4	5	6	7	8	9		
N	164	132	311	194	129	106	601	641	248	520	F	Sig.
% Second Homes 2000	1.19[a]	3.33[a]	2.47[a]	3.01[a]	3.57[a]	3.65[a]	6.19[b]	6.95[b]	9.28[c]	11.76[d]	50.23	.001
% Change Second Homes 1990–2000	.002[a]	.003[a]	.003[a]	.002[a]	.003[a]	.007[b]	.004[a]	.008[b]	.004[a]	.018[c]	17.76	.001
Social Capital Index, 2000	−.27[a]	−.48[a]	−.42[a]	−.03[b]	−.12[a]	.02[b]	−.28[a]	.28[c]	−.19[a]	.67[d]	28.07	.001
% Employment in Farming, Forestry, Fisheries 2000	.31[a]	.70[b]	.80[b]	1.00[b]	1.28[b]	1.40[c]	2.08[d]	2.63[e]	2.81[e]	4.55[f]	98.62	.001

* Values with different superscripts differ from each other at $p < .05$ (TukeyB).

of housing classified as second homes ranging from about 1 to 3 percent of all housing.

Did these figures change between 1990 and 2000? Table 13.3 also compares the percent change in second homes between 1990 and 2000 by county categorization. Only the counties at the opposite ends of the spectrum stand out from each other. Second home ownership is clearly becoming a "more rural" phenomenon, especially as indicated by percent growth rather than absolute numbers. The share of housing consisting of second homes gained an average of 1.87 percent in rural nonadjacent counties; counties in category 1 (high population metropolitan counties) lost second homes as a percent of all housing. Based on these findings, it is reasonable to summarize second home growth as a "rural phenomenon that is becoming more rural." This suggests that rural areas that are potentially less desirable from a second-home standpoint (i.e., more remote and harder to get to) will likely face increasing development pressure in the future.

Far from being a phenomenon confined to a single region of the country, second homes are more prevalent in rural areas throughout the country. Further analysis of change in the percent of second homes between 1990 and 2000 reveals that *growth* in second homes is fastest in rural, nonadjacent counties in every region but the West, where second home growth is occurring equally across counties independently of metropolitan and adjacency status (data available upon request). In all regions except the West, rural nonadjacent counties stand out as unique not just in the existence but in the continued growth of second homes.

IMPACTS OF SECOND HOMES ON SOCIAL CAPITAL AND EMPLOYMENT IN RESOURCE INDUSTRIES

Our primary task in this chapter is to examine the relationship between second homes and two phenomena rooted in traditional definitions of rural and rurality: social capital and employment in traditional resource-dependent industries. We ask two questions of each of these dependent variables: (1) to what extent is each really a "rural" phenomenon (are our images of rurality consonant with the current reality of rural places?), and (2) are these phenomena empirically linked to second home development?

Social Capital

We use *Social Capital* as a proxy for rural community cohesion. Although there is a lack of consensus on the meaning of social capital, many aspects of existing definitions indicate the utility of this approach. For example, Putnam (2000) describes social capital as social networks and associated expectations of reciprocity. Wollcock (2001) emphasizes the potential for social capital to facilitate collective action (see Lin, 2001, for an overview). Social capital is thus potentially consistent with traditional rural community attributes, such as dense networks of acquaintanceship that carry with them expectations of community-reinforcing behavior. In short, this is the small town where "everyone knows and looks out for each other." The measure of social capital used in this paper follows that developed in Rupasingha and others (forthcoming). It includes associational density variables: establishments per capita related to the creation of social capital, such as bowling alleys, civic organizations, etc.; voting behavior; county-level response rates to the U.S. Census; and density of non-profit organizations (see Rupasingha et al., forthcoming for additional information on the creation of the scale).

To what degree is social capital, as we measure it, a rural phenomenon? First, we examine the degree to which the county-level social capital index (2000 data) varies by adjacency and metropolitan status. We conduct a ONEWAY ANOVA of the social capital index by RUCCs to test for such differences (Table 13.3). In 2000, there is a fairly linear relationship between size and adjacency and the composite social capital index. Social capital levels are significantly higher in rural nonadjacent counties (RUCC = 9) than any other county type and lowest in metropolitan areas of over 250,000 (RUCC = 0, 1, 2). Although there is some noise in the middle categories, our measure of social capital is strongly associated with more rural places.

In terms of the relationship between second home ownership and social capital, a correlation analysis between the 2000 social capital index and percent second homes (2000) suggests a moderately positive association ($r = .226$). However, this is potentially misleading, as rural places are higher both in second home ownership and social capital. To further explore the relationship between second home ownership and social capital, we conduct a multiple regression analysis predicting county-level scores on the 2000 social capital index. We include variables associated with social capital, such as education (percent with a college degree), percent of female-heade households, and percent of residents ages 65 or over. We include a dummy variable for whether the county was rural/nonadjacent (RUCC = 9) to observe whether a rural effect remained after other variables were controlled for. We control for regional effects with dummy variables for each USDA-CSREES-defined regions, where the Northeast is used as the referent region, and we include two second home variables: the percent of housing classified as second homes in 1990, and the percent change between 1990 and 2000.

The regression equation predicting social capital explains 55 percent of the variation in the social capital index and reveals an interesting effect of second homes: increases in second home development between 1990 and 2000 have no impact on social capital (Table 13.4). However, high shares of second homes in 1990 are associated, all other factors equal, with lower social capital levels in 2000, essentially reversing the positive bivariate correlation observed earlier. This suggests that the positive bivariate relationship was primarily an artifact of rural areas being higher in the percentage of second homes and in social capital. The disappearance of the change in second homes variable is not due to collinearity with the share of second homes in 1990, as the correlation between these two variables is only .038. Consistent with Rupasingha et al. (forthcoming) and others, higher social capital is positively associated with education (share with a college

Table 13.4. Coefficients from a Model Predicting Social Capital Index, 2000

	Unstandardized Coefficients (B)	Standard Error	Beta	Sig
Intercept	−2.135	.119		
RUCC9 (See Table 13.2)	0.160	.046	.047	p < .001
Percent College Graduate, 1990	0.081	.003	.406	p < .001
Percent Age 65 or Over, 1990	0.102	.004	.346	p < .001
Percent Female Headed Household, 1990	−0.035	.003	−.144	p < .001
Region 2 (South)	−0.529	.058	−.205	p < .001
Region 3 (West)	−.0136	.066	−.036	ns
Region 4 (North Central)	0.699	.060	.261	p < .001
Percent Second Homes, 1990	−1.138	.187	−.084	p < .001
Change Percent Second Home 1990–2000	1.755	.640	.037	ns
Adjusted R Square	.551			

degree), an elderly population (percent over 65), and is negatively associated with the proportion of households that are headed by females. There are independent effects of region as well. Using the Northeast as the excluded category, there are strong negative effects on social capital in the South and strong positive effects in the North Central region. The rural effect noted above decreases when these other variables are controlled for, yet remains significantly positive; net of the variables identified above, more rural places remain higher in social capital. We can not ascertain from the data what dimension of rurality is associated with this relationship. Social interaction is one potential factor, but Brown and Cromartie (2004) note that interaction patterns do not differentiate urban and rural areas. Shared norms and cultural homogeneity are another possibility; although rural populations are becoming increasingly diverse, they remain more homogenous than urban populations (Brown & Cromartie, 2004). Bonding social capital in particular may be enhanced by expectations of similarity among one's interactional partners.

Employment in Natural Resource Industries

Perhaps the most salient image of rural America is based on what rural people do for a living. Despite the declining significance of occupations such as farming and forestry due to myriad factors such as economic segmentation and changing consumer preferences, these images remain strong. Associated with the strength of these images, especially in high-amenity areas where many second homes are located, is the tendency to see this form of development as potentially threatening to these traditional occupations and associated ways of life. Stereotypical views of these "outsiders" as hostile to traditional uses of resources and supportive of stringent environmental regulation may contribute to the hostility experienced by second home owners (e.g., Green et al., 1996).

Following the strategy laid out for social capital, we first assess the degree to which high dependence on resource employment (farming, forestry, and fisheries) really is a rural phenomenon. The answer is unequivocal: there is a pronounced linear effect of rurality—each size and adjacency category is a higher percentage than the one below it (ranging from 0.3 percent of employment in large metropolitan centers (RUCC = 0) to 4.5 percent in rural nonadjacent counties (RUCC = 9) (Table 13.3).

Does second home development actually threaten rural employment in natural-resource-based industries? Similar to the analyses for social capital, we conduct a multiple regression equation examining the shares of employment in 2000 in forestry, farming, and fisheries, net of other predictor variables. Based on this analysis, it appears that higher incidences of second homes do not threaten employment in natural resource industries. The model explains 23 percent of the variance in resource-based employment in 2000 (Table 13.5). Net of a county's

Table 13.5. Coefficients from a Model Predicting the Percent Employed in Farming, Forestry, and Fisheries, 2000

	Unstandardized Coefficients (B)	Standard Error	Beta	Sig.
Intercept	2.824	.263		
RUCC9 (See Table 13.2)	2.058	.119	.308	p < .001
Percent College Graduate, 1990	−0.044	.007	−.112	p < .001
Percent Age 65 or Over, 1990	0.030	.011	.052	p < .05
Percent Female Headed Household, 1990	−0.068	.008	−.143	p < .001
Change Percent Second Homes, 1990–2000	15.046	1.638	.161	p < .001
Percent Second Homes, 1990	0.513	.470	.019	ns
Adjusted R Square	.230			

rural, nonadjacent status (RUCC = 9), which continues to exert a strongly positive effect on resource employment (forestry, farming, and fisheries) increases in the percent of homes classified as second homes between 1990 and 2000 are associated with *higher* rather than lower employment in these industries. Also notable, the presence of second homes in 1990 is *not* a significant predictor of employment patterns in 2000, further suggesting that it really is the increase rather than the base level of second homes that is associated with increased employment. We were unable to model change in employment directly because of the incompatibility of the 1990 and 2000 measures of employment as collected by the Census.

SUMMARY AND CONCLUSIONS

Growth in second homes, at least as a percentage of all housing, continues to be a disproportionately rural phenomenon. More importantly, this growth continues to challenge traditional images of what kind of place rural settings entail and for whom these places ought to be. Our research examined the relationship between second home ownership and indicators corresponding to traditional images characterizing rural people and places: social capital as a measure of rural *gemeinschaft* community patterns, and natural-resource employment as an indicator of traditional economic patterns that emphasize land and resources as factors of production. We find that, consistent with popular images, social capital is indeed negatively impacted by second homes. When controlling for other variables typically thought to be associated with social capital, a higher incidence of second homes in 1990 is associated with lower social capital in 2000. These findings support concerns in the literature that rural settings with high proportions of second homeowners may embody less traditional social fabric thought to characterize rural communities. This may be tied to value differences, real or perceived, between year-round and seasonal residents, or the lack of social interaction between the two groups. However, another possible explanation for this finding is based on our measure of social capital which emphasizes civic participation somewhat more than interactional density. Simply put, second homeowners may not have the opportunity to participate in many civic behaviors. They may eschew membership in local civic organizations in their second home locales, viewing these locations instead as an opportunity to "escape" from everyday life (see Stedman, 2000). If the proportion of second homes is sufficiently large, civic organizations may suffer. Support for this latter contention is demonstrated by our finding that the percent *change* in second home ownership does not appear to be associated with decreased social capital. Places that already have a high proportion of second homes may lack the opportunities described above, while proportionate increases, even rapid increases, in second home development may not immediately threaten civic participation, especially if the increases are proportionately large because the baseline second home phenomenon is negligible. This is one of the important implications of the expansion of second home development into new areas: even with rapid increases, many may not yet be readily identifiable as "second home places." Yet, if current trends continue, they may face similar challenges in the future.

In contrast to concerns about social capital, employment in farming, forestry, and fisheries is generally a rural phenomenon but one that apparently is not particularly threatened by growth in second homes. Rather, we observe a fairly robust *positive* relationship between higher levels of resource employment and growth in second homes between 1990 and 2000. The causal mechanisms that underlie this relationship are somewhat elusive and difficult to parse out, and we are uncomfortable with the claim that increases in second home development *per se* are *causing* resource-industry employment. One likely explanation may be tied to the statement made earlier that second home development is a rural phenomenon that is becoming more rural. Non-metropolitan, non-adjacent counties with low populations—the most rural of all the counties in the nation—are those experiencing the most rapid growth in second home development. Simultaneously, these counties remain the traditional stronghold of employment in natural resource industries. Regardless of causality, however, our data clearly indicate that concerns about second home ownership crowding out resource employment appear unwarranted. Increases in second home development do not appear to pose grave threats to these employment opportunities.

Second homes have a strong presence in some places, especially high-amenity rural counties. While they are not a panacea for rural underdevelopment, they are also not a *de facto* threat to all that is cherished about rural life. These issues deserve further study, as the deconcentration of population to high-amenity places has been referred to as "a veritable suburbanization of rural areas" (Cromartie, 1995, p. 8). As rural communities in many regions continue to restructure, rapidly moving from production economies to consumption economies, land use and the effects of growth on the quality of rural life become critical issues generating substantial discussion and debate. The challenge often faced by these communities is whether they can maintain their preferred attributes in the face of population growth and its associated consequences. Bonds among members of traditional rural communities, defined by recurrent patterns of social interaction and shared goals, may be threatened by visitors and new residents who may be attached to these locales for other reasons. There is no evidence that these trends will decrease in the foreseeable future; understanding these tensions is key to understanding the future of many high-amenity areas of rural America.

ENDNOTE

1. Stefan Goetz acknowledges support from The Northeast Regional Center for Rural Development.

REFERENCES

Allen, L.R., Long, P.T., Perdue, R.R., & Kieselbach, S. (1988). The impact of tourism development on residents' perceptions of community life. *Journal of Travel Research, 27*, 16–21.

Beale, C.L., & Johnson, K.M. (1998). The identification of recreational counties in nonmetropolitan areas of the USA. *Population Research and Policy Review, 17*, 37–53.

Bealer, R.C., Willits, F.K., & Kuvlesky, W.P. (1965). The meaning of "rurality" in American society: Some implications of alternative definitions. *Rural Sociology, 30*(3), 255–266.

Bell, M.M. (1992). The fruit of difference: The rural-urban continuum as a system of identity. *Rural Sociology, 57*(1), 65–82.

Bennett, D.G. (1996). Implications of retirement development in high-amenity nonmetropolitan coastal areas. *Journal of Applied Gerontology, 15*(3), 345–360.

Beyers, W.B., & Nelson, P.B. (2000). Contemporary development forces in the non-metropolitan west: New insights from rapidly growing communities. *Journal of Rural Studies, 16*, 459–474.

Brown, D.L., & Cromartie, J.B. (2004). The nature of rurality in postindustrial society. In T. Champion & G. Hugo (Eds.), *New forms of urbanization: Beyond the urban-rural dichotomy* (pp. 269–283). Aldershot, UK: Ashgate.

Brown, R.J. (1970). *Economic impact of second-home communities: A case study of Lake Latonka, Pa* (ERS-452). Washington, DC: U.S. Department of Agriculture, Economic Research Service.

Buller, H., & Hoggart, K. (1994). The social integration of British homeowners into French rural communities. *Journal of Rural Studies, 10*(2), 197–210.

Buttel, F.H., Murdock, S.H., Leistritz., F.L., & Hamm, R.R. (1987). Rural environments. In E.H. Zube & G.T. Moore (Eds.), *Advances in environment, behavior, and design* (Vol. 1, pp. 107–128). New York: Plenum.

Chaplin, D. (1999). Consuming work/productive leisure: The consumption patterns of seasonal home environments. *Leisure Studies, 18*, 41–55.

Coppock, J.T. (1997). *Seasonal homes: Curse or blessing.* Toronto: Pergamon.

Cromartie, J. (1995, June). *The impact of growth on mountain communities.* Paper presented at the Boom in Mountain Living conference, Keystone, CO.

Cromartie, J.B., & Wardwell, J.M. (1999). Migrants settling far and wide in the rural West. *Rural Development Perspectives, 14*(2), 2–8.

Deller, S.C., Tsung-Hsiu, S.T., Marcouiller, D.W., & English, D. (2001). The role of amenities and quality of life in rural economic growth. *American Journal of Agricultural Economics, 83*(2), 352–365.

Duane, T.P. (1999). *Shaping the Sierra: Nature, culture, and conflict in the changing West.* Berkeley, CA: University of California Press.

Fortmann, L., & Kusel, J. (1990). New voices, old beliefs: Forest environmentalism among new and long-standing residents. *Rural Sociology, 55*(2), 214–232.

Fuguitt, G.V. (1991). The nonmetropolitan turnaround. *Annual Review of Sociology, 11*, 259–80.

Galston, W.A., & Baehler, K.J. (1995). *Rural development in the United States: Connecting theory, practice, and possibilities.* Washington, DC: Island Press.

Gartner, W.C. (1987). Environmental impacts of recreational home developments. *Annals of Tourism Research, 14*, 38–57.

Getz, D. (1983). Capacity to absorb tourism: Concepts and implications for strategic planning. *Annals of Tourism Research, 10*, 239–263.

Gilbert, J. (1982). Rural theory: The grounding of rural sociology. *Rural Sociology, 47*, 609–633.

Girard, T.C., & Gartner, W.C. (1993). Seasonal home second view host community perceptions. *Annals of Tourism Research, 20*, 685–700.

Gobster, P.H., Haight, R.G., & Shriner, D. (2000). Landscape change in the Midwest: An integrated research and development program. *Journal of Forestry, 98*(3), 9–14.

Godbey, G., & Bevins, M. (1987). The life cycle of seasonal home ownership: A case study. *Journal of Travel Research, 25*, 18–22.

Green, G.P., Marcouiller D., Deller, S., Erkkila, D., & Sumathi, N.R. (1996). Local dependency, land use attitudes, and economic development: Comparisons between seasonal and permanent residents. *Rural Sociology, 61*(3), 427–445.

Hay, R. (1998). Sense of place in developmental context. *Journal of Environmental Psychology, 18*, 5–29.

Huang, Y.-H., & Stewart, W.P. (1996). Rural tourism development: Shifting basis of community solidarity. *Journal of Travel Research, 34*(4), 26–31.

Jacob, S., & Luloff, A.E. (1995). Exploring the meaning of rural through cognitive maps. *Rural Sociology, 60*(2), 260–273.

Jordan, J.W. (1980). The summer people and the natives: Some effects of tourism in a Vermont village. *Annals of Tourism Research, 1*, 34–55.

Lin, N. (2001). *Social capital: A theory of social structure and action.* Cambridge, UK: Cambridge University Press.

Marcouiller, D.W., Kedzior, R., & Clendenning, J.G. (2002). Natural amenity-led development and rural planning. *Journal of Planning Literature, 16*(4), 515–542.

McGranahan, D.A. (1999). *Natural amenities drive rural population change* (Agricultural Economic Report No. 781). Washington, DC: U.S. Department of Agriculture, Economic Research Service, Food and Rural Economics Division.

Naples, N.A. (1994). Contradictions in agrarian ideology: Restructuring gender, race-ethnicity, and class. *Rural Sociology, 59*, 110–135.

National Association of Realtors. (2002). *The 2002 national associations of realtors profile of seasonal home owners.*

Putnam, R. (2000). *Bowling alone: The collapse and revival of American community.* New York: Simon and Schuster.

Radeloff, V.C., Hammer, R.B., Voss, P.R., Hagen, A.E., Field, D.R., & Mladenoff, D.J. (2001). Human demographic trends and landscape level forest management in the northwest Wisconsin Pine Barrens. *Forest Science, 47(2)*, 229–241.

Relph, E. (1976). *Place and placelessness.* London: Pion.

Ringholz, R.C. (1996). *Paradise paved: The challenge of growth in the new West.* Salt Lake City: University of Utah Press.

Rothman, R.A. (1978.) Residents and transients: Community reaction to seasonal visitors. *Journal of Travel Research, 16*, 8–13.

Rudzitis, G. (1999). Amenities increasingly draw people to the rural west. *Rural Development Perspectives, 14*(2), 9–13.

Rupasingha, A., Goetz S.J., & Freshwater, D. *The production of social capital in U.S. counties.* Paper under review at Journal of Socio-Economics.

Rural Sociological Society (Humphrey, C.R., Carrol, M.S., Geisler, C., Johnson, T.G., West, P.C., Berardi, G., Fairfax, S., Fortmann, L., Kusel, J., Lee, R.G., Macinko, S., Peluso, N.L., & Schulman, M.D.) (1993). Theories in the study of natural resource dependent communities and persistent rural poverty in the United States. In *Persistent poverty in rural America* (pp. 136–172). Boulder, CO: Westview Press, Rural Studies Series.

Schnaiberg, J., Riera, J., Turner, M.G., & Voss, P.R. (2002). Explaining human settlement patterns in a recreational lake district: Vilas County, Wisconsin, USA. *Environmental Management, 30*(1), 24–34.

Shumway, J.M., & Davis, J.A. (1996). Nonmetropolitan population change in the mountain west: 1970–1995. *Rural Sociology, 61*(3), 513–529.

Stedman, R.C. (2000). Up North: Toward a social psychology of place (Doctoral dissertation, University of Wisconsin-Madison, 2000).

Stedman, R.C. (2002). Toward a social psychology of place: Predicting behavior from place-based cognitions, attitude, and identity. *Environment and Behavior,* 34(5), 405–425.

Stedman, R.C. (2003). Is it *really* just a social construction: The contribution of the physical environment to sense of place. *Society and Natural Resources, 16*, 671–685.

Stewart, S.I., & Stynes, D.J. (1994). Toward a dynamic model of complex tourism choices: The seasonal home location decision. *Journal of Travel and Tourism Marketing, 3*(3), 69–88.

Stroud, H.B. (1985). Changing rural landscapes: A need for planning and management. *Land Use Policy, 2*(2), 126–134.

Stynes, D.J., Zheng, J., & Stewart, S.I. (1996). *Seasonal homes in Michigan.* Chicago: North Central Forest Experiment Station.

Tuan, Y.F. (1974). *Topophilia.* New York: Columbia University Press.

Wear, D.N., & Bolstad, P. (1998). Land-use and change in Southern Appalachian landscapes: Spatial analysis and forecast evaluation. *Ecosystems, 1*, 575–594.

Wear, D.N., Turner, M.G., & Naiman, R.J. (1998). Land cover along an urban-rural gradient: Implications for water quality. *Ecological Applications, 8*(3), 619–630.

Willits, F.K., & Bealer, R.C. (1967). An evaluation of a composite definition of "rurality." *Rural Sociology, 32*, 165–177.

Willits, F.K., & Luloff, A.E. (1995). Urban residents' view of rurality and contacts with rural places. *Rural Sociology, 60*(3), 454–466.

Wolfe, R.I. (1978). Vacation homes as social indicators: Observations from Canadian census data. *Leisure Sciences, 1*, 327–343.

Wollcock, M. (2001). The place of social capital in understanding social and economic outcomes. *Canadian Journal of Public Policy, 2*, 11–17.

Wright, J.B. (1993). *Rocky mountain divide: Selling and saving the West.* Austin, TX: University of Texas Press.

CHAPTER 14

HOUSING AFFORDABILITY AND POPULATION CHANGE IN THE UPPER MIDWESTERN NORTH WOODS[1]

ROGER B. HAMMER AND RICHELLE L. WINKLER

INTRODUCTION

The rate of change in rural society in the United States and other developed countries has increased in recent decades as new communications and transportation technologies, migration processes, and economic restructuring have contributed to the "urbanization" of rural communities. Migration from urban areas into the countryside (counterurbanization) and increasing residential and commercial development within rural areas (exurbanization) have served as important avenues through which rural neighborhoods have experienced profound change (Robinson, 1990); yet, little is known about the economic, cultural, and political impacts of these changes (Nelson, 2001). Rising housing values and the deterioration of housing affordability for low to moderate income residents in rural host communities constitutes just one possible unintended consequence of such counterurbanization/exurbanization. This chapter examines the effects of counterurbanization and exurbanization on housing affordability in a predominantly rural, natural amenity-rich region of the United States—the North Woods of Minnesota, Wisconsin, and Michigan.

Historically, rural areas in the United States have been heavily dependent on extractive and manufacturing industries that have declined as sources of stable employment and reasonable earnings during the last several decades due to changes in technology, declining demand, and international competition (Galston & Baehler, 1995). In response to this decline, leisure and recreation services have grown in economic importance in many rural areas. North Americans increasingly relate to nature primarily as a "place of leisure," and rural landscapes have become more valuable as recreation resources than as sources for raw material production inputs; rural space itself has become a commodity (Whitson, 2001). Consequently, many rural communities have shifted economic development

W.A. Kandel & D.L. Brown (eds.), Population Change and Rural Society, 293–309.

efforts away from traditional industries and toward service and amenity-based activities (Fawson et al., 1998; Frederick, 1993; Glasgow, 1990). Amenity-based development offers a niche for rural communities in a changing global economy in which they benefit from, and contribute to, idyllic visions of nature and rural space (Whitson, 2001). Tourism and recreation-promotion are increasingly used as community development strategies to rejuvenate local economies in rural areas throughout the United States. In attractive rural areas, new developments entice tourists, seasonal residents, in-migrants, and/or retirees to the area, and in this way, the rural experience, rather than raw materials, becomes the export mechanism (Rothman, 1998).

In the rural North Woods of Minnesota, Wisconsin, and Michigan, natural-amenity-based tourism, especially seasonal home development around lakes, has long been a source of local development. Many rural communities have initiated amenity-based economic development strategies in order to attract tourists, migrants, and businesses from more urban areas, yet little is known about the economic, cultural, and political impacts of this type of development (Nelson, 2001). In addition to the recognized benefits, such as population, employment, and earnings growth (Deller et al., 2001), tourism- and recreation-based development can also impose substantial costs (Marcouiller & Green, 2000; Power, 1996). One such cost may be that long-time residents are priced out of housing markets as housing demand increases. Power notes that "vacation homes and other tourism developments tend to drive up property values and the cost of living, driving out existing residents" (1996, p. 216). As Whitson explains, "the influx of outside money and population . . . is precisely what creates economic growth. . . . The result is that new developments are often priced beyond what people working in the local economy, or at least the old local economy, can afford" (2001, p. 150). In describing the social and economic changes generated by counterurbanization in amenity-rich areas, the popular press evokes images of "Aspenization" ruining previously rural communities (see Gates & Pryor, 1993; Janofsky, 1999). This study examines the relevance of these claims in a predominantly rural, natural-amenity-rich region, the North Woods of the U.S. Midwest.

Lack of quality, affordable housing is a critical issue facing many rural communities in the United States (Ziebarth et al., 1997). Housing is an important aspect of a local community's social structure, with numerous sociological implications. In addition to fulfilling basic human needs for shelter, it influences multiple aspects of individuals' lives, including employment opportunities, social status, education, health, family composition, and psychological well-being (Mutchler & Krivo, 1989). On a broader scale, housing conditions have been linked to the economic development and social well-being of neighborhoods, communities, and, by extension, the nation as a whole (Green & Malpezzi, 2000; Ziebarth, 2000). Affordability has become the central housing problem facing the United States as overcrowding has declined and substandard housing has been upgraded or replaced (Bogdon & Can, 1997; Bratt, 2002; Dolbeare, 1999). The percent of income that low and moderate income (LMI) households spend on housing costs affects their ability to provide other basic needs such as food, clothing, transportation, and health care. Housing affordability constitutes an important social equity issue and a critical indicator of general family and community well-being.

In this chapter we examine two aspects of amenity-based development and their influence on housing affordability in the rural North Woods. First, natural-amenity-led growth necessarily involves a migration process in which population is redistributed from urban to rural areas and urban populations move from larger to smaller places (Berry & Gillard, 1977; Dahms & McComb, 1999). This migration pattern, termed counterurbanization, represents the social transformation of a rural community. Second, economic development entails commercial and residential development, termed exurbanization, which represents the physical transformation of rural landscapes into a low-density, nebulous zone (Marx, 1964), not urban or suburban, but also no longer rural. Although counterurbanization and exurbanization have been associated with a variety of social, cultural, economic, and environmental effects, community conflicts have been most visible—and often most contentious—around affordable housing issues (Whitson, 2001). This research both furthers our sociological understanding of the socially and physically transformative processes of counterurbanization and exurbanization and, in a practical sense, offers rural communities pursuing amenity-based development information concerning the potential consequences.

THE NORTH WOODS STUDY AREA

The North Woods is an ecologically and culturally contiguous region that encompasses the northern tier of Minnesota, Wisconsin, and Michigan. Known for its forests and lakes, the region has a long history of attracting tourists and seasonal homeowners each summer who seek natural amenities, recreation, and escape from Chicago, Milwaukee, Minneapolis/St. Paul, Detroit and other nearby cities. Because the culture and economy have long been tied to the physical characteristics of the landscape through forestry and recreation, we define the rural "North Woods" for the purposes of this study in ecological terms based on pre-settlement vegetation. Ecologically, the region popularly referred to as the North Woods is known as the Laurentian Mixed Forest province (Atwood, 1940). It encompasses approximately the northern half of Minnesota and Wisconsin, as well as Michigan's Upper Peninsula and approximately one third of its Lower Peninsula. The metropolitan areas of Minneapolis-St. Paul, Milwaukee-Waukesha, Duluth-Superior, Eau Claire, Wausau, Green Bay, Appleton-Neenah-Oshkosh, Sheboygan, Grand Rapids, and Saginaw all fall, at least partially, within the Laurentian Mixed Forest province. We exclude the two largest of these metropolitan areas (Minneapolis-St. Paul and Milwaukee-Waukesha), as well as the three Wisconsin counties (Manitowac, Ozaukee, and Sheboygan) that extend from Milwaukee to Green Bay in a narrow band along Lake Michigan. These counties have been substantially altered from their pre-settlement vegetation patterns, the defining characteristic of ecoregions, and are therefore culturally and economically not considered part of the "North Woods."

Over much of the past century, economic activity in the rural Upper Midwest was concentrated in forestry and, to a lesser extent, agriculture and mining. Promotion of the tourism and recreation industry began relatively early in the North Woods (Schnaiberg et al., 2002) and has assumed a more significant role in the region's economy with the decline of extractive industries. Nearly half of the counties in the region (64 of 131) are classified by USDA as recreational counties (Johnson & Beale, 2002).[2] After decades of widespread population stability and decline in some counties, population growth in the North Woods proceeded at a relatively rapid pace throughout the "turnaround" decade of the 1970s, a period marked by faster growth in nonmetropolitan counties than in their metropolitan counterparts. (Fuguitt, 1995). Growth in the North Woods subsided after the 1970s but re-emerged with the "nonmetropolitan rebound" of the 1990s, especially in selected recreational counties (Johnson & Beale, 2002).

Neighborhoods of the North Woods

Studies of housing affordability tend to examine national, state, or county patterns and trends over time (Belden & Wiener, 1999; "Housing Assistance Council," 2002), yet housing markets are very local in nature (Ziebarth et al., 1997). Housing availability, household incomes, and housing costs vary significantly across space, and aggregate studies cannot detect important localized variation in housing affordability. To capture variation in counterurbanization and housing affordability across space, this study uses rural "neighborhoods" in the rural North Woods as the unit of analysis.

Neighborhoods can be defined in many different ways. Bogdon and Can (1997), in a study of housing affordability in a metropolitan area, defined their neighborhood unit of analysis as the Census block group, which includes up to 3,000 persons (with an optimum population of 1,500 (U.S. Census Bureau, 2003). In urban areas, block groups encompass a relatively small land area and represent homogeneous neighborhoods reasonably well. However, because block groups are an aggregation based at least in part on population criteria, rural block groups encompass much larger land areas and may include multiple "neighborhoods." For example, one rural block group might encompass either a small town or several small towns and the surrounding rural township, including different housing conditions and migration patterns. Block groups are not always coextensive with municipalities and urbanized areas, especially in rural areas. For block groups that are divided by a municipal, boundary, or congressional district boundary, the decennial census provides tabulations for the block group as a whole and for each part. All else being equal, household and personal characteristics within constituent parts of a block group would be more homogeneous than in the block group as a whole.

We use these "partial" block groups as the representation of rural "neighborhoods" in our study in order to improve geographical and statistical precision relative to using data for complete block groups.

Rural Areas of the North Woods

Just as there are different approaches to defining neighborhoods, there are different approaches to defining "rural." The Federal government essentially delineates "rural" from "urban" on two different scales. The Office of Management and Budget (2004) categorizes counties as metropolitan based on population size (i.e., a city with a population of 50,000 or an overall county population of 100,000) and secondarily on the commuting exchange with more populous adjacent counties. The Census Bureau categorizes census blocks as urban or rural based on population density and location. Urban areas are generally comprised of a cluster of blocks or block groups with a population of at least 1,000 persons per square mile, surrounding blocks with a population of at least 500 persons per square mile, and less densely settled blocks that form enclaves or indentations or that connect discontiguous urban areas (U.S. Census Bureau, 2003). We use both these scales to delineate the "rural" North Woods. First, we include all partial block groups in nonmetropolitan counties in the region. Second, since metropolitan counties in the region include substantial rural territory, we include all neighborhoods in metropolitan counties that are defined as rural by the U.S. Census Bureau and are located more than 30 miles from the metropolitan area's population center. St Louis County in Minnesota illustrates why rural portions of metropolitan counties must be included in our analysis. It's county seat, Duluth, makes the county metropolitan, but the county itself extends far north of Duluth to the Canadian border and encompasses portions of the extremely remote Boundary Waters Canoe Area Wilderness and the rural communities scattered along its well-known eastern access, the Gunflint Trail.[3]

COUNTERURBANIZATION IN THE NORTH WOODS

As described in the introduction, counterurbanization is a process in which population is redistributed from more urban to more rural areas. Counterubanizing areas undergo a variety of social and economic changes. Research suggests that counterurbanization engenders gentrification-like outcomes, increasing demand for housing in rural neighborhoods, driving up housing costs, and exacerbating housing affordability problems for LMI households (Shucksmith, 1991; Spain, 1993; Whitson, 2001). We expect that counterurbanization will increase housing cost burden for LMI households.

We measure counterurbanization as the percent of the rural neighborhood's 2000 population over the age of five that moved into the neighborhood from a metropolitan area during the previous five-year period (1995–2000). For

Figure 14.1. Counterurbanization 1995–2000

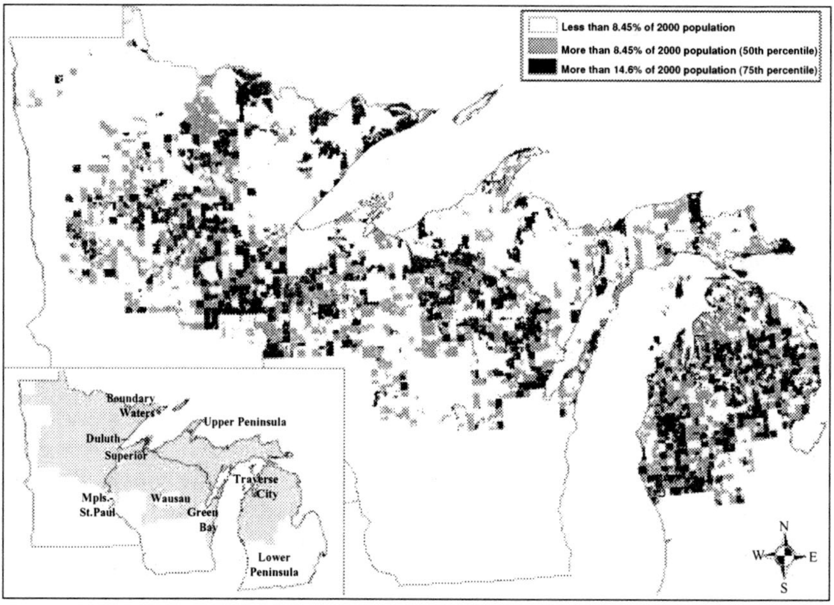

the rural neighborhoods located within a metropolitan county, we used the percent of in-migrants from both a central city (generally with a population of 50,000 or more) within the same metropolitan area and those from a different metropolitan area. Counterurbanization is widespread across the rural North Woods, especially in the Lower Peninsula of Michigan and the Minnesota/Wisconsin border area between the Minneapolis-St. Paul and Duluth-Superior Metropolitan Areas. It occurs less in central Wisconsin, most of Michigan's Upper Peninsula, and northwest and west central Minnesota.

EXURBANIZATION IN THE NORTH WOODS

Amenity-based development results in residential and commercial construction that transforms the rural landscape in a process of exurbanization. We measure exurbanization as the number of housing units constructed in each neighborhood of the rural North Woods during the 1990s and use housing growth as a viable proxy for the overall exurbanization process, given the lack of data on other types of land development across the region. In the neoclassical economic model, new housing construction should increase supply, reduce housing prices, and subsequently reduce LMI housing cost burden. However, the supply of housing in many rural areas experiencing amenity-based development may not meet the heightened

Figure 14.2. Exurbanization 1990–2000

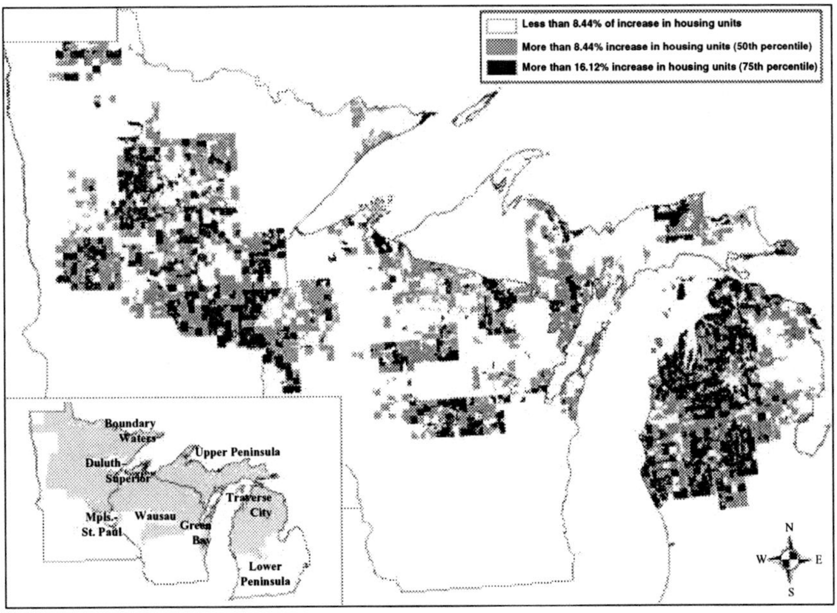

current demand. Under such conditions, housing developers seeking to maximize profits may choose to build more expensive new homes with higher internal rates of return (Myers, 2000). In this scenario, higher-income households demand new housing, middle-income households compete for a small supply of well-maintained older housing (driving up prices), and LMI households are left with disproportionately older and/or less well-maintained housing and/or are forced to incur cost burden (Thompson & Mikesell, 1981).

Across the rural North Woods, exurbanization is more spatially focused than counterurbanization. Large expanses of the region, especially in far north and northeast Minnesota and the eastern Upper Peninsula of Michigan experienced very low housing growth during the 1990s (less than 4 percent). Exurbanization was more concentrated in the western two-thirds of Michigan's Lower Peninsula, whereas counterurbanization encompassed more territory. Although counterurbanization was strong in the lake areas spanning the Wisconsin/Michigan border, exurbanization was not as extensive. However, central Wisconsin experienced exurbanization much more than counterubanization. Finally, the southern portion of Minnesota's rural North Woods exhibited similar levels of both counterurbanization and exurbanization. The Wisconsin neighborhoods along the Minnesota border experienced high levels of population influx from metropolitan areas, which is not surprising given the proximity of Minneapolis-St. Paul, but less exurbanization than neighborhoods across the St. Croix River in Minnesota. While counterurbanization and exurbanization are closely related processes, in the North Woods, they are spatially different.

HOUSING AFFORDABILITY IN THE NORTH WOODS

Over the past several decades, as housing quality improved and overcrowding declined, affordability became the predominant housing problem confronting rural households in the United States, as housing costs in many rural areas increased faster than incomes (Housing Assistance Council, 2002). During the 1990s, housing costs in nonmetropolitan areas grew considerably faster (59 percent) than in metropolitan areas (39 percent). Much of this increase has been attributed to increased demand from migration to nonmetropolitan counties, or what we term counterurbanization (Marcouiller et al., 2002; Mathur & Stein, 1991; Wills, 2002). Studies have demonstrated that population growth in rural areas is related to increasing housing costs and property taxes (Bennett, 1996; Marcouiller et al., 2002; Nelson, 2001). While real household *income* of homeowners in the nonmetropolitan Midwest grew 16.4 percent in the 1990's, constant-quality housing *prices* rose 55.2 percent (Wills, 2002).

Approximately one quarter of the 23 million nonmetropolitan households in the United States spend more than 30 percent of their gross income on housing and therefore incur a cost burden and lack affordable housing as defined by the Federal government. The U. S. Department of Housing and Urban Development considers households with incomes at or below 80 percent of the median income of the county in which they reside as low to moderate income. Cost-burdened LMI households are eligible for Federal housing assistance programs.

In this study, we emulate the Federal standard for housing affordability: a household at or below 80 percent of county median income (LMI) spending 30 percent or more of its income on housing. To compare housing affordability across the entire rural North Woods, we use the regional median household income instead of the county-level median in our definition of cost burden.[4] This modification of the Federal definition of housing cost burden does not alter the neighborhood scale of our analysis but does broaden the extent, enabling us to compare neighborhoods across the region rather than solely within single counties. Thus, LMI households are defined as households with gross incomes of less than $35,000 during 1999, the calendar year prior to the census.[5] In the rural North Woods, 488,230 or 48 percent of all households were LMI, and 128,864 or 13 percent experienced housing cost burden in 1999.

Mapping housing costs allows us to delineate the spatial variation that occurs within the North Woods region and to identify sub-regions where high housing costs tend to cluster. While the majority of rural neighborhoods in the region have relatively low housing costs, areas bordering metropolitan counties and

Figure 14.3. Median Housing Value 2000

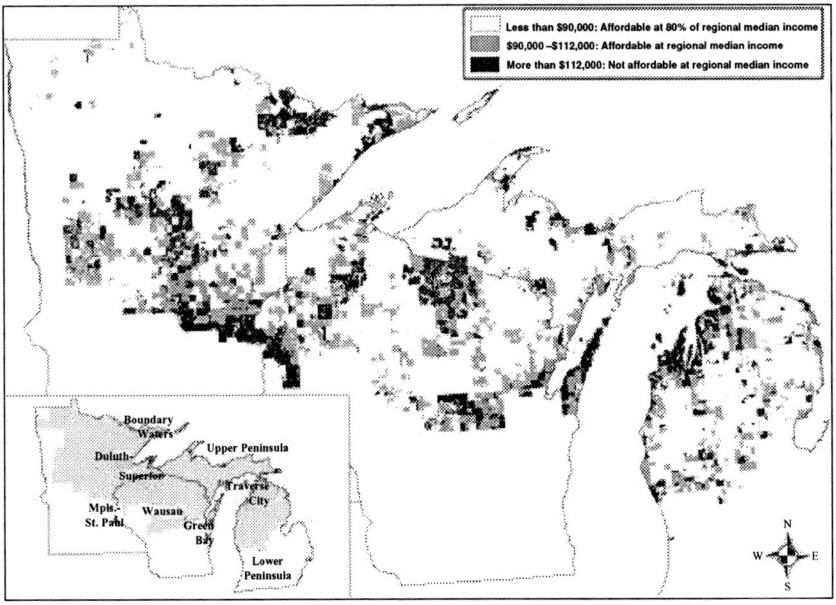

areas with natural amenities have high median home values that resemble values in metropolitan areas. Housing is much less affordable in a band of communities adjacent to the Minneapolis-St. Paul Metropolitan Area, in the Wisconsin River Valley of central Wisconsin just south of the Wausau Metropolitan Area, and in east central Wisconsin adjacent to the Green Bay Metropolitan Area. In these areas, median income households would be unable to afford a median-priced home in the neighborhood. Housing is similarly unaffordable in inland lake recreation districts across the rural North Woods, including the Brainerd Lakes area in the north-central part of Minnesota, the Hayward/Lac Courte Oreilles area in northwest Wisconsin, and the Northern Highlands Lake District of north central Wisconsin and extending into the Upper Peninsula. Housing values in several Great Lakes coastal areas are also high, especially in the boundary waters of far northern Minnesota, on the Door County, Wisconsin peninsula jutting into Lake Michigan, and the entire area in an around the Leelanau Peninsula that forms the Grand Traverse Bay of Lake Michigan.

Collectively, these maps illustrate problems with assessing housing affordability in terms of counties, states, or regions. Because housing markets are localized in space and restricted by employment opportunities and personal relationships, and because housing costs and household incomes vary drastically across space, a more localized and spatially-informed view of housing affordability is necessary to understand the nature of the problem in rural areas.

Although more spatially dispersed than either LMI households or affordable housing, LMI housing cost burden is not randomly distributed across the rural North Woods. The proportion of LMI households that experience housing cost burden is significantly spatially autocorrelated with a Moran's $I = 0.1107$, $p \geq 0.001$. As noted in chapter 19 on spatial demography, Moran's I is similar to the familiar Pearson correlation coefficient, except that rather than measuring the value similarity of two characteristics for single observations, it measures the value similarity of a single characteristic in neighboring observations. The level of housing cost burden in a given neighborhood is quite similar to the level in adjacent neighborhoods. This spatial clustering further disadvantages LMI households experiencing cost burden. If cost burden was spatially distributed in a random pattern, LMI households would be more likely to secure an affordable housing unit by simply moving to an adjacent unit. Due to the spatial clustering of cost burden, LMI households moving to nearby neighborhoods are likely to encounter a similar lack of affordable housing and thus continue to incur cost burden. Combined with the larger geographic size of rural neighborhoods, the quest for affordable housing might necessitate relatively long-distance moves for LMI households which increase the likelihood of disrupting employment, education, and social support.

ANALYSIS AND FINDINGS

We estimated a relatively parsimonious weighted least squares model[6] of housing affordability across the rural North Woods that included the factors described above, along with several control variables.[7] We weighted the 6,909 observations in the analysis based on the number of households in the neighborhood to prevent less populous neighborhoods from having a disproportionate effect on the results. The preponderance of LMI households and the rate of home ownership are important influences on housing affordability in rural neighborhoods and need to be considered in conceptual and statistical model development. Research in rural areas, including the Midwest, has attributed the lack of affordable housing to the prevalence of LMI households rather than to high housing costs (Dolbeare, 1999; Krofta et al., 1999). Low income restricts a household's capacity to secure affordable housing; very low income households may not be able to afford even the lowest-cost, market-rate housing. Therefore, neighborhoods with a prevalence of LMI households will experience relatively high rates of housing cost burden.[8]

Homeownership is also an important determinant of housing affordability. Homeownership reduces housing cost burden, as renters are more likely to suffer housing affordability problems than homeowners (Belden & Wiener, 1999; Dolbeare, 1999). Because renters generally have lower incomes and do not build equity through loan amortization and appreciation, as do homeowners, they are more likely to pay over 30 percent of their household income—a standard household

Table 14.1. Model of Housing Cost Burden

	Coefficient	Standard Error	t-Value	Standardized Coefficient
LMI	0.315	0.008	38.73	0.449
Owners	−0.133	0.007	−19.82	−0.226
Counterurbanization	0.153	0.013	12.11	0.118
Exurbanization	0.072	0.007	10.54	0.104
Intercept	11.095	0.851	13.03	

budget benchmark—for housing. Over time, housing costs incurred by homeowners are not as subject to inflation as rental expense, considerably reducing the relative incidence of cost burden among LMI homeowners. The incidence of LMI cost burden in the rural North Woods (18 percent) is low compared to national rates (25 percent), in part because rural North Woods residents predominantly own their homes. In 2000, 80 percent of the region's households owned their own home, compared to 66 percent nationally. This high rate is partially attributable to traditionally low housing costs for rural areas in the Midwest region in general (Krofta et al., 1999). However, a higher percentage of *homeowners* (14.1 percent) in the rural North Woods face housing cost burden than in the Midwest (11.4 percent) and the nation as a whole (13.0 percent).

Using these two control variables, the proportion of neighborhood households that are LMI, and the proportion of households that own their own home, we modeled the influence of counterurbanization and exurbanization on LMI housing affordability. We define counterurbanization as the percentage of the 2000 population that moved into the neighborhood from a more urban area between 1995 and 2000, and exurbanization as the growth of housing units in the neighborhood between 1990–2000 expressed as a percentage of housing units in the neighborhood in 1990. The model explains nearly 40 percent ($R^2 = 0.3963$) of the variance in the proportion of LMI households experiencing cost burden in neighborhoods of the rural North Woods. Jointly, the control variables explain nearly 37 percent ($R^2 = 0.3685$) of the variance. Although counterurbanization and exurbanization explain less than 3 percent of the variance after controlling for the percentage of households that are LMI and the percentage of homeowners, they contribute significantly to the fit of the model according to both the adjusted R^2 and the Akaike Information Criterion. F-tests also indicate that a model that includes counterurbanization and exurbanization either jointly or individually fits the data significantly better than a model with only the control variables. Moreover, the coefficient for each of the variables in the model was highly statistically significant ($p \leq 0.001$), and the sign of each coefficient was in the expected direction.

According to the model, a change in the composition of a neighborhood, in which an additional 10 percent of households have incomes at or below 80 percent of the regional median, would result in an additional 3 percent of LMI households experiencing housing cost burden. A concomitant increase of 10 percent in homeownership in a neighborhood would improve housing affordability, resulting in an additional 1.33 percent of the neighborhood's LMI households spending less than 30 percent of their income on housing. However, counterubanization, the proportion of persons moving into a neighborhood from a more urban area, can have a greater impact on LMI housing affordability than homeownership. Given two similar neighborhoods, if 5 percent of the residents in the first neighborhood recently moved in from a more urban area, while 10 percent had done so in the second neighborhood, 1.53 percent more of the LMI households in the second neighborhood would incur a housing cost burden. This represents slightly more than the difference produced by a similar proportional decline in homeownership and just under half the change associated with a similar proportional increase in LMI households. Although the impact of exurbanization is considerably lower than other variables, and just over half that of counterubanization, housing construction during the 1990s equal to 10 percent of the neighborhood's housing units in 1990 results in an additional 0.72 percent of LMI households experiencing cost burden. Although this difference might seem negligible, it demonstrates that exurbanization-driven growth, which is widely perceived as a positive development for rural communities, imposes costs on economically vulnerable households. The finding that housing growth in the rural North Woods contributed to the lack of affordable housing for LMI households rather than increase supply and ease housing affordability has important public policy implications.

CONCLUSIONS

Migration from urban areas into the countryside (counterurbanization) and increasing residential development in rural areas (exurbanization) have served as important avenues through which rural neighborhoods have experienced profound change. One consequence of such change, however, is rising housing values, which, in turn, affect housing affordability. Counterurbanization significantly affects LMI housing cost burden in neighborhoods of the rural North Woods, as does exurbanization to a lesser extent. The results of this study suggest that rural community development and planning efforts should consider impacts on housing affordability that amenity-based development strategies engender. They also indicate that increasing residential development in rural areas does not generally meet the housing needs of LMI households and, in fact, reduces housing affordability.

These findings have important implications for community development planners and affordable housing advocates, as LMI households may face severe affordable housing problems when confronted with an influx of migrants from urban areas and housing growth. Communities, experiencing counterurbanization and exurbanization, especially communities with high concentrations of low- and moderate-income households, should be aware of the need to provide affordable housing in the wake of population change. Planners should recognize these risks and devise plans for mediating the negative impacts of urbanization in host communities. Fortunately, the nature of this counterurbanization/exurbanization problem affords these communities considerable advantages for addressing housing needs of LMI households compared to rural communities in which affordable housing problems stem from long-term decline and neglect. Along with more diffuse advantages of an increasing tax base and vibrant economy, these communities may be able to harness the forces of counterubanizaiton and exurbanization and ameliorate negative impacts on housing affordability by adopting inclusionary zoning, a relatively new tool being used by increasing numbers of rapidly growing municipalities. Inclusionary zoning reverses the tendency of traditional zoning regulations to exclude affordable housing due to minimum lot-size standards and multi-family housing restrictions by establishing "mandatory set-asides" or minimum percentages of new housing units that must be affordable to households at a particular income level (Burchell & Galley, 2000). By definition, in communities experiencing counterurbanization/exurbanization new housing units are being constructed, thus providing the community with the capacity to produce a relatively permanent stock of affordable housing units provided by the private market. Moreover, to maintain long-term affordability and reduce administrative oversight, inclusionary zoning units are most often owner occupied. As demonstrated by this study, home ownership in and of itself reduces housing cost burden among low- and moderate-income households. In this way, inclusionary zoning programs can deliver a "one-two punch" to housing affordability problems in rural neighborhoods experiencing counterurbanization/exurbanization by both providing affordable housing and promoting homeownership.

The lack of in-migrant characteristics remains an important limitation of this study. Because income levels of in-migrants are not tabulated in these data, it remains unclear whether counterurbanization introduces low-income migrants who exacerbate poverty and increase demand for low-income housing or if in-migrants are relatively well-off financially and demand higher-quality housing, raising housing costs. The two processes may occur in different neighborhoods according to different temporal and spatial trajectories and have different effects on housing affordability. Subsequently, additional work using characteristics such as income of in-migrants to rural areas could be conducted to further examine the relationships between counterurbanization, gentrification, and housing cost burden.

As Federal and state governments in the United States review the efficacy of affordable housing programs, it is important that policy-makers understand the extent of housing cost burden in rural areas as well as in urban centers. Planners, policy-makers, and housing advocates can benefit from the fine-grained statistical and cartographic analysis provided by this study. Both housing service providers and policy-makers should have access to precise and detailed maps portraying the extent of housing cost burden by neighborhood in order to allocate resources to the problem more effectively.

ENDNOTES

1. The authors would like to acknowledge the very helpful comments of Gary P. Green, Paul R. Voss, Susan I. Stewart, and two anonymous reviewers. We also acknowledge data acquisition assistance from Daniel L. Veroff and the University of Wisconsin Applied Population Laboratory and Volker C. Radeloff and the University of Wisconsin Spatial Analysis for Conservation and Sustainability Laboratory, as well as the editorial and bibliographical assistance of Tracy Schmid. This research was funded by the USDA Forest Service North Central Research Station (00-JV-11231300-055). Earlier versions of this chapter were presented at the 10th International Symposium for Society and Resource Management in Keystone, CO, June, 2004, and at the Annual Meeting of the Rural Sociological Society in Montreal, July, 2003. The authors appear in alphabetical order and authorship is shared equally.
2. The USDA's Economic Research Service identifies recreational counties using indicators of recreational activity, including: 1) the percentage of employment in the entertainment and recreation, accommodations, eating and drinking places, and real estate sectors; 2) the percentage of wage and salary income in the same sectors; and 3) the percentage of housing units intended for seasonal or occasional use.
3. The rural Northwoods encompass 7,359 partial block groups. The census did not determine housing costs in 450 of these neighborhoods due to limited number of renter and/or owner households, forcing us to exclude those observations from our analysis. Since excluded neighborhoods had higher percentages of both LMI and renter households when compared with neighborhoods that are included in the analysis, this exclusion could be expected to bias our estimates downward for the regional rate of households experiencing cost burdens to a marginal extent. However, there is no reason to believe that these excluded neighborhoods systematically differ from other neighborhoods in other respects, and therefore this exclusion should not affect the results of our analysis.
4. We estimate the regional median income by calculating the household-weighted average of the county median income of all counties that are included in whole or in part in the rural North Woods. For the metropolitan counties that we partially include in the rural North Woods, the median income includes both the rural neighborhoods that are part of the study and the urban neighborhoods that we exclude.
5. Calculated as the weighted mean of the county median income of each county in the North Woods region.
6. The spatial autocorrelation of LMI housing cost burden necessitates caution in selecting an appropriate analytical approach. Spatial autocorrelation results in the violation of the independent and identically distributed assumption of standard statistical methods and can cause bias and/or inefficiency in analyses of spatially-aggregated data (Anselin, 1988). In the case of positive spatial autocorrelation, that is neighboring value similarity rather than dissimilarity, the value similarity among neighboring observations reduced

variance and the estimates of standard errors, exaggerating the statistical significance of the results. Including independent variables in a model that, at least partially, explain the spatial relationships of the dependent variable can serve to reduce the influence of spatial autocorrelation on the results. The success of this analytical strategy can be tested by calculating the Moran's I statistics for the residuals of the model and, if spatial autocorrelation persists, employing spatial regression techniques to alleviate such effects.

7. We also estimated more complex models that controlled for natural amenities, recreational activity, and the supply of affordable housing but found no significant improvement in the model's explanatory power.
8. Our definition of housing cost burden (a household must be both LMI and spend 30 percent or more of income on housing costs) is expected to exaggerate the explanatory power of LMI in the model.

REFERENCES

Anselin, L. (1988). *Spatial econometrics: methods and models*. Dordrecht, The Netherlands: Kluwer.

Atwood, W.W. (1940). *The physiographic provinces of North America*. Boston: Ginn.

Belden, J.N., & Wiener, R.J. (1999). *Housing in Rural America*. Thousand Oaks, CA: Sage.

Bennett, D.G. (1996). Implications of retirement development in high-amenity nonmetropolitan coastal areas. *Journal of Applied Gerontology, 15*(3), 345–360.

Berry, B.J.L., & Gillard, Q. (1977). *The changing shape of metropolitan America*. Cambridge, MA: Ballinger.

Bogdon, A.S., & Can, A. (1997). Indicators of local housing affordability: Comparative and spatial approaches. *Real Estate Economics, 25*(1), 43–80.

Bratt, R.G. (2002). Housing and family well-being. *Housing Studies, 17*(1), 13–26.

Burchell , R.W., & Galley, C.C. (2000). Inclusionary zoning: Pros and cons. *New Century Housing, 1*(2), 3–12.

Dahms, F., & McComb, J. (1999). "Counterurbanization," interaction, and functional change in a rural amenity area: A Canadian example. *Journal of Rural Studies, 15*(2), 129–146.

Deller, S.C., Tsung-Hsiu, S.T., Marcouiller, D.W., & English, D.B.K. (2001). The role of amenities and quality of life in rural economic growth. *American Journal of Agricultual Economics, 83*(2), 352–365.

Dolbeare, C.N. (1999). Conditions and trends in rural housing. In J. Belden & R. Wiener (Eds.), *Housing in rural America*. Thousand Oaks, CA: Sage.

Fawson, C., Thilmany, D., & Keith, J.E. (1998). Employment stability and the role of sectoral dominance in rural economies. *American Journal of Agricultural Economics, 80*, 521–533.

Frederick, M. (1993). Rural tourism and economic development. *Economic Development Quarterly, 7*, 215–224.

Fuguitt, G.V. (1995). Population change in nonmetropolitan America. In E.N. Castle (Ed.), *The changing American countryside*. Lawrence, KS: University Press of Kansas.

Galston, W.A., & Baehler, H.J. (1995). *Rural development in the United States: Connecting theory, practice, and possibilities*. Washington, DC: Island Press.

Gates, D., & Pryor, T. (1993, December 27). Chic comes to Crested Butte. *Newsweek, 122*(26), 45.

Glasgow, N.L. (1990). Attracting retirees as a community development option. *Journal of the Community Development Society, 21*(1), 102–114.

Green, R.K., & Malpezzi, S. (2000). *A primer on U.S. housing markets and housing policy.* Madison, WI: University of Wisconsin, Center for Urban Land Economics Research.

Housing Assistance Council. (2002). *Taking stock: Rural people, poverty, and housing at the turn of the 21st Century*. Washington, DC: Author.

Janofsky, M. (1999, September 5). Housing for poorer neighbors offends Vail's rich. *The New York Times*, p. 14.

Johnson, K.M., & Beale, C.L. (2002). Nonmetropolitan recreation counties: Their identification and rapid growth *Rural America, 17*(4):12–19.

Krofta, J.A., Crull, S.R., & Cook, C.C. (1999). Affordable housing in the rural Midwest. In J. Belden & Robert Wiener (Eds.), *Housing in rural America.* Thousand Oaks, CA: Sage.

Marcouiller, D.W., Clendenning, J.G., & Kedzior, R. (2002). Natural amenity-led development and rural planning: CPL Bibliography 365. *Journal of Planning Literature, 16(4)*, 515–542.

Marcouiller, D.W., & Green, G.P. (2000). Outdoor recreation and community development: Perspectives from the social sciences. In G.E. Machlis, D. Field, & W.H. Gardiner (Eds.), *National parks and rural development* (pp. 33–49). Washington, DC: Island Press.

Mathur, V.K., & Stein, S.H. (1991). A dynamic interregional theory of migration and population growth. *Land Economics, 67*(3), 292–298.

Marx, L. (1964). *The machine in the garden; Technology and the pastoral ideal in America.* New York: Oxford University Press.

Mutchler, J.E., & Krivo, L.J. (1989). Availability and affordability: Household adaptation to a housing squeeze. *Social Forces, 68*(1), 241–261.

Myers, D. (2000, November). *Building the future as a process in time.* Paper presented at the Lincoln Institute of Land Policy Annual Roundtable: Metropolitan Development Patterns, Cambridge, MA.

Nelson, P.B. (2001). Rural restructuring in the American West: Land use, family, and class discourses. *Journal of Rural Studies, 17* (4), 395–407.

Office of Management and Budget. (2004). *OMB bulletin N. 04–03: Update of statistical area definitions and additional guidance on their uses.* Washington, DC: Author.

Power, T.M. (1996). Marketing the landscape: Tourism and the local economy. In T. Power (Ed.), *Lost landscapes and failed economies* (pp. 213–234). Washington, DC: Island Press.

Robinson, G.M. (1990). *Conflict and change in the countryside: Rural society, economy, and planning in the developed world.* New York: Belhaven Press.

Rothman, H.K. (1998). *Devil's bargains: Tourism in the twentieth century American West.* Lawrence, KS: University Press of Kansas.

Schnaiberg, J., Riera, J., Turner, M.G., & Voss, P.R. (2002). Explaining human settlement patterns in a recreational lake district: Vilas County, Wisconsin, USA. *Environmental Management, 30*(1), 24–34.

Shucksmith, M. (1991). Still no homes for locals? Affordable housing and planning controls in rural areas. In T. Champion & C. Watkins (Eds.), *People in the countryside: Studies of social change in rural Britain* (pp. 53–66). London: Paul Chapman.

Spain, D. (1993). Been-heres versus come-heres. *Journal of the American Planning Association, 59*(2), 156–171.

U.S. Census Bureau. (2003). *2000 census of population and housing technical documentation, summary file 3.* Prepared by the U.S. Census Bureau.

Whitson, D. (2001). Nature as playground: Recreation and gentrification in the mountain west. In R. Epp & D. Whitson (Eds.), *Writing off the rural West* (pp. 145–164). Edmonton: University of Alberta Press.

Wills, D.S. (2002). Rural housing prices grew rapidly in the 1990s. *Rural America, 17*(3), 47–56.

Ziebarth, A. (2000). Local housing policy: The small town myth and economic development. *Rural America, 15*(2), 18–23.

Ziebarth, A., Prochaska-Cue, K., & Shrewbury, B. (1997). Growth and locational impacts for housing in small communities. *Rural Sociology, 62*(1), 111–125.

CHAPTER 15

SOCIAL CHANGE AND WELL-BEING IN WESTERN AMENITY-GROWTH COMMUNITIES

RICHARD S. KRANNICH, PEGGY PETRZELKA, AND JOAN M. BREHM

INTRODUCTION

Natural amenities involving a mild climate, topographic variation, and the presence of water areas are closely linked to population growth throughout the United States. From 1970 to1996 nonmetropolitan counties with high ratings on six natural amenity factors grew by an average of 125 percent, compared to just 1 percent among counties rated low on those same factors (McGranahan, 1999; also Beale & Johnson, 1998; Johnson & Beale, 1994; Rudzitis, 1999; Rudzitis & Johansen, 1989; Shumway & Davis, 1996). Amenity-based growth has been especially evident in nonmetropolitan portions of the American West, reflecting the widespread presence of public lands, national parks and monuments, wilderness areas, scenic vistas, and other natural amenity features. The development of major winter and summer resorts at places like Park City, Utah and Aspen, Colorado has driven both seasonal tourism and extensive land and housing development in many areas. Other areas without major resort developments, such as Idaho's Teton Valley, have also experienced substantial growth due to in-migration of retirees, telecommuting professionals, and urban refugees attracted to high-amenity locations.

Although the occurrence of amenity-based growth is well documented, its implications for social and community well-being are not clearly understood. From some perspectives, such growth represents a potential solution to difficulties associated with the deterioration of traditional rural economies such as farming, ranching, and resource extraction. From other perspectives, such growth has the potential to open a Pandora's Box of social and economic problems associated with rapid population growth, tensions and conflicts between established and in-migrant populations, and the transformation of valued rural cultures and traditions. Amenity-based growth has the potential to influence, both positively and negatively, residents' satisfaction with community conditions, their levels of

W.A. Kandel & D.L. Brown (eds.), Population Change and Rural Society, 311–331.

social integration, and their views and preferences regarding community change and development.

In this chapter we present a comparative case study focusing on four rural communities located across the Intermountain West that are characterized by widely varying experiences with amenity-based development and growth. Drawing upon survey data collected in each community, we examine how these diverse contexts, representing lower or higher levels of amenity-based development, may be associated with varying levels of social and community well-being. Specifically, we focus on relationships between residence in these varied settings and levels of community satisfaction, social integration and community participation, and attitudes regarding community change.

Declines in extractive and agricultural industries have affected nonmetropolitan areas throughout the western United States for decades. When combined with changes in federal development policies, these changes have placed increased pressures on local governments to address social and economic development needs. In some rural areas these joint occurrences have contributed to efforts by both public officials and community residents to pursue a variety of natural amenity-based development strategies as means of combating the problems accruing from economic restructuring and devolution of government responsibility.

Because economic development of virtually any type is ordinarily welcomed in areas affected by declines in traditional rural industries (Krannich & Luloff, 1991), we anticipate that residents of areas exhibiting higher levels of amenity-based development will be more satisfied with community conditions generally, and economic conditions and opportunities in particular, than those living where little or no such development has occurred. At the same time, the social and demographic changes associated with such development—including in-migration of new populations, increased presence of seasonal and episodic residents, and the potential for a "culture clash" between tradition-oriented long-term residents and more cosmopolitan newcomers—can be expected to produce lower levels of social integration and community participation in areas heavily affected by amenity-based growth (see Smith & Krannich, 2000). Moreover, at some point residents of high-growth areas are likely to develop more critical orientations regarding the consequences of unabated growth and become more concerned about the preservation of valued sociocultural as well as biophysical landscapes than residents of areas experiencing economic and demographic stagnation or decline (Smith & Krannich, 1998). In short, we expect that resident responses to extensive amenity-based growth will be mixed, depending on the specific dimensions of well-being under consideration.

ECONOMIC AND SOCIAL IMPLICATIONS OF AMENITY GROWTH

Both positive and negative consequences have been observed in amenity-rich settings where growth and development outcomes have occurred, reflecting a variety of economic and social changes. Analyses of economic consequences have highlighted a number of positive outcomes. One review of the economic effects of amenity-based growth concluded that "parks and park-related tourism generate millions of dollars of income, sizeable multiplier effects, and new jobs in neighboring regions" (Achana & O'Leary, 2000, p. 72). English and others (2000) found higher per capita income levels, faster population growth, and higher housing prices in counties economically dependent on tourism. In addition, Johnson and Fuguitt (2000) observed a strong tendency for older adults to represent a major component of the migration stream to high-amenity recreation counties, an outcome that prior research has shown to create new income and employment opportunities in destination communities (Glasgow & Reeder, 1990).

The population growth that often occurs in high-amenity rural areas also has multiple consequences for the social contexts of affected communities. On the positive side, the arrival of new residents can substantially alter the composition of local populations and possibly enhance a community's "human capital" when in-migrants bring occupational, organizational, and leadership experience and skills to their new communities. Population growth also has the potential to generate the critical mass of residents needed to reinvigorate or even create churches, civic organizations, and interest groups that are often moribund if not entirely absent in many rural areas. Similarly, increased populations as well as the presence of tourists and seasonal visitors may stimulate the development of an expanded array of public and private sector businesses and services that more effectively meet the needs of area residents. Thus, amenity-driven population growth has the potential to enhance community capacity to address the needs of local residents (Doak & Kusel, 1996; Flora & Flora, 1993; Kreitzmann & McKnight, 1993; also see Green, 2003).

However, amenity growth may also produce negative consequences. Places heavily dependent upon amenity-based development can be as vulnerable to economic downturns as places dependent on more traditional resource extraction economies. The inherent seasonality of tourism-based activity and second-home residency can result in employment fluctuations rivaling those that characterize traditional extractive industries but with a far greater frequency of upswings and downturns (Keith et al., 1996, p.105). Furthermore, a substantial leakage of income out of the local area often occurs, particularly when income and profits are siphoned away by non-local corporations that often control much of the development in such settings (Miles, 2000). Seasonal spikes in visitation can require an expansion of public services to levels far in excess of what would be needed to serve the needs of permanent populations. Similarly, large numbers of seasonal homes can generate substantial increases in public sector expenditures, while seasonal occupancy may limit revenues derived from property, sales, and local income taxes (Burchell et al., 1998; English et al., 2000). The result can be an increased tax burden to support public facilities and services that may exceed the needs or preferences of established local populations.

Job growth generated by amenity-based development can also be a mixed blessing. Rural residents often balk at working in amenity-based jobs that they consider inconsistent with the cultural traditions and lifeways associated with traditional rural occupations such as logging, mining, or agriculture (Carroll, 1995). Employment opportunities associated with amenity-based growth are often in lower-wage service-sector industries, often are part-time or seasonal, provide few if any benefits, and seldom generate incomes sufficient to fully support a family. In addition, service workers in major destination areas such as Aspen and Jackson Hole frequently must live in and commute from more affordable locations, often at a substantial distance. Commuting time has been shown by Putnam (2000, p. 213) to exert a strong negative influence on civic involvement.

The potential for enhanced community capacity may be further compromised when growth occurs at levels exceeding local preference or the ability of established social structures and institutions to respond. Excessive growth may strain informal social structures as well as public institutions and formal organizations. Increased population along with the presence of larger numbers of recently-arrived residents and seasonal visitors can reduce the "density of acquaintanceship," which tends to be high in more stable rural places and can contribute in important ways to social solidarity and informal social support processes (Freudenburg, 1986; Putnam, 2000). Rural population growth has also been associated with a so-called "culture clash" between traditional and newcomer values (Smith & Krannich, 2000). Prior research suggests that divergent views about growth and environmental protection can contribute to tensions between established and in-migrant populations (Beyers & Nelson, 2000; Blahna, 1990; Cockerham & Blevins, 1977; Graber, 1974; Jobes, 1995; Ploch, 1978; Rudzitis, 1999; Spain, 1993). Concerns that amenity-based growth will overwhelm and obliterate the customs and cultures of rural and indigenous communities have become a focal point of local efforts to resist or limit such growth in a variety of settings (Canan & Hennessy, 1989). Also, established residents may feel that the uses and symbolic meanings of natural settings are threatened by increased tourism, new residents, and altered land use patterns (Hiss, 1990; Martin & McCool, 1992; Mitchell et al., 1993). While some evidence does suggest that newcomers' and long-term residents' perspectives on such issues are more similar than is often assumed (Fortmann & Kusel, 1990; Smith & Krannich, 2000), the potential for civic engagement and collective action in pursuit of community interests is reduced when such divisions emerge (Wilkinson, 1991).

To summarize, the literature suggests that residents of non-metropolitan areas affected by amenity-based growth are likely to experience a mixture of positive and negative consequences. Satisfaction with community conditions may shift in a positive direction due to economic revitalization and service expansion. At the same time, such growth is likely to foster concerns about an erosion of social and cultural traditions. Levels of social integration and community participation are likely to decline, if only because of the tendency for newer residents to exhibit less expansive local social ties (Kasarda & Janowitz, 1974). Shifting and at times conflicting values and preferences regarding community change, resource management, and other local issues are likely to be reflected in tensions between established and in-migrant populations.

While many of these consequences are associated with growth and development in general, amenity-based growth may produce unique effects due to the seasonality of some economic activity and population fluctuations and the tensions that can arise between amenity-oriented and other types of land and resource use. In short, many questions remain about the effects of such growth and change. Accordingly, we turn next to an examination of how community satisfaction, social integration and participation, and attitudes about community change and development may be associated with varying amenity-growth conditions.

RESEARCH DESIGN AND APPROACH

This research centers on four small communities in the Intermountain West. At the time of data collection, one community (Star Valley) was in the midst of substantial social, economic, and demographic transformations associated with amenity-related growth and development. The second (western Wayne County) was also experiencing considerable amenity-related development, though the extent and pace of population growth and land use change were less extreme. The third (Escalante) was being affected by increased tourism associated with its location adjacent to a recently designated national monument, yet despite some expansion of tourism-related businesses and widespread anticipation of potential future growth, little in-migration or other amenity-based development activity had occurred. The fourth community (Caliente), while surrounded by public lands and proximate to several small state parks and a national park, had experienced long-term and persistent economic and demographic stagnation in spite of local development initiatives seeking to capitalize on surrounding landscapes.

Study Communities

Star Valley, Wyoming

Star Valley is located at the western edge of Wyoming in Lincoln County, approximately 50 miles southwest of Jackson. The area is comprised of a cluster of individual settlements, including the towns of Afton (1818 residents in 2000), Alpine (550 residents), Thayne (341 residents), Smoot (182 residents), Grover (137 residents), and Etna (123 residents). Star Valley is about 50 miles long, 5 to 10 miles wide, encircled by the Caribou, Salt River, Wyoming, and Gros Ventre mountain ranges and the Bridger-Teton, Caribou, and Targhee National Forests, and within 100 miles of both Grand Teton and Yellowstone National Parks. Dairy farming and dairy processing have historically been the primary sources of economic activity in the valley, but the local dairy industry has experienced substantial decline in recent decades. Timber harvesting and sawmills were also well-established during the 1960s, but as with the dairy industry this segment of the economy has declined significantly.

As the economy of Star Valley continues to change, tourism- and recreation-based services have become increasingly important. Due to the array of natural amenities surrounding the valley and the proximity of two National Parks and Jackson Hole, Star Valley is increasingly attracting new in-migrants. In addition to migrants attracted by natural amenities, service-sector workers in Jackson Hole have sought more affordable housing and a lower cost of living in the Star Valley area. The population of Alpine, located just 40 miles from the Jackson Hole area, grew by 194 percent between 1990 and 2000, and the towns of Afton and Thayne grew by approximately 30 percent and 25 percent, respectively, during the same period. A large residential subdivision located in an unincorporated portion of the county outside of Thayne has become developed with several hundred primarily seasonal recreation and retirement homes during the past decade, and extensive dispersed housing development is evident elsewhere in the valley.

Western Wayne County, Utah

The western Wayne County area includes several small towns located along a 15-mile-long section of State Highway 24. Moving from west to east, the study area includes the towns of Loa (252 residents in 2000), Lyman (234 residents), Bicknell (353 residents), and Torrey (171 residents), as well as adjoining unincorporated areas. Farming and ranching have historically been core elements of the local economy, but, as with many other parts of the rural West, the economic importance of agriculture has declined in recent decades. A small lumber industry that also contributed to the local economy has declined considerably with reductions in timber harvests on surrounding National Forest lands. Increasingly, tourism and recreation-based services have become key components of the local and regional economy.

Western Wayne County is bordered by the Dixie National Forest and the Escalante Grand Staircase National Monument to the south and the Fish Lake National Forest to the north. Capital Reef National Park is immediately east of the study area, near the "gateway" town of Torrey. These natural amenities have attracted increasing numbers of in-migrants and seasonal residents, as well as shorter-term visitors. Land use change associated with development of tourism-oriented businesses and seasonal residences is particularly evident in Torrey and nearby unincorporated areas surrounding Capitol Reef National Park. Between 1990 and 2000 the population of Torrey increased by 40 percent, while the town of Bicknell grew by over 17 percent. In contrast, the county seat of Loa lost population during the 1990s, falling 18 percent between 1990 and 2000. This reflects both the effects of declines in traditional resource-based industries during this period and the concentration of tourism-oriented developments and other amenity-based growth in the eastern-most portions of the western Wayne County study area.

Escalante, Utah

Escalante (population 818 in 2000) is located in Garfield County in southern Utah. The surrounding area is dominated by extensive tracts of public lands, with over 95 percent of the county's land area in federal and state ownership. Economic activity in this area has long been centered on timber and agriculture, particularly livestock grazing on public lands. While these are still important components of the local economy, both have experienced substantial declines in recent decades while tourism- and recreation-based services have become increasingly important contributors.

Beautiful natural amenities ranging from redrock deserts and slot canyons to forested mountains characterize the landscapes surrounding Escalante. In 1996 the Escalante-Grand Staircase National Monument was established on BLM lands that surround Escalante, bringing increased national and international attention to the area. The monument, coupled with the many other natural amenities in the region, has increasingly drawn tourists and recreationists to this remote rural area, and several new and expanded tourism-oriented businesses have developed in recent years. However, despite increased tourism and expectations of amenity-based growth and development following designation of the monument, Escalante has yet to experience the economic and demographic expansion often associated with the destination tourism. Indeed, unlike most other rural communities in the surrounding region, Escalante experienced a slight population decline during the 1990s, dropping from 838 residents in 1990 to 818 in 2000.

Caliente, Nevada

Caliente (population 1,123 in 2000) is located on the eastern edge of south central Nevada in Lincoln County, approximately 120 miles north of Las Vegas. The town was first established as a construction headquarters when railroad lines were extended from Salt Lake City to the Pacific coast, and Caliente remained an important transfer station along this route until the 1950s, when the shift from steam to diesel locomotives initiated a substantial decline in railroad-related employment (Cottrell, 1951). Mining was also an important historical economic activity throughout surrounding portions of Lincoln County, with over 250 active mines at the peak of mining activity. However, by 1999 only four small mining businesses remained active. Named for hot springs found in the area, Caliente is near several state parks, including Beaver Dam State Park, Cathedral Gorge State Park, Echo Canyon State Park, and Kershaw-Ryan State Park. Great Basin National Park is located approximately 100 miles to the north. The area is known for its abundance of desert climate amenities, including outdoor attractions such as hunting, fishing, camping, and ghost town explorations.

The economy in Caliente and Lincoln County has shifted from one heavily dependent on the railroad and mining industries to a more service-based economy that is highly dependent on government agency employment. A limited amount of primarily pass-through tourism is associated with the town's location on an access route to Great Basin National Park. However, despite long-standing efforts to promote tourism and other forms of economic development, Caliente and Lincoln County have experienced persistent economic stagnation, with little new business development, housing expansion, or in-migration occurring during recent decades. Between 1990 and 2000 Caliente's population increased by just 2 percent, from 1101 to 1123.

Data Collection

Survey data were collected during the summer of 2001 from adult residents in each of the study areas. Households were randomly sampled from public utility records and the resulting sample sizes were 200 in Western Wayne County and Star Valley, 203 in Caliente, and 166 in Escalante. The smaller sample in Escalante reflects both its smaller population and the presence of numerous unoccupied homes during the data collection period. Individual respondents within households were selected by having the adult whose birthday had occurred most recently complete the self-completion questionnaire. Questionnaires were administered using a "drop-off/pick-up" methodology (Steele et al., 2001); individuals unable to respond during the time that the research team was in the area were provided with a postage-paid envelope and asked to return the questionnaire by mail. These procedures produced response rates of 78 percent in Caliente, 81 percent in Escalante, 81 percent in Star Valley, and 85 percent in western Wayne County.

High numbers of seasonally or episodically occupied residences in the study areas and the use of a drop-off/pick-up method produced samples that inevitably under-represent seasonal populations in these communities. Seasonal residents and vacation home owners not occupying their second residence during the two-week period when questionnaires were delivered were not included in the study. Consequently, a limitation of this research is that it is more representative of the permanent populations of these communities than of seasonal or episodic residents.

Variable Measurement and Analysis

Community satisfaction was addressed using three indicators. "Global" community satisfaction was measured by asking respondents to indicate their overall satisfaction with the community "as a place to live;" responses were recorded on a numeric intensity scale ranging from 1 (completely dissatisfied) to 7 (completely satisfied). The second indicator measured satisfaction with local economic conditions by asking respondents to rate their satisfaction with the "opportunity to earn an adequate income" in the community; responses were recorded on the same 1–7 scale. Residents' views regarding recent patterns of community change were assessed by asking whether they thought the community had become more or less desirable as a place to live during the past five years; responses were recorded on a scale ranging from 1 (much less desirable) to 7 (much more desirable); the midpoint (4) represented a "no change" response.

Social integration and community participation were addressed through three distinct measures. Levels of social familiarity or acquaintanceship among neighbors were addressed by asking respondents to indicate the number of adults living in the 10 houses closest to theirs that they know on a first-name basis; because numerous respondents wrote in words like "most" or "all" rather than a numeric value, responses were collapsed into four ordinal categories (1 = 2 or fewer; 2 = 3 to 5; 3 = 6 to 10; 4 = 10 or more). Levels of interaction among neighbors were measured by asking respondents how often they join with neighbors for informal social activities like playing cards, going to dinner, or having picnics; responses were recorded in five ordinal categories (1 = never; 2 = less than once a month; 3 = 1 to 2 times a month; 4 = 3 to 4 times a month; 5 = 5 or more times a month). Involvement in community development activities was measured using an additive index of responses to four items asking respondents to indicate their degree of involvement in the local Chamber of Commerce, local planning groups, local economic development groups, and civic organizations such as Rotary or Lions; responses to each item were measured on a scale with values ranging from 1 (not involved at all) to 7 (highly involved), producing an index with potential values ranging between 4 and 28. The alpha coefficient of reliability for this index was .76, indicating a high degree of internal consistency.

Resident attitudes and preferences regarding community change and development were addressed using six survey questions. First, respondents were asked to indicate how important they thought it was to limit the rate of local population increase in order to maintain and improve the future quality of life in their community; responses were recorded on a scale ranging from 1 (not at all important) to 7 (extremely important). Using the same scale, respondents were also asked to rate the importance of "increasing tourism as a means of enhancing local economic opportunity." Respondents were then presented with several scenarios regarding future community change, and asked to indicate their views about each on a scale ranging from 1 (strongly support the change) to 7 (strongly oppose the change). This series of questions produced four measures focusing on residents' views regarding the scenario of having a 100 home subdivision proposed within one mile of their homes, the sale of 50 percent of local agricultural land for development, a 50 percent increase in the number of properties owned by seasonal residents, and a 50 percent increase in local visitation by tourists and recreationists.

Several of these measures involve ordinal rather than interval levels of measurement. Nevertheless, we have used general linear model procedures (analysis of variance and ordinary least-squares regression) that technically require dependent variables to be measured at the interval level. The decision to do so reflects both a recognition that these procedures are sufficiently powerful to produce generally valid results with ordinal measures (see Labovitz, 1967; also Berry, 1993) and the absence of multivariate analytic procedures producing readily accessible and interpretable results for quantitative ordered discrete dependent variables.

FINDINGS

Bivariate Comparison of Community and Social Well-being

An initial examination of response patterns indicates the presence of significant differences across the four study communities in most of the indicators used to evaluate community and social well-being (Table 15.1). Looking first at the measures of community satisfaction, the data reveal that overall satisfaction with the community as a place to live was lowest in Caliente, higher in Escalante, and highest in Star Valley and western Wayne County, the two areas most affected by amenity-based development. Although differences were not statistically significant, satisfaction with the opportunity to earn an adequate income was higher in Star Valley and western Wayne County than in the other two areas. In addition, residents of Star Valley and western Wayne County were significantly more likely to indicate that their communities had become more desirable during the past five years than were residents of Caliente or Escalante. On balance, these patterns are consistent with our research expectations and indicate a tendency across all three of the measures examined here for community satisfaction to be higher among residents of the areas most affected by amenity-based growth.

The measures of social integration and community participation tell a different story. While levels of acquaintanceship with neighbors were significantly lower in Caliente than in the other three areas, differences between Escalante, Star Valley and Western Wayne County were small and not statistically significant. For the measures focusing on levels of interaction with nearby neighbors and involvement in community development-oriented organizations, there were no significant differences across the study areas. Contrary to our research expectations, for this set of indicators there is no evidence of lower social integration and civic engagement when comparing residents of study communities most affected by amenity-based growth with those from areas not experiencing such growth.

In contrast, there were consistent differences across the study areas in the several measures focusing on residents' preferences about community change and development. When asked about the importance of limiting the rate of local population growth, residents of Star Valley were most likely to consider this highly important (mean = 5.21); average response values for this measure were somewhat

Table 15.1. ANOVA Results Examining Differences Across Study Areas in Mean Response for Measures of Community Satisfaction, Social Integration and Participation, and Attitudes Regarding Community Change

	Caliente	Escalante	Western Wayne	Star Valley	F
Community Satisfaction					
Satisfaction with community as a place to live	$5.03^{E,WW,SV}$	5.61^{C}	5.86^{C}	5.78^{C}	12.89*
Satisfaction with opportunity to earn an adequate income	2.82	2.82	3.15	3.22	2.41
Has community become more or less desirable in past 5 years?	$3.82^{E,SV}$	$3.41^{C,WW,SV}$	4.18^{E}	$4.31^{C,E}$	8.59*
Social Integration/Participation					
Acquaintance with neighbors	$3.13^{E,WW,SV}$	3.71^{C}	3.71^{C}	3.64^{C}	11.25*
Neighboring interactions	2.54	2.67	2.66	2.78	0.92
Involvement in community development organizations	7.39	7.80	7.12	7.19	0.55
Community Change Attitudes					
Importance of limiting population growth	$3.61^{E,WW,SV}$	$4.23^{C,WW,SV}$	$4.87^{C,E}$	$5.21^{C,E}$	19.12*
Opposition to 100-home subdivision	$3.65^{E,WW,SV}$	$5.08^{C,WW,SV}$	$5.60^{C,E}$	$5.82^{C,E}$	44.30*
Opposition to 50% increase in seasonal residents	$4.12^{E,WW,SV}$	$4.63^{C,WW}$	$5.02^{C,E}$	4.81^{C}	8.90*
Opposition to 50% increase in tourism/recreation visitation	$2.54^{E,WW,SV}$	3.53^{C}	3.63^{C}	3.93^{C}	18.60*
Importance of increasing tourism to enhance local economy	$5.58^{E,WW,SV}$	4.30^{C}	4.34^{C}	4.44^{C}	17.60*
Opposition to sale of 50% of local agricultural land for development purposes	$4.46^{E,WW,SV}$	5.52^{C}	5.70^{C}	5.62^{C}	16.81*

* $p < .001$

Superscript notations indicate which communities exhibit response means that are significantly different from those in a particular community; for example, different from Caliente (C), Escalante (E), Western Wayne County (WW), or Star Valley (SV), based on Fischer's Least Significant Difference test.

lower in western Wayne County (4.87), lower still in Escalante (4.23), and lowest in Caliente (3.61). Expressions of opposition regarding the scenario of a 100-home subdivision within one mile of respondents' homes were most evident in Star Valley (mean = 5.82), somewhat less widespread in western Wayne County (5.60) and Escalante (5.08), and least evident in Caliente (3.65). Concern about the prospect of a 50 percent increase in the number of properties owned by seasonal residents was highest in western Wayne County (mean = 5.02), slightly lower in Star Valley (4.81), lower still in Escalante (4.63), and lowest in Caliente (4.12). Respondents from Star Valley were most likely to express concern about the prospect of a 50 percent increase in tourist/recreation visitation (mean = 3.93), with somewhat less concern evident in western Wayne County (3.63) and Escalante (3.53), and substantially less concern evident in Caliente (2.54). Similarly, responses to the question about the importance of increasing tourism as a means of enhancing local economic activity indicated higher levels of support in Caliente (mean = 5.58), while residents in Star Valley (4.44), western Wayne County (4.34), and Escalante (4.30) expressed more ambivalence. Finally, residents of Caliente were least likely to express concern about the prospect of having 50 percent of local agricultural land sold for development purposes (mean = 4.46), while average responses in Escalante (5.52), Star Valley (5.62), and western Wayne County (5.70) revealed significantly more concern about such land use shifts.

Overall, responses to these six items indicate a clear tendency for residents of the communities most affected by amenity-based growth to express higher levels of concern about the prospect of additional population growth, expanded tourist visitation and tourism-based economic activity, and conversion of agricultural lands to residential use. This is consistent with our research expectations and supportive of prior research noting that extensive tourism-related growth can contribute to the development of negative attitudes toward such development. As Smith and Krannich (1998) observed, areas affected by high levels of tourism and similar amenity-based activity can become "saturated" to the point that both long-established residents and more recent in-migrants become disenchanted with and opposed to further development. In contrast, residents of areas experiencing little if any tourism/amenity-based growth along with limited alternative economic development prospects are often extremely anxious to encourage such development, even if that means sacrificing valued features of the local social milieu and surrounding physical landscapes.

Multivariate Analysis of Community and Social Well-being

To explore more fully differences in well-being indicators across the study areas, we turn next to a series of multivariate analyses designed to determine whether community differences in response patterns remain statistically significant once the confounding influences of individual-level socio-demographic variables are taken into account. Communities affected by amenity-based growth may be substantially transformed in terms of their socio-demographic composition, since in-migrants often differ from established residents with respect to characteristics such as age, income levels, religious orientation, and other personal background characteristics. To determine whether or not cross-community variation in well-being persists once these compositional differences are taken into account, we applied a form of analysis of covariance based on a dummy variable approach to ordinary least-squares regression (Neter & Wasserman, 1974). Here the analysis focuses on just four of the well-being measures as dependent variables: satisfaction with the community as a place to live; acquaintanceship with neighbors; attitudes regarding the importance of limiting local population growth; and opposition to/support for a hypothetical situation in which 50 percent of local agricultural land was sold for residential development. These measures were selected to represent each of the major categories of variables initially considered (community satisfaction, social integration and participation, and community change attitudes) and also because they are among the measures that exhibited statistically significant response variation across the study areas in the bivariate analysis.[1]

The four communities (coded as three dichotomous dummy variables, with Caliente assigned as a "reference" category) were treated as a "factor" in the multivariate analyses, reflecting our focus on variation in well-being across these distinct amenity-growth contexts. Community dummy variables are used in lieu of more explicit measures of contextual variation across the study areas for several reasons. Certainly it would be useful to examine the possible influence of specific types of contextual differences by incorporating into the analysis measures of such things as population size, recent population change, land use change, rates and spatial distribution of new housing construction, local economic base, and other factors that may distinguish these places. However, such measures could not be generated for the two aggregated study areas (Star Valley and western Wayne County) that are comprised of several proximate incorporated and unincorporated areas. Census and other data are not uniformly reported for each of the component areas in these locales, census tracts do not correspond closely with the areas comprised by these aggregations, and county-level data would be misleading due to the large geographic areas of these counties and the quite different growth and development patterns affecting other portions of the counties.

Several additional measures were added as control variables to account for the influence of factors such as socioeconomic status, length of residence, and specific contextual aspects that differentiate communities from one another. These included respondent age (in years), sex (female = 0, male = 1), household income (11 categories in \$10,000 increments, from under \$10,000 to \$100,000 or more), and size of community in which the respondent grew up (four categories, ranging from rural/very small town to large metropolitan city).

Length of residence was also included to account for the influence of recent in-migration to the communities. Many researchers have argued that an important factor in classifying newcomers and long-term residents in areas affected by substantial population change is the approximate year in which a major wave of in-migration began (Blahna, 1985; Graber, 1974; Smith & Krannich, 2000). For the communities examined here, as with many other areas of the rural West, much of the amenity-related growth began in earnest around 1990. Accordingly, length of residence was dichotomized to differentiate recently-arrived residents (10 years or less, coded 0) from longer-term residents (11 years or more, coded 1).

Finally, due to the dominance of the Church of Jesus Christ of Latter-Day Saints (LDS) faith within the study areas, religion was also included in the analysis. All four study sites are historic Mormon settlements, and the continued dominance of the LDS faith (overall, 68 percent of all respondents were Mormons) plays an important role in the social structure and context of these communities. For example, Toney and others (1997) found that membership in the Mormon Church provided an instant social connection for individuals living in the region, regardless of how long they had lived in a community or from where they had moved. Accordingly, religion was recoded into a dichotomous variable, with 1 = LDS and 0 = other.

Results of the regression analyses examining relationships between the well-being measures and the dummy variables used to measure community context differences along with the socio-demographic covariates are summarized in Table 15.2. Looking first at satisfaction with the community as a place to live, the results indicate that, net of the influence of control variables, the predicted community satisfaction score for Caliente residents is 3.76 (the constant term in the fitted regression equation). The predicted satisfaction score was significantly higher in Escalante at 4.2 (the constant term or "reference" value, plus the value of the partial regression coefficient associated with the dummy variable representing residence in Escalante). Predicted satisfaction scores were higher still in western Wayne County (4.37) and Star Valley (4.46). Admittedly, this community context measure provides only a crude representation of differences in amenity growth levels and inevitably incorporates the influence of other unmeasured conditions that differentiate these study areas. Nevertheless, it is clear that differences across the study communities remain significant even after controlling for variation in individual socio-demographic characteristics, with higher satisfaction still evident in the places most affected by amenity-based growth. Among the other independent variables, the only measures exhibiting significant relationships with this satisfaction measure were religion and age: Mormon respondents and older residents tended to express higher satisfaction than non-Mormon and younger individuals. In combination, community of residence and the socio-demographic variables accounted for only about 13 percent of variation in the community satisfaction measure.

As with the bivariate analysis, multivariate results revealed some significant differences across the study areas in levels of acquaintanceship with neighbors. The predicted value for the acquaintanceship measure was 2.59 in Caliente; values for Escalante (2.9) and Star Valley (2.89) were significantly higher ($p < .05$); the value for western Wayne County (2.83) was also higher than for Caliente, though

Table 15.2. Regression of Community of Residence[a] and Resident Socio-Demographic Characteristics on Satisfaction with Community, Acquaintance with Neighbors, Attitudes about Importance of Limiting Population Growth, and Opposition to Sale of 50 Percent of Agricultural Land for Development

Independent Variables	Community Satisfaction		Acquaintance With Neighbors		Limiting Population Growth		Opposition to Agricultural Land Development	
	b	*B*	b	*B*	b	*B*	b	*B*
Constant	3.760		2.585		3.268		4.264	
Dummy #1 (Escalante)	.441	.142**	.319	.124*	.765	.150***	1.197	.274***
Dummy #2 (Western Wayne)	.607	.204***	.249	.101	1.377	.287***	1.377	.332***
Dummy #2 (Star Valley)	.695	.239***	.300	.123*	1.597	.337***	1.287	.313***
Age[b]	.014	.180***	.002	.025	.009	.066	.009	.080
Sex[c]	−.002	−.001	−.054	−.025	.037	.009	−.050	−.014
Religion[d]	.364	.140**	.388	.180***	−.085	−.020	−.011	−.003
Length of Residence[e]	.007	.003	.478	.217***	.216	.050	−.277	−.075
Size of Community Growing Up[f]	.090	.080	.044	.047	−.049	−.027	−.032	−.020
Household Income[g]	.019	.038	.001	.003	−.024	−.030	−.008	−.012
Coefficient of Determination (R^2)	.133		.147		.116		.103	

* $p < .05$; * $p < .01$; * $p < .001$
b = unstandardized regression coefficients; *B* = standardized regression coefficients.
[a] Caliente is the reference category, represented when dummy variables representing the other communities all assume values of zero.
[b] Measured in years
[c] 0 = female; 1 = male
[d] 0 = not Mormon; 1 = Mormon
[e] 0 = 10 years or less; 1 = over 10 years
[f] 1 = large urban/metropolitan area; 2 = medium size urban area; 3 = small urban area; 4 = small town/rural area
[g] 1 = under $10,000; 2 = $10,000–$19,999; 3 = $20,000–$29,999; 4 = $30,000–$39,999; 5 = $40,000–$49,999; 6 = $50,000–$59,999; 7 = $60,000–$69,999; 8 = $70,000–$79,999; 9 = $80,000–$89,999; 10 = $90,000–$99,999; 11 = $100,000 or higher.

the regression coefficient for that community dummy variable fell slightly short of indicating a statistically significant difference ($p = .06$). In substantive terms the differences across study areas are relatively small, and the direction of the relationship is inconsistent with the expectation that social integration would be lower in areas most extensively affected by amenity-based growth. Control variables exhibiting significant relationships with the acquaintanceship measure included length of residence and religion, indicating that longer-term and Mormon residents tend to know more of their neighbors than do shorter-term and non-Mormon residents. However, none of the observed associations was particularly strong, and overall only a very small proportion (about 4 percent) of the variation in the acquaintanceship measure was accounted for by the combined set of independent variables.

Turning next to respondents' views about the importance of limiting population growth, the predicted response value on the 1–7 measurement scale for residents of Caliente was 3.27. Predicted values associated with residence in Escalante were significantly higher at 3.99, and higher still in both Star Valley (4.87) and western Wayne County (4.65). Thus, even after controlling for compositional differences, support for limiting population growth was substantially higher in the two areas most affected by recent patterns of amenity-based growth. In Escalante, where little increase in permanent population has occurred in recent years, the more moderately elevated support for limiting population growth likely reflects both anticipatory concerns that such growth may be imminent and a general aversion to change expressed by many residents of this culturally homogeneous and socially "closed" community. None of the socio-demographic control variables exhibited a significant partial association with this dependent variable. In combination the independent variables accounted for less than 12 percent of the variation in this measure of resident attitudes toward local population growth.

Finally, we examined the relationships of the community context measure and the compositional control variables with resident attitudes about the prospect of having 50 percent of local agricultural land sold for residential development. Net of the influence of other variables, the predicted value associated with residence in Caliente was 4.26. Significantly greater opposition to such land use change was evident in the other study areas: predicted response values were 5.46 in Escalante, 5.55 in Star Valley, and 5.64 in western Wayne County. Clearly, residence in the three areas that have experienced amenity-based growth and development is associated with heightened concern about land use transformations that would lead to the sale and development of agricultural lands. The observed differences may reflect the influence of several contextual features of these places, including recent local experience with fairly widespread agricultural land conversion in Star Valley and western Wayne County, anticipation of such changes in the face of mounting tourism visitation in Escalante, and the influence of stronger historical, economic, and cultural linkages to agricultural activity in each of these three areas than in Caliente. Again, none of the socio-demographic control variables was significantly associated with response to this measure, contributing to the fact that only about 10 percent of variation in the dependent variable is accounted for by the full set of independent variables.

DISCUSSION AND IMPLICATIONS

Our findings are consistent in several ways with patterns reported in a number of more broadly-focused analyses of rural social life. For example, acquaintanceship with neighbors and neighboring interactions are relatively high in all of the rural communities in this study. This is consistent with Putnam's (2000) finding that size of community makes a difference in terms of social integration, with smaller, more rural communities exhibiting higher social integration.

Differences between old-timers and newcomers found in this study are also consistent with other research on social integration. As Putnam argues (2000, p. 204), "Recent arrivals in any community are less likely to vote, less likely to have supportive networks of friends and neighbors, less likely to belong to civic organizations. People who expect to move in the next five years are 20–25 percent less likely to attend church, attend club meetings, volunteer, or work on community projects than those who expect to stay put." Similarly, Salamon's (2003a, 2003b) research on small towns in Illinois indicates that oldtimers' orientations to their town tend to reflect permanence and investment, while newcomers are more likely to have a transitory orientation, seeing the town from an instrumental perspective and focusing on traits such as good schools, rising property values, or being a good place to raise the kids (and then leave). Newcomers tend not to be highly integrated and do not feel a strong sense of community.

The role of religion observed in this study is also consistent with previous research on social integration. When examining traits and behaviors that are associated with community involvement, Putnam (2000, p. 67) notes church attendance and involvement have a particularly important role for the development of community participation in other arenas, citing studies that show those who attend church are more likely to vote and be active politically, to be involved in secular organizations, and to have more social connections than non-churchgoers. Such effects are particularly likely to be evident in places where a particular religion is dominant, as with the Mormon faith in our study areas.

In addition, our findings reinforce observations derived from earlier research on amenity growth communities. Residents of communities (in this case most obviously Star Valley) experiencing intensified pressures of in-migration and other aspects of amenity-based development are most likely to be concerned about population growth, land use change, and future expansion of tourism- and recreation-based visitation and economic activity—they are "saturated" with respect to their interest in and willingness to accommodate additional growth and change (Smith & Krannich, 1998). At the same time, we find that levels of social integration and community participation are not lower in these more rapidly-growing areas than in more stable communities, suggesting that they have not exhibited the "social disruption" observed in western "boomtowns" affected by extremely rapid growth (see Smith et al., 2001). More importantly, community satisfaction is highest in the study areas that have achieved substantial amenity-based growth, likely reflecting the broader array of facilities, services, economic opportunities, and perhaps increased social vibrancy of these growing and changing places.

While these findings regarding the social well-being consequences of amenity-based growth are mixed, we do not consider them to be contradictory. Rather, our results are indicative of the tension that exists between attaining the social and economic benefits that can result from amenity-based growth and trying to avoid the costs associated with rapid growth that can overwhelm local adaptive capacity and transform both social and physical landscapes in undesirable ways. The trick is to learn how to balance such growth in a way that issues of potential concern regarding the pace and trajectory of community change do not escalate to a point that satisfaction and other dimensions of well-being deteriorate.

An essay written by Bill Hedden, a County Commissioner from Southern Utah, provides some insight regarding this difficult balancing act (see Hedden, 1994). Speaking about amenity-based growth that occurred in and around Moab, Utah, he stated,

> The simplest way to describe what happened in Grand County is to say that, in 1986, our resilient community leaders got in their rowboat and went fishing for a little tourism to revive and diversify our economy. They hooked a great white shark. This monster has swamped the boat and eaten the crew, and those of us who have been thrust into the breach are struggling desperately to save some remnants of the valuable cargo.

While Hedden does acknowledge a number of positives that accompanied in-migration to the Moab area, he devotes much of his discussion to the negative effects of uncontrolled growth and development. At the same time, he notes that lessons learned in Moab and similar settings can provide direction for more successful future efforts to balance the forces of growth and community change. Specifically, he argues for the importance of partnerships involving a broad range of local agencies, organizations, officials, and stakeholders who need to "understand how a decision made by one of us affects all the rest" and who must learn to "share information and planning resources and work together to assure that individual decisions make collective sense for the land and human communities."

Although collaborative processes and broad-based engagement in community planning and decision-making do not represent a panacea for resolving concerns about the growth affecting many high-amenity communities, they do provide mechanisms for identifying strategies to address and manage the consequences of growth while taking into account the values and interests of a full range of local organizations and social groups. However, such processes can be effective only when discussions and decisions are based on accurate and accessible information rather than on emotion and hearsay. It is to be hoped that the findings of this and other recent studies on amenity growth can help to provide citizens with the knowledge they need to fully and effectively participate in these processes.

Finally, it is important to keep in mind that the variables incorporated in our multivariate models accounted for only a limited degree of variation in the four selected social well-being measures. Dummy variables used to address community context account for most of the explained variation, while socio-demographic variables exhibited inconsistent and in most cases insignificant relationships with the well-being measures. Although the models presented here encompass the full range of relevant socio-demographic measures available in our data, other measures (e.g., land ownership status or employment by industry) could prove useful in future efforts to identify correlates of these and other well-being dimensions. It would also be useful to develop measures that could help to disaggregate the array of community characteristics and conditions encompassed in our rather crude measure of community context differences. Future analyses that explicitly examine the influence of factors such as population growth trends, patterns of land use change, and shifts in local economic structures may be keys to understanding how and why community context variations are so important in accounting for well-being variation.

ENDNOTE

1. Details regarding multivariate results for well-being indicators are available from the authors.

REFERENCES

Achana, F.T., & O'Leary, J.T. (2000). The transboundary relationship between national parks and adjacent communities. In G. E. Machlis & D. R. Field (Eds.), *National parks and rural development* (pp. 67–87). Washington, DC: Island Press.

Beale, C.L., & Johnson, K.M. (1998). The identification of recreational counties in nonmetropolitan areas of the USA. *Population Research and Policy Review, 17*, 37–53.

Berry, W.D. (1993). *Understanding regression assumptions*. Newbury Park, CA: Sage.

Beyers, W.B., & Nelson, P.B. (2000). Contemporary development forces in the nonmetropolitan West: New insights from rapidly growing communities. *Journal of Rural Studies, 16*, 459–474.

Blahna, D.J. (1985). Turnaround migration and environmental conflict in northern Lower Michigan: The implications of social change for regional resource management (Doctoral dissertation, University of Michigan, 1985).

Blahna, D.J. (1990). Social bases for resource conflicts in areas of reverse migration. In R. G. Lee, D.R. Field & W.R. Burch, Jr. (Eds.), *Community & forestry: Continuities in the sociology of natural resources* (pp. 139–178). Boulder, CO: Westview.

Burchell, R.W., Shad, N.A., Listokin, D., Phillips, H., Downs, A., Seskin, S., Moore, T., Helton, D., & Gall, M. (1998). *The costs of sprawl—revisited* (Report 39, Transportation Research Board, National Research Council). Washington, DC: National Academy Press.

Carroll, M.S. (1995). *Community and the northwestern logger: Continuities and changes in the era of the spotted owl.* Boulder, CO: Westview.

Cockerham, W.C., & Blevins, A.L., Jr. (1997). Attitudes toward land-use planning and controlled population growth in Jackson Hole. *Journal of the Community Development Society, 8,* 62–73.

Cottrell, W.F. (1951). Death by dieselization: A case study in the reaction to technological change. *American Sociological Review, 16,* 358–365.

Doak, S., & Kusel, J. (1996). Well-being in forest dependent communities, part II: A social assessment focus. In *Sierra Nevada ecosystem project, final report to Congress, status of the Sierra Nevada. Vol. II: Assessments and scientific basis for management options* (Report No. 37, pp. 375–400). Davis, CA: Wildland Resources Center.

English, D., Marcouiller, D.W., & Cordell, H.K. (2000). Tourism dependence in rural America: Estimates and effects. *Society and Natural Resources, 13,* 185–202.

Flora, C., & Flora, J. (1993). Entrepreneurial social infrastructure: A necessary social ingredient. *Annals of the American Academy of Political and Social Science, 599,* 48–58.

Fortmann, L., & Kusel, J. (1990). New voices, old beliefs: Forest environmentalism among new and long-standing rural residents. *Rural Sociology, 55,* 214–232.

Freudenburg, W.R. (1986). The density of acquaintanceship: An overlooked variable in community research? *American Journal of Sociology, 92,* 27–63.

Glasgow, N., & Reeder, R.J. (1990). Economic and fiscal implications of nonmetropolitan retirement migration. *Journal of Applied Gerontology, 9,* 433–451.

Graber, E.A. (1974). Newcomers and oldtimers: Growth and change in a mountain town. *Rural Sociology, 39,* 504–513.

Green, G.P. (2003). What role can community play in local economic development? In D.L. Brown & L.E. Swanson (Eds.), *Challenges for rural America in the twenty-first century* (pp. 343–352). State College, PA: Pennsylvania State Press.

Hedden, B. (1994). Towns angling for tourism should beware of the great white shark. *High Country News.* Retrieved September 15, 2003, from http://www.hcn.org/servlets/hcn.Article?article_id=542

Hiss, T. (1990). *The experience of place.* New York: Vintage Books.

Jobes, P.C. (1995). Residential stability and crime in small rural agricultural and recreational towns. *Sociological Perspectives, 42,* 499–525.

Johnson, K.M., & Beale, C.L. (1994). The recent revival of widespread population growth in nonmetropolitan areas of the United States. *Rural Sociology, 59,* 655–667.

Johnson, K.M., & Fuguitt, G.V. (2000). Continuity and change in rural migration patterns, 1950–1995. *Rural Sociology, 65,* 27–49.

Kasarda, J., & Janowitz, M. (1974). Community attachments in mass society. *American Sociological Review, 39,* 328–339.

Keith, J., Fawson, C., & Chang, T. (1996). Recreation as an economic development strategy: Some evidence from Utah. *Journal of Leisure Research, 28,* 96–107.

Krannich, R.S., & Luloff, A.E. (1991). Problems of resource dependency in U.S. rural communities. In A. Gilg, D. Briggs, R. Dilley, O. Furuseth, & G. McDonald (Eds.), *Progress in rural policy and planning* (pp. 5–18). London: Belhaven Press.

Kreitzmann, J.P., & McKnight, J.L. (1993). Asset-based community development: Mobilizing an entire community. In J.P. Kreitzmann & J.L. McKnight (Eds.), *Building communities from the inside out* (pp. 345–354). Chicago: ATCA.

Labovitz, S. (1967). Some observations on measurement and statistics. *Social Forces, 46,* 151–160.

Martin, S.R., & McCool, S.F. (1992). *Attitudes of Montana residents toward tourism development* (Research Report 23). Missoula, MT: The University of Montana, School of Forestry, Institute for Tourism and Recreation Research.

McGranahan, D.A. (1999). *Natural amenities drive rural population change* (Agricultural Economic Report No. 781). Washington, DC: U.S. Department of Agriculture, Economic Research Service, Food and Rural Economics Division.

Miles, J.C. (2000). Three national parks of the Pacific northwest. In G.E. Machlis & D.R. Field (Eds.), *National Parks and rural development* (pp. 89–109). Washington, DC: Island Press.

Mitchell, M.Y., Force, J.E., Carroll, M.S., & McLaughlin, W.J. (1993). Forest places of the heart. *Journal of Forestry, 91*, 32–37.

Neter J., & Wasserman, W. (1974). *Applied linear statistical models*. Homewood, IL: Richard D. Irwin.

Ploch, L.A. (1978). The reversal in migration patterns—Some rural development consequences. *Rural Sociology, 43*, 294–303.

Putnam, R.D. (2000). *Bowling alone: The collapse and revival of American community.* New York: Simon & Schuster.

Rudzitis, G. (1999). Amenities increasingly draw people to the rural West. *Rural Development Perspectives, 14*, 9–13.

Rudzitis, G., & Johansen, H.E. (1989). Migration into western wilderness counties: Causes and consequences. *Western Wildlands, 15*, 19–23.

Salamon, S. (2003a). *Newcomers to old towns: Suburbanization of the heartland.* Chicago, IL: University of Chicago Press.

Salamon, S. (2003b). From hometown to nontown: Rural community effects of suburbanization. *Rural Sociology, 68*, 1–24.

Shumway, J.M., & Davis, J.A. (1996). Nonmetropolitan population change in the mountain west: 1970–1995. *Rural Sociology, 61*, 513–529.

Smith, M.D., & Krannich, R.S. (1998). Tourism dependence and resident attitudes. *Annals of Tourism Research, 25*, 783–802.

Smith, M.D., & Krannich, R.S. (2000). "Culture clash" revisited: Newcomer and longer-term residents' attitudes toward land use, development, and environmental issues in rural communities in the rocky mountain west. *Rural Sociology, 65*, 396–421.

Smith, M.D., Krannich, R.S., & Hunter, L.M. (2001). Growth, decline, stability and disruption: A longitudinal analysis of social well-being in four western communities. *Rural Sociology, 66*, 425–450.

Spain, D. (1993). Been-heres versus come-heres: Negotiating conflicting community identities. *Journal of the American Planning Association, 59*, 156–171.

Steele, J., Bourke, L., Luloff, A.E., Liao, P., Theodori, G.L., & Krannich, R.S. (2001). The drop-off/pick-up method for household survey research. *Journal of the Community Development Society, 32*, 238–250.

Toney, M.B., Stinner, W.F., & Byun, Y. (1997). Social and demographic characteristics of the Mormon culture region. In J.M. Wardwell & J.H. Copp (Eds.),*Population change in the rural West: 1975–1990.* Lanham, MD: University Press of America.

Wilkinson, K.P. (1991). *The community in rural America.* Westport, CT: Greenwood.

CHAPTER 16

COMMUNITY EVALUATION AND MIGRATION INTENTIONS

The Role of Attraction and Aversion to Place on the Northern Great Plains[1]

CHRISTIANE VON REICHERT

THE CONTEXT: POPULATION DYNAMICS OF THE NORTHERN GREAT PLAINS

This paper analyzes the migration intentions of Northern Great Plains residents. Much of that region, which encompasses North Dakota, South Dakota, Nebraska, eastern Montana and eastern Wyoming, has suffered remarkable and persistent population loss; roughly 70 percent of its counties have smaller populations today than 50 years ago (U.S. Bureau of the Census, 1995, 2000a). Sustained out-migration and slight in-migration account for part of that loss. Out-migration, typically of the young, leaves behind an aging population and a region with more deaths than births and therefore natural population loss. Population decline manifests itself in numerous ways. Hospitals, schools, and main street businesses that are taken for granted elsewhere are forced to close as populations shrink (Brown, 1981). Job opportunities dwindle, and even property values drop for lack of buyers. What the future will hold for communities of this region depends partly on the mobility of their current residents: continued out-migration, if not countered by in-migration, will further diminish the population base. For these rural communities, a central research and policy question centers on the factors influencing current residents' desire to stay in their community and motivations to move away.

Settlement Patterns and Population Dynamics

The Great Plains are among the most rural regions in America, with only a handful of areas within New England, Appalachia, and the Deep South comparably rural in character. In contrast to those regions, the Great Plains are much more sparsely settled and heavily affected by population decline (see chapter

W.A. Kandel & D.L. Brown (eds.), Population Change and Rural Society, 333–356.

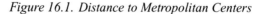

Figure 16.1. Distance to Metropolitan Centers

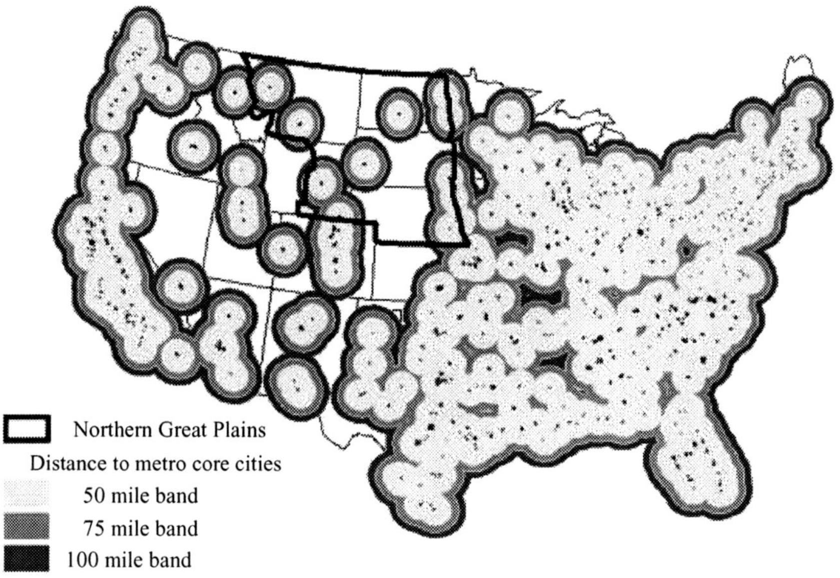

by Johnson and Rathge). The focus of this research is the Northern Great Plains, a five-state region, outlined in Figure 16.1, consisting of 267 mostly nonmetropolitan counties.

The Northern Great Plains can be seen as a homogenous sub-region distinct from the remaining Plains (Fuguitt, 1981; Fuguitt & Beale, 1978). Northern and Southern Plains have different temperature regimes and therefore fall into different agricultural zones. Additionally, the Northern Plains are geographically much more isolated, as shown in Figure 16.1 (Brunn & Ziegler, 1981). Dots on the map, which represent core cities of metropolitan areas in 1999, are surrounded by 50-mile, 75-mile, and 100-mile bands (U.S. Bureau of the Census, 1999). The map reveals that much of the Northern Great Plains lies beyond a 100-mile radius of metropolitan areas and in relative isolation from urban services and labor markets.

In the Northern Great Plains, the population dynamics are strikingly different from the rest of the United States. In the last 50 years, while the U.S. population soared by 86 percent from 151 million to 281 million, the population of the Northern Great Plains grew only 24 percent from 3.1 million to 3.9 million (U.S. Bureau of the Census, 1995, 2000a), as shown in Figure 16.2. In much of the nation, counter-urbanization in the seventies (Beale, 1975) and the "rural rebound" in the nineties (Johnson, 1999) reversed long-standing rural-urban population shifts, and this slowed metropolitan population growth. In the Northern Great Plains,

Figure 16.2. Population Change, United States the Northern Great Plains, 1950–2000

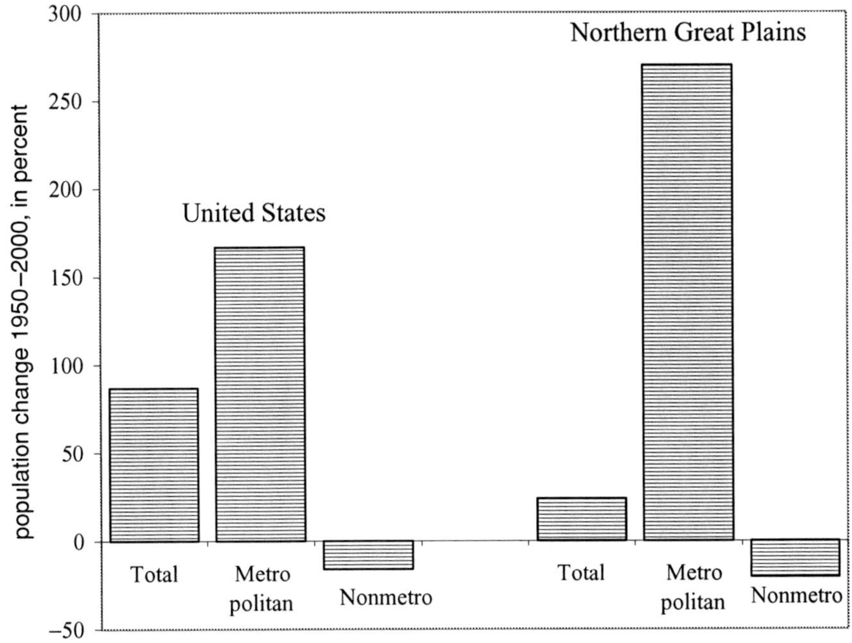

however, urbanization continues, as the population shifts from more rural to more urban areas and up the urban hierarchy (Cromartie, 1998). The population growth of existing metropolitan areas and reclassification of previous nonmetropolitan areas to metropolitan pushed metropolitan growth rates for the Northern Great Plains above 260 percent—at the same time as nonmetropolitan population declined (U.S. Bureau of the Census, 1953, 2002).

Figure 16.3 shows a breakdown of population change in counties of the Northern Great Plains according to their position on the rural-urban continuum scale (Beale, 1993). Unfortunately, no comparable continuum scale exists for 1950, the beginning of the half-century period considered. Organized by Beale code (as of 1993), the population data suggest the following: (1) in contrast to elsewhere, the location of nonmetropolitan counties adjacent to or not adjacent to metropolitan counties seems to have no long-term effect on population change in the Northern Great Plains, and (2) differences in rates of population change are pronounced and closely follow the rural-urban continuum. Metropolitan counties nearly doubled their populations, while nonmetropolitan counties with place populations above 20,000 grew at moderately high rates (between 35 and 45 percent). Smaller

Figure 16.3. Population Change of Northern Great Plains Counties by Rural-Urban Continuum Code, 1950–2000

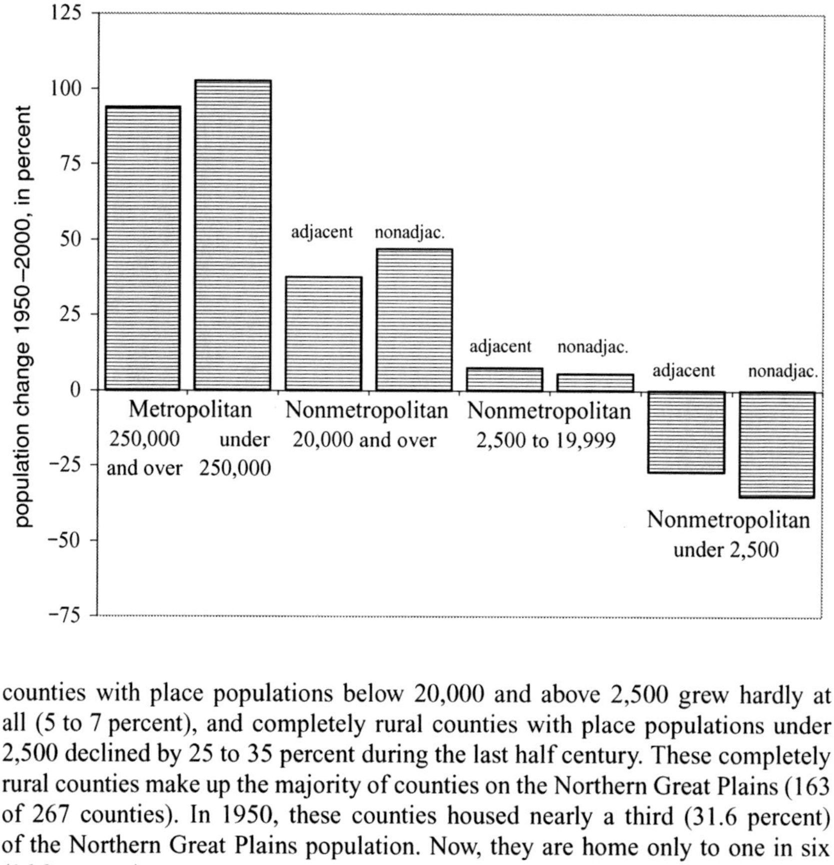

counties with place populations below 20,000 and above 2,500 grew hardly at all (5 to 7 percent), and completely rural counties with place populations under 2,500 declined by 25 to 35 percent during the last half century. These completely rural counties make up the majority of counties on the Northern Great Plains (163 of 267 counties). In 1950, these counties housed nearly a third (31.6 percent) of the Northern Great Plains population. Now, they are home only to one in six (16.9 percent).

A rural exodus has opened up a "new frontier" (Belsie, 2003), with more and more counties dropping to extremely low population densities. The most peripheral counties with the lowest populations were the most affected by out-migration and subsequent population loss (Fuguitt, 1981; Goudy, 2002; McGranahan & Beale, 2002; Rowley, 1998). The population spiral in sparsely settled, rural areas has shown a downward move.

Causes and Consequences of Rural Population Loss

The very rural parts of the Northern Great Plains strongly depend on agriculture, and many agriculturally dependent regions, especially if remote, suffer population decline (McGranahan & Beale, 2002). Agricultural technological advances allow fewer farmers to farm increasingly larger tracts of land. Given low commodity prices, those seeking a future in agriculture feel forced rather than enabled to "get big or get out." These economic forces driving farm consolidation have reduced the number of U.S. farm operations from over five million in 1950 to less than two million today, reducing, in turn, the farm population from nearly 20 percent to less than 2 percent of the U.S. population (Banker & Hoppe, 2002). The Northern Great Plains, where nearly a third (29 percent) of America's farm-dependent counties lie, are especially affected by that decline. Additionally, the region is ecologically quite vulnerable: these marginal lands suffer from periodic droughts, which challenge even the most dedicated large-scale farm and ranch operators.

A shrinking farm population reduces the demand for goods and services provided by farm communities, forcing businesses to close and employment to decline. The loss of employment plus the loss of service functions further diminishes the attractiveness of small places to the non-farm population, contributing to another round of population loss through out-migration. McGranahan and Beale (2002) recently noted that the lack of services, coupled with remoteness, has become a stronger determinant of population loss than farm dependence as such. Cromartie (1998) similarly observed that population loss in the Great Plains is no longer significantly affected by a decline in the farm population that has itself diminished greatly.

In rural areas, as elsewhere, those who move are the young and often the more educated. In growing areas, where in-migration exceeds out-migration, newcomers replenish the population pool. In areas of no growth or decline, however, selective out-migration leaves behind a sparsely populated region with an aging population and those with relatively low education levels (Rathge & Highman, 1998). An aging population is often rich in experience about the past but limited in skill and vision for an alternative future. At the same time, developing a future for sparsely populated parts of the Northern Great Plains represents a formidable challenge.

Some rural scholars view depopulation of the Plains as an opportunity for region-wide, long-term ecological-economic restoration: a region depopulated by humans would permit grassland restoration and re-population by bison (Popper & Popper, 1987, 1999). However, a large-scale return of the American bison to the "Buffalo Commons" is not a widely-embraced vision for the Plains, with opponents questioning its cost, the loss of the Plains as a food source, and the loss of rural communities as hearths of traditional culture (Froehlich, 2003). Rural life and rural values provide much sought stability in a fast-changing urban-suburban America (Horwath, 1997), and these local cultures vanish if rural communities disappear. Senator Dorgan from North Dakota, a staunch advocate of Great Plains population revival and sponsor of the *New 2003 Homestead Act*, argues that distressed rural areas, like distressed cities, are equally befitting of government support (Dorgan, n.d.). Yet, the need to preserve rural communities extends beyond equal treatment of rural and urban areas. In some parts of the Northern Plains people simply no longer have the freedom to relocate as assumed by free-market advocates who would argue against inefficient government intervention to revive depressed areas. A farmer who invested half a million dollars in his holdings cannot be considered free to move if he cannot sell his assets. Additionally, the skills of farmers are not readily transferred to other labor markets. Similarly, business owners, whether in retail or services, may find it equally hard to liquidate their assets if they wish to migrate elsewhere. Even individual homeowners could have difficulties in finding buyers for their homes. Additionally, the cost of a move might be relatively high so that people cannot easily relocate. One resident in a small eastern Montana town summed this situation up succinctly: "The ones who still live here are too poor to move."

RELEVANCE AND PURPOSE OF THIS RESEARCH

One of the challenges facing slow-growing or declining regions is population retention or "non-migration." It is therefore important to understand the factors influencing population retention. Demographic research based on aggregate data (Cromartie, 1998; Goudy, 2002; Rathge & Highman, 1998) tells an important part of the story of population change by pointing out, for instance, the areas most affected by population loss. The research presented below is survey-based, and findings derived from these micro-level data usefully complement findings from aggregate data. Survey data allow us to link attitudes (why), regional attributes (where), and individual attributes (who) when analyzing population change. This research uses attitudinal variables from survey data to assess the extent to which personal evaluations of community affect the propensity to out-migrate. Additionally, the effect of regional characteristics on migration intentions will be considered, as regions with different economic characteristics and of different population size show different rates of population change. Individual migration behavior further depends on individual socio-demographic attributes that must be controlled for as well.

The link, in particular, between people's evaluation of their community—what they like or dislike—and their inclination to stay may point toward policy variables and opportunities to enhance what makes rural areas attractive. Policy makers who wish to strengthen rural communities and stem population loss should therefore be cognizant of the forces underlying population retention and population loss.

FRAMEWORK AND RATIONALE FOR STUDYING MIGRATION INTENTIONS

From Aggregate to Micro Approaches to Studying Migration

Aggregate migration research has a long tradition of focusing on regional attributes, such as rural-urban characteristics or economic factors (Lowry, 1966; Ravenstein, 1885, 1889). Individual characteristics of the population, especially age, have been taken into account as well (Bogue, 1969). Rossi (1955), a pioneer of mobility studies at the micro level, discovered through a survey of Philadelphia households that dissatisfaction, a psychological component, significantly influenced mobility. His findings formed the basis of the stress-awareness or stress-threshold approach to mobility decisions (Speare et al., 1974; Wolpert, 1965).

The stress-threshold approach suggests that the decision to stay or move occurs in stages. The first stage, mainly of interest for this research, deals with the decision to consider a move. Stage 2 marks the search for alternative destinations, and stage 3 deals with choices among alternative destinations. While many empirical studies examine links between fertility intentions and actual fertility, only several studies examine the relationship between migration intentions and actual migration (Bach & Smith, 1977; Lu, 1999; Stinner et al., 1992; Waldorf, 1995). These studies basically look at the relationship between stages 1 and 3 of the stress-threshold model. Although not all households with migration intentions actually migrate, the behavior corresponds significantly enough with intentions that the latter serve as reasonably accurate predictors of mobility. Households consider a move (stage 1) if they are dissatisfied with where they are. Dissatisfaction depends on how individuals or households evaluate their current neighborhood or community and results from the sentiment that needs and preferences remain unmet at the current locale (Rossi, 1955; Speare et al., 1974). Considering a move is one possible response to dissatisfaction: the dissatisfied either make adjustments in place or search for destinations that better suit their needs (Stinner et al., 1992).

Variables Affecting Migration Decisions

Most studies of migration decisions include *socio-demographic* attributes. Therefore, a good deal is already known about the mobility behavior of different socio-demographic groups. Age, more than any other individual trait, is linked to mobility, with young adults exhibiting the highest mobility rates, and the propensity to migrate declining over the life span. Prior mobility is also known to affect future mobility, with greater recency serving as a stronger predictor of future mobility. A useful indicator of past mobility and the recency of mobility is a person's length of residence.

Regional characteristics also influence migration. As noted above, community growth varies by size. Differences exist, however, between trends at the national level and trends in the Northern Great Plains. At the national level, people frequently express preferences for nonmetropolitan locales. Medium-sized cities, especially if adjacent to metro areas, have proven to be popular destinations (DeJong, 1977; Fuguitt & Brown, 1990; Morgan, 1978). In contrast, larger communities in the Northern Great Plains have gained population, while smaller communities have suffered population decline (see Figure 16.3). The economic structure of communities tends to affect migration as well, with farm-dependent communities experiencing especially high out-migration and little in-migration.

The question is whether past patterns of regional population change are reflected in current migration intentions and possibly future migration.

Since Rossi (1955), research about migration decisions has also examined the effect of *psychological components* on mobility. Scholars have used measures of attachment to community (Fernandez & Dillman, 1979), community involvement (Stinner, 1992), and social bonds (Bach & Smith, 1977). These works have drawn on the community attachment research of Kasarda and Janowitz (1974) who tested the competing linear and systemic models (see also Goudy, 1990; Sampson, 1988; Stinner et al., 1990). The linear model of community attachment states that regional attributes, mainly community size and density, affect community attachment, with persons in more urban settings being less attached than persons in smaller, rural communities. The systemic model, on the other hand, attributes community attachment to socio-demographic attributes, in particular to a person's social position. Community attachment is also expected to influence mobility, with persons strongly attached to their community less inclined to move. However, Janowitz argued earlier that in a society of "limited liability" mobility may be little reduced by community attachment (Janowitz, 1951). The relationship between community attachment and mobility is therefore not entirely clear.

A Model of Migration Intentions

The process of migration decision-making is clearly multi-dimensional. The research presented here explores the extent to which regional characteristics, such as community size and economic structure, affect migration intentions, and it also takes into account effects of selected socio-demographic characteristics such as age and length of residence. The main focus of this study is the psychological dimension, namely community evaluation, and its effect on migration intentions. Figure 16.4 is a visual representation of expected linkages between community evaluation, regional and individual attributes, and migration intentions, a conceptual outline underlying the statistical model tested below.

Information about community evaluation comes from a survey of Northern Great Plains residents. Several open-ended questions were designed to capture both emotional dimensions (likes/dislikes) and rational dimensions (reasons for staying or leaving) of community evaluation. The questions were further phrased to obtain positive evaluation (what was liked most, and reasons for staying) and negative impressions (what was disliked most, and reasons for leaving). Positive evaluations reflect *attraction to place*, while negative evaluations represent *aversion*. Responses thereby serve as diagnostic tools with which to identify the shortcomings and strengths of areas as seen by residents of the Northern Great Plains. Shortcomings closely linked to migration intentions are of particular interest, especially if those shortcomings can be addressed by policies. Similarly, regional strengths closely linked to a desire to stay are important as well. Both help in

Figure 16.4. Model of Migration Intentions

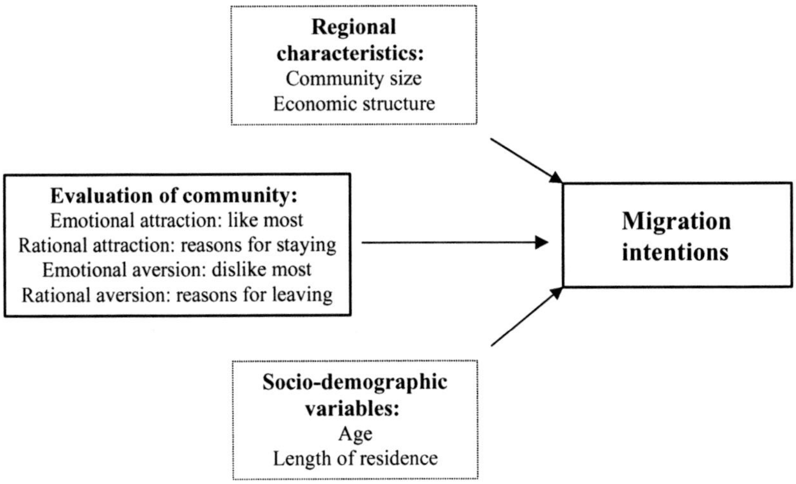

identifying opportunities for making and keeping the Northern Plains attractive to the current residents.

The following methods section describes the data and relevant variables. The subsequent results section shows (1) how migration intentions vary with socio-demographic and regional characteristics; (2) the association between community evaluation and migration intentions; and (3) the results of the model of migration intentions shown in Figure 16.4. The model goes beyond bivariate relationships and simultaneously takes into account how community evaluation, regional characteristics, and individual traits relate to migration intentions.

METHODOLOGY

The Northern Plains Survey

In spring and summer of 2001, the Bureau of Business and Economic Research (BBER) at The University of Montana contacted 2,931 randomly selected households of the Northern Great Plains to participate in a telephone questionnaire. The Northern Great Plains region as defined here consists of 267 mostly nonmetropolitan counties in North Dakota, South Dakota, Nebraska, and the eastern parts of Montana and Wyoming. This region is similar to Northern Great Plains subregion used by Fuguitt and Beale (1978) and the North section of the Great Plains used by Fuguitt (1981). From each state, there are roughly 400 responses, for a total of 2036 observations and a response rate of 69.5 percent.

The Dependent Variable: Migration Intentions

Information about migration intentions comes from the question "Do you expect to live in your community in five years?" Respondents identified their position on an ordinal or Likert scale ranging from "likely leave" to "50/50" to "likely stay" (Table 16.1). Survey responses show that in the foreseeable future, 12 percent will likely leave, and nearly 10 percent are uncertain about leaving or staying. Nearly four of five respondents (78.5 percent) expect to stay in their current community. This five-year rate of "non-migration intentions" is roughly equal to the national five-year rate of "non-migration" (U.S. Bureau of the Census, 2000b). This lends support to the argument that migration intentions reasonably well reflect actual migration behavior. Similarities between national non-migration rates and the regional rates obtained here further suggest that attachment to place, approximated by intentions to stay, is no weaker in the Northern Great Plains than in the nation at large. It also implies that relatively low rates of in-migration contribute to low or negative population growth as much as high rates of out-migration.

Independent Variables

Individual and Regional Characteristics

In addition to migration intentions, Table 16.1 shows individual characteristics considered (namely age and length of residence), their coding schemes, and their frequency distributions. Table 16.1 also shows regional characteristics, which capture population size and economic structure. To include the effect of a county's population size, I use the rural-urban continuum code (Beale, 1993) which is modified by combining nonmetro counties adjacent to and not adjacent to metropolitan areas due to no effect of adjacency on Northern Great Plains population change (see Figure 16.3). To capture county economic structure, I use the ERS typology of economic dependence of nonmetropolitan counties (Economic Research Service, 1995). For a minor modification, I merged responses from the small number of manufacturing counties with those from non-specialized counties to form the category "other nonmetropolitan."

Community Evaluation

Central to this study is the relationship between how people evaluate their community and how that influences their intention to move away or stay. Information about community evaluation comes from open-ended questions phrased to capture both emotional and rational dimensions in a positive and negative

Table 16.1. Coding Schemes of Variables and Frequency Distributions of Survey Responses

	Variable Name	Category/Coding Scheme	Frequency in Percent
Dependent Variable	Migration Intentions	all responses	100.0
		likely leave	12.0
		50/50	9.5
		likely stay	78.5
Independent Variables: Socio-Demographic	Age	under 35 years	30.9
		35 to 49 years	30.8
		50 to 64 years	19.7
		65 years or older	18.7
	Length of Residence	0–6 years	26.8
		7–20 years	24.3
		20s+ years	26.5
		never moved	22.3
Independent Variables: Regional	Rural-Urban Continuum[a]	metropolitan	42.6
		20,000 and more	12.6
		2,500 to 19,999	26.6
		under 2,500	18.3
	Economic Dependence[b]	metropolitan	42.6
		farm dependent	22.6
		government dependent	9.9
		mining dependent	3.1
		service dependent	14.2
		other nonmetropolitan	7.6

[a] The rural-urban continuum code is modified as follows: The Nebraska portion of the relatively large Omaha MSA (approximate population of 630,000) is combined with twelve smaller metropolitan areas with populations below 250,000. Responses from nonmetropolitan counties adjacent and non-adjacent to metropolitan areas are combined.

[b] The ERS nonmetropolitan county typology of economic dependence is modified as follows: Responses from few manufacturing-dependent counties (1.2 percent of responses) are grouped with non-specialized nonmetropolitan counties (6.4 percent) to form the category "other nonmetropolitan."

way (attraction versus aversion). To identify how people of the Northern Plains evaluate their community, several thousand survey responses were reviewed, and related responses were grouped into a limited number of categories, shown in Table 16.2. The nominal data obtained from open-ended responses are quite different from commonly used ordinal data of community satisfaction or

Table 16.2. Community Evaluation: Categories[a] and Frequency Distributions

	Emotional Community Evaluation		Frequency in Percent	Rational Community Evaluation		Frequency in Percent
+ Attraction +	What do you like most about living here?	nice place to live	32.0	What is the primary reason for staying here?	nice place to live	29.9
		rural character	15.7		family	26.5
		natural amenities	14.9		employment	24.5
		schools and services	13.2		schools and services	7.1
		family	9.0		rural character	4.0
		no disamenities	4.1		natural amenities	2.2
		economic opportunities	2.9		low cost living, housing	2.1
		low cost of living	0.5		no disamenities	1.2
		like nothing, other	7.7		other	2.5
− Aversion −	What do you dislike most about living here?	dislike nothing	20.1	What is the primary reason for leaving from here?[b]	lack of jobs, poor pay	40.2
		adverse natural condition	18.6		services (educ, medic, etc)	14.6
		infrastructure & services	17.5		family, return move	12.2
		adverse social climate	15.3		change, get away	11.0
		other disamenities	13.4		undesirable climate	8.0
		economic opportunities	6.7		retirement	5.8
		lack of contact	2.9		rural character, amenities	3.2
		dislike everything, other	5.5		other	5.1

[a]Evaluation categories derived from open-ended survey responses.
[b]Asked of those who thought about leaving.

dissatisfaction levels, or from closed questions with pre-defined options. In contrast to ordinal levels of community satisfaction or dissatisfaction, the information used here point toward the *source or nature* of place satisfaction or dissatisfaction. As opposed to closed questions with pre-defined options, open-ended questions reduce the possibility of inducing response biases (Sudman & Bradburn, 1982; Tourangeau & Raskinski, 2000), as survey respondents answer spontaneously and choose their own words. The categories and their frequencies are shown in the Table 16.2.

The majority (two thirds) of Northern Plains residents are emotionally attracted by place attributes: they like their community for being a nice place in which to live, for its rural character, for its natural amenities, and for the absence of disamenities. Respondents also mention schools and services, and family ties. While emotional attraction is decidedly one-sided in favor of place attributes, rational attraction (or reasons for staying) falls into one of three categories: respondents view their community as a nice place in which to live, they have employment, or family lives nearby. Emotional aversion is more multi-faceted than the other dimensions of community evaluation: while 20 percent of respondents dislike nothing, others dislike adverse natural conditions (mainly climate) and the lack of infrastructure and services.

A variety of responses such as "unfriendly people," "closed minds," "gossip," "local politics," and "favoritism" form the category "adverse social climate." Surprisingly, quite a few expressed their disenchantment with the social climate. This is contrary to how Great Plains people either see themselves or are viewed by others. The responses, shared in telephone interviews with a person outside the community and therefore in a somewhat anonymous setting, might be indicative of the stresses caused by economic change and population decline. In communities under such pressures, social and community relations may be put to a test, and the social fabric of Northern Plains communities may become stressed, as observed by Harder (2001) for Canadian communities of the Great Plains.

For the 50 percent of respondents who considered leaving, rational aversion (or reasons for leaving) is based on lack of employment. Dissatisfaction with services, a return move—often to be closer to family—or simply the desire to change lifestyles are also cited as reasons for leaving.

The following section shows how migration intentions vary by socio-demographic and regional characteristics, and how migration intentions depend on community evaluation. Results of the model of migration intentions, displayed in Figure 16.4 above, are discussed as well.

DETERMINANTS OF MIGRATION INTENTIONS

Socio-Demographic and Regional Variation in Migration Intentions

Figure 16.5 shows how migration intentions vary with socio-demographic attributes of individuals as well as characteristics of the regions. For age groups,

Figure 16.5. Migration Intentions by Socio-Demographic and Regional Characteristics

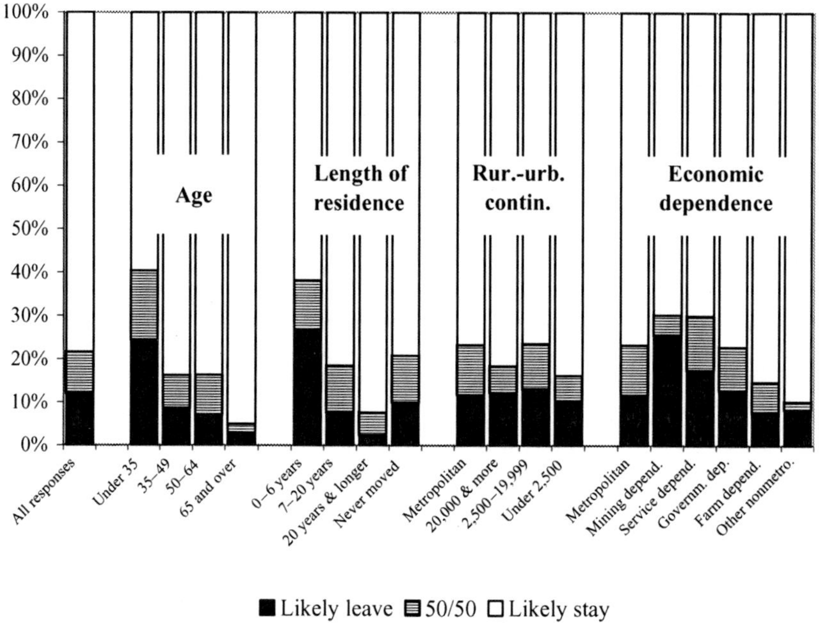

survey responses very much correspond to national data and confirm expectations: young adults under 35 are nearly twice as intent on leaving as the general population, while seniors are much less inclined to leave. Length of residence also influences mobility in anticipated ways: recent arrivals, who moved to their community within the last six years, express intentions to leave nearly twice as much as medium-term residents (7 to 20 years) or those who never moved. Long-term residents, who spent 20 or more years of their lives in their community, expect to be the least likely to leave it. Long-term residents typically possess more extensive social networks, while short-term residents, especially if chronic movers, have fewer local ties.

While migration intentions strongly depend on individual attributes, a county's population size has relatively little effect on migration intentions. Residents from metropolitan areas and from smaller urban counties (2,500–19,999) are somewhat less inclined to stay than those from the larger nonmetropolitan counties (20,000 and more) or from completely rural areas with place populations under 2,500. The higher expected mobility in metropolitan areas and the lower expected mobility in completely rural areas are partly explained by age differences—with relatively young populations in metropolitan areas and relatively old populations in completely rural areas. The somewhat stronger desire to leave the smaller urban counties could be a concern: towns between 2,500 and 20,000 form an important part of the Northern Plains urban system, and currently 25 percent of the Northern Great Plains population lives in these areas—down from 30 percent some 50 years ago. A continued population exodus from these towns would further weaken the settlement structure of the region.

Counties with different economic structures show much greater differences in migration intentions than counties of different population size but smaller differences than socio-demographic groups. Residents of mining-dependent counties express the highest inclinations to move. This is not surprising given the more migratory labor force in the mining sector and the cyclical swing of mining-dependent regions. For the Northern Plains region overall, the prospect of out-migration from the few mining-dependent counties (3.1 percent of survey responses) is not as relevant as the migration intentions of the much larger populations from service- and farm-dependent counties, with 14.2 and 22.6 percent of responses, respectively. Residents of service-dependent counties state lower intentions to stay, while the current population of farm-dependent counties is more inclined to stay. This suggests that smaller trade centers may continue to suffer from out-migration. For farm-dependent counties, which have been long plagued by out-migration, higher inclinations to stay suggest that out-migration may have reached bottom.

Effects of Community Evaluation[2] on Migration Intentions

Table 16.2 shows that Northern Plains residents assign great importance to place attributes, particularly for *emotional attraction*: people value their community for being a nice place in which to live, for its rural character, and for nearby natural amenities. Jobs and services, mainly education, and family ties also play a role. Figure 16.6, however, reveals that differences in what people like most do not translate into different intentions to move: 10 to 13 percent of respondents expect to leave, while 70 to 80 percent expect to stay. Migration intentions seem to be practically independent of differences in emotional attraction.

In contrast to emotional attraction, *rational attraction* affects migration intentions in significant ways. Differences in reasons for staying have strong differential effects on people's desire to leave or stay. Those attracted by place attributes express a much greater propensity to stay (nearly 90 percent) than those attracted by employment and infrastructure or by personal ties. The latter seem less inclined to stay (72 percent) and more inclined to leave or to be uncertain about leaving or staying.

Migration intentions are also influenced by *emotional aversion*. What people dislike significantly predisposes them to moving or staying. As expected, people who dislike nothing and like everything about their community are the most inclined to stay (90 percent), and those who dislike place attributes are nearly

Figure 16.6. Migration Intentions by Community Evaluation

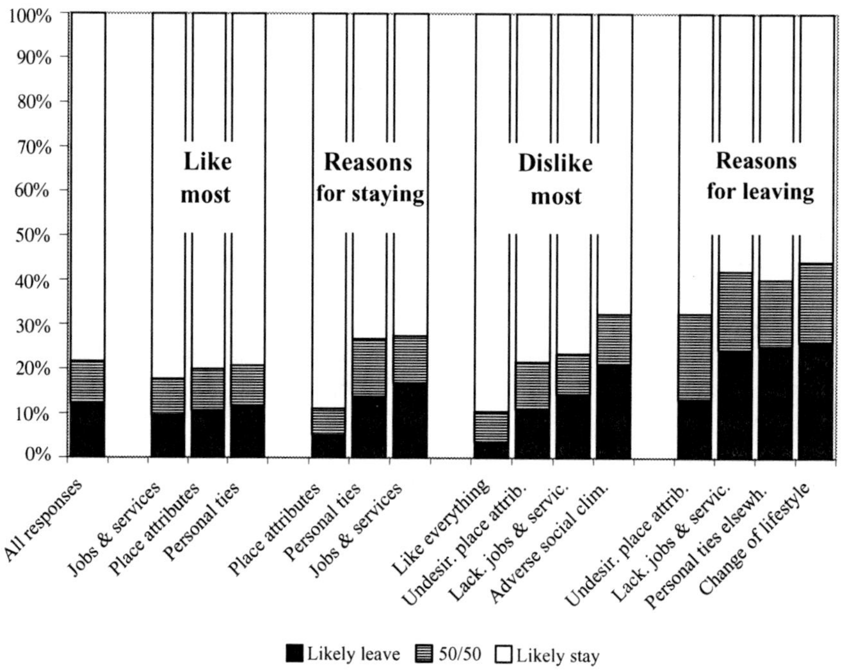

equally intent on staying as people who wish for better employment and services (77 percent). Those dissatisfied with the social environment have the highest intentions of leaving (20 percent) and the lowest intentions of staying (69 percent). Surprisingly, dissatisfaction with social relations so strongly raises inclinations to leave. Social alienation appears to be an important determinant of out-migration.

Respondents who at some time had thought about leaving their community were asked about the *primary reason for a move* (rational aversion). This group, roughly half of all respondents, has nearly twice the intention to leave as that of the entire sample population. Additionally, this group expresses more uncertainty about leaving or staying. Consequently, their stated propensity to stay is rather low (60 percent). Three broad categories—employment and services, personal ties, and change of lifestyle—have nearly equally strong effects on intentions to stay (60 percent or slightly less) or leave (roughly 25 percent). Dissatisfaction with place attributes, however, has a lesser effect on stated propensities to leave (10 percent).

The bivariate relationships examined suggest that associations between socio-demographic attributes, regional characteristics, and community evaluation on the one hand and migration intentions on the other are quite unequal. Differences in age, length of residence, economic structure and community evaluation, both rational attraction and emotional aversion, translate into differences in migration intentions. Only those variables are included in the following model explaining migration intentions, while remaining variables (population size, emotional attraction, and rational aversion) are left out. Fewer variables offer the advantage of increased cell frequencies, and higher cell frequencies provide for more reliable parameter estimates.

Logistic Regression of Migration Intentions

The model in Figure 16.4 sets out to assess the effect of community evaluation on migration intentions while simultaneously taking individual characteristics and regional attributes into account. Migration intention, the phenomenon to be explained, ranges from "likely leave" to "uncertain" to "likely stay." For such ordinal dependent variables, testing procedures for continuous measurements such as least squares regression are inappropriate. The procedure of choice is ordinal logistic regression, a procedure which essentially converts ordered choices into probabilities using a logistic function. Widely accepted is the cumulative or proportional odds specification of the model (Agresti, 1984; McCullagh & Nelder, 1989). For this model with three choices (j = 1 likely leave, j = 2 uncertain, j = 3 likely stay), there are two cumulative logistic regression equations of choice probabilities (prob) with two different intercept terms:

$$prob\,(j \leq 1) = prob\,(likely\ leave) = \frac{e^{a_1 - bx}}{1 + e^{a_1 - bx}} \qquad (16.1)$$

and

$$prob\,(j \leq 2) = prob\,(likely\ leave\ or\ uncertain) = \frac{e^{a_2 - bx}}{1 + e^{a_2 - bx}} \qquad (16.2)$$

An equation for the third choice (likely stay) is redundant as probabilities for all choices add up to one. Consequently, the probability for the third and last choice can be derived from probabilities for the previous (second and first) choices:

$$prob\,(j = 3) = 1 - prob\,(j \leq 2) = 1 - \frac{e^{a_2 - bx}}{1 + e^{a_2 - bx}} \qquad (16.3a)$$

or

$$prob\,(likely\ stay) = 1 - prob\,(likely\ leave\ or\ uncertain)$$
$$= 1 - \frac{e^{a_2 - bx}}{1 + e^{a_2 - bx}} \qquad (16.3b)$$

Table 16.3 shows model results which capture the simultaneous effects of individual characteristics, regional attributes, and community evaluation on migration intentions. The likelihood of staying is chosen as the reference category so that the first intercept term is an estimate of likely leaving, while the second intercept term is a cumulative estimate of likely leaving and uncertainty about leaving. Alternatively, the likelihood of leaving could be the reference category, in which case the positions of first and second intercept estimate would be reversed as well as the signs of all parameter estimates.

Table 16.3 shows parameter estimates, standard error, and significance levels, as well as summary information pertaining to the number of observations and model Chi squares. The intercept estimates are large and negative because intentions to leave or uncertainty about leaving are small when compared to intentions to stay.

Parameter estimates for independent variables show how migration intentions for a certain category compare to the last or reference category of the corresponding variable. For individual characteristics, the oldest age group and those without past migration experience are points of reference. For economic dependence of nonmetropolitan areas, metropolitan areas are the reference category. For the variables of community evaluation, place-related categories serve as the reference category.

Individual differences in both age and length of residence strongly affect migration intentions. Young adults are much less inclined to stay and more inclined to leave than older population groups, while those who moved recently are also much less likely to stay and more likely to leave again than those who never moved. Long-term residents who moved to their community 20 or more years ago are noticeably more inclined to stay than those who never moved.

Economic dependence, a regional attribute, exerts much more moderate effects on migration intentions than individual traits. When compared to metropolitan areas, the residents of government-dependent counties have similar inclinations to stay or move, as shown by a parameter estimate close to zero. Residents of mining-dependent communities, in contrast, have lower propensities to stay than metro residents. Residents of service-dependent counties are also slightly less inclined to stay than residents of metropolitan areas, but that difference is not significant. Residents of farm-dependent counties are marginally more inclined to stay than those of metropolitan counties, even when taking other factors into account.

The answer to the central question of this research—"Does community evaluation affect migration intentions?"—is *YES*. Rational attraction and emotional aversion significantly affect migration intentions. For *rational attraction*, a favorable evaluation of place attributes is more effective in holding people in place than other reasons. Those who stay for jobs and services, such as educational or medical services, are less inclined to stay than those who value their community and region for place qualities. Personal ties have very similar effects on migration intentions as employment and infrastructure. People who stay mainly for personal ties express greater inclinations to leave than those who value their community for place characteristics. This means that both jobs and family have a hold on people. However, that hold is not as strong as attractiveness of place.

Table 16.3. Ordinal Logistic Regression Coefficients of Migration Intentions

Variable	Categories	Estimate	Standard Error	Significance
Intercept	likely leave	−3.756	.405	.000
	likely leave or uncertain	−2.924	.398	.000
	likely stay (reference category)			
Age	under 35	−1.730	.347	.000
	35 to 64 years[a]	−.8475	.338	.012
	65 and over (reference category)			
Length of Residence	0–6 years	−.522	.202	.010
	7–20 years	.184	.226	.417
	more than 20 years	.666	.275	.015
	never moved (reference category)			
ERS Typology	mining dependent	−.665	.378	.078
	service dependent	−.352	.215	.102
	government dependent	−.068	.251	.786
	farm dependent	.388	.220	.078
	other nonmetropolitan	.729	.378	.054
	metropolitan (reference category)			
Reasons for Staying	jobs and services	−.730	.193	.000
	personal ties	−.730	.200	.000
	desirable place attributes (reference category)			
Dislike Most	like everything/dislike nothing	.460	.254	.071
	jobs and services	.015	.194	.938
	adverse social climate	−.540	.201	.007
	undesirable place attributes (reference category)			
N = 2036	Model Chi Squares (15 df)	225.6		.000

[a] Age groups 35–49 and 50–64 have similar migration intentions and are combined.

For *emotional aversion*, unfavorable views of place attributes and dissatisfaction with employment opportunities and service access are similar in their effects on migration intentions: this is shown by a small and insignificant parameter estimate for employment and services. Disenchantment with the social environment, however, decreases the expressed likelihood of staying a good deal: the parameter estimate is negative and highly significant. Disillusionment with the social climate is therefore a stronger repellent than dissatisfaction with the harsh, natural climate, which outsiders so often see as a main drawback of the region.

CONCLUSIONS

This research provides a micro-level insight into the complexities of community evaluation and migration intentions, and through it, community evaluation and attachment to place. It contains the following policy insights for community leaders and decision-makers:

- Nurturing and protecting the character of place is extremely important in retaining the population. Place attributes are clearly valued by Northern Great Plains residents, as these attributes dominate emotional community attraction.
- Economic development efforts are badly needed. Improved employment opportunities are critically important to people on the Northern Plains. People there tend to rate employment opportunities in the region as very poor, and better employment prospects elsewhere are closely linked to the intention to leave. However, development plans need to take carefully into account their effects on place character. Development efforts that fundamentally alter place character threaten to change what residents consider the biggest asset of the region.
- Access to services, whether education, medical, shopping or entertainment, is important. Peripheral, smaller communities are clearly disadvantaged by their geography and by difficulties in realizing economies of scale in smaller towns. New ways of providing services, possibly internet-based, need to be explored, and cooperative efforts between communities and counties may hold promise. Existing businesses may benefit from becoming more entrepreneurial to combat the appeal of larger metropolitan service centers. Local leaders also need to show strong commitment to retaining existing services.
- While dissatisfaction with the social environment is beyond the control of community and political leaders, they can take strides to improve social relations by fostering an atmosphere of respect, tolerance, neighborliness, and political fairness. These are exactly the kinds of concerns voiced by residents of the Northern Great Plains.
- More efforts need to be made to integrate young people and newcomers into the social fabric of Northern Great Plains communities.

While young people and recent migrants are generally known for their inclination to leave, members of these groups are at the same time over-represented among the socially alienated. Decision makers, especially at the local level, need to develop agendas inclusive of young adults and newcomers. The voices of these population groups need to be heard, and this in turn may foster more social involvement and community attachment of these groups.

This study of community evaluation and migration intentions also sheds light onto what could cause in- or out-migration. This means that stemming out-migration or fostering in-migration can support the same goal of stabilizing and increasing a region's population. Some efforts underway to attract in-migrants to declining areas include the *New Iowans* program (University of Northern Iowa, 2004) or the *2003 New Homestead Act* (Dorgan, 2003). These initiatives use different strategies in order to appeal to and attract population groups. The program in Iowa, a state adjacent to the Northern Great Plains, is designed to integrate immigrants, including Latinos, Asians, and Africans, by providing information about locally available resources, such as housing, job training and language instruction. The *2003 New Homestead Act* provides economic incentives geared toward younger, educated, and entrepreneurial persons to settle or conduct business for at least five years in counties that lost 10 percent or more of their population since 1980. Recent college graduates will receive repayment of 50 percent of their student loans up to $10,000 if they move to and stay at least five years in out-migration counties. These are efforts to counter population loss through out-migration by encouraging and fostering job growth and in-migration. This research suggests that it will take jobs and services, as well as social integration and attraction to place for recent arrivals to become permanent residents.

ENDNOTES

1. Funding for the survey used in this research was provided through a federal appropriation secured by Senator Byron Dorgan of North Dakota as part of the Great Plains Population Symposium Project. The survey was designed in cooperation with James T. Sylvester and John Baldridge and conducted by the Bureau of Business and Economic Research at the University of Montana.
2. Related categories of community evaluation are aggregated for better conceptualization and ease of interpretation. The residual categories of community evaluation 'other' are not considered further.

REFERENCES

Agresti, A. (1984). *Analysis of ordinal categorical data*. New York: Wiley.

Bach, R.L., & Smith, J. (1977). Community satisfaction, expectations of moving, and migration. *Demography, 14*(2), 147–167.

Banker, D., & Hoppe, B. (2002). *Farm structure: Number and size of farms*. Retrieved June 5, 2003, from U.S. Department of Agriculture, Economic Research Service Web site, http://www.ers.usda.gov/Briefing/FarmStructure/Gallery/numberoffarms.htm

Beale, C.L. (1975). *The revival of population growth in nonmetropolitan America* (ERS Report No. 605). Washington, DC: U.S. Department of Agriculture, Economic Research Service.

Beale, C.L. (1993). *Rural-urban continuum codes*. Retrieved June 16, 2003, from U.S. Department of Agriculture, Economic Research Service Web site, http://www.ers.usda.gov/Briefing/Rurality/RuralurbCon/code93.txt

Belsie, L. (2003, February 11). The dwindling heartland: America's new frontier. *Christian Science Monitor*, pp. 1, 10–11.

Bogue, D.J. (1969). *Principles of demography*. New York: Wiley.

Brown, D.L. (1981). Potential impacts of changing population size and composition of the Plains. In M.P. Lawson & M.E. Baker (Eds.), *The Great Plains. Perspectives and prospects* (pp. 35–51). Lincoln, NE: University of Nebraska Press.

Brunn, S.D., & Ziegler, D.J. (1981). Human settlements in sparsely populated areas: A conceptual overview, with special reference to the U.S. In R.E. Lonsdale & J.H. Holmes (Eds.), *Settlement systems in sparsely populated regions. The United States and Australia* (pp. 14–52). New York: Pergamon.

Cromartie, J.B. (1998). Net migration in the Great Plains increasingly linked to natural amenities and suburbanization. *Rural Development Perspectives, 13*(1), 27–34. Retrieved June 6, 2003, from U.S. Department of Agriculture, Economic Research Service Web site, http://www.ers.usda.gov/publications/rdp/rdp298/rdp298e.pdf

DeJong, G.F. (1977). Residential preferences and migration. *Demography, 14*, 169–178.

Dorgan, B.L. (2003). *Summary of S. 602*. Retrieved March 10, 2004, from http://dorgan.senate.gov/legislation/homestead/summary.cfm

Dorgan, B.L. (n.d.). *The case for a new homestead act*. Retrieved March 10, 2004, from http://dorgan.senate.gov/legislation/homestead/case.cfm

Economic Research Service, U.S. Department of Agriculture. (1995). *1989 ERS county typology codes*. Retrieved June 5, 2003, from http://www.ers.usda.gov/Briefing/Rurality/Typology/Data/TYP89.TXT

Fernandez, R.R., & Dillman, D.A. (1979). The influence of community attachment on geographic mobility. *Rural Sociology, 44*(2), 345–360.

Froehlich, P. (2003). Should the Great Plains be transformed into a vast ecological preserve?– No! *A New Paradigm, 3*(3), 32.

Fuguitt, G.V. (1981). Population trends in sparsely settled areas of the United States: The case of the Great Plains. In R.E. Lonsdale & J.H. Holmes (Eds.), *Settlement systems in sparsely populated regions. The United States and Australia* (pp. 125–147). New York: Pergamon.

Fuguitt, G.V., & Beale, C.L. (1978). Population trends of nonmetropolitan cities and villages in subregions of the United States. *Demography, 15*(4), 605–620.

Fuguitt, G.V., & Brown, D.L. (1990). Residential preferences and population redistribution 1972–1988. *Demography, 27*(4), 589–600.

Goudy, W. (2002). Population change in the Midwest. Nonmetro population growth lags metro increase. *Rural America, 17*(2), 21–29. Retrieved June 6, 2003, from http://www.ers.usda.gov/publications/ruralamerica/ra172/ra172d.pdf

Goudy, W.J. (1990). Community attachment in a rural region. *Rural Sociology, 55*(2), 178–198.

Harder, C. (2001). Overcoming cultural and spiritual obstacles to rural revitalization. In R. Epp & D. Whitson (Eds.), *Writing off the rural west. Globalization, governments, and the transformation of rural communities* (pp. 223–246). Edmonton: University of Alberta Press and Parkland Institute.

Howarth, W. (1997). The value of rural life in American culture. *Rural Development Perspectives, 12*(1), 5–10.

Janowitz, M. (1951). *The community press in an urban setting*. Chicago: University of Chicago Press.

Johnson, K.M. (1999). The rural rebound. *Reports on America, 1*(3), 1–21. Retrieved June 6, 2003, from http://www.prb.org/Content/NavigationMenu/PRB/AboutPRB/Reports on America/ReportonAmericaRuralRebound.pdf

Kasarda, J.D., & Janowitz, M. (1974). Community attachment in mass society. *American Sociological Review, 39*(3), 328–339.

Lowry, I.S. (1966). *Migration and metropolitan growth: Two analytical models*. San Francisco: Chandler.

Lu, M. (1999). Do people move when they say they will? Inconsistencies in individual migration behavior. *Population and Environment, 20*(5), 467–488.

McCullagh, P., & Nelder, J.A. (1989). *Generalized linear models* (2nd ed.). New York: Chapman and Hall.

McGranahan, D.A., & Beale, C.L. (2002). Understanding rural population loss. *Rural America, 17*(4), 2–11. Retrieved June 20, 2003, from http://www.ers.usda.gov/publications/ruralamerica/ra174/ra174a.pdf

Morgan, D.J. (1978). *Patterns of population distribution. A residential preference model and its dynamic*. Chicago: University of Chicago, Department of Geography.

Popper, D.E., & Popper, F.J. (1987). The Great Plains: From dust to dust. *Planning, 53*(12), 12–18.

Popper, D.E., & Popper, F.J. (1999). The buffalo commons: Metaphor as method. *Geographical Review, 89*(4), 491–510.

Rathge, R., & Highman, P. (1998). Population change in the Great Plains. A history of prolonged decline. *Rural Development Perspectives, 13*(1), 19–26.

Ravenstein, E.G. (1885). The laws of migration. *Journal of the Royal Statistical Society, 48*, 167–227.

Ravenstein, E.G. (1889). The laws of migration. Second paper. *Journal of the Royal Statistical Society, 52*, 241–301.

Rossi, P.H. (1955). *Why families move: A study in the social psychology of urban residential mobility*. Glencoe, IL: Free Press.

Rowley, T.D. (1998). Sustaining the Great Plains. *Rural Development Perspectives, 13*(1), 2–6. Retrieved June 20, 2003, from http://www.ers.usda.gov/publications/rdp/rdp298/rdp298b.pdf

Sampson, R.J. (1988). Local friendship ties and community attachment in mass society. *American Sociological Review, 53*(5), 766–779.

Speare, A., Goldstein, S., & Frey, W.H. (1974). A theory of geographic mobility. In Speare, Goldstein & Frey (Eds.), *Residential mobility, migration and metropolitan change* (pp. 163–205). Cambridge, MA: Ballinger.

Stinner, W.F., Tinnakul, N., Kan, S., & Toney, M.B. (1992). Community attachment and migration decision making in nonmetropolitan settings. In P. C. Jobes, W.F. Stinner, & J.M. Wardwell (Eds.), *Community, society and migration. Noneconomic migration in America* (pp. 47–84). Lanham, MD: University Press of America.

Stinner, W.F., VanLoon, M., Chung, S.-W., & Byun, Y. (1990). Community size, individual position, and community attachment. *Rural Sociology, 55*(4), 494–521.

Sudman, S., & Bradburn, N. (1982). *Asking questions: A practical guide to questionnaire design*. San Francisco: Jossey-Bass.

Tourangeau, R., & Raskinski, K. (2000). *The psychology of survey response*. Cambridge, UK: Cambridge University Press.

U.S. Bureau of the Census. (1953). *Statistical abstract of the United States*. Washington, DC: U.S. Government Printing Office.

U.S. Bureau of the Census. (1995). *Population of counties by decennial census: 1900 to 1990*. Retrieved June 16, 2003, from http://www.census.gov/population/cencounts/mt190090.txt

U.S. Bureau of the Census. (1999). *Metropolitan areas and components, 1999, with FIPS Codes*. Retrieved June 16, 2003, from http://www.census.gov/population/estimates/metro-city/99mfips.txt

U.S. Bureau of the Census. (2000a). *Census 2000 summary file 1 (SF 1) 100-percent data: Total population*. Retrieved June 16, 2003, from http://factfinder.census.gov/servlet/DatasetMainPageServlet?_program=DEC&_lang=en&_ts=

U.S. Bureau of the Census. (2000b). *Residence in 1995 for the population 5 years and over. Census 2000 summary file 3 (SF 3)—sample data*. Retrieved June 16, 2003, from http://factfinder.census.gov/servlet/DatasetMainPageServlet?_ds_name=DEC_2000_SF3_U&_program=DEC&_lang=en

U.S. Bureau of the Census. (2002). *Statistical abstract of the United States*. Retrieved June 16, 2003, from http://www.census.gov/prod/www/statistical-abstract-02.html

University of Northern Iowa. (2004). *New Iowans homepage*. Retrieved March 10, 2004, from http://www.bcs.uni.edu/idm/newiowans/

Waldorf, B. (1995). Determinants of international return migration intentions. *Professional Geographer, 47*(2), 125–136.

Wolpert, J. (1965). Behavioral aspects of the decision to migrate. *Papers of the Regional Science Association, 15*, 159–169.

CHAPTER 17

POVERTY AND INCOME INEQUALITY IN APPALACHIA

ELGIN MANNION AND DWIGHT B. BILLINGS

INTRODUCTION

With a population of 22,894,017 people, the federally defined region of Appalachia stretches from southern New York to northeastern Mississippi. When established, its boundaries were generously drawn to include hundreds of counties in ten states in order to insure adequate Congressional support for its designation and funding (Bradshaw, 1992). Today, Appalachia includes 410 counties. But the artificiality of its definition makes generalization about Appalachia difficult. Although many of its counties are rural, the region also includes metropolitan centers like Pittsburgh and Birmingham and is closely bordered by other large cities such as Atlanta, Cincinnati, and Columbus. Baltimore, Buffalo, New York, Philadelphia, and Washington, DC are all within an hour's drive. Its economy is diverse, incorporating farming, timbering, coal mining, steel making, automobile manufacturing, textiles and apparel, tourism and retirement communities, and, increasingly, a number of rural communities economically dependent on prisons.

Despite its obvious diversity, Appalachia has long been identified primarily as a region of persistent poverty. By the end of the American civil war, journalists and local color novelists had begun to identify the Mountain South as a "strange land and peculiar people" because it already seemed out of step with 19th-century American economic, industrial, and urban growth (Shapiro, 1978). A century later, Appalachian poverty was rediscovered when the President's Appalachian Regional Commission defined Appalachia in 1963 as "a region apart—geographically and statistically" and advocated federal programs to achieve "the introduction of Appalachia and its people into fully active membership in the American society" (quoted in Isserman, 1996). The passage of the Appalachian Regional Development Act (ARDA) in 1965 initiated one the most enduring regionally targeted federal development programs.

W.A. Kandel & D.L. Brown (eds.), Population Change and Rural Society, 357–379.

How effective have these programs been in reducing poverty and income differentials in the Appalachian region? This case study addresses a question that persists in rural, regional, and international development. Are policies that mainly enhance economic efficiency and economic growth adequate in reducing poverty in severely distressed, mainly rural sub-regions? Which development strategies are the most effective in the reduction of poverty remains subject to considerable debate nationally and internationally. Some approaches maintain that economic growth and expansion alone are sufficient in reducing poverty rates (Dollar & Kray, 2002), as expressed in the quote that "a rising tide lifts all boats." Development strategies, then, are generally confined to economic-efficiency-enhancing measures such as provision of "hard" infrastructure, openness to international trade, and stable, market-friendly macroeconomic policies (Kray, 2004). The well-known "equity versus efficiency" trade-off is posited (Okun, 1975); re-distributive efforts are viewed as potentially distorting and detrimental to overall growth. Alternative views of development find some type of re-distribution and income maintenance vital in achieving a reduction in poverty rates and positively related to long-term growth (Alesina & Rodrik, 1994; Bourguignon, 2003; Brown, 1998; van der Hoeven, 2000). While initially conceived as a poverty alleviation agency, the Appalachian Regional Commission was institutionalized as an economic development agency: "Public investments shall be concentrated in areas where potential for future growth will be greatest . . . the region will then be able to support itself by the workings of a strengthened free enterprise economy" (ARDA, 1965).

In this chapter, we examine the region currently and find, like other researchers (see especially Isserman, 1996), significant economic improvement in Appalachia since 1965, when one in three Appalachian people were impoverished (Appalachian Regional Commission, 2003a). But economic improvement is spatially uneven, reflecting, as we show below, both the legacy of long-standing structural differences in economic and urban development among subregions and the effects of federal policies that either have failed to overcome, or have even exaggerated, these differences. Many mining and industrial communities in Northern Appalachia are in economic decline, while Southern Appalachia is benefiting from economic expansion. Central Appalachia remains mired in poverty with little prospects for improvement. Developmental success is customarily assessed through rising per capita incomes. For this reason, after an overview of region-wide trends, we focus on income convergence and income inequalities in the Appalachian region from 1969 and 2001. We find not only persistent poverty in some areas but also income divergence and widening income inequalities between the north, south, and central Appalachian regions, and within central Appalachian state boundaries, as well as increasing income divergence between rural and metropolitan counties, with rural income inequalities that exceed initial 1969 levels. We argue that income divergence and increasing metro/nonmetro income inequalities are partly related to major public policy shifts.

POVERTY AND POLICY IN APPALACHIA

In her history of efforts to eradicate American poverty, Alice Cooper (1992) shows that most development specialists acknowledge the need for multi-dimensional approaches to anti-poverty policy that address three factors—culture, economics, and politics—even though these have not received equal emphasis by scholars, policy makers, or practitioners. In the case of Appalachia, some scholars have often attributed poverty to cultural and economic isolation, but critics charge that such accounts are based on stereotypes and victim-blaming. Sociologists have used attitude surveys to show that cultural values believed to define Appalachian culture and to keep the region in the grip of poverty are no more prevalent there than elsewhere in the rural South, including areas that have undergone significant economic, industrial, and urban growth (Billings, 1974). Critics of the theory of economic isolation contend that Appalachia has been deeply integrated into the wider American economy at least since the late 19th century and much earlier in some sub-regions (Billings & Blee, 2000; Dunaway, 1996; Lewis, 1998). Others stress the connection between poverty and the outside, corporate ownership of land and resources, referring to Appalachia as an "internal colony" (Eller, 1982; Gaventa, 1980). Finally, relationships among politics, political policy, and poverty have been least studied in Appalachia, but scholars have shown a connection between persistent poverty and the domination of the poor by local elites (Duncan, 1999), as well as how political corruption and patronage often negate the anti-poverty efforts of local governments (Billings & Blee, 2000; Perry, 1972). In this chapter, we evaluate the effects of *national* anti-poverty and economic development policy in Appalachia because it has received so little attention.

Internationally, the 1960s have been called the decade of development. That period was also the heyday of large-scale federal initiatives in Appalachia under the rubric of the "War on Poverty." When the President's Appalachian Regional Commission defined Appalachia as "a region apart" in 1963, it articulated the long-standing stereotype of the region as both culturally and economically isolated. The discovery of massive levels of poverty in Central Appalachia, including more than 50 percent of the population in some rural counties, prompted scholars influenced by Michael Harrington and Oscar Lewis to link the presumption of an Appalachian folk culture to the idea that Appalachia could be characterized by a region-wide culture of poverty (Ball, 1968; Weller, 1965). This approach to poverty found expression in county-level community action programs supported by the Office of Economic Opportunity under the rubric of "maximum feasible participation" of the poor. Designed to overcome the supposed cultural isolation and marginalization of the poor, these programs were complemented by the economic initiatives of the Appalachian Regional Commission that aimed at overcoming economic isolation. Millions of dollars were spent to improve physical infrastructure in Appalachia, such as highways, airports, sewers, and on human capital improvements, such as education, job training, and health care (though the latter received less funding).

Although the Appalachian states' governors who provided the initial impetus for the creation of the Appalachian Regional Commission had advocated a "least first" model that would have targeted federal funds for the neediest Appalachian counties, this approach was not enacted into federal legislation (Bradshaw, 1992; Hansen, 1970; Rothblatt, 1971). Fearing that the ARC would be viewed as a federal handout program benefiting only one section of the country, the Johnson Administration insisted that ARC funds be directed "efficiently" in ways that would benefit the national as well as regional economy. Non-Appalachian governors and House and Senate Republicans were hostile to the implementation of what was perceived to be yet another poverty program (Bradshaw, 1992; Rothblatt, 1971). As the first executive director of the ARC, Ralph Widner, recounts (1990), the growth-center strategy was the quid pro quo required in order to get the legislation to pass. The resulting focus of the act was therefore the congressional economic efficiency mandate rather than the desired poverty alleviation.

The ARC's growth-center approach to development was loosely bolstered by various economic development theories (Appalachian Regional Commission, 1970; Higgins & Savoie, 1988; Isard, 1956). Arthur Lewis's (1954) seminal dual-sector or expanding capitalist nucleus model advocated the transfer of labor and financial investments from the non-capitalist, subsistence sectors of developing economies to expanding nodes of capitalist activity. It assumed a strong role for the state in economic development. Robert Solow's (1956) neo-classical growth model postulated that capital would shift to labor-rich regions, and labor would shift to capital-rich regions as a consequence of diminishing marginal returns to capital in capital-rich regions. Development practitioners concluded from such highly theoretical studies that federal investments to rural areas showing the promise of growth would enhance such factor transfers and eventually bring about the inter-regional convergence of capital/labor ratios and growth rates. But many rural counties in central Appalachia lacked promising urban centers that could serve the function of an expanding capitalist nucleus. Consequently, small Appalachian cities and service centers were designated as growth areas, even though they clearly could not replicate the performance of the expanding capitalist nodes that had figured so centrally and effectively in the prior industrial history of Europe and non-Appalachian America.

We should also note that models favoring enhanced factor mobility did not address questions of income distribution and inequality. The ARC thus found itself in the same position as countless development agencies around the globe: the absorption of rural labor surpluses and poverty alleviation were desired goals, but once a development approach was chosen that focused on economic efficiency, lower priority was assigned to income distribution, health, and human capital development. Consequently, the resulting approach was not "distribution favorable." Labor flexibility and mobility were stressed, while equity concerns and redistribution policies that might impede labor transfers were discouraged. With growth rather than equity as its goal, the ARC was left without direct mechanisms to influence income distribution in the region. Instead, federal funds were concentrated on infrastructure improvement, most notably highways, and enhanced economic efficiency was expected to generate significant "trickle down" effects throughout Appalachia.

Whether developmental differentials are framed in terms of poverty or employment and access to an adequate income is a reflection of the theoretical and policy climate (Wuyts, 2001). The "classical surplus" approach (Serrano & Medeiros, 2001) of early, post World War II development theory placed great emphasis on overcoming underemployment. Economic policy in this demand-managed, Keynesian era similarly focused on the generation of full employment and the raising of income levels among all market participants. The Kennedy and Johnson administrations pursued both an aggressive growth strategy and income maintenance programs in its "War on Poverty." The institutionalization of the ARC was part of this strategy. Following the macroeconomic oil and debt crises of the 1970s and 1980s and the ensuing global "stagflation," the resurgence of neoclassical theory de-emphasized government supports for employment and income maintenance, and economic policy shifted towards anti-inflationary controls (Tobin, 1996). Public-sector contraction and declining support for re-distributive efforts undermined the income maintenance programs enacted under the Johnson administration. The late 1970s thus witnessed an erosion of cash-based transfers such as welfare and a reduction in non-cash benefits such as food stamps, a trend that accelerated in the early 1980s (Haveman, 2000). Theoretical as well as financial support for Federal intervention in regional development declined. State intervention in regional development began to be viewed as efficiency-distorting and detrimental to private investment initiatives (Lal, 1988). The first Reagan administration failed in its bid to eliminate ARC funding altogether, but the agency's appropriations have declined sharply ever since. Before examining how these major policy shifts, the decline of federal investment in lagging regions and greatly reduced transfer payments have impacted incomes, we examine recent economic and social trends in Appalachia.

OVERVIEW OF ECONOMIC AND SOCIAL TRENDS IN APPALACHIA

Developmental success according to the ARC's own measure—whether counties have moved out of distress—is a mixed bag. Currently, 91 out of 410 counties are classified as economically distressed (poverty and unemployment rates 150 percent above national averages, incomes below two-thirds of the national average) by the Appalachian Regional Commission. The majority of all economically distressed counties are located in the central Appalachian region and the remainder in northern Mississippi and Alabama. Notable here is that the central Appalachian counties have persistently remained in distress since 1965. Figure 17.1 shows the regional division by ARC into north, south, and central

Figure 17.1. Counties in Appalachia by Region

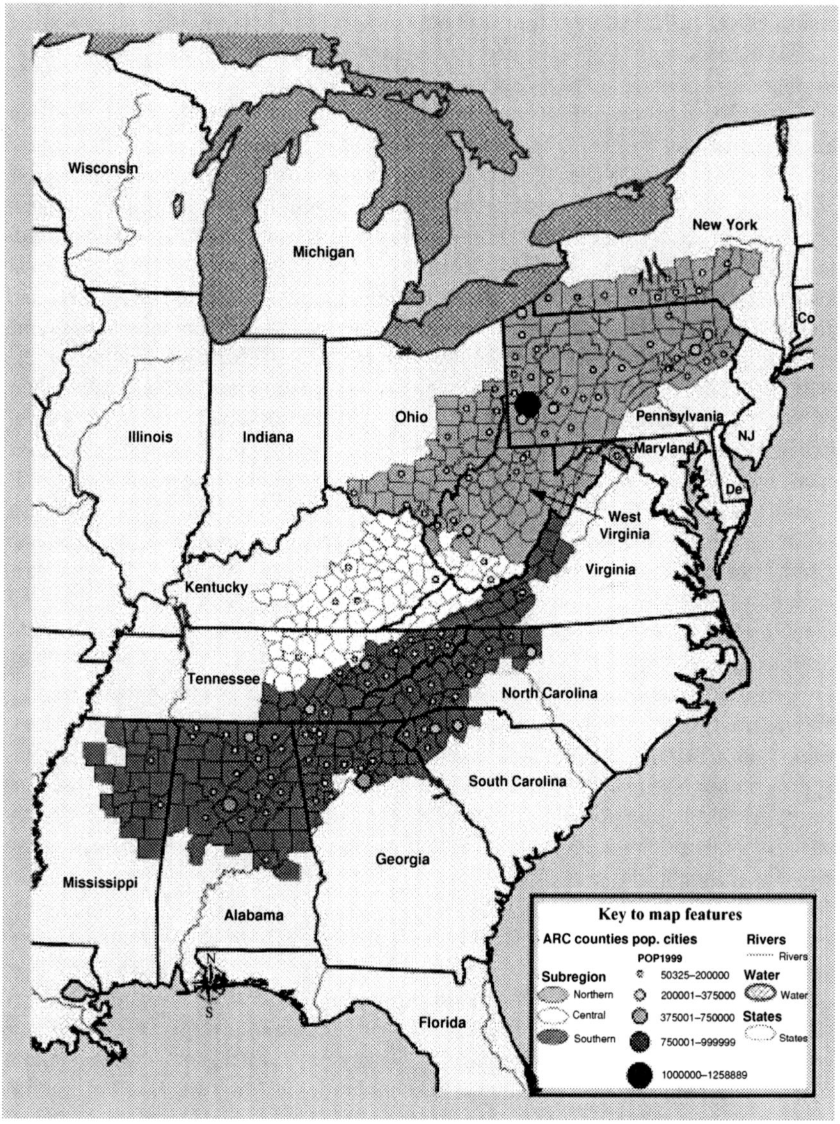

Table 17.1. Poverty and Income Levels in Appalachian Sub-Regions

Region	Poverty Rates 1970	Poverty Rates 1980	Poverty Rates 1990	Poverty Rates 2000	PCPI 2000	% U.S. PCPI 2000
United States	13.3	12.4	13.1	12.4	21,587	100
Appalachia	17.7	13.7	14.9	13.7	18,230	84
Metro Portion	13.5	11.2	12.3	11.7	19,860	92
Non/Metro Portion	21.7	15.9	17.3	16.5	16,002	74
Northern Appalachia	13.0	11.0	13.6	12.87	18,075	84
Metro Portion	11.7	9.4	12.0	11.9	19,131	89
Non/Metro Portion	15.8	12.8	15.3	14.5	16,340	76
Central Appalachia	34.0	22.3	25.3	22.2	14,343	66
Metro Portion	17.2	14.0	15.8	15.3	17,400	81
Non/Metro Portion	35.9	23.2	26.3	23.3	13,825	64
Southern Appalachia	20.2	14.9	13.9	12.9	19,162	88
Metro Portion	17.1	13.5	12.4	11.4	20,665	96
Non/Metro Portion	22.9	16.3	15.5	15.3	16,680	77

Source: 1970, 1980, 1990, Richard Couto (1994); for 2000, U.S. Census.

Appalachia and also illustrates the continued lack of sizable urban areas in the central Appalachian region.

Table 17.1 shows the percent of population in Appalachia below federally defined poverty levels from 1960 to 2000. Significant economic improvements were made throughout Appalachia between 1960 and 1980. After a slight increase in 1990, the level of poverty in Appalachian in 2000 remains stuck at roughly the 1980 level. Even so, with an overall poverty rate only 1.2 percentage points higher than the national level, Appalachia as a whole can no longer be thought of as a region of poverty if—indeed, it ever could. In fact, poverty in the metropolitan counties of Appalachia (where 58 percent of the region's population reside) is below the national average. The decline in poverty has been greatest in Central Appalachia. Yet with a poverty rate almost double that of the United States as a whole, economic performance in Central Appalachia still badly lags behind the nation and the rest of the region. In all subregions, nonmetropolitan poverty exceeds urban poverty.

Poverty rates also vary significantly across Appalachian states (Table 17.2). Poverty is greatest in Appalachian Kentucky, where one fourth of the population lives in poverty and almost one in three children is poor. The Appalachian counties of Mississippi, where one in four children are in poverty, rank

Table 17.2. Poverty and Income in the Appalachian Portion of States

Region	PCPI	% U.S. PCPI	Median Household Income	% Poor	% Poor under 18
United States	21,587	100	41,994	12.4	16.6
Appalachia	18,230	84	34,780	13.6	17.7
Alabama	18,901*	88	35,438*	14.4	21.5
Georgia	20,853	97	46,179*	9.2	10.9
Kentucky	13,738	64	24,529	24.4	31.8
Maryland	18,538	86	36,353	11.7	14.9
Mississippi	15,150	70	29,794	19.4	25.4
New York	17,730	82	35,004	13.6	17.6
North Carolina	19,262	89	36,090	11.7	15.3
Ohio	16,870	78	34,200	13.6	17.8
Pennsylvania	18,725	87	35,529	11.4	15.2
South Carolina	19,667*	91	38,423*	11.7	14.6
Tennessee	18,251	85	33,342	14.2	18.3
Virginia	16,656	77	30,449	15.7	18.1
West Virginia	16,477	76	29,696	17.9	24.3

Source: 2000 U.S. Census, *Higher than average for entire state.

second. In contrast, poverty in the Appalachian sections of Georgia, Maryland, North Carolina, Pennsylvania, and South Carolina is below the national level.

Per capita income is one of the best measures of economic performance, indicating rising productivity and output and the establishment of well-functioning labor markets. Here the economic lag between Appalachia and the nation is more evident than in the region's absolute level of poverty. Per capita income in Appalachia is only 84 percent of the national average, while in non-metropolitan Appalachia it is only 74 percent of the national level. Per capita income in Central Appalachia is drastically lower (Table 17.1). Economic performance as measured by per capita income also varies among Appalachian states (Table 17.2). Per capita incomes are lowest in the Appalachian counties of Kentucky, Mississippi, West Virginia, Virginia, and Ohio (in that order). Per capita income in Appalachian Alabama and Appalachian South Carolina, however, exceeds state averages, and the median household income in Appalachian Georgia is also above the state average. Except for these states, however, per capita and median incomes in all other Appalachian areas are lower than average for their states.

Table 17.3 reports additional demographic and economic variables across the region in 2000. It gives both a clear picture of the region's diversity and the

Table 17.3. Social and Economic Variables for Appalachian Sub-Regions

Region	% in Civilion Labor Force	% Unemployed	% College Educated	% Rural/ Urban
United States	59.7	5.8	24.4	100
Appalachia	56.6	5.7	17.7	100
Metro Portion	58.9	5.3	21.0	58
Non-Metro Portion	53.4	6.4	13.2	42
Northern Appalachia	55.5	6.2	17.7	100
Metro Portion	56.4	5.9	19.7	62
Non-Metro Portion	54.0	6.8	14.3	48
Central Appalachia	47.5	7.5	10.7	100
Metro Portion	54.5	6.1	16.2	14
Non-Metro Portion	46.3	7.8	9.8	86
Southern Appalachia	59.5	5.0	19.2	100
Metro Portion	61.6	4.7	22.6	62
Non-Metro Portion	56.1	5.5	13.7	48

Source: 2000 U.S. Census.

continuing economic deficits in some sections of Appalachia. As the Appalachian Regional Commission (2003a) notes, economic gains in Appalachia "have transformed the Region from one of almost uniform poverty to one of contrasts: some communities have successfully diversified their economies, some are still adjusting to structural changes in declining sectors, and some severely distressed areas still require basic infrastructure such as water and sewer systems." Several recent studies have attempted to explain these differences in economic performance across the region.

One frequently identified factor in the differential economic well-being of Appalachian counties is rurality. Incomes are lower in rural America than in urban America, and Appalachia, with a nonmetropolitan population of 42 percent, is significantly more rural than the nation as a whole, where 80 percent of the population lives in urban areas. Though comprising only 9.4 percent of the total Appalachian population, Central Appalachia is predominantly rural. Eighty-six percent of its population is nonmetropolitan. As Table 17.3 shows, poverty is greater in the nonmetropolitan counties of each of the Appalachian subregions than in their respective metropolitan counties. Several recent studies provide more elaborate information. The University of Wisconsin Applied Population Laboratory (2000) reports that poverty rates from 1979 to 1995 systematically increase along the ten categories of the Beale Code of the urban-rural continuum, from lowest in metropolitan core counties to highest in those nonmetropolitan counties that are not adjacent to metropolitan areas. Wood and Bishak (2000) report that Appalachian counties with improved economic performance are near, or have been incorporated into, expanding metropolitan areas, especially in Southern Appalachia, or have higher proportions of their populations in towns and small cities. Finally, Isserman (1996) demonstrates that standardizing for urbanization reduces the income deficit in Appalachia to 93 percent of the national level. Noting that "most of the Appalachian per capita income gap can readily be understood in terms of urbanization" (p. 5), he also points out that had the arbitrary regional boundaries of Appalachia been drawn differently to include nearly adjacent cities such as Atlanta, Cincinnati, and Columbus, the region's income and economy would appear dramatically improved. It would likely be less poor, more industrial, and more urban.

While rurality is a key factor in Appalachian poverty, economic performance varies across the non-metropolitan counties of the region. Differences in industry and occupational composition help to explain the income gap between Appalachia and the nation, as well as the very different developmental trajectories of Appalachia's states and subregions. Data from the 2000 census (Table 17.4) indicate that high-paying occupations such as professional and managerial jobs are scarcer in Appalachia than in the United States as a whole. They are even less prevalent in Appalachia's non-metropolitan counties. On the other hand, production and transportation jobs are more prevalent in the non-metropolitan counties of all three subregions than elsewhere and highest in non-metropolitan Southern Appalachia. Southern Appalachia leads the region in manufacturing employment and has the lowest level of service employment. Well-paying manufacturing jobs still exist throughout the region, but declining manufacturing wages have reduced income levels in many rural Appalachian communities, and employment in better-paying jobs in high-tech industries is largely confined to metropolitan counties (Appalachian Regional Commission, 2003b, 2003c; Couto, 1994). Nonetheless, along with highly diversified county economies, counties with higher shares of employment in manufacturing, especially in Southern Appalachia, tend to have improved their economic outlook over the past several decades (Wood & Bishak, 2000).

The advantages of urbanization and a strong manufacturing base continue to elude Central Appalachia. Employment in the primary sector in Central Appalachia is significantly higher than in the region as a whole or the nation. Coal mining accounts directly for 60,000 jobs in 118 Appalachian coal mining counties, and in Appalachian Kentucky for $ 50 million in annual earning in five counties alone, but employment continues to decline, despite high output, because of mechanization (Berger & Thompson, 2001). Although mining jobs often pay high wages in Appalachia, coal-dependent counties nonetheless perform more poorly than manufacturing counties. Mining-dependent counties are characterized by lack of a diversified economy and high poverty and unemployment rates. Income for many people in these counties is often dependent on low paying employment in service industries and the government sector and such employment is often distributed

Table 17.4. Employment Distribution by Occupation (Percent)

	Prof./Managerial	Production and Transport	Manufacturing	Services	Primary Production
United States	33.6	14.6	14.1	42.0	1.9
Appalachia	28.7	19.8	19.2	39.0	2.1
Metro Portion	31.1	17.0	16.9	40.6	1.0
Non-Metro Portion	25.0	24.1	22.6	36.5	3.8
Northern Appalachia	29.2	18.4	16.7	41.8	2.2
Metro Portion	30.6	16.5	15.3	42.8	1.2
Non-Metro Portion	26.7	21.8	19.1	39.9	3.8
Central Appalachia	24.4	22.0	17.3	37.2	6.0
Metro Portion	27.9	17.7	16.0	41.5	1.9
Non-Metro Portion	23.7	22.9	17.5	36.3	6.8
Southern Appalachia	28.9	20.7	21.7	36.8	1.5
Metro Portion	32.0	17.4	18.3	38.7	0.8
Non-Metro Portion	24.0	26.7	27.8	33.3	2.6

Source: 2000 U.S. Census.

through corrupt systems of political patronage and elite control (Duncan, 1992). Half of the Appalachian counties that have remained economically distressed since 1960 are coal-dependent (Wood & Bishak, 2000). They experience high rates of poverty, unemployment, and low average incomes. Good housing, healthcare, and education are also less available in mining counties than elsewhere (Couto, 1994; Tickamyer & Duncan, 1984; Tickamyer, 1992).

Education deficits are also associated with poverty and low incomes in Appalachia (Wood & Bishak, 2000). While the proportion of young people (18 to 24) with 12 or more years of schooling (77 percent) exceeded the national level (76 percent) for the first time in 1990 (Appalachian Regional Commission, 2003a), the educational gap between Appalachia and the nation persists in 2000 because of the lower educational levels attained by prior generations. While the proportion of adults who have graduated from high school in Appalachia and the nation as a whole are roughly similar, far fewer adults in Central Appalachia have done so. As Table 17.3 shows, the proportion of college graduates in Appalachia, lags behind the national average in nonmetropolitan Appalachia, and especially in Central Appalachia.

Unemployment and underemployment also lower incomes and point to weaknesses in local and regional Appalachian economies. Unemployment in 2000 was slightly lower in Appalachia than in the United States overall and even lower than the national average in Southern Appalachia including its non-metropolitan counties, yet unemployment far exceeded the national average in the non-metropolitan counties of Northern Appalachia and Central Appalachia. These rates, however, underestimate how many people have either become "discouraged" from seeking work or are under-employed. Thus, more indicative of economic performance is the ability of an economy to absorb population.

The percentage of the adult population in the civilian labor force in Appalachia in 2000 is three points lower than the national level. Only metropolitan Southern Appalachia exceeds the national average, another indicator of that subregion's relative economic strength. Fewer adults are employed in the non-metropolitan counties of Northern Appalachia than nationally and a smaller share of the working-age population is in the paid civilian workforce of Central Appalachia. The weakness of Appalachian Kentucky's economy is especially evident: it has been estimated that in some poor counties the "real" unemployment rate may be over 50 percent of the labor force (Keesler, 1991). Historically, transfer payments such as those for disability, Black Lung compensation, supplemental Social Security Income, Social Security retirement, and (until recently) Aid to Families of Dependent Children have only partially filled this gap. One study of ten of the poorest counties in Appalachian Kentucky found that even before "welfare reform," "only about half of those living below the poverty level in these distressed communities receive public assistance" (Eller et al., 1994). In the absence of such aid, anthropologists have documented "multiple livelihood strategies," known in folk idiom as "making ends meet the Kentucky way"' that help many Central Appalachians to sustain a livelihood despite very low monetary incomes, including subsistence gardening, bartering, temporary wage labor, and the informal economy (Halperin, 1990).

INCOME DISTRIBUTION IN APPALACHIA

Social scientists have grown increasingly critical of standard measures of poverty that indicate simply the percent of the population below defined thresholds of need. Often these standards are arbitrary and out of date. While absolute thresholds remain useful for measuring profound deficiencies in economic well-being, especially among populations in less developed societies, they fail to take into account variable depths of poverty among the poor (Brady, 2003). For this reason, some economists such as Amartya Sen have proposed alternative measures of relative poverty in order to evaluate not only absolute need but also the extent to which poverty results in "economic unfreedom" that limits the capacity of the poor for effective participation in society (Sen, 2000, p. 8). We believe, however, that measures of income equity better capture exclusion and marginalization in advanced industrial and postindustrial societies than measures of poverty alone (also see Tickamyer & Duncan, 1990). Subsistence needs in a market economy are mainly derived through market incomes, and inequalities among market participants can be discerned through income differentials. Moreover, since income inequality has a spatial as well as interpersonal dimension, inequalities between places can also be used to register their marginalization and exclusion.

Since the ARC was designed as an economic development rather than poverty alleviation agency, it seems appropriate to assess development success or failure in terms of income distribution. Economic development has as its aim raising levels of productivity, and it has become customary to assess development through the main available aggregate measure of production output, gross domestic product (GDP). Steadily rising per capita GDP is indicative of development success. For smaller developmental units such as counties, where share in GDP is not readily available, rising per capita personal income can serve as a proxy for increased output and labor productivity. Rising income levels indicate that economic development has been initiated through the process of economic expansion, the absorption of labor surpluses, and the ability of markets to compensate labor adequately. Per capita personal income includes income from all sources, including transfer payments and pensions and excluding contributions to social security. Per capita personal income therefore allows us to track the movement of wages as well as government income maintenance programs over time.

We ask the following questions about income distribution from 1969 to 2001: Are incomes across the Appalachian region converging? How do income convergence and income inequalities compare at different levels of aggregation, namely state, county, metro/nonmetro counties? Is the distribution of income across the region becoming more equal or less so? The "creative Federalism" proposed by the ARDA legislation left designation of Appalachian counties and design and implementation of the development plan to the authority of individual state governors. Development success therefore varies greatly within state boundaries. Are metro and non-metro incomes converging across the region and within state boundaries?

To assess income convergence over time, we apply a simple deviation measure, sigma convergence, also named the coefficient of variation (CV). The CV refers to the ratio of the standard deviation to the sample means, expressed as a percentage. For the assessment of income inequality, we apply the Gini Coefficient and the Theil Index. If development efforts in the Appalachian region have been successful in "plugging" (Widner, 1970) the Appalachian counties into the economy at large, we should expect over time for incomes to converge towards similar values and income inequalities to diminish. If convergence occurs, we can expect declining values of dispersion around the mean, meaning per capita incomes have pulled closer together, with poorer counties "catching up" with higher incomes.

Income Convergence

Incomes across the thirteen Appalachian states and the 410 Appalachian counties, as found in studies elsewhere (Barro & Sala-I-Martin, 1999; Williamson, 1967), do indeed converge, with declining values of dispersion over time, as shown in Figures 17.2 and 17.3:

Figure 17.2. All ARC States Income Convergence, 1969–2001 (Sigma Coefficient)

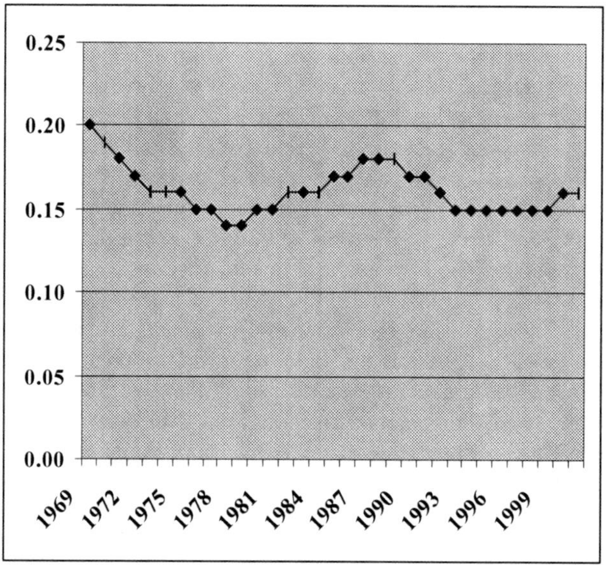

Source: Bureau of Economic Analysis.

Figure 17.3. All ARC Counties Income Convergence, 1969–2001 (Sigma Coefficient)

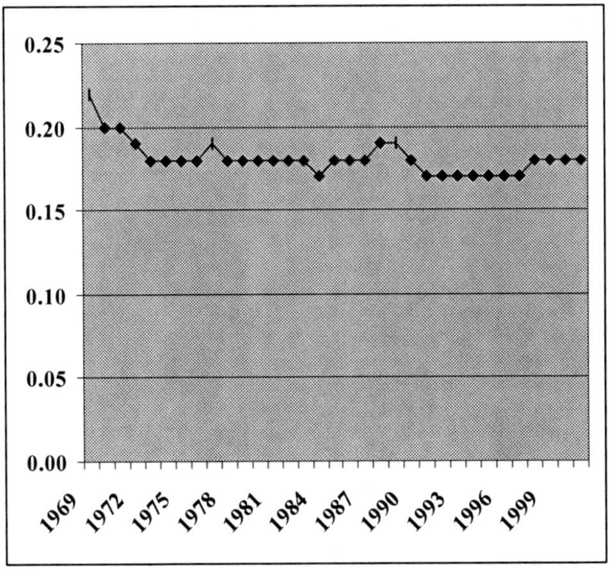

Source: Bureau of Economic Analysis.

Values for the coefficient of variation across both Appalachian states and counties are comparable to the United States overall (Bernat, 2001). After an initial disturbance, often attributed to the "oilshocks" of the 1970s and the ensuing international financial instability, there is a return to convergence in the economic expansion experienced in the 1990s. In contrast, if Northern, Southern and Central Appalachian regions are disaggregated, incomes show much higher values of dispersion, illustrating the persistence of large income differentials between the Southern, Northern, and persistently impoverished Central Appalachian regions. Initial values were much higher and have never been reduced to levels similar to those for all Appalachian states and counties, as can be seen in Figure 17.4. Have efforts to incorporate rural counties been successful, and have the hypothesized "trickle down" effects been sufficient to raise incomes in rural counties? As shown in Figure 17.5, after a brief period of convergence, metro/nonmetro incomes for all Appalachian states have been steadily diverging.

The ARDA legislation maintained individual state autonomy in the ARC development process. Each individual Appalachian state was responsible for designating Appalachian counties and designing and implementing the development

Figure 17.4. North-South Central Appalachia Income Convergence, 1969–2001 (Sigma Coefficient)

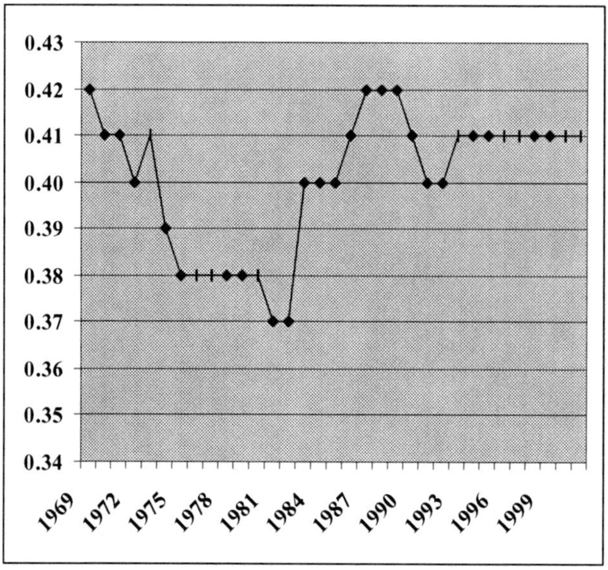

Source: Bureau of Economic Analysis.

Figure 17.5. Metro-Nonmetro Income Convergence for All ARC States, 1969–2001 (Sigma Coefficient)

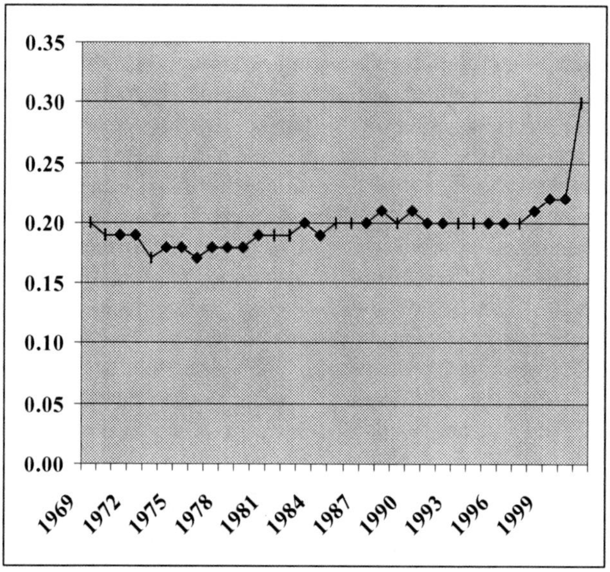

Source: Bureau of Economic Analysis.

process. How has income convergence played out in Kentucky and Tennessee, the two states with the largest number of counties that are part of the most persistently impoverished Central Appalachia region? Kentucky consists of 120 counties, of which 51, are designated as Appalachian and contiguously located in the eastern half of the state. Tennessee designated as Appalachian 50 out of 95 counties, similarly contiguously located in the eastern half of that state. Incomes in individual Appalachian states such as Kentucky and Tennessee tend towards convergence when the non-Appalachian counties and metro areas are included in the analyses, with a pattern similar to Figures 17.1 and 17.2. However, if metro and non-metro counties in Tennessee and Kentucky are disaggregated, incomes diverge, with 2001 values surpassing initial 1969 values, as shown in Figure 17.6 and 17.7. The strong return to convergence experienced in the 1990s by all Appalachian states and counties and within state boundaries is less pronounced, and it appears that rural counties in Kentucky and Tennessee did not benefit significantly from the economic expansion of the decade. It is notable that the initial disturbance of the 1970s appears to have affected non-metro counties and the central Appalachian region most adversely.

Figure 17.6. Metro-Nonmetro Income Convergence for All Tennessee Counties, 1969–2001 (Sigma Coefficient)

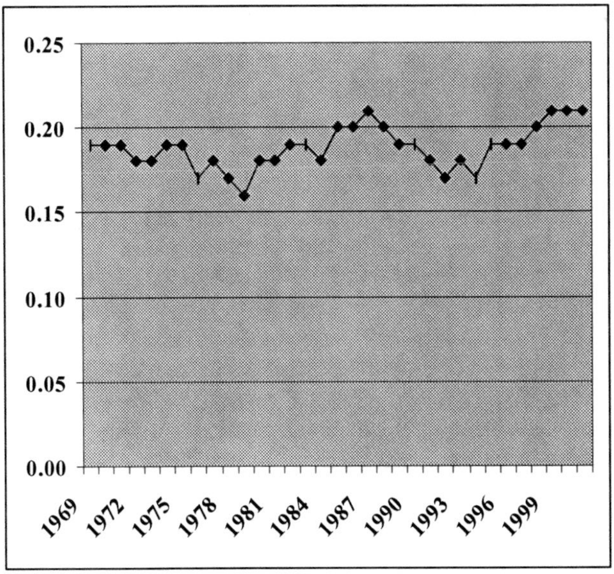

Source: Bureau of Economic Analysis.

Figure 17.7. Metro-Nonmetro Income Convergence for All Kentucky Counties, 1969–2001 (Sigma Coefficient)

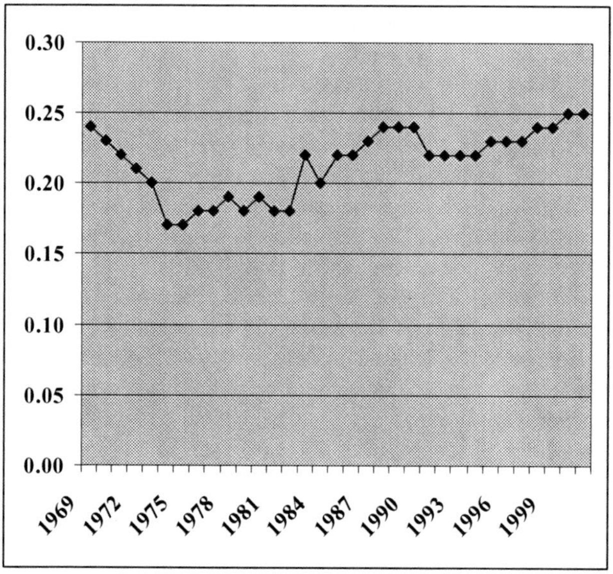

Source: Bureau of Economic Analysis.

Income Inequality

Did Appalachian income inequalities decline between 1969 to 2001? Applying two measures of inequality, the Gini Coefficient and the Theil Index, we see that PCPI income inequalities have actually been increasing, surpassing initial 1969 levels, as shown in Figure 17.8 and 17.9 for Appalachia and Kentucky. An initial period of declining income inequality was reversed in the early 1980's, and income inequality rose thereafter.

In the 1980s, sociologists and economists began to call attention to the impact of national economic restructuring, especially capital flight to locations outside the country and deindustrialization, on "poverty and economic deterioration in rural America" (Sechler, 1992). Others have pointed to heightened income inequalities in the United States and abroad that can be attributed in part to shifts in public policy, such as the decline in redistributive efforts and public service contraction (Cornia & Court, 2000; Galbraith, 2000; Muqtada, 2003; van der Hoeven, 2000). It is beyond the scope of this chapter to parcel out these effects on Appalachia, although it is clear that Appalachia's subregions have been unevenly affected by such changes. It is also apparent from the data analyzed here that initial trends

Figure 17.8. North-South Central Appalachian Region PCPI Income Inequality, 1969–2001 (Gini Coefficient)

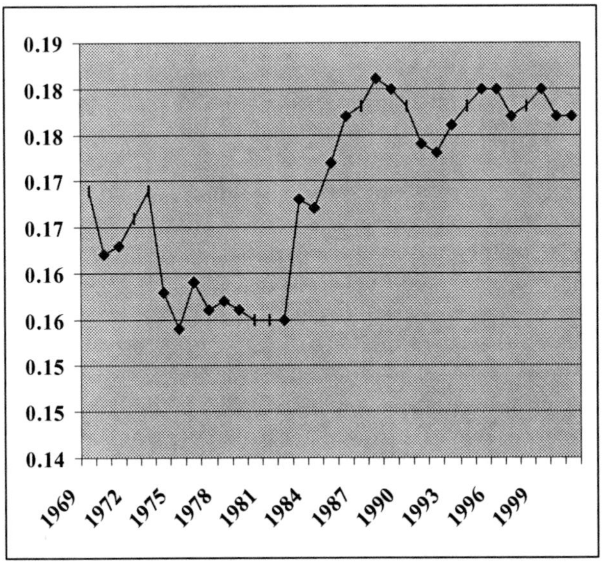

Source: Bureau of Economic Analysis.

Figure 17.9. Metro-Nonmetro Kentucky PCPI Income Inequality, 1969–2001 (Theil Coefficient)

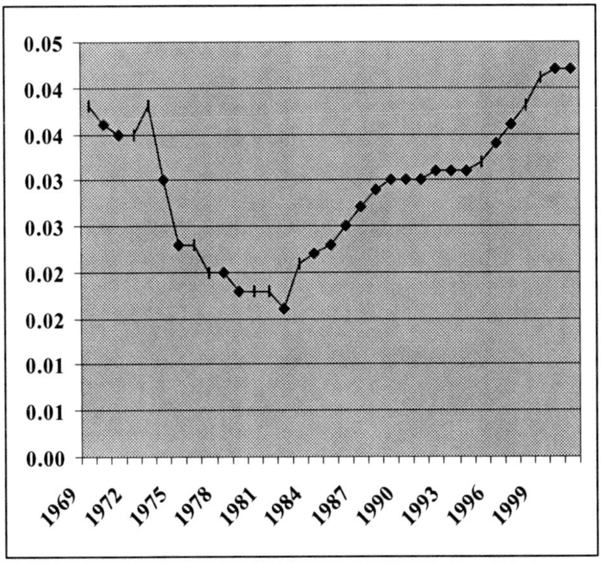

Source: Bureau of Economic Analysis.

toward the convergence of incomes between metropolitan and rural Appalachian communities in the 1970s have been reversed. Income disparities and inequalities between metropolitan and nonmetropolitan communities in Appalachia have continued to worsen throughout the past two decades, just as Central Appalachia has remained poor.

It is significant that the infusion of billions of dollars of federal investment in the region through the ARC and the jobs that this investment stimulated, alongside the income maintenance programs of the War on Poverty, correspond to the brief period of economic improvement in the region and that the decline or elimination of such support corresponds to income divergence between Appalachian subregions and increasing metro/nonmetro income inequities. It is also significant that income convergence and greater equity were achieved without directly overcoming Appalachia's "traditional" causes of economic distress. Improvements were made despite the continuation of unfavorable taxation and landownership patterns, agricultural decline, education deficits, the domination of extractive industry, and the lack of urbanization. The uninterrupted period of income convergence and declining levels of income inequality lends support to the assertion that "new causes" of economic distress (Cornia & Court, 2000) are at work, that is, effects that can be traced to a changed federal policy environment.

CONCLUSION

In a region that continues to be highly dependent upon federal spending (Gatrell & Calzonetti, 2003), public money matters. The contention that free market forces in and of themselves are sufficient to lift lagging regions out of poverty has gained great currency over the past two decades. Efficiency-enhancing measures and infrastructure investments have helped some Appalachian communities but not others. The abrupt reversal of declining income inequities between metro and nonmetro counties in the 1980s suggests that both income maintenance and investments in economic efficiency remain necessary for many rural Appalachian counties. In Central Appalachia, despite significant infrastructure investments, many communities still lack basic "nuts-and-bolts" infrastructure such as sewer and water systems. Continued federal involvement and income maintenance for rural counties are difficult propositions to advance in the current policy climate but appear to remain vital tools for the reduction of currently increasing subregional and metro/nonmetro economic differentials.

REFERENCES

Abramowitz, M. (1986). Thinking about growth: Catching up, forging ahead, and falling behind. *Journal of Economic History*, *46*, 385–406.

Alesina, R., & Rodrik, D. (1994). Distributive politics and economic growth. *Quarterly Journal of Economics*, *109*, 465–490.

Appalachian Regional Commission. (1970). *Urban-rural growth strategy* (Appalachian Regional Commission Staff Summary Report). Appalachian Regional Commission Archives, Internal Documents, University of Kentucky Libraries, Special Collections.

Appalachian Regional Commission. (2003a). *Appalachian Region economic overview*. Retrieved June 18, 2003, from www.arc.gov

Appalachian Regional Commission. (2003b). *Building on past experiences: Creating a new future for distressed counties*. Retrieved June 18, 2003, from www.arc.gov

Appalachian Regional Commission. (2003c). *An assessment of labor force participation rates and underemployment in Appalachia*. Retrieved June 18, 2003 from www.arc.gov

Appalachian Regional Development Act 1965. Washington, DC: Appalachian Regional Commission.

Ball, R. (1968). A poverty case: The analgesic subculture of the Southern Appalachians. *American Sociological Review*, *33*, 885–895.

Barro, R.J., & Sala-I-Martin, X. (1999). *Economic growth*. New York: McGraw-Hill.

Bernat, A. (2001). Convergence in state per capita income, 1950–1999. *Survey of current business*. Washington, DC: Bureau of Economic Analysis.

Billings, D.B. (1974). Culture and poverty in Appalachia: A theoretical and empirical analysis. *Social Forces*, *53*, 315–323.

Billings, D.B., & Blee, K.M. (2000). *The road to poverty: The making of wealth and hardship in Appalachia*. New York: Cambridge University Press.

Billings, D.B., Pudup, M.B., & Waller, A. (1995). Taking exception with exceptionalism: New approaches to the social history of Appalachia. In M.B. Pudup, D.B. Billings, & A. Waller (Eds.), *Appalachia in the making: The mountain South in the nineteenth century* (pp. 1–24). Chapel Hill, NC: University of North Carolina Press.

Billings, D.B., & Tickamyer, A. (1993). Uneven development in Appalachia. In T. Lyson & W.W. Falk (Eds.), *Forgotten places: Uneven development in rural America* (pp. 7–29). Lawrence, KS: University Press of Kansas.

Bourguignon, F. (2003). *The poverty-growth-inequality triangle*. Washington, DC: World Bank. Retrieved January 4, 2004, from http://econ.worldbank.org

Bradshaw, M. (1992). *The Appalachian Regional Commission: Twenty-five years of government policy*. Lexington, KY: University Press of Kentucky.

Brady, D. (2003). Rethinking the sociological measurement of poverty. *Social Forces*, *81*(3), 715–751.

Brown, D. (1998). Enhancing the spatial policy framework with ecological analysis. In M. Miklin & D.L. Poston (Eds.), *Continuities in sociological human ecology* (pp. 195–211). Dordrecht, Netherlands: Plenum.

Cappelen, A. (2000). *Convergence, divergence, and the Kuznets curve*. Paper sponsored by the European Commission for Program Technology, European Integration and Social Cohesion (TSER). Retrieved August 8, 2003, from http:/meritbbs.unimas.nl/tser/tser/html

Cooper, A. (1992). Modernization and the rural poor: Some lessons from history. In C.M. Duncan (Ed.), *Rural poverty in America* (pp. 215–233). Westport, CT: Auburn House.

Cornia, A., & Court, J. (2000). *Inequality, growth and poverty in the era of liberalization and globalization*. Policy brief for the United Nations project: Rising income inequality and poverty reduction: Are they compatible? Retrieved July 27, 2003, from the World Institute for Development Economics Research (UNU/WIDER) Web site, http://www.wider.unu.edu/publications/publications

Couto, R.A. (1994). *An American challenge: A report on economic trends and social issues in Appalachia*. Dubuque: Kendall/Hunt.

Dollar, D., & Kray, A. (2002). Growth is good for the poor. *Journal of Economic Growth*, *7*, 195–225.

Dunaway, W. (1996). *The first American frontier: Transition to capitalism in America 1700–1860*. Chapel Hill, NC: University of North Carolina Press.

Duncan, C.M. (1992). Persistent poverty in Appalachia: Scarce work and rigid stratification. In C.M. Duncan (Ed.), *Rural Poverty in America* (pp. 11–133). *Westport*, CT: Auburn House.

Eller, R. (1982). *Miners, millhands, and mountaineers: Industrialization of the Appalachian South, 1880–1930*. Knoxville, TN: University of Tennessee Press.

Eller, R., Jenks, P., Jasparro, C., & Napier, J. (1994). *Kentucky's distressed communities: A report on poverty in Appalachian Kentucky*. Lexington, KY: University of Kentucky Appalachian Center.

Gatrell, J., & Calzonetti, F. (2003). Growing competitiveness in Appalachia: Strategic science & technology planning in West Virginia. *Journal of Appalachian Studies, 9*, 293–321.

Gaventa, J. (1980). *Power and powerlessness: Quiescence and rebellion in an Appalachian valley*. Urbana, IL: University of Illinois Press.

Halperin, R. (1990). *The livelihood of kin: Making ends meet "the Kentucky way."* Austin, TX: University of Texas Press.

Haveman, R. (2000). Poverty and the distribution of economic well-being since the 1960s. In G. Perry & J. Tobin (Eds.), *Economics, events, ideas, and policies* (pp. 243–299). Washington, DC: Brookings Institution.

Higgins, B., & Savoie, D. (1988). *Regional economic development- Essays in honor of Francois Perroux*. Boston: Unwin Hyman.

Isard, W. (1956). *Location and space: A general theory relating to industrial location, market areas, land use, trade, and urban structure*. Cambridge, MA: MIT Press.

Isserman, A. (1996). *Appalachia then and now: An update of "The Realities of Deprivation" reported to the President in 1964*. Washington, DC: Appalachian Regional Commission. Retrieved June 18, 2003, from www.arc.gov

Keesler, W. (1991). *Jobs and economic development: Meeting the needs of Appalachian people*. Lexington, KY: University of Kentucky Appalachian Center Civic Leadership Project.

Kray, A. (2004). *When is growth pro-poor*. Washington, DC: World Bank. Retrieved February 25, 2004, from http://econ.worldbank.org

Lewis, A. (1954). Economic development with unlimited supplies of labor. *Manchester School of Economics and Social Studies, 22*, 139–191.

Lewis, R. (1998). *Transforming the Appalachian countryside: Railroads, deforestation, and social change in West Virginia, 1880–1920*. Chapel Hill, NC: University of North Carolina Press.

Muqtada, M. (2003). *Macroeconomic stability, growth and employment: Issues and considerations beyond the Washington consensus*. Geneva, Switzerland: International Labor Organization.

Okun, A. (1975). *Equity versus efficiency—The big trade-off*. Washington, DC: Brookings Institution.

Perry, H. (1972). *They'll cut off your project: A Mingo county chronicle*. New York: Praeger.

Raitz, K., Ulack, R., & Leinbach, T. (1984). *Appalachia: A regional geography*. Boulder, CO: Westview.

Rothblatt, D.R. (1971). *Regional planning: The Appalachian experience*. Lexington, MA: Heath.

Sechler, S. (1992). Foreword. In C. Duncan (Ed.), *Rural poverty in America* (pp. 13–17). New York: Auburn House.

Serrano, F., & Medeiros, C. (2001). *Economic development and the revival of the classical surplus approach*. Paper for the United Nations Research Institute for Social Development conference, The Need to Rethink Development Economics, Geneva, Switzerland.

Shapiro, H.D. (1978). *Appalachia on our mind: The Southern mountains and montaineers in the American consciousness 1870–1920*. Chapel Hill, NC: University of North Carolina Press.

Solow, R. (1956). A contribution to the theory of economic growth. *Quarterly Journal of Economics, 70*, 65–94.

Tickamyer, A. (1992). The working poor in rural labor markets: The example of the southeastern United States. In C.M. Duncan (Ed.), *Rural poverty in America* (pp. 41–61). Westport, CT: Auburn House.

Tickamyer, A., & Duncan, C.M. (1984). Economic activity and quality of life in eastern Kentucky. *Growth and Change, 15*, 43–51.

Tickamyer, A., & Duncan, C.M. (1990). Poverty and opportunity structure in rural America. *Annual Review of Sociology, 16*, 67–86.

Tobin, J. (1996). *Full employment and growth: Further Keynesian essays on policy*. London: Edward Elgar.

Van der Hoeven, R. (2000). *Poverty and structural adjustment: Some remarks on tradeoffs between equity and growth*. Geneva, Switzerland: International Labor Organization.

Waller, A. (1988). *Feud: Hatfields, McCoys, and social change in Appalachia, 1860–1900*. Chapel Hill, NC: University of North Carolina Press.

Weise, R.S. (2001). *Grasping at independence: Debt, male authority, and mineral rights in Appalachian Kentucky 1850–1915*. Knoxville, TN: University of Tennessee Press.

Weller, J. (1965). *Yesterday's people: Life in contemporary Appalachia*. Lexington, KY: University Press of Kentucky.

Widner, R. (1970). *Appalachia after five years: A progress report on Appalachia's experiment in regional development.* Appalachian Regional Commission Archives, University of Kentucky Libraries, Special Collections.

Widner, R. (1990). Appalachian development after 25 years: An assessment. *Economic Development Quarterly, 44*, 291–312.

Williamson, J. (1967). Regional inequality and the process of national development. *EDCC, 13*, 3–45.

Wuyts, M. (2001). *Inequality and poverty as the condition of labour*. Paper delivered at the United Nations Research Institute for Social Development conference, The Need to Rethink Development Economics, Geneva, Switzerland.

CHAPTER 18

WELFARE REFORM AMIDST CHRONIC POVERTY IN THE MISSISSIPPI DELTA

M.A. LEE AND JOACHIM SINGELMANN

INTRODUCTION

After almost one hundred years of welfare-state expansion that began with Bismarck's social legislation in the 1880s, welfare regimes have come under siege in all advanced industrial societies. Since the severe recession of the mid-1970s, high levels of unemployment accompanied by an aging population created fiscal pressures on governments to look for ways to curtail entitlement programs (Leisering & Leibfried, 1999). In the United States, with its non-integrated approach to social welfare, discussion about welfare limits led to implementation of a welfare-to-work approach to public assistance—namely, the Personal Responsibility and Work Opportunity Reconciliation Act (PRWORA). This legislation has been subject to three major criticisms: (1) only more qualified persons will be able to leave welfare (creaming hypothesis); (2) persons shifting from welfare to work, given low minimum-wage levels, will join the working poor; and (3) the inclusion of only minimal provisions for variation in regional and local economies will disproportionately burden states with low tax revenues and a greater proportion of residents in economically distressed areas. As a state with over half of its counties in the Mississippi Delta region, Louisiana allows us to compare welfare reform in distressed non-metro areas with relatively more vibrant metro communities in the region. Also, Louisiana's large urban and rural black population allows us to compare more readily metro and non-metro differences without the confounding effect of race present in many other states.

In this chapter, we analyze how welfare reform has played out in urban and rural areas in the Mississippi Delta's context of persistent poverty. To that end, we examine characteristics of Louisiana's welfare stayers (respondents still getting welfare cash assistance) and leavers (those no longer receiving cash assistance), as well as the labor market success of those working. Recent studies have examined the impact of location on welfare receipt. In general, state-level studies of caseload decline find relatively little difference in how local labor market

W.A. Kandel & D.L. Brown (eds.), Population Change and Rural Society, 381–403.

dynamics influence caseloads in metropolitan and non-metropolitan areas (Lee et al., 2002; Ziliak et al., 2001). However, analyses of individual or family outcomes found some significant effects for place of residence. Cancian, Haveman, Meyer, and Wolfe (1999) showed higher exit rates among families in large urban areas, and Knox, Miller, and Gennetian (2000) noted a greater impact of recent reforms on employment and earnings in urban counties. Cancian and others (1999) used demographic and economic factors to explain urban-rural differences in outcomes. Unfavorable local labor markets, high rates of poverty, and a large proportion of the population eligible for cash assistance may slow welfare exits and reduce potential earnings as the supply of low-wage labor outstrips demand in non-metro areas (The Lewin Group, 2001).

Stratification research has also shown that "where you live" matters. Locality and neighborhoods exert a strong influence on economic opportunities (Logan 1975; Logan & Molotoch, 1987; Massey & Denton, 1993; South & Crowder, 1997, 1998). In a weak local labor market, returns to education may be lower. In a poor neighborhood, social ties may be less useful in finding work. The 1996 Welfare Reform Act (PRWORA) has increased labor supply without necessarily affecting labor demand or access to jobs. For this reason, concerns have been raised about the impact of reform on economically distressed areas. In this analysis, we assess how welfare reform has turned out in Louisiana, one of the poorest states in one of the poorest regions in the nation.

The Lower Mississippi Delta competes with the Rio Grande Valley in South Texas for the dubious honor of being the poorest region in the United States. Both regions suffer from low income levels and poor health conditions. In the Delta, however, much of the existing poverty is due to lingering effects of the plantation economy. Although the Delta's agricultural land is of high soil value, in many counties the plantation economy concentrated land ownership among a few families. Frequently, these families actively resisted industrialization because competition would have raised the cost of labor (Duncan, 1999; Quadagno, 1994). As a result, many Delta residents left the region, but those who could not—or would not—often remained poor, especially if they are black.

In addition to a history of resistance to industrialization, the region has a history of resistance to public assistance. In fact, in the past, it has been the South's opposition to social welfare that shaped some key aspects of federal cash assistance programs. Local control of dollar amounts awarded can be traced back to the southern elite's reluctance to support the Social Security Act of 1935 (Quadagno, 1994). Despite the rise of other industries in the South, cheap labor continues to be used as an incentive to draw employers to the region. High levels of cash assistance would threaten the supply of cheap labor and undermine what has, until recently, been seen as a competitive advantage (LEDC, 1999, p. 7). The importance of cheap labor in Louisiana's economic history is one reason why the level of cash assistance offered to welfare recipients is so low. In 2002, a maximum monthly grant for a family of three was $190 in non-metro areas and $240 in designated metro areas. Louisiana's level of cash assistance is on par with what other Southern states provide to recipients of Temporary Assistance to Needy Families (TANF) but it is lower than the median level of cash assistance in the United States ($438) and far below cash assistance levels in states such as California ($645), Michigan ($792), or Massachusetts ($633). These state differences in monthly benefit levels exceed cost-of-living differentials, especially in non-metro areas.

Given Louisiana's history and the incentive structure under PRWORA, it is not surprising that Louisiana's state government narrowly defines successful reform as a reduction in caseload. Other states such as Illinois, Oregon, and Wisconsin, all place more emphasis on successful integration into the labor market. PRWORA instituted a new cash assistance program, Temporary Assistance for Needy Families (TANF). Under this program, federal entitlements ended, and states applied for TANF community block grants. Recipients now have a five-year lifetime limit on federally funded cash assistance, stricter work requirements, and tougher sanctions for non-compliance. TANF grants require states to implement cash assistance guidelines that include these basic provisions as well as requiring drug testing and cooperation in garnishing payments from absentee parents. Federal TANF regulations tie funding to a minimum level of caseload reduction and reward states for a reduction in caseloads by allowing them to finance ancillary activities with savings from decreasing cash assistance outlays. In the first year of welfare reform, a state's total TANF dollar amount was based on pre-reform levels of spending. Because Louisiana historically made small cash assistance payments, its initial TANF grant was low relative to states such as Massachusetts and Illinois. As a result, even with falling caseloads, Louisiana had little money to divert to programs designed to enhance the material well-being of welfare leavers.

Because economic opportunities differ among regions and localities, it is important to study regional as well as local differences in the effects of welfare reform. Brown and Lee (1999) discussed how opportunity structures affect returns to human capital. The Lower Mississippi Delta Region (LMD), as defined by the Lower Mississippi Delta Commission, is disproportionately poor and rural but contains some prosperous metropolitan areas such as New Orleans and Baton Rouge (LMDC, 1990; Reeder and Calhoun, 2002). Given the positive association between highly concentrated land ownership and extreme levels of poverty in the non-metro Mississippi Delta (Tomaskovic-Devey & Roscigno, 1996), we expected non-metro residents to be less successful in moving from welfare to work and in exiting poverty. Also, given economic disparities between Louisiana's metro and non-metro areas in the study, we expected to find stronger metro/non-metro differences. Using a panel study for the 1998–2001 period, we address differences between leavers and stayers (the creaming phenomenon), employment outcomes, and metro/non-metro differences. Although we identify some important metro/non-metro differences in socioeconomic outcomes, we do not find significant differences in exit rates and earnings as found in other states.

BACKGROUND: WELFARE REFORM AND CASELOAD DECLINE

Louisiana's implementation of TANF began in January 1997 and included two main programs: the Family Independence Temporary Assistance Program (FITAP) and the Family Independence Work Program (FIND Work). More recently Louisiana instituted two other cash assistance elements: in 2000, subsidies to children in the care of relatives other than their parents; and in 2002, a one-time lump sum payment to FITAP-eligible families with strong labor market attachment, provided these families agree not to enter FITAP for four months. Among state-specific aspects of FITAP are a 24-month time limit on receipt of cash assistance within 60 months, required drug testing for all recipients, and school attendance and immunization for children. For TANF purposes, Louisiana disregards up to $900 in monthly earnings for a 6-month period and provides transitional transportation payments for those leaving the program for work. This disregard is far less than what TANF participants can keep in some other states, such as Illinois. The 24-month limit encourages participants to "save" their time and is only applied when particular exceptions are not met. Most families can qualify for exceptions to the 24-month time limit, for example, by searching for work. However, exceptions to the 24-month limit still count toward the federal five-year lifetime limit (Bloom et al., 2002).

The emphasis in Louisiana is on accelerating the transition into work activities and not on improving recipients' earnings capacity. For example, federal TANF rules allow GED instruction for adults age 20 or older, and FITAP has adopted this policy. However, in practice, only FITAP participants under age 20 are assigned to GED preparation (Valvano & Abe, 2002, p. 27). Louisiana's FITAP program recognizes some barriers to employment, such as physical or mental incapacity, injury or illness, and domestic violence, but plans for mental health evaluations only began in 2002. Work exemptions are granted in the above circumstances and also when transportation or child care is not available. Although work-related expenses such as the cost of transportation, uniforms, or tools may be a barrier, FITAP includes provisions to help with these. Very few participants, however, make use of payments available for these expenses (Valvano & Abe, 2002, pp. 30–31). In almost every aspect, Louisiana's approach to welfare reform does less to promote higher-quality employment than many other states.

Sanctions for non-compliance with work requirements are progressive. The initial sanction is a reduction in cash assistance for three months or until the violation is remedied. If the partial sanction does not succeed in bringing the adult recipient into compliance, a family sanction follows, and the case is removed from FITAP. Although TANF legislation mandates sanctions for drug use and failure to assist in garnishing child support payments from absentee parents, most partial and family sanctions are for non-compliance with work requirements (Valvano & Abe, 2002, pp. 70–71).

Table 18.1. Caseload Trends in Study Parishes

	January 1997	January 2001	January 2003	Percent Change, 1/97–6/03
Delta Non-Metro	3477	1743	1476	−58.7%
Ouachita Parish	1922	823	618	−67.9%
Orleans Parish	16383	7400	6014	−64.8%
Louisiana	60266	25953	19943	−67.8%
United States (Thousands)	4114	2100	2032*	−50.6%

* June 2003 estimate used as Jan. 2003 estimate is not readily available. *Sources:* Louisiana's Department of Social Services, Office of Family Service at http://www.dss.state.la.us/offofs/html/statistics_2002–2003.html accessed on August 10, 2003 and electronic files of FITAP/AFDC reports 7/1989 to 3/1998; U.S. Dept. of Health and Human Services, Administration of Children and Families accessed on March 24, 2004 at http://www.acf.dhhs.gov/news/stats/index.html.

After implementation of FITAP in 1997, Louisiana's caseloads dropped 68 percent through June 2003 (Table 18.1). The rate of caseload decline in Louisiana outpaced the national decrease of 51 percent. In part, this is because several states began welfare-to-work initiatives prior to 1997, and the largest drop-off in cases occurs in the first couple of years. Another reason is the emphasis in Louisiana on reducing caseloads rather than improving TANF recipients' earning capacity. Although Table 18.1 shows little difference between metro (Ouachita and Orleans) and non-metro Delta caseload decline, there is variation within these areas. Among non-metro parishes in our study, Morehouse and Union parishes had the lowest rate of caseload decline from 1997 to June 2003 (38 percent and 32 percent, respectively). Since 2000, some parishes have had annual increases in caseloads—Union parish's caseload rose 30 percent from July 2002 to June 2003, and the Gentilly district in New Orleans had a similar increase from 2001 to 2002. After reviewing local newspaper accounts, we could not identify specific events that might have precipitated these caseload increases in particular locations. We suspect that variation in program administration may account for some of the local differences.

Despite the success of welfare reform in producing caseload decline, debate still surrounds the effects of mandated employment for nearly all TANF recipients. Only about 50 percent of Louisiana's FITAP participants find employment. Few are continuously employed in the year following their employment, and earnings among employed recipients fail to pull them out of poverty

(Valvano & Abe, 2002). Early on, critics attributed initial successes of welfare reform to robust economic conditions in the 1990s and "creaming," that is the quick exit of TANF recipients with better education, more job experience, and a family situation conducive to employment. The case for "creaming" was supported by the first U.S. Department of Health and Human Services report on TANF, which indicated that an increasing proportion of the caseload included long-term recipients (U.S. Department of Health and Human Services, 1998). Rising caseloads in several states since 2000 support another hypothesis—that the robust economy accelerated caseload decline.

Although welfare researchers have judged Louisiana's implementation of welfare reform as severe relative to other states, time limits are not as stringent as they may appear on the surface. In practice, Louisiana's regulations allow families to receive federally funded cash assistance continuously for up to five years and offers more generous earnings disregards than in the past. On the other hand, Louisiana's implementation of welfare reform provides virtually no state-funded supplement to federal funds. In other states, such supplements increase lifetime limits on cash assistance or allow higher earnings disregards. Louisiana also continues to pay relatively low monthly benefit levels. The greatest shortcoming of welfare reform in Louisiana may, however, be the failure to take advantage of existing provisions by *not* encouraging recipients over age 20 to use education to fulfill work requirements.

THE LOUISIANA WELFARE SURVEY

With funding from Louisiana's Office of Family Services, we began our Louisiana Welfare Survey in 1998. In order to compare different labor market areas, we drew samples from a major metropolitan area and from parts of the Mississippi Delta that have been persistently poor. For that reason, the survey is based on a stratified random sample of (then) current TANF recipients of cash assistance in three welfare districts in the city of New Orleans–Algiers, Gentilly, and Midtown—and 12 parishes in northeastern Louisiana. All 13 parishes are part of the LMD region (note: the city of New Orleans is synonymous with Orleans Parish). The 12 parishes in the Delta region form two contiguous labor market areas: one is centered on Monroe, the other is a non-metropolitan labor market (without a metropolitan core). Those two labor market areas stretch from around Monroe to the Louisiana-Arkansas border to the north, to the Mississippi river to the east, south to Ferriday and Vidalia, and from Sicily Island back to Monroe. When the survey began, the only metropolitan area in the two northeastern Delta labor market areas was Monroe, with a population slightly above 50,000. Union Parish has since been designated part of the Monroe metropolitan area but is not considered so in our analysis. The Delta parishes and New Orleans neighborhoods represented in this study have total poverty rates (Figure 18.1) and race-specific poverty rates well above the U.S. poverty rate. Despite having employment growth slightly better than the U.S. national rate of growth between 1989 and 1999, our study parishes still

Figure 18.1. Ratio of County-to-U.S. Poverty Rate, Lower Mississippi Delta, 1999

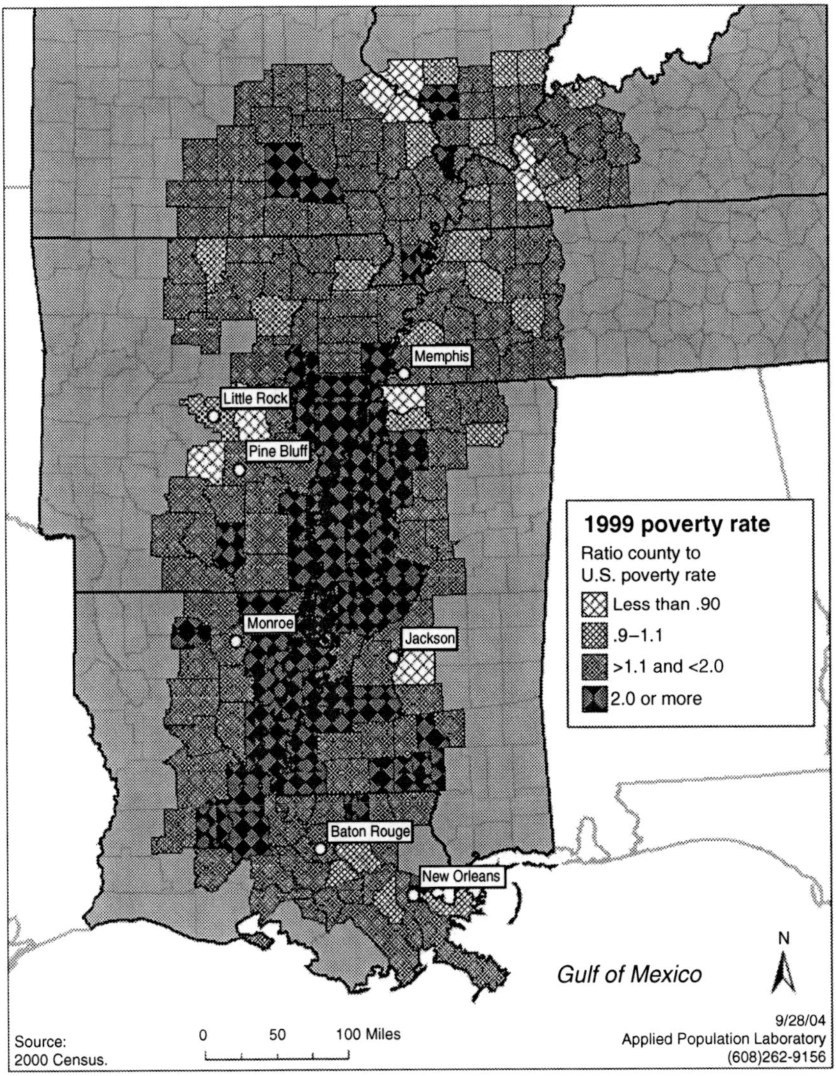

have employment ratios lower than the U.S. overall (Figure 18.2). Strictly speaking, our results are generalizable only to areas of Louisiana from which the sample was drawn. However, these are important areas to understand because they represent persistent pockets of limited economic opportunity located in predominantly black rural communities and inner city neighborhoods.

Figure 18.2. County-to-U.S. Employment Ratio, Lower Mississippi Delta, 1999

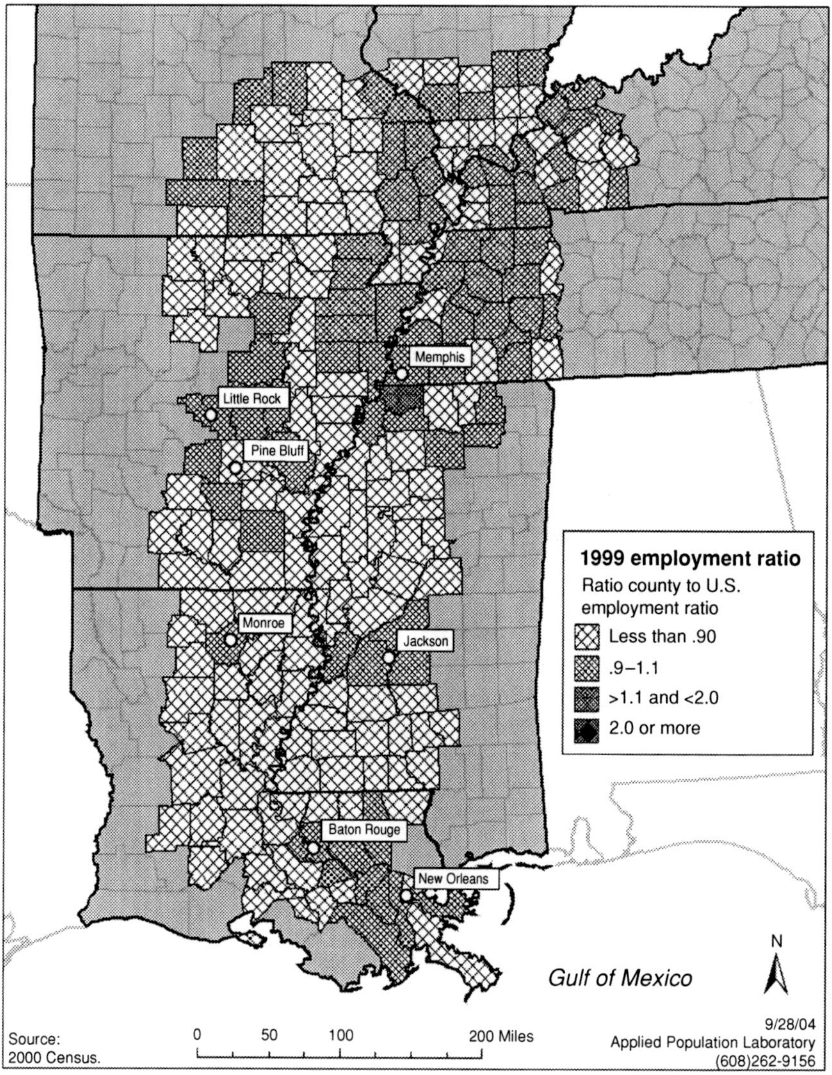

The initial survey population consisted of persons age 18 or older who, according to administrative records, received cash assistance payments as of March 1998. We augmented the survey population with another sample drawn in February 1999. Comparison of interviews for the initial sample and the supplement indicate no significant differences in the characteristics of the two samples. Contacts and interviewing over the 1998–2001 period were done mainly via CATI (Computer Assisted Telephone Interviewing) technology. However, since this population was not easily reached by telephone, we attempted to interview respondents face-to-face when they did not have a telephone. The baseline sample used for this analysis included 996 respondents, nearly equally divided among the northeastern Delta parishes and New Orleans districts (Table 18.2). As with the Louisiana FITAP caseload, all but a few (18) respondents were women.

The usefulness of survey panels which interview the same respondents over time relies on the representativeness of the sample. Increasing nonresponse over time is a potential source of bias. Discounting those individuals we could not reach, we had a response rate of over 60 percent for the initial interviews. As was done in more recent interviews for the PSID and the National Longitudinal Survey of Youth (NLSY), we tried to maximize long-term response rates by efforts to recontact respondents from the initial interview in each wave. Still, due to attrition, we were only able to complete interviews with 582 respondents in 2000 and 400 in 2001. Our response rate from initial interviews to 2001 was approximately 40 percent. This is comparable to recent results (30–49 percent) for the total PSID, not just the low-income sample (Fitzgerald et al., 1997; Weinberg, 1999). An examination of panel mortality showed that those who dropped out of the sample did not have significantly different socioeconomic characteristics in Wave 1 than those who remained in the panel survey.

Before we proceed with an analysis of stayers and leavers, we examine selected demographic characteristics of respondents in the baseline interviews (Table 18.2). In 1999, FITAP participants were overwhelmingly younger than 45 (over 92 percent), black (86 percent), and single (97 percent) (Louisiana Office of Family Services, cited in Weimer et al., 2001). A majority was unemployed and about half had less than a high school education. Over 90 percent of our baseline sample was black, ages 18 to 44, and single. Slightly more than 40 percent did not have a high school education, making our baseline more educated than expected.

In 1999, federal regulation required 40 percent of TANF recipients to be working, leaving 60 percent not employed. A slightly higher percent (67 percent) of our baseline sample was not employed. The initial differences between our sample and the general FITAP caseload suggests that we might observe better employment outcomes for our sample members. Also, because non-metro respondents have an education level more consistent with the FITAP caseload (46 percent with less than a high school education), results for non-metro stayers may be more comparable to results for the entire Louisiana caseload in later years. The characteristics of TANF participants in Louisiana are typical of what one finds in other states, except for the high percentage of blacks, which is specific to the South because of the concentration of the black population in that region.

We compare our results from 2001 with a description of Louisiana's caseload to determine whether characteristics of stayers in our sample correspond

Table 18.2. *Selected Characteristics of Baseline Sample in 1998–1999 and 2000 (Percent)*

	1998–1999			2001		
	All	Original Sample	Supplement	All	Stayers	Leavers
Place Of Residence	(N = 996)	(N = 427)	(N = 569)	(N = 400)	(N = 171)	(N = 227)
Delta LMA Non-Metro	33.0	38.2	29.2	39.3	35.7	41.4
Delta LMA Metro	16.8	19.7	14.6	14.0	14.0	14.1
New Orleans	50.2	42.2	56.2	46.8	50.3	44.5
Age	(N = 993)	(N = 424)	(N = 569)	(N = 399)	(N = 171)	(N = 227)
18–44	85.0	85.1	84.9	74.7	69.6	77.9
45 or Older	15.0	14.9	15.1	25.3	30.4	22.1
Black	(N = 991)	(N = 424)	(N = 567)	(N = 397)	(N = 170)	(N = 226)
	90.1	88.2	88.5	91.7	91.8	91.6
Case Type	(N = 996)	(N = 427)	(N = 569)	(N = 400)	(N = 171)	(N = 227)
Family	87.4	86.9	87.9	79.8	77.8	81.1
Child-Only	8.9	10.3	7.9	11.3	14.6	8.8
Other	3.6	2.8	4.2	9.0	7.6	10.1
Receives Cash Assistance	(N = 993)	(N = 425)	(N = 568)	(N = 398)	(N = 171)	(N = 272)
	78.5	72.2	83.3	43.0	100.0	0.0

Education	(N = 991)	(N = 422)	(N = 569)	(N = 396)	(N = 169)	(N = 226)
Less than H.S	41.2	42.7	40.4	35.6	38.5	33.3
H.S/GED	44.2	42.7	45.3	42.4	41.4	43.1
Some College	12.3	12.6	12.1	17.9	15.4	20.0
College Degree	2.1	2.1	2.1	4.0	4.7	3.6
Single	(N = 995)	(N = 427)	(N = 568)	(N = 398)	(N = 171)	(N = 227)
	93.4	92.3	94.2	90.9	91.8	90.7
Employment Status	(N = 988)	(N = 423)	(N = 565)	(N = 398)	(N = 171)	(N = 227)
No Work/No TANF	10.1	12.5	8.3	25.9	0.0	45.4
No Work/ TANF	57.3	52.5	60.9	29.4	68.4	0.0
Work and TANF	21.4	20.1	22.3	13.6	31.6	0.0
Work and No TANF	11.2	14.9	8.5	31.2	0.0	54.6

Note: For 2001, sample of stayers and leavers do not always add to the observations for all 2001 respondents because of missing information about TANF participation for four respondents.

to characteristics reported in Louisiana's TANF evaluation (Valvano & Abe, 2002, pp. 13–18). By March 2002, the FITAP caseload had fallen to about 20,000 cases, with 56 percent family cases and 44 percent child-only cases. This represented a doubling of child-only cases as a proportion of the caseload. Although child-only cases constitute a smaller proportion of our sample, we also observe a large increase in these cases as a percent of all respondents still receiving FITAP cash assistance. Ninety percent of adult heads of FITAP families were under 40 years of age in 2002. Ninety-seven percent were single, 82 percent non-Hispanic black. Forty-nine percent completed less than a high school education. Seventy-two percent were from urban parishes, with 32 percent from New Orleans and 2.8 percent from Ouachita. Despite geographic selectivity in our sample, in 2001, the percent in metropolitan areas (61 percent) is reasonably similar to that found in the FITAP caseload. However, respondents still in FITAP in 2001 are slightly older than those in Louisiana's caseload and more likely to be black.

In 2001 our survey provides a sample of FITAP recipients from selected parishes in Louisiana who had been on the rolls in 1998–1999. It differs from the FITAP caseload particularly with respect to education level. Stayers in the survey have a significantly higher proportion of respondents with a post-secondary education (20 percent vs. 0.4 percent in Louisiana's total FITAP caseload). TANF regulations required 50 percent of the caseload to be working by 2002. In our 2001 wave, significantly fewer than this percent of stayers were employed (32 percent). This is unexpected since education differences between our respondents and those in the overall Louisiana caseload would suggest that our findings will err on the side of being optimistic when applied to the caseload at large. However, high unemployment rates in our non-metro parishes may affect our results.

In the next section, we examine how the distribution of stayers changed over time, particularly with respect to background and human capital characteristics that might indicate "creaming." Given the dearth of economic opportunities in non-metro Delta parishes and the lower human capital in these areas, we do not expect to see as many indications of "creaming" as in metro areas. Finally, we examine characteristics of stayers and leavers and employment outcomes. Based on results from other state evaluations noted above and greater economic opportunities in metropolitan areas, we expect higher exit rates and better employment outcomes among metropolitan residents. Readers should note that our findings are based on a very short time period. Thus, results must be viewed as preliminary; only after several more years can we be certain about the longer-term effects of PRWORA.

FINDINGS

Do TANF Leavers Transition from Welfare-to-Work and Back?

In the baseline 1998–1999 survey, four of every five respondents reported that they participated in TANF. For subsequent survey waves, respondents' welfare-to-work transitions tracked trends in caseload decline. As noted in Table 18.1, even in Delta non-metro areas which had the smallest rate of decline, the number of active TANF cases dropped by almost 60 percent. In our total sample, there has been a decline in the percent solely reliant on TANF (57 to 31) and the percent partially dependent on TANF (21 to 14). While dependence on TANF has declined, reliance on work has increased (from 11 percent to 33 percent), as has the percent with no work and no cash assistance (10 to 22). With the downturn in the economy during 2000, the shift toward employment slowed, particularly in metropolitan areas, where the percentage working without TANF support decreased from 35 to 31 percent by 2001. However, the worsening economic situation did not result in a move back to TANF, as in previous recessions; instead, when former TANF recipients could not find work, our results indicate that they most likely remained unemployed without seeking TANF cash assistance. Having worked, some former participants might have qualified for unemployment insurance, which would have delayed their re-entry into TANF.

The economic downturn that started in 2000 affected non-metro areas differently than Monroe and New Orleans. In 1998–1999, non-metro respondents were less likely than their metro counterparts to be working only and more likely to be on TANF without working (Table 18.3). This difference persisted through 2000. By 2001, however, the percentage of non-metro respondents with welfare as their sole support (28 percent) had fallen below that of metro respondents (31 percent). We suspect that the non-metro Delta region had not participated much in the economic expansion of the 1990s and thus was less affected when the economy contracted. This supposition is supported by higher unemployment rates in our non-metro Delta parishes from 1998 to 2001 and the greater likelihood throughout the study period that non-metro respondents were without work and without TANF assistance. Despite the economic gains of the 1990s, the parishes from which respondents in our study are drawn remained poorer than most other parishes in the LMD (Figure 18.1: see parishes east of Monroe and north of Baton Rouge). Another reason why non-metro areas responded differently to the 2000–2001 economic downturn is the prominent role of government in employing current and former TANF recipients in non-metro labor markets. A greater proportion of non-metro respondents than metro respondents was employed in government jobs, with the metro/non-metro relationship reversed for jobs in the private sector. In 2001, the government employed almost as many non-metro respondents as did the private sector.

From 1998 to 2000, only about 7 percent of our respondents had returned to TANF. However, from 2000 to 2001, about 13 percent returned. These estimates are much lower than the recidivism estimates (18–36 percent) found in Louisiana's evaluation (Valvano & Abe, 2002). There are several possible reasons for this discrepancy. First, some recipients may have cycled on and off again within a year or two. Our survey had only annual interviews, whereas Louisiana's TANF records would show specific dates of welfare receipt, thereby capturing return to

Table 18.3 Employment and TANF status by Wave and Rurality

	Total (Percent)	Metropolitan (Percent)	Delta Nonmetro (Percent)
1998–99			
TANF Status/Employment	(N = 988)	(N = 662)	(N = 326)
TANF Only	57.3	56.9	58.0
TANF and Work	21.4	21.1	21.8
Work Only	11.2	12.4	8.9
No Work and No TANF	10.1	9.5	11.3
	(N = 317)	(N = 220)	(N = 97)
Self Employed	10.7	10.9	10.3
Private Non-Government	66.9	70.5	58.8
Government	22.4	18.6	30.9
2000			
TANF Status/Employment	(N = 582)	(N = 380)	(N = 202)
TANF Only	31.3	30.8	32.2
TANF and Work	13.7	13.9	13.4
Work Only	33.2	35.5	28.7
No Work and No TANF	21.8	19.7	25.7
	(N = 259)	(N = 179)	(N = 80)
Self employed	11.6	12.3	10.0
Private Non-Government	59.6	62.0	55.0
Government	28.6	25.7	35.0
2001			
TANF Status/Employment	(N = 398)	(N = 243)	(N = 155)
TANF Only	29.4	30.5	27.7
TANF and Work	13.6	14.8	11.6
Work Only	31.2	30.5	32.3
No Work and No TANF	25.9	24.3	28.4
	(N = 173)	(N = 106)	(N = 67)
Self Employed	19.7	17.9	22.4
Private Non-Government	53.2	60.4	41.8
Government	27.2	21.7	35.8

Note: Categories may not add to 100 percent due to rounding. Private non-government workers are predominantly wage-and-salaried employees and those workers (less than 1 percent) paid according to production, for example, by the piece.

TANF at any time during a given period instead of just at the endpoints. Second, our respondents have a higher level of education, making it likely that they will experience longer spells of employment.

Turning to TANF exits, we find that transitions from 1998 to 2000 show substantial proportions having left TANF (about 33 percent). However, we did not find the statistically significant differences in urban and rural exit rates that administrative studies in other states have found. The proportion leaving TANF declined to 15 percent for 2000 to 2001. Declining proportions leaving TANF and increasing proportions entering TANF likely reflect the deteriorating labor market conditions that started in 2000. *Trends in the magnitude of transitions on and off welfare support our hypothesis that the robust economy of the 1990s accelerated caseload decline after the 1996 welfare reforms were implemented in Louisiana.* An alternative explanation for declining exits would be that several years into welfare reform, TANF cases represent the hard-to-serve among the eligible population. However, we believe that if the economic conditions had remained favorable after 2000, caseloads would have declined further.

Do Trends in Characteristics of TANF Stayers Indicate "Creaming?"

Comparing characteristics of stayers in each wave, *we find little indication that more difficult cases remain on TANF, especially in non-metro areas*. Overall demographic characteristics of stayers such as age and education level do not vary significantly over time. However, trends in the proportion of stayers raised in welfare families support a "creaming" hypothesis. Trends in age of first AFDC/TANF receipt do not. Between 1998 to 1999 and 2001, the percentage of stayers raised in AFDC/TANF families increased, but relatively fewer stayers reported having received first-time AFDC/TANF at an early age.

In later waves, non-metro stayers were increasingly less likely never to have held a job and increasingly more likely to have held multiple jobs. The percent of non-metro stayers who never held a job went from 29 percent in 1998–1999 to 15 percent in 2001. Those with multiple jobs went from 56 percent to 76 percent. As stayers' education and job training levels did not change significantly over time, it is unlikely that this pattern in jobs-ever-held is a result of the most educated finding work first. *These findings suggest that early on, work requirements may provide job experience in non-metro areas but not job stability.* This interpretation would be consistent with the evidence of recidivism found in Louisiana's TANF evaluation (Valvano & Abe, 2002). It would also be consistent with long-time AFDC/TANF recipients having more difficulty getting and holding a job.

How are Stayers and Leavers Different?

Bivariate analyses suggest that TANF leavers do not differ significantly from respondents still on TANF. However, looking at leavers and stayers by residence-work categories reveals some differences. Working metro respondents are younger than those without a job. This holds for employed metro respondents on or off TANF. The oldest group tends to be metro women who neither work nor receive TANF, possibly because they have shifted to social security or other support programs. Neither metro nor non-metro areas show significant race differentials for the four TANF-work status groups (TANF only, TANF and work, work only, and neither TANF nor work). There are also no marital differences among the four groups in either metro or non-metro areas.

However, education matters. Metro as well as non-metro respondents with less than a high school education are far more likely either to remain on welfare or to be both without TANF and without work (see Table 18.2). In non-metro areas, for example, when comparing stayers without work and leavers with work, we find that 35–42 percent of stayers without work have less than a high school education and only 15–23 percent of working leavers have such low education levels. Similar differences exist in metro areas. By 2000, the education gap among TANF and non-TANF workers in metro and non-metro areas had all but closed. However, for non-metro areas, the education gap between non-working stayers and working leavers remained in 2001 (28 percent vs. 40 percent with a high school diploma).

How Well-Employed are Current and Former TANF Recipients?

We examine the first observed job that respondents had after being in AFDC or TANF (see Table 18.4). Even in non-metro areas, hardly any respondent had agricultural occupations. Table 18.4 shows that about 80 percent of all respondents worked in the lower-status occupations of sales, clerical, and service workers or as operators. Around one half of the respondents found work as service workers (mostly as waitresses, certified nurse assistants [CNAs], or domestic workers), with another 30 percent in sales, clerical, and operator occupations. Only 6 percent were professionals, technicians, or managers, with most respondents in those higher-status categories being teachers and registered nurses (RN). Non-metro respondents were more likely than metro respondents to be service workers, whereas metro respondents were more likely to be in professional, technical, managerial, sales, clerical, and operative occupations. This likely reflects the greater diversity of work available in metro areas and the higher education levels of metro respondents.

The industry composition of respondents' employment reflects occupations held. Very few respondents worked in extractive industries; those who did were all in agriculture. About three out of every four respondents worked in social or personal service industries. Four categories of service industries account for most of the employment: food services, retail trade, health services, and other services (e.g., personal services). The metro/non-metro differences in industrial composition is small: more metro respondents worked in food services, whereas more non-metro respondents worked in health and other services.

Table 18.4 Characteristics of First Job after TANF/AFDC by Rurality

	All (Percent)	Metro (Percent)	Non-metro (Percent)
Occupation (a)			
Service Worker	49.7	47.0	55.6
Sales/Clerk/Operator	29.3	34.7	17.5
Professional/Tech/Manager	5.9	5.4	6.9
Other	15.1	12.9	20.0
Industry (b)			
Extractive	1.2	0.3	3.3
Transformative	4.3	3.6	6.0
Distributive Services	18.1	17.9	18.5
Producer Services	6.0	7.5	2.6
Social Services	34.4	30.7	42.4
Personal Services	36.0	40.0	27.2
Hours Worked Per Week (c)			
1–19 hrs	36.7	35.5	39.1
20–39 hrs	24.4	26.0	21.2
40 or more hrs	38.8	38.5	39.7
Weeks Worked in Job Last Year			
1–4 weeks	18.6	17.8	20.3
5–11 weeks	13.9	13.1	15.9
12–49 weeks	52.4	54.8	47.1
50–52 weeks	15.0	14.3	16.7
Hourly Wage (d)			
Up to $5.15	47.0	40.1	62.5
$5.16–$7.99	40.3	45.3	28.9
$8 or more	12.7	14.5	8.6
Health Care Benefits			
Yes	23.9	24.4	22.8
No	76.1	75.6	77.2

Notes: (a) The few female operators in the sample perform work duties similar to sales and clerical workers. Other workers are primarily laborers and those not elsewhere classified. (b) Extractive industries include agriculture; six persons work in agriculture, five of whom are non-metro residents. (c) Cutoff points for hours of work were chosen based on number of hours usually associated with different levels of fringe benefits. (d) Less than 0.5 percent earn under minimum wage, and these are generally persons engaged in informal work arrangements where hourly wage estimates are highly inaccurate.

Clearly, many current and former welfare recipients already work 40 hours per week, as the current (2003) proposal for re-authorization of the Welfare Reform Act would mandate. Almost 40 percent of all working respondents reported that they worked 40 hours or more in the week preceding the interview. A similar percentage reported having worked less than 20 hours per week, and about 20 percent worked 20–39 hours. The number of hours worked per week did not differ significantly between metro and non-metro areas. It is unclear, at this point, if those women working fewer than 40 hours per week can find jobs that give them more hours and/or if their family situation permits them to be away from their children for more hours than at present. About one half of all working respondents worked at least three months during the year preceding the interview, with 15 percent reporting that they worked throughout the previous 12 months. Close to one fifth of respondents had been working for one month or less. In general, metro respondents reported more weeks worked than did non-metro respondents, which is likely to be a reflection of the greater scarcity or seasonality of jobs in non-metro areas. The work input reported by respondents suggests considerable labor force attachment.

Hourly earnings and health benefits are key indicators of job quality. Given the low educational attainment reported earlier in this chapter, it comes as no surprise that few women—if they worked full-time (40 hours per week) and throughout the year (at least 50 weeks per year)—have jobs paying enough to lift them out of poverty. Only 13 percent of all respondents reported a living wage (defined as at least $8.00 per hour). See Pollin and others (2002) for a discussion of living wage in New Orleans. On the other hand, 47 percent of all respondents earn a minimum wage or less; that percentage rises to 62 in non-metro areas. Three-quarters of the first jobs respondents held did *not* provide health benefits.

The work characteristics reported above pertain to the *first* job obtained after having been on TANF and not working. It is possible that with time respondents will be able to obtain better-paying jobs with health care benefits, even if their low educational attainment does not make such an outcome very likely. It is too soon after the welfare reform act for a comprehensive analysis of post-TANF job mobility. However, with a panel study, we can examine occupational mobility for the 1998–2001 period of the panel survey. We are less interested here in job changes if they were from, for example, one CNA job to another. Instead, the interest here is in job *status changes*. Preliminary analysis shows that about two out of every five working respondents, regardless of whether they were stayers or leavers, kept the same *kind* of job over more than one wave.

Examining mobility patterns in terms of stayers and leavers, metro stayers were more likely to remain in their occupational category than were non-metro stayers. Regarding leavers, the situation reversed: metro leavers were less likely to keep their occupational status and more likely to experience downward mobility than non-metro leavers. Among leavers, there was little difference in metro and non-metro mobility. A comprehensive interpretation of these patterns would have to take into account types of occupations for the various groups. For example, if non-metro respondents occupied much lower status jobs than metro respondents, a greater upward mobility would imply that non-metro workers might merely be catching up with their urban counterparts. However, since the occupational differences observed earlier between metro and non-metro areas were not particularly large, we believe that these mobility patterns reflect different conditions presented to stayers and leavers and in metro and non-metro areas.

CONCLUSIONS AND DISCUSSION

The Lower Mississippi Delta, especially in Mississippi and Louisiana, is one of the poorest regions in the United States. Persistent regional economic disadvantage has implications for recent welfare reform because historical and contemporary sources of poverty limit opportunities for social mobility. Indeed, one of the criticisms of the 1996 welfare reform was that it made little concession to the economic disadvantages recipients faced in some places. In this study, we compare outcomes for a sample of welfare recipients in selected metro and non-metro parishes in Louisiana. Among non-working respondents still on welfare in 2001, we observe significantly lower education levels than among working welfare leavers. We find that working respondents from non-metro parishes have significantly more employment in the government sector than in the private sector. Accordingly, in respondent's first observed jobs, a greater proportion of non-metro residents work in social service industries than do metro residents. Respondents' first jobs are generally low-paying and either offer no health care coverage or unaffordable coverage. Although the lack of health care coverage applies equally to metro and non-metro respondents, non-metro respondents are more likely to make just the minimum wage and not a penny above this rate.

Our analysis failed to find some metro/non-metro differences found in other studies. Exit rates did not differ significantly by place of residence, nor did the employment rate or earnings. Even though a significantly greater proportion of non-metro respondents earned the minimum wage or less, working metro respondents did not have significantly higher annual earnings because, on average, most employed metro respondents only had a slightly higher wage rate than non-metro respondents and worked a similar number of hours per week and weeks per year. This result is understandable if one considers the results of the 2002 Louisiana Job Vacancy Survey and the 2000 Louisiana Occupational Employment Statistics Wage Survey. Both indicated that health service, retail, and food service vacancies for which most current and former recipients qualify pay only pennies more in New Orleans than in other parts of Louisiana.

Also contributing to the problem of low wage rates in Louisiana is the structure of service industries in this state. Although some parts of the South benefited from growth of knowledge-based technical service jobs in both the private and government sector, Louisiana has not experienced growth in these types of jobs (LEDC, 1999). Historically, the plantation economy in the Lower Mississippi Delta concentrated land ownership and social benefits among the elite. This legacy left Louisiana with a school system inferior to that of most non-Delta states and with few industrial alternatives to agricultural employment. Thus, existing service industries in Louisiana mostly require low-status service employees such as waitresses, fast food workers, retail sales clerks, and nursing home service workers.

Even given the industrial structure in Louisiana, we expected to find a more pronounced employment disadvantage for non-metro respondents because metro areas generally provide far greater opportunities for education and employment. The absence of a metro/non-metro differential with respect to welfare exits, earnings, and employment could be due to several factors. First, the spatial concentration of race, poverty, and welfare could make metro TANF participants so isolated that their social and physical environment does not differ much from that in non-metro areas. As Massey and Denton (1988, 1993) have shown, concentration of poverty is associated with a lack of amenities and opportunities. Another explanation for the absence of metro/non-metro employment differentials in our analyses could be that metro and non-metro areas alike suffer from the consequences of structural poverty in the Lower Mississippi Delta. According to this hypothesis, the historical legacy of the LMD region does not provide metro TANF participants any more opportunities than their non-metro counterparts. We suspect that both explanations contribute to the absence of significant metro/non-metro differentials in welfare exits, employment, and earnings.

Low monthly benefit levels may be another reason we see little substantial difference in employment outcomes for metro and non-metro respondents. TANF participants in Louisiana receive only 25–30 percent of what other states like Wisconsin or Massachusetts pay out. For Louisiana TANF recipients, loss of cash assistance therefore has fewer consequences than it would in other states. The PRWORA provision that allows non-working adults only three months of food stamps is a far greater incentive to work than TANF requirements. Losing the cash portion of TANF is far less important than the potential loss of food stamps or access to Section 8 housing.

The region's historical legacy has also had implications for its political culture. The South, for the most part, has little experience with public policy making. At almost every major turn of social policy in the United States during the 20th century, be it the New Deal or Civil Rights, the South lagged behind and responded more often than it initiated. Reasons for the South's past position with respect to social policy included active opposition to both racial integration and the establishment of labor unions. Lack of experience with policy innovation has hurt the Delta region in an era of reforms based on devolution of authority from the federal government to states. States such as Illinois, Wisconsin, Minnesota, and Oregon have been using their new latitude to experiment with a variety of state-specific welfare measures that can be funded with federal TANF dollars. Louisiana, on the other hand, has focused narrowly on reducing the TANF caseload, failing to take advantage of TANF policies that allow education of recipients. Low education levels limit job opportunities, particularly among non-metro residents. With higher levels of education, recipients would have a better chance of sustaining labor force attachment and making a living wage. Also, a more educated labor force has the potential to stimulate labor demand, which will be important in addressing the lack of jobs and job instability in non-metro areas.

REFERENCES

Bloom, D., Farrell, M. & Fink, B. (2002). *Welfare time limits*. Report to the Department of Health and Human Services. Boston: The Lewin Group.

Brown, D.L. & Lee, M.A. (1999). Persisting inequality between metropolitan and nonmetropolitan America: Implications for theory and policy. In P. Moen & D. Dempster-McClain (Eds.), *A nation divided: Diversity, inequality, and community in American society* (pp. 151–170). Ithaca, NY: Cornell University Press.

Cancian, M., Haveman, R., Meyer, D. & Wolfe, B. (1999). *Before and after TANF: The economic well-being of women leaving welfare*. Madison, WI: University of Wisconsin, Institute for Research on Poverty.

Duncan, C.M. (1999). *A world apart*. New Haven, CT: Yale University.

Fitzgerald, J., Gottschalk, P. & Moffitt, R. (1997). An analysis of sample attrition in panel data: The Michigan panel study of income dynamics. *Journal of Human Resources 33*, 251–299.

Knox, V., Miller, C. & Gennetian, L. (2000). *Reforming welfare and rewarding work: A summary of the final report on the Minnesota family investment program*. New York: MDRC.

Lee, M.A., Harvey, M. & Neustrom, A. (2002). Local labor markets and caseload decline in Louisiana in the 1990s. *Rural Sociology, 67*(4), 556–577.

Leisering, L. & Leibfried, S. (1999). *Time and poverty in western welfare states*. Cambridge, UK: Cambridge University Press.

Logan, J. (1975). Growth, politics and the stratification of places. *American Journal of Sociology, 84*, 404–415.

Logan, J. & Molotoch, H. (1987). *Urban fortunes: The political economy of place*. Berkeley, CA: University of California Press.

Louisiana Economic Development Council (LEDC). (March 31, 1999). *Louisiana: Vision 2020*. Baton Rouge, LA.

Lower Mississippi Delta Commission (LMDC). (1990). *Delta initiatives: Realizing the dream . . . fulfilling the promise*. Memphis: Walker Freeman Advertising.

Massey, D. & Denton, N. (1988). The dimensions of residential segregation. *Social Forces, 67* (2), 281–315.

Massey, D. & Denton, N. (1993). *American apartheid: Segregation and the making of the underclass*. Cambridge, MA: Harvard University Press.

Pollin, R., Brenner, M. & Luce, S. (2002). Intended versus unintended consequences: Evaluating the New Orleans living wage ordinance. *Journal of Economic Issues, 36*(4), 843–875.

Quadagno, J. (1994). *The color of welfare: How racism undermined the war on poverty*. New York: Oxford University Press.

Reeder R. & Calhoun, S. (2002). Federal funding in the Delta. *Rural America 17*(4), U.S. Department of Agriculture, Economic Research Service.

South, S. & Crowder, K. (1997). Escaping distressed neighborhoods: Individual, community, and metropolitan influences. *American Journal of Sociology, 102*(99), 1040–1084.

South, S. & Crowder, K. (1998). Leaving the "hood": Residential mobility between black, white, and integrated neighborhoods. *American Sociological Review, 63*(1), 17–26.

The Lewin Group. (2001). *How well have rural and small labor markets absorbed welfare recipients* (Final Report for Assistant Secretary of Planning and Evaluation, Department of Health and Human Services)? Retrieved April 2001, from http://aspe.hhs.gov/hsp/rural-lm01/index.htm

Tomaskovic-Devey, D. & Roscigno, V.J. (1996). Racial economic subordination and white gain in the U.S. South. *American Sociological Review, 61*, 565–589.

U.S. Department of Health and Human Services, Administration of Children and Families. (1998). *TANF Caseload.* Retrieved March 24, 2004, from http://www.acf.dhhs.gov/news/stats/index.html

Valvano, V. & Abe, Y. (2002). *The state of Louisiana TANF final evaluation* (Vol. 1). Oakland, CA: Berkeley Policy Associates.

Weimer, B.J., Gavin, N.I., Rachel, J.V. & MacLain, B. (2001). *Substance abuse and treatment needs among Louisiana's family independence temporary assistance program (FITAP) Recipients, 1999*. Baton Rouge, LA: Final Report for Department of Health and Hospitals.

Weinberg, D. (1999). *Comparing response rates for SPD, PSID, and NLSY* (SPD Working Paper SPD99-2). Washington, DC: U.S. Department of Commerce, Census Bureau.

Wilson, W.J. (1987). *The truly disadvantaged.* Chicago: University of Chicago Press.

Ziliak, J., Figlio, D., Davis, E. & Connolly, L. (2001). Accounting for the decline in AFDC caseloads: Welfare or the economy? *Journal of Human Resources*, *35* (3), 570–586.

APPENDIX: GLOSSARY OF ABBREVIATIONS

AFDC: Aid to Families with Dependent Children was a means-tested welfare program for poor women and children. This program was structured by a framework of federal rules that guided state-level administration of cash assistance since the 1960s. It replaced the Aid to Dependent Children program enacted by the Social Security Act of 1935.

FIND-Work: Family Independence Work Program is the State of Louisiana's job search and training program implemented in 1997 to comply with requirements to qualify for federal matching funds of cash assistance under the federal Personal Responsibility and Work Opportunity Reconciliation Act of 1996.

FITAP: Families Independence Temporary Assistance Program is the State of Louisiana's cash assistance program for poor parents and children living with these parents. The program began in 1997 and complies with requirements of the Personal Responsibility and Work Opportunity Reconciliation Act of 1996 and associated amendments. It receives federal funds from the federal government's Temporary Assistance to Needy Families community block grant program.

GED: General Education Diploma

LMD: Lower Mississippi Delta includes 240 mostly contiguous counties or parishes in eight states along the Mississippi river from Illinois to Louisiana. This region was identified by the Lower Mississippi Delta Development Commission. The Commission was established in 1988 by Congress to develop a 10-year economic development plan for the region. The Commission completed its work in 1990. There is now a standing Delta Regional Authority (www.dra.gov).

PRWORA: Personal Responsibility and Work Opportunity Reconciliation Act of 1996 is the federal welfare reform act that abolished the Aid to Families with Dependent Children program and replaced it with a system of block grants. Under this legislation, the federal government no longer guaranteed matching funds for cash assistance to poor families and children, and allowed states to pursue a greater variety of policies.

PSID: Panel Study of Income Dynamics is a longitudinal study of U.S. families begun in 1963.

TANF: Temporary Assistance to Needy Families is the community block grant program under which states receive federal funds for cash assistance to poor families. It was enacted as part of the Personal Responsibility and Work Opportunity Reconciliation Act of 1996.

PART IV

NEW ANALYTIC DIRECTIONS AND POLICY IMPLICATIONS

CHAPTER 19

EXPLORATIONS IN SPATIAL DEMOGRAPHY[1]

PAUL R. VOSS, KATHERINE J. CURTIS WHITE,
AND ROGER B. HAMMER

INTRODUCTION

Social scientists in many disciplines have noted re-emerging interest in issues concerning social processes embedded within a spatial context (e.g., Messner & Anselin, 2004). In this chapter, we echo and emphasize the long-standing assertion, found in various forms across numerous disciplines, that special methods are necessary for the appropriate analysis of spatial data. Attributes of spatially referenced data generally violate at least one of the assumptions underlying the standard regression model, which necessitates both caution regarding these violations and attention to methods designed to correct for them. We discuss the nature of the problem, how it arises, how to identify it, and methods by which one can press forward appropriately with the investigation of such data. We present what we view as the most important and well-developed concepts of spatial data analysis and indicate for interested readers where greater detail can be found. Specifically, we have sought to minimize the presentation of technical material, including formulae and equations, and, instead, apply the concepts and methods to an analysis of population change in the Great Plains.

SPATIAL IS SPECIAL

When investigating population change for a large number of spatial units (e.g., counties), it is the natural inclination of sociologists and demographers to move from simple descriptive analyses to begin asking such questions as: How might these data be modeled? How well can I account for variability in attribute values among geographic units by identifying other covariates of our attribute of interest? Such analysts have traditionally turned to multivariate regression modeling to answer such questions. Regrettably, standard regression approaches to data for spatial units bring special complications that have not always been appreciated

W.A. Kandel & D.L. Brown (eds.), Population Change and Rural Society, 407–429.

or understood. The idea that somehow "spatial is special" is a notion that has begun only slowly to enter the awareness of quantitative demographers.

Over the past two decades, increasing attention has been drawn to the fact that spatial data require special analytical approaches. Many of the techniques documented in standard statistics textbooks and taught in our "methods" classrooms unfortunately confront significant difficulties when applied to the analysis of geospatial data. These problems are summarized by language more familiar to geographers and regional scientists than to demographers: spatial autocorrelation, the modifiable areal unit problem, and scale and edge effects. But the emphasis on "problems" fails to capture the fact that there also is a benefit arising from the special nature of spatial data. Aspects of space (e.g., distance, proximity, and interaction), when properly acknowledged and incorporated into one's model, can overcome complications of space and error dependence, improve specification of models based on spatial units, and provide estimates of parameters that are less subject to statistical bias, inconsistency, or inefficiency. Further, such approaches can contribute to theoretical notions regarding the role of space in social relationships and processes.

Although rural demography has long maintained a strong focus on patterns and trends that vary spatially (Voss, 1993, 2004), the field has not been very sensitive to these more recent analytical issues, and rural demographers have largely failed to adopt the methods of formal quantitative spatial analysis that have emerged in the fields of geography, regional science, and spatial econometrics during the past decade (Lobao & Saenz, 2002). It is encouraging that such neglect is waning, as evidenced by the spatial focus of a recent Rural Sociological Society presidential address (Lobao, 2004).

To illustrate some of these spatial concepts, we examine in this chapter the correlates of county-level population change in the Great Plains between 1990 and 2000. Details regarding the sample, measures, and theoretical motivations can be found in White (2003).

A thorough researcher will carefully begin an analysis by exploring the behavior of the variables of interest using the standard tools of exploratory data analysis (EDA)—and thus we begin. In the present example, one that will be used throughout the remainder of the chapter, interest is focused on population change (measured as the natural log of P_{2000}-P_{1990}/ P_{1990}) and a few potentially useful, theoretically derived covariates of population change: farm dependence, population age structure, climatological conditions, metropolitan status, county acreage (natural log) and initial county population (natural log). The latter two variables are of less substantive interest and are included in the model as possible controls for heteroskedasticity.

When undertaking initial EDA explorations of spatial data, in addition to examining the univariate statistical distributions of the attributes (for normality, outliers, etc.) and their bivariate relationships with the dependent variable (for linearity), it also is worthwhile to develop a sense of the spatial distributions of

Figure 19.1. Spatial Distribution of Population Change among Great Plains Counties, 1990–2000

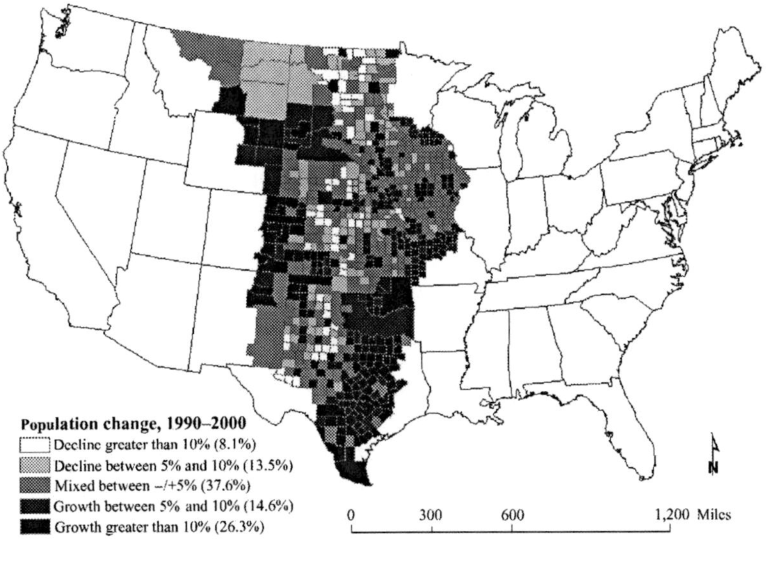

the attribute values. As illustrated in Figure 19.1, the map of population change indicates that roughly one-in-twelve Great Plains counties suffered population loss in excess of 10 percent over the decade of the 1990s, while more than one-in-four counties witnessed population growth of more than 10 percent during the same period.[2] Growth characterizes many of the east-west boundary counties, while loss is largely concentrated along a north-south axis among the central counties and along the northern edge of the region. These concentrations lead to two initial conclusions: First, there is sub-regional variation within the larger Great Plains region, something we discuss below as *spatial heterogeneity*. Second, there appears to be evidence of spatial clustering, such that counties experiencing growth seem to be near other counties experiencing growth while those suffering loss are near other counties undergoing loss, which we discuss below as possible evidence of *spatial dependence*. By mapping our data and reviewing the distributions of the variables across space, it becomes evident that spatial patterning, in the form of positive spatial autocorrelation, will have to be addressed in our modeling strategy.

SPATIAL AUTOCORRELATION

Those who have studied time-series analysis will recognize the parallels to temporal autocorrelation. Typically, when most social phenomena are mapped, locational proximity usually results in value similarity. High values tend to be located near other high values, while low values tend to be located near other low values, thus exhibiting *positive* spatial autocorrelation (Cliff & Ord, 1973, 1981). This appears to be the case with population change in the 1990s within the Great Plains. Less often, high values may tend to be co-located with low values or vice versa as "islands" of dissimilarity or in a spatial "checkerboard" pattern that exhibits *negative* spatial autocorrelation (see Tolnay et al., 1996). In either case, the units of analysis in spatial demography likely fail a formal statistical test of randomness and thus fail to meet a key assumption of classical statistics: independence among observations. With respect to statistical analyses that presume such independence, such as standard regression analysis, positive autocorrelation means that the spatially autocorrelated observations bring less information to the model estimation process than would the same number of independent observations. The greater the extent of spatial autocorrelation, the more severe is the information loss. Again, this fact has been known for several decades. For example, early recognition of this problem is found in a brief paper by census statistician Frederick Stephan, who, when referring to the use of census tract data in social research, introduced the problem by analogy to classical sampling theory: "Data of geographic units are tied together, like bunches of grapes, not separate, like balls in an urn" (1934, p. 165).

How Does Spatial Autocorrelation Arise?

We have pointed out that *positive* spatial autocorrelation is very commonly a property of mapped social and economic data, whereas negative spatial autocorrelation is much less commonly observed. A quick explanation for the presence of spatial autocorrelation can be found in the oft-cited "first law of geography," enunciated by Tobler (1970, p. 236): "Everything is related to everything else, but near things are more related than distant things." While useful as a shorthand reminder, Tobler's first law is somewhat unsatisfying because it doesn't tell us *why* this phenomenon arises in practice, or what difference it makes. Why, for example, do state sales tax levels tend to cluster regionally? Why does the percentage vote cast for presidential candidates show systematic geographic clustering? Why do high housing values cluster in some neighborhoods of a large city and low values in other neighborhoods? Or, as in the case of our example, why is relatively high growth concentrated in some sub-regions of the Great Plains and low growth or decline in others?

While helpful reviews exist on this topic (e.g., Brueckner, 2003; Wrigley et al., 1996, pp. 30–31), the answers to such questions can only be approximated with models of the spatial process that inevitably are imperfect. Such answers generally will be a function not only of the data being analyzed but will depend strongly on the analyst's theory about the process, as well as assumptions underlying both the data and the statistical model(s) selected to describe the nature of the relationships under investigation. For example, the four substantively interesting independent variables selected for our example (farm dependence, population age structure, climatological conditions and metropolitan status) and two additional control variables were not chosen at random but have been identified in earlier work addressing population change. Our task is to analyze appropriately the nature of their joint relationship with population change while simultaneously accounting (or correcting) for spatial process relationships at work in the data.

Exploratory Spatial Data Analysis

While much of the growing literature on spatial data analysis focuses on matters of specification tests, parameter estimation, and advanced tools such as Monte Carlo simulation, any proper empirical analysis must begin more simply by exploring and understanding one's data. Continuing our earlier discussion of EDA, many of the techniques first codified by John Tukey (1977) and later expanded by Tukey's colleagues (Hoaglin et al., 1983, 1985) are also appropriate for the exploration of spatial data. Once again, however, some of the unique aspects of spatial data make exploratory *spatial* data analysis (ESDA) a field that has attracted considerable attention in and of itself. The science of creating and interpreting maps of spatial data, for example, is the topic of a large literature fostered by the development over the past 30 years of powerful geographic information systems (GIS) (Chou, 1997). In addition, software for creating and testing a variety of neighborhood weights matrices, for generating various measures of spatial autocorrelation (both global and local), and for obtaining diagnostic results concerning error dependence in standard regression models are now widely available. This literature is large and dynamic. Perhaps the best citation that can be provided is to invite the reader's attention to the website of the Center for Spatially Integrated Social Science (CSISS), a center whose mission is to serve as an ongoing clearinghouse for software tools, literature, and training opportunities in spatial data analysis (http://www.csiss.org).

Global and Local Diagnostics

Global measurements—whether they are overall descriptions of attribute values, measures of statistical relationships, or model accuracy assessments—are derived using data for the entire study region. For example, a global Moran's I statistic is a single measure describing the general extent of spatial clustering of an attribute across the region, conditional on the specific neighborhood structure imbedded in the chosen weights matrix (Moran, 1950). The global Moran's I can be scaled to the interval $(-1, 1)$ where a strong positive value indicates value similarity among neighbors (clustering, or *positive* spatial autocorrelation), a strong negative value indicates value dissimilarity (dispersion, or *negative* spatial autocorrelation), and a value near zero suggests no spatial relationship. Tests for significance use z-scores and the standard normal distribution. As commonly applied to a full data set, Moran's I yields an indication of the extent of overall spatial clustering of similar values on a given attribute. It is a "global" measure of spatial autocorrelation and, as such, cannot by itself identify *where* "hot spots" of value clustering exist within the study region. Since spatial data are easily mapped, it is thus only natural that techniques have been developed for generating and mapping *local* counterparts to many global measurements.

Two useful ESDA tools in spatial data analysis are the Moran Scatterplot (Aneslin, 1996) and so-called LISA statistics (for Local Indicators of Spatial Association) such as the "local" Moran's I (Anselin, 1995). These devices are extremely valuable for understanding the localized extent and nature of spatial clustering in a data set. Their use logically should precede and inform the process of hypothesis construction, model specification, estimation, and statistical inference. Rather than producing a single global statistic or parameter, local analysis generates statistics or parameters that correspond with researcher-specified smaller-scale local areas (commonly called "neighborhoods"). It is helpful to re-emphasize that it is the researcher, not the data or some accommodating software program, who defines what is meant by a local neighborhood. As indicated earlier, this is done by specifying a matrix of weights (≤ 1) that characterizes the structure of local dependence. There exists a large literature on the topic of selecting a weights matrix, and Griffith (1996) is but one helpful resource.

Figure 19.2 shows the Moran scatterplot for the Great Plains dependent variable: log percent growth for counties from 1990 to 2000. In this exploratory view, the data are standardized so that units on the graph are expressed in standard deviations from the mean. The horizontal axis shows the standardized value of the log percent population change for each county. The vertical axis shows the standardized value of the *average* log percent population change for that county's "neighbors" as defined by the weights matrix. Neighbors for this illustration are defined under the "first-order queen" convention, meaning that the neighbors for any given county "A" are other counties that share a common boundary (or single point of contact) with "A" in any direction. Importantly, "A" is not considered a neighbor of itself and is excluded from the average. Counties on the border of the Great Plains region, as shown in Figure 19.1, are permitted only to have neighbors within the region. This restriction creates some boundary problems ("edge effects") in this analysis, but the topic is not addressed further in this overview. The reader is referred to any of several articles or texts on spatial data analysis for more information and ways of dealing with such problems (e.g., Martin, 1987).

The upper right quadrant of the Moran scatterplot shows those counties with above average growth which share boundaries with neighboring counties that also have above average growth (high-high). The lower left quadrant shows counties with below average growth and neighbors with below average growth (low-low). The lower right quadrant has counties with above average growth surrounded by counties with below average growth (high-low), and the upper right quadrant has the reverse (low-high). Anselin (1996) has demonstrated that the slope of the regression line through these points conveniently expresses the global Moran's

Figure 19.2. Moran Scatterplot of Population Change

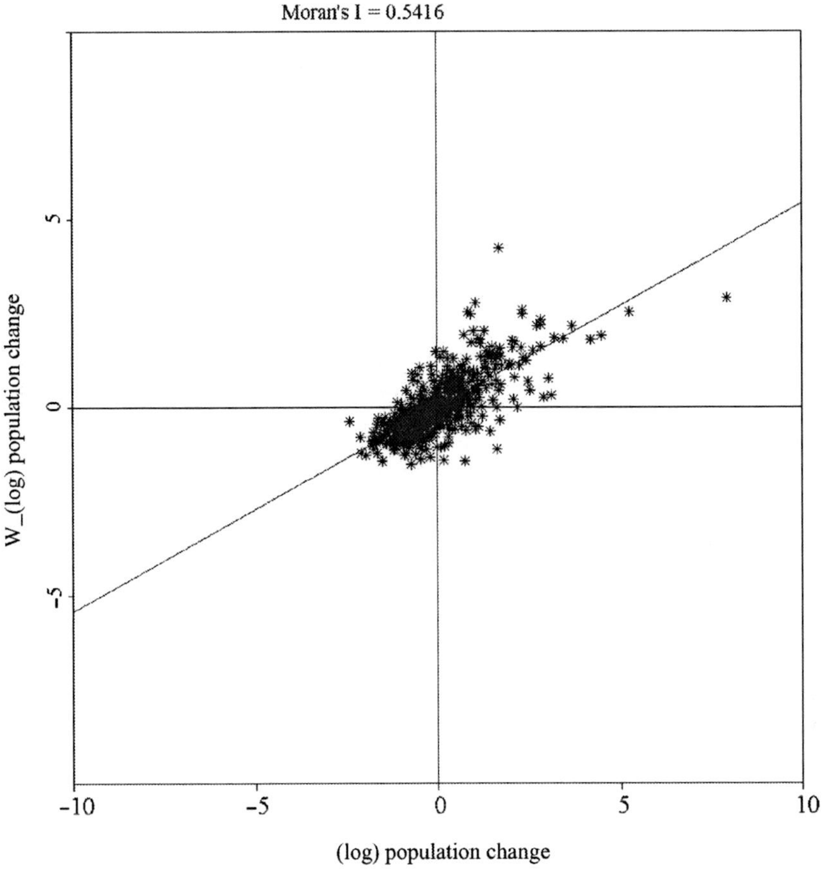

I value, which, for our Great Plains example, is 0.54. This statistic is strongly positive, indicating powerful *positive* spatial autocorrelation (clustering of like values). Most counties are found in the high-high or low-low quadrants.

Figure 19.3 shows a LISA cluster map which displays in a different way the same data as the Moran scatterplot of Figure 19.2. The map shows where in the Great Plains region the various combinations of high-high, low-high, etc. counties are found. Counties where the local Moran statistic is not significant (at the .05 level, based on a randomization procedure) are not shaded. Hotspot clusters of high growth counties surrounded by high growth counties are apparent in the sprawling east-central Texas region connecting metropolitan areas of Dallas-Fort Worth, Austin, San Antonio and Houston-Galveston. Another large

Figure 19.3. LISA Cluster Map of Population Change

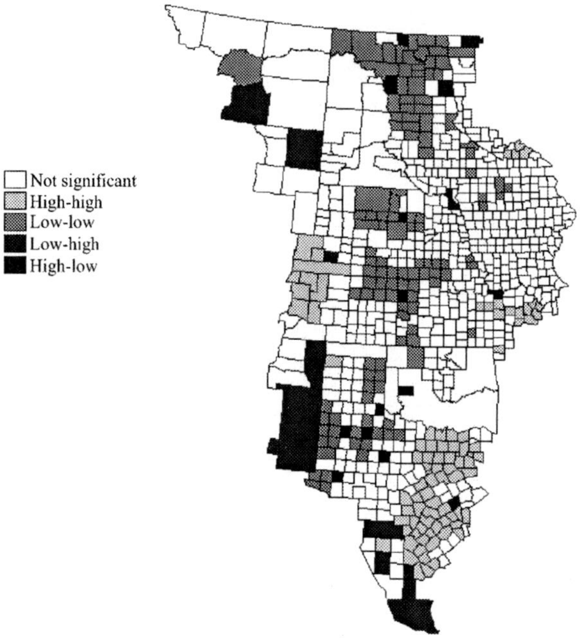

high-high cluster connects the Denver-Boulder, Colorado Springs, and Pueblo metropolitan areas, and a small high-high cluster is found mostly in the Missouri counties southeast of Kansas City. Coldspots include the (low-low) clusters of counties of central North and South Dakota, central Nebraska and Kansas, and two or three small clusters in the Texas Panhandle region and other areas of east-central Texas.

Individual high-low counties appear as islands throughout a central band running north-south through the Great Plains. Often these include small, somewhat isolated, metropolitan counties—for example, Burleigh County (Bismarck) and Cass County (Fargo) in North Dakota. A few statistically significant (at the .05 level) low-high counties are also present in the region. These defy easy summarization, save for the fact that they are largely found along or near the borders of the region, and thus may suffer from unknown but troublesome edge effects. While this exploratory view of the data may suggest hypotheses for the analyst to confirm in the inferential part of any further analysis, perhaps the principal message for us at this point is that, taken together, the maps in Figures 19.1 and 19.3 confirm that growth in the Great Plains in the 1990s has conspired somehow to partition the region into identifiable sub-regions of growth and decline. Such spatial heterogeneity must be addressed in any further analysis of the data, and we begin by examining whether there might be parameter regimes that can be associated with the patterns observed in Figures 19.1 and 19.3.

Geographically Weighted Regression

One of the more recent and fascinating developments in the design of local statistics is the theoretical/conceptual background and associated software to explore how regression parameters and regression model performance vary across a study region. Geographically Weighted Regression (GWR) is similar to a global regression model in that the familiar constant, regression coefficients, and error term are all present within the regression specification. There are two ways in which GWR differs from standard global regression, however. First is the fact that a separate regression is carried out at each location or observation using only the other observations that lie within a user-specified distance from that location. Second, the regression specification includes a statistical device that weights the attributes of nearby counties more highly than it does the attributes of distant counties. The result is a set of *local* regression parameters for each county. The precise implementation of GWR is controllable by the analyst and is far too detailed for discussion here (see Fotheringham et al., 2002). The important feature to emphasize, however, is that the output file enables the researcher to examine and map local parameter estimates and local regression diagnostics, thereby enabling assessment of the utility of the model for various portions of the larger study region.

Examples of such maps are illustrated in Figures 19.4 through 19.7. Local R^2 statistics are mapped across the region in Figure 19.4, illustrating those areas where the model performs well versus those where the model "fit" is less precise. The local R^2 statistic in this example ranges widely from 0.230 to 0.740. We note that the model's highest performance is found roughly in southern Oklahoma and in the northwestern Plains counties in western North Dakota and eastern Montana. Lower model fits are generally found among the boundary counties but specifically in the Texas Panhandle region, in southern Iowa, and, to a lesser extent, in western Nebraska. When referring back to the distribution of population growth (Figure 19.1), variation in model fit does not appear to associate closely with either areas of growth or areas of loss. For instance, the model fits relatively poorly (low R^2) both in the loss (Panhandle) and the growth (southeastern) clusters of Texas counties.

GWR parameter estimates can also be mapped and compared to gain further insight regarding spatial variation in relationships. We stress that these tools are exploratory in nature as opposed to explanatory. GWR can be a useful guide in showing where particular covariates of the response variable contribute strongly and where they do not. The parameters shown in Figures 19.5 through 19.7 are the

Figure 19.4. GWR Derived Distribution of Local R^2 Estimates

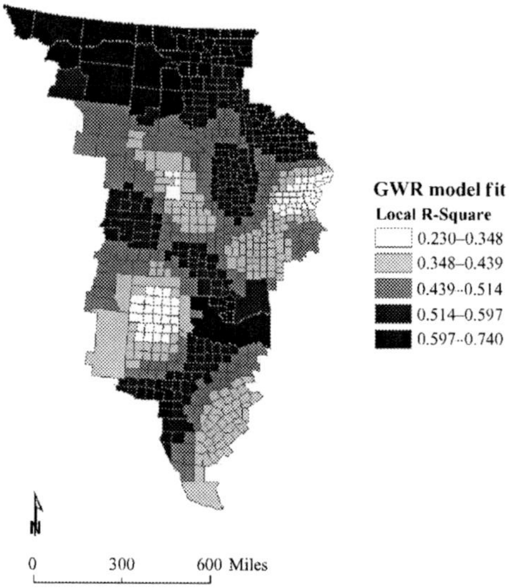

Figure 19.5. GWR Derived Distribution of Intercept Parameter Estimates

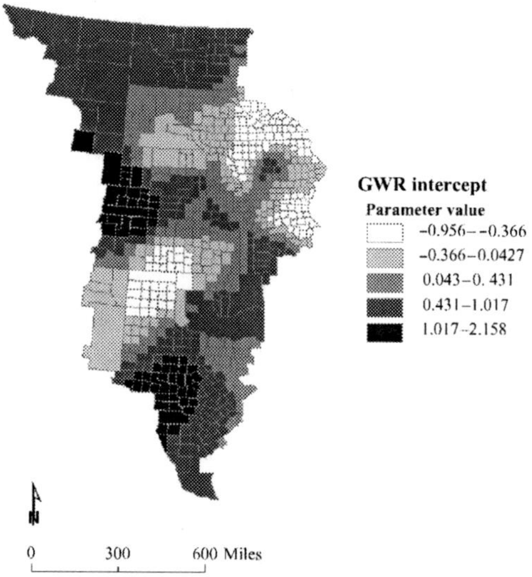

Figure 19.6. GWR Derived Distribution of Farm Employment Parameter Estimates

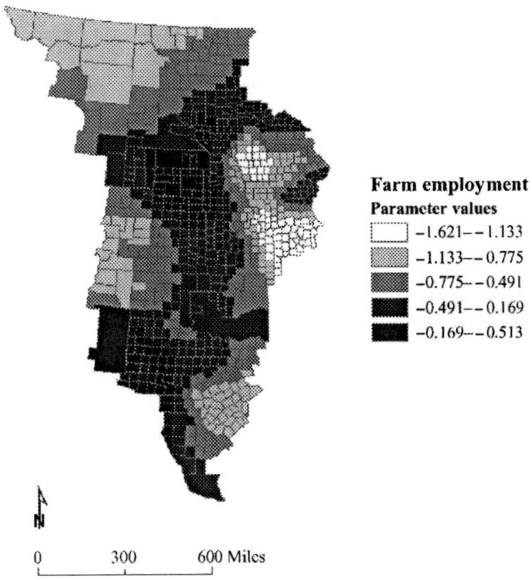

intercept term and those for two of the independent variables, farm employment and temperature range, respectively. Caution is advised when attributing statistical significance to the local parameter values because of the high degree of multiple hypothesis testing in GWR. Some type of Bonferroni-like adjustment to the critical values clearly is appropriate. Fotheringham and colleagues suggest rejecting the null only when t-values approach 4.5 and greater (2002, p. 135).

The map showing the distribution of the intercept parameter (Figure 19.5) indicates that, controlling for the response to predictive variation from the six independent variables, the level of the local intercept varies rather dramatically across the Great Plains (from negative .956 to positive 2.158). Such intercept heterogeneity suggests the likely presence of an unaccounted interaction in the model. For example, local intercept values are relatively high for the band of counties sweeping toward the northeast from southern Texas to northwestern Missouri. The intercept also is high in the higher growth area around (and north of) the Denver metropolitan area. Among these counties, the local parameters for a number of our variables are negative in value and moderately strong (e.g., see Figure 19.6, which shows local variation of the parameter for the farm employment variable). On the other hand, local intercept values are relatively low and negative in northern Texas, southwestern Kansas, and southern Minnesota. One variable appears to be contributing strongly to these lower local intercepts: the temperature range variable. For this predictor variable, the response of regional growth is strong and positive (Figure 19.7).

Figure 19.7. GWR Derived Distribution of Temperature Range Parameter Estimates

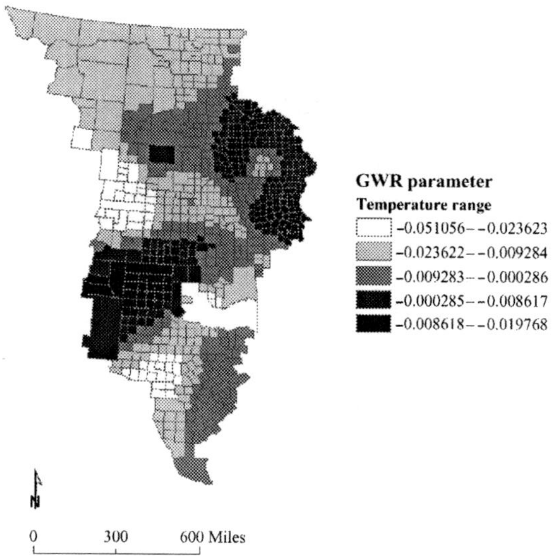

While visualizing a regression hyperplane in seven dimensions is challenging, to say the least, talking about it in general terms may be easier. An examination of the maps of the GWR-generated local parameters, of which only three are presented in Figures 19.5 through 19.7, suggests the following types of local interactions. In the areas of northern Texas, southwestern Kansas and southern Minnesota, our Ordinary Least Squares (OLS) regression hyperplane has a positive slope that is especially strong, marginally, on the temperature range dimension. The positive slope produces a negative intercept value in these portions of the region. On the other hand, in those portions of the region where the intercept is positive and relatively strong, in southern Texas to northwestern Missouri and in the vicinity of the Denver metropolitan area, the hyperplane likely has an overall negative slope. These implied interactions might well inform a re-specification of our model to accommodate the interactions. While this is a promising direction, we do not embark on this particular path in the remaining analysis reported here. Rather, we seek to deal directly with the implied spatial heterogeneity by fitting a trend surface to our data before tackling any spatial dependence that may remain after modeling the spatial heterogeneity.

Spatial Heterogeneity versus Spatial Dependence

As hinted at in the preceding section, large-scale regional differentiation among attribute values and/or among parameter values is an important component of spatial variation. Most treatments of spatial data analysis refer to such subregional variation as "spatial heterogeneity." We follow the usual convention of referring to spatial heterogeneity as the lack of stability across space of one or more attribute values, more formally expressed as lack of stability in the moments of the joint probability distribution of the attributes, or as lack of stability of relationships among the attributes as measured by correlation statistics or regression parameter values (see Anselin, 1988). Spatial heterogeneity often is a concept referred to somewhat casually or vaguely—as we are guilty of here. A more precise sense of what is captured in the notion of spatial heterogeneity is contained in the statistical concept of spatial stationarity in its various forms (Cressie, 1993). In essence, the term "heterogeneity" simply acknowledges the common observation that values of a variable, or values of relationships among variables, are not the same across space. Few social processes are spatially *homogeneous*.

In our example, the nature and extent of population change and its associations with correlated factors are distributed unequally across the Great Plains. In particular, the term spatial heterogeneity applies to large-scale trend or drift in a spatial process, where "large-scale" is taken to mean scales involving distances that extend well beyond any "neighborhood" structure imposed on the data, as discussed further below. Spatial heterogeneity often is also referred to as "first-order variation" or as "first-order spatial effects" in a spatial process (Bailey & Gatrell, 1995). The inclusion in a regression model of one or more variables might satisfactorily account for the observed spatial heterogeneity. If population growth is mainly concentrated in specific types of counties, for example, and if this is the spatial process dominating our data, then inclusion of a dummy variable to identify these counties would not only boost the explanatory value of the model but also would reduce the extent of spatial heterogeneity and, ideally, also reduce or eliminate heteroskedasticity and spatial autocorrelation among the residuals. Another approach to deal with large-scale trends is to fit a trend surface to the data, as we illustrate below.

"Spatial dependence" or "second-order variation" refers to small-scale spatial effects that manifest as a lack of independence among observations. The assumption is that dependence among observations derives from spatial interaction among the units of analysis which ideally can be defended theoretically and which can be statistically captured by a spatially lagged "neighborhood" effect in a model of the spatial process. Such spatial lags may involve the dependent variable, one or more of the independent variables, the error term, or some combination of all three. Properly specified and estimated, such a model with spatial lags is able to "borrow information" or "borrow strength" from neighboring observations precisely because of the spatial autocorrelation among the units of analysis (Haining, 2003, p. 36). We do not present the details, but once a spatial lag is included in a regression model to account for spatial dependence in the data, maximum likelihood estimation (MLE) is usually the appropriate estimator (see Anselin & Bera, 1998). In our example, a carefully selected variable to account for spatial heterogeneity in the data might boost the explanatory value of the model and largely remove the large-scale spatial process, but spatial autocorrelation would persist if a spatial dependence process also were indicated. In other words, there would remain in the data a more complicated, interactive spatial relationship among neighbors that suggests the requirement of some type of autoregressive term in the regression specification.

While the preceding discussion appears to present a sequential, orderly, step-by-step process, in practice the situation is more complex. Often the data suggest a combination of both first-order and second-order effects or fail to give unambiguous clues to one or the other. For example, the map of recent population change in the Great Plains (Figure 19.1) reveals an uneven gradation of population growth and decline in the 1990s that defies any simple and immediate explanation. Several clusters of counties with high growth are apparent: for example, east-central Texas, central Missouri, eastern Colorado—certainly very different counties in terms of topography, cultural history, and industrial base. Clusters of slow growth or population decline are apparent across the most northern Plains counties of Montana, North Dakota, and northwestern Minnesota, in much of Nebraska and Kansas, and in the Texas Panhandle. Might these clusters be accounted for by established historical or legacy effects, and might they be "explained" by a few well chosen independent variables? Or might there exist neighbor influences among these counties, such as spatial spillovers or diffusion, which account for the spatial pattern? The first question inquires about possible spatial heterogeneity, the second about possible spatial dependence. For whatever reasons, parts of the Great Plains reveal relatively high growth, while others exhibit population decline. The goal of the researcher is to identify potential covariates of population change in the region and to explain the variation in growth among Great Plains counties using a combination of traditional modeling approaches and newer spatial modeling approaches.

Regardless of the analyst's theoretical notions about the process giving rise to the observed spatial pattern, the analysis generally proceeds as follows. First, based on a combination of theory and review of the relevant literature, a defensible OLS regression model is fit to the data, and a variety of residual-based diagnostics are examined, including a test for spatial autocorrelation. Tests for spatial error dependence generally take two forms: (1) a general test for spatial autocorrelation of residuals against the alternative of no autocorrelation, and (2) a set of tests against a specific *form* of spatial process. The first such generalized test usually is the calculation of a region-wide or "global" measure of spatial autocorrelation, such as the Moran's *I* statistic, as discussed above. The second set of specific tests is based on the maximum likelihood principle (see Anselin, 2001; Anselin & Bera, 1998). We comment on these tests in interpreting the regression model results below.

Unfortunately, in the cross sectional context, no statistical tools exist to inform the analyst which spatial process, heterogeneity or dependence, has generated the data at hand (Bailey & Gatrell, 1995, pp. 32–33). That is, it is not mathematically possible to differentiate an independent heterogeneous spatial process from a dependent homogeneous spatial process. As mapped realizations, they may appear quite identical. Either process alone or both acting together could be responsible for the spatial pattern shown in Figure 19.1. The story is less bleak if repeated observations are available for cross sectional data. There may, under such conditions, be sufficient data to distinguish between the two spatial processes. Moreover, the distinction between large-scale variation and small-scale variation in an attribute is rarely easily determined. It depends in part on how the analyst has chosen to define "neighborhood" structure. As described earlier, the latter is expressed formally in a proximity or weights matrix. This matrix captures the researcher's view of the *nature* of neighboring influences. The actual *degree* of such influences is captured by the data and a spatial parameter to be estimated along with other parameters. A strong theoretical framework and some testing of alternatives should guide the choice of spatial weights, as they play a strong role in determining statistics or parameter values derived using a specific weights matrix. This matrix is required for the calculation of spatial autocorrelation statistics, such as the Moran's I, and for specifying and estimating regression models incorporating spatial dependence terms to account for spatial autocorrelation in the data.

Thus far in our discussion, spatial autocorrelation has been described as something that arises from a substantive spatial process. In the case of spatial heterogeneity, there are presumed forces (geophysical, cultural, social, or economic) that somehow work to constrain or otherwise serve as influences causing individuals, families, or counties with similar attribute bundles to find themselves physically near one another. In the case of spatial dependence, presumed *interaction* among individuals results in spatial clustering. The large body of literature springing from the theory of social adoption/diffusion (Rogers, 1962), for example, captures well the notion of spatial dependence.

Spatial autocorrelation, however, can also arise as a nuisance (Anselin, 1988). Most commonly this occurs when the underlying spatial process creates regions of value clustering that are much larger than the units of observation chosen by, or available to, the analyst. An example of such nuisance autocorrelation might be present in the distribution of population growth in the Great Plains. The large cluster of high growth counties in central Texas (Figure 19.1) is discussed above as a sub-region contributing to spatial heterogeneity, and this sub-region contributes heavily to the fairly high global Moran's I statistic. Stepping back from the data for a moment, one quickly observes that this sub-region of high growth is considerably more extensive than is the particular lens (counties) through which the process is viewed. When units of analysis are smaller than the boundaries of areas having high or low attribute values, spatial autocorrelation in the observations is inevitable. Such nuisance autocorrelation must somehow be recognized and eventually brought into the formal analysis of the data. Customarily this is handled in models of spatial heterogeneity with the use of dummy variables to identify different "spatial regimes" or through the incorporation of a "surface trend" as part of the regression model (Anselin, 1988).

The aim of the researcher is to specify and estimate a model that reasonably accounts for or incorporates the spatial effects present in the data. These effects can be modeled separately or jointly as spatial heterogeneity and spatial dependence. When first examining a spatial relationship, the researcher must ask whether the association appears to be a *reaction* or an *interaction*, characteristic of heterogeneity or spatial dependence, respectively. Anselin, referring to earlier studies, discusses this difference using the terms "apparent contagion" (spatial heterogeneity) and "real contagion" (spatial dependence) (1988, p. 15).

If the association is merely a reaction to some geophysical, cultural, social, or economic force that works to create spatial patterning, then a modeling strategy with a standard regression structure may be appropriate. Often it is discovered that independent variables in the model—themselves spatially autocorrelated—can account satisfactorily for the observed spatial autocorrelation in the dependent variable. In such a situation, regression residuals generally are found to be negligibly autocorrelated, and standard regression approaches are adequate. At other times, the researcher might introduce variables that capture the influence of the geophysical or other forces underlying the spatial effect. Fotheringham, Brunsdon and Charlton provide several examples—GWR among them—to approach this particular issue (2002, pp. 15–24). As a general matter, it is wise practice to model, perhaps with a simple regression specification, the heterogeneity of a spatial process before spatial dependence modeling is undertaken. The reason for this is that spatial dependence modeling assumes a homogeneous (technically, stationary) spatial process.

If, on the other hand, the association is an interaction suggesting some type of formal dependency among areal units, then a modeling strategy with a spatially dependent covariance structure is the way to proceed. In this instance, controlling for heterogeneity likely will not fully remove the spatial effects within the data. An alternative is needed—a spatially oriented approach that formally incorporates a spatially lagged dependent variable or spatially lagged error term. In a conceptual way, this approach is a spatial analogue to the treatment of temporal variables in time series analysis. The added dimensionality of geographic space and the absence of any form of natural order in spatial data, however, render many statistical procedures in time series analysis inappropriate in spatial analysis. For details on spatial dependence modeling, the reader is advised to begin with Anselin (1988), Anselin & Bera (1998), and Anselin (2003). This literature is expanding rapidly.

Concluding our discussion of population change in the Great Plains, we attempt to bring several of these thoughts together by presenting some regression results in Table 19.1. The table has four columns of regression parameter values and some useful diagnostic terms. In the table, we take the dependent variable, logged population growth in the 1990s, and regress this on several independent variables. The first column shows the results of a standard OLS regression. We take initial satisfaction in noting that the OLS model performs reasonably well. Several

Table 19.1. Non-Spatial and Spatial Regression Models of County Population Change, 1990–2000 Dependent Variable = log (Percent Population Change)

	(1) OLS	(2) Geographic Coordinates	(3) Spatial Error	(4) Spatial Lag
Farm Employment (β)	−0.332***	−0.342***	−0.459***	−0.420***
	(0.092)	(0.096)	(0.081)	(0.078)
Proportion of Pop <18 (β)	0.190	0.223	0.096	0.091
	(0.123)	(0.120)	(0.111)	(0.097)
Temperature Range (β)	−0.008***	−0.006*	−0.005	−0.004
	(0.001)	(0.002)	(0.003)	(0.002)
City Status (β)	0.014	0.007	0.011	0.012
	(0.012)	(0.012)	(0.010)	(0.001)
log County Acreage (per 100,000) (β)	−0.004	−0.026**	−0.006	−0.008
	(0.007)	(0.010)	(0.009)	(0.008)
log Initial Population (per 1,000) (β)	0.025***	0.026***	−0.001	0.004
	(0.006)	(0.007)	(0.006)	(0.006)
Intercept (β)	0.309***	0.041	0.011	0.020
	(0.049)	(0.076)	(0.081)	(0.061)
Latitude		0.00002	0.00003	0.00002
		(0.00001)	(0.00002)	(0.00001)
$Latitude^2$		0.000	0.000	0.000
		(0.000)	(0.000)	(0.000)

(cont.)

Table 19.1. (Continued)

	(1) OLS	(2) Geographic Coordinates	(3) Spatial Error	(4) Spatial Lag
Longitude		0.0002*	0.0002	0.0001*
		(0.00007)	(0.0001)	(0.0005)
Longitude^2		0.000	0.000	0.000
		(0.000)	(0.000)	(0.000)
Latitude*Longitude		0.000***	0.000***	0.000***
		(0.000)	(0.000)	(0.000)
Spatial Error Parameter (λ)			0.679***	
			(0.035)	
Spatial Lag Parameter (ρ)				0.651***
				(0.034)
Adjusted or Pseudo R^2	0.337	0.378	0.280	0.502
Moran's I (error)	0.363***	0.341***		
Likelihood	619	646	751	765
AIC	−1225	−1268	−1478	−1503
Heteroskedasticity	23.505***†	51.067***†	328.807***‡	335.155***‡
Robust Lagrange Multiplier (error)	2.895	0.327		10.924**
Robust Lagrange Multiplier (lag)	322.013***	41.174***	0.106	

* $p < .05$, **$p < .01$, ***$p < .001$ (two-tailed tests).
† Koenker-Bassett Test for Heteroskedasticity, ‡ Breusch-Pagan Test for Heteroskedasticity.

parameter estimates are strongly significant, parameter signs are as anticipated, and the adjusted R^2 statistic achieves a respectable level of 0.337. Having anticipated and checked for it, however, we quickly note a problem: regression residuals show strong spatial autocorrelation (Moran's $I = 0.363$), a clear indication that the model violates at least one of the assumptions underlying standard linear regression. The Moran test tells us that the residuals are not independent. Moreover, the Koenker-Bassett test for heteroskedasticity indicates that the residuals also are not distributed identically. Both are serious violations of OLS assumptions and suggest that inferences drawn from the model in column one could be seriously flawed.

Comparing the residual spatial autocorrelation ($I = 0.363$) with the spatial autocorrelation for the dependent variable (reported above, $I = 0.542$) tells us that spatial autocorrelation in one or more of our independent variables actually "explains" a portion of the spatial autocorrelation in the dependent variable. As indicated above, it frequently is the case that the independent variables in a regression model can almost completely account for the spatial autocorrelation in a dependent variable, thus removing a problematic spatially autocorrelated residual. However, in our case, the regressors have not satisfactorily accounted for obvious spatial heterogeneity and/or dependence in the data, and a correction to the model clearly is indicated. But what type of correction? At this point one's theory of the process under investigation is asked to do some heavy lifting. Does the residual dependence in the model likely stem from omitted variables on the right-hand side of the regression specification, thus suggesting the utility of a spatial error model? If so, we might pause to ask, what variables? On the other hand, might there be spillover influences among growing counties or declining counties that directly influence the growth rates of their neighbors? Fortunately, to supplement our theory about the process, however strong, we receive some additional guidance from other diagnostic statistics applied to the residuals in the OLS regression.

Two such regression diagnostics are shown at the bottom of the first column: Lagrange Multiplier test statistics which, for this example, suggest a preference for a spatial lag specification (a lagged dependent variable term on the right-hand side) over a spatial error specification (a lagged error term). While often very helpful, these diagnostic statistics are also known to be unreliable in the presence of unresolved heterogeneity in the model. We therefore have added a second-order polynomial trend surface to the OLS model in the hope of capturing at least a portion of the spatial heterogeneity in the data.

Using ESDA software we examined the shape of the north-south and east-west marginal distributions of the dependent variable, and on that basis we chose a second-order trend surface and added to our OLS model five variables expressing linear and nonlinear aspects of the geographic centroid of each county: latitude, longitude, latitude-squared, longitude-squared, and latitude-x-longitude (column two of Table 19.1). Few of the parameters of the added variables are statistically significant. Understandably, there is a correlation between latitude, a north-south variable, and the temperature range variable. The addition of the geographic variables thus reduces the significance of the latter, and latitude and its square are not significant contributors with the temperature variable in the model. Other parameters also change in the shift from column one to column two. Quite interestingly, after controlling for the geographic variables, county acreage assumes significance in the anticipated direction.

Yet the model in column two remains unsatisfactory. The Moran's *I* is modestly reduced, but it and the heteroskedasticity test both suggest the need to deal with spatial dependence. The model, when augmented with the trend surface variables (column two), unambiguously suggests dependence in the form of a spatially lagged dependent variable. Yet heteroskedasticity remains high, thus reducing our confidence in the Lagrange Multiplier tests. Consequently we present both a spatial error model (column three, Table 19.1) and a spatial lag model (column four), partly as a concession to our uncertainty about the process but partly also to see what additional understanding we might glean by examining both the spatial error and lag specifications.

We comment first on results of the spatial error model shown in column three. In this specification, the error variance-covariance matrix is assumed to have non-zero off-diagonal terms, thus permitting the extent of autocorrelation in the errors to be estimated by a parameter, λ. The underlying assumption in the model, apart from those assumptions justifying a linear specification and the particular set of selected independent variables, is that spatial autocorrelation in the dependent variable is caused by one or more spatially autocorrelated "omitted variables" on the right-hand side of the regression specification. Such a specification is often appropriate in the absence of a theoretical rationale for assuming interaction dependence in the dependent variable. If indeed a spatial error specification is the "correct" specification for the process, then estimated parameters from the OLS regression are unbiased but inefficient, with standard errors of parameter estimates downwardly biased in the presence of positive spatial autocorrelation. We note that the parameter estimates in column three are modestly different from those in column two. Most notably, both the initial population and acreage variables lose their significance, and the only remaining strong substantive parameter is that for our key independent variable, farm employment. A higher likelihood and lower (more negative) Akaike Information Criterion (AIC) score in column three are encouraging, but the pseudo R^2 statistic is considerably lower than achieved in the OLS models. We note two additional desirable features of this model: the spatial error parameter (λ) is strong, and the model has eliminated any diagnostic evidence of a remaining spatial lag influence, because the Lagrange Multiplier test for remaining lag specification is small and not statistically significant. Aside from the remaining heteroskecasticity, the model appears to be a plausible alternative to the OLS specification.

We now comment on the spatial lag model shown in column four, a model we anticipate from the OLS diagnostics to be the appropriate model. In this specification, a lagged version of the dependent variable appears on the right-hand side of the regression specification. As discussed above, the particular form of the spatial lag is determined by the researcher through a definition of "neighborhood," operationalized by a weights matrix. The strength of the lag effect is estimated by the lag parameter, ρ. A spatial lag specification is particularly appropriate when there is structured spatial interaction involving the dependent variable and when the analyst is concerned about measuring the strength of that interaction or is concerned about having "correct" estimates of the regression parameters which can be obtained only after removal of the effect of spatial autocorrelation in the process. If a spatial lag model is the "correct" specification for the data-generating process at hand, then the incorrect OLS specification will suffer from biased and inconsistent parameter estimates.

We note modest changes in the estimated regression parameters, including the observation that inclusion of the lag term has removed the importance of the initial population variable but has not reversed the sign of this parameter, as occurred with the spatial error model. The spatial lag parameter (ρ) is strong and significant and, of the four models, this specification has the highest likelihood and lowest AIC score. Some indication of residual error correlation is apparent in this model, and that is of some worry. It suggests that a model including both a lag and error specification may yet be a preferred fifth model. However, we do not pursue that route here. Our inclination at this point is to state a preference for the lag specification over the error specification. We are not uncomfortable with the implied theoretical position that sprawl and residential spillover growth into neighboring counties—and elsewhere, spillover influences of population loss—are likely the source of difficulty in the OLS misspecification.

SUMMARY AND CONCLUSIONS

In this chapter, we have discussed the role of geographic space in quantitative demography. A re-emerging interest in spatial demography is evidenced by an increasing number of demographers seeking to adopt the formal tools of spatial econometrics to improve on traditional regression models of demographic processes operating in space. The concept of spatial autocorrelation and ways to specify correctly multiple regression models in the presence of spatial autocorrelation are made more concrete through an illustration of spatial modeling of county-level growth in the U.S. Great Plains region during the 1990s.

It is our belief that we will have moved the science of spatial demography forward in very exciting ways as our own statistical models become more sophisticated, as spatial processes are brought into empirical demographic studies to correct for potential misspecification, and as our work begins to add significantly to the larger literature on spatial data analysis. The growing interest in the field of spatial econometrics among several disciplines in the social sciences, of which the re-emergence of interest in spatial demography is a part, suggests an exciting future for quantitative demographers.

ENDNOTES

1. Please direct all correspondence to Paul R. Voss at 316 Agriculture Hall, 1450 Linden Drive, Madison, WI, 53706, or voss@ssc.wisc.edu. The authors extend their appreciation to David Long and Nick Fisher for assistance and advice regarding the GIS applications and spatial modeling for the Great Plains working illustration, to Jeremy White for graphic support, and to Glenn Deane for extensive comments on earlier drafts. This research was supported in part by the U.S. Department of Agriculture, Hatch Grant WIS04536, by the National Institute for Child Health and Human Development, Center Grant HD05876 and Training Grant HD07014, and by the University of Wisconsin Center for Demography and Ecology, through its Geographic Information and Analysis Core.
2. The county boundaries used throughout this example refer to 1900 boundaries since the example is taken from a larger, historic project.

REFERENCES

Anselin, L. (1988). *Spatial econometrics, methods, and models*. Dordrecht, Netherlands: Kluwer.

Anselin, L. (1995). Local indicators of spatial association—LISA. *Geographical Analysis, 27*, 93–115.

Anselin, L. (1996). The Moran scatterplot as an ESDA tool to assess local instability in spatial association. In M. Fischer, H.J. Scholten, & D. Unwin (Eds.), *Spatial analytical perspectives on GIS* (pp. 111–125). London: Taylor & Francis.

Anselin, L. (2001). Rao's score test in spatial econometrics. *Journal of Statistical Planning and Inference, 97*(1), 113–139.

Anselin, L. (2003). Spatial externalities, spatial multipliers, and spatial econometrics. *International Regional Science Review, 26*(2), 153–166.

Anselin, L., & Bera, A. (1998). Spatial dependence in linear regression models with an introduction to spatial econometrics. In A. Ullah & D. Giles (Eds.), *Handbook of applied economic statistics* (pp. 237–289). New York: Marcel Dekker.

Bailey, T.C., & Gatrell, A.C. (1995). *Interactive spatial data analysis*. Harlow, UK: Longman Scientific & Technical.

Brueckner, J.K. (2003). Strategic interaction among governments: An overview of empirical studies. *International Regional Science Review*, 26(2), 175–188.

Chou, Y.-H. (1997). *Exploring spatial analysis in Geographic Information Systems*. Santa Fe, NM: OnWord Press.

Cliff, A.D., & Ord, J.K. (1973). *Spatial autocorrelation*. London: Pion.

Cliff, A.D., & Ord, J.K. (1981). *Spatial processes: models and applications*. London: Pion.

Cressie, N.A.C. (1993). *Statistics for spatial data*. New York: Wiley.

Fotheringham, A.S., Brunsdon, C., & Charlton, M.E. (2002). *Geographically weighted regression: The analysis of spatially varying relationships*. Chichester, UK: Wiley.

Griffith, D.A. (1996). Some guidelines for specifying the geographic weights matrix contained in spatial statistical models. In S.L. Arlinghaus (Ed.), *Practical handbook of spatial statistics* (pp. 65–82). Boca Raton, FL: CRC Press.

Haining, R. (2003). *Spatial data analysis in the social and environmental sciences*. Cambridge, UK: Cambridge University Press.

Hoaglin, D.C., Mosteller, F., & Tukey, J.W. (Eds.). (1983). *Understanding robust and exploratory data analysis*. New York: Wiley.

Hoaglin, D.C., Mosteller, F., & Tukey, J.W. (Eds.). (1985). *Exploring data tables, trends, and shapes*. New York: Wiley.

Lobao, L. (2004). Continuity and change in place stratification: Spatial inequality and middle-range territorial units. *Rural Sociology, 69*(1), 1–30.

Lobao, L., & Saenz, R. (2002). Spatial inequality and diversity as an emerging research area. *Rural Sociology, 67*(4), 497–511.

Martin, R.J. (1987). Some comments on correction techniques for boundary effects and missing value techniques. *Geographical Analysis, 19*, 273–282.

Messner, S.F., & Anselin, L. (2004). Spatial analyses of homicide with areal data. In M.F. Goodchild & D.G. Janelle (Eds.), *Spatially integrated social science* (pp. 127–144). Oxford: Oxford University Press.

Moran, P.A.P. (1950). Notes on continuous stochastic phenomena. *Biometrika, 37*, 17–23.

Rogers, E.M. (1962). *Diffusion of innovation*. New York: Free Press.

Stephan, F.F. (1934). Sampling errors and interpretations of social data ordered in time and space. *Journal of the American Statistical Association, 29*(Suppl. 185), 165–166.

Tobler, W.R. (1970). A computer movie simulating urban growth in the Detroit region. *Economic Geography, 46*, 234–240.

Tolnay, S.E., Deane, G., & Beck, E.M. (1996). Vicarious violence: Spatial effects on Southern lynchings, 1890–1919. *American Journal of Sociology, 102*(3), 788–815.

Tukey, J.W. (1977). *Exploratory data analysis*. Reading, MA: Addison-Wesley.

Voss, P.R. (1993). Applied demography and rural sociology. In D.L. Brown, D.R. Field, & J.J. Zuiches (Eds.), *The demography of rural life* (pp. 145–170). University Park, PA: Northeast Regional Center for Rural Development.

Voss, P.R. (2004). *Demography as a spatial social science*. Paper presented at the Annual Meeting of the Southern Demographic Association, Hilton Head, NC.

White, K.J.C. (2003). A century of population change in the U.S. Great Plains (Doctoral dissertation, University of Washington, 2003).

Wrigley, N., Holt, T., Steel, D., & Tranmer, M. (1996). Analysing, modeling, and resolving the ecological fallacy. In P. Longley & M. Batty (Eds.), *Spatial analysis: Modelling in a GIS environment* (pp. 23–40). Cambridge: GeoInformation International.

CHAPTER 20

POLICY IMPLICATIONS OF RURAL DEMOGRAPHIC CHANGE

LESLIE A. WHITENER

Rural regions and communities have changed dramatically over the last decade, affected by increased in-migration, changing age and ethnic composition, and related social and economic restructuring. Such trends encompass all components of demographic change and directly affect employment opportunities, human capital development, land use, and social and economic well-being in rural America. All Americans' well-being depends upon many things: availability of good-paying jobs; access to critical services, such as education and health care; technology; transportation and communication infrastructure; strong communities; and a healthy natural environment. But the challenges for achieving these goals differ considerably in rural and urban areas (Brown & Swanson, 2003; Center for the Study of Rural America, 2000; Christenson & Flora, 1991; Dillman & Hobbs, 1982; Economic Research Service, 1988, 1995; Southern Rural Development Center, 2003). The research presented in this volume focuses on population change and the diverse needs of rural areas in an effort to further social science research on population and society interdependencies and to provide federal, state, and local policymakers with sound empirical analysis to develop strategies that enhance social and economic opportunities of rural Americans.

This chapter summarizes some of the public policy implications of key findings presented in this volume as well as in other recent studies on rural communities. Population change and diversity of need underscore many of the economic, political, and geographic changes occurring in rural America. Declines in agricultural jobs, particularly in the Midwest, have forced many families to leave rural communities to seek new sources of income. Remaining small farmers now rely more on off-farm work than farm work for the largest share of their support. Declining populations and small-scale, low-density settlement patterns have made it more costly for some rural communities and businesses to provide critical services and infrastructure. And changes in the use of natural resources, such as the conversion of farmland to urban activities or the economic development of recreation and high-amenity areas, affect the people who earn a living from these resources,

W.A. Kandel & D.L. Brown (eds.), Population Change and Rural Society, 431–447.

as well as those who derive recreational and other benefits from these developments. Population growth from retirement and immigration is contributing to the revitalization of many small towns, but it is straining community resources in others. Some rural areas have met these challenges directly, achieved some degree of prosperity, and are prepared to advance into the new century. Other rural areas have fallen behind and are not positioned well for the future.

As rural America has changed, so have the rural policy questions, solutions, and choices. In 1950, 4 out of every 10 rural people lived on a farm, and almost a third of the nation's rural workforce was engaged directly in production agriculture. Because agriculture dominated the social and economic well-being of most of the rural population, public policy related to agriculture was a dominant force shaping rural life both on the farm and in rural communities. But rural America is different today than 50 years ago, and current commodity-based farm policies do not fully address the complexities of rural economies and populations. Today, less than 10 percent of rural people live on a farm and only 14 percent of the rural workforce is employed in agriculture. The major policy questions that frequently appear in much of the literature on rural economic sustainability and development today address how rural communities can build successfully on their economic base and other assets to retain and attract population and employment, as well as when, where, and under what circumstances rural development strategies are most successful. Demographic change, economic restructuring, changing land use patterns, and a diversity of rural needs are major factors affecting rural policy in the 21st century.

DEMOGRAPHIC CHANGE

This volume emphasizes four major demographic trends with important implications for the future of rural policy. First, population growth rebounded through most of the 1990s, recovering from the widespread population losses of the 1980s. Net migration from metro areas and an increasing flow of immigrants accounted for two-thirds of this nonmetro population increase (Johnson & Cromartie in this volume). Since the mid-1990s, however, nonmetro population growth has slowed, and the number of counties losing population rose from around 600 during the 1990s to well over 1,000 since 2000. Population loss affects all regions, but is particularly widespread in farming areas of the Great Plains and western Corn Belt that contend with declining agricultural employment, lack of replacement employment in other industries, and distance from metro areas (Cromartie, 2005; Johnson & Rathge in this volume; McGranahan & Beale, 2002). Maintaining the population base, improving off-farm job opportunities, and providing public services continue to challenge many of these traditional farming areas. In contrast, the fastest growing rural counties are often located in the Rocky Mountain West, the southern Appalachians, and the upper Great Lakes, areas rich in natural and recreational amenities and close to metropolitan areas. Tourism, recreation, second-home development, and retirement migration underlie rapid growth in many parts of the Upper Midwest and New England as well (Stedman et al., in this volume.).

Second, growing numbers of Hispanics are settling in rural America, accounting for over 25 percent of nonmetro population growth during the 1990s. With a younger population and higher fertility, Hispanics are now the fastest growing racial/ethnic group in rural America. And almost half of all rural Hispanics live outside of the traditional Southwestern settlement states (Kandel & Cromartie, 2004). In many places, new Hispanic settlement patterns are contributing to the revitalization of small towns; in others, the influx of residents is straining housing supplies and other community resources. The younger age, lower education, and larger family size of Hispanic households suggest increased demands for social services geared toward a younger population, including prenatal care, child care, schooling, health care, and affordable housing (Kandel & Parrado in this volume).

Third, nonmetro America is aging more rapidly and is notably older than metro America in all regions of the country (Kirschner et al. in this volume). The older population grew rapidly in many rural places in the 1990s, due largely to retirement opportunities. The Economic Research Service (ERS) has identified 277 nonmetro *retirement destination counties* (13.5 percent of all nonmetro counties) where the population age 60 and older grew by 15 percent or more in the 1990s through net in-migration (Figure 20.1). In contrast, only 36 nonmetro counties qualified as retirement areas from 1950–1960, when data were first available (Beale, 2005). Retirement areas are widely scattered across rural America. Warm winter areas have their appeal, but so too, do many counties in the cold winter climate of the Upper Great Lakes, the uplands of the Ozarks, and the southern Blue Ridge Mountains, especially around reservoirs. Other major destinations are the Texas Hill Country, both the Atlantic and Pacific coasts, and many parts of the inland Mountain West from Montana to New Mexico.

Although migration to retirement destination counties is primarily motivated by the presence of amenities, the opportunity for family reunification has become increasingly important (Glasgow & Brown in this volume). But in some rural places, particularly the agricultural areas of the Great Plains and Corn Belt, the growth of the older population slowed and in some places stopped altogether. In the 1990s, the older population declined in a third of all nonmetro counties. This pattern reflects the small size of the cohort now reaching age 65, a group that was depleted in many rural areas by low birth rates in the 1930s, an exodus to cities in the 1940s, and an exit from farming in the 1950s (Beale, 2003). These dual patterns of growth and decline suggest the need for different strategies. Areas with rapidly increasing older populations must be prepared to provide essential services, resources, and programs for the elderly. Areas with declining elderly populations must consider economies of scale when ensuring that necessary services are available and accessible.

Figure 20.1. Nonmetro Retirement Destination Counties, 2000

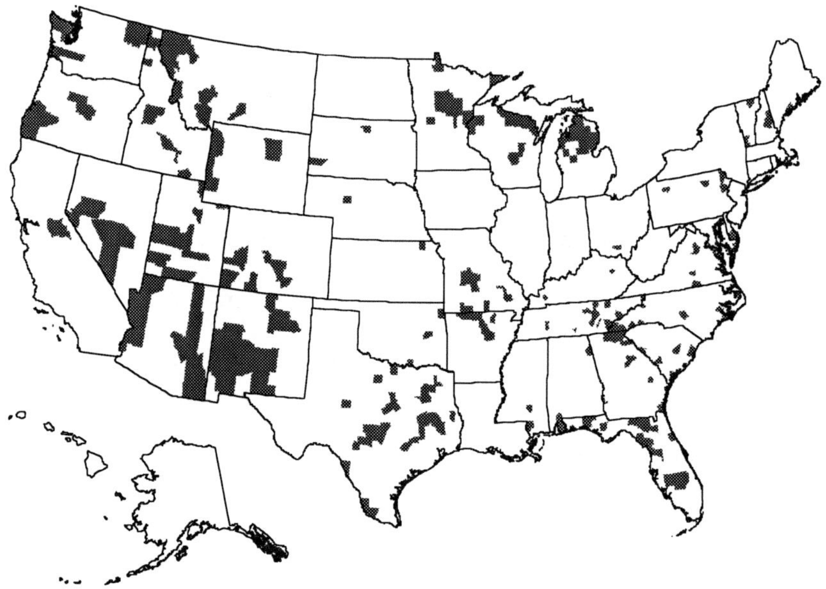

Retirement destination counties–number of residents 60 and older grew by 15 percent or more between 1990 and 2000 due to inmigration.

Source: Calculated by ERS based on Bureau of Economic Analysis data. See http://ers.usda.gov/briefing/rurality/typology.

Fourth, although not dealt with specifically in this volume, changing rural educational attainment suggests a brighter economic future for rural areas that retain their more educated workers. The educational attainment of rural Americans is higher than ever before, continuing a long upward trend (Gibbs, 2003). In 2000, nearly one in six rural adults had a four-year college degree, about twice the share of a generation ago, and the labor market rewards to a college degree have greatly increased in the past 20 years. Rural college graduates now make more than twice as much as rural high school dropouts and have far lower unemployment rates. College graduates still earn much more in cities, making it harder for rural counties to build and retain their human capital base. At the same time, the substantial growth in the college-educated population is not evenly distributed across rural areas, and low education levels still challenge many rural communities. Low-education counties, those with 25 percent or more of residents age 25 to 64 who had not completed high school, are concentrated in the South and Southwest (Figure 20.2). Strategies for raising educational levels and the quality of that education are essential to improving the economies of many rural of these communities (Beaulieu & Gibbs, 2005).

Figure 20.2. Nonmetro Low Education Counties, 2000

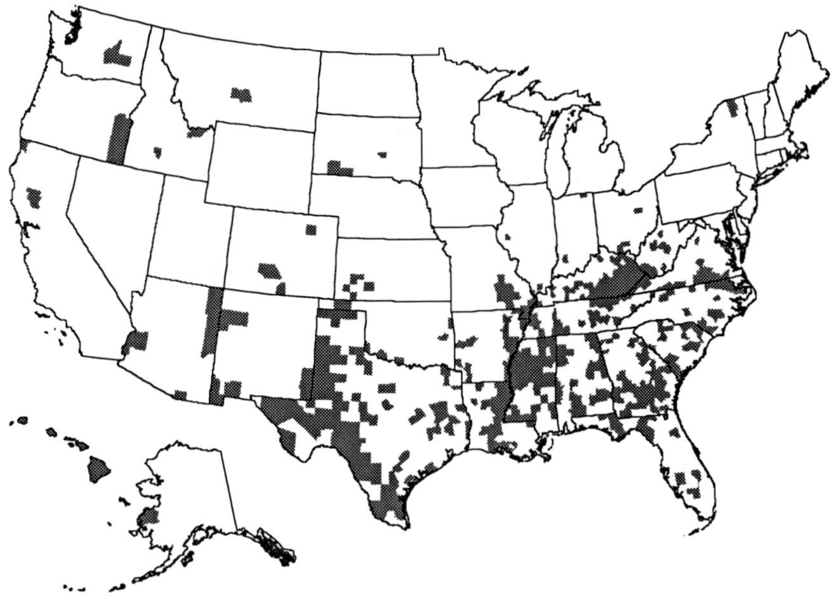

Low-education counties–25 percent or more of residents 25–64 years old had neither a high school diploma nor GED in 2000.

Source: Calculated by ERS based on Bureau of Economic Analysis data. See http:// ers.usda.gov/briefing/rurality/typology.

ECONOMIC RESTRUCTURING, GLOBALIZATION, AND ALTERED LIVELIHOODS

Industrial restructuring presents new opportunities and challenges in a more global economy. Farming no longer dominates most rural economies. Instead, four out of five rural counties are characterized by nonfarm activities, including manufacturing, services, mining, and government operations. This diversity means that global, macroeconomic, and financial events affect rural areas differently than in the past, resulting in new labor market conditions (Vias & Nelson in this volume). For example, trade liberalization is favorable to areas in the Northwest that manufacture aircraft (a U.S. export), but less so to communities in the rural South that produce apparel or footwear that are in direct competition with lower-cost foreign producers. Economic conditions vary widely based on each area's industry dependence. Those dependent on mining, manufacturing, and agriculture have shown slower employment growth over the last decade than areas dependent on services or federal and state government (Figure 20.3).

Figure 20.3. Employment Change by ERS County Economic Type, 1990–2000

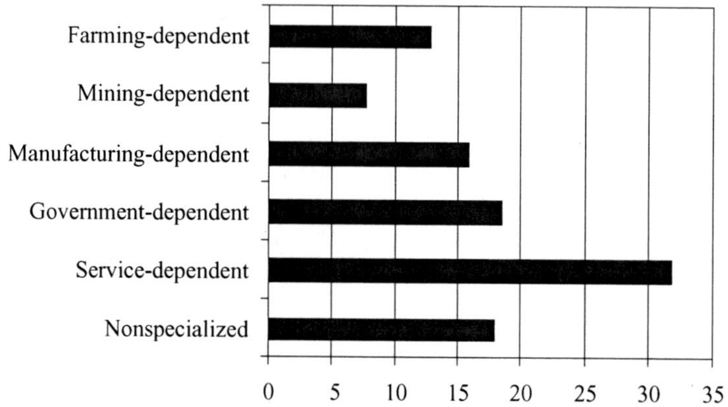

Note: Note: See http:\\ers.usda.gov\briefing\rurality\typology for definitions of economic types.
Source: Calculated by ERS from Bureau of Economic Analysis data.

Despite the relatively small number of people employed in agriculture, farming is an important income-producing sector in many rural areas, particularly in the Great Plains (Johnson & Rathge in this volume). ERS defines farming-dependent counties as those having either 15 percent or more of average annual earnings derived from farming during 1998–2000 or 15 percent or more of employed residents working in farm occupations in 2000 (Figure 20.4). These counties comprised 20 percent of all nonmetro counties and accounted for 10 percent of farm operators and 21 percent of total farm cash receipts in 2000. Employment and income growth in these areas is slow compared with other nonmetro counties. The challenge for farming-dependent rural counties, however, is not a weak agricultural economy. Rather, the nonfarm sectors in these counties have not been equally prosperous because economic development is often limited by remoteness from major urban markets and low population densities (McGranahan & Ghelfi, 2004).

Almost 30 percent of nonmetro counties depend on manufacturing for their economic base, defined by ERS as having 25 percent or more of average annual labor and proprietors' earnings derived from manufacturing during 1998–2000 (Wojan, 2005) (Figure 20.5). Manufacturers originally located in rural areas of the South to take advantage of lower labor and land costs. Although some manufacturers competed on the basis of low-cost production by shifting their production overseas, others began to take advantage of new technologies to compete on the basis of product quality. This shift resulted in a need for more highly skilled labor, and manufacturers began to move to rural areas with better schools and fewer high school dropouts. Areas with low high school completion rates, located

Figure 20.4. Nonmetro Farming-Dependent Counties, 1998–2000

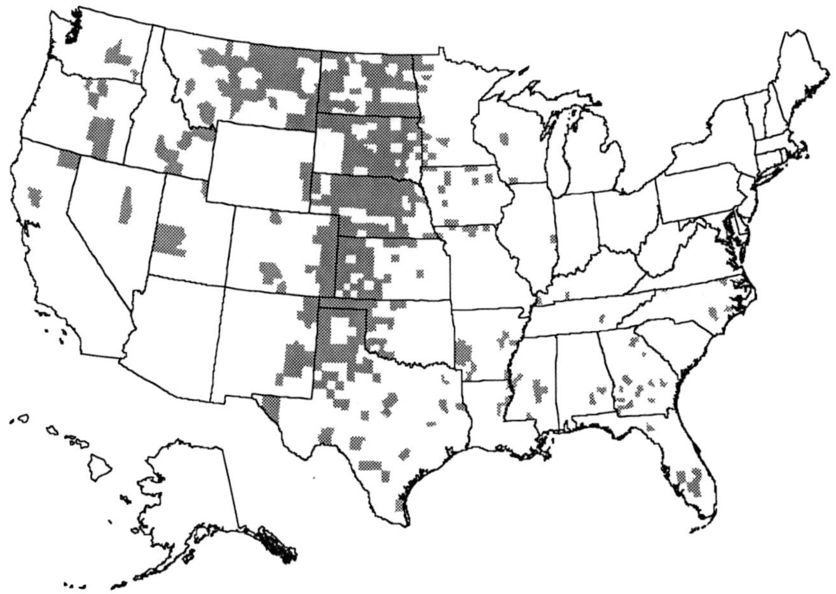

Farming-dependent counties–either an annual average of 15 percent or more of total county earnings derived from farming during1998–2000 or 15 percent or more of employed residents working in farm occupations in 2000.

Source: Calculated by ERS based on Bureau of Economic Analysis and Census Bureau data. See http:/ers.usda.gov/briefing/rurality/typology.

predominantly in the South, now face greater difficulties in attracting and retaining manufacturing employers. Manufacturing counties of the rural Great Plains and Midwest offer a more educated labor force and these areas have been most attractive to employers in recent years. But the loss of 2.6 million manufacturing jobs nationwide since 2000 suggests that manufacturing counties as a whole may be especially hard pressed to find alternative sources of economic growth (Hamrick, 2004).

CHANGING LAND USE PATTERNS

Changing rural population distribution calls for a new look at land use. The conversion of farmland to urban uses as well as the consequences of urban expansion into rural areas raises public concern on many fronts (Cromartie in this volume). How can competing interests be resolved to allow the most efficient use of rural lands while protecting rural amenities, local food supplies, water and air quality, natural resource-related jobs, and quality of life? Changes in land use are

Figure 20.5. Nonmetro Manufacturing-Dependent Counties, 1998–2000

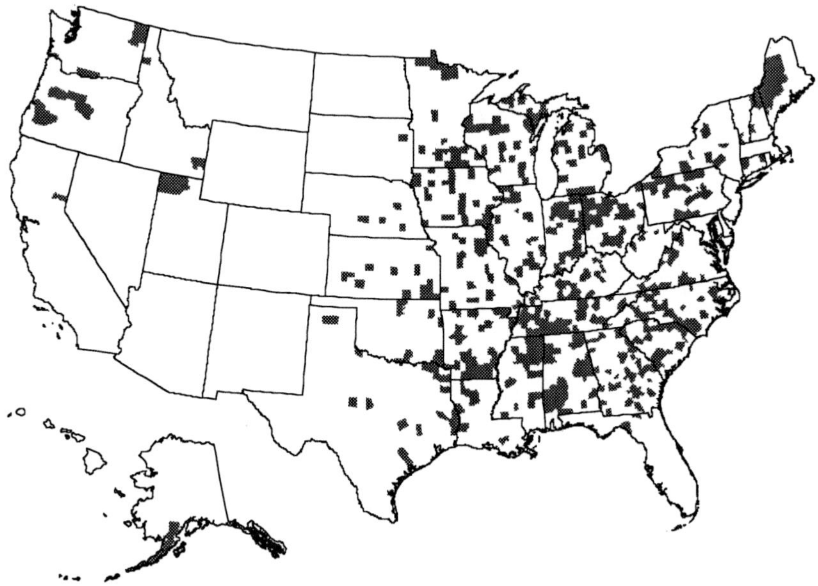

Manufacturing dependent counties–an annual average of 25 percent or more of total county earnings derived from manufacturing during1998–2000.

Source: Calculated by ERS based on Bureau of Economic Analysis data. See http:/ers.usda.gov/briefing/rurality/typology.

the end result of many forces that drive choices made by homeowners, farmers, businesses, and governments. The ultimate drivers are population growth, household formation, and economic development. Economic growth increases income and wealth, and housing and lifestyle preferences, enabled by new communications technologies and infrastructure development, spur new housing development and new land-use patterns. Metropolitan areas expand into the countryside, and more isolated large-lot housing development occurs, generally beyond the urban fringe.

A benefit is that growth in rural areas has allowed many people, including those who cannot afford city real estate, to buy single-family homes because land costs are cheaper on the urban fringe than in the core. While most people prefer the residence situation in which they are living, those who would rather live elsewhere are more likely (by a 2 to 1 margin) to prefer a less densely populated setting (Brown et al., 1997). Potential benefits from lower-density development at the city's fringe include access to employment, access to open-space amenities, lower crime rates, lower housing costs, better air quality, more flexible transportation by automobile, and preferred separation of residences from commercial and industrial activities (Gordon & Richardson, 1997; Peiser, 1989).

But development can impose costs as well—direct costs on the communities experiencing it and indirect costs in terms of the rural lands lost to it. Communities may fail to anticipate the results of development because they have not planned and zoned to provide an institutional framework within which development can proceed (Brown & Glasgow, 1991). Research shows that less dense, unplanned development requires higher private and public capital and operating costs than more compact, denser planned development (Axelrad, 1998; Burchell et al., 1998).

At the same time, public concern continues over the preservation of farming and conservation of rural land to protect against the worst effects of development (Pfeffer et al. in this volume). Research suggests that urban growth and development is not a likely threat to national food and fiber production or traditional uses of rural land (Jackson-Smith et al. in this volume). Agriculture has shown it can adapt to development, and farms in metro areas are an increasingly important segment of U.S. agriculture, making up 33 percent of all farms, 16 percent of cropland, and producing a third of the value of U.S. agricultural output (Heimlich & Anderson, 2001). Farmers trying to adapt to rising land values and increased contact with new residents may have to change their operations to emphasize higher-value products, more intensive production, and a more urban marketing orientation.

CHRONIC DISADVANTAGE, EMERGING OPPORTUNITIES

Also, demographic change points to the continued importance of recognizing the diversity of rural needs. The opportunities and challenges facing rural America are as diverse as rural America itself. Farming communities in the Great Plains (von Reichert in this volume) face different problems with different solutions than do poor, generally less educated areas of the South (Billings & Manion; Lee & Singelmann this volume) or high-amenity counties in the Intermountain West (Krannich et al. in this volume). There is no single recipe for rural prosperity. Rural diversity means that some areas have shared in the economic progress of the nation while others have not. One of the valuable lessons social scientists learned from the study of rural welfare reform is that the poorest and most rural areas were often the hardest to serve (Weber et al., 2002).

The Economic Research Service (2004) has developed a new set of county typologies that help to better understand the broad patterns of economic and social diversity in rural America. The 2004 County Typology identifies seven overlapping categories of policy-relevant themes that are of critical importance for developing public policies and programs at the beginning of the 21st century. These policy types identify both chronic disadvantage and emerging opportunities for rural places. They include population loss, persistent poverty, housing stress, low education, low employment, retirement destination, and recreation counties. Two policy types—persistent poverty and recreation—are discussed here as examples of areas with chronic disadvantage and emerging opportunities.

ERS defines 340 persistently poor nonmetro counties that have had poverty rates of 20 percent or higher over the last 30 years as measured by the 1970, 1980, 1990, and 2000 decennial censuses (Jolliffe, 2004). These counties contain almost one-fourth of the rural poor. They are heavily concentrated in the South, especially in Appalachia, the Ozarks, the Mississippi Delta, the Rio Grande Valley, and the Native American reservations of the Southwest and Northern Plains. These areas are characterized by the disproportionate number of economically at-risk people and the generally weak local economies. Population and employment growth are slower in these areas, and unemployment and underemployment are higher. Poverty in nonmetro America is spatially clustered and largely, though not exclusively, mirrors the geographic clustering of rural minorities in the South, West, and on Native American reservations (Beale, 2004; Jackson Smith et al. in this volume).

At the same time, some rural areas are characterized by emerging opportunities. Natural amenities are an economic development trump card for many rural areas. Rural areas with beautiful scenery, lakes, mountains, forests, and resorts increasingly attract permanent residents, and recreation has been one of the fastest growing rural industries (Krannich et al. in this volume) ERS identifies 334 nonmetro recreation counties using a combination of factors, including share of employment or share of earnings in recreation-related industries in 1999, share of seasonal or occasional-use housing units in 2000, and per capita receipts from motels and hotels in 1997 (Johnson & Beale, 2002). Recreation counties are most numerous in the Mountain West and Upper Great Lakes Areas. Research suggests that tourism and recreational development exert positive affects on rural well-being by contributing to local employment growth, higher income and wage levels, and improved social conditions, such as reduced poverty and improved health (Reeder & Brown, in press).

RURAL POLICY CHOICES FOR THE FUTURE

The goals of economic/community development programs and policies in rural areas vary widely, as do the resources and the opportunities and challenges communities face. Some areas will focus on strategies to stimulate economic and community growth to help address problems associated with population and employment decline. Other areas will seek to improve wages and living standards by changing the job market or by enhancing infrastructure and public services. Low-density settlement patterns often make it more costly for communities and businesses to provide critical public services. In contrast, other rural areas, particularly those rich in natural amenities, face growing pains borne out of economic transformation and rapid population increases. Community leaders in these areas are struggling to provide new roads, schools, and other community services and may actually want to stem growth in order to limit rural sprawl.

One point is clear—commodity-based farm policies as currently structured do not fully address the complexity of issues facing rural economies and populations. For example, the high level of farm payments in the late 1990s did little to eliminate the long-term outmigration from farming areas. Research shows that counties highly dependent on farm payments had some of the highest rates of population loss, even during periods when most other rural areas were gaining population (McGranahan & Sullivan, 2005).

Rural policy for the future will need to encompass a broader array of issues, and these different rural issues will require different mixes of solutions. Strategies to generate new employment and income opportunities, develop local human resources, and build and expand critical infrastructure hold the most promise for enhancing the economic opportunities and well-being of rural America.

New Economic Engines

Prosperity for many rural communities will depend on innovative income-generating strategies that attract people and jobs. Jobs are declining and incomes are eroding in rural areas that depend on natural resource-based industries, such as farming and mining. Many rural areas have successfully built on their assets and taken on new roles—providing labor for diverse industries, land for urban and suburban expansion, sites for prisons, and natural settings for recreation, retirement, and enjoyment. Enhancing rural communities as places to live, retire, and vacation may improve not only the quality of life for existing residents but also the possibility of attracting new businesses and residents. These rapidly growing areas can help sustain their successes by ensuring that the changing demand for essential services and infrastructure is adequately met.

Faced with continuing losses of farm jobs, some rural communities, particularly in the Midwest, have sought to offset shrinking employment by adding value to farm products. Focusing on the role of farms as a source of raw materials for food and fiber products, these communities seek to add value to agricultural commodities by luring food processing plants to rural areas, developing new consumer or industrial uses for agricultural products, or bypassing conventional wholesale-retail systems to sell food products directly to consumers. These strategies may prove successful for some communities, but research suggests that value-added strategies in general are not especially promising as an engine for rural job growth. Food retail and marketing are the largest and fastest growing value-added sectors, but these businesses usually choose to locate in urban areas for their more efficient access to consumers, non-agricultural suppliers, and distribution networks. Food manufacturing and other value-added activities account for a relatively small share of rural employment, and the amount of job growth from these value-added strategies has little impact on the general rural labor market (Gale, 2000).

Many rural communities are looking at other innovative ways of attracting and retaining high-paying industries and employment. The traditional way of attracting firms to a region by offering tax reductions and other subsidies may no longer be sufficient. New approaches, such as providing training and technical assistance by local educational institutions to clusters of similar types of firms, may be more successful than tax-based incentives because they help firms to adopt innovative production techniques (Rosenfeld, 2001). Training and business assistance programs can help new entrepreneurs in some rural areas enhance their business acumen and improve business communications skills (Drabenstott et al., 2000). Networks of small business can help build a more effective business infrastructure by coordinating marketing services, warehousing, business resources, and computer technology (Novack, 2001).

Capitalizing on new uses of the nation's natural resource base may be essential for ensuring the economic well-being of rural America. This resource base, which is primarily located in rural areas, can provide such uses as water filtration, carbon sequestration, and nontraditional energy sources, including methane utilization. Some rural areas may be well suited for the development of renewable energy as well as the production of more traditional fossil-fuel energy. Natural amenities, though, will be the most important advantage for some rural areas. Rural counties with varied topography, relatively large lakes or coastal areas, warm and sunny winters, and temperate summers have tended to reap large benefits from tourism and recreation, one of the fastest growing rural industries. Recent research finds that tourism and recreational development in rural areas lead to increased local employment, income, and wage levels, and improvements in social conditions such as poverty reduction, increased education, and improved health (Reeder & Brown, in press). These strategies have drawbacks, however, particularly in the form of higher housing costs in many of these nonmetro recreation counties. Native American groups have been particularly successful in capitalizing on the gaming industry as an innovative economic development strategy (Rudzitis in this volume). Revenue from tribal gambling rose from $121,000 in 1988 to $13 billion by 2002, although most of this success occurred in areas near urban and metro centers.

However, many of these approaches to capitalize on the natural resource base result in the conversion of farmland to alternative uses and raise issues of public concern on many fronts. Controlling and planning for area growth have historically been the domains of state and local governments. For example, some states have adopted "smart growth" strategies that actively direct transportation, infrastructure, and other resources to channel growth into appropriate areas. Others have turned to policies such as "adequate public facilities" ordinances, impact fees, zoning changes to allow mixed-use development, and partnerships with neighboring communities to develop compatible growth management plans. The federal government has no constitutional mandate to take action on urban growth and development issues, but it may be able to assist with building capacity to plan and control growth, providing financial incentives for channeling growth in desirable directions, coordinating local, regional, and state efforts, and providing trusted research-based information on growth dynamics (Heimlich & Anderson, 2001).

Human Resource Development

The wage gap between urban and rural workers reflects a rural workforce with less education and training than urban workers. In 2003, average weekly earnings for nonmetro workers ($555) were about 79 percent of the metro average ($699). In 2000, only 16 percent of rural adults age 25 and older had completed college, compared with 27 percent of urban adults. Moreover, the rural-urban gap in college completion has widened since 1990 (Gibbs, 2003). Today, employers are increasingly attracted to rural areas offering concentrations of well-educated and skilled workers. A labor force with low educational levels poses challenges for many rural counties seeking economic development. Rural areas with poorly funded public schools, few universities and community colleges, and very low educational attainment may find it hard to compete in the new economy. Recent studies document the direct link between improved labor force quality and economic development outcomes and find that increases in the number of adults with some college education resulted in higher per capita income and employment growth rates, although less so in nonmetro than metro counties (Barkley et al., 2005). Efforts to reduce high school drop out rates, increase high school graduation rates, enhance student preparation for college, and increase college attendance are all critical to improving local labor quality (Beauleau & Gibbs, 2005).

Rural human capital can also be improved by strengthening the quality of classroom instruction (Beaulieu & Gibbs, 2005). Technical assistance could ensure that best-practice models of distance learning are available to remote schools, where the benefits from such technologies are greatest. Instructional quality could be improved by promoting teacher recruitment and retention efforts in remote and poor rural areas. Efforts to facilitate school-to-work transitions of youth are particularly important in isolated and distressed rural communities (Green, 2005). The benefits of these strategies will be greatest in rural communities, where existing workforce development programs (especially the Workforce Investment Act) face special challenges due to high rates of high school dropout or limited demand for youth labor.

Infrastructure and Public Services

Telecommunications, electricity, water and waste disposal systems, and transportation infrastructures (such as highways and airports) are essential for community well being and economic development. But many rural communities are financially constrained in providing infrastructure because of a limited tax base, high costs associated with "dis-economies" of size, and difficulties adjusting to population growth or decline. Investments in needed infrastructure have increased in recent years, but high costs and deregulation pose considerable challenges.

Investment in rural infrastructure not only enhances the well-being of community residents, but also facilitates the expansion of existing businesses and the development of new ones. As an example, a recent study assessed the economic impacts of 87 water and sewer projects funded by the Economic Development Administration and found that these projects in general created or saved jobs, spurred private-sector investment, attracted government funds, and enlarged the property tax base (Bagi, 2002). But the average urban water/sewer facility, which costs only about one-third more than the average rural facility, generated two to three times the economic impacts of rural facilities. The rural-urban difference in economic benefit likely stems from the generally more abundant infrastructure of urban areas—easy access to highways, railroads, and airports, primary and secondary suppliers, input and output markets, community facilities and amenities, and skilled labor.

The federal government has helped rural communities finance public infrastructure, but many communities still lack infrastructure such as advanced telecommunications and air transportation services. Information and communication technology—abetted by financial and technical assistance—can help smaller communities enjoy the same benefits as larger cities, such as higher standards of health care and virtually unlimited educational opportunities. Federal financial assistance for deploying broadband access and/or the creation of incentives for state, private, and public partnerships to develop fiber optic or wireless capabilities are options for rural areas seeking to invest in a telecommunication infrastructure.

SUMMARY

In closing, the 1995 ERS report, Understanding Rural America, highlights a critical policy challenge for rural America.

> Understanding rural America is no easy task. It is tempting to generalize and oversimplify, to characterize rural areas as they once were or as they are now in only some places. Understanding rural America requires understanding the ongoing changes and diversity that shape it. The economies of individual rural areas differ, as do the resources upon which they are built and the opportunities and challenges they face. Some have participated in the economic progress of the Nation, while others have not. Even among those who have benefited in the past, many are not well positioned to compete in today's global economy (p 24).

Little empirical analysis is currently available on what strategies will be most effective in which areas under what circumstances, and there is no one formula for success. The findings reported in this volume discuss the determinants and consequences of demographic change, economic restructuring, changing land use patterns, and the diversity of needs. These four themes are important considerations for federal, state, and local policymakers charged with enhancing the economic opportunity and economic well being of rural Americans.

Many rural problems occur region-wide and some policies will need to address broader geographic implications. Agriculture, as a major source of income and employment, is concentrated in the northern Great Plains and western Corn Belt. Rural manufacturing is disproportionately located in the Midwest and Southeast. Mining and other extractive activities are conducted west of the Mississippi River and in Appalachia. All of these industries have experienced very slow job growth or job loss in recent decades. Regional or multi-community cooperative efforts, such as the Delta Regional Authority and the Northern Great Plains Regional Authority, may offer rural areas a better chance of success in responding to industry wide declines or problems associated with persistent poverty, population loss, or educational disadvantage. Job generation and human resource development will require close coordination to ensure that the skills possessed by workers will be appropriate for the new, largely service-based and information-dependent industries, and that the jobs will be available in the regional economy (Whitener, 2005).

Some rural community issues will be most effectively addressed at the local level. Devolution of federal programs, such as welfare reform, has allowed many local areas to better tailor assistance to local needs and improve program and service delivery. However, policy outcomes may be less successful in some local areas, particularly the smaller, poorer rural communities that lack the capacity to provide good jobs, offer critical work supports, and effectively target hard-to-serve populations. The federal government may have to play a stronger supportive or coordinating role in these areas.

In the future, policy analysts will do well to look to the areas that have achieved prosperity to help develop successful prototypes for areas that may be less well prepared to meet the challenges of the future. The most successful rural policies will build on unique partnerships among a wide range of American institutions, including different levels of government, the business community, public advocacy groups, and local organizations. Solid analysis of the inter-dependencies between population change and rural society will help policy makers at all levels understand the changing contexts that affect policy choices for the future.

REFERENCES

Axelrad, T. (1998). *The costs of sprawl: Summary of national literature review.* Denver, CO: Clarion Associates.

Bagi, F. (2002). Economic impact of water/sewer facilities on rural and urban communities. *Rural America, 17*(4), 44–49.

Barkley, D., Henry, M., & Li, H. (2005). Does human capital affect rural economic growth? Evidence from the South. In L. Beauleau & R. Gibbs (Eds.), *The role of education: Promoting the economic & social vitality of rural America* (pp. 10–15). Starkville, MS: Mississippi State University, Southern Rural Development Center.

Beale, C. (2003). Growth of older population slows in rural and small-town areas. *Amber Waves, 1*(5), 11.

Beale, C. (2004). Anatomy of nonmetro high poverty areas: Common in plight, distinctive in nature. *Amber Waves, 2*(1), 20–27.

Beale, C. (2005). Rural America as a retirement destination. *Amber Waves, 3*(3), 8.

Beaulieu, L., & Gibbs, R. (Eds.). (2005). *The role of education: Promoting the economic and social vitality of rural America.* Starkville, MS: Mississippi State University, Southern Rural Development Center.

Brown, D., Fuguitt, G., Heaton, T., & Waseem, S. (1997). Continuities in size of place preferences in the United States, 1972–1992. *Rural Sociology, 62*(4), 408–428.

Brown, D., & Glasgow, N. (1991). A capacity building framework for rural government adaptation to population change. In J. Christianson & C. Flora (Eds), *Rural policies for the 1990s* (pp. 194–206). Boulder, CO: Westview.

Brown, D., & Swanson, L. (Eds.). (2003). *Challenges for rural America in the 21st century*. University Park, PA: Penn State University Press.

Burchell, R., Shad, N., Listokin, D., Phillips, H., Downs, A., Seskin, S., Davis, J., Moore, T., Helton, D., & Gall, M. (1998). *The costs of sprawl—revisited.* Washington, DC: National Academy Press, Transportation Research Board.

Center for the Study of Rural America. (2000). *Beyond agriculture: New policies for rural America.* Kansas City, KS: Federal Reserve Bank of Kansas City.

Christenson, J., & Flora, C. (Eds.). (1991). *Rural policies for the 1990s*. Boulder, CO: Westview.

Cromartie, J. (2005). Population loss counties lack natural amenities and metro proximity. *Amber Waves, 3*(2), 8.

Dillman, D., & Hobbs, D. (1982). *Rural society in the U.S.: Issues for the 1980s*. Boulder, CO: Westview.

Drabenstott, M., Novack, N., & Abrahan, B. (2000). *Main streets of tomorrow: Growing and financing rural entrepreneurs.* Kansas City, KS: Federal Reserve Bank of Kansas City, Center for the Study of Rural America.

Economic Research Service. (1988). *Rural economic development in the 1980's*. Washington, DC: U.S. Department of Agriculture.

Economic Research Service. (1995). *Understanding rural America* (AIB No. 710). Washington, DC: U.S. Department of Agriculture.

Economic Research Service. (2004). *County typology codes*. U.S. Department of Agriculture. Retrieved February 26, 2005, from http://ers.usda.gov/briefing/Rurality/Typology/

Gale, F. (2000). Nonfarm growth and structural change alter farming's role in the rural economy. *Rural Conditions and Trends, 10*(2), 2–6.

Gibbs, R. (2003). *Rural education at a glance* (RDRR No. 98). Washington, DC: U.S. Department of Agriculture, Economic Research Service.

Gordon, P., & Richardson, H. (1997). Where's the sprawl? *Journal of the American Planning Association, 63*(2), 95–105.

Green, G. (2005). Employer participation in school-to-work programs in rural America. In L. Beauleau & R. Gibbs (Eds.), *The role of education: Promoting the economic & social vitality of rural America* (pp. 36–42). Starkville, MS: Mississippi State University, Southern Rural Development Center.

Hamrick, K. (Ed.). (2004). *Rural America at a glance: 2004* (AIB No. 793). Washington, DC: U.S. Department of Agriculture, Economic Research Service.

Heimlich, R., & Anderson, W. (2001). *Development at the urban fringe and beyond: Impacts on agriculture and rural land* (AER No. 803). Washington, DC: U.S. Department of Agriculture, Economic Research Service.

Johnson, K., & Beale, C. (2002). Nonmetro recreation counties: Their identification and rapid growth. *Rural America, 17*(4), 12–19.

Jolliffe, D. (2004). *Rural poverty at a glance* (RDRR No. 100). Washington, DC: U.S. Department of Agriculture, Economic Research Service.

Kandel, W., & Cromartie, J. (2004). *New patterns of Hispanic settlement in rural America* (RDRR No. 99). Washington, DC: U.S. Department of Agriculture, Economic Research Service.

McGranahan, D., & Beale, C. (2002). Understanding rural population loss. *Rural America, 17*(4), 2–11.

McGranahan, D., & Ghelfi, L. (2004). One in five rural counties depends on farming. *Amber Waves, 2*(3), 11.

McGranahan, D., & Sullivan, P. (2005). Farm programs, natural amenities and rural development. *Amber Waves, 3*(1), 28–35.

Novack, N. (2001). *Producer alliances in the new agriculture*. Kansas City, KS: Federal Reserve Bank of Kansas City, Center for the Study of Rural America.

Peiser, R. (1989). Density and urban sprawl. *Land Economics, 65*(3), 193–204.

Reeder, R., & Brown, D. (2005). *Recreation, tourism, and rural well-being.* Washington, DC: U.S. Department of Agriculture, Economic Research Service.

Rosenfeld, S. (2001). Rural community colleges: Creating institutional hybrids for the new economy. *Rural America, 16*(2), 2–8.

Southern Rural Development Center. (2003). *The rural South: Preparing for the challenges of the 21st century.* Starkville, MS: Mississippi State University, Southern Rural Development Center.

Weber, B., Duncan, G., & Whitener, L. (2002). *Rural dimensions of welfare reform.* Kalamazoo, MI: W.E. Upjohn Institute for Employment Research.

Whitener, L. (2005). Policy options for rural America. *Amber Waves, 3*(2), 28–35.

Wojan, T. (2005). Job losses in manufacturing counties. *Amber Waves, 4*(1), 8.

INDEX

Springer Series on Demographic Methods and Population Analysis

1. Robert Schoen: *Modeling Multigroup Populations*. 1987. ISBN 0-306-42649-8
2. David P. Smith: *Formal Demography*. 1992. ISBN 0-306-43869-0
3. Louis G. Pol and Richard K. Thomas: *The Demography of Health and Health Care*. 1992. ISBN 0-306-43981-6
4. S.S. Halli and K.V. Rao: *Advanced Techniques of Population Analysis*. 1992. ISBN 0-306-43997-2
5. Dudley L. Poston Jr. and David Yaukey (Eds): *The Population of Modern China*. 1992. ISBN Hb: 0-306-44235-3; Pb: 0-306-44138-1
6. Susan M. de Vos: *Household Composition in Latin America*. 1995. ISBN 0-306-44962-5
7. Oscar Harkavy: *Curbing Population Growth:* An insider's perspective on the population movement. 1995. ISBN 0-306-45050-X
8. Evert van lmhoff, Anton Kuijsten, Pieter Hooimeijer and Leo van Wissen (Eds): *Household Demography and Household Modeling*. 1995. ISBN 0-306-45187-5
9. Krishnan Namboodiri: *A Primer of Population Dynamics*. 1996. ISBN 0-306-45338-X
10. Michael Micklin and Dudley L. Poston Jr. (Eds): *Continuities in Sociological Human Ecology*. 1998. ISBN 0-306-45610-9
11. Alfred J. Lotka: *Analytical Theory of Biological Populations*. 1988. ISBN 0-306-45927-2
12. Leo J.G. van Wissen and Pearl A. Dykstra (Eds): *Population Issues*. An interdisciplinary focus. 1999. ISBN 0-306-46196-X
13. Louis G. Pol and Richard K. Thomas: *The Demography of Health and Health* Care. Second Edition. 2000. ISBN Hb: 0-306-46336-9; Pb: 0-306-46337-7
14. Stanley K. Smith, Jeff Tayman and David A. Swanson: *State and Local Population Projections*. Methodology and analysis. 2001. ISBN Hb: 0-306-46492-6; Pb: 0-306-46493-4
15. Samuel H. Preston, Irma T. Elo, Mark E. Hill and Ira Rosenwaike: *The Demography of African Americans, 1930–1990*. 2003. ISBN 1-4020-1550-X
16. William A. Kandel and David L. Brown (Eds): *Population Change and Rural Society*. 2006. ISBN Hb: 1-4020-3911-5; Pb: 1-4020-3901-8

Printed in the United States
82994LV00002B/97-99/A

9 781402 039010